PRICE AND QUANTITY TRENDS IN THE FOREIGN TRADE OF THE UNITED STATES

NATIONAL BUREAU OF ECONOMIC RESEARCH
STUDIES IN INTERNATIONAL ECONOMIC RELATIONS
NUMBER 2

Price and Quantity Trends in the Foreign Trade of the United States

BY

ROBERT E. LIPSEY

A STUDY BY THE
NATIONAL BUREAU OF ECONOMIC RESEARCH

PUBLISHED BY
PRINCETON UNIVERSITY PRESS
PRINCETON, NEW JERSEY
1963

382
L 76p

Printed in the United States of America

RELATION OF THE DIRECTORS TO THE WORK AND PUBLICATIONS OF THE NATIONAL BUREAU OF ECONOMIC RESEARCH

1. The object of the National Bureau of Economic Research is to ascertain and to present to the public important economic facts and their interpretation in a scientific and impartial manner. The Board of Directors is charged with the responsibility of ensuring that the work of the National Bureau is carried on in strict conformity with this object.

2. To this end the Board of Directors shall appoint one or more Directors of Research.

3. The Director or Directors of Research shall submit to the members of the Board, or to its Executive Committee, for their formal adoption, all specific proposals concerning researches to be instituted.

4. No report shall be published until the Director or Directors of Research shall have submitted to the Board a summary drawing attention to the character of the data and their utilization in the report, the nature and treatment of the problems involved, the main conclusions, and such other information as in their opinion would serve to determine the suitability of the report for publication in accordance with the principles of the National Bureau.

5. A copy of any manuscript proposed for publication shall also be submitted to each member of the Board. For each manuscript to be so submitted a special committee shall be appointed by the President, or at his designation by the Executive Director, consisting of three Directors selected as nearly as may be one from each general division of the Board. The names of the special manuscript committee shall be stated to each Director when the summary and report described in paragraph (4) are sent to him. It shall be the duty of each member of the committee to read the manuscript. If each member of the special committee signifies his approval within thirty days, the manuscript may be published. If each member of the special committee has not signified his approval within thirty days of the transmittal of the report and manuscript, the Director of Research shall then notify each member of the Board, requesting approval or disapproval of publication, and thirty additional days shall be granted for this purpose. The manuscript shall then not be published unless at least a majority of the entire Board and a two-thirds majority of those members of the Board who shall have voted on the proposal within the time fixed for the receipt of votes on the publication proposed shall have approved.

6. No manuscript may be published, though approved by each member of the special committee, until forty-five days have elapsed from the transmittal of the summary and report. The interval is allowed for the receipt of any memorandum of dissent or reservation, together with a brief statement of his reasons, that any member may wish to express; and such memorandum of dissent or reservation shall be published with the manuscript if he so desires. Publication does not, however, imply that each member of the Board has read the manuscript, or that either members of the Board in general, or of the special committee, have passed upon its validity in every detail.

7. A copy of this resolution shall, unless otherwise determined by the Board, be printed in each copy of every National Bureau book.

(Resolution adopted October 25, 1926, as revised February 6, 1933, and February 24, 1941)

Contents

CONTENTS

TABLES

CONTENTS

CONTENTS

CONTENTS

xv

CHARTS

CONTENTS

Acknowledgments

THE author's balance sheet, at the conclusion of this study, records a heavy weight of indebtedness to colleagues, assistants, and others.

Solomon Fabricant first suggested the subject for study and supplied advice and encouragement as the work progressed. Albert O. Hirschman and Ilse Mintz contributed many stimulating ideas regarding the questions to be asked and the organization of the answers. Other valuable comments and suggestions were made by Sally I. Lipsey, Harry McAllister, A. Maizels, and Jacob Mincer. My thanks are also due the Directors' reading committee, which was composed of Wallace J. Campbell, Harold Halcrow, and Lloyd G. Reynolds.

I am indebted to Carl P. Blackwell of the U.S. Department of Commerce for supplying unpublished data underlying the Commerce trade indexes and to Alexander D. Angelidis of the U.S. Department of Agriculture, Foreign Agricultural Service, for information on the Agriculture Department's export and import indexes.

Calculation of the many detailed annual and quarterly indexes would have been impossible without the help of the National Bureau's IBM unit under Martha Jones. The charts represent H. Irving Forman's customary craftsmanship. Joan Tron, as editor, patiently excised unnecessary detail and improved the clarity and style of the presentation.

The greatest debt is to my research assistants. Chief among these was Eleanor Silverman, whose calm efficiency and intelligence benefited every aspect of the study from the collection of the original data to the preparation of the manuscript. Amy Ferrara Hoagland also had an important share in several phases of the study. Many other assistants aided in the collection of the basic trade data and other aspects of the study, particularly Arlene Holen, Robert Kinsey, Anne Novick, Chandra Thakur, Joseph Viladas, and Lucille Wu. Doris Preston was responsible for the checking of the final manuscript.

PRICE AND QUANTITY TRENDS IN THE FOREIGN TRADE OF THE UNITED STATES

Introduction

THIS study grew out of the National Bureau's interest in two related aspects of the international economic relations of the United States: "long-term movements of men, commodities, services, and securities . . . examined against the background of secular movements in the domestic economy . . ."[1]; and the cyclical behavior of American international trade and finance.

In both trend and cycle studies, a major obstacle to the analysis of changes in commodity trade has been the lack of data needed in order to separate price from quantity changes over a long period. This investigation was undertaken mainly to provide comprehensive and detailed price and quantity indexes useful for long-term and for short-term analysis.

Data previously published consisted chiefly of official U.S. Department of Commerce indexes for total exports and imports and five major economic classes. These indexes provided annual figures for 1913 and 1919–28, and quarterly or monthly figures for later years. They are fairly satisfactory,[2] except that export coverage has recently become somewhat inadequate among finished manufactures. We accepted these Commerce indexes for the period after 1923, and have concentrated our attention on the earlier years for which the data were less reliable.[3]

The only existing indexes of total trade for 1879 to 1913 are those computed by Theodore J. Kreps.[4] These measured total exports and imports

[1] Arthur F. Burns, *The Cumulation of Economic Knowledge*, National Bureau of Economic Research, 28th Annual Report, May 1948, p. 22.

[2] The export and import price indexes of the Department of Commerce are appraised by the Price Statistics Review Committee of the National Bureau in *The Price Statistics of the Federal Government*, New York, National Bureau of Economic Research, 1961, Appendix A, pp. 79–86.

[3] For use in business cycle analysis, some provision must be made for filling the gap between the end of the NBER quarterly data in 1923 and the beginning of the Commerce quarterly data in 1929. A set of monthly export indexes constructed by Dudley J. Cowden in *Measures of Exports of the United States*, New York, 1931, can be used as an interpolator for the annual Commerce series for the 1924–28 period. On the import side, however, only a very inadequate American Tariff League index is available for intervals shorter than a year. We therefore produced a quarterly interpolating series for the five major economic classes of imports. The calculation of these is explained in Appendix D.

[4] "Import and Export Prices in the United States and the Terms of International Trade, 1880–1914," *Quarterly Journal of Economics*, August 1926.

A very crude pair of export and import price indexes was constructed from wholesale price data for 1866–78 by Frank D. Graham in "International Trade Under Depreciated Paper. The United States, 1862–79," *Quarterly Journal of Economics*, February 1922. These were extended back to 1860 by Matthew Simon in "The United States Balance of Payments, 1861–1900," in *Trends in the American Economy in the Nineteenth Century*, Studies in Income and Wealth 24, Princeton University Press for NBER, 1960. Douglass C. North presents new export and import price indexes for the U.S. in the period before 1860 in *The Economic Growth of the United States, 1790–1860*, Englewood Cliffs, N.J., 1961.

only, with no breakdown by commodity group. They were heavily over-weighted with primary, as against manufactured, products, and were available only annually for years ending June 30.

Our new indexes are intended to give a more detailed and a more accurate picture of the period covered by Kreps and the early estimates of the Department of Commerce. The requirement that the data be useful for business cycle analysis necessitated the computation of quarterly indexes. Since quarterly data on imports for consumption were not published, we followed the somewhat asymmetrical procedure of using general imports (rather than imports for consumption) in combination with exports of domestic products.

Because we accepted the Commerce figures for the later period, no important alterations were made in applying the Commerce classification system to earlier years, even where changes seemed desirable to make the categories more homogeneous or economically significant.

We have, however, subdivided the Department of Commerce economic classes considerably and constructed a number of combinations of the detailed indexes. For example, Export Class 207 (foodstuffs, excluding tobacco and products) matches the two Department of Commerce food classes (crude and manufactured), while Export Class 208 (foodstuffs, including tobacco and products) was constructed to fit more closely into the United Nations classification[5] or that used by the United Kingdom. Some of the minor classes of Appendix C fit fairly well into the industrial classification of domestic output, although not as well, of course, as if they had been specifically designed for that purpose.

Commodity prices and volumes describe a good deal, but by no means all, of what one might wish to know in order to analyze the changing size and composition of American trade. The American data, unlike those of many other countries, exclude ocean freight costs on both sides of the account, thus removing the need for an f.o.b.=c.i.f. adjustment to make export and import data comparable. This characteristic of the data leaves the development of transportation costs outside the area of this study, although these costs are of great importance. A forthcoming study by Douglass C. North[6] should make possible a combination of commodity prices and transportation costs for much of the period covered here.

Another missing variable, on both the export and import sides, is the tariff. There is no information readily available on tariff rates applicable

[5] United Nations, *Standard International Trade Classification*, Statistical Papers, Series M, No. 10, 2nd Edition, New York, 1951.
[6] Summarized in "Ocean Freight Rates and Economic Development, 1750–1913," *Journal of Economic History*, December 1958.

to exports; some kind of composite of the tariffs of importing countries would be the appropriate rate. For American imports there is a tariff index with U.S. wholesale price index weights covering the period 1907 through 1946.[7] There are also data, covering a much longer period, on the ratio of total tariffs collected to total dutiable imports, or total imports. These, as tariff indexes, have the obvious defect that the level of the tariff rate on a commodity influences the weight of the commodity in the index. A sufficiently high tariff could conceivably remove itself from the index by eliminating the import. Nevertheless, these ratios, which were used as tariff indexes by Humphrey[8] for example, were appraised by Lerdau as being "far less suspect than it would appear on theoretical grounds."[9] Neither of these indexes is altogether satisfactory, but Lerdau found that his had some net explanatory value in a correlation analysis in which the ratio of imports to gross national product was the dependent variable. Either of these indexes could be combined with our price indexes to produce a crude estimate of changes in the prices actually facing American purchasers of foreign goods.

A number of adjustments to the official series on the total value of U.S. exports and imports have been suggested, both in official customs reports and by independent scholars. We have incorporated into our indexes only those two adjustments which proved allocable by commodity, but it would be fairly simple to make other adjustments in the totals.

For example, exports by land, omitted from U.S. customs data before 1893, could be added. Matthew Simon, using Canadian import data,[10] made such an adjustment in the aggregate figures, but our attempt to break these down by commodity groups was frustrated by difficulties in matching Canadian and U.S. commodity classifications. For a number of products, exports reported by the U.S. were greater than the reported Canadian imports despite the presumed exclusion of exports by land from the U.S. data.

Simon also adjusted for a discontinuity in the prescribed method of valuation of imported commodities : he increased the 1884-91 values by 5 per cent to add certain inland freight and other costs. This followed a suggestion made by the Chief of the Bureau of Statistics.[11] We were not able to find any basis for applying this adjustment to individual com-

---

[7] E. Lerdau, "On the Measurement of Tariffs: The U.S. Over Forty Years," *Economia Internazionale*, May 1957.

[8] Don Humphrey, *American Imports*, New York, 1955.

[9] "On The Measurement of Tariffs," p. 239.

[10] "The United States Balance of Payments, 1861–1900."

[11] U.S. Bureau of Statistics, Treasury Department, *Annual Report and Statement of the Chief of the Bureau of Statistics on the Commerce and Navigation of The United States, 1884*, p. XI.

modities. Since it could have varied a great deal from one commodity to another, we did not take it into account at all.

We have tampered with the official value series in only two ways. The first was a correction for the overvaluation of imports from Brazil in the early 1890's which resulted from the depreciation of the paper milreis. The error was conspicuous and was concentrated in two important commodities, coffee and rubber. More realistic values were estimated by using official quantity data (which were not affected) in combination with outside data on rubber and coffee prices. A description of the adjustment is given in Appendix C.

Official values were further adjusted for changes in the U.S. customs area which took place in 1900. Here again the adjustment, which is described in Appendix F, rested on fairly reliable data and was concentrated in two commodities, exports of green coffee and imports of sugar.

Many fundamental questions about the meaning or validity of long-term comparisons of price levels and terms of trade have been ignored here, as in most empirical discussion of these problems. Except in Chapter 3, where several types of index numbers are compared, we have generally used the Fisher "ideal" indexes to represent "price" and "quantity" as if these terms were unambiguous and independent of the particular weights from which they were computed. It is also assumed that the shift after 1923 from one type of index to another, and the shifts from one base (or weighting pattern) to another before that date, do not by themselves make comparisons meaningless.

The first two chapters survey the outstanding changes in the foreign trade of the United States over the last eighty years. The remaining chapters deal primarily with the construction of the NBER indexes, appraisals of their quality, and an interpretation of the relations among the several types of indexes.

Chapter 1 sets forth the findings on U.S. export and import prices, and their relation to domestic prices and to the export prices of other countries. It describes the evidence relating to the terms of trade of the United States and the terms of trade of primary and agricultural products. Relations between price and productivity changes are also discussed.

Chapter 2 is concerned mainly with quantity trends in relation to domestic output and to the trade of foreign countries. Possible price-quantity reactions are also explored.

The method by which the NBER indexes were constructed is explained in Chapter 3, and comparisons of Paasche and Laspeyres indexes are used as evidence of the connections between price and quantity changes.

Characteristics of the basic data on export and import quantities and prices are discussed in Chaper 4, with particular reference to the problems involved in using unit value data as prices.

Chapter 5 contains an account of the use of sampling ideas in the construction and appraisal of index numbers and describes estimates of sampling error in the NBER indexes.

Finally the new price and quantity indexes are compared, in Chapter 6, with those of Kreps and the Department of Commerce, as well as with indexes of the Department of Agriculture and the Bureau of the Census.

CHAPTER 1

Trends in Prices and Terms of Trade

Summary View of U.S. Export and Import Prices and Terms of Trade

The history of the international trade of the United States during the last eighty years is divided into three segments by the two world wars. The "prewar period" covers the thirty-five years before World War I. For these years the NBER indexes presented here provide an extensive set of new data. The interwar period covers the twenty-one years from 1919 to 1939. For this segment, we use new NBER data only through 1923; Commerce Department estimates and other series are used for later years. The "postwar period", from 1946 through 1960, is discussed entirely in terms of data compiled originally by others.

In any analysis of long-term trends in this eighty-year period, the treatment of the 1930's poses a difficult problem. For many series, such as the terms of trade and import prices shown in Chart 1, the levels of the 1930's were unprecedented and seem unlikely to recur. Yet, because these years stand nearer to the end than to the beginning of our period, they exert a strong influence on estimated trends. (In the terms-of-trade series, for example, they impart a considerable upward slant to a fitted trend.) For this reason, we have frequently omitted consideration of the interwar period and compared the 1950's directly with the prewar years.

This period should not, however, be ignored completely. Much recent discussion of the terms of trade, ratios of trade to output, and price-quantity relations has been colored by, and can only be understood in terms of, the events of the depression years.

EXPORT AND IMPORT PRICES

In the prewar years, a period of declining prices before 1898 was followed by rising prices up to World War I (Chart 1). No substantial trend for the period as a whole can be discerned, although import prices in 1909-13 were below the level of thirty years earlier. At the end of World War I, and for two years thereafter, prices were far higher than before—in 1920, almost twice the prewar peak for imports and more than twice for exports. After 1920, however, the interwar period was characterized by devastating price declines and comparatively weak recoveries. In the single year 1921, and again in 1931-32, export and import prices fell a distance equal, or almost equal, to the whole range of their prewar fluctuations. The fall

8

CHART 1

U.S. Export and Import Prices and Terms of Trade

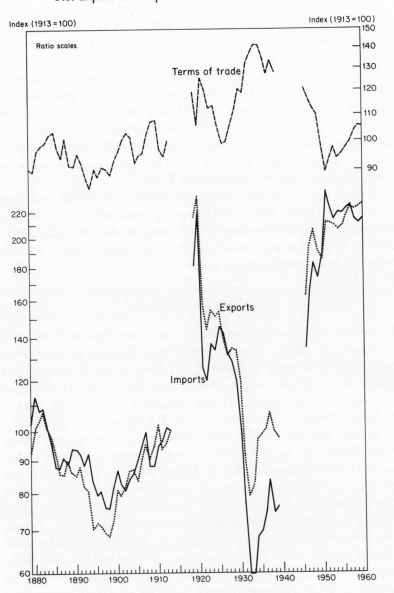

Source: Appendix Tables A-1, A-3, and H-1.

brought import prices in twelve years from the post-World War I peaks to a level substantially below that of the trough in the late 1890's. Even a sharp recovery after 1933 did not carry them much above the prewar low. For exports, the decline in prices was slightly less severe, but they too fell below the prewar average. The recovery in the late 1930's brought export prices back to the level of the higher prewar years.

The end of World War II again found prices far above the interwar levels. In contrast to the earlier experience, it was import prices that had risen the most. In even stronger contrast, the postwar rise was followed, not by a collapse, but by further price increases. These tapered off somewhat or, in the case of imports, were mildly reversed after 1951. The postwar peaks barely surpassed those of the early 1920's but were far above any of the longer-lasting prewar or interwar price levels.

A distinct shift took place also in the relative volatility of export and import prices. Before World War I, export prices underwent sharper fluctuations than imports, reaching a lower trough in the 1890's particularly. After 1918 prices of imports suffered the more violent changes, and continued to do so into the postwar period.

U.S. TERMS OF TRADE

Export and import prices determine the net barter terms of trade which have been the subject of much acrimonious discussion in the postwar period (the controversy is discussed in a later section of this chapter). Despite the suspicion, current since the late 1930's, that the developed countries have experienced very large long-term gains in their terms of trade, little trend can be discerned in the U.S. figures. This is illustrated by the fact that the 1949-58 terms of trade were close to most prewar levels. The average for all the postwar years, however, was slightly higher, and the 1959-60 indexes matched the highest prewar figures. But all except the first few postwar figures are far below the heights reached in the interwar period.

Much more definite changes have taken place in the pattern of short-term movements. The prewar fluctuations in the terms of trade roughly followed those of prices. After rising at first, they fell to a low point in the 1890's (earlier than prices), and then rose again. During World War I, the terms-of-trade index increased sharply, as did the price level; but there the resemblance ended. During both the interwar period and the postwar years, the movement in the terms of trade was closer to being inverse than conforming to the price level, particularly during sharp price fluctuations.

This switch in behavior is a reflection of the fact, mentioned above, that export prices fluctuated more violently than import prices before World War I, and import prices more sharply thereafter.

The greatest fluctuations in the terms-of-trade index took place during the interwar and early postwar period. In several instances, the index covered the whole span of prewar changes within two or three years.

The interwar period was the most "favorable" to the United States in the eighty years considered here. In the mid-1930's, the terms of trade briefly reached 40 per cent above the 1913 level and more than 50 per cent above the trough levels of the 1890's, but these levels were never reached again after World War II.

During World War II and for several years after, the terms of trade shifted sharply against the United States, falling briefly during the Korean War to the level of the 1890's before rising moderately again.

COMPARISON OF NBER AND KREPS INDEXES

The only previously available series on prewar United States foreign trade prices were those published by Kreps in 1926.[1] Our indexes differ substantially from his, as can be seen in Table 1.[2]

For export prices, the two series agree in showing virtually no change between 1880 and 1913. However, the Kreps index shows a rise more than double that of the NBER index between the 1880's as a whole and 1913. In addition, the Kreps index undergoes sharper fluctuations, particularly before 1900, and falls more steeply to the trough in the late 1890's.

TABLE 1
COMPARISON OF KREPS AND NBER INDEXES OF U.S. EXPORT AND
IMPORT PRICES AND TERMS OF TRADE
(1913 = 100)

	Fiscal Year 1880		Average of Fiscal Years 1880–89	
	Kreps	NBER	Kreps	NBER
Exports	100.0	99.7	91.3	95.9
Imports	131.7	109.3	108.9	98.1
Terms of Trade (E/I)	75.9	91.2	84.2	98.0

SOURCE: Appendix Tables G–1 and H–2.

[1] Theodore J. Kreps, "Export and Import Prices in the United States and the Terms of International Trade, 1880–1914," *Quarterly Journal of Economics*, August 1926, p. 708.

[2] A more detailed comparison of the two sets of indexes and some explanations of the discrepancies between them appear in Chapter 6.

11

The import price series differ even more radically; the Kreps index exhibits not only wider fluctuations but a much stronger downward trend. It declines by 24 per cent between 1880 and 1913, as compared with 8 per cent for the NBER series; and by 8 per cent from 1880-89 to 1913, when our series actually rises slightly.

These differences in opposite directions for export and import prices make the two terms-of-trade indexes diverge even more widely. Kreps shows a 32 per cent improvement in U.S. terms of trade from 1880 to 1913 and 19 per cent from the decade of the 1880's to 1913. The corresponding increases in the NBER index were 9 per cent and 2 per cent.

If we stretch this comparison, perhaps recklessly, to the 1950's, the Kreps indexes, linked to those of the Commerce Department suggest an improvement in the U.S. net barter terms of trade of about 15 per cent since the 1880's. Our indexes indicate virtually no change.

International Comparisons of Terms of Trade

TERMS OF TRADE OF INDUSTRIAL COUNTRIES

The NBER export and import price indexes for the United States provide new evidence in the controversy over long-run trends in the terms of trade. There are really two questions at issue, and an answer to one does not, as is sometimes assumed, necessarily provide a key to the other.

(1) Have long-run trends in the terms of trade been favorable to developed or industrialized countries[3] and by inference, unfavorable to underdeveloped countries?

(2) Have the terms of trade moved in favor of manufactured goods as compared to primary products? We attempt to develop some evidence on the first question here, and on the second in the next section, but much of the evidence is applicable to both questions.

There is a widely-held belief that the terms of trade have moved in favor of industrialized countries in the long run.[4] It is, therefore, of some interest to review the existing data and to observe the effect of introducing the new U.S. indexes.

One set of comparisons was made by K. Martin and F. G. Thackeray

---

[3] The terms are not, of course, interchangeable; an agricultural country could well be developed. Most of the comparisons have referred to countries which were both developed and industrialized.

[4] See, for example, United Nations, *Relative Prices of Exports and Imports of Under-Developed Countries,* (New York, 1949), pp. 21–23, where U.K. data are offered as evidence.

in 1948.[5] Of the three industrial nations for which they presented prewar data, Germany showed a decline in the terms of trade and the U.S. and U.K. a rise. The U.S. figures, however, were derived from Kreps' data. A substitution of the NBER indexes would put the U.S. in an intermediate position and shift the results toward a finding that no substantial change had taken place in the terms of trade of industrial countries between 1879 and 1913.[6]

For the interwar period, Martin and Thackeray show improved terms of trade for the U.S., the U.K., and Germany, and a deterioration only for Japan. But the final year of their study was 1938, almost the peak for terms of trade of industrialized countries. Extension of these data to 1960 would wipe out all the gains since 1920 for the U.S. and the U.K. and all since 1925 (the first year shown) for Germany. The U.K. terms of trade would remain, however, considerably above the 1913 level.[7]

Kindleberger's data showed that the improvement in U.K. terms of trade, from which the deterioration in underdeveloped countries' terms of trade had been inferred, was not characteristic of the rest of industrial Europe. For both 1870-1913 and 1870-1952, U.K. terms of trade improved while those of industrial Europe as a whole (including the U.K.) declined.[8] The implication is that there was a considerably larger decline in the terms of trade of continental industrial Europe (CIE).[9]

A positive relationship between stage of development and terms of trade does, however, emerge from other features of Kindleberger's data. The more developed countries within industrial Europe, such as Belgium, Sweden, and Switzerland, improved their long-run terms of trade by comparison with the less developed members of that group, France and Italy.

Kindleberger further found that, in its trade with industrial Europe, the area he calls "all other countries"[10] suffered a major deterioration in terms of trade, by as much as one-quarter between 1872 and 1952. This was the most unfavorable experience among all the areas he distinguished.[11]

[5] Bulletin of the Oxford Institute of Statistics, Vol. 10, No. 11, November 1948, pp. 373–398.
[6] Martin and Thackeray classify the United States as a primary producer before 1900 (Ibid., p. 374). It is true that the United States was at that time an exporter primarily of agricultural products, but it was already a developed, industrial country in terms of the distribution of the labor force or of income originating by sector.
[7] These statements are based on our data for the U.S. and on indexes for European countries from Charles P. Kindleberger, The Terms of Trade: A European Case Study, New York, 1956.
[8] Ibid., pp. 53–57.
[9] Industrial Europe excluding the United Kingdom.
[10] Mostly made up of underdeveloped countries but also including Japan.
[11] Kindleberger, "The Terms of Trade and Economic Development," in Problems in International Economics, Special Conference 9, New York, NBER, 1958.

13

COMPARISONS OF TERMS OF TRADE : U.S. AND OTHER COUNTRIES

Two features stand out in the comparison of U.S. terms of trade with those of the U.K. and with our crude estimates for "Continental Industrial Europe" (CIE) in Chart 2. One is that British terms of trade increased considerably relative to the other two over the period for which they can be compared. The other is that the behaviour of U.S. terms of trade,

CHART 2
Terms of Trade of U.S., U.K., and Industrial Europe

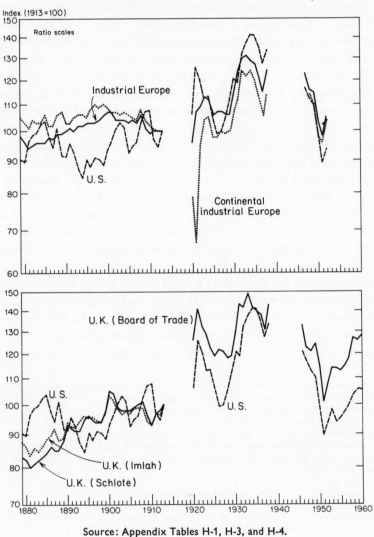

Source: Appendix Tables H-1, H-3, and H-4.

14

independent of or even inverse to that of Europe before 1920, became quite similar after that date.

Over the whole time span, as was pointed out earlier in this chapter, U.S. terms of trade did not change substantially. Those of industrial Europe rose somewhat, but most or all of this increase disappears if we make a very crude adjustment to remove the U.K. The reason for this effect is clear (see lower half of Chart 2): British terms of trade rose substantially from 1879 to the end of World War II. From the 1880's to the 1950's they gained by over 37 per cent according to Schlote's index for the period up to 1913—slightly less if Imlah's data are used.[12] The largest gains in the U.K. index, relative to CIE and the U.S., came in the prewar period and during World War I. The end of the war found U.K. terms of trade 20 per cent higher than in 1913, and those of CIE, 20 per cent lower.[13]

In the short-run behavior of U.S. terms of trade, a sharp shift may be noted. In the prewar years, as was pointed out earlier in this chapter, they moved with prices and were roughly inverse to the terms of trade of the U.K. and CIE. They reached a peak in the 1880's (but later than the trough in the other series) and a trough in the 1890's (earlier than the peak in the others). After World War I, when U.S. terms of trade became inverse to price changes, they conformed well to both British and CIE terms of trade. It might be said that the trade pattern matured, developing from one that is characteristic of a primary goods exporter to one characteristic of a nation exporting manufactured products.

The terms of trade may be resolved into export and import price components which are shown in Chart 3. After 1913, the rise in U.K. trade terms in relation to those of the U.S. is seen to be mainly on the export side, where American prices fell by 20 per cent relative to British prices. For the prewar period, there are two explanations for the behavior of U.K. terms of trade. In Schlote's estimates, most of the change relative to the U.S. (and to CIE as well) took place on the export side of the account; U.S. export prices fell by roughly 15 per cent relative to British prices between the 1880's and 1913. Imlah, on the other hand, finds U.K. export prices keeping pace with those of the U.S. over the same periods, and rising only slightly by comparison with CIE.

[12] Werner Schlote, *British Overseas Trade from 1700 to the 1880's*, Oxford, 1952, and Albert H. Imlah, *Economic Elements in the Pax Britannica*, Cambridge, Mass., 1958.

[13] There are some peculiarities in the CIE index in the first few years after World War I. Germany does not appear to be included in 1920 and then apparently enters at very low export-price and terms-of-trade levels in 1921 and 1922. See Kindleberger, *Terms of Trade*, pp. 13 and 23.

CHART 3

Ratio of U.S. Export and Import Prices to Those of the U.K. and Continental Industrial Europe
(1913 ratio = 100)

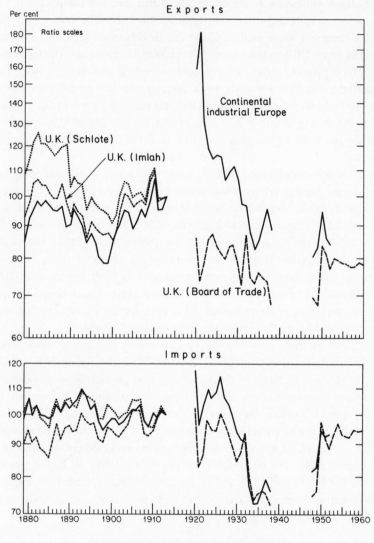

Source: Appendix Tables H-5 through H-8.

For imports, Schlote's estimates show the U.K.'s prices moving with those of both the U.S. and CIE, while Imlah's data show them falling relative to both by about 6 per cent. Both authors agree, however, in finding considerable improvement in U.K. terms of trade—Schlote, a somewhat greater one.

If U.S. prices are compared with those of CIE, they show a fall in both exports and imports with, perhaps, a slight relative decline in U.S. terms of trade.

To summarize, among the three industrialized areas compared, only one —the U.K.—showed evidence of substantial gains in its terms of trade. Neither our new indexes for the U.S. nor Kindleberger's data for continental industrial Europe confirm the belief that industrial countries as a whole have enjoyed large improvements in their trade terms since the 1870's or 1880's. The experience of the U.K. cannot be taken as typical of developed countries.[14]

Prices of Primary and Manufactured Products

OTHER STUDIES

The conviction has been widespread in the last twenty years that, compared to prices of manufactures, primary product prices inexorably decline in the long run and that they have, in fact, declined by a substantial amount since the 1870's or 1880's. This idea has become widely accepted despite its contradiction of the classical belief, dating back at least to Robert Torrens, that "the exchange value of manufactured articles, compared with the products of agriculture and of mines, have, as population and industry advance, a certain and decided tendency to fall."[15]

It was noted, during the British debate over the terms of trade in the 1920's, that the operation of this "law" seemed to have been suspended at

[14] Robert E. Baldwin in "Secular Movements in the Terms of Trade," *American Economic Review*, No. 2, May 1955 (Papers and Proceedings), suggests that differences in the type of index number used are sources of bias or of divergent interpretations. During the period covered by the NBER indexes, however, the U.S. terms of trade calculated from Laspeyres indexes diverged greatly from those calculated from Paasche indexes only during World War I. The difference between them widened from 2.5 in 1879 to 4.7 in 1923 (1913 as 100).

[15] John Stuart Mill, *Principles of Political Economy*, New York, 1909, Vol. II, Book IV, Chapter 2, p. 282.

The history of the debate over this proposition is reviewed extensively by Walt W. Rostow in *The Process of Economic Growth*, New York, 1952, pp. 173 and 182–192, and by J. M. Letiche, "The Relevance of Classical and Contemporary Theories of Growth to Economic Development," *American Economic Review*, May 1959.

various times, such as during the 1890's. But the fundamental tendency toward declining relative prices of manufactures was challenged only to the point of suggesting that agricultural productivity might possibly keep up with that of manufactures indefinitely. The participants in the argument generally assumed that relative productivity trends were the key to price trends.

It was Folke Hilgerdt who first turned the classical proposition upside down. He argued that, in the sixty years before 1938, primary product prices had fallen relative to prices of manufactures and that "the general trend of the relative movements . . . of the prices of these two classes of goods can scarcely be doubted."[16] The evidence for this contention consisted of League of Nations indexes for primary product and manufactured goods prices.[17] These, for the period before 1929 when most of the apparent fall in the relative prices of primary goods took place, rested entirely on two indexes : one, a combination of Schlote's indexes for British exports and imports of manufactures; the other, for primary products, the Sauerbeck wholesale price index.[18]

The theme of declining relative prices for primary products was taken up after the war in a series of United Nations documents.[19] None of these were primarily concerned with the prewar period; they treated the long-term deterioration in primary product prices as an established fact, relying on Hilgerdt and Schlote.

The view that primary producers have suffered from deteriorating terms of trade has been challenged, on both the facts and their interpretation. We shall not deal with the questions of interpretation except in discussing U.S. productivity trends in the next section of this chapter. Haberler, Viner, and Baldwin have pointed to the likelihood that price indexes of manufactures are biased upward because of the neglect of

[16] League of Nations, *Industrialization and Foreign Trade*, 1945, p. 16. It is ironic that, despite the classical tradition on this question, the only opposing view that Hilgerdt mentioned was that of the protectionist theorist, Manoilesco.

[17] *Ibid.*, p. 157.

[18] *Ibid.*, p. 154. The Schlote indexes appear in *British Overseas Trade.*

[19] For example, *Relative Prices of Exports and Imports of Underdeveloped Countries*, 1949, pp. 21–24, and several publications of the Economic Commission for Latin America, particularly *The Economic Development of Latin America and its Principal Problems* [by Raul Prebisch], 1950, pp. 8–10.

[20] Jacob Viner, *International Trade and Economic Development*, Glencoe, Ill., 1952, p. 143; Robert E. Baldwin, "Secular Movements in the Terms of Trade," *American Economic Review*, No. 2, May 1955 (Papers and Proceedings); Gottfried Haberler, "Introduction," in *Problems in International Economics*, pp. 73–81; and *International Trade and Economic Development*, Cairo, National Bank of Egypt, Fiftieth Anniversary Commemoration Lectures, 1959.

quality changes and underrepresentation of new commodities.[20] The same authors have made the additional point that one cannot, by simply inverting a country's terms of trade, derive the terms of trade for its partners. When exports are reported in trade statistics on an f.o.b. basis (excluding, among other things, freight costs) and imports are reported c.i.f. (including freight costs), as is the case with the U.K., it is possible for the terms of trade, measured in home prices, to improve for both countries simultaneously. The necessary condition for such an outcome is a fall in shipping costs relative to prices; this does seem to have occurred during the nineteenth century.[21]

We have already mentioned the likelihood that U.K. export prices and terms of trade, particularly in Schlote's data, were biased upward as a measure of the experience of industrial nations generally. Kindleberger[22] found no clear trend in the terms of trade of primary products vs. manufactures and suggested that the large country and product dispersion in the price indexes made the question almost meaningless.

A recent study by Theodore Morgan,[23] which examined prices of manufactured and agricultural products in seven countries, concluded that there was great diversity of experience but no evidence of declining relative prices for agricultural commodities.

From a review of Kindleberger's data, combined with U.S. price indexes for the period since 1913, Sarah S. Montgomery found signs of improvement rather than deterioration in world terms of trade for primary products.[24] This was especially the case when they were measured in terms of prices within primary producing countries. The decline in freight rates relative to commodity prices tended to make the price relationships in the industrial countries (where imports were valued c.i.f.) appear less favorable to the primary producers than they really were. In other words, at least part of the decline in relative prices of primary product imports represented a fall in transport costs rather than a decline in the return to the primary producer.

[21] See P. T. Ellsworth, "The Terms of Trade Between Primary Producing and Industrial Countries," *Inter-American Economic Affairs*, Vol. X, Summer 1956. Data on freight rates appear in Douglass North, "Ocean Freight Rates and Economic Development," *Journal of Economic History*, Dec. 1958, and in Sarah S. Montgomery, "The Terms of Trade of Primary Products and Manufactured Goods in International Trade, 1870–1952," unpublished Ph. D. dissertation, University of Wisconsin, 1960.

[22] *Terms of Trade*, p. 263, and "The Terms of Trade and Economic Development," pp. 73–81.

[23] "The Long-Run Terms of Trade Between Agriculture and Manufacturing," *Economic Development and Cultural Change*, October 1959.

[24] "The Terms of Trade of Primary Products."

EVIDENCE FROM NBER DATA

The NBER export and import price indexes may be viewed as a new set of observations bearing on the relative prices of manufactured and agricultural or primary products entering into international trade. Four measures of this relationship are described in Chart 4 and Appendix Table H-9.

The clearest trends relate to U.S. agricultural exports. Between the 1880's and the 1950's, the purchasing power of manufactured imports (foreign manufactures) over American exports of farm products fell by 20 per cent or more, mostly between the middle 1890's and the 1920's. Since then there has been no clear secular trend. Within U.S. exports, the change has been more violent : the price of manufactured products declined by almost half, in comparison with agricultural products. Here too, the largest drop came after 1894; another large fall during World War II was only partially reversed afterward.

Although the purchasing power of U.S. manufactured exports over agricultural imports rose during the 1930's to heights 60 to 90 per cent above 1879 or 1913, it has since declined to the point where no definite trend can be identified. The 1950's as a whole show some deterioration compared with the 1880's and 1913—in fact, with the whole prewar period. But the levels of the ratio for 1879-81, 1913, and 1958-60 are almost identical, and the verdict must be—probably no change, possibly a slight decline.

Only within imports do manufactured goods prices exhibit a relative gain. Manufactures imported into the U.S. increased in price by about 25 per cent between the 1880's and the 1950's, compared with foreign agricultural products. The gain took the form of a substantial increase before World War I followed by a great jump during the war and in the 1930's and then a retreat to the level of the 1920's.

Two price relationships are implied, but not stated, in these indexes. One was a great decline in the ratio of export to import prices of manufactured goods (from 1.24 in the 1880's to .78 in the 1950's);[25] the other was a large increase in the ratio of export to import prices among agricultural products—from .79 in the 1880-89 decade to 1.25 in 1950-59.

Not all primary products are agricultural, and the proportion which is has undoubtedly fallen over the last eighty years within both exports and imports. For the years through 1923, in addition to the index for finished manufactures, we have an NBER index for "all commodities other than manufactures"—a broad definition of primary products. But for the later

[25] From 1951 to 1959, however, there was a steady rise, pausing only in 1954.

CHART 4
Ratio of Manufactured to Agricultural Product Prices
(1913 ratio = 100)

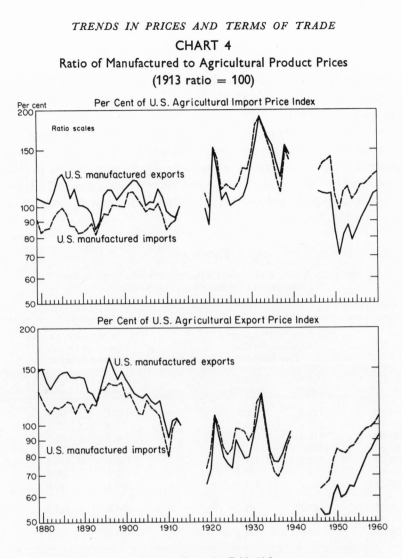

Source: Appendix Table H-9.

years, there is no similar index available. The direction of change in the ratio of manufactured to primary product prices can be calculated, however, by comparing manufactured to total export and import prices; the relation to total primary product prices would always be in the same direction, but stronger.

This comparison is made, using only prewar and postwar data, in Table 2. On the export side, the relation with agriculture is confirmed. U.S. export prices for manufactures fell by more than one quarter with

21

respect to both total export and total import prices, and thus even further with respect to primary prices.

For manufactured imports, however, prices rose by about 15 per cent compared with total prices on both sides of the trade account between the 1880's and the 1950's.

Until 1913, the comparison of manufactures with total trade confirmed the results of the comparison with agricultural product prices almost exactly. Manufactured exports fell substantially in price relative to total exports and imports, while manufactured imports hardly changed relative to total U.S. exports and rose very slightly in price only by comparison with total U.S. imports.

TABLE 2

RELATION BETWEEN MANUFACTURED PRODUCT AND TOTAL EXPORT
AND IMPORT PRICES, FIVE YEAR AVERAGES
(1913 = 100)

	Price Index for Manufactured Exports as Per Cent of Price Index for:		Price Index for Manufactured Imports as Per Cent of Price Index for:	
	Total Exports	Total Imports	Total Exports	Total Imports
1879–83	122.8	116.6	102.1	96.9
1884–88	125.4	125.2	99.4	99.2
1889–93	116.4	106.7	102.0	93.5
1894–98	125.7	111.5	114.2	101.4
1899–03	118.9	114.6	108.1	104.3
1904–08	110.7	107.7	102.8	100.0
1909–13	100.7	101.9	94.4	95.6
1949–53	87.7	85.2	116.8	113.5
1954–58	90.4	88.6	113.3	111.0
1959–60	95.9	101.3	109.9	116.1

SOURCE: Appendix Tables A–1 and A–3.

These shifts are investigated further by breaking down primary product prices into their four components : crude and manufactured foodstuffs, crude materials, and semimanufactures (Table 3). Manufactured exports and imports are compared with eight export and import primary classes. In relation to four of them, manufactured exports became a great deal cheaper—by almost 50 per cent. In the remaining four comparisons, three primary product classes rose somewhat in price relative to manufactured exports between the 1880's and the 1950's and one showed practically no

22

change. By 1959-60, however, all four had fallen slightly below the level of the 1880's. Manufactured imports rose in price relative to four groups and fell relative to the other four; the rises were generally stronger than the falls.

Before 1913, relative prices of manufactures clearly declined. U.S. exports of primary products rose in price compared to exports and imports of manufactures in all eight comparisons and U.S. imports of manufactures fell in price in five out of eight. Since 1913, manufactured imports have risen in price relative to seven out of eight primary product classes. Manufactured exports have gained compared to four primary classes and lost in comparison with four others.

What conclusion can now be reached regarding the terms of trade between primary and manufactured commodities? For the period before 1913, the weight of evidence indicates declining terms of trade for manufactured goods. This is particularly clear for American manufactures but also appears true for foreign manufactures. Over the whole eighty years the picture is not quite as clear. U.S. exports of manufactures declined in price relative to total primary imports and exports and to agricultural exports; compared with agricultural import prices, they changed very little, possibly falling slightly. Imported manufactures fell in price relative to U.S. agricultural exports but rose compared with total primary product imports and exports and agricultural imports.

In summary, comparisons with exports of U.S. manufactures strongly contradict the belief in declining relative primary product prices; comparisons with manufactures imported into the U.S. mildly confirm it. On the whole, there seem to be more instances of primary products relatively gaining in price than losing. The scatter around the relationships among totals is large, and supports Kindleberger's view that the primary vs. manufactured product distinction is not a particularly useful one for the analysis of changes in terms of trade.

We have used the terms "favorable change" or "favorable direction" frequently as a synonym for a rise in prices. From the cases mentioned, however, it should be clear that rising prices were often not really favorable to the producers concerned. Some instances clearly represented producers who were losing their world markets, perhaps because their productivity was lagging behind that of industries or countries with "unfavorable" changes in prices or terms of trade. Some evidence on the effect of productivity movements is discussed in the next section of this chapter, and Chapter 2 deals further with the interrelationships of price and quantity change.

TABLE 3

RELATION OF MANUFACTURED TO PRIMARY PRODUCT PRICES, BY
ECONOMIC CLASS, 5-YEAR AVERAGES

	Manufactured Products Price Index as % of Price Index For:			
	Crude Foodstuffs	Manufactured Foodstuffs	Crude Materials	Semi-Manufactures
U.S. Exports of Manufactures and Imports of Primary Products				
1879–1883	113.1	82.4	124.3	148.5
1884–1888	113.1	105.0	131.7	153.9
1889–1893	82.2	82.2	124.6	133.1
1894–1898	92.6	97.1	123.5	138.8
1899–1903	139.8	102.4	112.2	118.7
1904–1908	131.9	96.5	103.0	108.9
1909–1913	108.5	89.4	97.7	107.6
1949–1953	48.4	92.5	112.7	82.4
1954–1958	46.9	99.1	125.9	82.4
1959–1960	65.5	108.7	138.0	94.0
U.S. Exports of Manufactures and Exports of Primary Products				
1879–1883	122.8	133.0	145.7	140.4
1884–1888	132.4	138.5	144.2	135.0
1889–1893	117.5	125.6	134.6	123.6
1894–1898	126.2	129.7	159.6	126.2
1899–1903	122.6	125.4	137.9	110.5
1904–1908	112.4	120.8	120.1	101.2
1909–1913	96.8	99.5	101.8	102.3
1949–1953	95.8	103.4	74.4	82.8
1954–1958	120.5	117.1	81.9	80.9
1959–1960	136.8	140.0	95.6	91.2
U.S. Imports of Manufactures and Exports of Primary Products				
1879–1883	102.1	110.5	121.1	116.7
1884–1888	104.9	109.8	114.3	107.0
1889–1893	102.9	110.0	117.9	108.3
1894–1898	114.7	117.9	145.1	114.6
1899–1903	111.6	114.1	125.5	100.5
1904–1908	104.4	112.2	111.6	94.0
1909–1913	90.8	93.3	95.5	95.9
1949–1953	127.5	137.7	99.1	110.3
1954–1958	151.0	146.8	102.7	101.4
1959–1960	156.7	160.4	109.5	104.5
U.S. Imports of Manufactures and Imports of Primary Products				
1879–1883	94.0	68.5	103.3	123.4
1884–1888	89.6	83.2	104.4	122.0
1889–1893	72.0	72.1	109.2	116.6
1894–1898	84.2	88.3	112.2	126.1
1899–1903	127.2	93.1	102.1	107.9
1904–1908	122.6	89.6	95.7	101.2
1909–1913	101.8	83.8	91.6	100.9
1949–1953	64.4	123.1	150.0	109.8
1954–1958	58.8	124.2	157.8	103.2
1959–1960	75.1	124.6	158.2	107.7

SOURCE: Appendix Tables A–1 and A–3.

24

Price and Productivity Changes

Great divergences among price trends for different classes of commodities are among the central facts of economic history. Upon the interpretation of these trends rest many of our explanations for the growth and decline of nations, classes, and industries, and for the enrichment of one class or nation and the impoverishment of another.

One such interpretation (often referred to as the Singer-Prebisch thesis)[26] is based on the belief, discussed earlier, that the terms of trade of primary products vis-à-vis manufactured goods have deteriorated over the long run,[27] and that these trends have led to a widening of the gap in real income between primary and manufactured goods producers.[28] Crucial to this conclusion is the conviction that productivity changes have not been responsible for the deterioration in primary products' terms of trade—that in fact, they have tended in the opposite direction.

A great deal of data on productivity by sectors in many countries would be required to investigate thoroughly the influence of productivity changes on international price relationships. We have made no attempt to collect such data, and much of the necessary information is probably not available. But the development and refinement of productivity measures for various sectors of the American economy offer opportunities for analysis of price changes within American exports. We have, as an experiment, examined the long-term decline in the prices of U.S. exports of manufactures relative to those of U.S. exports of agricultural products.[29] A comparison of available productivity data with the list of export indexes in Appendixes A to C would probably suggest other candidates for investigation.

[26] See, for example, H. W. Singer, "The Distribution of Gains Between Investing and Borrowing Countries," *American Economic Review*, May 1950, pp. 477–478, and *The Economic Development of Latin America*.

[27] An alternative version of the thesis emphasizes the terms of trade of underdeveloped countries vis-à-vis the more advanced countries, which is not necessarily the same question, as Kindleberger and Singer himself have pointed out. Singer later stated a preference for the second version, "my original emphasis was too much on primary commodities and their characteristics and not enough on underdeveloped countries and their characteristics." (Comment on Kindleberger's "Terms of Trade and Economic Development," p. 88).

[28] Just as it is crucial to arguments for agricultural price parity programs within the industrial countries which attempt to keep parity ratios constant over long periods of time.

[29] Our findings regarding price changes within U.S. exports would not necessarily apply, of course, to changes between export and import prices or within imports. But Singer, in the comment on Kindleberger's paper quoted above, hints they are related: "I gladly accept this shift in emphasis (from primary products to underdeveloped countries) even though it leaves the chronic troubles of the primary producers within the industrial countries to be explained" (*ibid*).

As can be inferred from the preceding section of this chapter, the net barter terms of trade for agricultural and manufactured exports[30] showed very different trends (Chart 5). The purchasing power of agricultural exports rose by about 50 per cent between the 1880's and the interwar period, fluctuated around the interwar level during the early 1950's, and then declined to roughly 30 per cent above the 1880's level. The purchasing power of manufactured exports over imports, on the other hand, fell by 15 to 20 per cent before World War I, climbed to a peak in 1932, and then declined again to a postwar average below that of 1913. Only in 1959-60 did it regain the 1913 level.

It would be wrong, of course, to read into these figures a decline in welfare for the producers of manufactured products (measured in terms of ability to purchase imports). For this we would wish to know, not the purchasing power of a unit of output, which we have measured, but purchasing power per unit of input. This is estimated as the product of the net barter terms-of-trade index and a productivity index. It represents, for each of the two sectors, Viner's "single factoral terms of trade."[31]

We calculated this measure from the NBER and Commerce export and import prices indexes and Kendrick's indexes of output per manhour and total factor productivity.[32] These last take account not only of manhours worked but also of capital employed and, in the case of manufacturing, of changes in the composition of the labor force.

The results of this computation (Chart 5) give a far different impression from that implied by the net barter terms of trade. In terms of inputs, the purchasing power of both agricultural and manufacturing factors of production increased greatly. In the 1950's, it was four to five times the initial level, measured by output per manhour, and three to four times as high, measuring by "total factor productivity." The growth of purchasing

---

[30] We refer here to the ratio of their prices to total import prices or, in other words, their purchasing power over imports in general.

[31] Jacob Viner, *Studies in the Theory of International Trade*, New York, 1937, pp. 558–559.

[32] John W. Kendrick, *Productivity Trends in the United States*, Princeton for NBER, 1961, Appendixes B and D. Many doubtful aspects of this computation spring to mind immediately. For one thing, manufacturing and agriculture, as industries, do not coincide with what we call manufactured and agricultural exports. The main culprit in this incomparability is the class of manufactured foodstuffs, most of which we class as agricultural even though part of their value has been added in manufacturing and they are included in the manufactured products productivity index. Their price behavior, however, was similar to that of crude foods.

Weighting is another problem. The appropriate productivity indexes for such a computation would have export rather than domestic weights. There are also differences in valuation; a good part of the value of many exports, as reported in our data, was added by the transportation industry as well as by others which intervene between the producer and the exporter.

CHART 5
Terms of Trade for Agricultural and Manufactured Products:
Ratios of Export Prices and Export Value per Unit of
Factor Input to Total Import Prices

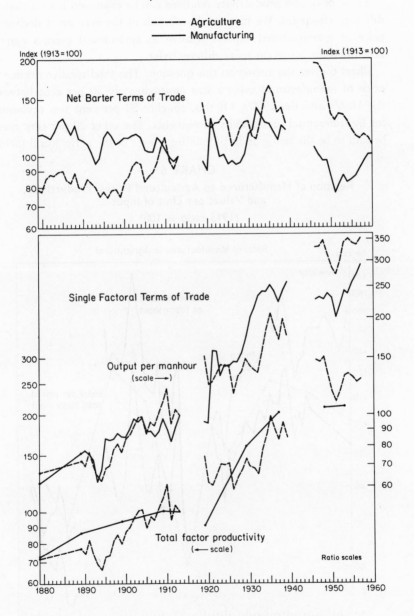

Source: Appendix Tables H-14, H-15, and H-16.

power over imports by manufacturing factors of production was quite similar to that for agricultural factors, although the latter retained some advantage.

These price and productivity relations can be examined from a slightly different viewpoint. We may ask how much of the very great decline in price of manufactured exports relative to agricultural exports can be accounted for by productivity differentials?

Chart 6 gives the answer to this question. The total relative decline in price of manufactured exports was approximately 50 per cent between the 1880's and the 1950's. Of this, roughly 30 per cent was accounted for by differential productivity movements. The other 20 per cent could be said to be the real gain in purchasing power of the agricultural factors

CHART 6

Relation of Manufactured to Agricultural Prices, Productivity, and Values per Unit of Input

(1913 ratio = 100)

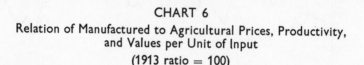

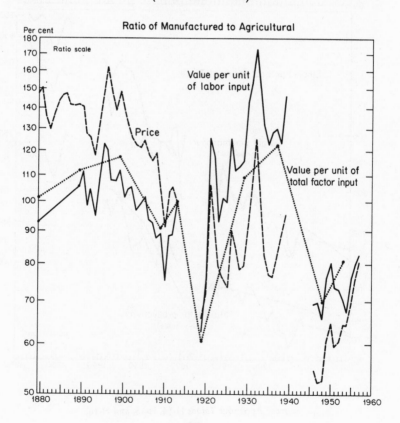

over the factors used in manufacturing production. If we compare the 1880's with 1913, all of the 25-30 per cent fall in purchasing power of manufactures can be explained by productivity differentials, measured by output per manhour; about two-thirds of it can be explained by using total factor productivity. Most of the unaccounted for long-term decline in the price ratio took place after 1913. This decline might represent the overstatement in agricultural productivity involved when only labor inputs are used, since there has been such a great increase in capital intensity in agriculture. To some extent, the price ratios may reflect the effects of U.S. price support policies in keeping up agricultural prices and terms of trade, or they may be affected by changes in inputs not covered by the indexes.

Since the end of World War II, there seems to have been some reversal

CHART 6 *(Concluded)*

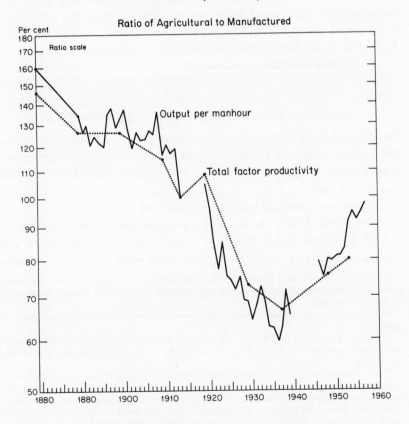

Ratio of Agricultural to Manufactured

Source: Appendix Tables H-9, H-17, and G-7.

29

of the long-term trends; manufactured goods prices have been gaining on agricultural export prices. This too is in line with productivity movements; output per manhour has recently been growing more rapidly in agriculture than in manufacturing.

We conclude then—to the extent that one can draw a conclusion from so crude a test—that differences in the rate of increase in productivity between manufacturing and agriculture, particularly before World War I, account for most of the long-run decline in price of manufactured goods relative to agricultural products within U.S. exports.[33]

The "ratios of value per unit of input"[34] in Chart 6 are informative in another respect. They reveal the severity of the depression of the 1930's for agriculture much more clearly than do the price ratios. The price ratio between agricultural and manufactured products turned sharply against agriculture after 1929, but it remained considerably more favorable than before 1900. The ratios of value per unit of input, however, were more unfavorable to agricultural factors in the 1930's than at any other time in the period covered here. They were far worse than in the depths of the depression of the 1890's, and the short-term swings were far larger than any conceivable estimate of the trend.[35]

Relation of Foreign Trade Prices to Domestic Prices

For the analysis of shifts in the flow of trade or the balance of payments, one is often interested not so much in absolute changes in export and import prices as in their relation to the domestic price level. In both exports and imports, a single large shift in this relationship occurred more than thirty years ago and has not been reversed.

Before World War I, the ratios of export and import prices to domestic prices[36] fluctuated within a narrow range (Chart 7). Both exports and imports exhibited a slight downward trend with respect to domestic

[33] Kendrick found (*ibid.*, Chapter 7) that productivity and price changes were highly correlated within manufacturing—productivity accounting for half or more of the variation in price movements.

[34] These ratios are, to some extent, analogous to Viner's "double factoral terms of trade."

[35] Singer has recently laid heavier stress on the importance of cyclical swings in prices and import earnings as compared to secular trends, in *Problems in International Economics*, pp. 85–86.

[36] For domestic prices, the implicit price index underlying GNP was used. Experiments were performed with variants, such as the index underlying the flow of goods to consumers plus gross producer durables, which, by virtue of its omission of services, might be considered more comparable to merchandise trade. The results were so similar to those using GNP that they have not been presented here. Some use is made of a variety of measures of domestic output, however, in Chapter 2.

prices, but at least part of the trend was a result of differences in index number construction.[37]

The first year of peace found export prices 10 per cent above their pre-war ratio to domestic prices, and import prices 10 per cent below. By the early 1930's, both sets of ratios had fallen about 35 per cent below the 1919 levels. Since then, neither exports nor imports have reached more than 80 per cent of the 1913 price ratio, except briefly, and both have hovered between 70 and 80 per cent through most of the postwar years.

CHART 7
Ratio of Export and Import Prices to Domestic Prices
(1913 ratio = 100)

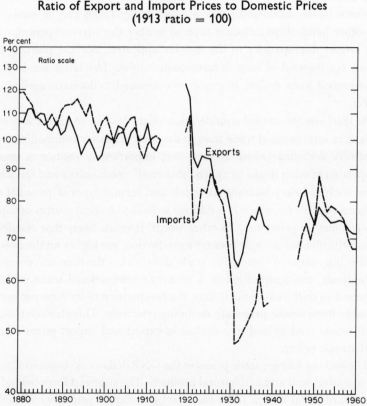

Source: Appendix Tables H-18 and H-19.

[37] The domestic price index is a Paasche price index, derived by dividing what is, in effect, a value index by a Laspeyres quantity index. The foreign trade indexes are Fisher "ideal" index numbers. If, for the period before World War I, we substituted our Paasche price indexes for the Fisher indexes, the downward relative trend in export prices would disappear and the relative decline in import prices would diminish considerably.

31

Neither export nor import prices have risen far enough to approach even the lowest points in their prewar relations to the domestic price level.

This decline in foreign trade prices could be explained in two ways. It is conceivable that there was considerable divergence between home and export or import prices for individual commodities. Alternatively, commodities that have fallen relatively in price might have greater importance in international trade than in the domestic economy.

The first explanation would be contrary to theoretical expectations regarding competitive markets. Furthermore, our experiments with prewar data (reported in Chapter 4) suggested that export and import prices conform closely to domestic prices where comparisons can be made. On the other hand, these measures covered neither the interwar period, when the largest discrepancies in the indexes appeared, nor the postwar programs for disposal of surplus farm commodities. The latter are likely to have caused some decline in export as compared to domestic agricultural prices.

At least one theoretical consideration might lead us to expect a heavier weight in international trade than in domestic trade for commodities with relatively declining prices. Exports and imports may contain a smaller proportion of what might be called "sheltered" commodities and services — items such as heavy building materials and certain types of personal and business services for which it is difficult to shift to foreign sources of supply when domestic prices rise. In other words, it seems likely that elasticities of substitution, for a single country's production, are higher on the average within international commodity trade than within the domestic economy. As a result, the composition of a country's international trade could be expected to shift more quickly than the composition of its domestic output towards items whose prices are declining relatively. This characteristic by itself would tend to lead to a decline in export and import prices relative to domestic prices.

The ratio of foreign trade prices to the GNP deflator is shown in Chart 8 for manufactured and agricultural products. The strongest force behind the downward trend is seen to be manufactured export prices, which fell by half relative to the domestic price level. Both manufactured and agricultural import prices also declined relatively, while prices of agricultural exports underwent large short-term fluctuations with no distinct trend. Prices of agricultural exports have been declining in most of the peacetime years since 1913, but large jumps during the two World Wars canceled out the years of decline.

A further breakdown into economic classes for the prewar and postwar years (Table 4) reveals even more impressively the pervasiveness of the decline in foreign trade prices. Every class but one has fallen in price relative to domestic output by the 1950's, some by only a little, others by almost 50 per cent or more. The contrary behavior of imports of crude

CHART 8

Ratio of Manufactured and Agricultural
Export and Import Prices to GNP Deflator
(1913 ratio = 100)

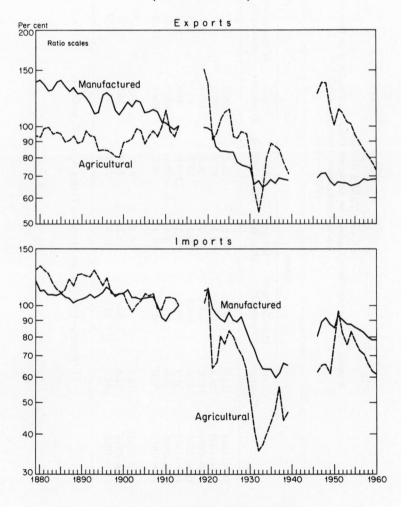

Source: Appendix Tables H-18 and H-19.

33

TABLE 4

EXPORT AND IMPORT PRICE INDEXES, BY ECONOMIC CLASS, AS PER CENT OF IMPLICIT PRICE
INDEX UNDERLYING DEFLATED GNP
(1913 = 100)

	Imports				Exports			
	Crude Foodstuffs	Manufactured Foodstuffs	Crude Materials	Semi-Manufactures	Crude Foodstuffs	Manufactured Foodstuffs	Crude Materials	Semi-Manufactures
1879–1883	118.4	162.4	107.7	90.2	109.0	100.7	91.9	95.3
1884–1888	118.4	127.5	101.7	87.0	101.2	96.7	92.9	99.2
1889–1893	147.2	147.1	97.0	90.8	103.0	96.3	89.9	97.9
1894–1898	131.0	124.9	98.3	87.4	96.1	93.6	76.0	96.2
1899–1903	85.3	116.5	106.3	100.6	97.3	95.1	86.5	108.0
1904–1908	85.4	116.7	109.4	103.4	100.2	93.2	93.7	111.3
1909–1913	92.8	112.7	103.1	93.6	104.1	101.2	98.9	98.5
1949–1953	138.4	72.4	59.4	81.2	69.9	64.7	89.9	80.8
1954–1958	142.8	67.6	53.2	81.3	55.6	57.2	81.8	82.8
1959–1960	104.5	63.0	49.6	72.9	50.1	48.9	71.7	75.1

SOURCE: Derived from Appendix Tables A–1, A–3, and G–8.

foodstuffs resulted from the great postwar increase in coffee prices. In 1959-60, however, even this class had fallen below the 1879-88 level.[38]

The substitution of Paasche price indexes for the Fisher indexes before 1913 would have had very little effect. It would have eliminated the slight rising trend of relative agricultural export prices and most, or all, of the very mild drop in relative prices of manufactured imports.

The fact that the relative decline in foreign trade prices was concentrated in the 1920's and 1930's might argue for an explanation related to that period alone, rather than one involving more fundamental characteristics of foreign trade. But it is also possible that the concentration of the aggregate trend within a few years, rather than the trend itself, is the "accidental" feature of the series.

The behavior of prices for agricultural and manufactured products casts some light on the timing of the decline in the total index. Manufactured export prices fell quite consistently, relative to the domestic price level, from the 1880's to the 1930's, and then leveled off. Agricultural export prices rose slightly (in relative terms) before 1913. This rise canceled out in the total index most of the fall in manufactures prices, since agricultural exports were so much more important at that time. Agricultural export prices jumped more than 45 per cent during both World Wars and then fell. In the 1913-19 increase, agriculture was still important enough to carry the aggregate index with it. The sharp fall in aggregate prices after World War I was the result of price declines in both agricultural and manufactured products.

On the import side, both manufactured and agricultural products declined in price compared with the domestic index from the 1890's to the 1930's, and aggregate import prices declined with them. There was some recovery in both import price indexes following the 1930's, but a renewed decline began after the Korean War.

It would appear, then, that declining foreign trade prices were fairly widespread among commodity groups and over time, and that the main reversals of this decline, particularly for primary products, occurred in wartime.

In Chapter 2, this fall in export and import prices relative to the domestic price level is shown to be important in the analysis of the relations between the volume and value of trade and measures of domestic output.

[38] As in other cases mentioned earlier, the long-term decline in export and import prices may be exaggerated slightly by the difference in formula between foreign trade and domestic price indexes. Substitution of the Paasche indexes (Appendix A—Basic Tables) in Table 4 would have lowered the 1879–83 figures to approximately:

Imports of crude foodstuffs	109	Exports of crude foodstuffs	103
Imports of semimanufactures	86	Exports of manufactured foodstuffs	93

CHAPTER 2

Trends in Values and Quantities

THE foreign trade of the United States, like almost every other aspect of its economic life, has been characterized by persistent growth (Chart 9 shows the data since 1869). There were, it is true, periods of retardation and decline as well as sudden spurts and reversals that marked war and reconstruction periods. But the only major peacetime interruption of the climb was the great depression of the 1930's which cut into international trade even more deeply than into other areas of the economy. The interwar experience was unique in at least two respects. The severity of the decline in both export and import values and quantities had never been approached in peacetime, even in the depression of the 1890's. The failure to recover previous peak levels after ten or fifteen years was also unprecedented.

In the postwar years the amplitude of fluctuations and the length of recovery periods have returned to prewar levels.

Trends in the Ratio of Total Trade to Output

BACKGROUND OF THE PROBLEM

It has often been said that the economic development of a country reduces its dependence on foreign trade and that the spread of industrialization throughout the world tends to diminish the importance of international trade by reducing those differences in economic structure and skill which are the basis for profitable exchange.

Pervading this discussion has been the belief that international trade consists mainly of the exchange of manufactured goods from the developed countries for crude materials and foods produced by the undeveloped areas. The importance of international trade in the nineteenth century was therefore considered to be a temporary phenomenon. The eventual industrialization of the backward areas would result in the diversion of their export staples to domestic uses and in the replacement of imported by domestically produced manufactured goods.

This line of reasoning is related to classical theorizing regarding the future terms of trade between agricultural and manufactured products. The link between them is exemplified by a frequently quoted statement from Torrens to the effect that the price of crude products relative to manufactured goods would eventually rise within developing countries, as

36

it already had in the older countries, thus destroying the basis for the most profitable trade between them.[1] These predictions were echoed more than a century later by D. H. Robertson, who considered it evident that "we must learn to accomodate ourselves permanently to a smaller relative volume of international trade. . . ." The fact that "the scope for advantageous exchange between nations is narrowing" would not only diminish the relative volume of international trade but also encourage trade restrictions because the "narrowing of the gap of Comparative Advantage" would make the welfare loss from a reduction in imports less important compared to advantages in terms of, for example, stability.[2]

Similar pessimism about the future scope of international exchange had been expressed by German economists around the turn of the century, and for much the same reasons.[3] Sombart, for example, stated that over a period of fifty or hundred years, civilized nations had become less interconnected through trade relationships, and less involved in world markets. Actually his evidence—very dubious estimates for Germany in 1830 and 1895—indicated no more than an unchanging trade-income ratio.[4]

---

[1] "As the several nations of the world advance in wealth and population, the commercial intercourse between them must gradually become less important and beneficial. . . . The species of foreign trade which has the most powerful influence in raising profits and increasing wealth, is that which is carried on between an old country in which raw produce bears a high value in relation to wrought goods, and a new country where wrought goods possess a high exchangeable power with respect to raw produce. Now, as new countries advance in population the cultivation of inferior soils must increase the cost of raising raw produce, and the division of labor reduce the expense of working it up. Hence, in all new settlements, the increasing value of raw produce must gradually check its exportation, and the falling value of wrought goods progressively prevent their importation; until at length the commercial intercourse between nations shall be confined to those peculiar articles, in the production of which the immutable circumstances of soil and climate give one country a permanent advantage over another." Robert Torrens, *Essay on the Production of Wealth*, London, 1821, pp. 288–289.

[2] "A narrowing of the gap of Comparative Advantage will not only diminish the volume of advantageous foreign trade, but will tend to produce a state of affairs in which there is a relatively large volume of foreign trade trembling, as it were, on the margin of advantageousness, and liable to be blown to one side or the other of that margin by small changes in the wind of circumstance. If, having been for some time just outside the range of profitableness, it is suddenly blown just within that range, great dislocation and distress will be caused to those who have laid their plans on the expectation of its remaining outside that range; and at the same time the benefit conferred on the community as a whole will be relatively small." D. H. Robertson "The Future of International Trade," *Economic Journal*, March 1938, pp. 7–8.

[3] See Jacob Viner, "The Prospects for Foreign Trade in the Postwar World," *Transactions of the Manchester Statistical Society*, Annual Meeting, June 19, 1946, reprinted in Viner, *International Economics*, Glencoe, 1951, and in American Economic Association, *Readings in the Theory of International Trade*, 1949. These arguments are more extensively discussed in Albert O. Hirschman, *National Power and the Structure of Foreign Trade*, Berkeley, University of California Press, 1945.

[4] Werner Sombart, *Die Deutsche Volkswirtschaft im Neunzehten Jahrhundert*, 7th ed., Berlin, 1927.

CHART 9
Value and Quantity of U.S. Exports and Imports, 1869-1960

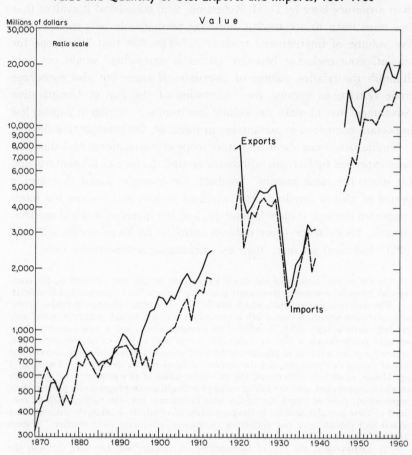

Millions of dollars   V a l u e

This line of argument has been attacked on several grounds. Viner attributed any fall in the importance of international trade since the 1870's to the effect of increased tariffs, import quotas, and other "deliberate obstacles to international trade" rather than to any "natural factors."[5] Other writers argued that the role of the "traditional" type of exchange—manufactured goods from industrial countries for foods and raw materials from undeveloped ones—had been exaggerated. They pointed to the importance of the exchange of agricultural products against other agricultural products and of manufactures against manufactures, or to the major importance of trade among industrial countries as compared to that between

[5] *International Economics*, pp. 316–317.

CHART 9 *(Concluded)*

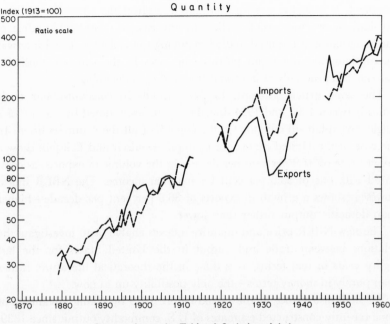

Source: Appendix Tables A-2, A-4, and A-6.

industrial and nonindustrial ones.[6] Eugene Staley presented national income and trade data (in current dollars) for several countries which showed little clear change in trade-income ratios before the 1930's.[7] Mainly interested in proving that there had been no absolute decline in trade, he accepted relative decline as a fact, attributing it to the shift in consumer demand from goods to services as income increases. But he may have been influenced in this by the data for the 1930's, the last period he covered.

In a recent article, Deutsch and Eckstein[8] reported that an increase in trade-output ratios during early stages of economic development, followed by a decrease in the later stages, has been a typical pattern. But their data for individual countries showed very diverse patterns. It is true that the

[6] For example, Hirschman, *National Power*, p. 146; League of Nations, *Industrialization and Foreign Trade* [by Folke Hilgerdt], New York, 1945; Eugene Staley, *World Economic Development*, Montreal, International Labor Office, 1945.

[7] *World Economic Development*, pp. 137–143.

[8] Karl W. Deutsch and Alexander Eckstein, "National Industrialization and the Declining Share of the International Economic Sector, 1890–1959," *World Politics*, January 1961.

latest years were not the highest of the whole period, but in several cases they were close to it. There was no rising period in the trade-output ratios for the U.S., and the rise for Germany rested on the virtually worthless Sombart figures mentioned earlier. In any case, a considerable effort of the imagination is required to discern among the violent war and interwar fluctuations and the rapid postwar increases in the ratio, a consistent pattern of a gradually rising trend followed by a declining one.

The same article attempts to assess trends in constant-dollar trade ratios between 1890 and 1954, but the results are vitiated by the use of a single (unexplained) deflator for the exports of all the countries listed. In the case of the United States, for example, Deutsch and Eckstein show a growth rate of 31.9 per cent per decade in the volume of exports, as compared with one of 33.8 per cent for national income. The NBER index, however, shows a growth in exports of 36.6 per cent per decade—higher than domestic output rather than lower.

The new NBER price and quantity indexes enable us to investigate the relations between trade and output in the United States for the last eighty years in real terms, as is done in the theoretical literature, rather than purely in money terms—the only possibility up to now.

We shall also glance at the period before 1879 by taking advantage of some recently constructed estimates of U.S. commodity output since 1839.

U.S. TRADE-OUTPUT RATIOS

When the export and import trade of the United States is compared with current-value gross national product or commodity output, the expansion that was so evident in Chart 9 vanishes completely. Instead, the data seem to confirm the pessimistic predictions about the course of world trade discussed earlier. Ratios of exports to GNP[9] (Table 5 and Chart 10), after fluctuating between 6 and 7 per cent during most years before World War I (slightly higher during the 1870's), dropped as low as half that

---

[9] Absolute levels of trade-output ratios cannot easily be translated into measures of the importance of foreign trade to the economy. There are differences in valuation, for example—foreign trade prices probably lying somewhere between the producers' prices of the Shaw data and the purchasers' prices of the Kuznets data. And there are difficulties in choosing a concept of output: for individual commodities and narrowly defined industries, gross output is the closest to exports and imports, but becomes inflated by duplication as these are combined into larger industries or total output. Exports and imports are free of duplication in the sense that a product exported in crude form will not be exported again as a manufactured item, although it is true that a product imported as a crude material may be exported in processed form. The use of an unduplicated total such as finished manufactures is an imperfect solution because many exports and imports are in a crude or semimanufactured state. Value added, another possible denominator, is an attribute of industries rather than commodities.

level during the 1930's and then recovered only to an average of about 5 per cent after World War II.

For imports the decline was even greater; the ratio to GNP in the 1870's ranged between 5½ and 9 per cent, averaging about 7 per cent. It fell in two sharp drops after 1871 and again after 1895, to a level of between 4½ and 5 per cent just prior to World War I. Another sharp drop after 1929 brought the ratio down to around 3 per cent, and the postwar recovery did not carry it much above 3½ per cent.

Values of international trade have been compared in the literature with several measures of output. Table 5 indicates that the conclusions drawn would not be substantially affected if any of three common measures were used. The ratios of trade to GNP (column 2) show the steepest decline, partly because GNP includes services, which were growing more rapidly than commodity output. From 1869-89 to 1930-39 the ratio of exports to GNP fell 47 per cent and that of imports 53 per cent.

TABLE 5

RATIOS OF EXPORTS AND IMPORTS TO DOMESTIC OUTPUT,
CURRENT DOLLARS

	Output of Finished Commodities and Construction Materials, Producers' Prices (Shaw)	GNP (Kuznets)	Flow of Commodities to Consumers plus Gross Producers' Durables, Purchasers' Prices (Kuznets)
	RATIO OF EXPORTS		
1869–1889	14.8[a]	7.0	11.0
1879–1889	15.3[b]	6.9	10.9
1889–1913	14.2	6.8	11.5
1922–1929	12.0	5.3	9.3
1930–1939	8.8	3.7	6.2
1948–1957		5.1	8.2
1958–1960		4.7	
	RATIO OF IMPORTS		
1869–1889	13.8[a]	6.6	10.3
1879–1889	13.6[b]	6.2	9.8
1889–1913	10.7	5.1	8.6
1922–1929	10.4	4.6	8.0
1930–1939	7.3	3.1	5.1
1948–1957		3.5	5.5
1958–1960		3.6	

SOURCES: See Table 6. Shaw data are total output through 1913 and "output destined for domestic consumption" thereafter. The 1869–89 ratio comparable to later years is 14.7.

[a] Exports and imports are average of 1869–89. Output data are average of 1869, 1879 and 1889.

[b] Exports and imports are average of 1879–89. Output data are average of 1879 and 1889.

41

CHART 10

Exports and Imports as a Percentage of Gross National Product,
Current and 1913 Dollars

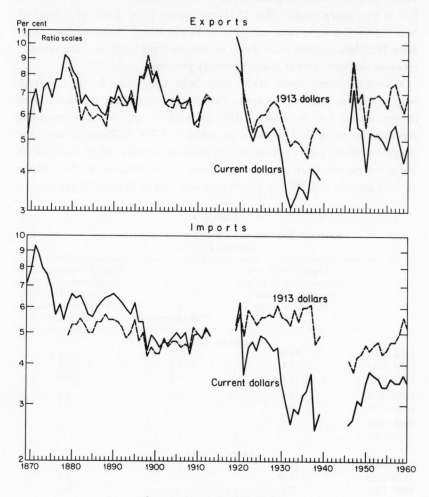

Source: Appendix Table G-11.

Ratios to the Kuznets commodity flow series (column 3) declined less rapidly—by 44 and 50 per cent during the same period—but by 1948-57 they had virtually caught up with the GNP percentages. Trade declined least when measured against the Shaw series, 41 per cent for exports and 47 per cent for imports from 1869-89 to 1930-39.

In the twenty years before the Civil War, export ratios (based on Gallman's recently published estimates of commodity output),[10] were somewhat lower on the average than in the rest of the years before World War I. Import ratios were, however, slightly higher before 1860 than after.

We may say, then, that there seems to have been a large and consistent decline, extending over a period of more than a century, in the ratio of the value of imports to the value of American domestic production. This decline has taken place mainly in several large jumps. Export ratios, comparatively stable before World War I, have been considerably lower ever since.[11]

When the effect of price change is removed, a very different picture emerges of the relation between the quantity of trade and output since 1879.[12] Export ratios in 1913 dollars were at approximately the same level during the 1920's as before World War I; they were cut sharply after 1929, but regained their earlier levels after World War II (Chart 10 and Table 6). The postwar ratios have been above those of the 1880's and approximately equal to those of the 1890-1913 period; no downward trend is evident.

The behavior of the import ratio, too, was strikingly different when constant-price figures were used. After some decline between the 1880's and the 1890's, the import ratio rose and maintained, during the 1920's, a higher level than in the whole prewar period (in sharp contrast to the current-dollar figures).[13] During the 1930's, when the current-dollar import

[10] Robert E. Gallman, "Commodity Output, 1839–1899," *Trends in the American Economy in the Nineteenth Century*, Studies in Income and Wealth, Vol. 24, Princeton University Press for NBER, 1960.

[11] The difference in trend between export and import ratios is a reflection of the shift in the international capital position of the United States.

[12] Lacking export and import price indexes for earlier years, we cannot study quantity relationships before 1879. Douglass C. North has recently published new export and import price indexes for the period 1790 to 1860 in *The Economic Growth of the United States, 1790–1860*, Englewood Cliffs, N.J., 1961. But the tasks of linking these to indexes for later years and filling the gap between 1860 and 1879 still remain. The existing indexes for these years, discussed in the Introduction, appear too weak to support any conclusions regarding long-term trends.

[13] This seems to contradict the general impression. For example, in Don D. Humphrey, *American Imports*, New York, 1955, a chart on p. 19 and a table in Appendix 1, p. 527, show a fall of 38 per cent between 1890 and 1919 in the ratio of imports to finished commodity output in constant dollars (Shaw's data). Our figures indicate virtually no change in this interval. The difference between the two findings arises mainly from Humphrey's use of the U.S. Wholesale Price Index to deflate imports. The Wholesale Price Index rose 147 per cent during these years, considerably more than the implicit index underlying his denominator (Shaw's series for finished commodity output destined for domestic consumption), which rose only 119 per cent. Our import price index, in contrast, rose less than the implicit deflator—only 85 per cent. Humphrey was aware of the possibility of bias in his deflator but apparently felt that the Kreps index (T. J. Kreps, "Import and Export Prices in the United States and the Terms of International Trade, 1880–1914," *Quarterly Journal of Economics*, August 1926), which was the only one available at the time he wrote, was overly dominated by coffee, sugar, and wool (see Humphrey, *American Imports*, note p. 20 and p. 99).

ratio fell to half the level of the 1880's, the quantity ratios were the highest since 1879. Only after 1937 did the constant-dollar import ratios drop sharply, falling by a third within five years, to the lowest levels in our record. After World War II, they began to climb sharply until, in the years 1958-60, they again reached a level similar to that of the 1880's.

Over the whole period, then, the only suggestions of a downward trend in the ratios of the quantity of trade to output were the low interwar export and postwar import ratios. Both now appear to have been temporary. It is clear, therefore, that the well-known decline in the value ratios has been largely a price phenomenon. It is a reflection of the fact, pointed out in Chapter 1, that both import and export prices have fallen, in the long run, compared with domestic prices.

Thus, although current value export ratios have followed roughly the pattern expected by Sombart (and others mentioned earlier), ratios for

TABLE 6

RATIO OF EXPORTS AND IMPORTS TO DOMESTIC OUTPUT,
1913 DOLLARS

	Output of Finished Commodities and Construction Materials, Producers' Prices (Shaw)	GNP (Kuznets)	Flow of Commodities to Consumers plus Gross Producers' Durables, Purchasers' Prices (Kuznets)
	RATIO OF EXPORTS		
1879–1889	14.3[a]	6.4	10.4
1889–1913	14.7	6.8	11.5
1922–1929	12.0	6.1	10.6
1930–1939	10.2	5.1	8.2
1948–1957		6.7	10.8
1958–1960		6.5	
	RATIO OF IMPORTS		
1879–1889	12.0[a]	5.3	8.7
1889–1913	10.5	4.8	8.2
1922–1929	11.2	5.7	9.9
1930–1939	11.1	5.5	8.9
1948–1957		4.5	7.2
1958–1960		5.3	

SOURCES: Kuznets data: Simon Kuznets, *Capital in the United States: Its Formation and Financing*, Princeton for NBER, 1961, and unpublished worksheets underlying that study. Shaw data: William H. Shaw, *Value of Commodity Output Since 1869*, New York, NBER, 1947, series entitled "Output destined for domestic consumption." Exports and imports are from Table A–6.

[a]Exports and imports are average of 1879-89. Output is average of 1879 and 1889.

current-dollar imports and constant-dollar exports and imports for the United States appear to contradict his thesis. It is in real terms that the pessimistic outlook for the future of international trade has usually been stated and theoretically justified.

Agricultural Trade and Output

BACKGROUND OF THE PREWAR AGRICULTURAL EXPORT TRADE

Despite increasing industrialization after the Civil War, agricultural exports were predominant in U.S. trade throughout the nineteenth century. For almost 100 years, until the early 1890's, agricultural products were 73 to 83 per cent of total exports,[14] and even at the beginning of World War I they still accounted for almost half. Thus, agricultural exports virtually kept pace with the rapid growth of industrial exports almost to the end of the nineteenth century. At that time, their share of total exports began a fifty-year decline, leveling off only during the last few years at a little over 20 per cent.

Since agricultural exports played so large a role, the development of American trade during this period must be studied against the background of shifting and interacting supply and demand conditions for agricultural production in the United States and her chief market—Europe. These supply and demand changes were interrelated; long-term shifts in supply conditions encouraged and yet depended on the changes in demand.

The changes on the demand side were such familiar economic events of the nineteenth century as the growth of cotton textile manufacturing, the urbanization and industrialization of Europe with the attendant growth of income and the decline of European agriculture.[15] The Eastern seaboard of the United States played the same role vis-à-vis the West that Europe played in relation to the United States as its population shifted from rural to urban areas and from agriculture into manufacturing.

On the supply side, the second half of the nineteenth century represented the climax in the development of American agriculture and the agricultural export trade. Farm output grew at a rapid and fairly constant rate throughout the nineteenth century,[16] but it slowed down at the

[14] *Foreign Commerce and Navigation of the United States,* 1902, p. 73.

[15] Some of these developments are summarized in Edwin G. Nourse, *American Agriculture and the European Market,* New York, 1924, pp. 8–42 and 239–276.

[16] Marvin W. Towne and Wayne D. Rasmussen, "Farm Gross Product and Gross Investment in the 19th Century," *Trends in the American Economy in the Nineteenth Century,* Studies in Income and Wealth, Vol. 24, Princeton University Press for NBER, 1960. Some of the constancy in the rate of growth may have been imparted by the estimating procedure.

beginning of the twentieth century and never regained its earlier rate.[17] Agricultural productivity and output per capita increased faster in the second half of the century than in the first; per capita output reached levels that were never attained again.[18]

The growth of farm output was associated with great expansions in the farming area of the United States. The land added to farms in the fifty years ending in 1900 was almost twice the 1850 acreage, and almost equaled that added in all other years. After 1900, growth in the farming area slowed considerably.[19]

The major increases in farm output, and particularly those in the major export products, involved not only expansions in the farming area but also large-scale migrations of production to new areas. In the first half of the century the major migration was that of cotton production from Georgia and South Carolina (the original producers and still responsible for more than half of the output in 1820), to Mississippi, Louisiana, Texas, and Arkansas, which accounted for most of the increase in output after the 1830's.[20]

The migration of grain and meat production was the outstanding feature of the second half of the century. In 1850 the North and South Atlantic states accounted for more than half the wheat and oats, almost half the cattle (other than dairy cattle) and over 30 per cent of corn output and swine. Only 14 per cent of the swine, 15 per cent of the cattle, and 12, 6, and 5 per cent of the corn, oats, and wheat, respectively, were accounted for by the states west of the Mississippi. By 1900 the share of the Atlantic states in all of these products had fallen to 10-13 per cent; west of the Mississippi it ranged from 48 per cent for oats to 65 per cent for wheat and 70 per cent for cattle.[21]

Accompanying the westward expansion of agriculture was the growth of railroad mileage, which more than doubled between the end of the Civil War and 1879, more than redoubled by 1899, but increased much more slowly thereafter.[22] With the forging of railroad connections both the eastern United States and Europe were brought economically closer to the

[17] Appendix Table G–9.

[18] Appendix Table G–6, and Towne and Rasmussen, "Farm Gross Product."

[19] U.S. Department of Agriculture, *Agricultural Statistics, 1957*, p. 520.

[20] U.S. Statistics Bureau, Treasury Department, "The Cotton Trade of the United States and the World's Cotton Supply and Trade," *Monthly Summary of Commerce and Finance of the U.S.*, March 1900, pp. 2545–2552.

[21] U.S. Census Office, *12th Census of the United States: 1900*, Vols. V and VI, and U.S. Bureau of the Census, *13th Census of the United States: 1910*, Vol. V.

[22] U.S. Bureau of the Census, *Historical Statistics of the United States*, 1949, pp. 200, 202.

West by falling freight rates. For example, rates for the shipment of wheat from Chicago to New York by lake and canal fell by more than 50 per cent between 1860 and 1879 and by another 50 per cent from 1879-1899; rail rates for the same product fell by 50 per cent between 1869 and 1879 and about 30 per cent more by 1899.[23] Ocean freight rates for American exports also fell drastically during the nineteenth century, particularly before 1850 and after 1870.[24]

With rapidly increasing production and falling prices and transportation costs, American grain and meat products invaded European markets. American wheat, for example, drove both German and Russian wheat from the English market during the 1860's and 1870's, and supplied more than half of British wheat imports to the end of the 1800's.[25] In a similar way American meat products captured the British market from European suppliers who had dominated it before the 1870's, although the newer exporting areas, such as Argentina and Australia, began to challenge the American position toward the end of the century.[26]

After the 1890's there was a sharp reversal in the agricultural situation. The expansion in the farming area slowed, and the increase of farm production, which had raced ahead of the growth of population in the 1870's and more than kept pace with it during the 1880's and 1890's, began to lag behind. The quantity of agricultural exports, which had multiplied several times since the Civil War, began to fall slightly, while agricultural prices recovered from their long post-Civil War decline and began to rise more rapidly than other prices. European countries turned to new sources of food : Canadian, Indian, and Australian wheat; Argentine beef; and Canadian and Danish bacon, for example, all began to supplant American products in the British market.

TRENDS IN U.S. EXPORTS AND OUTPUT OF AGRICULTURAL PRODUCTS

Values of U.S. agricultural exports after World War II were ten times those of the post-Civil War period and triple those of the years just before World War I (Chart 11). Only the depression of the 1930's reversed the

[23] U.S. Bureau of Statistics, Treasury Department, "The Grain Trade of the United States and the World's Wheat Supply and Trade," *Monthly Summary of Commerce and Finance of the U.S.*, January 1900, p. 1973.

[24] Douglass North, "Ocean Freight Rates and Economic Development, 1750–1913," *The Journal of Economic History*, December 1958.

[25] U.S. Bureau of Statistics, Treasury Department, *Monthly Summary of Commerce and Finance of the U.S.*, January 1900, p. 2058.

[26] U.S. Bureau of Statistics, Treasury Department, "The Provision Trade of the United States and the World's Provision Supply and Trade," *Monthly Summary of Commerce and Finance of the U.S.*, February 1900, pp. 2328–2336.

trend for any length of time, slashing export values to 40 per cent of those in the 1920's and reducing them below the average value of the decade before World War I. The advance in general was an uneven one, slowing during the 1880's and 1890's and accelerating during the two wars.

The quantity of agricultural exports showed no such growth. Its rapid increase until the late 1890's—much faster than the values—was followed

CHART 11
Value of U.S. Agricultural Exports, Current and 1913 Dollars

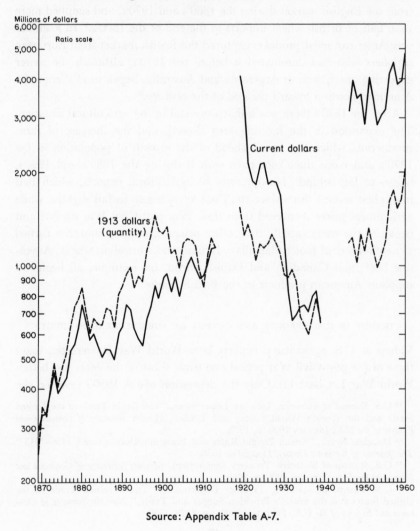

Source: Appendix Table A-7.

by a long period of stagnation. The levels just after World War II were no greater than those of the 1890's, more than fifty years earlier. Only recently have exports of agricultural products come to life again, growing, at least for a few years, at a rate reminiscent of the nineteenth century.

Because of this lack of growth over so many years, the quantity of agricultural exports declined relative to total national output. The extent of this fall is shown in Chart 12. Before 1900 agricultural exports were almost always above 5 per cent of deflated GNP—slightly higher in the 1870's than in the eighties and nineties. By the 1930's, a long, steady decline had carried them below $1\frac{1}{2}$ per cent of GNP. They have remained roughly at this level since that time. Data for current-value ratios, not shown in the chart, tell much the same story.

There are two possible explanations for this reduction in the importance of agricultural exports. It might have reflected the shifting of resources out of agriculture within the domestic economy, or it might have implied a shift within U.S. agriculture away from dependence on foreign markets and toward reliance on domestic consumption.

Over the period as a whole, as can be seen in Chart 12, the first factor was the crucial one. The decline in agriculture's share of gross national product is much steadier than, but roughly parallel to, the decline in the ratio of agricultural exports to GNP. This rough, long-run agreement is reflected in the fact that the ratio of agricultural exports to agricultural gross product shows no long-term trend.[27]

Despite the fact that the fall in agriculture's share of gross output explains the long-run fall in the ratio of agricultural exports to GNP, some very substantial shorter-term changes in the ratio remain to be accounted for. There is, in particular, the contrast between the steady decline in the domestic position of agriculture since 1869, and the failure of agriculture's share of exports, measured in constant or current dollars, to decline until the 1890's. This contrast reflects a considerable shift toward foreign markets for farm products; agricultural exports rose from about one-eighth of agricultural gross output just after the Civil War to a peak of roughly one-quarter at the end of the 1890's. After that, however, the

[27] This ratio is only a crude measure of the importance of export trade to farm income. On the one hand it tends to overstate the importance of exports because an agricultural product will have a higher value at the port of shipment than at the farm. Even if the product has not been processed, the export price includes value added by the transportation and, perhaps, the wholesale trade or service industries. Processed farm products contain value added in manufacturing as well.

On the other hand, the export ratio tends to understate the role of international trade because many products of agricultural origin, such as textiles and leather goods, drop out of the agricultural class between the farm and the port of export.

CHART 12
Relations of Agricultural Exports, Agricultural Gross Product, and GNP, 1913 Dollars

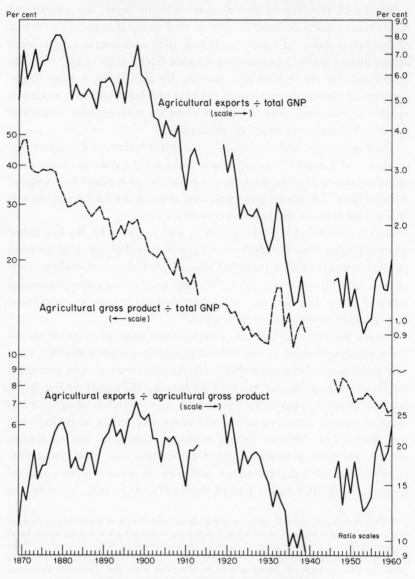

Source: Appendix Tables G-10, G-12, and G-14.

foreign share began to fall; following a brief rebound during World War I, it plummeted during the thirties to the lowest level since before 1869. World War II again lifted the ratio, which has continued to rise erratically toward the prewar levels.

The high ratio of exports to gross income within agriculture in the 1890's represented a peak not only for the post-Civil War years but apparently for the nineteenth century as a whole, judging from current-dollar data on agricultural production. A comparison of agricultural exports with the Towne-Rasmussen output series,[28] shows that the ratio rose from 11 and 12 per cent in 1800 and 1810 to 13 per cent or more in 1840 and 1850, almost 18 per cent in 1860, and between 20 and 23 per cent in 1880-1900.

The significance of the foreign market to American agriculture is only partially indicated by the level of these ratios, even apart from the ambiguities in them mentioned earlier. Exports were much more important for some crops than for others and were particularly important to individual products when their output was expanding most rapidly. It might be said that the existence of a broad foreign market made possible some of the great spurts in production by providing an incentive to produce goods which could have been sold on the domestic market only at much lower prices.

Cotton, which dominated U.S. agricultural exports before 1860, is the prime example of an export-dependent commodity. During the period of the most rapid growth in cotton production, between about 1815 and 1840, the export ratio rose to almost 80 per cent and remained near that mark. From 1870 to World War I output grew somewhat less rapidly than before the Civil War, and the export ratio fell to 65-70 per cent. Production leveled off after that, and the export ratio continued to fall, until in recent years it has rarely been above 40 per cent.

After supplying 80 per cent of the increase in agricultural exports between 1800 and 1860, cotton lost its leading role and provided only 14 per cent of the growth over the last forty years of the century. The main role then shifted to grain and meat products, which accounted for over 70 per cent of the increase between 1856-60 and 1895-99. Production data show that the growth in cotton output slackened after the middle of the century; the growth of output of food grains, feed grains, and livestock accelerated.[29] Per capita output of food and feed grains and livestock hardly changed from 1800 to the 1850's. After that all three rose until the 1890's and then declined until the beginning of World War I. Except for cotton,

[28] "Farm Gross Product."   [29] *Ibid.*, pp. 282, 292.

the peak in exports and export ratios coincided with that brief period when production ran ahead of the increase of population. The peak in cotton export ratios coincided with the most rapid increase in per capita output.

The story can be put in another way. The pattern of exports for the major food items can be at least roughly inferred from the output data by assuming constant per capita consumption. This stability in consumption, in the face of changing farm prices and growing real incomes, suggests that domestic price and income elasticities were low, as might be expected. These low elasticities imply that the absorptive ability of the foreign market was a prerequisite for the great expansion in American agriculture after the Civil War.[30]

Some further data on individual commodities emphasize the role of export trade in the expansion of agricultural output after the Civil War. Exports of pork products were never very high relative to farm income from hogs : less than 7 per cent in 1869-73, 21 per cent in 1899-1903, and 17 per cent in 1904-8. But of the increment in gross income between the first and last of these periods, exports supplied 57 per cent; and the increase in exports between the first and second periods was greater than the growth in gross income. Corn exports rose from a little over 10 per cent of production entering gross income in 1869-73 to over 20 per cent in 1899-1903, and the addition to exports was about 26 per cent of the addition to production. Exports were always important relative to wheat output—some 24 per cent in 1869-73 and 36 per cent in 1894-98. But they were still more important in the increment to production—almost 50 per cent in the same period.

For some commodities, foreign trade, then, quickly provided an extensive market which could only have been created much more slowly by the growth of the American economy itself. In this respect American development depended on the willingness of the older industrial nations, particularly the U.K., to permit their domestic resources to be shifted out of agriculture by the influx of cheaper products from the developing areas.

TRENDS IN U.S. AGRICULTURAL IMPORTS

Agricultural imports, like exports, have shown a large long-term increase in values (Chart 13). The short-run similarity between the two value series, however, is mainly imposed by large price movements such as those

---

[30] It should be noted that the crude assumption of constant per capita consumption will not serve at all for cotton. The export ratio fell after 1840 while output per capita was still increasing.

CHART 13

Value of U.S. Agricultural Imports, Current and 1913 Dollars

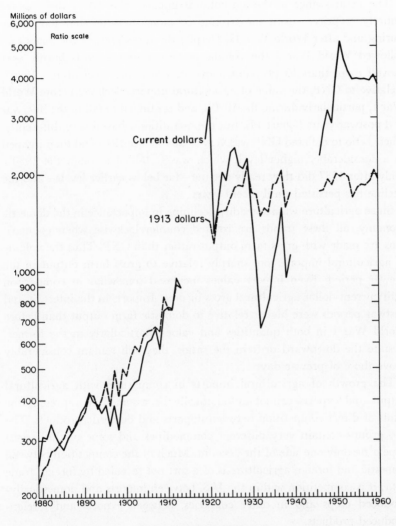

Source: Appendix Table A-7.

during the two world wars. Over the long run, agricultural exports rose much more than imports in price, but rose much less in quantity.

Agricultural imports in 1913 dollars increased rapidly, and at a remarkably steady rate, before World War I. They showed none of the sharp fluctuations that were present in exports and no retardation after the 1890's. The interwar period found them between 50 and 100 per cent above the prewar level, even during the 1930's,[31] and they remained in this range after World War II.

The great swings in the agricultural import value series were almost entirely in prices—even the tripling or more in value that took place during and after World War II. Despite the turbulence of the years that followed World War I the volume of agricultural imports hardly ever moved more than 15 per cent above or below the level of the 1920's. Relative to GNP, the value of agricultural imports declined before World War I, particularly during the 1890's, and continued to fall in the interwar and postwar years (Chart 14). But the quantities behaved very differently. Their ratio to deflated GNP was very steady before 1913 and then jumped to a considerably higher level, which was sustained through the 1930's. Only after 1937 did they really decline—far below earlier levels—and the decline has persisted until recent years.

Since agriculture was so steadily declining in importance in the domestic economy, all these trends are rotated counterclockwise when comparisons are made with gross farm output rather than GNP. Thus the volume of agricultural imports rose sharply relative to gross farm output in the prewar period. Even import values increased somewhat in comparison with current-dollar agricultural gross income. Imports in the interwar and postwar periods were higher relative to domestic farm output than before World War I in both quantities and values, particularly in the former. Despite the downward drift in the ratios, they still remain considerably above those of prewar days.

The growth of agricultural imports in comparison with agricultural output and exports cannot automatically be assumed to represent the result of direct competition between imports and domestic products. The two groups contain very different commodities and some of the largest appear on only one side of the account. Much of the competition between domestic and foreign agriculture is of a sort not revealed by foreign trade data; it is competition within the U.S. between imports and domestically-produced crops and in other countries, between exports and foreign-produced products.

Trade in Manufactured Articles

It is difficult to date the end of agricultural predominance in exports and the beginning of the rise of manufactures. Our series indicate that the

[31] There is some evidence that agricultural imports in the 1930's were sustained by the severe drought which afflicted the grain-growing areas of the United States. See John H. Adler, Eugene R. Schlesinger, and Evelyn Van Westerborg, *The Pattern of United States Import Trade Since 1923*, Federal Reserve Bank of New York, 1952.

share of agricultural products in total exports remained almost unchanged from 1800 through the early 1890's (despite the relative decline of agriculture in the labor force and in national income).

Only after the 1890's did it begin to fall steadily. This constancy in the share of agricultural products in exports is partly conceptual : we consider

CHART 14
Agricultural Imports as a Percentage of Farm and Total GNP, Current and 1913 Dollars

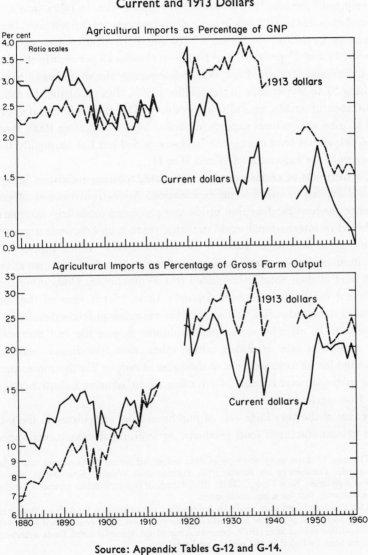

Source: Appendix Tables G-12 and G-14.

as agricultural a number of manufactured foods, such as flour and meat, which are treated in income and labor force statistics as products of manufacturing. Ideally, the export values should be divided among the sectors (including transportation) in proportion to their contribution to value added up to the point of export.[32]

It is possible to roughly estimate the effect of applying the domestic industry classification to the trade figures. Excluding manufactured foods, the share of agricultural products in total exports ranged from 60 to 70 per cent until the late 1870's,[33] and then began to fall. In other words, the share of manufactured foods in agricultural exports (as defined here) began to increase in the 1870's. Between 1820 and 1870 it had varied generally between 14 and 25 per cent, and had been close to 15 per cent in the years just before and after the Civil War. Subsequently the share began to rise, reaching 37 to 39 per cent in the middle 1890's, thus offsetting the falling importance of crude agricultural products. The ratio of manufactured food to total agricultural exports fell below 30 per cent after 1908. It was again below that level during the interwar period but has frequently been higher since the beginning of World War II.

The inclusion of certain products of manufacturing industries in agricultural exports requires some explanation. Aside from reasons of convenience, such as the fact that crude and processed foods are customarily combined in international trade statistics, there is an economic argument as well. As illustrated in Table 7, the food industries which supplied the main items of exports, meat packing and flour milling, had a comparatively small part of their total value added in manufacturing. Costs other than purchased materials accounted for only 12 to 16 per cent of the total output in these industries, and most of the materials purchased came from agriculture. In all other industries combined, despite the fact that some food industries are included, costs other than purchased materials accounted for 41 to 49 per cent of the value of output. Furthermore, many of the materials were obtained from other manufacturing industries rather than from agriculture.

Because of the very large role of purchases from agriculture in the total value of manufactured food products, agricultural developments appear

[32] This can be done using the type of data assembled for an input-output table. See, for example, Conference on Research in Income and Wealth, *Input-Output Analysis, Technical Supplement,* New York, NBER, 1954, Chap. 3. But such tables would be needed, not for one year, but for a historical series.

[33] This is a rough estimate made by subtracting manufactured foods from total agricultural products. It is too low by amounts between 1 and 5 per cent, judging from the evidence of the period after 1879, because some of the manufactured foods subtracted had never been included in the agricultural total.

more relevant for understanding the trade in manufactured foods than changes within manufacturing.

Despite the industrial development of the United States, exports of manufactures (nonfood manufactured products) had not, by the late 1890's, encroached substantially on the overwhelming share of agricultural products. In the next fifty years, however, manufactures became the leading export, accounting for more than all the other classes combined (Chart 15). Since World War II, the share of manufactures in total exports seems to have leveled off at about 60 per cent.

TABLE 7

MATERIALS AND OTHER COSTS IN RELATION TO VALUE OF PRODUCT:
COMPARISON OF MAIN FOOD INDUSTRIES WITH OTHERS,
1880–1900
(dollar figures in thousands)

	Value of Product	Cost of Materials	Other Costs	Other Costs as Per Cent of Value of Product
Slaughtering and meat packing excl. retail butchering				
1900	790,253	686,861	103,392	13.1
1890	564,667	482,897	81,770	14.5
1880	303,562	267,739	35,823	11.8
Flour and grist mill products				
1900	560,719	475,826	84,893	15.1
1890	513,971	434,152	79,819	15.5
1880	505,186	441,545	63,641	12.6
All other industries				
1900	11,653,428	6,182,727	5,470,701	46.9
1890	8,293,799	4,244,995	4,048,804	48.8
1880	4,560,831	2,687,540	1,873,291	41.1

SOURCE: U.S. Census Office, *Twelfth Census of the United States: 1900*, Manufactures, Part 1 (1902), pp. 3, 8, and 14.

The ratio of manufactured exports to deflated GNP behaved similarly; it grew rapidly over the period as a whole, reaching its highest levels in the postwar period. But again, there is no evidence of a rising trend within the postwar years.

The rise of manufactures to a leading role in exports was partly a reflection of the increasing importance of manufacturing in the economy, as exemplified by its growing share of the labor force and of national income. But the share of manufactures increased much more rapidly in exports than in the domestic economy as the growth of manufactured exports outstripped that of manufacturing output.

This difference in rate of growth is reflected in the ratio of exports to gross manufacturing output,[34] which more than doubled between the early years

CHART 15

Trade in Manufactures Compared with Total Exports
and Imports and GNP

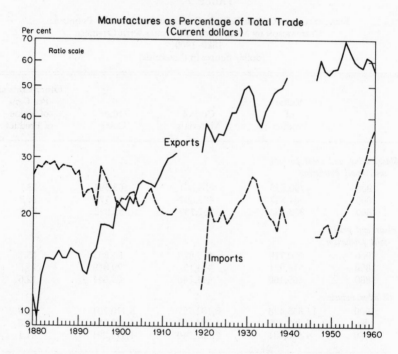

[34] This calculation is more hazardous for manufactured than for agricultural products because the valuation questions are more important (see footnote 10). We have evaded the problem posed by valuation by comparing only indexes of export and import quantities and manufacturing output.

The ratio of value added to value of product is much higher in agriculture than in manufacturing. Therefore, the comparison of exports, which are a value-of-product measure, with gross output, which is a value-added measure, is more appropriate for the farm sector. Comparisons of exports and imports with value of production, by industry, were made in an unpublished study by Phyllis A. Wallace, reported on briefly by Solomon Fabricant in the National Bureau's 33rd Annual Report, May 1953, pp. 77–78. Some of the results of this study were published in an article by Irving B. Kravis on "Wages and Foreign Trade" in *The Review of Economics and Statistics,* February 1956.

of our period and 1911-13 and rose another 50 per cent by the postwar period (Chart 16).

Manufactured products are an enormously varied collection of commodities, ranging from the simplest transformation of agricultural or mineral products to complex machinery or scientific equipment in which the cost of the original raw material is insignificant. The composition

CHART 15 (*Concluded*)

Manufactures as Percentage of GNP
(1913 dollars)

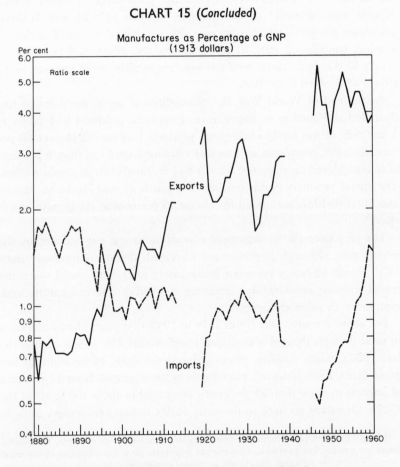

Source: Appendix Tables A-6, A-8, A-10, and G-13.

of manufactured exports has been changing ceaselessly since 1879 in a fairly consistent direction—away from products of animal or vegetable origin and toward those of mineral origin. Among those of mineral origin, the trend has been away from commodities closely tied to the production of raw materials, such as petroleum products, to metal products, including machinery and vehicles; and within the metal products group the shift has been to the more complex machinery and vehicles.

In 1879-81, manufactured petroleum products and articles of animal or vegetable origin (mainly textiles, wood, and tobacco products) represented more than 65 per cent of American exports of manufactures, while all metal products accounted for only 21 per cent. But the leading commodities of 1879 contributed very little to the great surge in manufactured exports that followed : of the increase between 1879-81 and 1910-13, petroleum products, which were over 40 per cent of the total at the beginning, contributed only 13 per cent; textiles, which had been 16 per cent, added only 8. Metal products were responsible for 73 per cent of the gain, and doubled their share.

By the end of World War II, commodities of agricultural origin had dwindled still further in importance. Petroleum products had fallen to 5 per cent of the total, while metal products had soared to over 60 per cent. By 1957, petroleum and textiles combined were less than 8 per cent of manufactured exports, and textiles had declined even in absolute terms. The metal products group reached two-thirds of manufactured exports and, in 1949-1957, accounted for almost 75 per cent of the growth in this class.[35]

The very steep rise in exports of manufactures was not matched on the import side, although imports have increased almost continuously since 1870. Rapid advances occurred immediately after both world wars, the recent increase considerably surpassing the earlier one in quantity and, even more, in value and length.

For about seventy years (from 1879 to 1950), the share of manufactures in total imports showed a declining trend (Chart 15), except during the late 1920's, when skidding prices reduced the share of agricultural imports. Since 1950, however, manufactures have jumped from 17 per cent of imports to more than 35 per cent—considerably above the levels of the 1880's. One must go back to the early 1870's to find percentages as high.

---

[35] Many complex phenomena are buried in this summary. For example, the United States has steadily lost ground as a supplier of petroleum products according to the usual international trade statistics. But American-owned companies continue to supply capital, entrepreneurship, and technical skills for petroleum production abroad.

Another interesting case is that of rubber products exports, the main component of which was automobile and truck tires. Despite the growth in use of automobiles outside the United States between 1949 and 1957, this class did not even keep up with total manufactured exports. But exports of synthetic rubber, which appears among semimanufactures, grew more than tenfold in the same period. Both groups consist of rubber products which are the output of domestic manufacturing industry and which contain a large technological component, but the shift from a finished to a semifinished product reduces the manufactured goods category.

The ratio of manufactured imports to GNP in 1913 dollars also suffered a great decline from the 1880's to the late 1940's. It has recovered strongly since then, reaching the level of the 1880's in 1959 and 1960.

By comparison with domestic gross output in manufacturing, imports of manufactures had dwindled by the early postwar years, to less than one-quarter of the 1880-89 level (Chart 16). Since then they have recovered to the level of the 1920's but not to that of the prewar period.

CHART 16

Ratio of Manufactured Export and Import Quantity Indexes
to Manufacturing Output Index
(1913 ratio = 100)

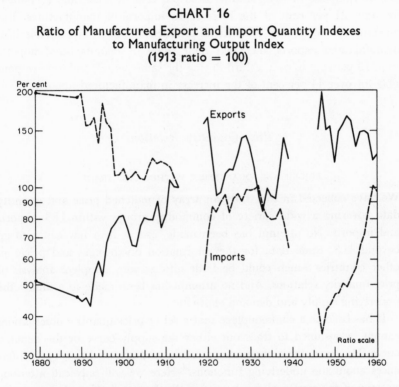

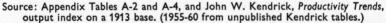

Source: Appendix Tables A-2 and A-4, and John W. Kendrick, *Productivity Trends*, output index on a 1913 base. (1955-60 from unpublished Kendrick tables.)

Imports of manufactures, like exports, have changed radically in composition. In both 1879-81 and 1890-94, textile products alone accounted for more than two-thirds of the total; by 1910-13 they had fallen to a half, and by 1949 to 20 per cent. Paper and paper products rose from 6 to more than 36 per cent, and metal manufactures from 8 to 13 per cent between 1910-13 and 1949.

The postwar resurgence of manufactured imports is of interest for a number of reasons. One is that reversal of the long-standing trend away from manufactures would have implications for the stability of import demand and prices and for the U.S. balance of trade with other industrial nations. Another is that the changing composition of imports since 1949 has involved shifts almost identical with those in exports—away from products of agricultural or organic origin and towards products of mineral origin, particularly metal products (including machinery and vehicles). Textile and paper products, which constituted 60 per cent of all manufactured imports in 1949, shrank to 35 per cent by 1958, and accounted for only 22 per cent of the increase in imports of manufactures. But machinery, vehicles, and other metal products, the mainstays of American manufactured exports, increased their share of manufactured imports from 13 per cent to over a third during the same period, and were responsible for over 44 per cent of the increase in manufactured imports.

Price-Quantity Relations

PRICES AND QUANTITIES WITHIN U.S. TRADE

We have collected in this study an array of matched price and quantity data covering a wide variety of commodity groups within U.S. exports and imports. No attempt has been made, except in a few cases, to go beyond U.S. trade data for the information on incomes and prices in other countries which could be built into a more complete analysis of price-quantity relations. And no attempt has been made to estimate the underlying supply and demand elasticities.

It has become a commonplace that a set of price-quantity observations cannot be assumed to trace out either the supply curve or the demand curve. However, these observations can be and are used to suggest inferences about the underlying functions.[36] Here we will only call attention to some of the empirical regularities in the data, and offer a few tentative explanations or interpretations of them. In particular we shall note the pervasiveness and strength of negative relations between prices and quantities, particularly over the long run.

This section deals only with evidence for commodity aggregates. Some inferences concerning price-quantity relations for individual commodities are drawn in Chapter 3. By examining the relation between Paasche and

---

[36] A recent example is an attempt to infer supply elasticities from price and acreage data for British wheat in the prewar period. See Mancur Olson, Jr., and Curtis C. Harris, Jr., "Free Trade in 'Corn': A Statistical Study of the Prices and Production of Wheat in Great Britain from 1873 to 1914," *Quarterly Journal of Economics*, February 1959.

Laspeyres price indexes, we find that substitution in favor of commodities with relatively declining prices was an almost universal feature in total exports and imports and within virtually all of the commodity classes.

The expectation of inverse price-quantity relations usually involves the response to relative price changes of relative quantities sold. But before 1913 there are quite clear examples of inverse relations between absolute volumes and prices for total exports and individual commodity classes. Total exports, for example, showed a rising trend from 1879 to 1913 (Chart 17). But there was a noticeable slackening in the rate of growth after 1898—the year in which export prices ended their long post-Civil War decline and turned upward. Before 1898 the only marked reversal in the growth in quantity was in the early 1880's. This was accompanied by a corresponding temporary reversal in the price decline.

Over shorter time periods, some parallel, instead of inverse, price and quantity movements emerge. Two sharp increases in export quantities (which occurred in 1888-92 and 1895-98, during the long-term downswing in prices) were accompanied by pauses in the price decline rather than by severe price cuts.

Exports of agricultural products and manufactured foods exhibit negative price-quantity relations more clearly, without the obscuring presence of strong trends. The period of rising agricultural exports coincides with the period of falling prices between 1882 and 1897-98, after which time, quantities declined slightly until World War I. It was as if the rising prices after 1898 (which, as noted in Chapter 1, were associated with a slowing in the growth of output and a decline in per capita output) choked off the growth of exports. Once again, however, short, sharp rises in export quantities temporarily stabilized prices in the course of the long-term decline.

For manufactured food exports, the period of rising prices before World War I was clearly associated with a decline in quantities rather than a retardation or cessation of growth. Again, short spurts in export quantities seemed to bring a slight increase in prices.

The difference between the long- and short-term patterns of price-quantity behavior suggests that the long-term changes represented shifts mainly in the supply function and the short-term changes, shifts mainly in the demand function. One would expect a negative price-quantity relation from the former and a positive one from the latter.

In the sphere of relative, instead of absolute, price-quantity relations a striking illustration was given by Folke Hilgerdt[37] of the inverse relation between the relative prices of primary and manufactured products and

[37] *Industrialization and Foreign Trade,* p. 18.

CHART 17

Price and Quantity Indexes for U.S. Total, Agricultural, and Manufactured Food Exports

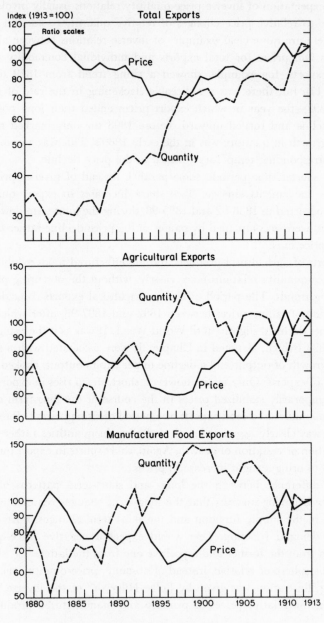

Source: Appendix Tables A-1, A-2, and A-5.

their relative quantities in international trade. Using three- to five-year averages, he showed that prices of primary products relative to those of manufactured goods fell between 1876-80 and 1896-1900, between 1911-13 and 1921-25, and between 1926-29 and 1931-35; they rose between 1896-1900 and 1911-13, between 1921-25 and 1926-29, and between 1931-35 and 1936-38. In each case the relative quantities moved in the opposite direction.

Hilgerdt's method of estimating quantities was probably biased in favor of an inverse price-quantity relationship. He constructed his estimates by deflating the value of world trade in manufactured goods by a price index. This price series, which related to Great Britain alone during much of his period, was probably a poor approximation of the true world price index, as we have suggested in Chapter 1. To the extent that it was, Hilgerdt introduced in his quantity estimates spurious changes inverse to those in the price index.[38]

However, we have encountered similar inverse relations in many instances where the likelihood of such bias was much smaller. A purely technical explanation, therefore, seems inadequate; an economic one is required.

Over short periods, changes in demand might be expected to outweigh those in supply. Yet, inverse price-quantity relations between primary (or agricultural) products and manufactured goods are frequent. One explanation is that supply elasticities are lower for agricultural than for manufactured products. As a result, the effects of changes in demand will appear mainly in prices for primary products, but in quantities for manufactured goods. Thus, in both world wars prices of agricultural products far outdistanced those of manufactured goods, but quantities lagged behind. In the early 1930's, prices of manufactured goods fell much less than agricultural prices but quantities dropped more sharply. Some of these inverse movements go beyond short periods and encompass swings of ten or twenty years' duration.[39] Presumably these represent changes in supply conditions.

Along the same lines as Hilgerdt we have compared manufactured and agricultural products within exports and within imports. The export and import price trends differed markedly, as has been mentioned earlier. Within exports, manufactured goods became cheaper by comparison with

[38] The danger of spurious correlation is discussed further in Chapter 4.

[39] The influence of differences in supply elasticities may persist over longer periods because of differences in ease of entry and exit between agriculture and manufacturing. See Kindleberger, *The Terms of Trade*, pp. 227–231.

agricultural products; within imports they became more expensive. Since the 1930's, the direction of the import trend has been reversed.

Changes in export quantities have been broadly the opposite of those in prices (Chart 18). Over the long run the quantity of manufactured exports has increased rapidly relative to that of agricultural products, while the price of manufactured goods has fallen. Even the rate of growth of manufactured exports seems to have been related to price changes. After 1882, both quantity and price ratios were comparatively stable for ten or twelve years. Between the 1890's and 1913, manufactures prices fell and quantities rose rapidly relative to agricultural products. The interwar period was dominated by large fluctuations in the price and quantity ratios, mostly in opposite directions. Relative quantities of manufactures fluctuated about a higher level, and prices about a lower level, in the interwar period than in prewar years. In the postwar period manufactured exports were again much higher, relative to agricultural exports, while the price ratios hovered around the lowest level of the interwar period. Postwar short-term fluctuations, in relative quantities and prices, however, seem to have been completely independent.

The shares of manufactured and agricultural products in total exports have fluctuated inversely to the price ratios. Like the quantity and price ratios, they were stable for a time after 1882. Between the 1890's and 1913, the share of manufactures rose from 20 to over 30 per cent, while the relative price of manufactured exports declined.

Within imports, inverse behavior of prices and quantities was much less visible; even quite large movements in one variable were without reflection in the other (Chart 19). But taking whole periods at a time, one can observe the phenomenon here too.

The strength of the inverse relationship in Chart 18 is not easy to explain, since agricultural and manufactured exports do not, to an important extent, compete with one another for markets. There are some elements of competition, however : all industries compete for some resources and, to some extent, all commodities compete for the consumer's dollar. In addition, there may be a choice as to whether a particular product should be exported before or after processing. The decision would be affected by changes in the productivities of processing industries. For example, in the last half of the nineteenth century a larger and larger proportion of wheat was exported as flour. The change presumably was linked to the increasing efficiency in the U.S. flour milling industry.

Within agricultural products, where substitution between exports and

66

CHART 18
Ratio of Manufactured to Agricultural Export Price and Quantity Indexes
(1913 ratio = 100)

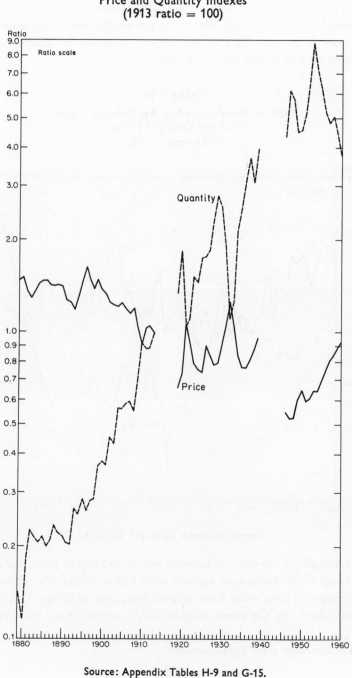

Source: Appendix Tables H-9 and G-15.

imports is plausible,[40] no trend appears in the quantity or price ratios before 1900 (Chart 20). But from then until the late 1930's, agricultural export prices rose steeply in comparison with imports, and export quantities fell even faster. After World War II the price ratio reversed direction and fell most of the way back to the 1913 level, while the quantity ratio regained most of its loss since that date.

CHART 19

Ratio of Manufactured to Agricultural Import Price and Quantity Indexes
(1913 ratio = 100)

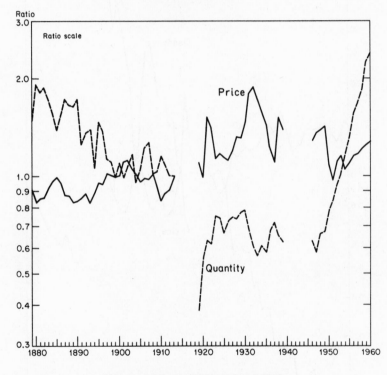

Source: Appendix Tables H-9 and G-15.

At first glance the relation between export and import price and quantity ratios for manufactures appears weak before World War II because the changes in price ratios were so small compared with those in quantity ratios (Chart 21). On closer examination, however, it is clear that the

[40] Although a large proportion of agricultural imports are considered by the Department of Agriculture to be "complementary."

changes were definitely inverse. A period of comparative stability, until about 1886, was followed by a drop in the price ratio and a sharp increase in the quantity ratio. From 1898 to 1910 there was another period of stability for both, followed by another drop in price and jump in the quantity ratio. Only the very great rise in the quantity ratio between

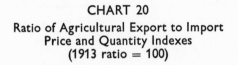

CHART 20
Ratio of Agricultural Export to Import
Price and Quantity Indexes
(1913 ratio = 100)

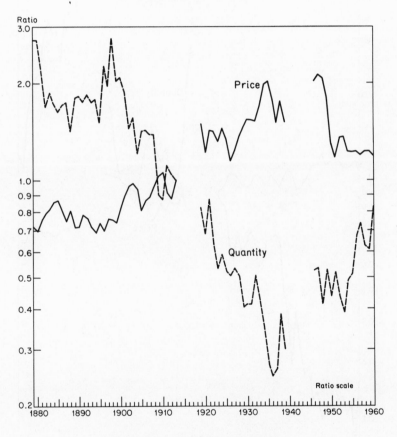

Source: Appendix Tables H-20 and G-16.

1894 and 1898 seems eccentric; it might have been a product of the sharp increase in tariffs that took place at that time.

A surprisingly high elasticity of substitution between exports and imports of manufactures is implied by the fact that quantity-ratio fluctuations

CHART 21

Ratio of Manufactured Export to Import
Price and Quantity Indexes
(1913 ratio = 100)

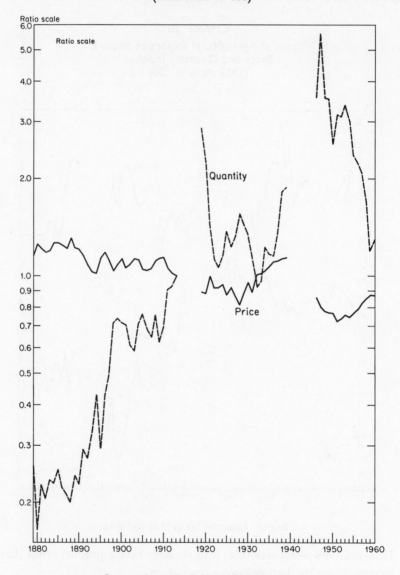

Source: Appendix Tables H-20 and G-16.

were so much larger than price-ratio movements.[41] If our data had ended with the interwar period, the negative price-quantity relation might be attributed to a spurious correlation between two series with trends in opposite directions. But the reversal of the price-ratio trend after 1950—the rise in manufactured export prices relative to import prices—was accompanied by a great relative increase in imports of manufactures. This fact suggests that the large implied response of quantity to price ratios may have been quite genuine.

COMPARISON OF U.S. AND FOREIGN PRICES AND QUANTITIES

The rise in world trade of a new country, a new commodity, or a new supplier of a commodity is often accompanied by declining prices and terms of trade. We might think of the lowering of price as the way in which the newcomer forces its way into world markets. Or, perhaps more appropriately for a competitive economy, we might say that technological advances or the opening of new lands to cultivation have, by reducing prices, pushed the new country or commodity into world trade.

This phenomenon has often been noted in such cases as the growth of American raw cotton and British cotton goods exports in the first half of the nineteenth century, and in the rise of the American provision trade in the second half. The inverse movement of the volume of British exports with the terms of trade was commented on by Schlote,[42] for example, and we noted (in Chapter 1) the relative fall in American export prices and terms of trade as the United States overtook and passed Great Britain as an exporter.

For the years covered by our new indexes it is possible to examine the behavior of some components of the major import and export classes. A few of many possible comparisons for the period before World War I are discussed below.

American exports of manufactures have been the main force behind the rise in this country's foreign trade since the 1890's. If we compare U.S. export prices and quantities with those of Great Britain (Chart 22), we note that both ratios were steady until the late 1880's. Between the 1890's and 1913, the ratio of American to British prices fell by almost a third, while the quantity ratio increased almost four times. Two brief reversals of the

[41] See, however, the substantial elasticities of substitution (of the order of 2½-3) between U.S. and U.K. exports of manufactures found in G. D. A. MacDougall, "British and American Exports: A Study Suggested by the Theory of Comparative Costs," *Economic Journal*, December 1951. Our "elasticity of substitution" here is a somewhat strange construction, since exports and imports of manufactures are sold in different markets.

[42] Werner Schlote, *British Overseas Trade*, pp. 46–47.

price ratio decline were reflected in interruptions of the rise in quantity ratios.

Similarly, U.S. import prices for manufactures declined relative to British export prices, even though Great Britain supplied an important part of U.S. manufactured imports. Unless British export prices of manufactures to the U.S. fell relative to those of exports to other countries,[43] this means that U.S. import prices from countries other than Great Britain fell by

CHART 22

Ratio of U.S. to U.K. Export and Import Price and Quantity Indexes, Total Manufactures and Textiles

(1913 ratio = 100)

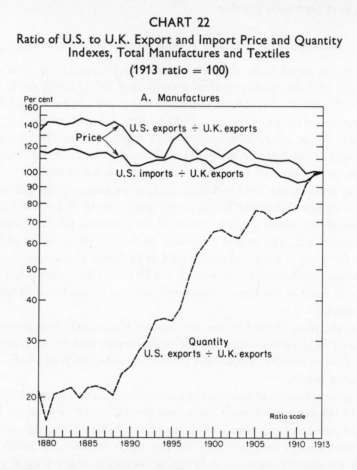

[43] Kindleberger's figures (*The Terms of Trade*, p. 33) do not suggest that they do. He gives export unit values indexes for total United Kingdom exports and exports to the U.S. for 1900/1876 and 1913/1900 which can be combined into the following indexes (1872 = 100) for the two main manufactured goods categories.

Exports To:	Metals and Manufactures	Textiles
U.S.	133	72
World	130	74

more, and probably substantially more, than the 15 per cent decline in total import prices.

A narrower comparison[44] can be made of British and American exports of textile products. Again the fall in relative prices for U.S. exports over the period as a whole was accompanied by a great relative expansion in exports (Chart 22). Short reversals of the fall in prices were clearly reflected in the quantities. Relative prices of American textile exports rose in 1881-83, 1885-89 and 1903-07; relative quantities fell in 1881-84, 1886-89 and 1902-07.[45]

CHART 22 *(Concluded)*

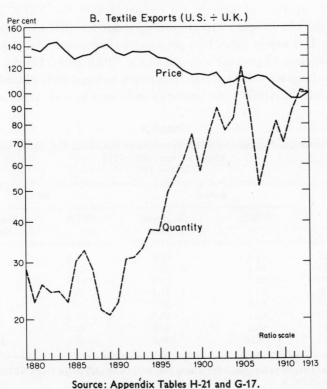

Source: Appendix Tables H-21 and G-17.

[44] One of many possible such comparisons using the data in Appendixes A to C.

[45] A number of other comparisons could be made between groups of British and American exports, using the indexes of Schlote (*British Overseas Trade*) and A. G. Silverman ("Monthly Index Numbers of British Export and Import Prices, 1880–1913," *Review of Economic Statistics,* August 1930). Textiles could be subdivided further, and comparisons might also be made of groups of metal products. The range of comparison could be widened a great deal by using domestic price data for narrow classes of commodities and both price and unit-value data for individual commodities.

These observations on American import and export prices of manufactures cast further doubt on the representativeness of British export prices of manufactured goods. By showing the decline in Great Britain's share in world trade, the quantity trends illustrated here, as well as those shown by Hilgerdt,[46] reinforce the impression that British export prices of manufactures must have been rising relative to those of other countries. Thus, the improvement in Great Britain's terms of trade before World War I may have been more a reflection of the decline in the competitive position of her exports than a source of increasing real income.

The use of U.K. data to represent the whole world results in errors, which can be seen when the League of Nations indexes for U.S. manufactured exports and imports are compared with the NBER indexes (Table 8). The League's export-quantity index for 1881-85, derived by dividing U.S. export values by a price index constructed from U.K. data, was more than 40 per cent higher than the NBER index. On the import side the League's index falls by 11 per cent between 1881-85 and 1896-1900, while the NBER import-quantity index rises by over 30 per cent.

TABLE 8

LEAGUE OF NATIONS AND NBER ESTIMATES OF VOLUME OF U.S. TRADE IN
MANUFACTURES, 1881-1913
(1913 = 100)

	Exports		Imports	
	NBER	League of Nations	NBER	League of Nations
1881–1885	11.8	16.8	52.8	59.2
1886–1890	14.1	18.9	64.2	63.2
1891–1895	19.4	21.9	57.8	61.1
1896–1900	35.2	34.4	70.3	52.6
1901–1905	47.5	52.1	70.3	69.1
1906–1910	62.1	65.6	91.5	87.6
1911–1913	93.1	90.2	98.7	94.7
1913	100.0	100.0	100.0	100.0

SOURCE: League of Nations indexes from *Industrialization and Foreign Trade*. NBER indexes from Appendix A.

SIGNIFICANCE OF PRICE-QUANTITY RELATIONS

We have discussed a number of cases in which price and quantity changes showed a strong negative correlation. The direction of the relation is in

[46] *Industrialization and Foreign Trade*, pp. 157–158. Because of Hilgerdt's method of estimating quantity, these are essentially value trends.

accord with the hypothesis that the changes represent shifts in supply functions. However, two questions arise. Should it be possible to observe the effects of supply changes through price changes? And why are these price-quantity relations often characteristic of commodity aggregates even when not of the individual commodities?

If product A exported by country X is a perfect substitute for product A exported by country Y, their prices in country Z must, by definition, be equal. If there are no transportation costs, the export unit values for commodity A from the two countries will be equal also. An increase in productivity in country X, which results in a fall in the export price of commodity A, will cause a fall in the export price of A from country Y, if Y is to remain in the market. No interrelations between price and quantity changes will be observable.[47]

What then accounts for the many negative price-quantity relationships that were found? It is the incomplete adjustment of prices in the two countries, because of such factors as transportation costs and imperfect substitutability. If transportation costs are introduced in the example above, the fall in X's export price of A will widen X's market area and contract Y's market area. After the adjustment they will still be selling at the same c.i.f. price in any market they share, but Y's export price need not have fallen to the same degree as X's price.

Imperfect substitutability operates in the same manner. The fall in X's price of commodity A_1 will drive Y's exports of A_2 out of some uses or reduce its share in some areas, but will not eliminate it completely. One can therefore observe a fall in X's export price relative to Y's associated with a rise in X's relative quantity of exports.

Even where there are no frictions (and every decline in X's export price for A is matched by Y, but accompanied by a decline in Y's volume of exports) a negative price-quantity relation may be observed for commodity aggregates or total trade. A will gain in importance among X's exports and lose in importance among Y's exports. In a price index which reflects this shift, the price of X's exports will decline relative to that of Y's exports. The quantity index of country X will rise correspondingly.

We conclude, then, that these negative price-quantity relations are not freaks or accidents. While they may not directly measure elasticities of substitution, they reflect them and may serve as approximations to them.

---

[47] Several attempts were made in the early stages of this study to explain the growth of particular U.S. food exports in terms of changes in export price relations between the U.S. and foreign competitors. Most of them failed because of the similarity between U.S. and foreign price movements.

Summary of Main Findings

Before going into some of the more technical aspects of the NBER indexes, it may be worthwhile to recapitulate the main findings of the first two chapters.

Two widely held beliefs regarding net barter terms of trade found no confirmation in the data for the United States. One is that there has been a substantial long-term improvement in the terms of trade of developed countries, including the United States; the other, that there has been a significant long-term deterioration in the terms of trade of primary as compared to manufactured products.

Although there have been very large swings in U.S. terms of trade since 1879, no long-run trend has emerged. The average level of U.S. terms of trade since World War II has been almost the same as before World War I. However, the terms of trade have been improving quite steadily since 1951.

The preponderance of our data appeared to be contrary to the accepted view regarding the terms of trade between primary and manufactured products. Manufactured products in U.S. trade became cheaper relative to primary products, particularly before World War I. The purchasing power of U.S. manufactured exports fell with respect to both exports and imports of primary products; export prices of primary products rose compared with those of imported manufactures.

Neither of these findings prove that less developed or primary producing countries have experienced favorable shifts in their terms of trade. Like most of the original evidence on this question, ours is indirect. A regional or country breakdown of trade would be required to ascertain the course of U.S. terms of trade vis-à-vis particular areas or countries.

For only one of the comparisons of agricultural and manufactured prices—that within exports—was it possible to test roughly whether the trend represented mainly productivity or real income changes. It appeared that most of the long-run relative decline in export prices of manufactures could be accounted for by the fact that manufacturing productivity advanced at a more rapid rate than agricultural productivity, particularly before World War I. The reversal of the productivity relation since World War II has been accompanied by a reversal of the price relation as well. However, it was evident that the price ratio understated the plight of the agricultural sectors in the 1930's. By comparison with manufactured exports, agricultural exports suffered a drop in purchasing power per unit of input not only back to the prewar level, as indicated by the price ratio, but far below any level we have observed here.

The productivity data suggest that declining long-run net barter terms of trade are far from a certain sign of declining real income—they may well represent growing productivity and competitiveness. This impression is confirmed by the frequency with which declines in relative prices are associated with growth in relative quantities. This negative price-quantity relation appeared not only between agricultural and manufactured exports but between agricultural and manufactured imports, between exports and imports of agricultural products, and between exports and imports of manufactures. Similarly, the growth of U.S. exports of manufactured products (for example, textiles) relative to those of the U.K. was accompanied by a relative decline in U.S. export prices. These events, in conjunction with other evidence that negative relations between price and quantity changes are quite pervasive, suggest that productivity changes were the most frequent cause of long-term relative price movements.

A comparison of the value of exports and imports with the value of domestic output confirmed the view that there has been a decline in the ratio of trade to output. Import ratios have been falling for more than a century, while export ratios reached something of a peak in the last half of the nineteenth century before receding.

The volume of trade, however, shows no such long-run decline in importance. Recent export ratios have been among the highest since 1879; import ratios, very low just after World War II, have recently recovered strongly, reaching the pre-World War I levels in 1958-60. However, they have not repeated the higher levels of the interwar years.

The contrasting behavior of current- and constant-dollar trade ratios, caused by the substantial decline in the ratio of export and import prices to domestic prices, demonstrates how misleading the common practice of using them interchangeably can be. Most of the decline in this ratio occurred during the interwar period. The subsequent recovery in foreign trade prices fell far short of restoring the prewar relations.

Although no long-term trend was observed in aggregate trade-output ratios, there was evidence of a connection between export ratios and rates of growth in output for the agricultural sector, as well as for agricultural products individually. It took the form of a peak in the importance of the foreign market when the growth rate of domestic output was at its highest. Foreign markets took large shares of additions to output, even for commodities in which their initial share was not so great. In such commodities as cotton, grains, and meats it appeared that the wide extent and penetrability of the foreign market was a prerequisite for the rapid growth of

77

American agriculture, particularly in view of the presumably low elasticity of demand for agricultural products. American economic growth was thus aided not only by the frequently cited size of the domestic market but by the opportunity the foreign market provided for rapid expansions in specialized fields of production.

CHAPTER 3

NBER Indexes: Methods of Construction and Comparisons Among Them

CHAPTERS 1 and 2 summarize long-term trends in the foreign trade of the United States as they are described by the new NBER indexes in conjunction with data previously available for later years. The remaining chapters deal mainly with the NBER indexes themselves, and thus with the period they cover : 1879 to 1923. The process of studying the technical characteristics of the indexes uncovers additional substantive findings relevant to the earlier chapters.

How the NBER Indexes Were Constructed

The NBER price and quantity indexes used in Chapters 1 and 2 are Fisher "ideal" index numbers. Paasche and Laspeyres indexes, employed later in this chapter, were an intermediate product in the computation of the Fisher indexes.

All the indexes were constructed in four segments : 1913-23, 1899-1913, 1889-99, and 1879-89, using the final year of each as the base. The segments were then linked at the overlapping years. The use of a single base for a period of ten or fifteen years has great computational advantages over annual linking, and also simplifies the interpretation of changes extending over several years. While avoiding the arbitrary character of bases far removed from the period studied, it does introduce into year-to-year comparisons some elements extraneous to the years compared.

A change in the price of an article which is of negligible importance in both of two years being compared could cause a substantial change in the Laspeyres index if the article were important in the base year. The Paasche index comparing two years can change even when all individual prices have remained the same, if the importance of the commodities has altered. Neither of these somewhat odd phenomena could occur in a direct comparison between two years.[1]

[1] In a direct comparison between years 1 and 2 the Laspeyres price index is $\frac{\Sigma P_2 Q_1}{\Sigma P_1 Q_1}$. In an indirect comparison of years 1 and 2 with year 0 as a base, the Laspeyres index is $\frac{\Sigma P_2 Q_0}{\Sigma P_1 Q_0}$. The Paasche index under indirect comparison, is

$$\frac{\Sigma P_2 Q_2}{\Sigma P_0 Q_2} \bigg/ \frac{\Sigma P_1 Q_1}{\Sigma P_0 Q_1} \left(\text{or } \frac{\Sigma P_2 Q_2}{\Sigma P_1 Q_1} \bigg/ \frac{\Sigma P_0 Q_2}{\Sigma P_0 Q_1} \right),$$

instead of, as in direct comparison,

$$\frac{\Sigma P_2 Q_2}{\Sigma P_1 Q_2} \left(\text{or } \frac{\Sigma P_2 Q_2}{\Sigma P_1 Q_1} \bigg/ \frac{\Sigma P_1 Q_2}{\Sigma P_1 Q_1} \right)$$

Comparison of years from different segments is conceptually quite complicated, since it involves different sets of base year weights. It may be thought of as implying the assumption that the index for one period, if extended, would be roughly parallel to the index of the adjoining period.

The main advantage of the backward-looking character of the index — the property that the base is the final year of a period rather than the initial year — is that it permits the fullest use of the steadily increasing detail in which trade data were published. In the first quarter of 1879, for example, there were slightly over 200 import commodities and 230 export commodities listed in the official trade returns; in 1923 there were more than 800 import and 1200 export commodities.

Indexes constructed with the terminal year instead of the initial year as the base have a number of peculiarities which must be kept in mind when the different types of indexes are compared. For example, the substitution effects which are expected on theoretical grounds (price and quantity changes negatively correlated), will cause our Paasche price indexes to rise relative to the Laspeyres indexes, the opposite of the usual case with initial-year weights. On the other hand, where quantity and price changes are positively correlated, the Laspeyres price index will rise in comparison with the Paasche, again the reverse of the results with initial-year weights.[2]

The commodity classification used here is the result of compromise among several objectives : comparability with other indexes, the isolation of economically significant classes of commodities, and reliability.

We constructed the classification to fit, with the proper combining of indexes, into the classifications used by the U.S. Department of Commerce. Thus, none of our minor groups were entered in more than one of the five economic classes or the eleven commodity groups of the Department of Commerce.[3] The distinction between agricultural and nonagri-

---

[2] This is the phenomenon of "weight bias." Mills suggests that it is characteristic of short and medium periods, including business cycles, while the substitution relationship may prevail over long periods. (Frederick C. Mills, *Statistical Methods*, 3rd Ed., New York, 1955, p. 452 n). It is, of course, the substitution relationship that is familiar from theoretical discussions of index numbers assuming constant tastes.

We could interpret these phenomena in another way. Substitution relationships are more likely to be observed when supply conditions are changing rapidly and demand is relatively stable; and "weight bias" when demand is shifting more rapidly (the 1913–23 period for many commodities).

[3] The five economic classes are: crude materials; crude foodstuffs; manufactured foodstuffs and beverages; semimanufactures; and finished manufactures. The eleven commodity groups are: animals and animal products, edible; animals and animal products, inedible; vegetable food products and beverages; vegetable products, inedible, except fibers and wood; textile fibers and manufactures; wood and paper; nonmetallic minerals; metals and manufactures, except machinery and vehicles; machinery and

cultural products was also maintained. Classes were set up for groups that seemed interesting from an economic point of view, or that demanded separate treatment on sampling grounds. The latter groups would otherwise have been combined with others exhibiting substantially different price behavior. The separation of such groups both improves estimates of the price behavior of larger classes, and narrows the margins of doubt surrounding these estimates (see Chapter 5). The next step was the selection of "covered" commodities—those for which unit values were accepted as representing prices or for which price data could be obtained from other sources.[4] The other commodities are referred to as "uncovered."

The list of covered commodities rarely remained constant throughout a period. It was therefore often necessary for the index computation to have several base-year value totals $[\Sigma P_0 Q_0$ (covered items)], each comparable in commodity composition to a different segment of the period.

When the selections had been made and matching base-year values computed, Paasche, Laspeyres, and Fisher "ideal" price indexes were calculated for the covered items in each minor class.

Following this, value indexes were calculated for each minor class, encompassing both covered and uncovered items. These indexes compare the total value of all commodities in the class with the base-year value for the same commodities. As was true of the covered items, the total list of commodities in a class changed during a period, mainly because items disappear from the published listing as one goes back in time. Such items were assumed to fall into the catchall class "all other articles."[5] As a result of these shifts, several base-year values—$\Sigma P_0 Q_0$ (All items)—often were required for a minor-class value index, as well as for the price index.

Quantity indexes for minor groups were computed by dividing value indexes by the Fisher price indexes. The assumption underlying this operation was that changes in the prices of items not covered were parallel to those of covered items.[6]

vehicles; chemicals and related products; miscellaneous. See U.S. Department of Commerce, Bureau of the Census: *Schedule A, Statistical Classification of Commodities Imported into the United States*, January 1, 1954, pp. VII and XVII and *Schedule B, Statistical Classification of Domestic and Foreign Commodities Exported from the United States*, Part II, January 1, 1949, pp. XXIV and XXVII.

[4] The selection of covered commodities and the use of outside price data are discussed in Chapter 4.

[5] Sometimes a commodity disappeared by merger with another. In most such cases we placed them both in the same class during that period to minimize shifts in composition within periods.

[6] This is identical to the "coverage adjustment" used, for example, in Solomon Fabricant, *The Output of Manufacturing Industries, 1899–1937*, New York, NBER, 1940. See *ibid.* pp. 362–372 and Chapter 5, below, for a justification of this procedure in terms of the sampling assumptions used.

Price indexes for larger groups (the intermediate classes of Appendix B) were computed from data for the minor classes, giving each class the weight of both its covered and uncovered commodities. In effect, each minor class was treated as a commodity, with $\Sigma P_0 Q_0$ (All items) as its $P_0 Q_0$ and $\Sigma P_1 Q_1$ (All items) as its $P_1 Q_1$ The $P_1 Q_0$'s were calculated by multiplying $P_0 Q_0$'s by the Laspeyres price indexes, and $P_0 Q_1$'s were calculated by dividing $P_1 Q_1$'s by the Paasche price indexes. Those minor classes for which price indexes were computed were considered "covered" classes, analogous to covered items within minor classes. The calculated cross-products were summed across the minor classes to give the price and quantity indexes for intermediate classes, and these, in turn, were used to build the indexes for major classes and total exports and imports.

The base-year dates were selected on a number of grounds. The final year of the study—1923—was selected as the base year for the last period, because we felt that Cowden's indexes for exports[7] and an interpolation of the annual Department of Commerce series for imports could adequately fill the gap between that date and the beginning of the quarterly Department of Commerce series in 1929. The year 1913, the last year unaffected by the beginning of the European war, has been used as a base for many other prewar series. The years 1899 and 1889 which divided up the remaining period fairly evenly, were United States Census years, and therefore convenient for comparisons with domestic data.

Some other characteristics of the base years may be of interest. Three of them—1923, 1913, and 1899—are peak years in the NBER business cycle chronology, while the fourth, 1889, is roughly midway between a trough in April 1888 and a peak in July 1890. Against the more specific background of trade fluctuations, 1923 comes just after the trough in exports and imports following World War I, but is considerably above 1913. The latter comes at the end of a period of rising values, prices, and quantities for both imports and exports. The two decades from 1879 to 1899 mark something of an interruption in the very great rise in import and export values which characterized the post-Civil War period as a whole—an interruption resulting from a combination of increasing quantities and declining prices. The base year 1899 is situated just after the upturn in prices and import values, but several years after the upturn in export values. For import quantities, 1899 is in the middle of a fairly steady increase which covered the whole period 1879-1913; for export quantities it follows a period of very rapid growth and precedes a decade of retardation.

[7] Dudley J. Cowden, *Measures of Exports of the United States,* New York, Columbia University Press, 1931.

Comparison of Paasche and Laspeyres Indexes

The Paasche and Laspeyres indexes shown in Appendix A are of interest for two reasons. One is that they show the range of error arising from the comparison of our Fisher indexes with Paasche and Laspeyres price and quantity indexes from other sources. The second, discussed later in this chapter, is that the differences between the two types of indexes shed some light on relations between price and quantity changes.

Many series with which one might compare export or import prices (such as the GNP deflator, the wholesale price index, and most foreign indexes) are Paasche or Laspeyres price indexes. It is not immediately clear, therefore, to what extent the apparent differences between the U.S. indexes and other series, such as those discussed in Chapter 1, represent real divergences in behavior or only the results of comparing dissimilar types of index numbers. The computation of Paasche and Laspeyres indexes permitted us to judge, in any specific case, whether the latter was the case, and to note that fact in the text. Even where no specific comparisons are made, the extent of Paasche-Laspeyres differences indicates whether any relations found are strong enough to make this type of "formula error" unimportant.

Ratios of Paasche to Laspeyres indexes, which measure the percentage differences between them, fluctuated much more violently between 1913 and 1923 than before, according to the data for agricultural products, nonagricultural products, and the five Department of Commerce economic classes (Table 9). In ten out of sixteen cases the swings were wider in those ten years than in the previous thirty-four. All the cases in which the range was over 21 per cent occurred in the later period.

The most spectacular range was in manufactured goods exports, where the Paasche index reached a level 50 per cent higher than the Laspeyres in 1916 (on a 1913 base). Most of this great discrepancy can be traced to manufactured chemical products (Export Class 075 in Appendix C), in which the Paasche index soared to twice the Laspeyres in 1916 and remained almost as high in 1917. Within this class the responsibility can be placed on one commodity: smokeless and other powder (item 6 in class 075). Its price rose much more than the average for all chemicals, while the value of its exports, less than one million dollars in 1913 and 1923, reached 262 million in 1916 and 338 million in 1917.

This one commodity was thus of negligible importance in the 1913-23 comparison and in the Laspeyres index for 1916 (weighted by 1923 values), but was of overwhelming importance in the Paasche index for 1916. Its influence in total manufactured exports was reinforced by the weight of exports of fuses and explosive shells and projectiles (items 25, 26, and 28 in class 075), which were uncovered commodities in the same class. They amounted to only $652,000 in 1913 and $663,000 in 1923, but reached $394 million in 1916 and $256 million in 1917.

TABLE 9

RANGE OF VARIATION OF RATIOS (IN PER CENT) OF PAASCHE TO LASPEYRES
PRICE INDEX
(1913 = 100)

Major Class[a]	1879–1913	1913–1923	1879–1923
Exports, total	12.3	31.2	43.5
Agricultural prod. (209)	12.1	17.2	21.0
Nonagricultural prod. (222)	17.3	37.7	55.0
Crude foodstuffs (201)	20.6	11.4	27.3
Manuf. foodstuffs (203)	18.4	10.3	23.2
Crude materials (212)	4.8	8.6	12.9
Semimanufactures (213)	12.8	20.7	33.5
Manufactures (215)	13.2	50.5	63.7
Imports, total	11.4	12.3	23.7
Agricultural prod. (209)	8.8	20.4	29.2
Nonagricultural prod. (223)	10.4	7.9	15.3
Crude foodstuffs (201)	20.9	13.1	34.0
Manuf. foodstuffs (203)	8.6	7.0	10.1
Crude materials (212)	6.0	24.3	30.3
Semimanufactures (213)	11.3	19.9	19.9
Manufactures (220)	9.3	6.3	14.9

SOURCE: Tables A–20—A–23.

[a] Numbers following class titles are NBER major class designations as shown in Table A–30.

Because of the growth of these commodities, manufactured chemicals accounted for over a third of the total weight of covered classes in "manufactured products of mineral origin and rubber" (Export Class 147 in Appendix B) in 1916 and over 30 per cent in 1917, as compared with roughly 4 per cent in 1913 and 4½ per cent in 1923. The wide fluctuations in the Paasche-Laspeyres ratio, illustrated by this extreme case, are the direct result of wartime changes. At no other time does an insignificant commodity became a staple of international trade in a few months.

The Paasche-Laspeyres ratios were higher in 1923 than in 1879 for every major export and import class; for all but two of forty-five classes, they were higher in 1913 than in 1879 and higher in 1923 than in 1913 (Table 10). The only exceptions in the prewar period were two closely related export classes: agricultural products (Class 209) and products of animal or vegetable origin, except printed matter and rubber products (Class 210). The two exceptions in 1913-23 were Import Classes 203 and 204 (manufactured foods, including and excluding tobacco products).

Column 3 of Table 10 shows how different the changes in price would appear if measured by a Paasche instead of a Laspeyres index.[8] The Paasche index always shows a larger change, ranging from 2.7 per cent greater for Import Class 203 (manufactured foodstuffs) to more than 40 per cent for Import Class 202 (crude foodstuffs, including tobacco products).

Differences between Paasche and Laspeyres indexes not only shed light on the range of possible "errors" in comparisons of one type of index with another, but provide economic information as well. Both indexes are averages of identical price relatives for individual commodities, differing only in the weights they assign to each. In the Laspeyres indexes the price relatives are weighted by base-year values—those of the last year of each period in our indexes. (Alternatively, one could say that the prices are weighted by base-year quantities.) In the Paasche indexes each price relative is weighted by P_0Q_1, the base-year price multiplied by the given (earlier) year quantity; each price is weighted by the given-year quantity. The Paasche index thus gives more weight than the Laspeyres to those commodities which have declined in quantity relative to the average—those for which Q_1/Q_0 was greater than the average.

What does this difference in weighting imply as to the meaning of discrepancies between the two indexes?[9] Suppose, for example, that the Laspeyres index for a class is higher than the Paasche. Since the base year in our indexes is at the end, this means that the Laspeyres index has declined relative to the Paasche. It follows that the base-year weights were heavier than given-year weights for those commodities with the highest P_1/P_0—those for which prices fell the most or rose the least. There was a shift in quantity terms toward those commodities that fell relatively in price.[10] If, on the other hand, the Paasche index is higher, the base-year weights were lower for commodities with high P_1/P_0, that is, there was a shift in quantity terms toward those commodities that rose most in price or fell least.

It is clear, then, that a higher (relatively falling) Laspeyres index suggests that substitution (or changes in supply conditions) was of predomi-

---

[8] The Fisher index is of course closer to each of them than they are to each other.

[9] It is simplest, in this connection, to think in terms of the original indexes for the four periods prior to linking.

[10] This does not imply a shift in value terms. Evidence of such a shift could be found by comparing the Laspeyres index to an index with given-year value weights.

TABLE 10
RELATION OF PAASCHE TO LASPEYRES PRICE INDEXES
1879 AND 1923, MAJOR CLASSES
(1913 = 100)

Class	Paasche Index as % of Laspeyres		1923 Ratio	
	1879 (1)	1923 (2)	As % of 1879 Ratio (Col. 2 ÷ Col. 1) (3)	Minus 1879 Ratio (Col.2 minus Col.1) (4)
EXPORTS				
201	95.0	100.6	105.9	5.6
202	98.4	101.6	103.3	3.2
203	82.7	104.8	126.7	22.1
204	82.1	105.4	128.4	23.3
205	97.1	103.3	106.4	6.2
206	97.3	104.9	107.8	7.6
207	92.3	103.6	112.2	11.3
208	92.4	105.5	114.2	13.1
209	108.3	113.1	104.4	4.8
210	104.2	112.5	108.0	8.3
211	95.0	105.1	110.6	10.1
212	96.0	103.7	108.0	7.7
213	96.6	105.6	109.3	9.0
214	91.3	123.4	135.2	32.1
215	91.0	123.6	135.8	32.6
216	95.7	108.4	113.3	12.7
217	95.9	107.1	111.7	11.2
218	97.8	111.0	113.5	13.2
219	92.2	116.7	126.6	24.5
220	92.2	116.7	126.6	24.5
221	91.3	117.5	128.7	26.2
222	84.9	116.4	137.1	31.5
IMPORTS				
201	82.7	106.2	128.4	23.5
202	77.4	108.5	140.2	31.1
203	95.9	98.5	102.7	2.6
204	93.7	99.0	105.7	5.3
205	91.5	103.5	113.1	12.0
206	88.8	103.9	117.0	15.1
207	89.8	104.8	116.7	15.0
208	86.2	105.2	122.0	19.0
209	93.8	117.2	124.9	23.4
210	89.7	114.4	127.5	24.7
211	99.0	120.0	121.2	21.0
212	97.9	120.6	123.2	22.7
213	91.0	104.7	115.1	13.7
214	95.1	115.2	121.1	20.1
215	94.5	115.5	122.2	21.0
216	90.3	113.1	125.2	22.8
217	91.7	105.5	115.0	13.8
218	91.1	105.6	115.9	14.5
219	89.7	112.0	124.9	22.3
220	91.0	105.6	116.0	14.6
221	89.7	112.0	124.9	22.3
222	90.9	104.7	115.2	13.8
223	89.6	104.9	117.1	15.3

SOURCE: Tables A–20—A–23.

nant importance, while the higher Paasche index implies that changes on the demand side were a stronger influence.[11]

The difference between these indexes and conventional formulations (with the base year at the beginning) should be kept in mind. In both cases a higher Laspeyres index implies substitution in response to relative price changes. But in our indexes, Laspeyres>Paasche means that the Laspeyres index is declining relative to the Paasche, while in the usual formulation, the reverse is true.

The interpretation of the Paasche-Laspeyres ratios is more complicated when the indexes are placed on a 1913 base by linking (Tables 9 and 10). For example, in the 1913-23 period the shifting of the base to 1913 transforms the situation as follows.

The interpretation must be reversed : the higher Paasche index implies substitution and the higher Laspeyres index, changes in demand. A preferable procedure is to concentrate attention on changes in the Paasche-Laspeyres ratio between any year and its matching base year. A relatively declining Laspeyres index, or a rising Paasche-Laspeyres ratio, implies shifts toward commodities becoming relatively cheaper. A decreasing ratio implies a shift in the opposite direction.

These relationships suggest that the upward drift of the Paasche-Laspeyres ratios, evident in most of the series (Table 10), is the result of substitution in favor of commodities with relatively falling prices. Although, strictly speaking, each year can be compared only with the base year of its period, a steady drift in the ratio can be identified with a gradual change in composition.

Several of the exceptions to the upward trend are associated with changes in demand. Most of the substantial declines in the Paasche-Laspeyres ratio occurred between 1916-18 and the 1923 base year (see basic tables, Appendix A). This means that high relative prices in 1916-18

[11] The observed price predominance does not necessarily imply a larger shift in the schedule, since the slopes of the supply and demand curves also influence the direction of the price-quantity relation.

were positively correlated with high relative quantities; many of the highest wartime prices were for those commodities (for example, gunpowder) which experienced spectacular increases in demand.

The cause of the downward trend in the Paasche-Laspeyres ratio for agricultural exports before 1913 is less clear. The relative increase in tobacco exports may be responsible. Tobacco was one of the few commodities whose prices increased even between 1879 and 1899, and one of the few to show a strong positive correlation between price and quantity relatives. These relations, together with the rapidly increasing consumption per capita, particularly of cigarettes, suggest that there were large increases in demand for tobacco products. A similar explanation can account for the fall in the Paasche-Laspeyres ratio for imports of manufactured foodstuffs. Here the main influence was the relative growth of sugar imports in the face of relatively increasing prices.

One of the sharpest declines in the ratio occurred in exports of crude foodstuffs after 1880-81. The high level during the first three years was clearly a demand phenomenon, when "a failure during the years 1879, 1880, and 1881, of the cereal crops of Europe and most other countries of the world, with the exception of the United States—a failure for which, in respect to duration and extent, there has been no parallel in four centuries—occasioned a remarkable demand on the latter country for all the food products it could supply at extraordinary prices."[12]

The information on price-quantity relations provided by the NBER indexes can be put in more formal terms. The Paasche-Laspeyres ratio, since it involves the extent and direction of responses of quantity changes to price changes, could be expected to bear some relation to the covariance between the two. And, in fact, a weighted covariance can be calculated from the two indexes.

The weighted covariance between price and quantity relatives for any year "1" is

$$Cov_w = \sum \left[\frac{P_0Q_0}{\Sigma P_0Q_0} \left(\frac{P_1}{P_0} - \frac{\Sigma P_1Q_0}{\Sigma P_0Q_0} \right) \left(\frac{Q_1}{Q_0} - \frac{\Sigma P_0Q_1}{\Sigma P_0Q_0} \right) \right]$$

If we use the following abbreviations:

Value index	$(\Sigma P_1Q_1/\Sigma P_0Q_0)$	=	V
Laspeyres price index	$(\Sigma P_1Q_0/\Sigma P_0Q_0)$	=	L_p
Laspeyres quantity index	$(\Sigma P_0Q_1/\Sigma P_0Q_0)$	=	L_q
Paasche price index	$(\Sigma P_1Q_1/\Sigma P_0Q_1)$	=	P_p
Paasche quantity index	$(\Sigma P_1Q_1/\Sigma P_1Q_0)$	=	P_q

[12] David A. Wells, *Recent Economic Changes*, New York, 1890, p. 6.

Then,

$$Cov_w = \sum \left[\frac{P_0 Q_0}{\Sigma P_0 Q_0} \left(V - \frac{P_1}{P_0} L_q - \frac{Q_1}{Q_0} L_p + L_p L_q \right) \right]$$

$$= V \sum \frac{P_0 Q_0}{\Sigma P_0 Q_0} - L_q \sum \frac{P_1 Q_0}{\Sigma P_0 Q_0} - L_p \sum \frac{P_0 Q_1}{\Sigma P_0 Q_0} + L_p L_q \sum \frac{P_0 Q_0}{\Sigma P_0 Q_0}$$

$$= V - L_q L_p - L_p L_q + L_p L_q$$

$Cov_w = V - L_p L_q$[13] or $\Sigma P_1 Q_1 / \Sigma P_0 Q_0 - (\Sigma P_1 Q_0 / \Sigma P_0 Q_0)(\Sigma P_0 Q_1 / \Sigma P_0 Q_0)$[14]

The weighted covariance, then, is the value index minus the product of the Laspeyres price and quantity indexes. Since we do not list the Laspeyres quantity indexes in Appendix A, the covariances can be computed for the NBER indexes as $Cov_w = V(1 - L_p / P_p)$.

The covariances are related to the Paasche-Laspeyres ratios as follows :

$$\frac{P_p}{L_p} = \frac{V}{V - Cov_w}$$

We have not computed covariances for many of the classes in Appendix A. From the Paasche-Laspeyres ratios, it can be inferred that those for the major classes, at least, were almost all negative once the effect of linking to a 1913 base is removed. The covariances, in combination with the variances among price ratios calculated in Chapter 5 and Appendix E, permit one to estimate the slope of the relationship between price and quantity relatives, comparing each year with the corresponding base year. Thus

$$\text{Slope} = \frac{Cov_w}{\sigma_w}$$

where σ_w is the weighted variance of the price relatives.

To summarize, this chapter gives further evidence of the pervasiveness of negative relations between price and quantity changes. To the comparisons among countries and among major classes in Chapters 1 and 2, it adds indirectly derived information on price-quantity relations within

---

[13] This expression is Irving Fisher's factor-reversal test. The Laspeyres index passes this test (the expression is equal to zero) only when the covariance of price and quantity relatives (weighted by base year values) is zero, that is, when there is no correlation between price and quantity changes.

[14] A recent paper by Victor Zarnowitz, "Index Numbers and the Seasonality of Quantities and Prices," in *The Price Statistics of the Federal Government*, New York, NBER, 1961, points out that these relationships between the Paasche and Laspeyres price indexes and the covariance of price and quantity changes were originally derived by Ladislaus von Bortkiewicz in *Nordisk Statistisk Tidskrift*, II, 1922, pp. 374–379, and III, 1924, p. 218.

major classes. It suggests, furthermore, that these indirect methods, using the differences between Paasche and Laspeyres indexes, could reveal more information on these relationships within intermediate and minor classes, and could, in addition, be applied to problems outside the area of international trade wherever the two types of indexes are available.

CHAPTER 4

Characteristics of Basic Foreign Trade Data

Nature and Testing of Customs Data

THE raw materials for this study, as for almost all investigations into international commodity trade, are the official monthly, quarterly, and annual reports on foreign commerce published first by the Treasury Department and in later years by the Commerce Department.[1] These reports show the value of exports and imports under several hundred (thousands in recent years) commodity titles. For some of them, quantities (and therefore, by implication, unit values) are also given.

The need for quarterly series, particularly for business cycle analysis, led to our use of imperfectly matching concepts of imports and exports. Exports of domestic (rather than domestic and foreign) merchandise were used because they seemed more logically related to the development of the domestic economy and because the inclusion of re-exports would have necessitated an extensive additional compilation of data. However, the corresponding import concept, imports for consumption, could not be used because quarterly data were available only for general imports.[2]

The principal type of import valuation required by the customs regulations is foreign selling price (the actual transaction price or wholesale price) plus expenses necessary before shipment to the U.S. Exports are valued at American selling price plus freight and other expenses between the source and the border of the United States. For some import items other value concepts are used, such as the price of comparable merchandise produced in the United States ("American valuation") or foreign cost of production. It is clear that, despite the regulations, many exporters and importers make up their own valuation rules.[3]

These customs data, compiled from declarations filed by exporters and importers or their agents, have not generally received very high marks for

---

[1] A detailed list of these reports is given in Appendix C.

[2] General imports are those coming directly through customs from foreign countries plus those entering customs warehouses. They exclude imports withdrawn from customs warehouses for domestic use. Imports for consumption include the same directly imported goods, but exclude those going from foreign countries into customs warehouses, and include withdrawals from warehouses for domestic consumption. For more extended discussions see R. G. D. Allen and J. Edward Ely, *International Trade Statistics*, New York, 1953, pp. 44–50, and Lawrence F. Schmeckebier, *The Statistical Work of the National Government*, Baltimore, 1925, pp. 327–329.

[3] For an extensive discussion of import valuation, see R. Elberton Smith, *Customs Valuation in the United States*, Chicago, 1948.

accuracy from scholars who have examined them closely. They are often prepared carelessly, especially for duty-free goods. Where tariff questions do arise, there is often incentive for undervaluation or incorrect description of merchandise. Furthermore, requirements for valuation change from time to time, are often ambiguous, and in some cases differ among classes of commodities.

In the period covered by the NBER indexes, the effects of respondents' errors were compounded by the procedures of the collecting agencies. When these agencies fell behind on the processing of reports, shipments were sometimes entered in the data for the months in which they were processed rather than the month of entry into the country.[4]

The only study which examined in any detail the accuracy of traders' reports to the customs authorities was one published by the Department of Commerce in 1939.[5] Values on more than 12,000 invoices, a sample of imports of nine commodities between 1913 and 1937, were compared with those of corresponding customs reports. In terms of numbers the results were discouraging; 60 per cent of the entries were incorrect (by balance of payments standards, but not necessarily according to customs regulations) and another 20 per cent lacked data necessary for the comparison. The most frequent discrepancies involved transportation costs : the failure to include the cost of transport to the customs border of the exporting country or the incorrect inclusion of the cost of ocean freight to the U.S. Other differences involved the inclusion, in whiskey import values, of taxes payable by British consumers but not paid by American importers.[6]

There is, however, a brighter side to the results of this study. The discrepancies, although frequent, were not usually very important in value terms. This was partly because positive and negative errors cancelled each other out to some extent. The net discrepancy was very important only in the case of whiskey (47.5 per cent); in all the other commodities it was below 5 per cent. It should be noted, however, that in all of the transactions in petroleum and most of those in bananas (both of which involved

---

[4] Questions of the accuracy of the data are discussed in more detail in the following sources: Schmeckebier, *Statistical Work*, pp. 335–339, 355; Dudley J. Cowden, *Measures of Exports of the United States*, New York, 1931, pp. 18–21; Eliot G. Mears, "The Foreign Trade Statistics of the United States," *Journal of the American Statistical Association*, pp. 501–516; Frank R. Rutter, "Statistics of Imports and Exports," *Publications of the American Statistical Association*, March 1916, pp. 16–34; and Smith, *Customs Valuation*.

[5] U.S. Bureau of Foreign and Domestic Commerce, *Merchandise Import Statistics in the Balance of International Payments* (Report on Office Project No. 365–97–3.20 conducted under the auspices of the W.P.A.), mimeo, 1939.

[6] This was correct according to customs regulations but did not, of course, represent purchase prices.

intracompany rather than real commercial transactions), as well as roughly a quarter of those in rubber, sugar, and whiskey, the information needed for assessing the reports was not available.

Although we are aware of the frequency of these errors, we are unable to measure their direction and importance and therefore cannot correct for them. We are, however, able to test the data indirectly by methods described later in this chapter.

The sources of error listed thus far are probably of secondary importance, since they are likely to be random in relation to price changes. The fundamental difficulty, even if all the declarations and compilations were made correctly, is that we are attempting to construct a price index without price data. The unit values used instead apply to commodities defined in terms of the requirements of tariff legislation. They usually lack the precise specification typical of price quotations.

Most of the commodity titles in the export and import classifications are broad enough to include items of widely varying unit value. Where this is true, we cannot be sure whether a change in the unit value represents a change in price or merely a shift in importance among the items included.[7]

It cannot be assumed that differences between the movements of unit values and those of prices are scattered randomly over the commodity universe. The downward bias caused by a shift to a lower grade of product (see footnote 7), probably occurs more frequently among crude products than among manufactured goods. It seems likely that an upward bias would be more frequent among manufactured goods, as consumers, with secularly rising incomes, shift toward higher-quality goods within, as well as between, commodity categories.[8]

The problem posed by heterogeneity within commodity titles is not

---

[7] Crude petroleum exports illustrate this problem. Unit values fell by about 25 per cent between 1902 and 1923, while the export unit value of illuminating oil, the BLS price for "refined petroleum for export," and the BLS price for Pennsylvania crude petroleum all rose by 40 per cent or more. The divergent behavior of the crude oil unit value was due to a shift from high-grade, high-priced Pennsylvania crude to cheaper grades from other fields.

[8] Several examples of striking changes in quality, perhaps associated more with fashion than with rising incomes, can be found among the commodities listed in imports for consumption. For example, in the narrowly defined category "ladies' or children's gloves, lamb or sheep, glacé finish, unlined," the unit value increased by 29 per cent from 1899 to 1913. But the increase was not a change in price. It was caused principally by a shift from short gloves (under 14 inches in length), whose unit value rose by 8 per cent, to much more expensive long gloves (over 17 inches in length), whose unit value fell by 16 per cent. The shift was even larger between 1899 and 1907, when total unit value rose by 77 per cent, while that for gloves 14 inches or shorter rose by only 12 per cent and that for gloves over 17 inches fell by 11 per cent.

solved by avoiding the word "price" and replacing it by "unit value" as the Department of Commerce does. Prices are unit values, and unit values are of interest only to the extent that they do represent prices.[9] Nor is the problem avoided by computing a quantity index instead of a price index. If nonhomogeneity makes the unit values economically meaningless, the quantities are made equally so.

Our solution was to compare each series with price and unit value data from sources other than customs reports.[10] In many cases we examined the components of a commodity aggregate to see if their behavior cast doubt on the total. Each export series was compared with related domestic price series. Where agreement was close, the unit value series was accepted for the index; where discrepancies in movement were large, the series was rejected. Doubtful cases were resolved by examining unit values for commodities disaggregated by country of destination or customs district of shipment; or comparisons were made with foreign prices and unit values. Import unit values were compared with data from the more detailed commodity list shown annually for imports for consumption and with prices and export unit values in the country of origin and other countries. They were also broken down by country of origin and customs district of entry. In addition, unit values of closely related commodities were compared with each other. None of the series was subjected to the full battery of tests listed, but none was accepted without passing at least one of them.

For many articles, particularly finished manufactures, no quantity data and therefore no unit values were available. Those for which no corresponding domestic or foreign price series was obtainable were put into the uncovered category. Where a price series was available, it was necessary to choose between two assumptions : (1) that the export or import price movements of that commodity were parallel to those of the outside price series, or (2) that the price movements were parallel to the average of those of the other commodities in the same group. Generally, the first assumption was chosen since it was usually confirmed when both sets of data were obtained.

Some of the outside price or unit value series used were available only on an annual basis. Since quarterly data were needed to combine these commodities or groups with others, they were estimated by freehand interpolation of unit values, following, where possible, the quarterly

[9] It would be difficult to imagine much use (except perhaps in connection with shipping problems) for a series showing the total value of exports divided by the total tonnage.

[10] These, along with imports-for-consumption series, are referred to here as "outside data."

movements of related price or unit value series. Groups in which such interpolations played an important part have been indicated in the appendixes. They cannot, of course, be used for quarterly analysis.

Comparison of Customs Data with Price Series

Throughout this study two types of data have been used as equivalents : foreign trade unit values for broadly defined commodities and domestic prices for narrowly defined commodities. Both have appeared in previous studies of export and import prices,[11] but there has been little discussion of their relationship or of the consequences of using one instead of the other.

We have made some crude tests of these data to answer two questions : (1) How well do price and unit-value data agree in the prices they report?, and (2) when they do agree on price levels, how close is their agreement on the dating of transactions? The second question is of interest partly because timing discrepancies between value and price data might produce spurious quantity movements and partly because a knowledge of possible leads and lags might aid in interpreting cyclical behavior. The answer to the first question provides information on the accuracy of the foreign trade indexes. Although neither type of data is wholly satisfactory (the customs data are not prices and the prices are not foreign trade data), we have assumed that where two such different kinds of information agree closely, the truth cannot be far away.

Fluctuations in Prices and Unit Values

The question of agreement between price and unit value records, aside from timing, is a complicated one. Our confidence in the usefulness of the unit values rests mainly on the general agreement of hundreds of pairs of price and unit value series charted against each other. On the other hand there were many instances of violent disagreement. Because the degree of agreement was the main criterion for accepting or rejecting the unit

[11] Kreps used import unit values to represent import prices and U.S. wholesale prices to represent export prices (Theodore J. Kreps, "Import and Export Prices in the United States and the Terms of International Trade, 1880–1914," *Quarterly Journal of Economics*, August 1962). The currently published indexes of the U.S. Department of Commerce rely completely on customs data, as do most of the indexes for European countries used by Kindleberger in *The Terms of Trade*, pp. 322–333. Silverman's index numbers for the U.K. were based almost entirely on domestic market prices (A. G. Silverman, "Monthly Index Numbers of British Export and Import Prices, 1880–1913," *Review of Economic Statistics*, August 1930), as were some indexes mentioned by Kindleberger.

values, formal comparisons are made here only for commodities whose unit values were not discarded.

There have been no comprehensive comparisons of the two types of data. Mitchell[12] did make one test in which he compared two indexes of British prices for the years 1871-1902. The indexes were arithmetic means of equally weighted price relatives, one set made up of export and import unit values and the other of Sauerbeck's market prices. He found that the unit values "pursue a more even course than market-price series" and, in particular, that the market price series fell more steeply during the price decline from 1871-72 to the trough in 1897.

CHART 23

Market Price and Unit Value Indexes for 25 Commodities,
Great Britain, 1871-1902
(1890-99 = 100)

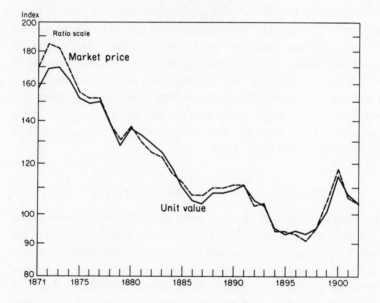

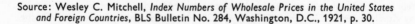

Source: Wesley C. Mitchell, *Index Numbers of Wholesale Prices in the United States and Foreign Countries*, BLS Bulletin No. 284, Washington, D.C., 1921, p. 30.

[12] Wesley C. Mitchell, *Index Numbers of Wholesale Prices in the United States and Foreign Countries*, B.L.S. Bulletin No. 284, Washington D.C., 1921.

It is clear in Chart 23 that the two indexes agree quite closely, except in 1871-74, despite the fact that the set includes some pairs of prices and unit values (particularly coffee, tea, and bacon) so poorly matched that by our standards the unit values would have been discarded. There is very little indication that the market price index is more volatile than the unit value index except during the first few years.

The differences between the two indexes, taken as percentages of the

CHART 24

Difference Between Market Price and Unit Value Indexes,
Great Britain, 1871-1902
(1890-99 = 100)

Differences are taken as a percentage of the unit value index.

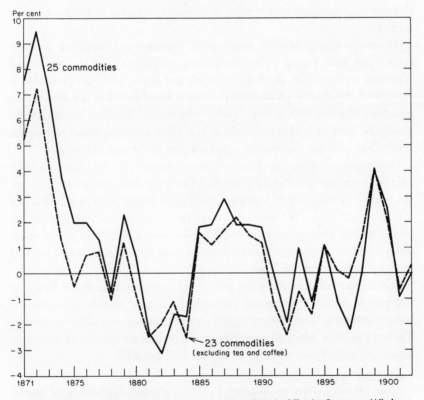

Source: Mitchell, *Index Numbers*; United Kingdom Board of Trade, *Report on Whole-•ale and Retail Prices in the United Kingdom in 1902 with Comparative Tables for a Series of Years*, London, 1903; A. Sauerbeck, 'Movement of Wholesale Prices in Great Britain,' *Monthly Summary of Commerce and Finance of the United States*, Bureau of Statistics, U.S. Department of Commerce and Labor, June 1904, pp. 4686-4692; and *Journal of the (Royal) Statistical Society*, Vol. XLIX, 1886, pp. 642-647.

unit value index, are shown in Chart 24. It is clear again that they fall within a narrow range, except in 1871-74, particularly when the tea and coffee series are removed. No downward trend of the market price index relative to the unit value index is visible after the first three years.

A comparison by Kindleberger[13] of postwar Swedish unit value and price indexes indicates some very wide discrepancies. The largest of these occurred in 1951, when the export price index was 27 per cent higher than the unit value index, even though "the indexes for Sweden based on price are weighted by the value of the commodities going into exports and imports. . . ." But this evidence is not as good as it appears : the price series is a Laspeyres index on a 1935 base, while the unit value series are Fisher "ideal" indexes on a 1948 base.[14] It is not clear therefore, what is responsible for the differences between the two indexes; the type of data used, as Kindleberger implies, or divergent weights and index number formulas.

There are several possible measures of the degree of similarity between prices and unit values. The correlation coefficient and the associated standard error would, in their conventional form, give too favorable a picture of the degree of similarity. This is because the usual correlation equation includes both a slope and a y-intercept. The two types of data would be perfect substitutes only if the ratio between them were constant; that is, if the correlation equation passed through the origin.

One could compare the ratios of the two series with the base-year ratio (as the index number formally does). In other words, one could measure the scatter around a line passing through the origin with slope equal to the base-year ratio. We have not used this measure because it gives no weight to intraperiod comparisons. For example, a price and a unit value series might be considered poorly matched even though they were identical in every year except the base.

Our method of examining the price/unit value relation was to fit to the two sets of data a line passing through the origin; that is, to study the scatter around a "best" estimate of the ratio between unit value and price. These lines were fitted to prices and unit values for eleven of the most important export commodities in the 1913-23 period.[15]

[13] *Terms of Trade*, p. 318.

[14] The Swedish indexes are described in United Nations, *Supplement to the Monthly Bulletin of Statistics*, 1954, pp. 114 and 140.

[15] The unit values were: wheat grain; wheat flour; hams and shoulders, cured; lard; leaf tobacco; unmanufactured cotton; bituminous coal; gasoline, 1913–21, extrapolated to 1923 by gasoline, naptha, and other light products; illuminating oil; and refined copper in ingots, bars, rods, or other forms. (For sources see Appendix C.)

The BLS price series were—wheat: Cash, No. 2, red winter, Chicago; wheat flour:

In nine of the eleven cases the relationship was close, the "explained variance," or r^2, being over 92 per cent. For two commodities, bituminous coal and leaf tobacco, it was only 71 per cent and 21 per cent respectively. When 1920 was dropped from the coal series and 1920 and 1921 from the tobacco series, the figures rose to 88 and 62 per cent.

More relevant for our purposes than the proportion of variance explained, is the relative error involved in estimating unit values from prices. This is measured by comparing "unexplained variation" in unit values with the unit values themselves.

For eight of the eleven commodities the ratio of the standard error of estimate[16] to the mean of the unit values was less than 8 per cent. The ratio for lubricating oil was 10.4 per cent; for bituminous coal, 24.8 per cent; and for leaf tobacco, 45.7 per cent. When 1920 was removed from the coal comparison and 1920 and 1921 from that for leaf tobacco, the figures became 12.9 per cent and 28.4 per cent.

The leaf tobacco unit value and price series were the only badly matched pair in the group, and even these two series were consistent before 1913. Because of the wide range of wartime price changes, both the level of r^2 and the unexplained variation in the 1919-23 period were probably greater than would have been obtained in earlier years. In a more tranquil period, an unchanging price might serve as an excellent approximation to a slightly fluctuating unit value even though the r^2 were 0.

The distribution of the deviations around average unit value/price ratios is of interest because it reveals the frequency with which these ratios differed substantially from their mean in this sample of commodities. Most of the large discrepancies were concentrated in bituminous coal and leaf tobacco (Table 11). Half the deviations in these commodities were greater than 15 per cent, as compared with one out of ninety-eight in other commodities.

Chart 25 shows the similarity in time pattern of the wide deviations in leaf tobacco and bituminous coal. These follow, in general, the movements of the unit value series themselves. This is particularly true around the peaks of the two series and is a reflection not only of differences in timing

standard patents, Minneapolis; hams: smoked, Chicago; Lard: prime contract, New York; tobacco: leaf, average warehouse sales, Kentucky; cotton: Middling upland, New York; bituminous coal: Pocahontas, f.o.b. Norfolk, Va.; gasoline: motor, New York; petroleum: refined, standard white, 110° fire test, New York; lubricating oil: paraffin, 903 gravity, New York; Copper: ingot, electrolytic, refinery. These were all taken from U.S. Department of Labor, *Wholesale Prices, 1890 to 1923*, BLS Bulletin No. 367, 1925, and earlier issues.

[16] Allowing for the loss of only one degree of freedom in the fitting of the line because only one constant was used.

CHART 25
Percentage Variation in Ratios of Unit Values to Prices:
11 Commodities, 1913-23
(average ratio for 1913-23 = 100)

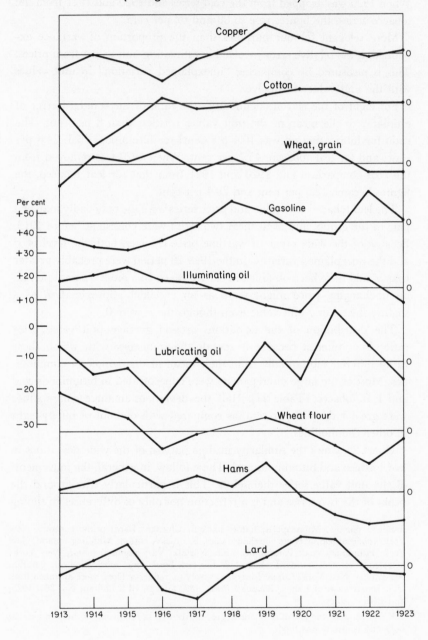

CHART 25 (Concluded)

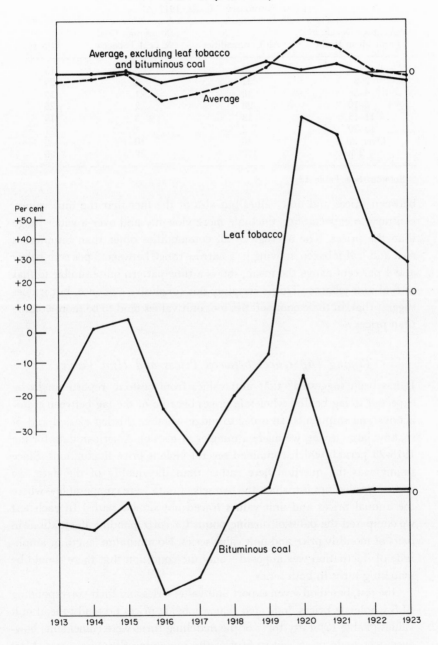

Source: See Chapter 4, footnote 15.

TABLE 11

RATIOS OF UNIT VALUES TO PRICES: DEVIATIONS
FROM COMMODITY MEANS, 1913–23

Percentage Deviation From Mean Ratio	All Commodities	Bituminous Coal & Leaf Tobacco	Others
1 or less	18	3	15
2–3	31	2	29
4–5	18	1	17
6–10	28	2	26
11–15	13	3	10
16–20	2	1	1
Over 20	10	10	0
Total	120	22	98

SOURCE: See Table 12.

between prices and unit values but also of the fact that the unit values, contrary to expectations, fluctuate more violently and over a wider range than the prices. The average of all commodities other than bituminous coal and leaf tobacco, moving in a narrow range between 3 per cent below and 4 per cent above the mean, shows a time pattern quite similar to that of coal and tobacco. This is certainly not conclusive evidence, but it does suggest that, in these commodities too, unit values tend to be more volatile than prices.

Timing Differences between Prices and Unit Values

It has been suggested[17] that unit values from customs reports might be expected to lag behind wholesale prices because of the lag between transactions and shipments. In order to judge whether this lag existed and, if so, how large it was, we made a number of tests on American data for the 1913-23 period, which contained several violent price fluctuations. Since timing was the question here rather than the quality of the data, we chose commodities for which the two sets of data were comparable—where the annual prices and unit values traced out similar paths. In each test we compared the dates of turning points for corresponding fluctuations in pairs of monthly price and unit value series. No minimum length or amplitude of fluctuation was imposed—only the condition that there should be matching turns in both series.

One test, based on seven export unit value series and their corresponding BLS wholesale prices, indicated that wholesale prices do tend to lead unit values (Table 12). Fifty-three of the matching turns were coincident; however, wholesale prices led in fifty of the remaining fifty-nine cases. Most

[17] For example, by Kindleberger, *Terms of Trade*, pp. 317–318.

TABLE 12
TIMING RELATION OF EXPORT UNIT VALUES[a] AND WHOLESALE PRICES[b]
(monthly data)

	Cotton	Copper	Illuminating Oil	Corn	Oats	Rye	Wheat	Total
No. of corresponding turns	23	20	7	13	16	17	16	112
Wholesale price leading	14	7	2	6	8	5	8	50
Coincident	9	12	4	4	5	11	8	53
Unit value leading	0	1	1	3	3	1	0	9
Average lead of wholesale price (months)								
All turns	1.04	.45	−.29	.15	.38	.29	.81	.51
Turns with wholesale price leading	1.71	1.29	1.00	1.17	1.38	1.20	1.62	1.46

SOURCE: For BLS data, *Wholesale Prices, 1890 to 1923* and earlier issues. For NBER data, see sources in Appendix C.
a Cotton, unmanufactured; refined copper in ingots, bars, rods, and other forms; illuminating oil (kerosene); corn, grain; oats, grain; rye, grain; and wheat, grain. b BLS series for cotton, middling, upland, New York; copper, ingot, electrolytic; refined petroleum, for export; corn, cash, contract grades; oats, cash; rye, No. 2, cash; wheat, cash, Chicago, No. 2, red winter.

TABLE 13
TIMING RELATION OF IMPORT UNIT VALUES[a] AND WHOLESALE PRICES[b]
(monthly data)

	Tin	Cocoa	Sugar	Coffee	Silk	Rubber	Total
No. of corresponding turns	11	10	23	18	19	12	93
Wholesale price leading	9	5	14	13	15	9	65
Coincident	1	4	8	3	2	1	19
Unit value leading	1	1	1	2	2	2	9
Average lead of wholesale prices (months)							
All turns	2.09	.50	.65	.78	1.11	1.33	1.01
Turns with wholesale price leading	2.67	1.80	1.14	1.31	1.53	2.56	1.78

SOURCE: See Table 12.
a Tin in bars, blocks, pigs, etc.; cocoa or cacao beans; cane sugar; coffee; rubber, crude; and raw silk. b BLS series for tin, pig; cocoa beans, Arriba; sugar, 96° centrifugal; coffee, Rio, No. 7; raw silk: Japanese—filatures, special, and extra extra; rubber, Para island, fine, N.Y.

of these leads were quite short: forty-six of the fifty were one or two months; the average lead for all turns was half a month. For those cases in which wholesale prices led, the average was a month and a half.[18]

The results of a similar test, comparing U.S. wholesale prices with import unit values, are given in Table 13. Unit values lag more consistently than for exports (sixty-five of ninety-three turns) and by a longer interval — a month on the average. The average lead of wholesale prices, for those turns in which they do lead, is 1.78 months. Wholesale prices lead in a majority of turns for every commodity in the list except one. Furthermore, these leads are not only more frequent than in exports, they are longer on the average; there are thirteen leads of more than two months as compared to only four among exports.

On the assumption that monthly data reveal the true leads of wholesale prices, an experiment was conducted to determine the extent to which our consolidation of the data into quarters hides or exaggerates these leads. Imports were used rather than exports because they showed longer, and therefore more troublesome, leads. The results, in Table 14, indicate that one effect of the consolidation, as might be expected, is to convert many of the leads into coincident turns. There are thirty-six in the quarterly data as compared with nineteen in the monthly data, despite the fact that there are fewer matching turns in the former. Those leads which still remain have increased in length because of the increase in the minimum size of lead; the average lead is now 1.20 months as compared with 1.01 in the monthly data. All but one of the leads in the quarterly data are one quarter; the average is 3.06 months.

Leads and coincidences are almost equally represented in the quarterly data, but the leads are more frequent in four of the six commodities. Except for silk and rubber, where three of four price lags were eliminated, the lags were not erased by the shift to quarterly data.

The turning points that appear in Table 13 differ from those in Table 14. Some were eliminated by averaging in the shift from monthly to quarterly data; almost all of these were coincidences or one-month price leads. Other turns appearing in the quarterly series had not been identifiable in the more volatile monthly data. The effect of shifting from monthly to quarterly data on an identical set of turns is shown in Table 15 for sixty-eight matched turning points.

---

[18] It would have been desirable to extend this analysis to manufactured goods, but because many of their prices are constant for several months at a time, the selection of a monthly turning point is arbitrary and small leads and lags disappear. In addition manufactured-goods prices exhibit fewer and much milder fluctuations than prices of crude and semimanufactured products.

TABLE 14

TIMING RELATION OF IMPORT UNIT VALUES AND WHOLESALE PRICES

(quarterly data)

	Tin	Cocoa	Sugar	Coffee	Silk	Rubber	Total
No. of corresponding turns	12	13	15	15	17	9	82
Wholesale price leading	5	7	5	8	9	6	40
Coincident	6	6	9	5	8	2	36
Unit value leading	1	1	1	2	0	1	6
Average lead of wholesale price (quarters)							
All turns	0.33	0.43	0.27	0.40	0.53	0.44	0.40
Turns with wholesale price leading	1.00	1.00	1.00	1.00	1.00	1.17	1.02
Average lead of wholesale price (months)							
All turns	1.00	1.29	.81	1.20	1.59	1.32	1.20
Turns with wholesale price leading	3.00	3.00	3.00	3.00	3.00	3.51	3.06

SOURCE: See notes to Table 13.

TABLE 15

EFFECT OF SHIFTING FROM MONTHLY TO QUARTERLY
DATA ON LEAD OF WHOLESALE PRICES

	Lead in Monthly Data (Months)	Average Lead in Quarterly Data (Months)	Number of Cases
	5	3.0	1
	4	2.4	5
	3	2.14	7
	2	1.71	14
	1	1.50	22
	0	.27	11
	−1	.50	6
	−2	−3.0	1
	−6	−9.0	1
Total	82	81	68
Average	1.20	1.19	68

SOURCE: See notes to Table 13.

The longer leads of wholesale prices were reduced, on the average, by the conversion. One-month leads were stretched slightly, and coincidences and one-month lags were turned into short leads. The longer lags, however, were extended. The conversion to quarterly data thus altered the distribution of leads and lags, but it had no effect on the average length.

The Combination of Price and Unit Value Data as a Source of Error

"Outside" prices may behave differently from unit values for a number of reasons : the domestic commodity might be very different from the export commodity, even though they travel under the same name; when the commodities are the same, market conditions might be such that domestic and export prices move differently; even if the price movements are similar, the domestic price might lead or lag behind the export price. Any of these phenomena could lead to misconceptions not only about prices but about the behavior of quantities as well, since quantities are not estimated indepently of prices.

Table 16 and Chart 26 illustrate the effect of using an estimated price which is identical to the true one except that it leads the true price by one period.[19] The distortion of the quantity series is marked, although the timing is not altered. The amplitude is doubled and artificial accelerations are introduced into both the expansion and the contraction.

The estimation and interpretation of price-quantity relations may also

[19] Periods two through six in Table 11 may be viewed as a business cycle divided into five stages.

106

be affected by such errors. If, for example, a series of arbitrary numbers called "value" is divided by another arbitrary series called "price" to get "quantity," the price-quantity relation will not be random. Since prices and values are independent, high prices will tend to be associated with low quantities, and vice versa. The price elasticity will tend toward one, and the level of the correlation between price and quantity will depend on the relation between the variance in value and the variance in price. The larger the latter compared to the former the higher the price-quantity correlation will be.

In terms of the indexes calculated here, there is some possibility that a spurious negative price-quantity relation has been introduced or that a positive relation has been obscured by such errors. At least the direction of bias, if not the extent, is clear.

CHART 26

Effect on Estimated Quantities of Using Estimated Prices Leading Actual Prices by One Period

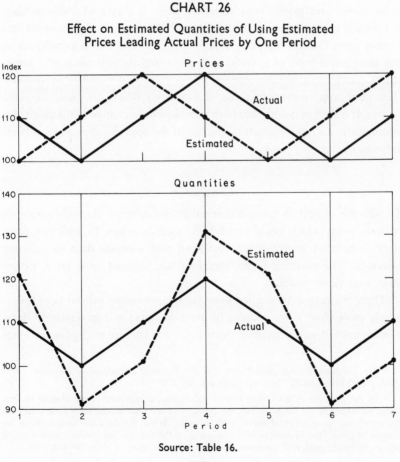

Source: Table 16.

TABLE 16

EFFECT ON ESTIMATED QUANTITIES OF USING ESTIMATED PRICES
LEADING ACTUAL PRICES BY ONE PERIOD.

	Period						
	1	2	3	4	5	6	7
Actual							
Price	110	100	110	120	110	100	110
Quantity	110	100	110	120	110	100	110
Value	121	100	121	144	121	100	121
Estimated from leading price series							
Price	100	110	120	110	100	110	120
Quantity	121	91	101	131	121	91	101
Value	121	100	121	144	121	100	121

These difficulties, most evident where quantities are derived directly from values and prices, exist wherever there is a lack of independence between the estimation of price and that of quantity. For example, an output series that includes a coverage adjustment in which parallelism in the price movements of covered and uncovered items is assumed,[20] introduces an element of interdependence in price and quantity estimation. The same applies even to those of our series which are based on unit values. If a shift in quality has been mistaken for a change in the price of a commodity, a spurious quantity change in the opposite direction has been introduced.[21]

Conclusion

Despite the defects of customs unit values, we selected, through a number of tests, many which could properly be used as prices. In addition, price data from other sources were combined with customs data to improve coverage. The resulting series, therefore, are referred to as price, rather than unit value, indexes.

There is strong evidence for some lag of unit values behind prices. It is rarely more than a few months in monthly data; and in quarterly data, seldom more than one quarter. Although these lags are negligible for long-

[20] See, for example, Solomon Fabricant, *The Output of Manufacturing Industries: 1899–1937*, New York, NBER, 1940, especially pp. 362–372.

[21] In the example of the gloves mentioned earlier, acceptance of the change in unit value indicated in the totals for 1899 to 1907, +77 per cent, would have meant an estimated change in quantity of about +40 per cent. When the data are broken down by length of glove, the highest possible estimate of the increase in average unit value is about + 10 per cent, and the lowest increase in quantity, more than 100 per cent.

term analysis, they may affect short-term comparisons of foreign trade prices with quantities or domestic prices.

Earlier studies indicating much greater sluggishness in unit values than in prices were examined and found to rest on weak foundations. A comparison of the two types of data in our period indicated little difference in most series. The differences that were observed pointed to the contrary finding : unit values may have been more volatile than prices.

CHAPTER 5

Sampling Characteristics and Accuracy
of Index Numbers

Sampling Problems in the Construction of Price Indexes[1]

QUESTIONS of sampling procedure almost always arise in the construction of price and other index numbers, but are rarely treated explicitly. They are, in fact, obscured by the use of index number terminology. Our consideration of sampling problems first arose in setting up standards for commodity classification. We also wished to say something about the accuracy of our indexes beyond the usual warnings that they must be used with care. Many of the decisions to be made in designing the indexes and the questions to be answered in appraising them were closely analagous to problems of sampling design and the measurement of sampling error. We have attempted, therefore, to translate our problems into a simplified sampling terminology.

A THEORETICAL DESCRIPTION OF SAMPLING FOR A PRICE INDEX

Suppose that, ignorant of the vast index number literature and unable to collect every price, one set out to measure the average change in prices between two dates.

The first procedure to come to mind might be to list all the commodities, choose from among them in some random fashion and strike an average of the price ratios, weighting them all equally. But this method is clearly unsatisfactory—the classification of commodities is arbitrary, and, there-

---

[1] The first part of this chapter is an expanded version of a paper on "Some Sampling Problems in the Construction of Price Indexes" read at the Annual Meeting of the American Statistical Association, December 1955. Several substantial discussions of this subject have since appeared, each treating it from a slightly different viewpoint and, in some cases, giving evidence that random sampling is a practical possibility. The following are some of the main contributions: Irma Adelman, "A New Approach to the Construction of Index Numbers," *The Review of Economics and Statistics*, August 1958; K. S. Banerjee, "Calculation of Sampling Errors for Index Numbers" *Sankhya*, January 1960, and "A Comment on the Sampling Aspects in the Construction of Index Numbers," *The Review of Economics and Statistics*, May 1960; two staff papers of the NBER Price Statistics Review Committee: Philip J. McCarthy, "Sampling Considerations in the Construction of Price Indexes with Particular Reference to the United States Consumer Price Index," and Victor Zarnowitz, "Index Numbers and the Seasonality of Quantities and Prices," published in *The Price Statistics of the Federal Government*, New York, National Bureau of Economic Research, 1961.

fore, the frequency with which any group of commodities is represented in such a selection depends on the fineness with which the group has been broken down, rather than on its importance. Each commodity would have an equal chance of being represented, but not each dollar of trade. If each commodity is thought of as a cluster of transactions, this procedure is one in which samples of equal size are drawn from each commodity cluster, even though some clusters are much larger than others. The probability of inclusion in the sample for a given dollar of trade, as well as the sampling fraction, would be inversely proportional to the size of the cluster.

What is needed is a method by which we can dip at random into the stream of trade, giving each dollar of transactions an equal opportunity to be represented in the sample, and, therefore, giving each commodity or group of commodities representation in proportion to the value of its trade. This might be achieved if the number of times a commodity appeared on the list was proportional to its importance (as measured by base-year value, given-year value, or some combination of the two, the choice depending on the type of index number used). Such a method would be equivalent to choosing from a list of dollars of trade, rather than commodities, and it would give each dollar of trade an equal chance of inclusion.

Of course this would be even more impractical than our first list of commodities. The same results could be achieved by selecting commodities from the first list and then weighting each price ratio by the importance of the commodity it represents. If we assume that all of the price ratios for a given commodity are identical (or that the sample of dollars of trade in that commodity would give an unbiased estimate of the mean or index for that commodity), the weighting achieves the same result as taking equal sampling fractions for each commodity. The equality of sampling fractions insures equal probability of inclusion for each dollar of trade.

The size (or importance) measure can be easily described for the Paasche, Laspeyres, Marshall-Edgeworth, and several other indexes. In the case of the Laspeyres price index, for example, it is the base-year value of (trade or exports in) the commodity. For the Paasche index it is the base-year price multiplied by the quantity in the year being compared with the base year. And for the Marshall-Edgeworth index it is the average of the Paasche and Laspeyres weights. Each of these can be put in the form : index $= \Sigma ab$, where a is the weight, the ratio of the size (e.g., value) of the commodity to the total for all commodities, and b is the ratio of given-year price to base-year price. The Fisher index cannot be represented in this way,[2] but its weights can be approximated by those of the Marshall-Edgeworth index.

We have discussed, so far, only simple sampling procedure, but we know, from such studies as those of Mitchell and Mills,[3] that prices can be divided into groups which show distinctly different cyclical or trend characteristics. For this reason, a stratified rather than a simple random sample would improve the accuracy of our estimate of the mean. We should distinguish, to cite Mitchell's classification, crude from manufactured, agricultural from nonagricultural, animal from vegetable and from mineral, and consumer from producer goods. It is advisable to make even finer distinctions if groups within these strata differ significantly in the characteristics which interest us.

Stratification involves breaking the universe into several subuniverses, sampling within each as before, and then giving each mean (that is, price index) the weight of the subuniverse, or stratum, to which it refers, instead of the weight of the commodities selected. Stratification will increase the precision of our estimate of the mean even if we take a proportional sample (which, on the average, produces the same sampling fractions as a simple random sample) by insuring the proper weight for each stratum in each sample, instead of only on the average among all samples. Stratification also opens another avenue towards increased precision: the more variable groups can be sampled more heavily than the less variable ones.

Proportionate sampling can be described as that in which $\dfrac{n_h}{\Sigma n_h} = \dfrac{N_h}{\Sigma N_h}$, where n_h is the number in the sample from a stratum and N_h is the total number in the stratum. Optimum sampling, cost factors aside, is such that $\dfrac{n_h}{\Sigma n_h} = \dfrac{N_h S_h}{\Sigma N_h S_h}$, where S_h is the standard deviation for the stratum.[4] An optimum allocation shifts the sample from the less to the more variable strata.

ACTUAL SAMPLING PROCEDURES IN PRICE INDEX CONSTRUCTION

It is obvious that the preceding paragraphs are not a description of the way in which price indexes are presently computed. In particular, the

[2] The Fisher index is a square root and can therefore be irrational. But Σab must be rational, because the a's and b's are fractions, and their products and the sums of their products must therefore be rational.

[3] Wesley C. Mitchell, "Index Numbers of Wholesale Prices in the United States and Foreign Countries," BLS *Bulletin 284*, 1921; and Frederick C. Mills, *The Behavior of Prices*, New York, NBER, 1927.

[4] Morris H. Hansen, William H. Hurwitz, and William G. Madow, *Sample Survey Methods and Theory*, New York, 1953, Vol. I, p. 209.

selection of prices for inclusion in the indexes is not made by random methods. Instead commodities are chosen to obtain the greatest coverage at the least cost. A selection may be made, for example, of a number of the most important items,[5] or of those in which trade is greater than a given amount, or perhaps of a sufficient number of items to reach a specified portion of the total.

Such methods may rest on the assumption that the value of trade in a commodity is not correlated with price behavior. Unfortunately, this is not true. Most of the commodities of large value are crude or semimanufactured materials or foodstuffs. Commodity classes for manufactures tend to be relatively small.[6] Since the price behavior of manufactured goods differs from that of foods and materials, selection by amount of trade tends to bias the index towards the behavior of crude products.

Random selection is hampered, even for those agencies which collect their own price data, by ignorance of those properties of the universe which would be needed to guide sampling procedure.[7] For those working with already collected data such as foreign trade reports, the problem of nonresponse is the main obstacle. That is, for the great majority of commodities listed in the U.S. customs returns, either no data on quantities (and unit values) are given at all, or the commodity titles are amalgamated into groups so heterogeneous that the unit values cannot be treated as prices. Because most commodity categories give no information on price changes, index number compilers are often led to use whatever is available without worrying about possible biases.[8]

[5] This was the case, for example, with the import and export price indexes computed by Theodore J. Kreps, "Import and Export Prices in the United States and the Terms of International Trade, 1880–1914" *Quarterly Journal of Economics* August 1926. The Department of Commerce indexes are described as including directly "all leading commodities for which quantities are available and which show a reasonable degree of homogeneity . . .," U.S. Department of Commerce, Bureau of Foreign and Domestic Commerce, *Foreign Trade of the United States, 1936–49*, GPO, 1951, note to Table 10, p. 6. See also Dorothy S. Brady and Abner Hurwitz, "Measuring Comparative Purchasing Power" *Problems in the International Comparison of Economic Accounts*, Studies in Income and Wealth, Volume Twenty, Princeton University Press for the NBER, 1957.

[6] Since the commodity classification is arbitrary, these manufactured goods categories could be amalgamated into larger classes only at the cost of grouping together dissimilar articles. These groups would be so heterogeneous that changes in unit values could not be interpreted as price changes. Thus the selection problem would have been solved by producing what could be described in sampling terminology as a nonresponse problem. The large manufactured goods classes so created would not yield any meaningful price data. One reason for this difficulty is that in the manufacturing process a few types of raw cotton, for example, can be made into many types of cloth and these into uncountable varieties of clothing.

[7] See Brady and Hurwitz in, *International Comparison of Economic Accounts*, pp. 310–311. Their discussion relates mainly to international comparisons of price levels, but could apply almost as well to comparisons over time.

[8] See, however, the articles by Adelman, Banerjee, and McCarthy, referred to in Note 1.

113

The problem of nonresponse would not be troublesome if it were spread evenly over the commodity universe. But we find differences in price behavior between manufactured goods and crude materials, and between goods whose method of production is changing technologically and those whose technology is stable. The former of each pair are likely to show high rates of nonresponse which threaten to bias the index.[9]

STRATIFICATION TO MINIMIZE SELECTION AND NONRESPONSE BIAS

The possibilities of bias inherent in nonrandom sampling methods and in extensive nonresponse cannot be eliminated completely, but we can attempt to minimize their effects. As in reducing sampling error, the method is to stratify the universe by those attributes of commodities which we know to be related to price behavior. In addition, stratification by attributes which are related to nonresponse or selection bias, would eliminate some bias due to differences in nonresponse among strata, although not bias due to within-strata differences.[10]

There is no way of being agnostic with regard to the price behavior of any commodity. If the stratification has any validity, every commodity should be placed within some stratum. Omitting a commodity from the price index is equivalent to assuming that its behavior is that of the average of all included commodities. It would be illogical, for example, to treat machinery, which we know to be a durable, nonagricultural, producers' good as behaving like the average of all commodities if we have a durable vs. nondurable or a producers' vs. consumers' or an agricultural vs. nonagricultural product classification which reveals significant differences in price behavior.

[9] Some of these shortcomings in the BLS Wholesale Price Index of that period are discussed in Morris A. Copeland, "Some Suggestions for Improving our Information on Wholesale Commodity Prices," and Robert W. Burgess, "The General Structure of Wholesale Prices," both in *Proceedings of the Ninety-second Annual Meeting of the American Statistical Association*, 1931.

[10] The sampling problems involved in the construction of price indexes from data collected for other purposes are similar to those dealt with in Appendix G of *Statistical Problems of the Kinsey Report*, by William G. Cochran, Frederick Mosteller, and John W. Tukey (American Statistical Association, Washington, 1954). In both .cases, the sample has not been drawn randomly, and it is therefore difficult to know exactly what the parent population is. The stratification described here is parallel, if it is performed after the sample has been drawn, to the process of "adjustment" of sample means described in that report. It can be thought of as a process by which the characteristics of the sample are compared with those of the population and the sample mean reweighted in accordance with the characteristics of the population. The constructor of price indexes has one advantage: there have been studies of the price universe which give some guidance as to which characteristics are significant for pre-sampling stratification or post-sampling adjustment.

It would be ideal to design the stratification scheme in advance, using knowledge about the behavior of prices gained from other studies. Such a stratification would reveal many empty classes, classes containing only commodities for which we have no price data, and would illuminate the areas where bias is most likely. We have usually made the best guess possible by amalgamating many such classes with those which seemed most closely related.

THE MEASUREMENT OF THE PRECISION OF PRICE INDEXES

Published price indexes have rarely been accompanied by estimates of sampling error, but some independent estimates have been attempted. With the exception of those in the articles by Adelman and Banerjee mentioned earlier, they have probably exaggerated the accuracy of the indexes.

A. L. Bowley, in 1924[11] made some measurements of the sampling error of Sauerbeck's index, published in the *Statist*. His method indicated coefficients of variations (standard error ÷ mean), of 1.6 to 3.4 per cent for the 1899-1913 period (forty "independent" price series), and 4.6 to 6.0 per cent for the 1913, 1919-22 period (thirty-nine "independent" price series).[12] Frederick C. Mills[13] made more extensive investigations of this subject, estimating coefficients of variation for eight of his own index numbers. The coefficients for the fixed-base indexes, which were in every case larger than those for the corresponding link relatives, had the following ranges:

	1891–1913	1914–26
Unweighted arithmetic mean	.8-2.1	.7-4.7
Unweighted geometric mean	.8-1.8	.6-1.8
Weighted arithmetic mean	1.4-3.4	.9-3.0
Weighted geometric mean	1.4-3.4	1.0-3.1

If the confidence interval is measured by twice the coefficient of variation, these figures indicate ranges of error of 3 to 12 per cent for the *Statist* index. For the Mills indexes, the ranges are 1.5 to 7 per cent in the prewar period and 1.2 to 9.5 per cent in the later years (even though the series covers 200 to 400 commodities).

---

[11] *Relative Changes in Price and Other Index-Numbers*. London and Cambridge Economic Service, Special Memorandum No. 5, Feb. 1924, pp. 6–8.

[12] Bowley computed probable errors of the means for only one year. We extended the computation to the remaining years using his method and his data, and increased the probable errors by 50 per cent to approximate standard errors.

[13] *Behavior of Prices*, pp. 240–274.

Fisher did not publish any extensive calculations on actual index numbers, although he recognized the existence of sampling problems. For a 200-commodity index he compiled from *Dun's Review,* he suggested a probable error of 1.5 per cent,[14] which would imply a standard error of slightly over 2 per cent. Mudgett[15] presents the formulas for the standard error of the mean (i.e., the index), both weighted and unweighted, with and without the finite sampling correction, and for stratified as well as unstratified sampling. He points out that stratification can be effective in reducing the sampling variability of the average, but he does not discuss its use to minimize the effects of bias in selection.[16] He is therefore led to say of the BLS Wholesale Price Index, which has for some years contained over 800 items, "It might even be possible to say that such a comprehensive index is practically devoid of sampling error."[17] Since Mudgett mentions the total number of items, it would appear that for this purpose he is treating the BLS index as if it were constructed from a simple random sample.

STRATIFICATION AND THE MEASUREMENT OF SAMPLING ERROR

We suspect that most of the preceding estimates of sampling error are too low because they assume simple random sampling, and, therefore, probability of representation proportional to size. In fact, there are serious differences in representation, and the groups which are poorly represented are not necessarily those with low dispersion.[18] The total number of items included in an index is clearly not significant without some information about the distribution (consider, for example, a 100-item index where ninety-eight of the items were drawn from one identifiable half of the population and only two from the other).

The error caused by combining in the same stratum groups which differ in the extent of coverage (or nonresponse) can be illustrated by the following example. Suppose that we can stratify a population into two groups that are equal in size (N_h) but differ in the extent of coverage (or probability of inclusion in the sample). Let us say that they differ to the extent that the number of commodities in the sample from one group (Kn_h) is K times the number from the other group (n_h).

[14] Irving Fisher, *The Making of Index Numbers,* Boston, 1922, p. 340.
[15] Bruce D. Mudgett, *Index Numbers,* New York, 1951, pp. 51–54.
[16] Mudgett does observe that it is often exceedingly difficult to draw a random sample. *Ibid,* p. 53.
[17] *Ibid.,* p. 54.
[18] It might be that the poorly covered groups, since they are frequently manufactured products, have a large proportion of sticky prices and therefore small dispersion of price changes over short periods. But this would not be likely for price trends over longer periods.

The variance of the sample mean $(\sigma_{\bar{x}}^2)$ from a stratified sample can be written as $\frac{1}{N^2}\Sigma\left[N_h^2 \frac{S_h^2}{n_h}\right]$ where $N = \Sigma N_h$ and S_h^2 is the variance within a stratum.[19] In our example, with the two strata described above, this variance $(\sigma_{\bar{x}}^2)$ becomes

$$\frac{1}{(2N_h)^2}\left[N_h^2 \frac{S_h^2}{n_h} + N_h^2 \frac{S_h^2}{Kn_h}\right]$$

which reduces to $\frac{S_h^2}{n_h} \cdot \frac{1+K}{4K}$.

But suppose we had combined these two strata into a single one and had treated the stratified sample as if it were a simple random sample. Our estimate of the variance of the mean would have been $\frac{S^2}{n}$ where

$$S^2 = \frac{n_h S_h^2 + Kn_h S_h^2}{n_h + Kn_h} \text{ and } n = n_h + Kn_h$$

This estimate of the variance reduces to $\frac{S_h^2}{n_h} \cdot \frac{1}{1+K}$. The ratio of the first, correct, estimate of the variance of the mean to the second, incorrect, one is $\frac{(1+K)^2}{4K}$. Or, in other words, the valid estimate of the standard error of the mean (or index) would be $\frac{K+1}{2\sqrt{K}}$ times the estimate derived by treating the sample as random, as was done by Bowley and Mills and, implicitly, by some of the others mentioned above.

For small values of K the understatement of the standard error is not large; at $K=2$ it is about 6 per cent. It rises to 14 per cent for $K=3$, 20 per cent for $K=4$, and 40 per cent for $K=9$.

This ratio would be higher if it took into account the case where n in one stratum is so small that it should be treated as a small sample.

Thus another important reason for stratification emerges : without it we cannot make any reasonable estimate of the sampling error of the index. It is true that the stratification which would be optimum for increasing the precision of the estimate of the mean and for reducing bias in that estimate (one based on homogeneity with respect to the mean, or price behaviour) would not be the optimum stratification for estimating the sampling error of the mean. The latter would be one which revealed the greatest differences in coverage (probability of inclusion) among strata;

[19] Hansen, Hurwitz, and Madow, *Sample Survey Methods*, p. 189.

that is, which grouped together types of commodities whose degree of coverage was similar. But a detailed stratification for the former purpose is likely to reveal many of the differences in coverage relevant to the latter.

MEASURES OF VARIABILITY AND SAMPLING ERROR IN THE NBER INDEXES

We have performed measurements of variability and sampling error in two ways. The first is appropriate when a weighted index is used to deflate the value of the uncovered items. It treats the covered items as if they had actually been picked with probability proportional to size. In other words, it assumes that the commodity distribution of the covered items is representative of the uncovered ones as well — that a large item represents a greater number of observations of the mean than a small one. The variance and other measures (Appendix Tables E-1 through E-3) are computed by weighting each price ratio by the size of the commodity.

There are certainly grounds for uneasiness about this method of estimation, since we are not sure of the representativeness of the sample. If, for example, the covered items in a class are dominated by a single large item which is not outstandingly important among the uncovered commodities, we are likely to have underestimated the margins of error. This danger is increased by the fact that we assume no within-commodity variance even though we know there must be some.

For these reasons, we computed, as a rough check, a second estimate of the standard error which treats each commodity, regardless of size, as a single observation. The standard error is thus estimated from an unweighted variance of the price ratios. Only the first step in these computations, the calculation of unweighted standard deviations, is shown here (Table E-1), but the relation between unweighted and weighted standard errors can be inferred from this table. The counterpart of this assumption in the index computations would be the deflation of the uncovered items by an unweighted rather than a weighted index of the covered items.

It would be possible to find from such computations that the margins of error surrounding the indexes were tolerably small even where only a small fraction of all the items were sampled, provided we were willing to assume the randomness of the sampling, and had sufficiently large numbers of items included. However, given our assumption that the covered items are free from sampling variation, these measurements exaggerate the range of error, for sampling error applies only to that part of each class which consists of uncovered items. To estimate the variability of the whole group we made a finite sampling adjustment, multiplying the variance of the mean by one minus the coverage ratio. These computations yield the adjusted measures in Appendix Tables E-2 and E-3.

The coverage ratio itself is often used as a measure of the reliability of an index.[20] The usual practice is to set a minimum level of coverage below which an index is considered too unreliable for use.[21] The logic of this criterion is that, given the degree of variation among the covered items, the standard error of the index varies directly with the noncoverage ratio.

Measures of sampling error take account of both the coverage ratio and the variability of the covered items. Thus a maximum level of error, rather than minimum coverage which is only a proxy for it, can be established as a criterion for acceptance of the index.[22] One index with a fairly low coverage may be acceptable if the price behavior is homogeneous and there are many items, while another with higher coverage may be rejected because it contains heterogeneous price behavior and few items.

Table 17 summarizes the sampling error measurements for NBER minor classes. It is evident from the coefficients of variation how important the finite sampling (or coverage) adjustment is to the reliability of the indexes. The unadjusted coefficients were frequently quite high; almost a third of the export and half of the import classes which contained more than one covered commodity showed coefficients of more than 10 per cent, and more than one out of ten had coefficients above 20 per cent. These figures exclude, however, all the classes in which there is no variability (those consisting only of one commodity) and those in which variability is unknown because none or only one of the commodities is covered.

Once the coverage adjustment is made (Columns 2 and 4) the minor class indexes appear more reliable. Of the 120 cases where unadjusted coefficients were over 10 per cent, only eight of forty-six remain on the export side and sixteen of seventy-four on the import side. If completely covered one-commodity classes are included, approximately 40 per cent of all the coefficients are zero and over half are 2 per cent or less.

The sampling variability of the five major classes which correspond to

---

[20] For example, in John H. Adler, Eugene R. Schlesinger, and Evelyn Van Westerborg, *The Pattern of United States Import Trade Since 1923*, Federal Reserve Bank of New York, 1952; in descriptions of the official Department of Commerce quantity and unit value indexes for U.S. exports and imports; and in Solomon Fabricant, *The Output of Manufacturing Industries*, New York, NBER, 1940.

[21] Fabricant, for example, did not accept indexes whose coverage was less than 40 per cent (*Ibid.*, pp. 34–35).

[22] Fabricant in *Output of Manufacturing Industries*, pp. 362–367, presented some calculations showing the effects on his indexes of various degrees of divergence between the price movements of covered and uncovered items, but gave only very general indications of the likelihood of each degree of divergence.

TABLE 17

SIZE DISTRIBUTION OF WEIGHTED COEFFICIENTS OF
VARIATION: MINOR CLASSES (EARLIEST YEAR OF EACH PERIOD)

Coefficient of Variation	Exports		Imports	
	Unadjusted (1)	Adjusted (2)	Unadjusted (3)	Adjusted (4)
	Classes Containing More Than One Covered Commodity			
0	3	47	1	36
.001 – .020	17	41	9	28
.021 – .040	23	28	20	22
.041 – .060	27	14	17	23
.061 – .080	18	9	14	13
.081 – .100	18	5	15	12
.101 – .120	6	3	16	3
.121 – .140	4	1	14	5
.141 – .160	9	1	7	2
.161 – .180	7	0	10	2
.181 – .200	4	2	9	0
.201 – .250	8	1	6	2
.251 – .300	2	0	4	0
.301 – .400	3	0	3	2
.401+	3	0	5	0
Total	152	152	150	150
	Classes Containing Only One Covered Commodity			
Complete coverage	43	43	68	68
Incomplete coverage	22	22	39	39

SOURCE: Appendix Table E–3.

Commerce Department economic classes is summarized in Table 18 (and described in greater detail in Appendix Table E-4). Coefficients of variation for imports are larger than those for the corresponding export classes —sixteen out of twenty times. The coefficients for finished manufactures are generally high; those for food classes are low, with the exception of Import Class 201 (crude foods) in 1899. The size of this coefficient is due mainly to one small minor class, Import Class 006 (spices), in which the three covered items were so divergent in behavior as to give a standard error of estimate of .44 before finite sampling adjustment and .23 even after coverage is taken into account.

On the whole, the errors seem tolerable. None of the coefficients of variation exceeds 3.5 per cent; none outside of manufactures is greater than 2.3 per cent. Seventy per cent of the total and 80 per cent of those outside finished manufactures were under 2 per cent. The coefficients are large enough, however, to suggest that it would be useful to experiment with random selection to produce more valid variability estimates.

120

TABLE 18

COEFFICIENTS OF VARIATION FOR SELECTED MAJOR CLASS PRICE INDEXES[a]

Economic Class	Year	Exports (%)	Imports (%)
Crude foods	1879	.1	1.0
	1889	.5	.6
	1899	.8	2.3
	1913	.8	1.1
Manufactured foods	1879	.5	1.4
	1889	.7	.9
	1899	1.2	.9
	1913	.9	.7
Crude materials	1879	1.3	1.4
	1889	.8	1.0
	1899	.8	1.2
	1913	1.3	1.5
Semimanufactures	1879	2.3	1.7
	1889	2.1	2.3
	1899	1.0	2.1
	1913	1.1	1.0
Finished manufactures	1879	1.8	2.4
	1889	2.0	3.5
	1899	2.0	3.3
	1913	2.6	2.7

SOURCE Variances from Appendix Table E–4; indexes can be calculated from Tables A–1 and A–3.

[a] The classes included are those equivalent to the five Department of Commerce economic classes.

Extent of and Changes in Coverage

Coverage ratios are interesting not only as crude measures of accuracy but also because they reflect differences, between covered and uncovered items, in price behavior and in supply and demand elasticities. Although it is rarely possible to disentangle these factors, radical changes in coverage, when the commodity list is unchanged, are grounds for suspecting heterogeneity in a commodity class. This is especially true where the changes in the coverage ratios are correlated with changes in the price index; it would appear likely in such a case that the price changes in the covered items were not duplicated in the uncovered ones. This correlation is not conclusive evidence of divergences in price behavior, however. It could result from differences in elasticity of demand. Suppose, for example, a group in which covered and uncovered commodities were identical in price behavior but the former were subject to a much more elastic demand. Coverage would then decrease every time the group's prices rose and increase every time they fell. By the same reasoning we could say that differing elasticities could conceal the expected influence of differing price behavior on coverage ratios.

COVERAGE IN NBER FOREIGN TRADE INDEXES

Coverage ratios for minor classes are summarized in Table 19 below. There are almost 6,900 class-years (numbers of classes multiplied by the number of years each is available) for which indexes might have been computed (over 5,500 indexes actually were calculated). Of the 6,900 class-years over 40 per cent consisted almost completely (more than 95 per cent) of covered commodities, and could therefore be said to suffer from virtually no sampling error. At the other extreme, for over 19 per cent of the class-years no coverage was possible or so little that no indexes were calculated. This group of empty classes was particularly important in the earliest period : 31 per cent for exports and 29 per cent for imports. Another 7.5 per cent of the class-years are of marginal quality, with coverage of less than 50 per cent. Most of these, particularly in the lowest ranges, occur in periods in which the majority of years had adequate coverage.

In every period, the proportion of classes more than 95 per cent covered was slightly higher in exports than in imports. But the better coverage in exports disappears at a somewhat lower standard : imports show a higher proportion with coverage above 60 per cent, and a smaller proportion completely uncovered in every period.

Among those groups for which indexes were calculated, over half the class-years had coverage ratios above 95 per cent. Exports had a higher proportion than imports in that class in every period, but even for imports, at least 45 per cent of the class-years had coverage ratios over 95 per cent.

Measurements based on numbers of class-years do not take into account differences in the importance of individual classes. They therefore present a very conservative assessment of the indexes, since many of the largest classes (for example, cotton, grain, and tobacco exports, and coffee, tea, cocoa, and sugar imports) consist entirely or almost entirely of covered items. Measured by number or value, the coverage ratios tend to be exaggerated in classes where prices were used in place of unit values. The price series describe narrowly defined commodities but are applied here to much

TABLE 19

COVERAGE RATIOS FOR MINOR CLASSES

Coverage ratio (%)	Exports and Imports — All Periods	Exports					Imports				
		1879–88	1889–98	1899–1912	1913–23	All Periods	1879–88	1889–98	1899–1912	1913–23	All Periods
				PERCENTAGE DISTRIBUTION							
95 to 100	42.5	39.6	45.6	45.7	46.9	44.7	38.5	42.6	41.7	39.3	40.6
90 to 95	4.7	2.9	4.6	4.4	6.5	4.7	4.2	5.1	3.6	6.1	4.7
80 to 90	8.5	8.4	6.1	9.4	8.4	8.2	6.8	8.1	8.5	10.6	8.7
70 to 80	7.3	4.8	3.0	8.0	7.6	6.2	8.2	7.2	8.2	9.0	8.2
60 to 70	6.1	2.3	3.4	4.4	5.8	4.1	5.0	5.5	9.4	9.5	7.7
50 to 60	4.1	4.1	4.4	2.3	4.5	3.7	3.2	2.7	5.9	4.6	4.3
40 to 50	3.8	4.3	4.2	6.1	3.8	4.7	1.1	3.1	4.6	2.4	3.1
30 to 40	2.2	1.0	2.4	1.7	1.8	1.7	2.2	1.4	3.3	3.3	2.7
1 to 30	1.5	1.6	1.2	1.5	0.1	1.2	1.9	1.2	2.0	1.7	1.8
0	19.5	31.2	25.1	16.6	14.5	20.8	28.8	23.0	12.9	13.4	18.3
Total	100.0	100.0	100.0	100.0	100.0	100.0	100.0	100.0	100.0	100.0	100.0
				NUMBER OF CLASS-YEARS							
Total	6,887	657	676	1,014	844	3,191	694	827	1,195	980	3,696

123

broader categories. For example, a BLS series on "Cattle, steers, good to choice," is used here to deflate values of an export commodity defined only as "cattle". The price series, therefore, apply only to a part of the export values, and an unknown part at that. It would be more appropriate (but much more laborious) to use a combination of several cattle series for the price index, attaching some measure of dispersion to it. Alternatively, one could count only part of the cattle series as contributing to the coverage in the class. Instead, as with the unit values, we assumed no variance within a commodity, and treated its whole value as a covered item.[23]

With these limitations in mind we may examine the coverage ratios for total exports and imports which appear in Table 20. These ratios were computed only for the earliest year in each period and for the comparable base-year figure. The earliest year of each period was used because it is generally the one with the poorest coverage.[24] For exports, coverage was above 85 per cent in each of the four periods, and for imports it fell no lower than 72 per cent.[25] Coverage of exports was highest in the earlier years and then declined as the improvement in commodity detail and in the availability of price data was offset by the decline in the importance of agricultural commodities for which both price and unit value data were plentiful. In the case of imports the shift in composition away from manufactured goods and the improvement in data led to a slight increase in coverage.

---

[23] This difficulty is involved in the problem of estimating from "composite commodities" discussed by Banerjee, "Calculation of Sampling Errors for Index Numbers."

[24] This may seem puzzling in view of the fact that the base year coverage shown in Table 20 is generally worse than that for the earliest year. Coverage is shown for a list of commodities that is unchanged during a period, and thus no advantage is taken of the availability of more data in later years. It is true that those commodities which were covered in 1879, for example, were a larger proportion of the total then than they were ten years later. But the commodities covered in 1888 were usually a larger proportion of the total in 1889 than were those covered in 1879. In other words, total coverage increased through time but the importance of the group of commodities covered initially usually decreased.

[25] Coverage of the Department of Commerce import indexes has been close to 70 per cent except for a fall to 60–65 per cent in 1957–59. That of the export indexes was 55–67 per cent before World War II. Since then it has ranged between 35 to 50 per cent, averaging about 45 per cent (U.S. Department of Commerce, *Business Statistics, 1957 Biennial Edition*, p. 251, and later editions). The Federal Reserve Bank indexes covered 64 to 69 per cent of the value of imports (Federal Reserve Bank of New York, *The Pattern of United States Import Trade Since 1923*, by John H. Adler, Eugene R. Schlesinger, and Evelyn Van Westerborg, May 1952, p. 64). The degree of coverage in Fabricant's output indexes ranged from 52 to 70 per cent of total value added (Solomon Fabricant, *The Output of Manufacturing Industries*, p. 602).

TABLE 20

COVERAGE RATIOS FOR TOTAL EXPORTS AND IMPORTS

| | 1913–23 | | 1899–1913 | | 1889–99 | | 1879–89 | |
	1923 (Comp. with 1913)	1913	1913 (Comp. with 1899)	1899	1899 (Comp. with 1889)	1889	1889 (Comp. with 1879)	1879
Exports	83.2	85.6	80.3	87.5	83.3	90.7	88.3	91.5
Imports	81.8	76.0	72.7	78.6	68.8	71.7	70.4	74.7

Appendix Tables E-5 to E-8 show intermediate and major class coverage ratios for the earliest year and the base year of each period. The base year coverage ratios shown include only those commodities covered in the earliest year. It is clear that the covered items are unevenly spread over the commodity universe. In exports, for example, the first twelve major classes, including all foods, crude materials, and agricultural exports, do not show a single case of coverage below 90 per cent. Import coverage was somewhat lower, but the first nine classes, consisting of foods and other agricultural products, included no cases under 86 per cent.

No major export class had less than 50 per cent coverage, and of those with between 50 and 70 per cent, twenty-six of twenty-seven cases were in classes 214, 215, 221, and 222.[26] One important component of all of these was Export Class 146 (manufactured metal products, including machinery and vehicles), whose coverage ranged between 33 and 66 per cent, mostly below 50 per cent. Among the 372 intermediate export classes listed in Table E-5, only eighteen had coverage ratios below 50 per cent (eleven among manufactured metal products) and nine others between 50 and 60 per cent.

Major import classes were more sparsely covered. There were thirteen cases below 50 per cent (as against none for exports) and nineteen between 50 and 60 per cent. But here again they were concentrated in the same area : thirty of thirty-two were in five classes.[27] Only once did coverage dip even slightly below 40 per cent.

The main sources of this poor import coverage are Import Class 150 (manufactured products of mineral origin) and its component, Import Class 147 (manufactured metal products), both of which contain very few covered items. Almost all the coverage of manufactured imports is in textiles and wood and paper products (Import Classes 064, 066, and 126).

[26] Manufactures, including tobacco products; manufactures, excluding tobacco products; mineral products; and nonagricultural products.

[27] (1) Nonagricultural products; (2) products of mineral origin; and (3) three classes of manufactured products.

Changes in the coverage ratios are of interest because they can suggest some inferences about the price behavior of uncovered items. They do this by virtue of the fact that they measure the relative rates of growth in value of covered and uncovered commodities. Where coverage is rising the covered commodities are growing more rapidly.

Especially among exports, relative value changes for major classes of commodities have tended to move in the opposite direction from relative price changes. Groups whose prices have fallen relatively have tended to gain in importance, for example, manufactured products in general and automobiles in particular. If this relationship is typical we can use these changes in coverage to draw some inferences as to the probable direction of bias in our indexes.

Some change in coverage arises from shifts in the importance of classes. For example, as we have seen, the rise within exports of the lightly covered manufactured goods class tended to lower total coverage. This change in coverage does not imply bias; it is taken account of in the construction of the index, as are any such changes arising from shifts in importance among minor classes. Shifts in importance within minor classes might suggest bias, however, because the method of constructing the indexes assumes that within each minor class prices of uncovered commodities move with those of covered commodities.

We therefore ask the following question: How does the value of covered commodities at the end of each period compare with what it would have been if the coverage in each minor class had remained constant at the earliest year's level? If actual coverage is greater, we know that covered commodities have increased in value more rapidly; if it is smaller, the uncovered items have been growing more rapidly.

Tables E-9 to E-12 show, for each intermediate and major class, actual coverage at the end of each period as a per cent of that which would have existed if there had been no changes within minor classes during the period. For total imports and total exports actual coverage is less than expected in three out of four periods, but never by more than 5 per cent. More significant lags in the growth of covered items appear among the major classes. In four major export classes, all among manufactures, non-agricultural products, and products of mineral origin, coverage within minor classes fell by more than 10 per cent. These classes, which fell in price and increased in value relative to other exports, show evidence of upward bias in the price index. That is, there is some ground for suspicion that their prices fell even more, relative to those of other classes, than is revealed by our indexes. The loss in coverage in these classes was concentrated particularly in Export Class 146 (manufactured metal products), and its main component, Export Class 143 (manufactured iron and steel products). These lost close to 50 per cent of their coverage over the four periods.

Changes in coverage among major import classes were much more scattered. There were six instances in which the growth of covered items exceeded that of uncovered items by more than 10 per cent and three over 20 per cent. (Only once did an export class show the value of covered items gaining on that of uncovered items by more than 4 per cent during one period.) All of these were among manufactured goods imports, as were three cases in which covered items fell behind by more than 20 per cent. The very low coverage in these classes left room for large increases and decreases, but in contrast to the situation on the export side, the net change in coverage was very close to zero.

CHAPTER 6

Comparison of NBER Indexes with Others

U.S. Department of Commerce Indexes

SINCE the NBER and Department of Commerce indexes have been combined to obtain the long series used in Appendix A and Chapters 1 and 2,
it is of interest to check their consistency for the years in which they overlap, 1913 and 1919-23. Perfect agreement between the indexes could not
be expected, even though both are Fisher "ideal" indexes. The Commerce
series were computed with annual linking, each year serving as the base
for the following year, while the NBER indexes use 1923 as a base for all the
years compared. Furthermore, the value series are slightly different : we
have attempted to use the 1949 classification of commodities throughout,
and shown overlaps wherever there are changes in the composition of a
class, while the Commerce Department used the contemporary classification
and ignored small changes in composition. In addition, there are differences
in weighting : the Department of Commerce in its computations, moves
directly from individual commodities to its five economic classes; the
NBER indexes are built up from individual commodities through minor
and intermediate classes to major groups, in an attempt to give each class,
rather than just each commodity, its proper weight.

Despite all these possible sources of disagreement the two indexes match
very well in most years—so well that they could hardly be distinguished
on a chart. We therefore compare them, in Table 21, by examining the
ratios of the Commerce to the NBER series, year by year and for the
period as a whole. Between 1913 and 1923 the Commerce indexes for
total exports and imports increased slightly faster than our own. The
ratio of 1923 to 1913 was 3 per cent greater in the Commerce series for
imports and only 0.3 per cent for exports. In none of the year-to-year
indexes for the totals was the divergence more than 5 per cent.

Among the ten comparisons for economic classes (five import and five
export) there were three cases where the ratio of the Commerce to the
NBER index increased by 6 to 7 per cent over the period as a whole.
Among the fifty year-to-year comparisons there were three where the
difference was greater than 10 per cent. One of these three was imports of
manufactured foods, 1920/1919, for which the Commerce index was 207.8
and our index 184.8. The most important commodity in this class was cane
sugar, weighted in the Commerce index[1] at 78 to 93 per cent. This is

[1] Unpublished details of the commodity composition of the Department of Commerce
indexes were supplied to us by Mr. Carl P. Blackwell, Director of the International
Economic Analysis Division, Bureau of Foreign Commerce.

considerably greater than its importance in the NBER index.[2] The role of sugar prices in the discrepancy between the indexes is confirmed by the fact that whenever the price relative for sugar was above the two indexes the Commerce index was higher; whenever it was below, the NBER index was higher.[3]

A similar case is the crude materials export index which contains the largest 1923/1913 discrepancy and the third largest year to year discrepancy. The commodity responsible is raw cotton, which Commerce weights 9 to 18 per cent more heavily than we do. Here again the Commerce index is higher when the cotton price relative is higher than the two indexes and lower when the cotton price is lower.

In both of these instances the greater number of commodities in the

TABLE 21

RELATION OF COMMERCE TO NBER PRICE INDEXES, 1913–23, YEAR-TO-YEAR COMPARISONS

	Commerce Index as Per Cent of NBER Index					
	1919 / 1913	1920 / 1919	1921 / 1920	1922 / 1921	1923 / 1922	1923 / 1913
Exports						
Total	102.3	100.6	95.7	101.4	100.0	100.3
Crude materials	102.9	95.9	93.6	110.6	104.4	106.8
Crude foodstuffs	100.0	100.2	99.8	103.2	99.2	102.2
Manuf. foodstuffs	101.3	100.5	97.8	99.9	99.4	98.9
Semimanufactures	99.6	101.3	101.2	100.8	98.9	101.8
Finished manufactures	112.6	100.3	95.1	97.6	96.1	100.7
Imports						
Total	103.6	97.7	98.4	100.7	102.8	103.1
Crude materials	100.5	99.8	100.0	103.1	102.8	106.3
Crude foodstuffs	97.6	98.7	98.0	101.7	100.9	96.9
Manuf. foodstuffs	100.7	112.4	91.3	97.8	105.4	106.6
Semimanufactures	94.7	103.0	102.1	98.5	100.8	98.9
Finished manufactures	96.8	100.6	102.3	99.2	104.7	103.5

SOURCES: Commerce indexes: U.S. Department of Commerce, *Foreign Trade of the United States, 1936-49*, International Trade Series No. 7, 1951, Table 10, p. 6 and Table 13, p. 9. NBER indexes: Appendix Tables A–1 and A–3.

[2] It is difficult to measure the weight of a single commodity in the NBER indexes. The weight of a commodity is amplified by the coverage adjustments as minor and intermediate classes are combined. But even if we estimate a maximum weight for sugar by adding the weight of all uncovered items in manufactured foods to that of sugar, clearly an overestimate, its weight in our index remains below that in the Commerce index. The greatest discrepancy is in the 1919/1913 comparison where the Commerce weight is more than 25 per cent larger than even our maximum.

[3] The sugar price relative was never between the two indexes.

129

NBER sample as well as the method of weighting tend to reduce the importance of the single dominant commodity.

The discrepancy for exports of manufactured products, 1919/1913, the largest in Table 21, has a different origin : the heavier weight in the NBER index of two groups with below-average price increases. These are vehicles, with a lower price ratio in the NBER index as well as a greater weight (perhaps double),[4] and machinery, heavily weighted in our index while virtually omitted from the Commerce series. The machinery component of the NBER index was constructed entirely from outside price data.

The measures listed in Table 21 might be said to understate the differences between the two series because they are comparisons of index numbers themselves, rather than of changes in them. In two classes the Commerce and NBER import price indexes moved in opposite directions in 1923 : crude foods, where NBER showed a decline of 0.2 per cent and Commerce a rise of 0.7 per cent; and finished manufactures, where the NBER index fell 1.1 per cent and the Commerce index rose 3.5 per cent.

In other instances the changes were much more divergent than the indexes themselves. In 1923 again, the ratio of export price indexes for finished manufactures was 96.1 per cent. But the Commerce price index fell by 4.5 per cent and the NBER index by only 0.6 per cent; the Commerce index thus declined by 7.5 times as much. Another example, not so dependent on the smallness of the denominator, was in exports of crude materials in 1922. Here the Commerce index rose 25 per cent, almost twice as much as ours.

Kreps Indexes for Exports and Imports

The only comprehensive indexes duplicating the NBER series for an extended period are those compiled by Theodore J. Kreps.[5] These are annual Marshall-Edgeworth price indexes for total exports and imports covering fiscal years 1879 through 1916, on a 1903-13 base. Kreps used unit values as import prices and U.S. wholesale prices as export prices. The import index included twenty-nine commodities, covering 30 to 40 per cent of total imports; the export index, twenty-eight commodities covering 40 to 45 per cent of total exports.

A comparison of the Kreps and NBER export price series (Chart 27)

---

[4] Our index was constructed from price data instead of the unit values used in the Commerce index. By both measurements the price ratio for vehicles was very low.

[5] "Import and Export Prices in the United States and the Terms of International Trade, 1880–1914," *Quarterly Journal of Economics*, August 1926.

CHART 27

U.S. Export and Import Price Indexes: Kreps and NBER, Fiscal Years
(calendar 1913 = 100)

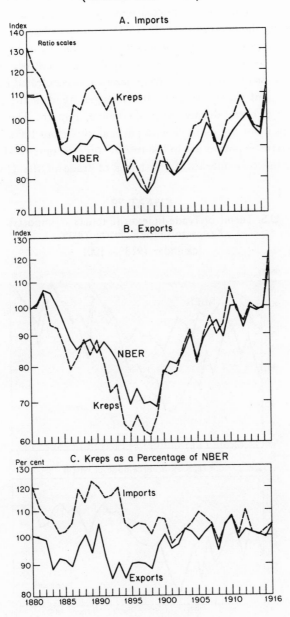

Source: Appendix Table G-1.

131

shows a fairly similar trend between 1880 and 1913 if only the first and last years are taken into account. But the Kreps index was generally below ours before 1900 and could be said to have shown some upward trend by comparison. In addition, its fluctuations were sharper, particularly the decline during the depression of the 1890's and the subsequent rise.

The import price series reveal larger disagreements, as high as 20 per cent or more compared with a maximum of 15 per cent between the two export series. As in exports, the divergences are concentrated in the period before 1900. But there is a somewhat stronger trend in the ratio of the Kreps index to ours—downward in the case of imports. The fluctuations in the Kreps index are more violent, particularly before 1900.

Since Kreps' export price index rose relative to ours, and his import index fell, the two indexes of the terms of trade of the United States

CHART 28

U.S. Terms of Trade Indexes (Exports ÷ Imports), Kreps and NBER, Fiscal Years

(calendar 1913 = 100)

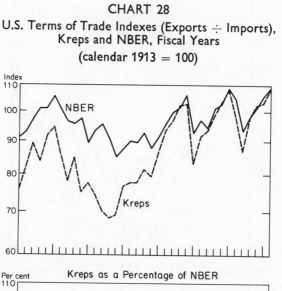

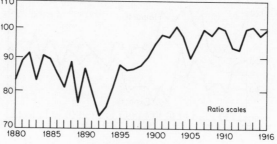

Source: Appendix Table H-2.

132

showed a greater divergence than either of the components. The disagreement is considerable; as can be seen in Chart 28, the Kreps index fell as far as 27 per cent below ours, on a 1913 base.

The Kreps indexes give a much more favorable picture of the development of the terms of trade, showing an improvement of almost a third between 1879 and 1913 instead of the 10 per cent indicated by the NBER indexes, and more than 40 per cent between 1894 and 1913 instead of less than 20. Furthermore, the NBER terms of trade series fluctuates less violently, even after 1900.

The distribution of weights among economic classes in the two indexes is compared in Table 22. Weights in the base period of the Kreps index, 1903-13, are compared with those of the 1899 base for the NBER index, and a similar comparison is made of 1892 weights for exports and 1890 weights for imports (these are the years in which the two indexes were furthest apart).

The main source of the differences in export indexes must have been the much heavier weighting of raw cotton by Kreps. This was a massive 42.7 per cent of the base-year weight of the Kreps index,[6] and only between 15 and, at the very most, 25 per cent of the 1899 base in the NBER index.[7]

In 1892 the two sets of export weights show a large discrepancy only in one class, manufactured products, but the base-year data show that Kreps weighted both crude foodstuffs and manufactured products less than half as heavily as the NBER indexes and gave crude materials more than twice as much weight.

No single commodity stands out on the import side as did raw cotton among exports. The main differences are the much higher weights assigned by Kreps to crude foodstuffs and the much lower ones assigned to manufactured products. Prices for the latter group in our calculations were below the average of all other commodities relative to 1899 and considerably smoother in their fluctuations.

USDA Index of Agricultural Export Prices

The United States Department of Agriculture has published several indexes of agricultural export quantities and values. The one which best matches the NBER index is a Laspeyres quantity index on a fiscal 1909-14 base. We have converted it into a Paasche price index, for comparison with our series, by dividing it into the Agriculture Department's value series.

---

[6] Given-year weights could be assumed to be more similar for the two series.

[7] It was during the 1889–99 period that the greatest gaps between the two indexes appeared.

TABLE 22

DISTRIBUTION OF WEIGHT BY MAJOR CLASS, NBER AND KREPS EXPORT
AND IMPORT PRICE INDEXES

	Base Year			Given Year		
	Kreps: Fiscal 1903–13 (1)	NBER: Calendar 1899 (2)	Col. (1) ÷ Col. (2) (3)	Kreps: Fiscal 1892 (4)	NBER: Fiscal 1892 (5)	Col. (4) ÷ Col. (5)
Exports						
Crude foodstuffs	9.1	18.5	49.2	28.8	25.9	112.2
Manuf. foodstuffs	16.6	25.0	66.4	20.6	24.3	84.8
Crude materials	46.8	22.8	205.3	39.5	32.1	123.1
Semimanufactures	16.9	11.6	145.7	4.7	5.5	85.5
Manufactured products	10.6	22.1	48.0	6.4	12.2	52.5
Total	100.0	100.0		100.0	100.0	

	Base Year			Given Year		
	Kreps: Fiscal 1903–13	NBER: Calendar 1899	Col. (1) ÷ Col. (2)	Kreps: Fiscal 1890	NBER: Fiscal 1890	Col (4) ÷ Col (5)
Imports						
Crude foodstuffs	22.1	12.9	171.3	27.2	16.9	160.9
Manuf. foodstuffs	16.2	18.2	89.0	19.2	17.1	112.3
Crude materials	43.6	30.4	143.4	25.6	21.0	121.9
Semimanufactures	12.5	17.3	72.3	12.2	16.5	73.9
Manufactured products	5.6	21.2	26.4	15.8	28.5	55.4
Total	100.0	100.0		100.0	100.0	

SOURCE: Kreps figures from "Import and Export Prices."

Comparison with the NBER Fisher indexes reveals a remarkable similarity despite the use of different base years and index number formulas. When both indexes are placed on a 1913 base they never differ by as much as 10 per cent and, before World War I, only once by more than 5 per cent (Chart 29). The ratio of the USDA index to ours shows no trend. It is almost a straight line, but droops slightly at the ends. The 1899 to 1913 period, when the base periods for the two indexes are very close and fluctuations in the ratio are at a minimum, is also the one where the ratio is at its highest.

134

CHART 29
U.S. Agricultural Export Price Indexes: U.S. Department of Agricultural and NBER, Fiscal Years
(calendar 1913 = 100)

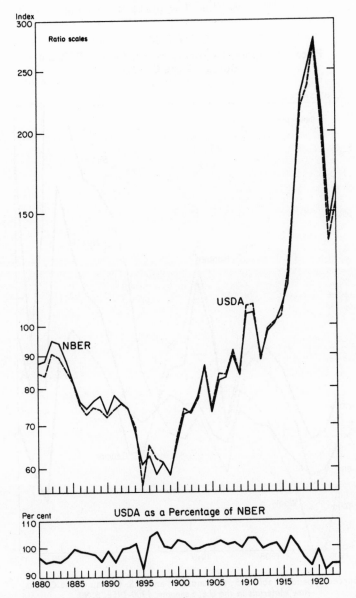

Source: Appendix Table A-24; and USDA, Foreign Agricultural Service, *United States Farm Products in Foreign Trade*, Statistical Bulletin No. 112, 1953, p. 7, divided by quantity indexes, p. 9, converted to 1913 base.

135

Census Bureau Price Index for Foreign Agricultural Materials

The Bureau of the Census has published a Laspeyres index of U.S. prices of foreign agricultural materials[8] on a 1935-39 base, with U.S. consumption rather than import weights. The prices are not import unit values

CHART 30
Prices of Imported Agricultural Products: NBER and
Bureau of the Census

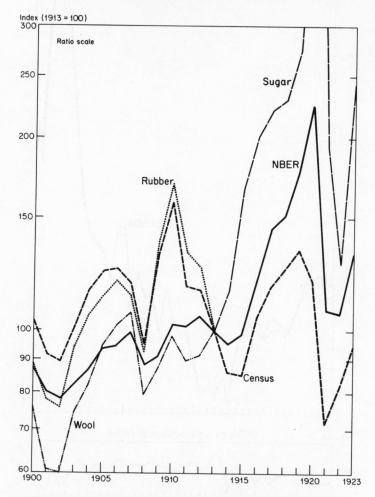

Source: Appendix Table A-5; Appendix C; and U.S. Bureau of the Census, *Raw Materials in the U.S. Economy, 1900-1952,* p. 90.

[8] *Raw Materials in the U.S. Economy, 1900–1952,* Bureau of the Census Working Paper No. 1, Washington, 1954.

but are prices "quoted on organized exchanges or markets" at a stage representing "the first important commercial transaction in the commodity after arrival in this country."[9]

The NBER series closest in coverage to the Census index is Import Class 209 (agricultural products). This class is, however, more comprehensive than the Census series because it covers all agricultural products while the Census excludes those which are produced to a substantial extent in the United States, no matter how important they are among imports.

Discrepancies between the two indexes arise not only from differences in coverage, but from the Census Bureau's use of a later base period, consumption rather than import weights, and prices rather than unit values (this last is probably of little significance).

It is clear in Chart 30, that the discrepancies between the two series are very large. The Census index has a strong downward trend by comparison with the NBER series and, in the earlier part of the period, quite different fluctuations as well. After 1913 most of the difference between the two indexes can clearly be attributed to sugar which is the second most important commodity in the NBER index but is excluded from the Census index because it is considered a domestic agricultural product. Other, but less important, factors in these years are the lighter weight of silk and the absence of wool in the Census index. Both commodities rose in price faster than the average.

In the years before 1913 the fluctuations in the Census series follow those of rubber fairly closely, while the NBER index does not. That is because the weight of rubber in the Census index is almost three times that in ours. The falling trend of the Census index relative to our own can be explained mainly by the absence from it of wool prices, which rose sharply. The Census Bureau considered wool, like sugar, a domestic agricultural product.

[9] *Ibid.,* p. 84.

APPENDIXES

Appendix A

Indexes and Values for Total Exports and Imports and Major Classes,
1879-1960

This appendix includes the following two sets of data :

(1) Tables A-14 through A-29 (basic tables) present price and quantity indexes and values for the period 1879-1923 for the NBER major classes. These data provide information on total exports (Export Class 220) and total imports (Import Class 221), on the five major economic classes into which the Department of Commerce divides foreign trade, and on selected combinations and variations of them.

Annual Fisher price and quantity indexes and dollar values are presented for all of the 22 export classes and 23 import classes. In addition, for 12 selected major classes, the basic tables include annual Paasche and Laspeyres price indexes, quarterly Fisher price and quantity indexes, and quarterly dollar values. (See Table A-30.)

(2) In Tables A-1 through A-11 the NBER data for 1879-1923 are combined with statistics of the Department of Commerce and the Department of Agriculture to extend certain series forward to 1960 and several back to 1869. For the period 1879-1960, annual price and quantity indexes and dollar values are presented for total exports and imports, for the five major economic classes used by the Department of Commerce, and for agricultural products. The NBER major classes which are used for these breakdowns for the period 1879-1923 are indicated in the individual table notes.

The correspondence between the major economic classes of the Department of Commerce and the comparable NBER classes is not exact because of the way in which miscellaneous articles, not elsewhere specified, are handled. The Department of Commerce includes this group with manufactured products and its five groups therefore sum to the total. The NBER series, on the other hand, include these articles in the total, but they are not assigned to any of the five major economic classes. The difference in value figures for 1879-1923 between total exports or imports and the sum of the five economic classes is therefore attributable to these miscellaneous articles.

Certain adjustments in price and quantity indexes and in value figures have been incorporated in Tables A-1 through A-11, to take into account the change in the United States customs area in 1900. The specific adjustments are indicated in the individual table notes. For a detailed explanation of the adjustments, see Appendix F.

Two additional tables are presented to show the classification scheme of exports and imports :

Tables A-12 and A-13 show the main components, by value, of the five major classes in the NBER series which correspond to the Department of Commerce economic classes.

Table A-30 shows, for each major class, the composition in terms of intermediate, minor or other major classes.

TABLE A-1

PRICE INDEXES FOR U.S. DOMESTIC EXPORTS, BY ECONOMIC CLASS
(1913 = 100)

Calendar Year	Total (1)	Crude Foods (2)	Manuf. Foods (3)	Crude Mater. (4)	Semi-Manuf. (5)	Manuf. Prod. (6)
1879	92.5	93.6	76.7	80.1	79.3	119.3
1880	101.5	96.3	86.6	89.4	87.5	132.4
1881	103.8	102.9	97.6	86.8	92.1	124.8
1882	107.0	109.2	106.8	88.3	93.0	123.3
1883	101.4	104.2	99.7	82.1	90.8	121.8
1884	97.6	91.6	92.2	83.3	86.4	122.3
1885	91.0	85.6	80.9	80.2	83.7	115.5
1886	85.7	80.6	76.3	74.9	80.5	109.0
1887	85.5	81.8	76.3	74.5	82.2	106.1
1888	89.7	86.2	81.3	78.1	84.7	110.9
1889	86.0	75.5	76.7	77.5	81.9	106.7
1890	85.0	76.8	73.6	78.5	82.5	104.4
1891	87.9	100.3	76.7	74.1	81.7	100.3
1892	81.9	86.8	77.7	67.8	78.7	91.8
1893	80.2	77.9	85.6	66.4	71.8	87.0
1894	70.5	67.8	74.2	55.3	67.7	82.0
1895	71.8	69.5	69.5	56.7	71.7	91.4
1896	71.0	63.6	63.5	61.0	70.1	96.8
1897	69.1	71.5	64.8	54.3	69.6	88.1
1898	68.4	76.9	68.0	48.9	70.4	82.6
1899	72.3	73.2	66.9	55.1	84.9	90.3
1900	81.0	74.4	71.3	72.2	89.5	98.9
1901	79.4	77.4	76.0	67.9	86.0	94.2
1902	81.4	82.0	83.8	69.1	83.5	94.0
1903	86.6	81.4	81.8	81.0	87.3	98.9
1904	86.9	80.3	77.8	84.3	85.9	98.8
1905	83.7	82.4	75.7	75.6	93.6	94.5
1906	89.9	81.7	80.7	83.8	105.9	97.5
1907	95.2	95.0	86.5	87.4	109.9	102.2
1908	90.1	99.8	87.9	79.8	92.4	100.5
1909	94.3	104.2	93.7	91.4	91.0	97.4
1910	102.1	98.7	107.3	108.4	93.4	98.7
1911	93.5	97.9	93.3	90.9	93.2	95.5
1912	95.5	104.2	97.0	89.3	100.3	97.2

(continued)

142

TABLE A-1 (concluded)

Calendar Year	Total (1)	Crude Foods (2)	Manuf. Foods (3)	Crude Mater. (4)	Semi-Manuf. (5)	Manuf. Prod. (6)
1913	100.0	100.0	100.0	100.0	100.0	100.0
1914	97.7	114.5	103.3	87.9	97.6	94.3
1915	105.1	133.8	106.5	86.0	113.2	100.9
1916	135.5	144.2	118.4	115.5	156.5	130.6
1917	177.0	214.8	170.5	166.8	198.4	150.4
1918	206.1	234.6	214.2	219.0	202.8	169.7
1919	215.7	241.7	237.4	241.3	199.5	174.4
1920	232.5	268.2	217.2	285.3	210.5	197.7
1921	157.5	155.7	136.2	156.4	143.5	163.9
1922	143.8	127.3	120.8	176.6	126.9	137.8
1923	154.2	129.2	123.5	214.8	138.4	137.1
1924	151.1	150.4	124.5	200.5	132.8	135.3
1925	153.2	174.2	147.8	181.2	139.5	137.1
1926	140.8	149.6	142.0	140.5	138.4	137.1
1927	131.6	149.6	130.3	136.4	130.6	124.2
1928	134.7	140.2	126.4	155.8	129.5	122.4
1929	133.6	134.3	126.4	150.7	137.3	121.5
1930	119.2	120.7	115.7	117.1	119.4	115.9
1931	91.5	83.3	90.4	79.4	97.1	92.9
1932	79.2	71.4	69.0	67.2	80.4	84.7
1933	82.2	69.7	72.0	78.4	82.6	80.1
1934	96.6	81.6	81.7	103.8	94.9	87.4
1935	98.7	85.0	95.3	104.9	93.8	88.3
1936	100.7	89.2	97.2	106.9	100.5	89.3
1937	106.9	96.9	104.1	104.9	121.7	93.9
1938	99.7	79.0	89.5	92.6	107.1	92.9
1939	97.7	66.3	83.6	91.6	107.1	92.0
1940	104.9	76.5	85.6	96.7	113.8	99.4
1941	112.1	90.1	101.1	112.0	125.0	103.1
1942	136.8	108.0	140.0	129.3	135.1	126.1
1943	150.1	134.3	149.8	143.5	139.5	140.8
1944	171.7	153.0	169.2	149.6	144.0	164.7
1945	171.7	166.6	166.6	151.6	141.3	163.3
1946	162.5	183.3	171.8	171.5	146.7	142.9
1947	193.3	210.6	212.8	199.5	189.3	167.4
1948	205.7	216.6	216.8	227.4	204.3	177.0
1949	191.3	190.9	173.2	215.4	193.4	168.8
1950	185.1	165.1	146.7	223.4	189.3	164.7
1951	211.9	183.3	183.7	265.3	233.1	182.4
1952	210.8	198.4	173.2	249.3	229.0	183.8
1953	209.8	186.3	178.5	235.4	223.5	185.1
1954	206.7	166.6	178.5	239.4	222.2	182.4
1955	208.8	160.6	162.6	239.4	235.9	185.1
1956	217.0	162.1	158.6	237.4	261.9	193.3
1957	224.2	160.6	165.2	239.4	256.5	205.5
1958	222.1	159.8	168.1	235.3	229.7	209.2
1959	223.2	158.1	155.5	227.1	236.4	213.8
1960	226.3	157.2	152.6	224.1	236.4	217.4

SOURCE: See sources following Table A-4.

TABLE A–2
QUANTITY INDEXES FOR U.S. DOMESTIC EXPORTS, BY ECONOMIC CLASS
(1913 = 100)

Calendar Year	Total (1)	Crude Foods (2)	Manuf. Foods (3)	Crude Mater. (4)	Semi-Manuf. (5)	Manuf. Prod. (6)
1879	33.1	134.1	74.4	37.0	10.1	9.7
1880	35.0	146.5	80.1	41.1	9.5	8.7
1881	31.8	106.3	67.2	39.8	10.4	11.6
1882	28.4	73.5	51.7	40.4	11.7	12.1
1883	31.1	74.7	64.1	43.7	12.1	12.6
1884	30.5	69.7	64.8	43.4	12.3	11.8
1885	30.0	64.0	73.8	39.0	12.1	12.1
1886	33.1	80.4	70.6	46.6	12.0	12.8
1887	33.4	77.0	72.4	46.6	12.8	13.1
1888	30.7	51.2	63.6	46.7	13.7	13.0
1889	38.4	77.6	82.9	55.4	15.8	15.6
1890	40.4	87.2	97.1	52.3	16.1	16.3
1891	44.2	107.6	94.5	60.1	18.3	17.1
1892	45.8	127.1	108.6	53.8	17.2	17.5
1893	43.3	97.3	89.6	54.7	23.1	19.7
1894	46.5	87.7	100.8	62.8	25.6	20.7
1895	45.7	83.1	100.5	59.0	25.5	22.2
1896	56.4	141.4	114.3	65.6	34.5	25.6
1897	63.4	178.6	121.8	67.2	39.6	30.6
1898	73.2	197.1	139.8	82.0	41.8	36.3
1899	70.3	183.9	148.2	66.8	41.8	41.4
1900	72.8	168.4	142.9	75.7	48.6	42.2
1901	74.0	182.7	143.4	77.0	40.0	42.9
1902	66.9	112.1	120.6	73.8	44.4	43.6
1903	68.8	123.1	123.1	77.2	46.0	43.2
1904	67.0	73.2	113.4	73.1	60.2	48.4
1905	78.0	108.8	129.8	84.7	58.4	58.5
1906	80.5	126.1	131.8	84.2	60.0	61.8
1907	81.3	118.2	121.8	89.3	62.6	62.5
1908	78.4	98.3	114.6	91.3	64.5	56.4
1909	73.7	65.1	94.3	83.5	69.8	60.7
1910	73.1	55.1	73.6	79.4	77.0	69.0
1911	90.0	68.5	103.2	96.2	89.7	84.0
1912	101.1	79.4	97.8	115.3	97.9	95.5
1913	100.0	100.0	100.0	100.0	100.0	100.0
1914	86.6	140.0	93.0	74.9	87.4	86.0
1915	135.7	200.6	160.5	103.1	111.7	163.6
1916	163.3	168.6	164.8	90.9	155.8	252.0
1917	142.2	134.4	147.0	64.4	168.5	225.0
1918	119.7	132.8	203.9	57.0	129.5	153.4
1919	146.6	156.3	257.6	86.7	126.4	179.9
1920	141.8	192.2	161.2	84.8	120.8	202.2
1921	113.4	252.8	153.9	81.3	72.2	125.6
1922	106.8	210.6	148.5	72.7	81.8	119.5
1923	108.2	116.9	144.1	73.0	95.8	138.0
1924	121.0	151.8	140.9	85.7	109.0	150.0

(continued)

TABLE A-2 (concluded)

Calendar Year	Total (1)	Crude Foods (2)	Manuf. Foods (3)	Crude Mater. (4)	Semi-Manuf. (5)	Manuf. Prod. (6)
1925	128.0	106.5	117.7	101.0	112.3	174.0
1926	137.3	131.0	108.2	116.3	112.3	182.0
1927	147.8	164.0	108.2	112.9	127.7	206.0
1928	153.6	122.6	111.9	107.8	131.0	238.0
1929	158.2	116.9	116.7	97.6	125.5	268.0
1930	130.3	86.7	95.5	91.7	102.4	212.0
1931	105.9	88.6	83.4	92.5	77.1	154.0
1932	81.4	73.5	67.0	99.3	58.4	94.0
1933	82.6	40.5	65.5	97.6	68.3	98.0
1934	88.4	42.4	62.3	81.5	85.9	128.0
1935	93.1	40.5	50.1	84.0	88.1	144.0
1936	97.7	37.7	44.9	80.6	93.6	166.0
1937	125.7	63.2	52.3	90.0	129.9	222.0
1938	125.7	183.8	62.3	84.0	109.0	212.0
1939	131.5	98.0	73.9	77.2	132.1	234.0
1940	153.6	56.6	59.6	62.0	188.3	302.0
1941	182.7	54.7	125.6	41.6	146.5	422.0
1942	239.7	36.8	201.6	41.6	161.9	578.0
1943	350.3	47.1	316.2	59.4	185.0	860.0
1944	337.5	50.9	294.5	47.5	180.6	840.0
1945	229.3	151.5	228.6	75.1	131.0	490.1
1946	239.7	207.3	270.3	108.0	144.7	451.6
1947	320.0	235.9	213.8	102.8	217.6	659.7
1948	249.0	340.2	186.9	85.5	158.4	514.8
1949	254.9	408.4	158.7	107.1	165.8	500.9
1950	224.6	269.4	133.1	109.7	140.5	448.5
1951	287.4	445.7	147.9	121.8	169.0	593.4
1952	291.1	401.0	131.8	103.6	166.9	652.0
1953	306.1	300.4	131.8	89.8	151.0	755.2
1954	296.7	259.5	143.9	103.6	194.3	679.7
1955	301.4	336.4	192.3	104.5	231.3	639.6
1956	357.3	478.0	244.7	138.2	250.3	733.7
1957	377.0	481.7	216.5	170.1	298.9	738.3
1958	327.0	465.7	201.1	118.8	233.8	672.3
1959	318.9	530.5	212.8	111.1	247.1	630.3
1960	366.6	608.5	223.9	150.4	352.9	676.3

SOURCE: See sources following Table A-4.

TABLE A–3

PRICE INDEXES FOR U.S. IMPORTS OF MERCHANDISE, BY ECONOMIC CLASS
(1913 = 100)

Calendar Year	Total (1)	Crude Foods (2)	Manuf. Foods (3)	Crude Mater. (4)	Semi-Manuf. (5)	Manuf. Prod. (6)
1879	102.4	114.3	132.4	95.0	78.0	102.8
1880	113.1	123.3	158.7	104.2	91.1	105.4
1881	107.7	112.4	157.6	99.3	83.8	103.2
1882	108.3	105.2	159.6	104.5	84.9	103.6
1883	101.8	94.6	145.8	96.9	80.8	101.6
1884	95.4	95.5	116.6	91.9	80.1	96.1
1885	87.7	88.3	105.0	84.6	71.8	90.7
1886	87.5	87.3	107.4	84.5	73.1	87.4
1887	90.9	118.9	97.6	85.8	71.8	87.5
1888	88.8	108.4	110.1	81.3	69.5	85.1
1889	93.9	112.4	131.6	83.0	72.5	87.6
1890	93.2	123.7	113.3	82.2	75.3	86.4
1891	92.0	122.8	116.1	77.6	74.3	86.1
1892	88.4	113.7	112.7	74.9	72.4	84.8
1893	92.0	123.9	122.4	75.6	73.7	84.6
1894	83.5	114.8	101.7	68.5	65.2	80.4
1895	79.5	111.6	80.7	70.0	63.4	80.3
1896	80.7	99.5	94.3	71.0	64.9	81.2
1897	75.9	81.8	84.7	71.4	63.4	79.4
1898	75.7	68.4	92.6	76.2	60.8	79.4
1899	81.5	66.4	99.1	83.2	73.4	82.8
1900	86.7	72.9	101.4	87.7	82.7	87.4
1901	82.6	66.1	96.0	82.0	82.4	88.6
1902	80.8	67.9	80.5	83.0	80.0	86.0
1903	84.0	67.3	88.2	88.5	82.9	87.6
1904	85.8	73.0	93.7	89.2	83.4	87.7
1905	90.6	74.2	113.2	93.5	85.4	90.1
1906	94.7	75.9	97.1	100.7	97.4	93.2
1907	99.2	78.2	101.8	106.2	103.1	97.1
1908	88.0	72.8	105.8	89.7	83.9	90.4
1909	88.0	71.1	104.3	95.3	81.2	86.3
1910	94.6	80.9	113.8	104.8	85.7	86.5
1911	96.1	94.5	109.7	99.9	90.4	90.2
1912	101.0	104.0	119.0	100.4	96.9	95.4
1913	100.0	100.0	100.0	100.0	100.0	100.0
1914	93.7	91.1	110.7	92.8	93.3	90.7
1915	97.2	89.9	142.9	89.7	99.8	90.3
1916	120.2	98.7	172.3	113.1	128.1	112.2
1917	145.3	106.7	196.9	139.8	160.4	136.1
1918	161.3	110.5	216.5	147.3	180.4	180.1
1919	181.0	159.4	255.7	161.6	183.1	195.2
1920	219.1	166.4	472.4	179.1	204.2	223.5
1921	125.2	101.1	179.0	99.8	135.0	164.6
1922	119.6	110.4	128.8	106.2	125.3	149.4
1923	136.6	110.2	206.0	123.2	136.8	148.7
1924	133.5	130.7	184.6	119.3	132.0	143.6

(continued)

146

TABLE A-3 (concluded)

Calendar Year	Total (1)	Crude Foods (2)	Manuf. Foods (3)	Crude Mater. (4)	Semi-Manuf. (5)	Manuf. Prod. (6)
1925	145.1	159.8	128.4	147.1	136.8	156.3
1926	142.0	158.2	119.5	145.1	136.8	148.7
1927	131.9	148.0	141.8	121.9	135.8	142.8
1928	128.1	159.8	125.7	110.9	129.1	149.5
1929	119.5	150.3	107.9	103.2	132.9	136.0
1930	98.6	111.0	89.2	81.9	113.7	121.5
1931	76.8	86.6	80.3	55.5	90.6	103.7
1932	59.8	73.2	66.0	39.3	72.3	84.1
1933	59.8	66.9	68.7	40.6	76.1	79.0
1934	68.3	76.4	76.7	48.4	90.6	84.1
1935	69.9	71.6	84.7	51.6	90.6	82.4
1936	74.5	74.8	91.9	60.6	91.5	80.7
1937	83.8	88.9	93.6	72.2	103.1	84.1
1938	74.5	72.4	82.0	60.6	93.4	90.1
1939	76.1	70.8	80.3	66.4	93.4	88.4
1940	81.5	67.7	76.7	72.2	103.1	98.6
1941	87.0	83.4	83.8	75.5	108.9	102.8
1942	100.9	111.0	113.3	85.1	119.5	113.9
1943	109.5	120.4	122.2	94.2	124.3	126.6
1944	117.3	133.0	124.8	100.6	128.1	139.4
1945	121.1	137.0	131.7	104.5	129.4	143.9
1946	134.3	172.9	150.8	105.8	144.3	166.4
1947	165.4	243.4	185.5	117.6	183.4	208.4
1948	182.5	268.7	188.9	132.0	209.0	226.3
1949	173.9	259.4	180.3	126.7	190.1	218.8
1950	188.7	356.4	182.0	138.5	186.1	214.3
1951	236.8	401.7	197.6	202.5	234.6	251.8
1952	224.4	404.3	199.3	167.2	237.3	248.8
1953	214.3	407.0	197.6	150.2	225.2	244.3
1954	219.8	486.8	194.1	145.3	219.8	244.3
1955	219.0	417.6	192.4	154.2	237.3	239.8
1956	222.9	403.0	194.1	158.1	252.2	244.3
1957	225.2	396.3	202.8	163.3	248.1	248.8
1958	214.3	375.9	201.0	152.9	226.9	245.4
1959	211.2	331.8	200.1	153.6	226.9	244.6
1960	214.3	326.3	196.5	158.8	231.8	249.6

SOURCE: See sources following Table A-4.

TABLE A-4
QUANTITY INDEXES FOR U.S. IMPORTS OF MERCHANDISE, BY ECONOMIC CLASS
(1913 = 100)

Calendar Year	Total (1)	Crude Foods (2)	Manuf. Foods (3)	Crude Mater. (4)	Semi-Manuf. (5)	Manuf. Prod. (6)
1879	26.7	38.8	28.4	17.9	28.9	37.4
1880	32.8	36.8	31.5	22.9	41.4	52.8
1881	33.1	42.9	32.4	21.5	38.4	51.3
1882	37.0	46.1	37.7	23.0	43.8	59.1
1883	35.9	45.0	38.9	23.1	41.0	54.0
1884	35.1	46.1	42.4	23.4	36.0	51.5
1885	35.6	46.9	43.8	25.3	37.0	48.0
1886	40.3	48.2	45.7	29.7	43.7	57.9
1887	41.4	43.9	44.8	29.7	50.5	61.7
1888	43.4	49.4	45.8	32.2	47.6	64.8
1889	43.6	48.4	43.1	35.2	47.3	64.7
1890	46.9	49.0	49.6	36.4	49.7	71.6
1891	47.7	49.9	63.7	38.6	50.7	58.8
1892	50.4	52.1	54.4	42.9	50.3	64.0
1893	44.7	48.2	54.6	37.1	45.4	59.5
1894	44.4	52.5	58.2	37.6	40.9	48.2
1895	55.7	55.8	53.2	50.6	50.8	75.8
1896	46.6	53.2	56.6	35.7	40.7	60.4
1897	54.0	64.9	56.4	51.9	44.1	62.3
1898	46.3	59.3	49.3	40.7	43.6	50.9
1899	54.1	67.5	61.4	48.6	50.6	56.0
1900	53.2	64.2	58.8	47.7	48.8	58.8
1901	59.4	77.5	64.0	56.6	52.0	60.8
1902	67.0	79.0	67.6	61.8	66.2	71.5
1903	66.1	78.8	63.1	58.6	66.6	73.7
1904	67.3	89.9	73.6	62.4	60.3	68.3
1905	72.6	81.6	70.9	70.0	70.5	76.9
1906	77.8	79.6	75.0	71.0	78.8	90.2
1907	80.0	86.7	78.7	70.7	77.0	96.1
1908	70.7	87.0	74.8	65.6	64.2	74.5
1909	93.5	106.4	82.7	90.4	94.6	96.9
1910	92.2	85.6	86.0	85.1	102.4	99.7
1911	89.0	90.8	83.5	83.2	95.8	92.7
1912	100.4	103.2	87.8	104.6	97.0	103.0
1913	100.0	100.0	100.0	100.0	100.0	100.0
1914	106.5	117.5	117.1	106.0	87.1	110.2
1915	102.1	120.6	96.6	126.6	77.3	79.3
1916	111.0	117.0	98.1	144.9	96.8	75.2
1917	113.4	154.9	89.5	149.1	96.1	69.7
1918	104.9	132.4	92.9	137.2	92.3	63.4
1919	120.4	150.6	112.4	171.7	86.5	63.0
1920	134.4	155.7	133.3	159.9	112.7	89.9
1921	111.8	135.8	100.7	140.3	75.8	86.6
1922	145.1	136.3	145.4	182.7	122.4	106.1
1923	154.8	148.3	126.2	186.5	145.0	129.6
1924	151.2	146.3	136.5	173.0	136.4	129.6

(continued)

TABLE A–4 (concluded)

Calendar Year	Total (1)	Crude Foods (2)	Manuf. Foods (3)	Crude Mater. (4)	Semi-Manuf. (5)	Manuf. Prod. (6)
1925	163.7	138.5	163.4	194.2	152.2	126.8
1926	174.4	154.2	169.6	201.9	162.2	147.9
1927	177.9	154.2	155.2	215.3	152.2	155.0
1928	179.7	156.1	157.2	215.3	162.2	152.1
1929	206.4	162.0	190.3	246.1	182.3	183.1
1930	174.4	162.0	159.3	200.0	146.4	156.4
1931	153.0	158.1	134.5	188.4	113.4	132.4
1932	122.8	142.4	128.3	150.0	81.8	101.4
1933	135.2	144.4	142.8	167.3	104.8	101.4
1934	133.4	150.3	165.5	153.8	93.3	104.2
1935	163.7	202.9	182.1	184.6	124.9	122.6
1936	181.5	208.8	204.8	196.1	146.4	143.7
1937	202.8	208.8	227.6	219.2	169.4	164.8
1938	145.9	162.0	184.1	155.7	113.4	116.9
1939	167.3	185.4	190.3	182.7	143.6	124.0
1940	176.2	189.3	175.9	226.9	149.3	104.2
1941	208.2	202.9	186.2	298.0	183.8	102.8
1942	154.8	140.5	117.9	203.8	146.4	101.4
1943	172.6	218.5	167.6	178.8	149.3	132.4
1944	186.9	284.9	202.7	175.0	152.2	132.4
1945	190.4	227.1	169.8	184.2	196.7	142.5
1946	201.1	212.6	161.9	267.1	176.6	126.1
1947	192.2	188.0	171.1	245.0	186.7	117.3
1948	218.9	212.6	186.9	265.3	213.9	143.7
1949	213.6	231.4	197.4	239.5	205.3	141.2
1950	259.8	221.3	239.6	289.2	314.5	175.3
1951	256.3	232.8	250.1	270.8	287.2	187.9
1952	268.7	229.9	264.6	285.5	295.8	209.3
1953	281.2	241.5	271.1	281.8	325.9	223.2
1954	261.6	203.9	276.4	268.9	288.6	224.4
1955	290.1	215.5	280.4	300.3	321.6	269.8
1956	315.0	227.1	292.2	318.7	327.4	327.8
1957	322.1	229.9	304.0	320.5	323.1	351.8
1958	334.6	231.8	365.6	297.6	321.7	396.5
1959	398.7	245.5	388.2	328.1	399.2	524.9
1960	384.2	237.7	386.2	305.2	366.2	523.5

NOTES TO TABLES A–1 THROUGH A–4

The NBER major classes which correspond to the economic classes used in these tables are as follows:

Economic Class	NBER Export Class	NBER Import Class
Total	220	221
Crude foods	201	201
Manufactured foods	203	203
Crude materials	212	212
Semimanufactures	213	213
Manufactured products	215	220

NOTES TO TABLES A-1 THROUGH A-4 *(continued)*

SOURCES ARE AS FOLLOWS:

Table A–1, cols. 1, 3–6;
Table A–2, cols. 3–6;
Table A–3, cols. 1–2, 4–6;
Table A–4, cols. 2, 4–6   *1879–1900:* Tables A–14 through A–17.

Table A–1, col. 2;
Table A–2, cols. 1–2;
Table A–3, col. 3;
Table A–4, cols. 1, 3   *1879–1900:* Figures in Tables A–14—A–17 multiplied by 1899 ratio of adjusted figures to unadjusted figures in Appendix F.

All tables and cols.   *1901–23:* Tables A–14 through A–17.

All tables, col. 1   *1924–39:* Extrapolated from 1923 by U.S. Department of Commerce, *Foreign Trade of the United States, 1936–1949*, pp. 6 and 9.

1940–60: Extrapolated from 1939 by Department of Commerce, World Trade Information Service (WTIS), *Statistical Reports*, Part 3, January 1960–February 1961, Table 2.

All tables, cols. 2–6   *1924–44:* Extrapolated from 1923 by *Foreign Trade of the United States, 1936–1949*, pp. 6 and 9.

1945–57: Extrapolated from 1944 by U.S. Bureau of the Census, *Historical Statistics of the U.S., Colonial Times to 1957*, pp. 540–541.

1958–60: Extrapolated from 1957 by WTIS, *Statistical Reports*, Part 3, January 1960–February 1961, and earlier issues, Table 3.

TABLE A-5

PRICE AND QUANTITY INDEXES FOR U.S. AGRICULTURAL
EXPORTS AND IMPORTS
(1913 = 100)

Calendar Year	Exports		Imports	
	Price (1)	Quantity (2)	Price (3)	Quantity (4)
1879	80.7	68.1	112.4	25.1
1880	88.1	74.3	126.5	27.4
1881	91.4	63.1	120.5	28.4
1882	95.2	53.2	120.4	31.4
1883	89.0	59.1	109.8	31.6
1884	85.2	56.9	99.6	32.9
1885	79.0	56.2	91.4	34.6
1886	73.8	64.0	91.9	37.5
1887	74.9	62.7	100.0	35.9
1888	78.5	55.5	97.7	38.9
1889	75.2	70.7	105.3	39.3
1890	74.1	75.5	103.4	41.5
1891	78.6	82.6	100.9	47.0
1892	73.0	86.4	95.8	46.8
1893	73.7	74.5	102.6	42.6
1894	62.6	81.2	91.0	45.4
1895	61.9	78.1	84.1	51.5
1896	59.9	98.3	86.0	43.6
1897	59.3	108.9	78.3	55.3
1898	59.5	126.8	78.9	46.2
1899	61.0	113.8	82.6	56.1
1900	71.3	111.9	87.3	53.5
1901	71.1	116.2	80.2	61.4
1902	74.8	96.2	78.1	66.2
1903	80.7	99.5	82.4	63.5
1904	81.2	86.0	86.5	71.4
1905	75.7	104.2	93.6	73.3
1906	82.0	106.0	94.5	74.1
1907	88.1	105.3	99.2	75.6
1908	84.4	101.6	88.5	73.5
1909	93.7	85.0	91.0	94.1
1910	108.2	75.0	102.0	86.0
1911	92.5	95.0	101.6	85.5
1912	92.4	107.6	105.3	102.5
1913	100.0	100.0	100.0	100.0
1914	100.8	86.7	95.2	116.0
1915	107.3	131.3	98.5	123.7
1916	130.0	117.9	119.6	131.3
1917	195.2	88.6	144.1	140.8
1918	249.2	96.4	151.2	133.1
1919	265.5	134.6	177.5	163.8
1920	273.1	110.1	225.2	161.1
1921	154.2	119.6	107.7	137.1
1922	151.6	108.5	106.2	171.6
1923	173.3	91.6	131.1	172.6

(continued)

TABLE A-5 (concluded)

Calendar Year	Exports Price (1)	Exports Quantity (2)	Imports Price (3)	Imports Quantity (4)
1924	178.7	102.9	122.6	174.6
1925	185.8	99.8	136.7	190.9
1926	152.4	103.5	132.3	203.6
1927	147.6	110.9	119.1	207.9
1928	156.3	103.5	113.8	205.7
1929	152.9	96.1	104.1	237.6
1930	126.8	82.2	82.2	199.4
1931	88.7	80.4	57.6	195.1
1932	67.7	85.0	44.4	167.6
1933	77.7	77.6	45.8	178.2
1934	106.0	60.1	53.3	171.8
1935	115.0	56.4	57.0	210.0
1936	116.9	52.7	65.4	212.1
1937	115.2	60.1	76.2	231.2
1938	105.1	68.4	59.8	178.2
1939	96.2	59.1	63.2	197.3
1940	103.4	43.4	65.0	220.6
1941	149.7	38.8	70.2	265.1
1942	208.9	49.0	89.2	159.1
1943	263.3	68.4	100.7	167.6
1944	294.1	61.9	111.2	182.4
1945	268.1	73.0	113.8	167.6
1946	261.2	104.4	128.5	199.4
1947	320.7	107.2	152.4	201.5
1948	336.5	89.6	162.4	216.4
1949	280.1	110.9	153.7	210.0
1950	254.6	98.0	197.8	224.8
1951	306.1	114.6	259.4	222.7
1952	303.9	98.0	224.2	224.8
1953	287.8	85.9	211.6	220.6
1954	284.2	93.3	232.1	190.9
1955	266.0	104.4	218.1	203.6
1956	257.7	140.5	210.4	210.0
1957	255.1	153.4	212.7	207.9
1958	249.7	134.0	203.2	214.2
1959	240.9	142.3	195.9	233.3
1960	233.6	179.3	195.2	218.5

NOTES TO TABLE A-5

Col. 1   *1879–1923:* Table A-14, Export Class 209.

1924–25: Extrapolated from 1923 by U.S. Department of Agriculture, Foreign Agricultural Service, *United States Farm Products in Foreign Trade,* 1953, p. 6, dividing value index by quantity index.

1926–60: Extrapolated from 1925 by quantity indexes divided into calendar year values from the following sources:

1926–28—U.S. Department of Commerce, *Survey of Current Business, 1942 Supplement,* p. 93

1929–57—U.S. Department of Commerce, *Business Statistics, 1959,* p. 110.

Notes to Table A–5 (continued)

1958–60—WTIS *Statistical Reports,* Part 3, March 1960, p. 5, and December 1961, p. 5.

Cols. 2, 3, and 4

1879–1900: Tables A–15 through A–17, Export Class 209 and Import Class 209, adjusted for change in customs area by the 1899 ratio: col. 2, .99912; col. 3, .97636; col. 4, .96558.

1901–23: Tables A–15 through A–17.

1924–25: Extrapolated from 1923 by same source as col. 1.

Cols. 2 and 4

1926–60: Extrapolated from 1925 by U.S. Department of Agriculture, Foreign Agricultural Service, *Quantity Indexes of U.S. Agricultural Exports and Imports,* revised January 1960, pp. 15–6 and 28–9; and U.S. Department of Agriculture, Foreign Agricultural Service, *Foreign Agricultural Trade of the United States,* Statistical Report for July 1961, issued October 1961, pp. 24–5.

Col. 3

1926–60: Extrapolated from 1925 using quantity indexes with calendar year values from the following sources:

1926–34—Department of Agriculture, Foreign Agricultural Service, *United States Farm Products in Foreign Trade,* 1953, p. 23.

1935–57—*Business Statistics, 1959,* p. 114.

1958–60—Same source as column 1 for this period.

TABLE A-6

VALUE OF U.S. EXPORTS AND IMPORTS, CURRENT AND 1913 DOLLARS
(in millions of dollars)

Calendar Year	Exports		Imports	
	Current Dollars (1)	Constant (1913) Dollars (2)	Current Dollars (3)	Constant (1913) Dollars (4)
1869	324		438	
1870	388		461	
1871	446		573	
1872	452		656	
1873	550		595	
1874	554		562	
1875	497		503	
1876	576		427	
1877	608		480	
1878	723		432	
1879	755	810	514	479
1880	876	857	697	588
1881	814	778	670	593
1882	750	695	753	663
1883	778	761	687	644
1884	734	747	629	629
1885	674	734	588	638
1886	700	810	663	723
1887	703	818	709	742
1888	680	752	725	778
1889	814	940	771	782
1890	846	989	823	841
1891	957	1,082	828	855
1892	923	1,121	841	904
1893	855	1,060	776	801
1894	807	1,138	673	796
1895	808	1,119	802	999
1896	987	1,381	682	836
1897	1,080	1,552	743	968
1898	1,234	1,792	635	830
1899	1,253[a]	1,721	799[a]	970
1900	1,453[a]	1,782	829[a]	954
1901	1,438	1,812	880	1,066
1902	1,333	1,638	969	1,200
1903	1,458	1,684	995	1,185
1904	1,426	1,640	1,036	1,207
1905	1,599	1,909	1,179	1,302
1906	1,773	1,971	1,321	1,395
1907	1,895	1,990	1,423	1,435
1908	1,729	1,919	1,116	1,268
1909	1,701	1,804	1,476	1,676
1910	1,829	1,789	1,563	1,652
1911	2,058	2,203	1,533	1,595
1912	2,363	2,475	1,818	1,800
1913	2,448	2,448	1,793	1,793

(continued)

TABLE A-6 (concluded)

Calendar Year	Exports		Imports	
	Current Dollars (1)	Constant (1913) Dollars (2)	Current Dollars (3)	Constant (1913) Dollars (4)
1914	2,071	2,120	1,789	1,909
1915	3,492	3,322	1,779	1,830
1916	5,423	3,998	2,392	1,990
1917	6,170	3,481	2,952	2,033
1918	6,048	2,930	3,031	1,881
1919	7,750	3,589	3,904	2,159
1920	8,080	3,471	5,278	2,410
1921	4,379	2,776	2,509	2,004
1922	3,765	2,614	3,113	2,602
1923	4,091	2,649	3,792	2,776
1924	4,498	2,962	3,610	2,711
1925	4,819	3,133	4,227	2,935
1926	4,712	3,361	4,431	3,127
1927	4,759	3,618	4,185	3,190
1928	5,030	3,760	4,091	3,222
1929	5,157	3,873	4,399	3,701
1930	3,781	3,190	3,061	3,127
1931	2,378	2,592	2,091	2,743
1932	1,576	1,993	1,323	2,202
1933	1,647	2,022	1,450	2,424
1934	2,100	2,164	1,636	2,392
1935	2,243	2,279	2,039	2,935
1936	2,419	2,392	2,424	3,254
1937	3,299	3,077	3,010	3,636
1938	3,057	3,077	1,950	2,616
1939	3,123	3,219	2,276	3,000
1940	3,934	3,760	2,541	3,159
1941	5,020	4,472	3,222	3,733
1942	8,003	5,868	2,780	2,776
1943	12,842	8,575	3,390	3,095
1944	14,317	8,262	3,887	3,351
1945	10,309	5,613	4,098	3,414
1946	9,950	5,868	4,827	3,606
1947	15,160	7,834	5,670	3,446
1948	12,532	6,096	7,095	3,925
1949	11,936	6,240	6,594	3,830
1950	10,142	5,498	8,743	4,658
1951	14,879	7,036	10,817	4,595
1952	15,049	7,151	10,747	4,818
1953	15,652	7,493	10,779	5,042
1954	14,981	7,263	10,240	4,690
1955	15,421	7,378	11,337	5,201
1956	18,940	8,747	12,516	5,648
1957	20,671	9,229	12,951	5,775
1958	17,745	8,005	12,786	5,999
1959	17,438	7,807	14,994	7,149
1960	20,300	8,974	14,652	6,892

NOTES TO TABLE A–6

SOURCES

Cols. 1 and 3

1869–78: (Specie values) U.S. Department of Commerce, *Statistical Abstract of the United States,* 1919, pp. 758–759.

1879–1923: Table A–18, Export Class 220 and Table A–19, Import Class 221.

1924–38: From U.S. Bureau of the Census, *Historical Statistics of the United States, Colonial Times to 1957,* Series U61 and U67, p. 544.

1939–60: WTIS, *Statistical Reports,* Part 3, February 1961, Table 1.

Cols. 2 and 4

1879–1960: 1913 current values multiplied by quantity indexes from Tables A–2 and A–4.

[a]These are published current dollar values. Figures from Appendix F, adjusted to make customs area comparable with later years, are as follows:

	Exports	Imports
1899	1,245	780
1900	1,445	821

TABLE A–7

U.S. EXPORTS AND IMPORTS OF AGRICULTURAL PRODUCTS, IN CURRENT AND
CONSTANT DOLLARS
(in millions of dollars)

Calendar Year[a]	Agricultural Exports		Agricultural Imports	
	Current Dollars (1)	Constant (1913) Dollars (2)	Current Dollars (3)	Constant (1913) Dollars (4)
1869	297	248		
1870	330	349		
1871	333	327		
1872	396	405		
1873	454	484		
1874	389	405		
1875	411	473		
1876	435	518		
1877	532	631		
1878	557	732		
1879	626	777	251	223
1880	747	848	308	244
1881	657	720	304	253
1882	579	607	336	279
1883	601	674	309	281
1884	552	649	292	293
1885	506	641	281	308
1886	539	730	307	334
1887	536	715	319	319
1888	497	633	338	346
1889	606	807	368	350
1890	639	861	382	369
1891	741	942	422	418
1892	720	986	399	416
1893	626	850	388	379
1894	580	926	367	404
1895	551	891	386	458
1896	672	1,122	334	388
1897	737	1,243	385	492
1898	860	1,447	324	411
1899	788	1,298	412	499
1900	910	1,277	414	476
1901	943	1,326	432	546
1902	822	1,098	454	589
1903	917	1,135	461	565
1904	798	981	545	635
1905	901	1,189	605	652
1906	994	1,209	618	659
1907	1,060	1,201	662	673
1908	980	1,159	574	654
1909	910	970	756	837
1910	926	856	775	765
1911	1,003	1,084	768	761
1912	1,137	1,228	957	912

(continued)

157

TABLE A-7 (concluded)

Calendar Year[a]	Agricultural Exports		Agricultural Imports	
	Current Dollars (1)	Constant (1913) Dollars (2)	Current Dollars (3)	Constant (1913) Dollars (4)
1913	1,141	1,141	890	890
1914	997	989	982	1,032
1915	1,608	1,498	1,084	1,101
1916	1,756	1,345	1,403	1,169
1917	1,980	1,011	1,813	1,253
1918	2,749	1,100	1,799	1,185
1919	4,091	1,536	2,598	1,458
1920	3,441	1,256	3,241	1,434
1921	2,113	1,365	1,319	1,220
1922	1,883	1,238	1,628	1,527
1923	1,819	1,045	2,020	1,536
1924	2,110	1,174	1,911	1,554
1925	2,136	1,139	2,340	1,699
1926	1,817	1,181	2,416	1,812
1927	1,885	1,265	2,220	1,850
1928	1,863	1,181	2,099	1,831
1929	1,693	1,097	2,218	2,115
1930	1,201	938	1,469	1,775
1931	821	917	1,008	1,736
1932	662	970	668	1,492
1933	694	885	732	1,586
1934	733	686	821	1,529
1935	747	644	1,073	1,869
1936	709	601	1,243	1,888
1937	797	686	1,579	2,058
1938	828	780	956	1,586
1939	655	674	1,118	1,756
1940	517	495	1,285	1,963
1941	669	443	1,668	2,359
1942	1,179	559	1,273	1,416
1943	2,074	780	1,514	1,492
1944	2,096	706	1,819	1,623
1945	2,254	833	1,710	1,492
1946	3,140	1,191	2,298	1,775
1947	3,960	1,223	2,754	1,793
1948	3,473	1,022	3,150	1,926
1949	3,578	1,265	2,894	1,869
1950	2,873	1,118	3,987	2,001
1951	4,040	1,308	5,179	1,982
1952	3,431	1,118	4,519	2,001
1953	2,847	980	4,185	1,963
1954	3,054	1,065	3,973	1,699
1955	3,198	1,191	3,982	1,812
1956	4,170	1,603	3,961	1,869
1957	4,506	1,750	3,965	1,850
1958	3,855	1,529	3,903	1,906
1959	3,949	1,624	4,099	2,076
1960	4,824	2,046	3,825	1,945

APPENDIX A

Notes to Table A–7

Sources

Col. 1   *1869–78:* U.S. Department of Agriculture, Foreign Agricultural Service, *United States Farm Products in Foreign Trade,* 1953, p. 7.

Cols. 1 and 3   *1879–1900:* 1913 value (Table A–18, Export Class 209 and Table A–19, Import Class 209) multiplied by value index. The value index is the product of the price and quantity indexes (Table A–5).

1901–1923: Tables A–18 and A–19 (class 209).

1924–34: Department of Agriculture, *United States Farm Products in Foreign Trade,* 1953, pp. 11 (exports) and 23 (imports).

1935–57: Business Statistics, 1959, p. 110.

1958–60: WTIS, *Statistical Reports,* Part 3, No. 60–6, March 1960, p. 5, and Part 3, No. 61-42, December 1961, p. 5.

Col. 2   *1869–78:* Extrapolated from 1879 by U.S. Department of Agriculture, Foreign Agricultural Service, *Quantity Indexes of U.S. Agricultural Exports and Imports,* revised January 1960, p. 11.

Cols. 2 and 4   *1879–1960:* 1913 value multiplied by Table A–5, cols. 2 and 4.

[a]1869–78 are years beginning July 1; 1879–1960 are calendar years.

TABLE A-8

(in millions of dollars)

Year	Crude Foods (1)	Manufactured Foods (2)	Crude Materials (3)	Semi-manufactures (4)	Manufactured Products (5)
1879	230	175	229	30	85
1880	258	212	284	31	84
1881	200	201	266	36	105
1882	147	170	275	42	110
1883	142	197	277	43	114
1884	118	186	279	42	106
1885	101	186	241	40	103
1886	119	167	270	38	103
1887	116	172	268	42	103
1888	81	161	282	46	107
1889	108	198	331	50	124
1890	123	222	317	51	127
1891	199	225	343	58	128
1892	203	262	282	52	120
1893	140	239	280	64	128
1894	110	233	268	67	126
1895	106	217	258	72	151
1896	166	226	309	95	185
1897	235	247	282	109	201
1898	279	297	310	117	223
1899	230[a]	311	283	144	276
1900	217[a]	319	420	176	308
1901	247	342	401	140	298
1902	160	317	392	150	303
1903	175	315	481	163	316
1904	103	277	474	210	353
1905	157	309	492	221	408
1906	180	334	542	258	445
1907	196	331	601	279	472
1908	171	317	561	242	420
1909	118	278	588	258	445
1910	95	248	663	293	514
1911	117	303	673	340	614
1912	145	299	795	400	713
1913	172	318	771	420	759
1914	275	306	507	358	615
1915	461	544	686	531	1,252
1916	417	628	813	1,040	2,518
1917	496	807	831	1,427	2,600
1918	535	1,406	971	1,121	2,008
1919	649	1,968	1,619	1,077	2,422
1920	885	1,127	1,872	1,086	3,084
1921	676	675	984	442	1,588
1922	461	577	994	445	1,274
1923	259	573	1,214	568	1,463
1924	393	573	1,333	611	1,588
1925	318	574	1,422	662	1,843

(continued)

TABLE A-8 (concluded)

Year	Crude Foods (1)	Manufactured Foods (2)	Crude Materials (3)	Semi-manufactures (4)	Manufactured Products (5)
1926	335	503	1,261	656	1,957
1927	421	463	1,193	700	1,982
1928	295	466	1,293	716	2,260
1929	270	484	1,142	729	2,532
1930	179	363	829	513	1,898
1931	127	247	567	318	1,120
1932	89	152	514	197	624
1933	48	155	591	237	617
1934	59	168	653	342	879
1935	59	157	683	350	994
1936	58	144	670	393	1,154
1937	105	178	731	669	1,617
1938	249	184	607	494	1,523
1939	111	202	545	599	1,667
1940	74	167	464	900	2,330
1941	84	418	362	771	3,385
1942	68	925	418	920	5,672
1943	109	1,551	662	1,089	9,431
1944	134	1,633	554	1,097	10,744
1945	432	1,246	871	780	6,257
1946	648	1,522	1,416	895	5,019
1947	849	1,483	1,579	1,734	8,607
1948	1,266	1,366	1,488	1,371	7,041
1949	1,342	908	1,780	1,356	6,551
1950	760	634	1,886	1,121	5,741
1951	1,401	881	2,471	1,665	8,462
1952	1,369	736	1,982	1,619	9,341
1953	962	759	1,626	1,423	10,881
1954	741	832	1,899	1,819	9,691
1955	930	1,012	1,907	2,309	9,260
1956	1,332	1,264	2,515	2,775	11,054
1957	1,332	1,163	3,110	3,242	11,823
1958	1,280	1,102	2,139	2,278	10,930
1959	1,444	1,076	1,914	2,462	10,486
1960	1,648	1,117	2,589	3,524	11,441

SOURCE: See notes following Table A-10.

aThese are published current dollar values. Figures from Appendix F, adjusted to make customs area comparable with later years, are 235 for 1899 and 219 for 1900.

161

TABLE A-9

Exports, by Economic Classes, in 1913 Dollars
(in millions of dollars)

Year	Crude Foods (1)	Manufactured Foods (2)	Crude Materials (3)	Semi-manufactures (4)	Manufactures (5)
1879	230	237	285	42	74
1880	252	255	317	40	66
1881	183	214	307	44	88
1882	126	164	312	49	92
1883	128	204	337	51	96
1884	120	206	335	52	90
1885	110	235	301	51	92
1886	138	225	359	50	97
1887	132	230	359	54	99
1888	88	202	360	58	99
1889	133	264	427	66	118
1890	150	309	403	68	124
1891	185	301	464	77	130
1892	218	345	415	72	133
1893	167	285	422	97	149
1894	151	321	484	107	157
1895	143	320	455	107	168
1896	243	364	506	145	194
1897	307	387	518	166	232
1898	339	445	632	176	275
1899	316	471	515	176	314
1900	289	455	584	204	320
1901	314	456	594	168	326
1902	192	384	569	186	331
1903	211	392	595	193	328
1904	126	361	564	253	367
1905	187	413	653	245	444
1906	217	419	649	252	469
1907	203	387	689	263	474
1908	169	365	704	271	428
1909	112	300	644	293	461
1910	95	234	612	323	524
1911	118	328	742	377	637
1912	136	311	889	411	725
1913	172	318	771	420	759
1914	240	296	578	367	653
1915	345	511	795	469	1,241
1916	290	524	701	654	1,912
1917	231	468	497	707	1,707
1918	228	649	440	544	1,164
1919	268	819	669	530	1,365
1920	330	513	654	507	1,534
1921	434	490	627	303	953
1922	362	472	561	343	907
1923	201	458	563	402	1,047
1924	261	448	661	458	1,138
1925	183	374	779	472	1,320

(continued)

TABLE A-9 (concluded)

Year	Crude Foods (1)	Manufactured Foods (2)	Crude Materials (3)	Semi-manufactures (4)	Manufactures (5)
1926	225	344	897	472	1,381
1927	282	344	871	536	1,564
1928	211	356	831	550	1,806
1929	201	371	753	527	2,034
1930	149	304	707	430	1,609
1931	152	265	713	324	1,169
1932	126	213	766	245	713
1933	70	208	753	287	744
1934	73	198	629	361	971
1935	70	159	648	370	1,093
1936	65	143	622	393	1,260
1937	109	166	694	545	1,685
1938	316	198	648	458	1,609
1939	168	235	595	555	1,776
1940	97	190	478	791	2,292
1941	94	400	321	615	3,203
1942	63	641	321	680	4,387
1943	81	1,006	458	777	6,527
1944	87	937	366	758	6,376
1945	261	727	579	550	3,720
1946	357	860	833	608	3,428
1947	406	680	793	914	5,007
1948	585	594	659	665	3,907
1949	702	505	826	696	3,802
1950	463	423	846	590	3,404
1951	767	470	939	710	4,504
1952	690	419	799	701	4,949
1953	517	419	692	634	5,732
1954	446	458	799	816	5,159
1955	579	612	806	971	4,855
1956	822	778	1,066	1,051	5,569
1957	829	688	1,311	1,255	5,604
1958	801	639	916	982	5,103
1959	912	677	857	1,038	4,784
1960	1,047	712	1,160	1,482	5,133

SOURCE: 1913 current values (Table A-8) multiplied by quantity indexes (Table A-2).

TABLE A–10

IMPORTS, BY ECONOMIC CLASSES, IN CURRENT DOLLARS
(in millions of dollars)

Year	Crude Foods (1)	Manufactured Foods (2)	Crude Materials (3)	Semi-manufactures (4)	Manufactured Products (5)
1879	102	82	85	77	136
1880	104	110	120	129	196
1881	111	112	107	110	187
1882	116	133	125	130	218
1883	102	125	117	116	196
1884	101	109	117	101	183
1885	95	102	116	93	161
1886	97	109	136	112	18
1887	120	97	139	127	200
1888	123	112	143	116	204
1889	123	128	160	124	205
1890	137	128	164	136	224
1891	139	167	167	137	187
1892	134	139	179	132	200
1893	135	151	156	121	186
1894	136	134	143	97	143
1895	141	97	199	116	225
1896	120	121	142	95	181
1897	120	108	208	101	182
1898	92	105	176	96	149
1899	100	141[a]	237	134	168
1900	105	126[a]	245	146	186
1901	114	118	272	155	195
1902	120	104	300	192	225
1903	119	107	305	200	234
1904	147	132	333	183	219
1905	136	154	392	218	253
1906	136	140	428	279	307
1907	152	154	451	288	341
1908	142	152	355	196	246
1909	170	165	521	279	305
1910	156	188	538	320	315
1911	193	177	502	315	307
1912	243	203	636	342	363
1913	231	191	608	355	374
1914	247	248	598	293	368
1915	250	264	691	278	264
1916	266	328	1,002	455	317
1917	382	342	1,275	565	356
1913	338	390	1,236	610	429
1919	554	557	1,697	581	462
1920	598	1,221	1,752	843	755
1921	317	350	856	375	535
1922	347	363	1,185	562	596
1923	377	504	1,404	727	724
1924	425	522	1,258	656	749

(continued)

APPENDIX A

TABLE A–10 (concluded)

Year	Crude Foods (1)	Manufactured Foods (2)	Crude Materials (3)	Semi-manufactures (4)	Manufactured Products (5)
1925	495	433	1,748	755	796
1926	540	418	1,792	804	877
1927	505	451	1,601	750	879
1928	550	406	1,467	763	906
1929	539	424	1,559	885	994
1930	400	293	1,002	608	757
1931	305	222	642	372	549
1932	233	174	358	217	341
1933	216	201	418	292	322
1934	254	264	461	307	350
1935	322	319	582	410	406
1936	349	386	733	490	466
1937	413	440	971	634	551
1938	260	311	576	385	418
1939	291	313	745	487	440
1940	285	277	1,011	559	409
1941	376	322	1,376	724	423
1942	349	275	1,061	640	457
1943	584	421	1,037	678	670
1944	841	521	1,078	706	741
1945	693	462	1,183	928	832
1946	814	504	1,729	931	847
1947	1,017	656	1,766	1,245	983
1948	1,272	731	2,147	1,633	1,309
1949	1,333	741	1,854	1,418	1,246
1950	1,750	898	2,465	2,126	1,504
1951	2,077	1,022	3,365	2,459	1,896
1952	2,068	1,083	2,937	2,566	2,094
1953	2,185	1,108	2,613	2,678	2,194
1954	2,200	1,117	2,413	2,313	2,196
1955	1,998	1,118	2,845	2,777	2,599
1956	2,036	1,167	3,087	3,005	3,221
1957	2,020	1,272	3,211	2,920	3,527
1958	1,942	1,516	2,783	2,661	3,917
1959	1,823	1,599	3,093	3,305	5,168
1960	1,732	1,564	2,998	3,092	5,259

a These are published current dollar values. Figures from Appendix F, adjusted to make customs area comparable with later years, are 117 for 1899 and 114 for 1900.

NOTES TO TABLES A–8 AND A–10

For the NBER major classes which correspond to the economic classes used in these tables, see notes to Tables A–1—A–4.

SOURCES

1879–1923: Tables A–18 and A–19.
1924–56: Historical Statistics of the U.S., p. 544.
1957–60: WTIS *Statistical Reports,* Part 3, Nos. 60–6, 61–1 and 61–11, Table 3, p. 5.

TABLE A-11

IMPORTS, BY ECONOMIC CLASSES, IN 1913 DOLLARS
(in millions of dollars)

Year	Crude Foods (1)	Manufactured Foods (2)	Crude Materials (3)	Semi-manufactures (4)	Manufactured Products (5)
1879	90	54	109	103	140
1880	85	60	139	147	197
1881	99	62	131	136	192
1882	106	72	140	156	221
1883	104	74	141	146	202
1884	106	81	142	128	193
1885	108	84	154	131	180
1886	111	87	181	155	217
1887	101	86	181	179	231
1888	114	87	196	169	242
1889	112	82	214	168	242
1890	113	95	221	177	268
1891	115	122	235	180	220
1892	120	104	261	179	239
1893	111	104	226	161	223
1894	121	111	229	145	180
1895	129	102	308	180	283
1896	123	108	217	144	226
1897	150	108	316	157	233
1898	137	94	248	155	190
1899	156	117	296	180	209
1900	148	112	290	173	220
1901	179	122	344	185	227
1902	182	129	376	235	267
1903	182	120	356	237	276
1904	207	141	380	214	255
1905	188	135	426	250	288
1906	184	143	432	280	337
1907	200	150	430	273	359
1908	201	143	399	228	279
1909	246	158	550	336	362
1910	198	164	518	364	373
1911	210	159	506	340	347
1912	238	168	636	345	385
1913	231	191	608	355	374
1914	271	224	645	309	412
1915	278	184	770	275	297
1916	270	187	881	344	281
1917	357	171	907	341	261
1918	306	177	835	328	237
1919	348	215	1,044	307	236
1920	359	255	973	400	336
1921	313	192	853	269	324
1922	315	278	1,111	435	397
1923	342	241	1,134	515	485
1924	338	261	1,052	484	485

(continued)

TABLE A-11 (concluded)

Year	Crude Foods (1)	Manufactured Foods (2)	Crude Materials (3)	Semi-manufactures (4)	Manufactured Products (5)
1925	320	312	1,181	541	474
1926	356	324	1,228	576	553
1927	356	296	1,310	541	580
1928	360	300	1,310	576	569
1929	374	363	1,497	647	685
1930	374	304	1,217	520	585
1931	365	257	1,146	403	495
1932	329	245	912	291	379
1933	333	273	1,018	372	379
1934	347	316	936	331	390
1935	468	348	1,123	444	459
1936	482	391	1,193	520	537
1937	482	435	1,333	602	616
1938	374	352	947	403	437
1939	428	363	1,111	510	464
1940	437	336	1,380	530	390
1941	468	356	1,813	653	384
1942	324	225	1,240	520	379
1943	504	320	1,088	530	495
1944	657	387	1,064	541	495
1945	525	324	1,120	699	533
1946	491	309	1,624	627	472
1947	434	327	1,490	663	439
1948	491	357	1,613	760	537
1949	535	377	1,456	729	528
1950	511	458	1,758	1,117	656
1951	538	478	1,646	1,020	703
1952	531	505	1,736	1,050	783
1953	558	518	1,713	1,157	835
1954	471	528	1,635	1,025	839
1955	498	536	1,826	1,142	1,009
1956	525	558	1,938	1,162	1,226
1957	531	581	1,949	1,147	1,316
1958	535	698	1,809	1,142	1,483
1959	567	741	1,995	1,417	1,963
1960	549	738	1,856	1,300	1,958

SOURCE: 1913 current values (Table A-10) multiplied by quantity indexes (Table A-4).

TABLE A–12

MAJOR COMPONENTS OF SELECTED EXPORT CLASSES,[a] 1879–1923

(thousands of dollars)

Class Composition	1879	1889	1899	1913	1923
201 Crude foodstuffs, excl. tobacco	229,839	107,900	229,823	171,753	259,488
001 Crude animal foods, agric.	10,058	27,009	33,077		
(live animals and crude dairy prods.)					
005 Grains	217,469	76,389	188,780	132,981	192,581
007 Fruits				16,323	35,912
Total accounted for	227,527	103,398	221,857	149,304	228,493
203 Manuf. foods, excl. tobacco prod.	174,706	197,737	310,791	318,140	572,799
106 Meats	70,581	71,787	115,972	72,899	154,281
011 Lard, oleo and related products	25,641	34,634	53,093	82,489	148,061
012 Dairy products	17,813	12,705	9,067	2,640	27,294
014 Flour and other grain products	37,716	53,300	76,908	64,456	118,721
015 Vegetable oil, cake and meal	8,155	10,437	28,597	45,753	25,129
018 Canned and dried fruits			5,896	17,386	33,385
019 and 020 Sugar and related products	7,308	3,275	7,390	9,890	39,503
Total accounted for	167,214	186,138	296,923	295,513	546,374
212 Crude materials, incl. tobacco	228,559	331,092	283,094	771,329	1,214,201
025 Crude tobacco, agric.	14,229	21,974	29,986	52,938	153,439
030 Furs, unmanufactured	6,086	5,634	3,338	16,416	18,763
042 Cotton textiles, crude	186,519	266,649	191,765	575,496	807,103
057 Coal, crude		6,420	15,713	67,410	154,124
059 Petroleum, crude		6,134	5,958	8,448	23,112
Total accounted for	206,834	306,811	246,760	720,708	1,156,541

213 Semimanufactured products	29,693	50,044	143,846	419,882	568,457
028 Hides, leather and products, semimfd.	5,762	10,957	22,104	37,370	42,739
040 (part) Spirits of turpentine and rosin	3,743	6,974	11,517	21,724	23,362
052 Wood and products, semimfd.	10,576	20,465	31,122	88,634	115,168
060 Petroleum and products, semimfd.		2,288	7,650	18,168	47,137
066 Nonferrous metals, semimfd.	3,707	2,152	43,986	159,426	145,119
069 Iron and steel products, semimfd.			8,800	43,959	69,467
074 Chemicals and allied products, semimfd.	3,399	3,297	10,278	20,910	66,373
Total accounted for	27,187	46,133	135,457	390,191	509,365
215 Manufactured products, incl. tobacco prod.	84,674	123,561	275,706	758,786	1,463,351
026 Tobacco products	2,219	3,833	5,201	6,756	25,769
029 Hides, leather and products, manufactured					22,079
036 Rubber products, manufactured				22,635	35,883
053 Wood and products, manufactured			9,911	21,068	26,126
061 Petroleum products	35,166	47,159	60,084	133,963	296,183
070 Manuf. iron and steel products	5,882	9,183	47,356	119,107	160,065
071 Machinery	10,029	22,903	77,876	217,588	323,580
072 Automotive vehicles and parts			200	33,301	166,347
075 Manuf. chemicals				21,204	47,802
077 Misc. uncovered items	6,628	7,494	9,043	50,615	72,727
121 Manuf. textiles	13,468	12,957	30,725	68,547	177,004
Total accounted for	73,392	103,529	240,196	694,784	1,353,565

SOURCE: Tables A–18, B–5, C–5, and unpublished NBER data on minor classes.
a These classes correspond to the five economic classes used by the Department of Commerce.

TABLE A-13

MAJOR COMPONENTS OF SELECTED IMPORT CLASSES,[a] 1879–1923

(thousands of dollars)

Class Composition	1879	1889	1899	1913	1923
201 Crude foods, excl. tobacco	102,030	123,389	100,274	230,784	377,260
001 Crude animal foods, agric. (live animals)				16,121	
004 Grains				10,737	19,945
007 Fruits and nuts, excl. bananas	11,737	11,011	10,560	27,058	38,581
008 Tea	19,866	11,953	10,934	16,404	29,683
009 Coffee	55,589	77,938	56,069	104,672	190,232
010 Cocoa or cacao beans			5,250	19,683	33,807
011 Bananas			6,598	15,394	19,739
Total accounted for	87,192	100,902	89,411	210,069	331,987
203 Manuf. foods, excl. tobacco prod.	82,446	128,487	141,295	190,970	504,162
012 { Dairy products				12,465	36,445
{ Meat products				8,019	23,949
013 Processed fish	2,698	3,471	5,793	13,337	13,701
014 Flour and other grain products	2,531	3,239	4,489	13,153	
016 Veg. oil, cake and meal				10,453	17,686
019 Sugar and related products, agric.	68,426	102,086	107,935	98,831	384,795
021 Beverages, agric.	5,526	9,595	9,003	14,162	
Total accounted for	79,181	118,391	127,220	170,420	476,576
212 Crude materials, incl. tobacco	85,358	160,467	236,840	608,262	1,404,090
024 Crude tobacco	3,615	13,774	11,790	36,321	57,158
026 Hides, leather and products, crude	19,981	22,377	51,088	105,893	118,917
029 Furs, unmanufactured				14,080	79,639
036 Rubber and related gums, crude	8,200	12,503	34,397	84,902	188,472
038 Oilseeds, crude				10,322	65,475
045 Cotton, crude			6,608	19,480	49,443

Class						
051 Crude vegetable fibers, excl. cotton and jute		7,638	20,817	18,562	39,660	37,024
054 Wool, crude		10,788	18,696	11,660	28,776	129,711
057 Silk, crude		11,099	21,472	42,781	89,770	392,299
062 Wood and products, crude		6,188	9,908	8,087	25,778	40,219
069 Petroleum and related prods., crude					11,525	63,295
145 Crude metals			2,754	7,715	36,657	58,092
Total accounted for		67,509	122,301	192,688	503,164	1,279,744
213 Semimanufactured products		76,841	124,252	134,495	355,161	726,611
027 Hides, leather and products, semimfd.		5,377	5,864	5,751	9,292	16,742
039 Veg. oils, expressed, and fats			10,330	3,472	17,694	50,228
063 Wood and products, excl. paper, semimfd.		4,633	13,559	9,260	22,726	70,684
065 Paper and related products, semimfd.				16,135	15,936	74,401
073 Precious stones					33,931	68,117
078 Nonferrous metals, semimfd.		4,982	10,516	32,889	107,946	172,182
081 Iron and steel products, semimfd.		5,207	31,795	8,814	14,576	26,215
086 Semimfd. chemicals		26,195	29,663	35,950	85,381	111,273
123 Semimfd. fibers		24,803	9,007	7,494	24,538	65,101
Total accounted for		71,197	110,734	119,765	332,020	654,943
220 Manuf. products, incl. tobacco and art works		135,591	205,283	167,838	373,547	724,000
147 Manuf. metal products		8,860	13,457	9,302	31,194	58,255
064 Wood and products, excl. paper					9,920	28,973
066 Paper and products, manufactured					25,191	125,038
076 Manuf. of stone, glass, and clay		10,260	14,861	13,171	18,690	45,904
088 Miscellaneous					23,599	53,389
089 Art works					35,054	29,496
126 Manufactured fibers		96,956	142,512	108,553	196,043	318,234
Total accounted for		116,076	170,830	131,026	339,691	659,289

Source: Tables A-19, B-6, C-6, and unpublished NBER data on intermediate and minor classes.
[a] These classes correspond to the five economic classes used by the Department of Commerce.

TABLE A-14

ANNUAL FISHER PRICE INDEXES,
MAJOR EXPORT CLASSES
(1913=100)

YEAR	201	202	203	204	205	206	207	208	209	210	211
1879	93.4	89.6	76.7	77.5	82.6	81.7	84.5	83.8	80.7	80.4	81.4
1880	96.1	92.4	86.6	87.3	89.0	87.0	91.3	90.4	88.1	87.8	91.1
1881	102.6	98.2	97.6	98.2	97.5	96.0	100.6	98.6	91.4	91.1	88.0
1882	109.0	102.8	106.8	107.2	105.1	102.7	107.6	105.3	95.2	94.8	89.7
1883	104.0	98.5	99.7	100.2	98.6	96.8	101.3	99.6	89.0	89.1	83.0
1884	91.4	90.1	92.2	91.4	89.2	88.9	91.9	91.0	85.2	85.1	83.4
1885	85.4	84.3	80.9	81.4	79.7	79.8	82.3	82.5	79.0	79.2	80.2
1886	80.4	79.9	76.3	76.8	77.1	77.4	77.8	78.2	73.8	74.7	74.6
1887	81.6	79.4	76.3	76.8	77.6	77.1	78.2	77.9	74.9	74.7	75.0
1888	86.0	84.0	81.3	81.9	82.2	81.7	82.8	82.6	78.5	78.0	78.4
1889	75.4	74.7	76.7	77.3	75.4	75.2	76.1	76.2	75.2	74.9	78.0
1890	76.6	75.8	73.6	74.2	74.1	74.0	74.8	75.0	74.1	74.0	79.2
1891	100.1	95.4	76.7	77.3	85.2	84.6	85.9	85.5	78.6	78.1	74.1
1892	86.6	84.9	77.7	78.2	80.3	80.1	81.0	81.0	73.1	72.8	67.4
1893	77.7	77.1	85.6	86.0	81.7	81.4	82.2	82.1	73.7	73.1	65.8
1894	67.7	68.3	74.2	74.7	71.2	71.3	71.8	72.1	62.6	62.9	54.0
1895	69.4	69.6	69.5	70.0	68.8	69.0	69.5	69.9	61.9	62.3	55.5
1896	63.5	64.0	63.5	64.0	68.5	62.9	63.2	63.9	59.9	60.4	60.4
1897	71.3	71.0	64.6	65.4	66.6	66.8	66.8	67.7	59.3	59.9	53.1
1898	76.7	76.5	68.0	68.5	70.6	71.0	71.3	71.9	59.5	60.1	46.9
1899	74.2	74.0	66.9	67.4	68.9	69.3	69.6	70.2	61.0	62.0	53.6
1900	74.1	74.2	71.3	71.7	71.5	71.8	72.3	72.7	71.3	71.5	72.1
1901	77.0	76.8	76.0	76.2	82.8	82.7	83.2	76.5	71.1	70.9	67.4
1902	82.0	80.1	81.8	83.9	81.1	81.0	81.6	83.1	74.9	74.6	68.2
1903	81.6	81.0	81.8	81.9	81.3	78.1	78.8	81.6	80.7	80.4	81.1
1904	80.3	79.4	77.8	78.0	77.3	77.6	78.0	78.0	81.2	81.0	84.9
1905	82.5	81.4	75.7	75.9	80.7	80.8	81.1	81.0	75.7	76.4	75.4
1906	81.7	81.7	80.7	80.8	89.7	89.2	89.5	89.2	82.0	83.0	83.9
1907	95.8	93.4	86.5	86.5	91.7	91.6	92.0	91.8	88.1	88.9	87.4
1908	99.8	97.8	87.9	87.9	96.8	96.0	97.1	96.1	84.4	84.8	79.1
1909	104.2	100.3	93.7	93.5	104.3	103.1	104.5	103.8	93.7	93.3	91.6
1910	98.7	99.1	107.3	106.9	94.2	94.3	94.7	94.7	108.2	106.7	109.5
1911	97.9	97.4	93.3	93.2	99.1	98.8	99.4	99.0	92.5	93.3	90.5
1912	104.2	102.2	97.0	96.9					92.4	93.5	88.9
1913	100.0	100.0	100.0	100.0	100.0	100.0	100.0	100.0	100.0	100.0	100.0
1914	114.5	117.4	103.3	103.2	102.2	108.4	107.5	108.6	100.8	106.5	86.2
1915	133.8	134.2	106.5	106.1	116.0	117.5	116.1	117.2	107.3	106.6	84.5
1916	144.2	141.8	118.5	118.0	126.9	127.8	126.8	127.2	130.1	128.5	116.4
1917	214.9	215.5	170.5	168.3	184.9	188.6	184.4	186.0	195.2	186.5	167.9
1918	234.6	244.7	214.2	210.4	220.7	228.5	220.5	224.7	249.2	239.2	217.2
1919	241.7	249.5	237.4	233.6	239.5	245.4	238.7	242.2	265.5	259.3	238.1
1920	268.2	311.6	216.2	213.6	243.1	254.4	234.8	250.4	273.1	269.1	270.2
1921	155.7	195.1	136.2	135.8	142.5	159.0	143.3	158.6	154.3	152.9	137.7
1922	127.3	161.6	120.8	121.2	122.4	136.3	123.0	136.5	151.6	150.4	165.9

Year	1	2	3	4	5	6	7	8	9	10	11
1379	102.9	117.3	92.5	92.5	84.9	85.0	86.6	119.3	119.0	79.3	80.1
1880	114.3	131.4	101.5	101.5	93.0	94.7	96.8	132.4	132.4	87.5	89.4
1881	112.7	124.8	107.5	103.8	96.2	92.9	94.5	124.8	124.9	92.0	86.8
1882	113.1	122.6	107.0	107.0	100.0	94.3	96.1	123.3	123.9	93.0	88.8
1883	111.4	121.6	101.4	101.4	94.0	88.3	89.7	121.8	121.9	90.8	82.1
1884	109.4	115.0	97.6	97.6	89.8	88.9	89.4	122.3	122.6	86.4	83.3
1885	103.7	107.7	91.0	91.0	83.6	85.6	86.0	115.5	115.8	83.7	80.2
1886	99.9	104.4	85.7	85.7	78.7	80.3	80.5	109.0	109.2	80.5	74.9
1887	94.8	104.4	85.5	85.5	78.8	80.1	81.1	106.1	106.2	82.0	74.5
1888	99.7	112.3	89.7	89.7	82.8	83.8	84.6	110.1	110.0	84.7	78.1
1889	95.7	104.9	86.0	86.0	79.3	82.8	83.8	106.7	106.7	81.9	77.5
1890	95.1	104.5	85.0	85.0	78.6	83.7	84.8	104.4	104.4	82.5	78.5
1891	92.4	101.1	87.9	87.9	82.6	73.8	80.4	100.3	100.1	81.7	74.1
1892	86.1	92.9	81.9	80.2	77.2	70.7	73.9	91.8	91.6	78.7	67.4
1893	80.4	84.6	80.2	80.2	76.3	70.6	70.5	87.0	86.6	71.9	65.4
1894	76.3	79.5	70.5	70.5	66.1	62.5	59.9	82.0	81.5	67.7	55.3
1895	83.0	90.4	71.8	71.0	65.9	65.4	62.0	91.4	92.2	71.7	56.7
1896	85.6	94.7	71.0	71.0	64.0	65.8	65.2	96.8	96.9	70.1	61.0
1897	80.6	87.8	69.1	69.1	63.4	59.8	59.2	88.1	88.0	69.6	54.3
1898	77.6	83.2	68.4	68.4	63.6	55.7	54.6	82.6	82.4	70.4	48.9
1899	87.3	95.4	72.3	72.3	66.7	64.1	63.6	90.3	90.2	84.9	55.1
1900	94.4	102.3	81.0	81.0	75.7	77.5	77.6	98.9	99.0	89.5	72.2
1901	90.5	99.1	79.4	79.4	74.9	73.3	73.2	94.2	94.3	86.0	67.9
1902	89.0	95.7	81.4	81.4	77.2	73.5	73.0	94.1	94.1	83.5	69.1
1903	94.0	100.9	86.6	86.9	82.5	83.0	83.3	98.9	99.1	87.3	81.0
1904	93.6	98.6	86.9	83.7	83.1	84.8	85.3	98.8	98.9	85.9	84.3
1905	93.5	97.2	83.7	87.2	79.0	81.1	81.3	94.5	94.6	93.6	75.6
1906	99.4	103.2	89.9	89.9	87.2	90.7	91.7	97.5	97.7	105.9	83.8
1907	103.6	106.6	95.2	90.2	92.7	94.4	94.7	102.2	102.4	109.9	87.4
1908	96.7	99.9	90.1	90.1	86.4	83.7	83.4	100.4	100.7	91.0	79.8
1909	94.9	97.0	94.3	94.3	93.0	91.8	91.4	97.4	97.6	93.4	91.4
1910	96.6	96.8	102.1	102.1	103.6	103.3	103.7	98.7	98.8	100.3	108.4
1911	94.5	93.9	93.5	93.5	94.7	92.9	92.8	95.5	95.6	95.5	90.9
1912	98.4	98.6	95.5	95.5	94.7			97.3	97.3	97.3	89.3
1913	100.0	100.0	100.0	100.0	100.0	100.0	100.0	100.0	100.0	100.0	100.0
1914	95.3	94.7	97.7	97.7	99.7	92.3	91.6	94.3	94.2	97.6	87.9
1915	103.5	103.7	105.1	105.1	107.3	97.2	96.0	100.6	101.0	113.2	86.0
1916	135.8	137.5	135.5	135.5	135.9	137.6	139.2	130.6	130.8	156.5	115.5
1917	161.7	160.2	177.0	177.0	193.0	192.4	192.0	150.4	150.8	198.1	166.8
1918	176.9	171.1	206.1	206.1	227.8	221.0	219.5	169.7	170.6	202.8	211.9
1919	179.7	166.6	215.7	215.7	240.3	227.5	225.4	174.4	174.0	199.5	241.3
1920	204.7	187.6	232.5	232.5	253.6	257.7	247.8	197.7	198.6	210.5	285.3
1921	158.6	158.6	157.5	157.5	153.6	157.6	139.4	163.8	164.5	164.5	156.4
1922	138.4	133.6	143.8	143.8	147.4	157.0	150.4	137.8	137.8	176.9	176.6
1923	140.0	132.0	154.2	154.2	164.1	185.2	180.7	137.1	137.3	138.4	214.8

TABLE A-15

ANNUAL FISHER PRICE INDEXES,
MAJOR IMPORT CLASSES
(1913=100)

YEAR	201	202	203	204	205	206	207	208	209	210	211	212
1879	114.3	112.8	141.9	139.2	131.4	129.6	127.0	124.2	115.1	104.5	95.8	95.0
1880	123.3	121.5	170.2	166.0	149.8	147.3	144.4	140.7	129.6	114.1	105.4	104.2
1881	112.5	111.6	169.0	164.8	142.1	140.0	137.4	134.2	123.4	110.0	100.1	99.3
1882	105.2	104.7	171.2	167.1	137.8	135.8	134.1	131.1	123.3	110.8	105.8	104.5
1883	94.6	94.8	156.4	152.8	125.1	123.5	121.9	119.4	112.4	104.0	98.2	96.9
1884	95.5	95.7	125.0	122.9	111.1	110.4	108.9	107.5	102.0	96.2	92.3	91.9
1885	88.3	89.2	112.5	110.9	101.2	101.0	99.3	98.6	93.6	88.7	84.6	84.7
1886	87.3	88.1	115.1	113.0	101.7	101.4	99.9	98.0	94.1	88.5	84.5	84.5
1887	118.9	117.3	104.7	103.0	101.4	113.7	112.2	110.5	102.4	93.5	85.6	85.8
1888	108.4	107.9	118.1	115.6	114.5	113.9	112.9	111.1	100.0	91.3	80.7	81.3
1889	112.5	111.6	141.1	137.6	127.6	126.2	125.5	122.8	107.8	97.2	82.6	83.1
1890	123.7	121.0	121.5	119.5	124.3	122.9	122.1	119.7	105.9	95.0	81.5	82.2
1891	122.8	121.2	124.5	123.3	123.0	122.1	121.3	119.9	103.3	93.7	77.5	77.6
1892	113.7	111.4	120.8	119.7	117.7	116.3	116.0	114.3	98.1	94.0	74.5	74.9
1893	123.9	122.1	131.3	130.0	128.1	126.9	126.0	124.4	105.0	94.7	74.9	75.6
1894	114.8	113.7	109.0	108.3	112.4	112.0	110.9	110.2	93.2	86.4	67.1	68.5
1895	111.6	109.6	86.5	86.3	100.6	100.3	99.4	99.1	86.1	81.7	69.2	70.0
1896	99.5	99.8	101.1	100.0	86.7	100.6	99.1	99.1	88.1	83.2	70.2	70.1
1897	81.8	85.1	90.8	90.6	82.7	88.0	86.0	87.2	80.2	77.4	69.8	71.4
1898	68.4	72.4	99.3	99.1	82.7	84.2	82.5	84.0	80.8	77.9	74.7	76.2
1899	66.4	70.7	106.3	105.9	84.3	85.9	84.6	86.1	84.6	82.1	81.8	83.2
1900	72.9	76.2	106.1	105.6	88.1	89.0	87.8	88.7	88.4	86.5	86.9	87.7
1901	66.1	69.1	96.0	96.0	78.8	79.8	78.8	79.9	80.2	80.8	81.4	82.1
1902	67.9	69.9	80.5	80.9	72.6	73.7	73.3	74.4	78.4	79.6	82.8	83.0
1903	67.3	69.7	88.2	88.3	75.3	76.2	76.2	77.2	87.4	83.5	88.6	88.5
1904	73.0	74.9	93.7	93.5	81.3	81.9	81.9	82.5	86.5	85.9	89.2	89.2
1905	74.3	76.4	113.2	112.4	91.3	91.4	91.4	91.4	93.6	91.3	93.6	93.5
1906	75.9	80.1	97.1	96.9	84.8	86.7	85.5	87.2	94.5	93.6	100.3	100.7
1907	78.2	82.7	101.8	101.8	87.0	90.0	88.7	90.7	99.2	98.3	105.6	106.2
1908	72.8	77.7	105.8	105.7	86.9	88.9	87.3	89.2	88.5	89.3	88.2	89.7
1909	71.1	74.8	104.3	104.3	84.9	86.2	85.2	86.6	91.0	90.2	94.9	95.3
1910	80.9	83.7	113.8	113.5	96.3	96.8	96.0	96.7	92.0	90.3	104.9	104.8
1911	94.5	96.5	109.7	109.6	101.8	102.4	101.4	102.0	101.6	98.4	99.3	99.0
1912	104.0	104.2	119.0	118.5	111.4	110.9	110.7	110.1	105.3	102.3	100.1	100.4
1913	100.0	100.0	100.0	100.0	100.0	100.0	100.0	100.0	100.0	100.0	100.0	100.0
1914	91.1	92.3	110.7	110.3	99.1	99.2	99.5	99.6	99.5	95.2	92.6	92.9
1915	89.9	91.2	142.9	141.3	113.1	112.1	113.0	111.7	98.5	97.2	89.3	89.7
1916	98.7	100.2	172.3	169.7	130.6	129.3	130.2	128.5	119.6	118.5	112.9	113.1
1917	106.7	110.0	196.9	193.5	145.4	144.6	145.7	144.2	144.1	144.1	139.6	139.8
1918	100.5	115.5	216.5	212.5	153.6	154.0	155.7	154.9	151.3	159.7	146.7	147.3
1919	159.4	162.7	255.7	251.6	199.9	201.2	201.4	199.3	177.5	186.0	160.6	161.6
1920	166.4	169.5	472.4	461.0	297.3	291.2	296.6	288.2	225.2	233.0	178.4	179.1
1921	101.1	109.5	179.0	177.6	132.9	135.9	134.6	137.4	107.7	125.8	96.8	99.8
1922	101.4	115.6	128.0	128.4	115.3	117.9	117.7	119.6	106.2	121.1	104.2	106.7
1923	110.2	117.0	206.0	202.8	150.0	151.5	151.1	151.8	131.1	140.3	121.2	123.2

YEAR	213	214	215	216	217	218	219	220	221	222	223
1879	78.0	87.7	87.7	101.6	107.6	102.8	102.4	102.8	102.4	93.9	89.4
1880	91.1	89.2	99.0	115.4	106.3	104.4	113.1	102.4	113.1	107.6	96.9
1881	83.8	92.7	92.7	108.8	104.1	103.2	107.7	103.2	107.7	98.2	92.3
1882	84.6	96.0	95.8	109.4	104.1	101.6	108.3	101.6	108.3	97.9	93.3
1883	80.8	90.2	90.0	101.2	102.5	101.7	101.8	101.7	101.8	92.8	90.4
1884	80.1	87.2	87.2	94.4	96.9	96.1	95.4	96.1	95.4	91.6	87.5
1885	71.8	79.1	79.4	86.1	91.4	90.7	87.5	90.7	87.7	83.9	80.9
1886	73.1	79.7	79.7	86.9	88.2	87.4	87.5	87.4	87.5	82.2	79.9
1887	71.8	79.8	80.0	91.7	88.3	87.4	90.9	87.5	90.9	80.5	79.3
1888	69.5	75.9	76.5	89.7	85.0	86.1	88.8	85.1	88.8	79.1	77.5
1889	72.5	78.4	78.9	95.8	88.3	87.6	93.9	87.6	93.9	81.2	80.3
1890	75.3	79.2	79.6	95.4	86.9	86.4	92.2	86.4	92.2	86.0	80.5
1891	74.3	76.8	76.6	93.7	86.2	86.0	92.0	86.0	92.0	85.3	79.9
1892	72.4	73.8	74.1	89.6	84.6	84.8	88.5	84.8	88.5	82.5	78.3
1893	73.7	74.6	75.1	94.4	84.6	84.5	92.0	84.6	92.0	81.6	78.6
1894	65.2	66.5	67.4	84.4	80.4	80.4	83.5	80.5	83.5	72.0	72.7
1895	63.4	66.9	67.4	79.2	80.4	80.4	79.5	80.3	79.5	70.3	72.2
1896	64.9	68.1	68.6	80.7	81.2	81.2	80.7	81.2	80.7	71.1	72.8
1897	63.4	67.3	68.3	74.9	79.5	79.5	75.9	80.2	75.9	69.8	71.0
1898	60.8	69.0	70.1	74.7	79.3	79.5	75.7	79.4	75.7	67.3	70.0
1899	73.4	78.4	79.4	81.2	82.7	82.8	81.5	82.8	81.5	79.4	78.0
1900	82.7	85.2	85.8	86.5	87.4	87.4	86.7	87.4	86.7	87.3	84.8
1901	82.4	81.8	82.2	81.1	88.9	89.0	82.6	88.6	82.6	89.0	85.2
1902	80.0	81.7	81.8	79.1	87.7	87.8	84.0	87.6	84.0	85.8	83.4
1903	82.9	86.2	86.3	83.0	87.8	87.8	85.8	87.7	85.8	85.7	85.6
1904	83.4	87.0	87.0	85.3	90.1	90.1	90.6	90.0	90.6	88.3	85.0
1905	85.4	90.4	90.4	90.7	90.1	91.1	94.7	93.2	94.7	98.3	87.5
1906	97.4	99.1	99.4	95.1	93.1	93.1	99.2	97.1	99.2	102.4	95.0
1907	103.1	104.6	105.0	99.8	90.3	97.0	88.1	90.4	88.1	83.8	87.5
1908	83.9	86.5	87.5	87.5	85.8	90.5	88.0	86.3	88.0	80.9	97.4
1909	81.2	89.5	90.0	88.6	85.4	86.1	94.6	86.5	94.6	82.6	84.8
1910	85.7	97.0	97.2	96.9	89.4	85.8	96.1	90.2	96.1	89.2	87.1
1911	90.4	95.7	96.2	97.8	94.4	85.7	101.0	95.4	101.0	96.9	90.4
1912	96.9	98.9	99.1	102.5		94.6					96.3
1913	100.0	100.0	100.0	100.0	100.0	100.0	100.0	100.0	100.0	100.0	100.0
1914	93.3	92.8	93.0	94.6	90.4	90.6	93.7	90.7	93.7	90.3	91.7
1915	99.8	92.7	92.8	98.3	89.9	90.2	97.2	90.2	97.2	97.2	94.6
1916	128.1	118.0	117.9	121.3	112.1	111.9	120.2	112.2	120.2	127.5	120.9
1917	160.4	146.5	146.4	146.1	136.7	135.9	145.3	136.1	145.3	147.6	146.1
1918	183.1	157.6	157.7	156.0	183.6	181.2	161.3	180.1	161.3	167.1	175.2
1919	204.2	167.9	168.4	177.1	197.8	196.5	181.0	195.3	181.0	163.0	186.4
1920	135.0	186.8	187.0	217.1	225.3	224.2	219.1	223.5	219.1	167.3	209.5
1921	125.3	108.1	110.0	116.8	167.3	166.9	125.2	164.6	125.2	124.3	150.1
1922	136.8	110.9	112.1	113.4	151.6	151.1	119.7	149.4	119.7	114.9	138.3
1923		126.3	127.5	133.8	150.2	149.5	136.6	148.7	136.6	124.2	144.2

175

APPENDIX A

TABLE A-16

ANNUAL FISHER QUANTITY INDEXES, MAJOR EXPORT CLASSES
(1913=100)

YEAR	201	202	203	204	205	206	207	208	209	210	211
1879	148.5	124.7	74.4	73.0	105.2	98.9	101.4	94.5	68.1	61.6	36.6
1880	162.3	136.9	80.1	78.5	113.5	107.1	109.2	102.2	74.4	67.0	40.5
1881	117.7	101.9	67.3	66.1	88.1	84.0	85.0	80.4	63.1	57.5	39.2
1882	81.4	73.8	51.7	51.3	64.2	67.5	62.2	60.3	53.3	49.6	39.8
1883	82.7	75.5	64.1	63.2	72.2	70.9	70.6	68.0	59.2	54.3	43.1
1884	77.2	69.4	64.8	64.0	70.5	67.8	69.1	66.1	56.9	53.1	43.2
1885	70.0	68.8	73.8	72.9	76.4	74.1	72.8	71.3	56.2	51.8	37.2
1886	89.0	84.1	70.6	69.9	80.7	79.4	77.0	75.7	64.0	58.1	44.9
1887	85.3	78.4	72.4	71.8	78.7	76.4	77.0	74.5	62.8	58.1	45.8
1888	56.8	54.2	63.7	63.3	62.0	60.3	61.2	59.6	55.6	52.1	46.6
1889	85.9	79.1	82.9	82.1	85.0	82.1	84.0	80.9	70.7	66.2	55.1
1890	96.5	86.7	97.1	95.9	98.8	94.3	96.7	92.0	75.6	69.9	51.9
1891	119.1	103.4	94.5	93.5	105.6	100.2	103.3	97.6	82.7	75.9	60.6
1892	140.7	120.6	108.6	107.1	123.1	116.1	120.2	112.8	86.5	79.2	57.7
1893	107.8	96.4	89.6	88.8	97.6	93.6	96.2	92.0	74.5	69.6	54.2
1894	97.1	90.2	100.9	99.6	100.8	97.3	99.7	95.8	81.2	75.8	62.4
1895	92.0	85.8	100.5	99.1	99.1	95.6	97.3	93.7	78.2	73.5	58.5
1896	156.6	135.0	114.3	113.3	132.6	125.6	129.5	122.4	98.4	91.4	65.6
1897	197.7	165.4	121.8	120.7	153.6	144.0	149.5	139.7	109.0	100.8	67.8
1898	218.2	180.3	139.8	138.2	173.4	161.4	168.5	156.2	126.9	115.9	84.8
1899	186.5	160.3	148.2	146.4	166.7	157.3	151.9	152.2	113.9	105.6	65.9
1900	176.6	150.3	142.9	141.6	158.5	149.0	154.7	145.2	112.6	105.7	76.3
1901	122.7	156.6	143.4	142.2	160.9	151.7	157.6	148.2	116.2	108.9	77.6
1902	112.1	104.8	120.7	120.1	119.2	115.4	117.6	113.8	96.2	91.8	73.3
1903	123.1	111.1	123.1	122.3	125.6	120.1	123.1	117.6	95.2	95.2	77.7
1904	73.2	74.3	113.4	112.8	99.6	97.5	98.6	96.5	86.0	83.9	72.7
1905	108.8	99.0	129.8	128.9	124.1	118.3	122.7	116.3	104.2	99.1	86.2
1906	126.1	114.1	131.8	131.0	132.1	126.3	129.7	124.0	106.0	101.8	84.9
1907	118.2	107.6	121.8	121.2	122.5	117.4	120.4	115.4	105.3	101.0	90.6
1908	98.3	91.6	114.6	114.0	110.2	106.0	108.5	104.3	101.6	97.4	93.1
1909	65.1	68.0	94.3	94.1	83.9	83.4	83.4	83.0	85.0	83.7	83.8
1910	55.1	59.3	73.6	73.6	67.1	67.7	67.2	67.9	75.0	76.2	79.8
1911	68.5	71.8	103.2	102.7	91.5	90.7	90.7	89.8	95.0	94.4	97.2
1912	79.4	82.3	97.8	97.6	91.7	91.7	91.1	91.2	107.6	106.1	117.1
1913	100.0	100.0	100.0	100.0	100.0	100.0	100.0	100.0	100.0	100.0	100.0
1914	140.0	121.0	93.0	93.3	111.3	106.5	110.4	105.9	86.7	85.7	74.8
1915	200.6	176.3	164.5	159.6	178.5	167.0	176.6	165.3	131.3	125.0	104.1
1916	168.6	150.8	164.8	164.9	168.4	159.8	166.9	159.0	117.9	114.4	89.4
1917	134.5	111.9	147.0	148.9	144.4	132.1	143.1	132.6	88.6	86.8	64.9
1918	132.9	119.7	203.9	207.8	180.8	167.5	178.6	168.5	96.4	92.3	54.1
1919	156.3	162.2	257.6	262.6	222.9	215.6	222.0	218.3	134.6	132.1	79.1
1920	192.2	161.5	161.2	166.7	174.5	163.4	173.6	166.1	110.1	107.4	83.5
1921	252.8	201.0	153.9	156.0	195.4	182.1	190.9	179.8	119.6	111.3	78.4
1922	210.6	167.2	148.5	151.7	174.1	161.0	170.9	160.2	108.5	104.2	70.8

YEAR	212	213	214	215	216	217	218	219	220	221	222
1879	37.0	10.1	9.6	9.7	25.6	26.4	47.9	34.3	33.3	7.0	10.2
1880	41.1	9.5	8.5	8.7	27.9	28.8	51.8	36.3	35.2	6.0	9.4
1881	39.8	10.4	11.4	11.6	27.3	28.2	44.8	33.0	32.0	8.2	11.5
1882	40.4	11.7	11.9	12.1	28.1	29.0	36.8	29.3	28.6	8.6	12.2
1883	43.7	12.1	12.5	12.6	30.2	31.2	42.8	32.1	31.3	9.7	12.8
1884	43.6	12.3	11.6	11.8	30.4	31.1	42.3	31.4	30.7	9.7	13.2
1885	39.0	12.1	11.8	12.1	26.7	28.3	41.4	30.9	30.2	9.6	12.9
1886	46.5	12.0	12.5	12.8	31.3	33.0	46.0	34.1	33.3	9.6	12.8
1887	46.6	12.8	12.8	13.1	32.1	33.2	46.2	34.4	33.6	10.3	14.0
1888	46.7	13.7	12.7	13.0	32.9	33.6	41.9	31.6	30.9	10.9	14.4
1889	55.4	15.8	15.2	15.6	38.8	39.7	52.9	39.6	38.7	13.1	17.3
1890	52.3	16.1	15.9	16.3	37.0	37.9	55.4	41.5	40.7	13.4	17.1
1891	60.1	18.3	16.8	17.1	42.9	43.4	60.9	45.5	44.5	14.8	18.6
1892	53.8	17.2	17.1	17.5	38.2	39.1	63.2	47.1	46.0	14.8	18.8
1893	54.7	23.1	19.4	19.7	41.1	42.1	57.7	44.5	43.5	18.7	22.5
1894	62.8	25.6	20.4	20.7	46.7	47.7	62.5	47.8	46.8	19.1	23.6
1895	59.0	25.5	21.8	22.2	44.3	45.3	66.4	47.0	46.0	19.6	24.4
1896	65.6	34.5	25.2	25.6	52.4	53.0	75.7	57.9	56.8	23.6	28.9
1897	67.2	39.6	30.2	30.6	55.8	56.0	83.6	65.0	63.8	28.0	33.3
1898	82.0	41.9	35.9	36.3	66.0	65.4	95.6	74.9	73.7	32.8	37.6
1899	66.8	41.8	41.0	41.4	55.7	56.7	87.8	71.9	70.8	35.7	41.3
1900	75.0	48.6	41.8	42.2	65.5	65.6	90.7	74.4	73.2	40.0	42.5
1901	77.0	48.0	42.5	42.9	62.0	62.9	90.8	74.0	74.0	36.1	42.3
1902	73.8	44.4	43.2	43.7	62.0	62.9	79.7	67.7	66.9	37.5	44.3
1903	77.2	46.0	42.9	43.2	65.9	66.1	82.7	69.8	68.8	38.0	44.9
1904	73.1	60.2	48.0	48.4	68.2	68.6	77.7	67.9	67.0	46.9	52.3
1905	84.7	58.4	58.2	58.5	75.4	74.9	88.7	79.0	78.0	51.5	58.1
1906	89.3	60.0	61.5	61.8	79.7	75.1	90.6	81.4	80.5	55.0	61.0
1907	91.3	62.6	62.2	62.5	82.2	79.3	91.2	82.1	81.3	60.0	62.6
1908	83.5	64.5	56.2	56.4	78.9	81.6	89.7	79.0	78.4	57.0	59.8
1909	79.4	69.8	60.5	60.7	94.4	78.8	80.2	74.0	73.1	60.5	64.1
1910	96.2	77.0	84.1	84.0	78.9	78.6	75.2	73.3	73.1	68.8	71.7
1911	96.2	89.7	84.1	84.0	94.4	93.9	92.9	90.1	90.0	84.1	85.9
1912	115.3	97.9	95.6	95.5	109.9	109.1	103.6	101.1	101.1	94.1	95.5
1913	100.0	100.0	100.0	100.0	100.0	100.0	100.0	100.0	100.0	100.0	100.0
1914	74.9	87.4	85.2	86.0	78.6	78.7	86.4	86.6	85.7	85.2	86.0
1915	103.1	111.7	164.2	163.6	105.3	104.9	122.9	135.4	135.4	141.5	139.0
1916	90.9	155.8	252.7	252.0	117.1	112.2	125.9	162.6	163.3	231.8	205.6
1917	64.4	168.5	224.8	225.0	97.8	97.8	109.0	141.3	142.2	231.5	196.3
1918	57.0	129.5	151.6	153.4	78.2	78.2	104.9	118.8	119.7	160.7	140.3
1919	86.7	126.4	177.5	179.9	94.2	98.7	131.1	145.4	146.6	155.3	152.2
1920	84.8	120.8	200.2	202.2	95.4	95.6	116.3	140.4	141.8	187.2	169.7
1921	81.3	72.2	124.5	125.6	76.3	78.9	107.4	112.4	113.4	117.5	105.4
1922	72.7	81.8	118.0	119.5	74.8	75.9	99.8	105.5	106.8	105.9	100.9
1923	73.0	95.8	136.6	138.0	78.4	80.0	94.5	107.0	108.2	132.2	121.0

TABLE A-17

ANNUAL FISHER QUANTITY INDEXES,
MAJOR IMPORT CLASSES
(1913=100)

YEAR	201	202	203	204	205	206	207	208	209	210	211	212
1879	38.8	35.1	32.0	32.5	35.5	33.6	35.6	34.0	26.0	30.6	18.4	17.9
1880	36.6	33.8	35.6	36.1	36.2	34.5	36.3	35.0	28.3	35.6	23.4	22.9
1881	42.9	33.0	36.6	37.2	39.7	37.7	39.8	38.2	29.4	36.0	21.9	21.5
1882	46.0	42.1	42.8	43.2	44.6	42.4	44.4	42.7	32.5	39.9	23.8	23.0
1883	45.0	42.2	43.8	44.5	44.6	42.9	44.6	43.4	32.7	39.2	22.5	23.1
1884	46.1	43.6	47.8	48.1	48.5	45.1	47.1	45.3	34.1	40.6	23.5	23.3
1885	46.9	44.5	49.4	50.1	48.8	46.7	48.3	46.3	35.8	41.2	25.1	25.3
1886	48.2	44.5	51.6	52.4	50.8	46.4	50.1	48.4	38.8	45.4	25.0	29.7
1887	43.9	41.9	50.5	51.5	47.6	46.0	47.1	46.3	37.1	44.9	30.0	29.3
1888	49.4	46.0	51.6	52.7	51.5	49.2	50.7	49.2	40.3	48.4	32.5	32.2
1889	48.4	46.7	48.6	49.7	49.4	48.2	48.7	48.3	40.7	48.8	34.6	35.2
1890	49.0	48.9	56.0	57.0	53.2	52.4	52.6	52.8	43.0	52.4	34.8	36.4
1891	49.9	46.2	71.9	71.5	62.7	59.4	61.3	58.3	48.6	53.4	39.3	38.6
1892	52.1	50.6	61.4	61.3	57.9	56.4	57.2	55.8	48.4	54.8	42.6	42.9
1893	48.2	45.7	61.6	61.3	55.9	53.2	55.2	53.2	44.1	50.3	37.1	37.1
1894	52.5	53.7	65.6	65.0	59.3	58.2	59.2	57.5	46.9	49.2	36.7	37.6
1895	55.8	54.3	60.0	59.5	58.0	55.6	57.9	56.3	53.3	61.8	50.6	50.6
1896	53.2	49.7	63.8	63.3	58.0	55.6	58.8	56.3	45.1	51.0	55.7	35.7
1897	64.9	57.9	63.6	62.9	63.9	60.0	64.5	60.5	47.2	61.5	54.2	51.9
1898	59.3	52.7	55.6	55.0	57.9	54.4	57.4	53.9	47.8	60.5	42.2	40.7
1899	67.5	61.0	69.2	68.5	70.0	66.0	68.8	64.9	58.1	56.9	50.1	48.6
1900	64.2	60.4	61.7	61.2	63.3	61.2	63.1	60.6	54.2	56.7	48.3	47.7
1901	77.5	72.8	64.0	63.4	70.5	68.5	70.0	68.6	61.4	62.6	57.2	56.6
1902	79.0	75.1	67.6	66.8	71.9	70.3	73.6	71.3	66.2	69.0	62.5	61.8
1903	78.9	83.9	63.1	62.9	71.9	80.1	71.2	69.0	63.5	66.6	58.9	58.6
1904	89.0	77.6	73.6	73.7	83.0	74.7	82.0	79.4	71.4	71.6	63.1	62.4
1905	81.6	77.7	70.0	71.1	76.4	76.4	76.2	74.6	73.3	75.7	70.9	70.0
1906	79.6	81.8	75.0	75.2	76.4	80.5	77.3	76.0	74.1	79.8	71.2	71.1
1907	86.7	82.3	78.7	78.5	83.3	78.9	82.9	80.4	77.6	82.9	71.6	70.7
1908	87.0	81.8	74.7	74.7	81.0	78.0	80.0	78.6	73.5	74.8	66.1	65.6
1909	106.4	82.3	82.7	82.4	94.4	92.0	94.6	92.0	94.1	95.4	91.9	90.4
1910	85.7	82.6	86.0	86.3	85.5	83.7	85.9	84.4	86.0	90.1	86.3	85.1
1911	90.8	89.3	83.3	83.5	87.1	86.5	87.7	86.7	85.5	87.7	83.4	83.2
1912	103.2	100.9	87.8	88.2	96.2	95.4	95.9	95.2	102.5	100.7	105.8	104.7
1913	100.0	100.0	100.0	100.0	100.0	100.0	100.0	100.0	100.0	100.0	100.0	100.0
1914	117.5	114.2	117.1	116.0	119.3	117.3	117.8	115.5	116.0	113.4	106.5	106.0
1915	120.6	111.4	96.6	96.3	108.7	105.8	107.9	104.0	123.7	111.7	131.1	126.7
1916	117.0	109.5	98.1	98.2	108.3	105.0	107.2	104.2	131.3	118.2	150.2	144.9
1917	154.9	141.5	89.5	93.8	118.9	114.9	116.7	113.2	140.8	122.4	154.6	149.1
1918	132.4	126.3	92.9	93.4	134.7	111.8	109.9	108.8	143.1	110.2	140.2	137.2
1919	150.6	144.9	112.4	113.0	150.0	132.8	129.8	128.5	163.8	132.2	175.6	171.7
1920	155.7	149.7	133.3	134.2	119.7	146.8	144.3	142.2	161.1	140.1	162.8	159.9
1921	135.8	126.8	100.7	100.1	147.6	116.3	116.4	113.0	137.6	118.2	144.1	140.7
1922	136.3	133.9	145.4	144.5	—	145.1	142.6	140.2	171.6	150.0	187.0	182.7

YEAR	213	214	215	216	217	218	219	220	221	222	223
1879	28.9	22.4	22.0	27.0	40.6	40.9	29.5	37.4	27.0	26.2	34.1
1880	41.5	30.5	29.8	31.6	57.6	57.7	36.5	52.8	33.1	40.8	48.1
1881	38.4	28.3	27.7	31.9	55.8	56.0	36.4	51.3	33.4	39.1	46.2
1882	43.8	31.2	30.6	35.4	64.2	64.4	40.8	59.1	37.4	43.0	52.4
1883	41.1	29.8	29.7	34.9	58.0	59.2	38.5	54.0	36.3	38.6	48.6
1884	36.0	28.7	28.0	34.8	56.0	56.2	38.8	51.6	35.0	35.5	45.5
1885	37.0	29.1	29.6	36.2	52.1	52.6	39.1	48.0	36.0	32.4	43.5
1886	43.7	35.3	34.8	40.0	62.8	63.3	44.3	57.9	40.7	40.9	51.5
1887	50.5	37.5	37.3	40.3	66.0	67.4	45.3	61.7	41.9	48.1	56.4
1888	47.6	38.3	37.8	42.1	70.5	71.1	47.4	64.8	43.9	44.7	56.9
1889	47.3	39.5	39.7	42.3	70.3	71.0	47.6	64.7	44.1	44.0	56.8
1890	49.7	40.6	41.3	44.8	78.1	78.5	51.0	71.6	47.4	46.5	61.8
1891	50.7	43.8	43.2	48.9	64.5	64.4	51.8	58.9	48.2	46.9	56.1
1892	50.5	45.7	45.7	48.9	70.1	69.0	53.0	64.0	50.0	47.0	59.0
1893	45.5	40.4	40.3	44.8	65.4	65.2	48.7	59.5	45.2	43.7	55.1
1894	40.9	38.4	38.6	45.4	52.3	52.2	46.7	48.2	44.9	38.3	46.6
1895	50.8	50.7	50.7	52.3	82.9	82.2	58.3	75.9	56.3	46.2	64.9
1896	40.7	37.6	37.5	44.4	65.6	65.2	48.6	60.4	47.1	40.5	53.1
1897	44.1	50.4	49.1	53.7	68.2	67.6	56.6	62.3	54.6	39.7	56.1
1898	43.7	42.8	41.8	46.6	55.8	55.3	48.4	50.9	46.8	41.5	49.3
1899	50.6	50.3	49.4	55.3	61.2	60.9	56.5	56.0	54.7	48.4	54.7
1900	48.8	48.5	48.1	52.7	64.5	64.1	54.9	58.8	53.4	49.1	55.8
1901	52.0	55.1	54.8	59.7	66.5	65.8	61.0	60.9	55.5	55.8	60.7
1902	66.6	63.9	63.5	66.4	78.0	77.3	67.6	71.5	67.0	57.4	71.4
1903	60.3	61.9	61.6	67.7	80.8	80.3	69.0	73.7	65.1	70.0	72.0
1904	70.5	62.0	70.2	72.0	74.3	74.3	74.2	68.3	66.3	60.5	66.3
1905	78.8	70.7	74.0	74.9	83.4	83.3	79.4	76.9	72.6	69.2	75.1
1906	77.0	74.2	73.0	75.8	98.4	98.1	81.4	90.2	77.8	78.0	84.9
1907	64.2	73.7	65.1	69.8	105.7	105.1	72.0	96.1	80.0	76.6	87.7
1908	94.6	65.3	91.9	92.6	81.4	80.9	94.4	74.5	70.7	63.0	70.5
1909	102.4	92.9	91.2	89.6	102.2	101.6	92.3	96.9	93.5	90.9	94.9
1910	95.8	88.1	87.8	87.6	104.5	104.3	88.8	99.7	92.0	99.8	92.6
1911	97.0	102.4	101.8	99.9	94.2	94.0	99.1	103.0	100.4	94.0	95.3
1912					95.5	95.6					
1913	100.0	100.0	100.0	100.0	100.0	100.0	100.0	100.0	100.0	100.0	100.0
1914	87.1	99.1	99.1	105.3	115.3	114.5	107.2	110.2	106.5	85.7	98.1
1915	77.3	90.7	107.8	108.3	82.5	82.4	103.3	79.3	102.1	74.6	81.9
1916	96.8	128.8	126.6	120.4	77.4	77.7	112.0	75.2	111.0	91.9	91.9
1917	96.1	131.1	128.6	124.8	72.6	73.3	114.6	69.7	113.4	89.2	87.6
1918	92.3	121.0	119.8	116.8	67.6	68.5	106.6	63.4	104.9	94.2	80.3
1919	86.5	139.4	138.4	136.3	65.1	66.0	121.5	63.0	120.4	84.5	77.7
1920	112.7	143.0	142.0	144.9	94.1	90.3	134.6	89.9	134.4	114.9	106.5
1921	75.8	115.7	114.5	115.7	91.1	90.7	110.5	86.6	111.8	83.6	85.8
1922	122.4	161.2	159.6	154.3	110.9	110.8	145.2	106.1	145.1	129.0	119.2
1923	145.0	174.7	171.2	160.4	136.6	136.7	155.7	129.6	154.8	141.1	137.8

TABLE A-18

ANNUAL VALUES, MAJOR EXPORT CLASSES (MILLIONS OF DOLLARS)

YEAR	201	202	203	204	205	206	207	208	209	210	211
1879	230	244	175	177	398	412	405	421	617	653	214
1880	258	276	201	214	463	481	470	491	735	776	265
1881	200	219	212	203	393	412	401	421	647	691	248
1882	147	166	170	172	309	328	316	338	570	621	256
1883	142	162	197	200	333	352	340	362	593	640	257
1884	118	137	186	188	291	311	303	326	548	601	259
1885	101	127	167	189	279	305	286	316	502	546	215
1886	119	148	186	171	281	309	287	318	535	576	241
1887	116	137	172	175	283	304	288	312	532	577	247
1888	81	100	161	165	236	254	243	265	494	541	263
1889	108	130	198	202	297	319	306	331	602	661	309
1890	123	144	225	226	339	360	346	371	634	689	296
1891	199	219	225	230	417	438	424	449	735	789	323
1892	203	225	262	266	458	480	465	491	715	768	260
1893	140	163	239	243	370	393	378	406	621	678	256
1894	110	134	233	236	332	358	342	372	575	634	242
1895	106	135	217	221	316	341	324	352	547	610	233
1896	166	131	226	231	384	408	392	420	667	735	285
1897	235	190	247	252	475	498	482	510	733	805	259
1898	279	258	297	302	569	593	576	605	856	929	286
1899	230	260	311	316	534	564	541	576	788	874	253
1900	247	244	319	325	526	553	536	569	910	1009	394
1901	160	274	342	347	579	606	588	621	943	1037	375
1902	175	195	317	323	467	502	477	518	822	921	358
1903	103	205	315	321	482	512	490	525	917	1028	451
1904	157	134	277	283	457	401	380	417	798	914	442
1905	180	183	309	314	457	484	465	498	901	1018	465
1906	196	212	334	340	505	537	514	552	994	1138	510
1907	171	229	331	337	519	551	527	565	1060	1208	568
1908	118	204	317	322	479	512	488	525	980	1111	529
1909	95	155	278	282	385	422	396	438	910	1051	551
1910	117	131	248	253	332	368	343	384	926	1094	627
1911	117	159	303	307	409	451	420	466	1003	1185	631
1912	145	192	299	304	431	478	443	496	1137	1336	748
1913	172	225	318	325	475	528	490	550	1141	1344	718
1914	275	319	306	313	566	610	581	632	997	1158	464
1915	461	514	544	550	983	1035	1005	1064	1608	1787	633
1916	417	480	628	639	1020	1083	1046	1119	1756	1983	751
1917	496	542	807	823	1276	1321	1303	1365	1980	2208	786
1918	535	658	1406	1436	1907	2030	1941	2094	2749	2978	848
1919	649	909	1968	2015	2551	2811	2617	2924	4091	4619	1359
1920	885	1131	1127	1170	1960	2206	2012	2301	3441	3899	1627
1921	676	881	675	696	1330	1536	1351	1577	2113	2293	779
1922	461	607	577	604	1018	1164	1038	1211	1883	2113	848
1923	259	413	573	599		964	832	1011	1810	2051	1051

YEAR	212	213	214	215	216	217	218	219	220	221	222
1879	229	30	82	85	244	258	665	747	755	75	129
1880	284	31	82	84	296	315	787	869	876	72	131
1881	266	36	103	105	284	302	705	808	814	93	159
1882	275	42	108	110	299	318	637	744	750	98	171
1883	277	43	111	114	300	320	662	773	778	109	178
1884	279	42	104	106	301	321	627	731	734	109	180
1885	241	40	100	103	255	282	571	671	674	103	166
1886	270	38	100	103	279	308	598	697	700	96	159
1887	268	42	100	103	289	310	601	701	703	100	165
1888	282	46	103	107	309	328	574	677	680	114	180
1889	331	50	120	124	359	381	691	810	814	128	205
1890	317	51	123	127	347	368	718	840	846	129	202
1891	343	58	123	128	381	401	830	953	957	139	214
1892	280	52	116	128	312	334	803	919	923	127	201
1893	280	64	124	126	320	344	726	850	855	147	225
1894	268	67	122	128	309	335	681	803	807	141	224
1895	258	72	146	151	305	330	657	804	808	165	252
1896	309	95	180	185	380	404	800	980	987	209	309
1897	282	109	196	201	368	391	877	1073	1080	229	335
1898	310	117	218	223	403	427	1008	1226	1234	255	365
1899	283	144	271	276	397	427	973	1243	1253	318	451
1900	420	176	302	308	570	597	1139	1441	1453	382	526
1901	401	140	293	298	514	541	1135	1428	1438	334	479
1902	392	150	297	303	508	543	1025	1323	1333	335	495
1903	481	163	310	316	614	643	1139	1449	1458	358	528
1904	474	210	348	353	652	683	1078	1416	1426	432	613
1905	492	221	403	408	687	714	1185	1587	1599	471	681
1906	542	258	445	445	768	800	1320	1759	1773	534	760
1907	601	279	466	472	848	880	1413	1879	1895	599	814
1908	561	242	416	420	771	803	1296	1712	1729	535	727
1909	588	258	440	445	809	846	1246	1687	1701	558	772
1910	663	293	509	514	919	955	1303	1812	1829	634	881
1911	673	340	609	614	971	1013	1437	2046	2058	760	1039
1912	795	400	707	713	1148	1195	1643	2351	2363	897	1208
1913	771	420	752	759	1138	1191	1688	2440	2448	973	1292
1914	507	358	609	615	822	866	1454	2062	2071	784	1058
1915	686	531	1246	1252	1165	1217	2228	3475	3492	1430	1861
1916	813	1040	2507	2518	1791	1854	2910	5417	5423	3136	3651
1917	971	1427	2583	2600	2213	2258	3578	6161	6170	3649	4164
1918	1619	1121	1978	2008	1970	2092	4064	6042	6048	2713	3263
1919	1872	1077	2375	2422	2436	2696	5360	7735	7750	2553	3598
1920		1086	3041	3084	2712	2958	5013	8054	8080	3466	4570
1921	984	442	1567	1588	1221	1426	2798	4365	4379	1838	2231
1922	994	445	1247	1274	1293	1439	2504	3751	3765	1402	1841
1923	1214	568	1438	1463	1629	1783	2641	4078	4091	1729	2234

TABLE A-19

ANNUAL VALUES,
MAJOR IMPORT CLASSES
(MILLIONS OF DOLLARS)

YEAR	201	202	203	204	205	206	207	208	209	210	211	212
1879	102	106	82	85	180	183	184	190	252	392	82	85
1880	104	109	110	112	209	214	214	222	309	498	115	120
1881	111	116	112	115	217	222	223	231	305	486	102	107
1882	116	122	133	136	242	247	249	258	343	519	120	125
1883	102	110	125	128	219	228	227	238	315	518	109	117
1884	101	108	109	113	204	210	211	220	299	491	110	116
1885	95	104	102	105	191	199	197	209	288	459	108	136
1886	97	104	109	112	200	207	205	216	314	507	129	139
1887	120	131	97	100	210	221	217	231	327	528	128	143
1888	123	132	112	115	228	237	235	247	348	556	134	
1889	123	137	128	132	245	259	252	270	381	603	147	160
1890	137	156	128	128	257	275	265	288	395	633	146	164
1891	139	147	167	170	299	307	306	317	436	638	158	167
1892	134	148	139	142	264	278	273	290	412	630	165	179
1893	135	147	151	154	278	289	287	301	402	608	144	156
1894	136	152	134	136	261	276	270	288	379	543	128	143
1895	141	156	97	99	227	242	238	266	399	646	183	199
1896	120	130	121	123	226	237	241	253	346	542	131	142
1897	120	129	108	110	215	224	228	239	399	608	199	208
1898	92	100	105	106	187	195	196	207	338	506	168	176
1899	100	112	141	144	230	242	242	256	431	626	225	237
1900	105	120	126	128	218	233	230	248	421	635	230	245
1901	114	131	118	121	217	233	232	251	432	655	256	272
1902	120	136	104	107	210	226	224	243	454	711	284	300
1903	119	137	107	110	211	229	226	247	461	724	288	305
1904	147	164	132	136	263	280	280	300	545	800	317	333
1905	136	155	154	158	273	291	290	313	605	900	373	392
1906	136	162	140	144	257	283	275	307	618	972	402	428
1907	152	177	154	158	285	309	306	335	662	1062	426	451
1908	142	167	152	155	275	299	294	322	574	871	330	355
1909	170	196	165	170	313	339	335	366	756	1123	496	521
1910	156	180	188	194	321	346	343	374	775	1154	514	538
1911	193	225	177	182	347	379	370	407	768	1126	470	502
1912	243	276	203	209	422	455	446	485	957	1349	603	636
1913	231	267	191	197	396	432	422	464	890	1312	572	608
1914	247	282	248	252	468	503	495	534	982	1413	564	598
1915	250	271	264	268	491	512	514	539	1084	1424	669	691
1916	266	293	328	334	565	592	594	627	1403	1845	975	1002
1917	382	415	342	349	690	724	723	764	1813	2338	1241	1276
1918	338	390	390	399	699	751	728	789	1799	2322	1183	
1919	554	630	557	569	1075	1150	1812	1198	2598	3241	1622	1697
1920	598	680	1221	1238	1780	1862	1819	1918	3241	4317	1670	1752
1921	317	371	350	356	635	689	666	727	1319	1967	802	856
1922	347	413	363	371	679	745	711	784	1628	2392	1119	1185
1923	377	434	504	514	854	912	881	948	2020	2957	1347	1404

YEAR	213	214	215	216	217	218	219	220	221	222	223
1879	77	159	162	349	132	134	481	136	514	89	226
1880	129	244	249	465	191	194	657	196	697	158	346
1881	110	212	217	443	181	184	624	187	670	138	316
1882	130	250	256	508	212	215	720	218	753	160	373
1883	116	225	233	463	191	194	654	196	687	137	336
1884	101	212	218	432	178	181	610	183	629	119	307
1885	93	201	210	410	156	159	566	161	588	107	274
1886	112	241	249	457	182	185	639	187	663	132	321
1887	127	255	266	486	194	197	680	200	709	152	349
1888	116	250	259	497	198	202	696	204	725	139	344
1889	124	271	285	541	199	203	740	205	771	137	355
1890	136	281	300	569	218	222	787	224	823	153	388
1891	137	295	303	612	182	184	794	187	828	156	355
1892	132	297	310	586	195	197	781	200	841	151	366
1893	121	266	277	566	181	183	747	186	776	139	343
1894	97	225	240	512	138	140	650	143	673	107	268
1895	116	299	314	555	218	220	772	225	802	127	371
1896	95	226	237	480	174	176	654	181	682	112	306
1897	101	299	308	539	177	179	716	182	743	108	315
1898	96	263	272	470	145	147	615	169	635	110	276
1899	134	360	371	615	163	165	778	168	799	152	344
1900	146	376	391	624	181	183	805	186	829	169	382
1901	155	411	427	662	189	192	851	195	880	196	417
1902	192	476	492	719	218	231	937	225	969	226	480
1903	200	488	505	734	228	231	962	234	995	237	498
1904	183	499	516	800	211	215	1011	219	1036	211	462
1905	218	592	610	905	243	247	1148	253	1179	248	539
1906	279	681	707	987	296	301	1284	307	1321	312	661
1907	288	715	739	1049	332	336	1381	341	1423	319	715
1908	196	526	550	848	238	242	1086	246	1116	215	508
1909	279	775	801	1140	284	288	1424	305	1476	301	664
1910	320	833	858	1208	289	296	1497	315	1563	342	716
1911	315	786	818	1193	274	279	1467	307	1533	340	693
1912	342	944	977	1429	296	302	1725	363	1818	377	762
1913	355	927	963	1391	332	338	1724	374	1793	412	828
1914	293	857	892	1391	341	346	1732	368	1789	318	745
1915	278	948	969	1487	243	247	1730	264	1779	306	641
1916	455	1430	1457	2057	289	295	2346	317	2392	501	937
1917	565	1806	1840	2570	331	338	2901	356	2952	563	1081
1918	610	1794	1846	2583	413	421	2995	429	3031	673	1187
1919	581	2203	2278	3401	429	441	3830	462	3904	589	1221
1920	843	2513	2595	4431	709	726	5139	755	5278	822	1882
1921	375	1177	1231	1904	508	514	2412	535	2509	445	1087
1922	562	1681	1747	2465	561	569	3026	596	3113	634	1391
1923	727	2074	2131	3022	685	695	3707	724	3792	750	1677

TABLE A-20

ANNUAL PAASCHE PRICE INDEXES,
SELECTED MAJOR EXPORT CLASSES
(1913=100)

YEAR	201	203	205	207	209	212	213	215	217	218	220	222
1879	91.1	69.8	81.5	81.2	83.9	78.5	77.9	113.9	83.2	84.0	88.9	94.8
1880	93.1	79.0	87.1	87.0	91.1	87.3	84.9	126.3	92.5	91.2	96.7	103.9
1881	96.8	89.5	99.2	94.0	94.2	85.0	91.0	119.4	91.0	94.3	99.0	103.6
1882	97.1	98.5	96.3	98.6	96.3	86.3	91.1	118.1	92.2	96.0	100.4	103.6
1883	96.4	91.7	94.3	94.2	90.9	80.5	89.0	115.6	86.5	91.1	95.8	102.6
1884	82.3	83.4	83.7	83.4	86.0	81.9	84.6	117.4	87.2	86.1	91.4	100.3
1885	79.0	73.1	75.4	75.3	80.0	78.8	82.1	110.9	84.0	80.5	85.6	95.0
1886	73.6	69.1	71.2	71.3	75.0	73.8	79.6	106.5	79.1	75.9	80.7	92.0
1887	75.8	72.1	73.9	73.1	76.3	73.4	81.4	102.0	78.9	77.2	81.5	91.1
1888	79.2	77.2	78.0	78.1	79.7	76.8	85.1	107.0	82.5	80.9	85.5	96.2
1889	70.7	73.3	72.5	72.7	76.9	76.3	81.6	101.6	81.6	77.9	82.2	91.5
1890	71.8	71.2	71.5	71.7	75.4	77.5	81.7	99.3	82.5	77.1	81.1	91.5
1891	94.1	74.3	82.3	82.3	73.6	73.0	78.5	95.5	77.7	80.4	83.7	87.7
1892	82.0	75.5	78.0	78.1	74.1	66.4	76.7	86.7	71.4	75.0	77.8	81.7
1893	73.2	82.1	78.8	78.8	62.8	64.8	68.0	81.0	67.6	73.4	75.3	75.2
1894	62.1	71.9	68.7	68.8	63.0	54.3	64.2	76.9	58.0	63.6	66.2	72.1
1895	65.8	67.9	67.4	67.6	61.2	55.8	68.8	89.0	60.1	64.2	68.3	80.4
1896	61.2	62.1	61.3	61.6	60.4	60.1	65.7	94.0	62.3	62.3	67.3	81.4
1897	69.1	63.2	65.3	65.5	61.2	53.7	66.2	86.6	57.1	61.7	65.8	77.8
1898	74.8	66.4	69.6	69.9	60.4	48.0	66.7	81.5	52.9	61.8	65.2	75.3
1899	72.0	65.5	67.9	68.1	62.2	54.4	81.3	87.5	61.3	65.0	68.9	84.2
1900	73.3	69.8	70.7	71.2	70.7	71.2	86.9	97.4	75.2	75.2	77.3	92.1
1901	76.3	74.8	75.2	75.4	71.4	67.0	81.0	92.0	70.2	72.9	76.1	87.4
1902	80.4	83.3	79.8	80.1	75.2	68.1	80.6	92.1	71.2	76.0	79.1	86.7
1903	78.2	81.2	79.8	76.0	80.0	80.2	85.1	96.8	81.4	80.9	84.6	91.3
1904	74.2	76.6	74.5	74.7	79.6	83.8	86.9	97.8	84.1	81.8	81.0	92.1
1905	79.0	72.7	74.4	74.4	74.2	74.8	92.2	93.3	79.4	77.5	84.1	97.9
1906	79.1	79.7	79.2	79.5	81.2	83.2	104.2	96.6	89.0	89.0	87.7	102.6
1907	90.8	85.8	87.4	87.6	87.4	87.2	108.8	101.4	93.1	90.9	93.3	95.5
1908	96.7	87.1	90.0	90.3	83.9	79.2	91.2	99.8	82.5	85.3	88.4	94.2
1909	101.2	92.7	94.8	95.0	92.9	91.3	90.7	96.6	91.1	92.3	93.4	95.9
1910	97.1	103.8	101.6	101.9	107.3	108.6	93.1	97.8	103.3	103.3	101.4	94.1
1911	96.1	91.2	92.0	92.5	91.4	90.6	93.2	95.2	91.5	91.8	92.8	95.9
1912	103.6	96.6	98.5	98.8	91.8	89.0	100.1	97.1	92.4	94.1	95.0	98.2
1913	100.0	100.0	100.0	100.0	100.0	100.0	100.0	100.0	100.0	100.0	100.0	100.0
1914	115.0	102.0	107.1	107.5	102.8	87.8	99.4	96.9	93.5	101.6	100.1	97.7
1915	136.8	105.5	117.4	117.7	114.1	89.5	115.7	113.2	100.2	112.4	113.4	112.6
1916	144.3	117.6	126.9	127.0	138.2	119.4	167.4	160.2	149.8	146.4	155.1	159.3
1917	213.0	165.7	181.6	181.1	207.9	170.8	217.9	178.8	217.0	211.0	200.2	187.6
1918	233.8	214.2	220.1	219.8	269.7	220.6	209.8	190.5	232.8	243.9	225.9	193.6
1919	240.9	231.1	234.9	234.1	281.0	244.1	204.0	190.2	234.8	252.7	231.4	191.0
1920	277.0	217.1	242.6	239.7	292.3	290.0	210.8	217.1	264.5	266.6	249.5	217.6
1921	153.0	136.2	142.6	143.7	164.1	156.3	146.5	151.7	151.4	159.9	166.3	170.4
1922	124.3	118.8	120.1	120.9	158.6	176.5	129.1	151.1	160.2	152.4	152.6	147.8
1923	129.6	126.5	126.2	127.6	184.4	218.7	142.2	152.4	191.7	172.9	166.6	151.1

TABLE A-21

ANNUAL PAASCHE PRICE INDEXES,
SELECTED MAJOR IMPORT CLASSES
(1913=100)

YEAR	201	203	205	207	209	212	213	215	216	220	221	223
1879	104.0	139.0	125.7	120.3	111.5	94.0	74.4	85.2	96.5	98.1	96.9	84.6
1880	112.8	167.3	143.9	137.3	126.5	103.8	87.4	96.9	110.7	101.9	108.3	93.1
1881	103.3	166.6	136.2	130.7	120.1	98.8	79.6	90.2	103.8	99.2	102.7	88.1
1882	96.5	170.5	132.4	128.3	119.6	103.7	79.9	92.5	104.2	99.5	103.0	89.0
1883	87.0	155.2	119.6	115.9	108.1	95.0	76.4	86.7	95.8	97.9	96.6	86.4
1884	79.2	124.9	106.6	104.2	97.9	90.1	76.2	84.4	89.4	92.3	90.3	83.8
1885	79.1	112.2	96.3	94.3	89.4	82.4	68.1	76.4	81.1	87.1	82.6	77.2
1886	81.1	114.6	97.3	95.3	90.8	83.2	69.3	77.4	82.6	83.7	83.0	76.2
1887	108.3	104.3	109.0	106.6	98.0	84.1	68.0	77.0	87.1	83.6	86.3	75.5
1888	99.0	118.2	110.1	108.3	97.1	79.8	65.7	73.8	85.7	82.0	84.7	74.3
1889	102.8	141.3	122.9	120.5	104.8	81.4	69.4	76.5	91.9	84.7	89.9	77.5
1890	110.1	127.8	117.9	115.4	101.7	79.7	72.0	76.9	90.8	84.0	88.8	77.8
1891	112.8	127.2	117.6	115.8	100.9	76.5	71.9	75.1	90.2	83.8	89.1	77.4
1892	104.7	122.6	113.6	111.7	95.4	73.9	68.9	71.9	86.3	82.9	85.4	75.5
1893	111.9	133.8	122.2	120.0	102.0	73.9	69.7	72.5	90.6	82.5	88.4	75.6
1894	103.7	111.2	107.2	105.5	91.0	67.9	62.0	65.6	81.8	78.5	81.0	70.1
1895	101.1	88.4	97.2	95.9	83.2	69.2	60.3	67.1	76.2	79.1	76.8	70.3
1896	91.1	103.3	97.2	95.6	86.5	70.1	62.5	67.1	78.7	80.3	79.0	71.2
1897	76.1	92.4	85.2	84.0	79.2	71.1	61.1	67.6	73.5	78.3	74.5	69.2
1898	64.0	101.1	81.2	80.8	79.3	74.3	57.8	67.6	72.6	77.9	73.8	67.6
1899	62.3	108.5	82.8	82.9	83.1	81.0	70.2	76.7	79.1	81.5	79.6	75.5
1900	69.1	106.4	85.9	85.5	86.0	85.2	79.0	83.1	84.0	86.5	84.5	83.0
1901	66.1	95.8	75.5	75.2	78.2	81.5	80.0	80.7	78.7	87.5	80.5	82.9
1902	65.1	79.7	70.8	71.1	76.4	81.5	78.5	80.3	77.3	85.7	79.1	81.7
1903	64.4	88.0	72.9	73.8	80.2	87.1	81.8	84.9	81.2	86.7	82.4	84.5
1904	71.2	94.6	80.1	80.6	93.5	88.0	81.0	85.4	83.7	88.9	84.3	83.0
1905	73.8	114.8	91.0	91.0	93.7	92.4	83.5	89.0	89.6	92.0	89.5	85.7
1906	75.5	97.0	84.4	85.1	97.2	104.4	95.8	98.0	94.0	95.6	97.4	93.3
1907	71.4	101.9	86.2	87.1	97.3	88.8	101.9	103.4	86.3	89.3	86.9	97.6
1908	69.3	106.0	85.3	85.8	88.4	92.8	82.6	86.5	86.4	85.8	86.2	86.5
1909	80.4	104.2	82.6	83.0	101.4	103.2	79.8	87.8	96.1	86.4	93.9	83.7
1910	94.6	113.9	96.2	95.4	101.4	99.4	85.3	96.1	97.4	90.2	95.8	86.8
1911	104.0	109.9	101.8	101.4	104.6	99.8	90.4	95.7	102.1	95.5	100.7	90.4
1912	104.0	118.9	111.0	110.3	104.6	99.8	96.7	98.7	102.1	95.5	100.7	96.1
1913	100.0	100.0	100.0	100.0	100.0	100.0	100.0	100.0	100.0	100.0	100.0	100.0
1914	91.5	111.5	113.0	106.6	98.7	97.4	93.6	96.2	97.2	90.5	95.7	91.7
1915	90.6	139.7	130.7	113.7	102.8	93.6	99.0	95.4	100.9	91.4	99.7	94.2
1916	98.9	167.6	149.5	130.3	124.9	120.5	118.0	119.4	123.2	115.0	122.8	119.1
1917	113.5	191.7	157.8	149.9	155.9	153.0	153.9	153.6	152.7	137.0	151.6	144.1
1918	117.5	212.8	202.2	160.6	165.9	164.2	179.4	169.3	166.7	184.6	170.3	176.2
1919	163.7	250.7	302.0	205.0	190.8	178.7	185.3	181.1	188.1	194.0	190.5	186.7
1920	173.0	464.7	302.2	302.7	246.6	196.5	205.3	199.6	231.5	226.7	232.2	209.7
1921	103.7	177.6	135.0	137.6	116.7	107.8	137.0	115.7	122.5	165.1	130.2	150.1
1922	113.2	125.2	113.9	116.7	113.5	116.0	127.8	119.8	119.1	152.6	124.9	140.5
1923	113.6	204.5	152.6	154.7	141.9	135.3	139.9	137.0	142.3	152.8	144.6	147.7

TABLE A-22

ANNUAL LASPEYRES PRICE INDEXES, SELECTED MAJOR EXPORT CLASSES
(1913=100)

YEAR	201	203	205	207	209	212	213	215	217	218	220	222
1879	95.9	84.4	83.8	87.9	77.5	81.8	80.7	125.1	86.8	85.8	96.4	111.7
1880	99.2	94.8	91.0	95.8	85.2	91.4	90.3	136.7	97.1	94.8	106.5	125.6
1881	108.8	105.9	100.5	106.5	86.6	88.7	93.2	130.5	94.8	98.3	106.6	122.6
1882	122.3	115.7	111.5	117.3	94.2	90.3	94.9	128.6	96.6	104.1	114.2	123.5
1883	112.2	108.3	103.1	109.0	87.2	83.8	92.6	127.3	90.2	97.0	107.3	121.3
1884	101.5	102.0	95.0	101.2	84.3	84.8	88.2	127.5	90.6	93.7	104.2	119.3
1885	92.3	89.5	84.3	90.0	77.9	81.5	85.3	120.4	87.1	86.8	96.8	112.6
1886	87.9	84.2	79.2	85.0	72.6	76.0	81.3	113.8	81.5	81.6	91.1	108.3
1887	87.7	80.8	81.5	82.5	73.6	75.7	83.1	110.2	81.5	80.6	89.7	98.5
1888	93.3	85.7	86.5	87.8	77.3	79.4	84.4	114.9	85.1	84.8	94.2	103.4
1889	80.3	80.2	78.4	79.7	73.5	78.7	82.1	112.1	84.1	80.6	89.9	100.0
1890	81.8	76.1	76.7	77.9	72.8	79.5	83.2	109.7	85.0	80.1	89.0	98.8
1891	106.4	79.8	88.3	89.5	77.6	75.2	85.1	105.2	82.0	85.0	92.4	97.2
1892	91.4	84.4	82.7	84.0	72.3	69.3	80.8	97.3	76.2	79.4	86.2	90.7
1893	82.5	89.2	84.8	86.0	73.3	66.3	75.9	93.4	73.9	79.4	88.5	86.0
1894	73.7	76.5	73.8	74.9	62.4	56.3	71.4	87.4	63.3	68.8	75.2	80.8
1895	73.1	71.0	70.3	71.4	60.8	57.5	74.7	93.8	65.0	67.6	75.4	85.8
1896	65.9	65.0	63.8	64.9	58.6	61.9	74.7	99.7	68.6	65.7	74.8	90.0
1897	73.7	66.5	67.9	69.0	58.2	55.0	73.3	89.6	62.6	65.2	72.5	83.5
1898	78.7	69.6	71.7	72.8	58.6	49.9	74.2	83.7	58.7	65.5	71.7	80.0
1899	76.5	68.4	70.0	71.2	59.8	55.8	88.5	93.2	67.1	68.4	76.0	90.4
1900	75.0	72.7	72.3	73.5	71.9	73.7	92.2	100.5	79.8	78.1	84.9	96.6
1901	78.5	77.2	77.0	77.7	70.9	68.7	91.3	96.4	76.5	76.9	82.9	93.8
1902	83.6	84.4	83.7	84.1	74.5	70.2	86.5	96.1	75.8	78.3	83.7	92.1
1903	84.8	82.3	82.5	83.2	81.3	81.8	89.6	101.1	84.5	84.2	89.4	96.7
1904	87.0	78.9	81.0	81.8	82.8	84.9	87.0	99.9	85.6	84.5	89.2	95.1
1905	86.1	78.8	81.0	81.4	77.2	76.4	95.0	95.7	82.8	82.4	86.5	95.0
1906	84.4	81.7	82.2	82.7	82.9	84.3	107.6	98.4	92.4	89.5	92.3	100.9
1907	99.3	87.3	91.3	91.6	91.6	87.7	110.9	103.0	95.7	94.4	97.1	104.6
1908	102.9	88.8	93.4	93.8	85.0	80.4	93.6	101.2	84.9	87.5	97.1	98.0
1909	107.2	94.8	98.9	99.2	94.5	91.5	91.3	98.2	91.4	93.7	95.1	95.7
1910	100.3	110.8	106.9	107.1	109.1	108.2	93.7	99.6	101.9	104.3	92.9	97.4
1911	99.7	95.4	96.4	97.0	93.5	91.1	93.3	95.9	91.9	94.3	94.2	94.9
1912	104.8	97.5	99.7	100.1	93.1	89.6	100.5	97.4	93.4	95.3	96.0	98.6
1913	100.0	100.0	100.0	100.0	100.0	100.0	100.0	100.0	100.0	100.0	100.0	100.0
1914	114.1	100.6	107.3	107.5	98.8	87.9	95.7	91.7	91.2	97.8	95.3	92.0
1915	120.9	107.6	114.6	114.6	100.0	82.6	110.7	89.9	94.4	102.3	97.3	95.0
1916	144.0	119.3	126.8	126.7	122.4	111.8	146.2	106.5	126.5	126.2	118.1	115.7
1917	216.7	175.4	188.4	187.8	183.3	162.8	180.6	126.4	170.6	176.5	156.4	139.4
1918	235.3	214.2	221.6	220.5	230.2	219.2	196.1	151.2	220.5	212.7	188.1	161.5
1919	242.6	243.7	244.3	243.5	250.9	238.5	195.1	160.0	220.7	228.5	201.0	169.1
1920	259.7	217.2	230.0	229.9	255.1	280.6	210.1	179.0	261.2	241.1	216.7	197.6
1921	158.4	136.2	142.5	142.9	145.0	156.5	140.4	151.8	150.0	146.7	149.1	197.4
1922	130.4	122.8	124.8	125.1	145.0	176.7	124.7	125.8	154.0	142.6	135.6	152.0
1923	128.9											129.6

TABLE A-23

ANNUAL LASPEYRES PRICE INDEXES, SELECTED MAJOR IMPORT CLASSES
(1913=100)

YEAR	201	203	205	207	209	212	213	215	216	220	221	223
1879	125.7	145.0	137.4	134.0	118.8	96.0	81.7	90.2	106.9	107.7	108.1	94.4
1880	134.9	173.2	156.0	151.9	132.7	104.7	94.9	101.1	120.4	109.1	118.1	101.0
1881	122.4	171.4	148.2	144.5	126.8	99.9	88.1	95.3	114.0	107.9	113.0	96.7
1882	114.7	157.6	143.4	140.2	127.3	105.4	90.1	99.2	115.0	107.9	113.8	97.7
1883	104.3	125.2	130.8	128.1	116.9	98.8	85.4	93.4	106.8	105.0	107.3	94.6
1884	104.9	112.8	115.8	113.8	106.3	92.7	84.2	90.1	99.7	100.0	100.7	91.4
1885	98.5	115.6	106.3	104.6	98.0	86.9	75.8	82.5	91.5	94.4	93.2	86.8
1886	96.3	105.6	106.3	104.8	97.5	85.9	77.2	82.6	91.5	91.4	92.3	83.8
1887	130.6	105.0	120.0	118.0	106.0	87.6	75.8	82.9	96.4	91.6	95.8	83.7
1888	118.7	117.9	119.1	117.7	103.0	82.9	73.5	79.3	94.0	88.4	93.1	80.0
1889	123.0	140.9	132.5	130.7	110.9	84.7	75.7	81.3	100.0	90.7	98.0	83.2
1890	139.1	120.3	131.1	129.1	110.3	84.7	78.7	82.5	100.1	89.0	97.8	83.4
1891	133.7	121.8	128.0	127.1	105.7	78.8	76.8	78.1	96.7	88.0	94.9	82.5
1892	123.4	119.0	122.0	120.5	100.9	76.4	76.0	76.3	93.0	86.7	91.7	81.2
1893	137.0	128.8	134.2	132.2	108.1	77.4	76.0	77.7	98.4	88.6	95.9	81.8
1894	127.0	106.0	118.0	116.6	95.4	69.2	68.6	69.1	87.1	88.6	86.1	75.4
1895	123.3	84.6	104.0	104.0	89.2	70.8	66.7	69.3	87.4	81.6	82.2	74.4
1896	108.7	98.0	104.1	103.3	89.6	71.9	65.9	70.2	87.1	82.1	82.6	74.4
1897	88.0	89.3	88.3	88.0	81.2	71.6	65.9	69.4	76.4	80.6	77.3	72.8
1898	73.1	97.6	84.2	88.3	82.4	78.2	63.9	72.7	76.9	80.9	77.7	72.4
1899	70.9	104.1	85.7	86.2	86.2	85.4	76.7	82.1	83.4	84.1	83.5	80.6
1900	76.9	105.8	90.4	90.2	90.9	90.3	85.6	88.5	85.0	88.4	88.9	86.6
1901	70.8	96.3	82.3	82.6	82.2	83.1	85.0	83.8	81.1	88.2	84.8	87.5
1902	70.8	81.2	74.9	75.6	79.9	84.5	81.5	87.7	85.0	89.0	82.5	85.2
1903	70.4	88.4	77.8	78.7	84.7	89.5	84.0	88.7	88.6	88.6	85.7	86.7
1904	74.8	92.9	82.6	83.2	87.6	94.7	85.8	88.6	89.3	89.3	87.4	87.1
1905	74.8	111.7	91.6	91.8	95.3	95.1	87.3	91.9	91.8	94.4	91.7	89.4
1906	76.3	97.1	85.3	85.9	101.2	101.9	99.1	100.8	96.3	98.7	95.9	96.6
1907	80.5	101.8	89.7	90.3	101.2	107.9	104.3	106.6	101.7	98.7	101.0	100.0
1908	74.3	105.6	88.4	88.7	89.8	90.5	85.2	88.5	90.8	91.6	89.2	88.4
1909	72.8	104.4	87.2	87.4	93.5	97.9	82.6	92.2	88.9	86.6	86.9	85.9
1910	81.4	113.6	96.5	96.2	102.6	105.7	86.0	98.2	97.7	90.3	95.4	87.5
1911	94.4	109.5	101.8	101.4	101.9	100.4	90.4	96.7	98.0	90.3	96.5	90.6
1912	103.9	119.2	111.7	111.0	105.9	100.9	97.2	99.5	103.0	95.3	101.4	96.5
1913	100.0	100.0	100.0	100.0	100.0	100.0	100.0	100.0	100.0	100.0	100.0	100.0
1914	90.7	109.9	98.2	98.5	91.8	88.5	93.0	89.8	92.0	90.9	91.8	91.8
1915	89.3	146.2	112.6	112.3	94.5	85.9	100.6	90.3	89.2	89.2	94.7	95.0
1916	98.4	177.0	130.5	130.1	114.4	106.1	139.1	116.0	119.4	109.1	117.8	122.8
1917	100.3	202.3	141.4	141.5	133.2	127.7	167.1	139.5	139.9	135.5	139.3	148.2
1918	103.9	260.9	151.0	151.0	137.9	132.1	181.0	146.9	147.7	195.7	152.7	174.2
1919	155.3	480.2	197.6	197.9	162.4	146.2	181.0	156.6	166.8	220.4	171.9	185.8
1920	160.1	480.2	292.7	289.9	205.4	163.2	203.1	175.1	203.5	164.1	206.7	209.1
1921	98.5		130.8	131.6	99.3	92.4	132.9	104.6	111.4		120.5	150.1
1922	107.7	132.6	116.0	117.6	99.4	97.2	122.8	104.8	108.1	146.3	114.7	136.1
1923	106.9	207.6	147.5	147.6	121.0	112.2	133.6	116.6	125.8	144.7	129.1	140.8

TABLE A-24

QUARTERLY FISHER PRICE INDEXES,
SELECTED MAJOR EXPORT CLASSES
(1913=100)

YEAR Q	201	203	205	207	209	212	213	215	217	218	220	222
1879 1	87.3	75.3	77.8	79.6	74.2	73.7	77.7	125.3	78.8	78.9	87.3	106.4
1879 2	85.2	75.6	78.2	80.1	78.7	81.4	77.9	122.0	85.5	82.8	91.0	104.1
1879 3	92.5	74.0	82.4	84.2	83.3	82.6	79.1	115.4	86.8	87.0	94.1	99.7
1879 4	107.8	82.9	92.3	94.3	87.7	85.6	85.0	119.7	91.1	92.3	99.6	105.7
1880 1	108.6	86.1	93.0	95.2	91.0	91.4	87.8	128.6	96.8	95.7	103.7	112.7
1880 2	97.6	84.2	88.5	90.7	88.6	91.0	86.5	128.3	95.5	93.3	101.4	111.5
1880 3	91.7	87.2	88.0	90.2	87.7	88.4	86.5	132.9	93.5	92.4	101.0	114.0
1880 4	93.9	89.7	89.5	91.7	87.1	87.5	91.2	136.8	93.5	92.3	101.2	118.2
1881 1	98.1	91.9	91.8	94.1	88.0	86.9	88.7	129.2	92.6	93.0	101.2	114.1
1881 2	100.5	96.7	96.4	98.9	90.0	84.7	92.0	122.4	90.9	95.0	102.3	111.6
1881 3	105.1	100.5	100.7	103.1	94.7	87.1	93.3	122.6	93.3	99.1	106.1	111.3
1881 4	108.7	105.4	104.5	106.9	94.7	88.2	95.0	125.4	94.5	99.6	107.0	114.1
1882 1	108.4	103.3	102.6	105.0	93.6	88.2	92.1	124.7	94.4	98.6	106.0	114.2
1882 2	116.0	105.7	107.5	109.4	97.3	89.7	92.8	123.7	95.5	101.2	108.1	112.6
1882 3	111.7	111.9	109.2	111.6	100.9	90.1	94.8	119.0	96.3	104.9	110.8	110.8
1882 4	103.8	108.4	103.5	106.4	92.8	87.1	93.8	124.8	93.3	98.0	105.5	114.7
1883 1	105.8	103.4	101.5	104.3	90.1	82.9	90.2	124.0	89.0	95.2	102.7	112.5
1883 2	109.8	103.7	103.3	106.0	92.2	83.2	91.4	121.9	89.4	96.8	103.9	111.7
1883 3	101.0	96.8	95.7	98.5	90.0	83.4	92.4	120.0	90.0	94.9	101.9	110.8
1883 4	99.6	96.9	95.2	97.8	86.2	81.4	90.8	120.8	87.6	91.4	98.8	110.7
1884 1	100.8	96.9	95.4	98.2	87.1	82.9	87.3	126.8	88.6	92.0	100.1	112.9
1884 2	99.3	93.8	93.2	95.7	90.1	87.8	86.1	123.8	92.4	94.1	101.7	110.6
1884 3	90.4	91.0	88.2	90.7	86.3	86.0	89.4	120.7	91.7	90.9	98.4	109.0
1884 4	80.2	89.1	83.1	85.7	81.3	81.9	84.2	118.6	87.3	86.0	93.6	106.2
1885 1	83.5	83.7	81.1	83.6	80.9	82.7	81.0	115.7	87.5	85.2	92.5	102.8
1885 2	89.7	80.8	80.8	83.5	80.9	83.1	85.0	114.5	88.3	85.4	92.6	103.8
1885 3	87.5	79.8	79.6	82.2	79.6	81.5	85.0	115.2	86.8	84.1	91.6	103.8
1885 4	82.3	79.5	77.6	80.3	76.4	77.6	84.0	117.1	83.2	81.4	89.0	104.8

YEAR	Q	201	203	205	207	209	212	213	215	217	218	220	222
1886	1	81.8	76.2	75.6	78.3	74.6	75.9	78.3	112.7	80.9	79.3	86.6	100.9
1886	2	81.0	76.3	75.4	78.2	74.9	76.0	81.5	108.8	82.1	79.8	86.8	100.2
1886	3	80.0	76.3	75.0	77.7	74.4	76.4	81.5	107.9	81.7	79.3	86.2	99.4
1886	4	78.8	76.7	74.6	77.4	72.5	73.2	81.9	107.0	78.8	77.7	84.4	99.5
1887	1	83.4	74.8	77.3	77.9	74.0	73.3	81.5	107.2	78.9	77.9	84.8	95.3
1887	2	84.0	75.5	78.4	78.9	76.3	75.0	81.7	106.6	80.7	79.9	86.5	94.4
1887	3	78.5	77.2	77.0	77.7	75.1	74.8	82.0	104.6	80.4	79.0	85.5	93.8
1887	4	80.4	77.8	77.7	78.5	75.1	75.5	84.9	106.6	81.3	79.4	86.0	96.4
1888	1	85.3	79.2	80.3	81.1	77.2	77.6	83.5	111.5	83.1	81.7	88.7	100.3
1888	2	88.2	79.8	81.6	82.3	78.5	78.1	83.1	113.0	83.6	82.6	89.9	100.1
1888	3	86.0	81.4	82.2	82.9	79.8	79.3	84.9	109.8	85.0	83.9	90.5	98.8
1888	4	86.3	85.7	85.3	85.8	79.4	78.2	88.5	109.9	84.2	83.8	90.6	100.5
1889	1	80.3	81.3	80.3	80.9	78.5	78.0	89.1	109.4	85.2	83.3	89.9	99.7
1889	2	75.0	76.6	75.4	75.9	73.4	76.5	82.3	105.9	80.8	77.4	84.1	95.2
1889	3	73.6	75.7	74.0	74.8	71.3	72.8	78.9	104.8	77.1	75.2	82.0	94.4
1889	4	74.1	74.6	73.7	74.5	76.4	79.3	81.4	107.0	85.3	80.7	87.6	95.8
1890	1	73.3	73.9	72.8	73.5	73.6	79.4	80.0	106.6	84.3	78.1	84.9	95.6
1890	2	75.7	73.3	73.2	74.0	70.9	76.9	81.8	105.3	80.1	75.5	82.3	94.6
1890	3	80.7	73.0	75.3	76.0	72.8	75.4	84.1	102.2	80.6	77.3	83.5	94.3
1890	4	84.3	74.8	78.2	78.8	79.3	79.6	84.8	104.2	86.3	83.8	89.7	95.6
1891	1	89.3	74.3	79.6	80.2	78.4	79.0	82.8	103.3	84.6	82.5	88.4	94.2
1891	2	105.3	77.6	87.3	88.0	80.9	76.6	79.9	102.1	80.4	84.0	89.1	92.7
1891	3	102.7	78.1	87.8	88.5	78.3	69.8	82.5	98.0	75.0	82.4	87.2	91.6
1891	4	100.6	77.7	86.5	87.1	78.2	71.6	82.3	97.5	78.8	82.9	88.0	91.0
1892	1	92.4	77.6	82.8	83.5	75.4	70.4	79.7	94.9	76.5	79.7	84.8	88.3
1892	2	86.3	76.0	79.3	79.9	71.9	66.6	80.2	93.4	72.5	76.0	81.0	88.2
1892	3	85.9	77.3	79.9	80.6	70.5	61.7	77.7	90.1	67.7	74.6	79.2	85.1
1892	4	82.4	79.9	80.1	80.7	73.6	68.4	77.6	90.0	74.7	77.6	82.1	84.7

YEAR	Q	201	203	205	207	209	212	213	215	217	218	220	222
1893	1	82.0	88.2	85.0	85.6	78.8	74.4	77.3	89.3	78.7	81.9	85.4	84.0
1893	2	81.2	88.3	84.7	85.2	75.1	65.2	76.5	88.2	70.3	77.9	81.5	82.6
1893	3	74.8	84.2	79.5	80.0	70.4	60.8	70.3	85.6	64.6	72.8	76.8	78.6
1893	4	74.0	82.5	78.8	79.3	71.7	65.2	67.9	85.6	69.9	74.5	78.6	78.5
1894	1	70.4	78.6	74.8	75.4	68.0	62.9	68.3	83.5	67.1	71.1	75.3	77.6
1894	2	68.3	72.8	70.6	71.1	64.2	60.4	70.1	82.0	64.4	67.7	71.7	77.0
1894	3	69.6	73.2	71.5	72.1	63.6	56.6	66.7	80.4	60.5	66.5	70.4	75.3
1894	4	70.8	72.1	71.4	72.1	60.0	49.8	66.4	82.4	56.1	63.7	68.5	75.9
1895	1	69.1	69.2	68.7	69.4	57.9	48.6	67.7	83.3	55.1	62.0	67.1	77.0
1895	2	77.4	70.3	72.5	73.1	62.4	53.1	69.1	91.4	58.7	65.9	71.8	82.1
1895	3	72.4	70.6	70.6	71.6	63.1	57.0	74.4	92.8	62.5	67.0	73.0	84.6
1895	4	64.3	68.2	65.9	66.6	65.0	66.4	75.5	98.3	72.0	69.3	75.9	88.4
1896	1	64.3	67.4	65.2	65.9	62.7	63.4	71.6	98.2	68.0	66.7	73.0	86.5
1896	2	64.1	63.5	62.8	63.6	59.5	61.1	69.4	98.9	64.0	64.4	71.0	86.6
1896	3	59.8	60.3	59.1	59.8	56.4	59.1	69.5	95.3	62.9	60.8	68.2	85.1
1896	4	66.0	63.3	63.5	64.1	60.7	60.5	70.4	95.3	65.9	65.0	71.5	84.8
1897	1	64.8	63.9	63.3	63.9	59.2	58.3	70.2	92.6	63.2	63.3	69.7	83.2
1897	2	64.7	63.1	62.8	63.5	58.4	58.6	69.7	89.0	61.8	62.4	68.8	81.6
1897	3	75.1	64.2	57.9	68.6	60.8	56.2	68.2	86.6	59.8	64.4	69.8	79.3
1897	4	76.2	67.6	70.3	70.9	59.7	50.8	71.1	85.0	57.8	64.2	69.3	79.4
1898	1	75.4	67.7	69.9	70.6	59.5	50.0	70.0	81.5	56.6	63.6	68.2	76.7
1898	2	87.3	70.7	76.9	77.6	64.9	51.8	70.3	82.5	57.6	68.4	72.4	77.6
1898	3	72.8	67.4	68.7	69.4	61.5	50.0	70.2	82.1	56.0	62.0	67.8	77.3
1898	4	72.1	66.7	67.9	70.3	61.1	47.1	71.7	84.6	54.6	61.3	66.6	79.4
1899	1	77.5	66.4	69.8	70.4	58.7	49.9	78.7	86.9	58.0	63.3	68.6	82.4
1899	2	76.1	64.9	68.6	69.0	60.5	53.8	83.5	98.1	64.1	66.5	72.0	86.5
1899	3	73.5	66.7	68.6	69.4	61.5	56.5	88.1	91.6	67.1	68.2	74.0	80.6
1899	4	72.8	68.8	69.4	70.3	61.1	59.3	89.7	95.7	67.5	68.9	75.0	92.4

YEAR	Q	201	203	205	207	209	212	213	215	217	218	220	222
1900	1	72.1	69.2	69.4	70.2	67.0	66.1	91.7	100.7	73.3	72.4	78.9	95.4
1900	2	76.8	70.3	72.1	72.7	71.3	72.2	90.8	101.6	78.3	76.2	82.5	96.5
1900	3	76.2	72.5	73.1	73.9	74.4	77.2	88.4	96.8	81.3	78.2	83.3	94.5
1900	4	74.5	73.2	72.7	73.7	73.8	75.4	88.7	95.5	79.0	77.3	81.2	92.4
1901	1	75.0	72.6	72.9	73.5	72.6	72.8	86.2	96.3	76.8	75.8	80.4	91.4
1901	2	78.6	75.1	75.9	76.5	71.0	67.4	84.8	94.2	73.3	75.0	79.8	90.4
1901	3	78.4	76.9	77.2	77.6	72.1	68.2	86.8	92.2	74.3	75.0	80.3	90.4
1901	4	79.3	80.1	79.4	79.8	70.2	65.2	87.4	94.8	70.8	74.0	78.6	91.4
1902	1	83.4	81.0	81.6	81.9	72.8	66.4	81.4	92.8	70.7	74.6	79.1	87.0
1902	2	86.7	83.9	84.6	84.9	78.8	73.5	83.9	94.9	77.2	80.3	84.4	90.1
1902	3	82.2	86.0	84.2	84.5	77.1	71.4	83.9	94.4	75.6	79.1	83.2	99.9
1902	4	81.5	85.5	83.6	84.0	74.1	68.7	85.1	96.4	72.9	76.8	81.3	91.8
1903	1	82.8	84.3	83.6	83.7	77.4	73.0	85.9	97.6	76.5	79.2	83.6	91.3
1903	2	80.8	82.2	81.8	82.1	81.4	82.0	89.6	98.4	84.7	83.6	87.8	94.6
1903	3	81.6	80.1	80.3	80.7	82.1	85.4	87.4	98.5	86.1	81.9	88.1	94.7
1903	4	80.5	79.4	79.0	79.8	82.8	84.3	87.7	101.4	86.5	84.3	88.1	96.3
1904	1	80.7	79.5	79.6	80.1	92.5	103.5	86.6	100.9	97.7	91.0	79.3	94.4
1904	2	77.1	76.6	76.9	77.2	86.8	97.8	85.9	100.4	94.1	86.9	90.8	94.7
1904	3	81.0	77.7	78.6	79.0	79.9	82.6	84.7	98.3	83.4	81.9	86.4	93.0
1904	4	83.3	77.5	79.0	79.5	75.3	74.3	87.2	97.0	77.7	78.3	82.7	93.2
1905	1	83.6	72.1	75.6	76.0	67.6	63.3	90.8	95.0	71.5	73.0	78.4	92.4
1905	2	87.6	74.7	78.7	78.9	71.4	67.8	92.3	94.5	75.8	76.8	81.6	93.0
1905	3	83.5	77.7	79.6	79.7	80.1	81.8	93.7	93.1	85.9	83.6	86.3	92.9
1905	4	82.6	78.3	79.5	79.8	82.8	86.2	97.5	95.7	89.4	86.0	88.4	96.1
1906	1	83.2	79.4	80.3	80.8	83.1	85.8	101.1	95.2	90.7	86.8	89.0	95.9
1906	2	82.2	80.3	80.9	81.1	83.3	86.2	103.9	97.8	92.4	88.0	90.9	98.9
1906	3	82.4	80.8	81.1	81.3	79.1	79.1	106.5	98.7	89.0	85.9	89.6	100.5
1906	4	82.2	83.3	82.5	82.9	82.6	83.4	112.3	99.5	91.0	88.5	91.1	103.1
1907	1	83.2	84.4	83.8	84.0	83.8	84.3	118.8	100.6	93.8	90.7	93.1	105.0
1907	2	80.3	85.5	86.7	87.2	86.9	87.7	110.6	102.5	99.2	94.6	92.8	107.7
1907	3	97.6	87.5	90.0	91.0	92.2	94.2	113.0	103.5	101.6	97.2	99.1	105.7
1907	4	103.9	89.6	95.0	95.1	91.2	88.6	97.5	102.4	91.2	92.4	94.8	99.5

191

YEAR Q	201	203	205	207	209	212	213	215	217	218	220	222
1908 1	99.0	86.1	90.5	90.7	89.7	88.5	94.7	103.1	90.4	90.4	93.6	98.4
1908 2	99.1	86.2	90.1	90.4	86.9	84.4	91.8	101.8	87.2	88.2	92.6	97.2
1908 3	102.9	89.3	94.0	94.3	85.2	78.8	90.5	99.8	83.0	86.9	90.6	96.0
1908 4	101.8	90.9	94.3	94.7	80.1	73.5	92.9	97.7	78.4	83.1	86.4	95.8
1909 1	103.4	88.7	93.3	93.3	82.3	76.4	92.4	98.5	81.0	84.8	88.5	95.8
1909 2	109.2	92.6	98.0	97.9	88.6	82.6	89.3	97.5	85.1	88.9	91.6	94.2
1909 3	106.8	94.8	98.7	98.8	96.5	94.4	90.5	96.4	92.9	94.7	95.3	94.2
1909 4	102.2	99.3	99.8	100.4	104.7	106.1	92.6	97.8	102.2	101.7	100.8	96.0
1910 1	104.9	101.9	102.9	103.0	108.1	110.1	94.0	99.3	104.2	103.8	102.4	97.5
1910 2	100.9	105.5	104.3	104.1	107.6	107.1	94.5	98.9	102.3	102.7	101.5	97.0
1910 3	102.6	106.3	105.1	105.2	106.2	104.5	92.6	99.1	100.8	101.4	100.7	96.4
1910 4	92.4	104.9	100.1	100.6	107.8	109.6	93.0	97.9	104.8	103.8	102.4	95.9
1911 1	91.9	98.1	95.6	96.0	104.6	108.2	94.6	98.1	103.7	101.4	100.4	95.4
1911 2	95.8	91.6	92.6	93.0	100.2	105.2	92.9	94.8	100.1	97.7	96.8	93.9
1911 3	104.5	90.4	94.1	94.7	91.8	89.9	92.8	94.5	91.0	92.1	92.8	93.7
1911 4	103.9	94.5	96.7	97.3	84.8	79.4	93.4	95.2	83.3	86.9	89.0	94.3
1912 1	108.5	94.1	97.8	98.2	87.2	82.9	96.2	96.3	86.7	89.7	91.5	96.5
1912 2	112.1	97.0	100.8	100.9	93.1	88.9	100.3	96.9	93.5	95.6	96.1	98.1
1912 3	105.6	97.6	100.2	100.4	95.6	92.3	102.0	97.7	96.1	97.4	97.5	99.9
1912 4	100.0	100.7	100.4	100.7	96.0	94.3	103.4	98.2	96.9	97.9	97.9	100.3
1913 1	97.4	97.2	97.1	97.2	99.9	99.1	101.5	100.2	101.0	100.8	100.4	101.4
1913 2	100.7	99.8	100.2	100.1	100.7	97.0	99.7	101.4	100.5	100.2	101.6	100.6
1913 3	104.0	103.8	103.5	103.6	104.0	99.9	97.9	98.4	100.5	102.4	101.0	97.9
1913 4	102.3	100.5	101.5	101.1	98.3	101.4	101.4	96.7	98.7	97.7	96.4	97.9
1914 1	105.1	100.9	102.3	102.2	97.2	97.1	99.8	96.4	97.3	97.7	97.0	97.9
1914 2	104.0	101.6	102.4	102.6	101.1	96.4	96.8	94.7	99.2	100.7	98.6	95.2
1914 3	110.9	106.7	107.8	108.1	116.2	93.1	94.3	91.8	97.9	107.7	102.2	91.7
1914 4	123.0	103.3	110.7	111.3	96.1	72.3	97.5	92.1	80.2	95.0	93.6	93.6
1915 1	142.2	108.2	120.7	121.1	99.4	76.1	102.8	92.6	82.4	98.1	95.5	95.7
1915 2	145.8	110.1	122.7	122.7	114.4	88.1	109.0	96.6	98.5	111.4	106.0	99.4
1915 3	123.6	104.5	110.9	111.0	113.1	96.0	116.1	100.4	108.1	112.6	108.4	103.7
1915 4	118.8	103.3	108.3	108.4	110.4	98.3	125.2	106.5	110.9	112.8	111.2	110.5

TABLE A-24 (concluded)

YEAR Q	201	203	205	207	209	212	213	215	217	218	220	222
1916 1	131.4	107.4	115.3	115.3	117.9	103.6	143.9	116.6	124.0	123.7	122.1	123.0
1916 2	130.8	115.3	120.1	120.3	121.8	104.1	156.1	129.0	132.0	130.1	131.6	134.3
1916 3	142.7	120.4	127.4	127.6	128.9	112.6	157.7	136.6	138.3	136.3	138.9	140.1
1916 4	171.9	133.2	146.7	146.1	149.2	134.9	166.9	135.6	151.1	151.8	146.6	142.4
1917 1	186.3	144.7	158.7	158.2	166.9	144.9	182.3	144.9	172.9	170.9	162.2	154.1
1917 2	237.8	170.2	192.6	192.2	197.9	146.6	198.1	147.0	186.2	194.1	175.7	158.9
1917 3	233.7	181.2	196.8	196.1	205.4	177.3	212.1	153.3	201.2	202.3	183.6	166.0
1917 4	217.9	196.3	203.9	203.0	216.5	191.3	205.1	155.2	207.6	208.6	188.3	167.6
1918 1	228.2	208.9	214.8	214.0	239.6	215.9	206.2	159.9	221.5	224.0	199.7	172.6
1918 2	232.6	203.2	219.1	218.6	251.6	215.9	199.1	162.9	219.3	229.2	203.2	170.8
1918 3	234.2	218.7	223.7	223.6	252.9	219.8	202.1	178.6	221.0	229.2	210.7	182.3
1918 4	232.8	218.5	224.3	223.5	250.7	226.2	205.1	178.2	222.4	230.2	211.1	183.1
1919 1	236.6	225.5	230.5	228.7	251.0	226.3	206.4	172.4	221.6	232.9	210.4	181.1
1919 2	246.9	239.4	241.8	241.6	261.9	218.7	182.1	170.9	207.6	233.8	210.4	173.0
1919 3	243.9	251.9	250.8	249.8	273.8	236.8	199.1	177.3	226.4	243.5	218.7	180.4
1919 4	239.3	232.1	234.6	234.2	272.6	273.7	208.2	178.9	248.9	248.2	222.2	185.3
1920 1	242.4	224.0	231.1	229.4	282.0	302.1	206.1	184.6	265.5	255.1	228.5	190.6
1920 2	278.6	219.1	236.7	236.7	294.1	312.3	215.1	198.9	275.8	265.2	239.7	205.1
1920 3	290.3	214.9	248.0	247.6	299.9	313.5	214.1	206.5	275.6	271.4	246.1	217.6
1920 4	253.3	210.6	227.6	228.3	233.7	229.9	204.6	200.8	220.6	228.3	219.0	207.4
1921 1	193.3	160.8	171.6	172.5	181.0	176.3	173.3	183.4	176.1	180.5	183.7	183.9
1921 2	158.1	131.7	140.6	141.6	145.9	142.2	143.3	165.5	141.3	147.1	154.8	162.2
1921 3	143.2	129.9	134.2	134.8	144.2	138.7	128.5	148.5	133.9	141.9	143.6	145.4
1921 4	131.1	121.3	123.6	124.4	144.0	162.1	126.9	142.4	147.9	141.2	141.0	140.6
1922 1	119.1	115.7	115.8	116.4	142.0	165.0	126.3	140.1	150.9	140.7	140.1	139.0
1922 2	138.8	119.9	125.8	126.4	146.7	158.7	123.1	137.0	145.7	142.1	140.3	135.7
1922 3	128.8	125.1	125.7	126.3	157.2	180.7	128.9	137.6	161.5	151.9	146.9	138.9
1922 4	128.8	125.7	126.0	126.5	160.1	192.6	131.7	136.9	165.6	154.5	148.0	139.7
1923 1	132.8	124.7	126.1	127.2	173.4	216.2	137.9	139.1	185.9	165.3	155.7	142.5
1923 2	133.9	124.8	126.4	127.6	169.2	204.6	143.6	139.9	182.2	163.4	155.0	143.5
1923 3	125.7	120.8	121.2	122.3	164.2	199.4	133.3	136.8	174.1	156.2	149.3	137.8
1923 4	125.6	125.5	124.5	125.7	181.5	226.9	130.6	132.8	189.8	167.1	154.5	134.4

TABLE A-25

QUARTERLY FISHER PRICE INDEXES,
SELECTED MAJOR IMPORT CLASSES
(1913=100)

YEAR	Q	201	203	205	207	209	212	213	215	216	220	221	223
1879	1	107.9	146.4	129.2	125.0	111.9	91.3	79.1	86.4	99.9	107.3	102.9	93.0
1879	2	106.2	137.1	124.3	120.6	108.7	91.1	78.4	86.0	97.6	101.0	98.5	88.5
1879	3	111.2	135.6	127.5	122.5	111.6	92.2	77.1	85.7	98.8	102.3	100.6	88.9
1879	4	125.4	154.9	145.6	140.0	127.1	101.8	78.4	91.1	108.9	100.7	107.0	87.9
1880	1	127.5	173.7	152.7	148.3	132.2	105.3	90.0	99.0	117.1	103.2	113.4	95.7
1880	2	118.7	173.8	150.3	145.4	131.3	108.5	96.8	104.1	118.9	107.2	116.1	100.8
1880	3	127.7	169.1	153.6	146.5	131.2	103.1	88.6	97.1	115.1	107.7	113.6	96.9
1880	4	120.5	157.3	142.8	137.5	123.0	98.2	86.3	93.6	109.3	104.0	108.2	93.4
1881	1	110.8	165.1	139.3	134.9	124.0	104.0	84.5	96.0	109.6	103.1	108.3	92.0
1881	2	105.7	169.9	140.1	135.8	121.7	99.7	84.1	93.2	108.1	102.3	106.8	92.2
1881	3	115.7	175.8	149.0	142.5	126.3	96.7	82.0	90.3	109.4	103.8	108.5	91.0
1881	4	115.9	164.6	141.5	137.3	123.1	97.9	84.4	92.4	108.7	103.4	107.6	92.2
1882	1	105.9	165.7	135.1	132.2	121.3	103.6	88.2	97.2	109.6	103.1	108.3	94.6
1882	2	132.6	177.6	161.0	156.3	136.3	104.8	86.3	96.7	118.1	104.6	114.7	94.3
1882	3	108.2	177.0	140.8	136.2	124.3	102.1	83.0	93.4	108.9	103.1	107.9	92.0
1882	4	102.7	163.5	130.9	127.8	120.5	106.6	82.0	95.3	106.9	103.8	106.4	92.2
1883	1	88.7	167.3	123.9	121.5	114.6	102.8	81.4	93.4	103.4	102.5	103.8	91.9
1883	2	91.4	157.1	126.3	122.8	112.8	96.4	80.6	89.8	101.2	99.7	101.7	88.2
1883	3	91.4	156.0	124.5	120.4	111.8	96.1	79.7	88.8	100.1	102.9	101.7	90.2
1883	4	104.1	145.5	125.1	122.1	110.7	92.9	80.3	87.8	99.9	101.0	100.4	89.5
1884	1	100.3	141.0	121.1	119.0	109.8	96.1	82.1	90.4	100.3	98.9	100.5	90.3
1884	2	95.8	125.3	111.9	109.6	104.3	86.5	81.2	89.6	95.5	95.8	95.7	87.9
1884	3	93.5	114.2	104.2	102.9	97.7	85.3	79.5	85.6	91.5	93.2	93.5	86.5
1884	4	97.6	111.9	103.8	101.9	96.1	87.3	77.7	83.6	89.7	88.2	90.9	84.7
1885	1	84.8	106.9	96.5	94.9	90.8	85.4	76.1	81.8	85.3	93.0	88.1	84.0
1885	2	85.3	109.0	98.3	96.4	91.1	84.0	71.6	79.4	84.2	90.2	85.6	86.2
1885	3	89.1	120.3	105.2	103.4	96.3	84.9	70.6	78.9	87.7	91.5	89.5	81.1
1885	4	92.3	119.3	106.8	104.6	97.1	83.9	70.7	78.5	88.1	88.2	88.4	79.0

194

YFAR O		201	203	205	207	209	212	213	215	216	220	221	223
1886	1	81.4	125.8	103.2	101.3	93.8	82.3	74.2	79.2	87.1	87.1	87.6	80.3
1886	2	83.8	117.2	101.7	99.7	92.0	81.4	72.8	78.1	85.3	86.5	85.9	79.1
1886	3	87.3	109.0	98.7	97.1	92.9	85.9	72.2	80.1	85.9	88.6	87.3	80.0
1886	4	97.2	106.0	103.8	102.3	97.7	89.1	73.5	82.0	89.5	87.8	89.5	80.5
1887	1	104.3	104.0	106.2	104.5	97.3	86.1	74.0	81.2	89.4	88.1	89.6	80.8
1887	2	116.0	101.6	109.3	107.2	98.5	85.0	71.3	79.2	88.9	87.3	88.8	78.8
1887	3	131.1	104.8	121.4	118.6	106.5	84.9	70.8	78.9	93.5	88.0	92.8	79.5
1887	4	129.7	112.5	126.7	123.9	110.3	87.5	70.8	80.4	96.3	85.1	93.5	77.8
1888	1	112.4	118.0	116.8	115.0	101.3	81.5	75.2	79.3	92.3	84.2	90.6	79.5
1888	2	109.6	118.7	115.0	113.0	99.4	80.4	69.5	76.0	89.3	84.2	88.2	77.0
1888	3	103.4	118.8	111.9	110.4	97.7	79.8	66.1	73.9	87.2	85.1	87.2	76.3
1888	4	107.2	118.9	114.9	113.4	101.5	83.2	67.9	76.8	90.2	86.6	89.5	77.6
1889	1	107.6	122.0	116.1	114.8	100.9	83.6	71.9	78.8	91.3	87.7	90.4	80.5
1889	2	116.9	148.6	132.3	130.4	111.7	83.2	73.7	79.4	99.0	87.7	96.7	80.8
1889	3	115.8	168.1	142.6	139.5	116.7	83.3	73.4	79.3	101.2	86.9	97.4	80.2
1889	4	113.1	115.6	118.3	116.1	101.8	82.3	74.9	79.5	92.6	88.5	91.8	81.6
1890	1	120.6	124.7	123.2	121.6	104.9	81.7	76.7	79.9	95.8	86.3	92.8	81.1
1890	2	130.5	123.3	127.4	125.4	108.1	82.1	74.3	79.2	96.8	85.6	94.2	79.8
1890	3	119.3	119.6	121.4	118.9	104.3	83.1	74.5	79.8	93.9	86.5	92.1	80.4
1890	4	123.3	117.5	124.1	121.4	105.7	81.8	76.4	79.9	95.4	87.6	93.5	81.2
1891	1	128.3	129.9	128.7	126.9	106.4	80.5	76.3	79.0	96.9	87.3	94.1	81.5
1891	2	135.7	127.2	127.5	126.1	109.0	80.4	75.8	79.2	97.9	85.7	95.5	80.5
1891	3	122.2	121.9	121.6	119.6	102.3	77.4	71.3	75.1	92.1	85.3	90.3	78.4
1891	4	109.4	117.7	115.2	113.4	96.3	73.8	73.4	73.7	88.9	86.2	88.3	79.5
1892	1	116.6	125.6	121.9	120.2	98.9	73.3	73.7	73.5	90.7	86.4	89.5	79.8
1892	2	115.4	118.0	115.8	114.4	97.2	74.0	71.3	73.2	88.7	84.6	87.8	77.6
1892	3	108.0	120.4	114.6	113.0	97.3	75.0	71.6	73.9	88.6	83.8	87.3	77.4
1892	4	115.0	118.2	118.9	116.7	98.8	76.5	74.1	75.7	90.6	84.5	89.2	78.9

YEAR Q	201	203	205	207	209	212	213	215	216	220	221	223
1893 1	128.6	127.1	128.2	126.5	104.4	78.0	75.8	77.3	95.0	84.9	92.4	79.8
1893 2	124.8	135.2	129.3	127.6	107.3	79.0	74.3	77.6	95.8	84.2	93.3	78.0
1893 3	120.5	141.3	132.1	129.3	106.8	73.1	70.2	72.2	94.3	84.6	91.6	77.3
1893 4	121.5	122.3	123.2	121.1	101.5	69.5	70.6	70.1	91.6	84.4	90.1	76.9
1894 1	126.6	114.8	119.8	118.4	99.6	70.8	69.2	70.2	90.2	82.6	88.5	75.5
1894 2	120.8	110.1	113.3	112.1	95.7	70.4	65.2	68.8	86.6	79.9	85.2	72.7
1894 3	112.3	108.0	111.2	109.8	92.0	66.7	63.2	65.5	82.8	81.5	82.5	72.4
1894 4	100.7	95.9	102.1	100.3	84.6	67.0	64.0	65.9	78.1	78.7	78.3	71.3
1895 1	113.7	84.8	102.2	101.1	84.0	65.6	63.4	64.7	77.9	80.4	78.5	72.5
1895 2	115.6	84.7	98.9	98.0	84.2	67.3	63.2	65.7	77.9	79.1	78.2	71.3
1895 3	110.6	85.6	100.0	99.0	86.3	71.5	62.3	67.9	78.8	80.5	79.3	71.9
1895 4	107.6	91.5	103.1	102.0	90.1	75.1	64.3	70.9	82.2	81.4	82.0	73.0
1896 1	106.0	101.5	103.8	102.7	90.3	74.4	66.4	71.2	83.0	81.3	82.5	74.1
1896 2	110.2	106.7	106.8	105.3	91.8	70.2	64.9	68.3	83.1	80.9	82.7	72.6
1896 3	97.4	97.4	97.6	96.4	85.6	66.6	63.6	65.8	78.2	80.9	78.8	72.1
1896 4	88.2	93.8	93.1	92.0	83.9	71.0	64.5	68.4	77.6	81.7	78.5	72.3
1897 1	86.0	88.6	88.6	87.8	80.9	71.4	64.7	68.8	75.9	80.4	76.9	72.4
1897 2	85.5	88.7	85.3	84.4	80.2	72.0	64.4	69.1	75.0	78.8	75.8	70.9
1897 3	77.0	100.0	90.5	89.2	80.6	69.4	63.1	67.0	74.7	79.8	75.8	70.6
1897 4	76.6	92.7	86.0	85.6	79.5	71.4	62.2	67.8	74.2	79.0	75.2	70.2
1898 1	67.1	95.8	80.5	80.3	78.4	74.1	60.9	69.0	73.1	79.1	74.4	70.0
1898 2	71.0	99.5	84.2	83.9	81.9	76.6	60.1	70.0	75.3	79.2	76.1	69.3
1898 3	73.0	104.7	87.9	87.4	83.7	76.1	59.4	69.3	75.9	79.0	76.0	69.0
1898 4	64.1	97.4	79.0	79.3	79.8	78.2	62.7	72.1	74.8	80.4	76.0	71.6
1899 1	67.4	101.1	82.1	82.0	83.0	81.6	65.8	75.8	77.9	83.1	79.0	74.3
1899 2	70.9	108.4	89.4	88.9	86.4	80.8	71.3	77.0	81.5	81.5	81.4	75.6
1899 3	66.5	112.7	88.0	88.2	85.1	80.9	74.1	78.0	81.5	82.4	81.7	78.2
1899 4	60.5	100.9	76.8	78.2	83.7	88.7	80.3	85.6	83.1	83.9	83.2	82.7

YEAR Q	201	203	205	207	209	212	213	215	216	220	221	223
1900 1	69.8	105.8	84.9	84.9	89.8	91.8	80.6	87.7	86.8	86.8	86.8	83.4
1900 2	76.3	112.8	95.4	94.6	92.7	88.5	83.1	86.5	86.2	86.3	88.6	84.1
1900 3	77.9	102.5	90.3	89.5	88.6	85.3	83.2	84.4	86.2	88.2	86.7	85.4
1900 4	70.6	100.5	82.9	83.1	82.4	82.7	83.7	83.1	83.0	88.7	84.2	86.2
1901 1	68.8	96.3	81.7	81.4	81.7	82.0	83.1	82.5	82.1	88.4	83.4	85.3
1901 2	73.6	102.2	87.6	86.7	84.2	81.7	83.5	82.4	83.8	89.0	84.8	85.3
1901 3	65.6	94.4	77.6	77.6	78.9	80.7	81.3	81.0	79.8	89.2	81.8	84.7
1901 4	59.6	89.1	69.9	70.8	76.3	83.6	83.0	83.4	79.0	88.0	80.8	85.7
1902 1	66.9	81.3	72.1	72.5	76.7	80.6	80.2	80.5	78.1	87.5	80.1	83.8
1902 2	71.0	80.3	75.0	75.1	78.5	81.2	80.0	80.9	79.1	86.4	80.6	82.6
1902 3	66.6	80.2	72.2	72.8	77.7	83.3	80.0	81.9	78.8	87.3	80.6	83.6
1902 4	67.2	81.1	72.3	73.5	79.8	86.7	80.4	84.2	80.8	86.7	82.0	84.3
1903 1	67.0	88.5	75.4	76.0	83.0	88.9	81.0	85.9	83.0	88.2	84.1	85.1
1903 2	70.6	89.0	78.2	79.2	82.2	86.1	83.2	84.9	83.2	86.6	83.9	84.2
1903 3	68.2	87.1	75.2	76.2	82.2	88.6	84.5	86.9	83.4	88.8	84.7	87.2
1903 4	66.1	88.1	73.1	74.6	82.7	90.9	83.1	87.8	83.2	87.1	84.0	85.4
1904 1	73.1	90.4	79.9	80.4	86.1	89.7	82.9	87.2	84.9	86.7	85.3	84.5
1904 2	78.4	96.3	87.3	87.2	88.6	87.5	82.6	86.5	86.2	86.0	86.3	83.6
1904 3	72.1	97.6	82.6	83.1	86.6	88.5	83.6	86.9	86.4	89.0	86.2	85.8
1904 4	70.9	90.2	77.4	78.3	85.6	91.5	84.5	88.9	85.3	89.0	86.0	86.3
1905 1	73.7	128.9	98.9	97.9	97.2	93.6	83.4	90.0	92.4	89.5	91.8	85.8
1905 2	77.8	124.0	99.1	98.6	96.0	92.1	85.5	89.6	92.2	89.4	91.6	87.0
1905 3	75.2	105.2	89.4	89.8	92.4	93.9	87.9	91.4	90.9	90.9	90.9	89.7
1905 4	71.8	94.3	80.0	81.0	88.8	95.1	85.5	91.4	87.9	90.8	88.5	88.1
1906 1	76.3	95.3	84.6	85.0	92.8	97.2	93.5	95.8	92.7	91.9	92.5	97.2
1906 2	79.9	96.7	88.1	88.3	94.2	97.6	95.3	96.7	94.2	92.4	93.8	93.2
1906 3	77.2	97.2	85.7	86.6	95.1	101.8	98.4	100.4	96.1	94.4	95.7	96.5
1906 4	73.7	97.6	82.4	83.5	96.2	106.8	102.0	104.8	97.8	94.5	97.1	98.0
1907 1	75.5	101.1	86.6	87.2	99.8	107.3	105.1	106.5	100.6	95.1	99.4	99.0
1907 2	80.8	103.6	91.3	91.6	100.8	105.6	106.2	105.8	101.3	98.0	100.6	100.4
1907 3	77.6	104.5	88.1	89.0	99.7	107.4	101.9	105.1	100.2	98.6	99.8	99.8
1907 4	79.1	96.8	85.2	86.4	95.9	103.8	97.2	101.3	96.3	96.7	96.4	96.9

YEAR Q	201	203	205	207	209	212	213	215	216	220	221	223
1908 1	74.7	105.5	87.7	88.2	90.8	92.4	85.6	89.9	89.4	94.2	90.5	90.1
1908 2	78.2	117.0	96.3	96.2	91.4	86.1	83.3	85.1	88.9	91.1	89.3	86.8
1908 3	72.7	101.0	84.9	85.2	86.6	88.7	86.7	87.9	87.1	88.7	87.4	88.2
1908 4	68.5	97.2	79.3	80.3	85.7	91.1	81.8	87.5	85.3	88.1	85.8	85.8
1909 1	67.2	101.4	80.7	80.8	86.6	91.1	79.6	86.8	85.0	86.2	85.2	83.5
1909 2	78.6	107.1	92.8	92.3	92.4	91.8	81.3	87.9	89.4	86.6	88.7	84.6
1909 3	72.2	105.8	86.6	87.1	92.1	96.1	81.2	90.3	89.4	86.3	88.7	85.3
1909 4	69.3	100.3	80.1	81.1	92.8	101.7	82.8	94.5	90.5	86.8	89.7	86.2
1910 1	76.5	111.1	93.9	93.4	101.6	105.9	84.3	97.7	96.5	86.1	94.3	86.5
1910 2	83.8	117.6	102.6	101.7	104.4	103.9	85.2	96.4	97.9	84.7	95.1	85.8
1910 3	79.6	116.7	95.7	95.9	104.9	109.8	86.2	100.0	98.8	88.0	96.4	88.3
1910 4	84.1	106.7	93.1	93.2	98.8	102.0	87.7	96.3	95.4	87.5	93.6	88.3
1911 1	91.1	102.8	97.2	96.5	101.1	102.1	89.7	97.2	97.0	88.8	95.3	89.3
1911 2	94.8	109.1	102.4	101.8	102.5	100.6	90.8	96.8	98.4	88.7	96.1	89.8
1911 3	93.9	113.9	102.9	103.0	100.8	98.0	90.6	95.1	97.4	91.6	96.1	91.5
1911 4	98.6	116.0	106.4	105.8	103.1	98.9	91.1	95.9	99.0	92.2	97.5	91.5
1912 1	101.0	129.8	115.0	113.8	106.9	100.1	92.9	97.5	102.4	92.3	100.3	92.6
1912 2	107.3	119.9	113.7	112.9	106.5	100.2	94.8	98.3	102.7	93.3	100.9	94.3
1912 3	103.6	111.5	108.3	108.2	103.3	99.5	97.9	98.9	101.6	96.5	100.5	97.5
1912 4	104.7	111.4	108.1	107.7	104.3	101.8	101.7	101.7	103.5	98.7	102.4	100.4
1913 1	108.1	99.7	102.6	102.3	105.0	105.2	101.8	104.2	103.7	98.4	102.8	99.8
1913 2	103.1	95.8	97.3	97.3	99.7	100.7	98.1	100.0	99.3	99.9	99.5	99.2
1913 3	95.6	98.5	95.1	95.4	96.0	98.2	100.4	98.9	97.8	101.3	98.4	101.2
1913 4	94.8	110.5	104.9	104.9	98.5	94.8	98.3	95.9	98.6	100.7	98.8	99.3
1914 1	96.1	99.1	97.5	98.1	97.1	96.4	96.6	96.4	96.7	94.2	96.1	94.8
1914 2	92.6	98.1	92.9	93.3	94.4	95.8	94.7	95.4	94.3	90.5	93.6	92.7
1914 3	90.8	123.7	103.9	104.2	96.4	92.0	88.9	90.9	94.5	89.0	93.3	89.1
1914 4	85.1	138.8	109.1	109.1	94.0	85.4	94.2	88.2	94.0	88.6	92.7	91.3
1915 1	89.8	135.3	109.5	109.6	94.9	86.0	94.8	88.8	94.5	86.9	93.1	90.0
1915 2	90.4	148.3	115.2	115.0	98.3	88.3	97.0	91.0	97.7	88.6	96.5	92.6
1915 3	90.8	145.8	114.9	114.6	99.1	90.2	107.4	95.6	100.8	95.2	99.8	100.4
1915 4	90.5	141.0	113.7	113.8	101.3	93.4	107.8	97.8	102.2	95.2	101.3	100.6

TABLE A-25 (concluded)

YEAR Q	201	203	205	207	209	212	213	215	216	220	221	223
1916 1	95.8	146.5	117.2	117.2	111.8	107.8	115.8	110.6	112.5	105.1	111.8	111.1
1916 2	98.8	176.5	132.8	132.0	122.5	116.0	129.9	120.5	123.6	109.4	121.7	120.4
1916 3	100.0	188.1	138.9	137.6	120.9	112.1	128.0	117.2	122.6	114.8	122.7	122.9
1916 4	98.9	190.3	137.2	137.7	124.2	117.4	136.5	123.5	127.2	120.4	126.5	129.5
1917 1	102.7	169.3	131.0	131.9	134.2	133.5	151.3	139.3	137.0	129.7	136.5	138.7
1917 2	110.6	194.9	147.0	147.1	143.3	138.4	160.2	146.3	146.2	133.1	145.1	146.3
1917 3	104.6	220.0	154.7	153.5	150.3	143.2	160.1	148.6	149.9	137.1	148.7	145.8
1917 4	106.6	233.0	156.8	158.1	152.1	144.0	167.1	151.3	153.3	145.7	152.7	153.5
1918 1	105.6	216.1	150.6	152.6	148.1	143.4	173.8	152.9	152.1	163.3	154.7	163.4
1918 2	108.9	216.7	151.6	153.0	148.7	144.5	178.0	155.1	153.8	172.8	157.7	169.6
1918 3	109.1	217.0	153.3	154.8	151.8	149.5	184.0	160.4	159.0	189.8	164.4	182.3
1918 4	122.4	227.9	165.0	167.5	156.9	151.6	188.2	163.3	164.7	198.5	170.8	180.8
1919 1	134.7	244.9	179.4	181.9	161.8	150.9	188.1	162.4	167.2	187.4	161.6	183.9
1919 2	144.2	245.8	185.8	187.5	161.3	147.5	169.1	154.9	163.6	183.6	160.3	173.5
1919 3	169.0	252.9	205.4	206.5	176.3	161.2	178.0	166.5	177.2	191.9	173.6	184.5
1919 4	183.4	269.4	222.2	223.0	196.3	180.0	194.5	184.7	194.8	211.4	198.0	200.0
1920 1	179.9	374.8	263.0	263.0	218.1	189.9	194.5	191.8	210.4	214.7	212.2	201.2
1920 2	176.6	499.1	316.9	315.5	242.4	194.4	203.4	197.3	229.9	229.6	231.0	213.2
1920 3	159.4	575.1	341.3	339.1	240.1	170.8	213.6	184.3	229.0	229.2	229.6	215.6
1920 4	144.9	408.1	254.8	254.5	183.9	140.7	200.7	160.2	187.1	215.8	192.5	204.2
1921 1	102.4	221.7	151.2	152.8	122.3	113.6	170.7	129.8	136.3	195.6	146.4	180.9
1921 2	96.8	193.0	136.1	137.6	108.6	99.7	140.5	111.4	118.8	170.9	127.9	155.8
1921 3	98.2	150.2	118.7	120.6	98.1	93.0	126.4	102.7	107.1	154.1	116.2	141.2
1921 4	107.0	135.9	118.8	121.0	101.2	95.0	117.7	101.8	107.2	148.3	114.4	132.5
1922 1	106.3	107.0	102.0	103.9	99.0	106.1	124.1	111.6	108.7	148.9	115.5	140.1
1922 2	111.6	119.5	110.4	112.3	102.0	104.9	125.3	111.2	110.9	145.1	116.9	137.0
1922 3	113.9	147.2	124.2	126.0	109.5	105.9	125.0	111.8	115.8	153.3	122.1	139.1
1922 4	111.4	162.9	133.2	135.0	115.5	108.2	126.7	114.0	119.6	152.9	125.5	138.8
1923 1	113.1	175.7	138.1	139.5	123.2	118.7	134.1	123.5	127.8	152.6	132.3	145.0
1923 2	116.2	233.1	165.7	166.6	140.6	128.3	139.5	131.8	141.0	149.1	142.7	145.5
1923 3	107.4	213.2	151.4	152.5	129.3	119.3	138.8	125.5	132.7	147.8	135.6	143.9
1923 4	106.1	213.3	150.0	151.1	132.5	125.9	135.2	128.8	134.7	146.2	136.9	142.9

TABLE A-26

QUARTERLY FISHER QUANTITY INDEXES,
SELECTED MAJOR EXPORT CLASSES
(1913=100)

YEAR Q	201	203	205	207	209	212	213	215	217	218	220	222
1879 1	95.8	84.7	91.9	88.8	74.8	53.6	11.4	7.6	37.2	52.2	35.1	9.0
1879 2	132.3	71.4	96.4	93.1	51.6	19.1	11.0	9.7	15.4	37.4	26.8	10.4
1879 3	215.2	66.9	125.7	121.1	58.3	13.5	9.5	10.8	11.4	42.0	30.0	11.0
1879 4	148.3	73.7	105.4	101.5	85.3	61.1	8.3	10.6	41.0	58.6	40.2	10.3
1880 1	105.3	71.2	86.8	83.8	66.1	44.5	9.4	8.1	30.9	46.2	31.6	8.8
1880 2	169.6	83.5	118.8	114.4	69.2	30.7	10.4	7.9	22.5	48.6	33.0	9.0
1880 3	219.0	77.4	131.6	126.7	68.5	23.3	8.9	9.7	17.4	48.3	33.4	10.4
1880 4	152.3	87.3	114.5	110.0	92.5	66.0	9.3	9.1	44.3	63.4	42.4	9.6
1881 1	105.8	90.0	99.2	95.6	75.7	50.6	9.8	8.6	34.8	52.5	35.7	9.2
1881 2	131.9	60.1	88.3	85.2	59.6	34.2	11.6	11.9	25.1	42.7	30.9	11.9
1881 3	138.4	62.9	92.2	89.3	54.0	24.6	10.0	13.3	18.6	39.2	29.2	13.1
1881 4	93.3	55.5	71.3	68.8	62.7	49.5	10.2	12.5	34.2	44.4	32.1	11.9
1882 1	63.4	58.2	61.9	60.0	53.4	40.8	11.3	10.7	29.1	38.3	27.7	10.7
1882 2	48.4	42.7	45.8	44.8	38.0	29.5	13.8	13.1	22.9	29.4	23.2	13.4
1882 3	129.2	49.4	79.5	77.4	45.1	19.5	11.1	13.2	15.8	34.2	25.9	13.5
1882 4	82.6	55.7	67.8	65.1	76.1	71.9	10.4	11.8	48.2	53.0	37.2	11.3
1883 1	85.1	66.4	75.9	72.9	70.4	57.8	11.8	11.2	39.9	49.5	35.0	11.4
1883 2	65.3	51.8	58.1	56.6	45.5	33.2	12.7	13.8	24.9	34.3	26.4	13.9
1883 3	100.2	70.1	83.7	80.6	46.9	19.5	11.6	13.1	16.0	35.0	26.5	13.3
1883 4	81.5	67.5	75.0	72.4	73.4	63.6	12.1	12.6	43.5	52.0	37.1	12.8
1884 1	58.8	54.9	58.4	56.3	59.1	53.6	11.7	10.6	37.2	42.8	30.6	11.3
1884 2	71.1	63.0	66.6	65.8	39.1	19.7	12.0	12.3	16.3	30.8	23.7	13.6
1884 3	95.5	69.9	79.1	78.8	45.1	22.1	12.1	12.0	17.8	35.6	26.6	14.4
1884 4	82.3	71.1	77.2	74.9	83.6	77.8	13.3	12.3	52.8	59.5	41.6	13.5
1885 1	93.6	76.6	85.5	82.5	62.1	40.9	12.8	10.9	29.7	45.1	32.1	12.0
1885 2	70.2	81.4	81.0	77.5	45.3	20.0	11.9	12.4	16.4	34.1	25.8	12.8
1885 3	58.7	66.5	66.0	63.8	39.5	21.3	12.5	12.9	17.5	31.0	24.0	13.7
1885 4	60.3	70.2	68.4	66.8	77.5	73.7	11.4	12.2	49.6	55.1	38.7	12.9

YEAR Q	201	203	205	207	209	212	213	215	217	218	220	222
1886 1	76.4	61.8	69.8	66.9	58.6	44.4	11.3	11.2	31.4	41.9	30.2	11.3
1886 2	94.3	67.7	81.0	77.1	55.8	34.8	12.1	13.1	25.7	40.7	30.2	13.0
1886 3	98.6	76.6	88.4	84.3	52.3	26.5	11.9	13.8	20.5	39.1	29.4	14.1
1886 4	87.0	75.8	83.5	79.7	89.1	80.5	12.3	13.1	54.0	61.9	43.4	12.9
1887 1	84.0	76.6	81.2	79.2	72.0	57.0	12.1	12.1	39.1	51.3	36.4	12.4
1887 2	96.9	65.9	79.0	77.0	42.7	17.1	14.0	13.2	15.4	33.2	25.5	14.2
1887 3	108.3	74.0	87.8	86.0	53.3	28.5	12.5	13.4	21.9	40.5	30.1	14.7
1887 4	51.9	73.2	67.0	65.7	82.9	83.5	12.3	13.9	55.9	59.4	42.1	14.7
1888 1	49.6	62.9	59.4	58.1	56.8	49.0	14.4	11.9	35.3	42.3	30.8	13.2
1888 2	40.9	62.7	56.0	54.9	40.9	29.2	14.6	12.8	21.1	32.5	25.0	14.4
1888 3	71.6	65.9	68.3	67.9	40.6	22.0	13.6	13.7	18.3	32.8	25.4	15.4
1888 4	64.3	62.5	63.4	63.2	83.4	86.4	12.1	13.6	57.6	59.7	42.3	14.5
1889 1	69.9	70.1	71.1	70.0	67.7	60.0	13.5	14.1	41.3	49.7	36.2	15.2
1889 2	82.3	73.2	77.0	76.4	50.5	29.3	15.4	15.3	23.7	39.4	30.3	16.6
1889 3	94.8	89.9	93.2	91.7	57.7	32.3	15.6	16.8	26.1	45.7	34.7	19.4
1889 4	96.2	97.9	98.2	97.2	106.5	99.3	16.3	16.1	66.7	75.9	53.1	17.7
1890 1	113.1	99.0	106.8	104.1	81.9	55.3	15.7	13.0	39.7	58.8	41.5	14.5
1890 2	120.0	93.3	105.8	102.9	57.8	21.2	17.2	16.4	19.4	44.1	33.9	17.2
1890 3	83.9	94.9	92.7	90.4	59.4	33.0	15.7	17.5	26.1	45.2	34.7	18.1
1890 4	64.7	100.2	86.8	86.0	100.4	99.2	15.7	18.2	66.1	71.6	51.5	18.7
1891 1	63.2	103.7	88.8	87.1	79.7	66.6	18.0	15.3	47.3	58.9	42.5	17.4
1891 2	70.0	81.6	77.6	76.0	55.0	36.5	19.0	17.4	29.5	43.3	33.5	19.0
1891 3	172.3	90.2	124.7	121.5	71.2	28.0	19.5	17.8	24.5	53.8	40.3	19.5
1891 4	168.8	101.7	129.9	126.9	124.1	108.6	16.8	18.2	71.6	86.9	61.2	18.7
1892 1	173.2	112.7	138.9	135.0	100.8	64.0	17.3	16.2	45.3	71.8	51.0	17.4
1892 2	140.3	104.6	120.7	111.5	75.1	38.4	17.5	17.3	30.0	56.2	41.6	19.0
1892 3	120.0	106.8	113.9	111.3	66.5	28.4	16.4	17.1	23.5	50.2	37.7	19.5
1892 4	125.4	109.7	117.2	115.3	103.0	84.7	17.3	19.3	57.7	74.1	53.6	20.2

YEAR Q	201	203	205	207	209	212	213	215	217	218	220	222
1893 1	92.5	80.0	86.4	84.5	63.8	43.7	16.9	16.7	33.0	48.2	36.5	17.8
1893 2	103.3	82.9	91.7	90.2	60.7	37.1	20.0	20.5	30.2	48.1	37.7	22.2
1893 3	141.0	104.3	119.1	117.4	71.4	34.7	20.5	21.1	31.7	57.5	44.3	25.5
1893 4	94.0	91.2	93.0	92.4	102.7	103.4	27.6	20.6	73.3	77.2	55.6	24.4
1894 1	102.8	101.1	103.8	101.9	83.9	63.7	25.9	18.8	48.6	63.9	47.0	22.1
1894 2	103.1	103.7	104.7	103.6	65.2	33.5	24.1	20.9	29.8	51.9	40.3	23.5
1894 3	88.9	101.4	97.0	96.8	60.8	32.4	27.1	21.1	30.2	50.1	39.2	24.8
1894 4	82.3	97.3	92.6	91.5	109.8	120.5	24.7	21.9	81.0	80.5	58.5	24.1
1895 1	81.2	100.1	95.3	93.0	88.3	79.9	22.9	19.8	56.3	65.8	48.5	21.9
1895 2	77.4	94.7	90.0	87.8	65.0	45.2	26.8	22.4	37.8	52.3	41.1	21.9
1895 3	82.9	93.7	90.6	89.6	54.7	27.7	27.8	22.6	27.9	46.4	37.4	25.6
1895 4	123.4	113.2	118.5	117.0	103.5	83.0	24.4	23.4	59.3	76.4	56.3	25.0
1896 1	137.4	107.3	121.5	118.1	94.1	66.1	29.7	21.8	51.4	71.1	52.4	24.7
1896 2	123.2	100.0	111.4	108.3	69.4	36.2	34.6	26.4	35.5	57.2	45.8	29.3
1896 3	161.2	117.4	136.7	133.2	83.9	41.5	35.7	26.6	39.2	66.0	51.8	29.9
1896 4	202.9	132.4	160.3	158.0	145.1	118.2	37.8	27.6	85.4	106.7	76.7	31.6
1897 1	167.3	116.8	138.6	134.8	103.6	69.2	36.2	27.9	55.8	79.1	59.9	30.5
1897 2	145.1	108.2	125.2	121.9	78.5	39.4	45.5	32.3	42.0	65.8	53.4	35.8
1897 3	228.5	125.7	168.5	163.7	96.0	35.9	41.5	30.7	38.4	76.0	59.1	34.1
1897 4	249.7	136.5	182.4	178.0	156.1	122.8	35.0	31.1	86.0	112.1	81.9	32.3
1898 1	205.7	142.4	171.1	165.4	133.1	93.5	39.9	33.7	71.2	98.4	74.5	34.9
1898 2	242.6	129.3	177.2	171.7	110.2	49.6	42.5	38.2	47.0	84.7	67.6	38.5
1898 3	177.3	121.5	145.9	141.7	87.5	39.0	42.7	37.2	41.1	71.4	58.8	38.8
1898 4	241.3	165.5	197.2	193.0	175.8	145.3	41.9	36.0	101.4	126.9	93.1	37.8
1899 1	170.9	156.8	166.5	161.7	123.4	79.2	41.8	37.8	64.1	94.0	73.4	38.8
1899 2	156.9	136.8	148.3	144.1	91.0	43.1	41.0	43.9	42.1	72.6	61.9	42.1
1899 3	215.2	143.1	174.3	168.9	106.2	49.9	41.3	41.8	46.2	82.3	67.2	41.3
1899 4	197.1	157.5	175.7	171.5	125.2	95.2	42.9	41.5	74.4	102.5	80.1	42.3

YEAR C	201	203	205	207	209	212	213	215	217	218	220	222
1900 1	150.4	142.2	148.8	145.0	119.2	91.4	46.7	42.8	74.2	94.3	75.5	44.7
1900 2	172.2	142.8	157.6	153.3	93.5	47.8	50.2	45.2	48.7	78.4	66.2	46.5
1900 3	172.8	134.1	152.1	147.7	86.8	42.3	49.4	41.3	44.9	73.6	73.6	43.1
1900 4	202.7	152.3	172.2	169.8	149.2	120.8	47.1	39.9	93.7	114.9	88.6	43.1
1901 1	191.3	150.2	169.5	165.0	118.6	77.2	41.7	40.4	64.1	92.9	74.4	41.2
1901 2	191.2	142.6	164.8	160.2	102.8	54.2	43.0	46.3	49.8	82.5	69.6	44.9
1901 3	199.8	132.0	160.3	156.0	96.8	48.4	35.6	42.7	43.4	77.0	64.8	40.8
1901 4	145.6	148.0	148.2	147.1	144.9	127.8	39.2	41.7	93.7	109.0	85.9	41.6
1902 1	90.4	121.3	111.9	110.0	99.2	84.2	44.1	43.4	69.3	81.9	68.2	44.4
1902 2	88.8	115.6	107.6	105.1	70.4	43.0	47.1	45.5	44.4	63.2	56.8	46.2
1902 3	126.4	102.6	112.7	111.1	79.0	51.3	44.4	42.4	48.7	67.9	58.8	43.1
1902 4	136.7	141.7	140.9	140.0	134.3	116.5	41.9	42.1	88.8	104.4	82.5	42.8
1903 1	139.9	126.3	134.1	131.2	116.5	96.7	43.4	41.3	77.2	93.3	74.9	43.1
1903 2	119.6	110.6	116.3	113.8	69.0	38.1	43.4	45.8	40.0	61.6	55.7	45.6
1903 3	101.2	111.8	110.3	107.9	64.3	35.8	46.8	42.0	39.6	59.3	52.9	44.4
1903 4	131.5	144.8	141.3	140.0	147.4	137.1	49.6	43.3	106.6	116.0	90.8	45.8
1904 1	99.5	132.1	121.8	120.2	85.9	61.3	59.4	43.4	60.7	77.1	65.5	48.8
1904 2	59.4	98.9	85.9	84.4	52.8	35.0	56.4	47.9	42.0	53.9	51.4	51.0
1904 3	53.6	92.5	78.9	78.0	64.2	53.9	63.2	48.4	57.1	63.4	57.7	53.3
1904 4	78.8	129.1	110.5	110.4	136.6	140.5	61.3	53.3	111.7	111.2	91.0	55.6
1905 1	114.4	131.4	127.7	125.2	105.0	81.5	54.5	52.6	71.2	87.6	75.1	53.2
1905 2	75.8	117.4	103.5	101.5	89.1	75.8	64.3	60.0	71.4	80.6	73.2	61.6
1905 3	81.0	111.3	101.2	100.1	78.4	61.2	58.4	60.0	60.1	71.8	67.3	59.0
1905 4	156.6	158.3	159.6	157.6	142.6	119.5	56.5	60.7	96.7	113.9	95.7	58.5
1906 1	170.7	149.4	160.6	157.1	110.4	75.0	58.2	62.6	68.9	93.8	82.9	61.8
1906 2	91.6	124.7	114.5	112.6	81.9	58.9	61.1	64.1	59.7	74.9	70.7	62.4
1906 3	98.4	122.2	115.9	113.6	79.5	54.5	61.7	59.2	57.2	73.6	68.2	60.1
1906 4	138.5	129.5	134.5	132.7	151.5	148.3	58.9	60.7	114.1	119.2	99.4	59.4
1907 1	121.0	134.5	132.2	129.6	128.5	116.4	54.5	61.1	92.3	102.7	88.6	58.5
1907 2	103.7	123.8	119.1	116.4	83.5	59.1	58.8	64.0	58.9	75.2	71.0	61.8
1907 3	93.6	110.4	106.2	104.2	64.9	40.6	59.2	63.9	47.5	63.8	63.3	62.6
1907 4	157.1	117.9	133.8	132.6	143.9	140.0	74.2	60.9	116.4	121.1	101.0	65.9

YEAR Q	201	203	205	207	209	212	213	215	217	218	220	222
1908 1	125.4	140.9	137.8	134.9	121.2	103.7	69.0	58.7	91.5	104.2	88.9	62.5
1908 2	60.4	101.3	87.6	85.9	64.0	50.1	69.2	58.7	56.9	65.6	63.1	62.7
1908 3	96.7	91.3	94.7	93.2	70.0	53.1	59.5	54.4	55.4	67.1	62.6	57.0
1908 4	106.7	124.2	118.3	117.7	148.8	157.3	60.0	53.5	121.1	120.0	97.7	56.6
1909 1	66.9	114.4	98.1	96.5	100.2	96.3	58.2	57.6	82.4	86.7	76.8	58.0
1909 2	37.8	85.7	68.1	67.2	61.0	57.5	76.3	62.2	64.2	65.2	64.0	66.6
1909 3	62.0	77.3	72.1	71.6	61.2	55.5	72.5	59.9	61.3	64.4	62.8	64.5
1909 4	92.4	99.9	95.6	97.2	117.5	124.2	71.8	62.7	106.9	104.0	90.7	66.7
1910 1	56.8	78.3	70.9	70.5	63.1	59.4	70.1	63.7	62.9	65.2	64.5	66.1
1910 2	38.1	65.9	56.3	56.2	49.8	49.5	71.4	71.2	56.8	56.7	61.1	71.6
1910 3	46.1	69.2	61.2	61.1	59.3	59.5	81.1	70.0	66.7	65.1	66.4	73.4
1910 4	78.2	88.5	83.9	85.0	129.6	149.5	85.1	70.7	128.3	115.4	101.5	75.7
1911 1	82.3	91.0	89.3	87.9	94.5	94.5	80.3	78.4	89.8	89.2	85.7	78.0
1911 2	54.4	101.6	86.0	84.4	58.9	45.5	93.3	89.9	61.9	68.0	74.6	90.2
1911 3	68.6	94.8	86.3	85.2	75.7	71.6	90.9	82.5	78.3	80.3	81.0	85.8
1911 4	66.2	124.0	101.9	102.7	146.9	170.2	93.8	85.2	142.6	130.1	115.5	89.2
1912 1	62.5	115.7	97.3	95.9	131.3	146.4	88.9	87.1	125.7	116.5	107.0	86.8
1912 2	26.2	85.7	63.9	63.3	62.2	63.7	101.6	100.5	77.3	73.1	81.8	98.7
1912 3	76.0	80.6	79.3	78.9	67.8	65.5	105.6	96.7	80.0	79.7	85.2	100.1
1912 4	152.2	108.4	123.8	124.1	167.4	183.8	94.6	97.4	152.0	143.6	129.1	96.1
1913 1	122.6	115.6	119.5	118.3	95.9	83.3	100.7	99.5	88.6	96.1	97.0	98.2
1913 2	77.8	92.6	88.3	87.4	69.9	66.7	106.3	105.3	78.8	80.9	88.0	105.2
1913 3	124.3	83.7	99.2	98.2	80.4	75.9	101.6	97.0	83.8	87.3	90.4	100.0
1913 4	70.9	107.8	91.5	94.7	152.8	174.5	91.1	101.3	149.1	135.2	125.8	98.3
1914 1	55.4	91.4	77.8	78.6	97.6	105.5	91.3	89.7	101.2	95.2	93.9	89.4
1914 2	62.9	72.1	68.9	68.9	59.2	58.4	100.2	95.6	71.2	70.4	77.9	96.3
1914 3	206.1	74.1	124.1	121.6	57.3	29.9	71.9	71.3	42.8	63.3	65.9	73.8
1914 4	234.9	135.0	174.6	172.4	133.4	105.8	87.5	89.1	99.4	118.2	110.2	86.2
1915 1	261.3	165.8	208.3	203.7	185.8	159.7	95.4	117.8	137.4	154.8	145.5	103.0
1915 2	198.5	150.5	172.7	170.1	117.6	87.7	113.2	154.8	94.9	114.1	126.7	134.6
1915 3	160.6	146.7	153.6	152.5	95.8	68.9	116.8	175.2	83.7	100.7	122.9	149.2
1915 4	180.3	179.5	179.5	180.4	123.2	68.3	118.3	211.9	99.7	119.8	147.4	170.2

YEAR Q		201	203	205	207	209	212	213	215	217	218	220	222
1916	1	187.8	179.7	185.0	183.5	120.1	82.3	126.9	227.0	96.7	118.4	150.8	179.1
1916	2	168.5	175.0	176.1	173.1	114.6	82.7	151.8	262.0	105.9	122.7	164.1	209.9
1916	3	147.9	149.7	151.4	149.6	108.4	88.6	172.2	281.3	116.4	124.5	170.9	229.3
1916	4	171.0	154.6	161.2	161.8	129.2	110.7	170.0	243.2	129.8	137.5	168.8	206.1
1917	1	166.6	163.1	166.7	165.5	100.9	67.3	182.7	268.8	104.9	119.9	162.9	223.5
1917	2	169.4	164.6	171.4	167.9	90.8	53.3	181.7	247.9	95.8	113.7	152.0	213.9
1917	3	80.1	117.3	105.2	103.8	73.0	63.3	131.1	180.1	85.1	89.2	115.9	158.8
1917	4	117.0	139.5	130.6	131.6	89.6	74.1	178.5	208.2	106.8	112.8	139.5	192.1
1918	1	84.9	192.6	154.6	154.0	88.0	55.1	136.7	154.2	79.9	99.1	115.8	141.7
1918	2	87.3	257.7	198.5	196.4	95.1	48.0	135.6	155.4	74.3	106.1	121.1	144.7
1918	3	166.2	185.1	182.2	178.6	94.9	56.5	133.1	157.4	79.5	105.7	121.0	144.7
1918	4	197.9	178.9	188.4	185.7	107.8	68.5	112.2	145.8	81.7	108.7	120.6	129.5
1919	1	124.3	268.1	216.5	217.0	128.7	79.1	112.4	170.8	89.3	122.8	137.9	141.1
1919	2	203.1	340.2	296.9	291.7	159.7	83.9	140.6	206.0	100.8	151.6	169.1	170.7
1919	3	148.0	212.2	190.7	189.9	114.2	76.1	138.0	159.5	94.5	119.5	132.3	146.5
1919	4	148.2	212.4	187.9	189.9	137.7	107.5	118.2	182.3	111.4	132.6	148.2	150.6
1920	1	106.9	212.7	170.8	175.0	133.4	109.5	133.9	196.1	117.3	133.0	153.0	165.9
1920	2	136.6	182.2	167.7	165.9	96.0	68.5	132.8	210.1	86.8	107.7	137.2	176.6
1920	3	249.5	104.2	163.8	160.7	79.4	56.7	108.4	181.3	71.5	94.7	119.7	158.6
1920	4	275.6	142.1	194.9	191.8	130.9	106.7	109.0	221.2	107.7	130.0	157.7	179.9
1921	1	223.4	157.5	187.0	182.7	114.4	77.7	86.8	187.0	80.5	107.2	131.6	144.9
1921	2	248.1	144.4	189.4	183.9	109.7	74.5	56.0	115.0	68.6	98.0	103.6	97.1
1921	3	368.8	181.8	257.5	250.5	140.4	79.5	65.1	96.0	75.3	119.0	113.4	86.1
1921	4	169.5	131.2	146.9	145.5	117.3	95.9	78.6	103.5	91.8	106.0	106.1	92.3
1922	1	183.3	155.3	168.9	165.8	98.7	64.0	84.1	104.9	70.2	94.1	98.3	94.5
1922	2	178.9	156.4	168.2	165.0	107.6	70.9	90.3	129.0	77.0	99.6	109.4	106.6
1922	3	287.1	135.2	193.4	189.2	99.0	50.5	77.7	120.0	58.5	90.5	100.0	97.4
1922	4	183.4	144.1	160.5	158.2	127.7	105.9	74.1	124.1	98.6	114.4	119.1	105.2
1923	1	124.7	153.0	145.1	143.1	87.6	62.7	87.7	128.9	70.2	88.5	101.2	111.4
1923	2	113.8	138.3	132.2	129.6	68.7	49.4	97.1	143.3	63.0	80.0	99.0	126.2
1923	3	131.6	127.3	131.8	129.0	83.6	67.4	99.1	141.8	76.8	90.8	106.6	125.8
1923	4	96.3	155.3	135.6	134.5	126.7	112.8	105.7	137.8	112.8	120.7	127.6	122.3

TABLE A-27

QUARTERLY FISHER QUANTITY INDEXES,
SELECTED MAJOR IMPORT CLASSES
(1913=100)

YEAR Q	201	203	205	207	209	212	213	215	216	220	221	223
1879 1	32.1	26.9	29.8	29.6	22.2	15.3	17.9	16.3	21.4	39.5	23.1	29.9
1879 2	31.9	50.5	41.9	41.4	28.6	16.2	24.5	19.2	27.7	26.4	25.4	26.4
1879 3	34.2	28.5	30.9	31.5	22.6	16.1	29.1	20.9	24.7	47.6	27.5	40.1
1879 4	56.4	22.1	38.9	39.3	30.4	24.1	43.8	31.3	33.7	35.7	31.7	40.1
1880 1	33.2	32.2	33.1	32.8	28.8	26.7	42.5	32.6	31.7	61.0	34.4	51.8
1880 2	31.1	56.7	44.9	44.4	33.9	25.9	51.9	35.6	38.2	49.0	37.0	51.0
1880 3	30.6	30.2	29.8	30.5	22.2	17.2	39.3	25.4	26.8	62.4	31.6	52.4
1880 4	52.6	23.2	37.3	37.7	28.5	22.0	32.1	25.7	29.9	38.4	29.5	37.0
1881 1	36.0	33.4	34.9	34.8	26.0	18.6	30.6	23.0	27.2	54.0	30.5	43.4
1881 2	41.8	60.0	52.2	51.6	36.0	21.8	38.2	27.8	36.6	41.4	34.9	41.1
1881 3	32.9	28.1	29.6	30.4	23.4	20.5	44.3	29.4	28.9	63.0	33.6	55.2
1881 4	61.4	24.9	42.3	42.5	32.1	24.7	40.7	30.7	34.7	46.9	34.6	45.3
1882 1	42.1	37.8	40.6	40.0	30.4	22.2	39.3	28.5	32.4	66.6	36.6	53.4
1882 2	34.9	64.3	49.6	48.8	35.9	23.8	44.9	31.6	38.0	46.6	37.0	46.4
1882 3	41.9	38.6	39.9	40.3	29.0	21.6	48.3	31.4	34.2	72.5	38.8	61.6
1882 4	56.2	29.4	41.8	42.3	32.0	24.6	43.0	31.3	34.9	50.7	35.6	47.8
1883 1	43.9	33.2	38.8	38.3	30.1	23.2	39.4	29.1	32.1	64.6	36.0	52.3
1883 2	40.4	65.8	54.7	54.0	38.7	24.7	41.2	30.7	39.3	47.0	37.9	44.5
1883 3	36.7	40.1	37.9	38.7	27.1	19.5	44.2	28.5	31.9	59.2	35.2	53.5
1883 4	58.6	36.2	46.9	47.5	34.8	25.1	40.0	30.6	36.7	45.3	36.0	44.5
1884 1	41.5	49.2	46.4	45.6	34.2	24.4	32.1	27.3	33.8	60.3	36.4	47.7
1884 2	43.2	70.1	58.1	56.9	39.4	23.2	38.7	28.9	39.0	41.3	36.5	40.6
1884 3	36.8	42.8	39.5	40.0	29.3	23.1	39.0	28.3	32.2	64.5	36.1	53.2
1884 4	63.3	79.3	46.5	46.6	33.5	23.5	34.5	27.5	34.2	39.8	32.9	38.6
1885 1	42.3	48.4	46.2	45.5	33.3	22.6	27.3	24.4	31.9	51.2	33.5	40.7
1885 2	45.1	72.0	59.7	58.7	40.3	23.2	38.9	28.9	39.7	36.0	36.1	37.8
1885 3	38.8	41.6	40.7	40.4	30.5	24.3	40.6	29.6	33.1	58.2	36.1	50.3
1885 4	61.4	35.2	48.3	48.3	38.7	32.1	41.1	35.5	39.7	46.0	38.1	44.8

YEAR	Q	201	203	205	207	209	212	213	215	216	220	221	223
1886	1	46.9	47.0	48.1	47.2	38.8	31.4	38.2	33.9	38.3	63.1	40.3	51.3
1886	2	44.2	68.0	58.3	56.9	41.9	28.4	47.4	35.4	43.0	49.2	41.1	48.8
1886	3	44.1	55.2	50.3	49.9	36.7	26.5	45.1	33.3	38.9	67.1	41.8	57.1
1886	4	56.1	35.3	46.4	46.2	38.0	32.7	44.2	36.9	39.7	52.1	39.7	48.6
1887	1	47.1	46.7	47.8	47.1	36.3	26.9	45.3	33.6	38.2	69.4	41.7	57.2
1887	2	46.5	79.3	63.3	61.7	45.2	29.9	57.0	39.7	47.5	47.8	44.5	51.8
1887	3	34.7	41.2	37.4	37.7	31.3	29.4	54.2	38.4	37.1	71.6	41.3	51.8
1887	4	46.6	34.9	41.3	41.4	35.2	32.6	46.0	37.5	38.1	58.1	39.8	53.1
1888	1	45.6	49.4	48.5	47.6	39.9	33.9	42.1	36.9	40.3	75.2	44.7	59.3
1888	2	49.0	69.5	60.6	59.2	45.5	32.4	51.1	39.3	46.3	54.1	44.9	52.5
1888	3	42.0	45.6	44.2	43.9	33.3	26.5	50.0	35.0	37.7	74.0	42.4	64.4
1888	4	61.4	41.1	52.1	51.7	42.4	35.7	47.4	40.0	43.8	55.7	43.4	52.3
1889	1	49.3	42.9	47.2	46.2	41.6	38.1	49.2	41.8	43.0	75.0	46.8	61.6
1889	2	50.5	64.4	60.1	58.3	45.1	33.6	47.2	38.7	45.2	50.8	43.4	49.6
1889	3	37.6	46.5	42.9	42.6	34.5	29.6	46.6	35.9	37.6	73.5	42.0	60.9
1889	4	54.9	41.3	47.8	48.1	42.0	39.3	44.9	41.4	43.3	59.5	42.9	53.7
1890	1	42.5	50.8	47.9	46.9	39.9	34.6	41.2	37.1	40.1	77.7	44.8	60.0
1890	2	53.0	70.1	63.3	61.7	48.9	37.8	52.5	43.2	49.2	67.6	49.6	60.4
1890	3	46.5	53.6	50.0	50.2	41.7	37.4	55.9	44.2	45.8	80.3	50.1	60.4
1890	4	54.0	49.5	51.6	51.9	41.4	35.7	49.0	40.7	43.9	60.8	45.3	57.0
1891	1	43.7	58.9	53.0	51.7	45.6	40.8	49.1	43.9	45.8	67.4	46.9	58.8
1891	2	50.4	103.1	80.0	77.1	55.4	35.6	64.4	46.3	56.4	47.1	50.8	55.9
1891	3	42.2	63.5	54.0	53.1	41.6	33.9	47.3	38.9	43.2	65.9	46.1	58.4
1891	4	63.4	61.9	63.1	62.8	51.4	33.7	42.0	43.1	49.4	54.9	48.8	51.2
1892	1	52.2	55.7	55.4	54.3	48.0	43.3	43.6	43.4	46.5	70.2	51.4	58.5
1892	2	51.6	72.5	64.5	62.6	51.2	42.3	55.0	47.1	51.7	51.0	52.9	54.3
1892	3	49.2	63.2	57.5	56.7	45.1	38.1	52.0	43.3	47.3	73.8	50.2	65.2
1892	4	54.9	55.0	54.3	55.1	49.6	48.3	50.0	48.9	50.1	60.9	49.2	57.9

YEAR C	201	203	205	207	209	212	213	215	216	220	221	223
1893 1	51.4	63.4	59.0	57.7	53.4	50.7	52.6	51.4	52.6	80.9	54.4	67.9
1893 2	49.0	70.9	62.1	60.5	49.0	41.8	63.8	50.1	52.7	58.4	51.1	63.0
1893 3	41.2	50.3	46.1	46.1	34.3	28.6	37.0	31.8	36.3	62.5	39.9	53.8
1893 4	50.8	62.2	56.3	56.6	39.7	26.9	29.4	27.9	37.9	36.3	35.9	36.1
1894 1	51.7	71.5	63.5	62.0	46.2	31.8	30.8	31.4	42.0	45.7	41.7	40.1
1894 2	48.0	86.4	68.9	67.1	49.3	34.7	41.5	37.3	47.3	35.5	43.7	41.2
1894 3	53.3	61.3	57.9	57.4	44.1	35.0	43.3	38.1	44.2	53.5	45.4	51.0
1894 4	57.3	44.4	49.7	50.9	48.6	48.9	47.8	48.5	48.4	57.5	49.3	53.9
1895 1	56.5	53.2	56.1	55.3	51.7	47.9	45.2	46.9	49.0	84.5	55.5	65.6
1895 2	55.0	80.0	68.4	67.2	58.7	51.0	50.9	51.0	55.7	62.0	56.1	58.7
1895 3	50.7	54.5	51.8	52.6	51.2	52.7	58.6	54.9	52.9	85.0	59.0	73.2
1895 4	60.8	52.4	55.4	56.7	51.9	51.0	48.8	50.3	51.6	70.9	54.6	62.7
1896 1	50.9	62.3	56.9	56.8	50.4	45.2	41.7	44.0	47.7	79.1	53.4	62.1
1896 2	46.5	82.8	63.6	64.9	46.6	34.0	43.7	37.5	46.6	49.4	46.4	50.0
1896 3	48.8	59.3	53.5	54.3	35.9	24.0	39.8	29.9	38.0	63.5	43.1	54.7
1896 4	67.1	52.0	58.1	59.5	47.7	39.2	37.7	38.7	45.3	49.4	45.4	45.6
1897 1	68.2	59.3	64.1	63.9	58.5	52.6	37.7	47.1	52.2	67.0	54.2	54.7
1897 2	69.0	126.7	98.0	98.9	83.5	70.9	54.5	64.9	75.5	95.9	78.2	79.6
1897 3	53.2	29.6	39.2	40.5	37.6	38.9	41.3	39.8	39.5	43.6	40.0	45.3
1897 4	70.5	39.1	53.2	53.9	49.0	45.8	42.5	44.7	47.3	42.6	45.7	44.9
1898 1	60.6	50.2	55.6	55.0	50.7	45.8	42.5	44.7	47.7	60.1	49.6	52.5
1898 2	64.2	67.2	67.7	66.1	52.3	41.1	44.4	42.3	49.7	42.6	47.1	45.5
1898 3	46.6	46.2	46.5	46.6	39.6	36.4	46.7	40.0	41.7	51.3	43.5	51.2
1898 4	65.4	59.1	61.6	62.1	48.7	39.7	41.2	40.2	47.1	40.3	46.9	47.8
1899 1	73.5	64.3	70.6	69.2	59.6	49.4	43.4	47.3	54.1	58.2	54.0	52.1
1899 2	68.1	81.9	77.1	75.3	59.8	46.4	50.7	48.0	56.6	47.9	54.0	51.3
1899 3	57.7	66.6	63.8	62.7	52.5	44.5	56.7	49.1	53.3	59.2	53.9	59.1
1899 4	71.4	65.0	68.6	68.4	60.7	53.9	52.2	53.2	57.7	58.6	57.1	56.7

YEAR	Q	201	203	205	207	209	212	213	215	216	220	221	223
1900	1	73.2	55.5	65.5	64.3	62.8	59.0	51.5	56.3	58.6	66.6	59.5	60.2
1900	2	51.1	70.4	62.1	61.0	54.3	49.2	50.4	49.7	53.2	53.1	52.4	54.2
1900	3	51.4	56.9	53.3	54.1	44.2	37.2	46.9	40.9	45.0	59.8	47.7	55.3
1900	4	81.0	65.0	72.7	73.4	56.9	45.9	46.4	46.1	54.5	55.4	54.3	53.8
1901	1	65.6	67.6	66.9	66.8	57.8	52.8	45.0	49.8	54.9	60.8	56.1	56.7
1901	2	69.8	71.8	71.2	71.0	65.0	62.1	52.6	58.4	62.2	51.5	58.9	57.2
1901	3	75.0	57.0	64.6	66.2	55.6	51.7	54.5	52.8	56.8	64.5	58.1	63.7
1901	4	99.0	59.8	79.0	79.7	66.8	59.8	55.4	58.1	64.5	66.6	64.6	64.8
1902	1	81.4	50.7	67.2	66.7	68.0	69.3	52.1	62.7	63.6	70.7	64.6	65.3
1902	2	70.1	63.3	66.3	66.9	61.3	60.1	62.9	61.1	62.7	62.5	62.2	66.9
1902	3	81.6	78.2	80.6	80.0	63.3	51.8	76.2	59.8	65.7	77.9	68.0	76.1
1902	4	83.0	77.5	80.3	80.3	72.0	66.1		69.8	72.8	74.8	72.7	76.7
1903	1	72.3	57.6	66.0	65.3	67.6	70.0	68.7	69.5	68.3	79.4	70.0	76.9
1903	2	68.1	75.5	70.2	71.8	64.1	59.5	73.9	64.9	66.6	65.1	66.2	71.9
1903	3	79.1	59.2	76.7	69.8	59.0	52.4	64.4	56.9	60.6	78.7	64.8	72.6
1903	4	93.6	59.4		77.0	62.7	52.4	59.5	55.0	61.4	71.2	62.8	66.4
1904	1	92.1	73.6	84.9	83.3	74.6	65.2	56.6	62.1	68.3	74.2	68.8	66.7
1904	2	62.6	80.2	72.1	71.2	66.1	61.9	61.3	61.7	64.6	60.6	63.5	63.6
1904	3	84.5	69.1	77.3	76.9	62.5	52.0	58.9	55.1	61.6	69.0	62.9	66.1
1904	4	120.0	71.9	97.2	96.7	81.9	69.0	64.6	67.4	76.0	68.8	73.9	68.6
1905	1	84.2	74.8	80.7	79.6	82.2	80.5	65.8	75.1	76.5	76.7	75.8	73.0
1905	2	64.8	60.4	62.7	62.6	68.7	73.0	68.4	71.3	68.7	65.9	67.7	69.7
1905	3	65.3	74.1	69.8	69.5	63.5	59.3	73.2	64.5	65.1	82.4	69.3	78.0
1905	4	112.6	75.8	94.1	94.5	78.6	66.8	73.7	69.3	76.6	82.2	77.4	79.2
1906	1	74.9	66.7	71.1	70.9	77.6	79.9	73.2	77.4	75.5	92.2	78.3	83.4
1906	2	62.5	83.1	73.4	72.5	71.7	71.2	78.0	74.1	73.6	77.8	74.5	80.4
1906	3	67.9	70.7	69.5	69.3	63.0	59.3	77.0	66.0	66.9	93.7	72.6	84.9
1906	4	111.4	79.9	95.7	96.1	83.7	73.6	85.8	78.2	83.3	96.2	85.5	90.5
1907	1	84.9	84.3	85.2	84.7	86.2	84.3	81.3	83.2	83.5	98.3	85.9	90.5
1907	2	83.8	96.1	91.3	89.9	80.3	74.2	79.8	76.3	80.0	88.8	81.7	87.0
1907	3	86.1	65.4	75.7	75.9	67.7	63.8	84.1	71.3	72.7	103.7	79.8	94.3
1907	4	91.6	69.8	80.2	81.3	68.5	60.5	63.3	61.5	67.4	93.6	72.9	79.5

YEAR Q	201	203	205	207	209	212	213	215	216	220	221	223
1908 1	75.0	66.7	70.9	71.0	63.7	57.9	50.6	55.2	59.9	78.9	63.8	66.6
1908 2	80.2	87.1	85.3	83.9	73.1	60.2	57.0	59.4	67.1	61.7	65.8	60.6
1908 3	83.1	72.0	77.5	77.5	72.0	64.6	65.1	64.8	68.5	77.4	70.5	71.4
1908 4	108.3	73.8	90.1	91.1	85.6	79.1	83.4	80.7	83.6	79.8	82.7	83.0
1909 1	125.6	82.8	105.6	104.1	101.3	92.4	87.7	90.7	94.5	89.5	93.0	88.8
1909 2	92.1	110.6	101.2	101.3	96.2	89.3	88.5	89.0	92.6	86.4	91.2	90.1
1909 3	78.6	70.0	73.8	74.3	80.1	83.3	95.6	87.6	83.6	103.3	88.2	97.9
1909 4	128.5	68.5	96.7	98.3	98.9	97.0	106.1	100.2	99.7	107.8	101.2	102.2
1910 1	77.6	97.9	87.6	87.9	100.6	104.8	108.4	106.1	100.7	104.2	101.0	104.7
1910 2	61.5	106.2	84.4	83.9	81.7	80.0	100.4	87.1	86.3	87.6	87.4	94.9
1910 3	91.0	77.0	83.7	84.0	73.1	68.8	99.6	79.4	80.7	101.1	86.3	100.2
1910 4	111.4	63.7	86.4	87.8	87.8	85.4	100.9	91.0	90.1	105.3	93.1	97.9
1911 1	82.5	85.7	83.3	84.0	88.8	89.4	103.2	94.4	91.2	92.8	91.6	96.1
1911 2	81.9	98.7	91.0	90.0	86.6	87.6	90.7	85.5	86.8	82.6	86.3	87.5
1911 3	82.1	76.7	79.8	79.5	78.3	78.9	97.4	85.6	83.7	91.8	85.7	94.4
1911 4	114.8	71.8	92.3	93.9	87.4	81.7	91.6	85.3	88.1	103.0	91.6	92.2
1912 1	100.7	88.1	95.4	94.5	102.4	102.5	89.9	97.9	96.7	96.2	96.7	89.0
1912 2	108.8	98.7	106.6	104.0	102.1	108.8	96.1	104.1	104.0	83.2	99.4	90.7
1912 3	88.2	89.9	89.6	89.0	95.6	98.9	98.7	98.9	95.9	113.8	99.7	99.6
1912 4	114.2	74.9	93.8	95.6	103.1	107.7	103.2	106.0	102.9	118.6	105.7	101.4
1913 1	90.1	106.6	100.1	99.1	105.3	108.3	102.5	106.0	103.8	95.8	101.5	99.9
1913 2	77.4	104.2	92.1	91.3	91.6	95.0	102.8	97.8	95.8	79.9	92.2	96.0
1913 3	87.0	106.6	97.5	97.5	93.0	92.3	104.8	97.1	97.3	113.2	101.7	106.4
1913 4	147.3	80.4	109.5	111.2	110.6	105.2	90.4	99.8	103.6	110.6	105.1	98.1
1914 1	122.4	111.4	118.9	116.6	120.5	115.0	93.5	107.1	110.0	121.1	112.7	105.7
1914 2	116.2	155.5	140.8	137.1	135.1	122.1	97.0	112.8	120.5	109.5	118.1	104.4
1914 3	105.2	128.9	120.9	119.4	111.4	96.2	83.0	91.4	101.1	107.7	102.6	95.3
1914 4	126.1	69.3	92.2	93.8	95.4	90.7	73.5	84.5	88.2	102.5	91.3	86.7
1915 1	113.3	98.1	107.8	105.6	116.5	111.0	68.7	94.9	99.1	90.4	97.1	79.4
1915 2	111.8	128.6	127.1	123.2	138.2	133.0	75.6	111.0	115.8	73.2	106.5	77.4
1915 3	110.8	90.6	101.5	100.2	115.2	121.7	80.0	105.9	104.4	72.1	97.6	81.5
1915 4	144.7	68.7	101.4	101.3	125.1	140.9	77.5	116.2	111.7	79.5	105.0	84.6

YEAR	Q	201	203	205	207	209	212	213	215	216	220	221	223
1916	1	106.6	109.5	111.7	109.7	147.8	170.0	94.2	140.7	130.7	72.5	118.1	90.7
1916	2	118.7	132.6	132.0	129.1	154.2	164.1	111.1	143.8	139.2	78.7	126.9	101.3
1916	3	100.5	78.9	88.3	88.8	109.2	126.3	95.7	114.9	106.5	74.9	100.2	92.2
1916	4	143.4	70.0	99.9	100.0	114.1	119.4	88.1	107.5	105.5	72.9	98.9	83.6
1917	1	148.6	102.4	125.7	122.7	146.0	152.5	94.8	130.1	127.8	72.9	116.4	87.4
1917	2	172.3	118.3	146.8	141.7	167.1	171.9	103.7	145.2	144.2	74.4	129.4	94.6
1917	3	134.8	91.9	109.5	109.8	133.6	143.8	97.8	126.2	121.1	64.7	109.5	87.4
1917	4	166.0	42.4	90.4	89.2	115.4	129.4	88.1	113.6	105.9	66.8	97.9	81.5
1918	1	144.0	89.7	115.7	112.0	126.9	128.2	79.7	109.2	110.4	56.8	98.7	73.4
1918	2	146.6	129.2	145.3	138.3	164.7	166.2	95.2	137.9	138.4	66.2	122.0	84.6
1918	3	134.1	83.6	108.1	104.6	128.2	133.9	101.1	121.7	116.3	67.8	105.4	86.5
1918	4	104.1	68.0	84.8	83.4	113.6	121.3	91.5	110.0	101.8	60.8	92.6	74.7
1919	1	123.9	103.0	117.7	113.0	121.4	115.7	72.8	98.9	104.2	52.2	98.8	66.9
1919	2	144.6	141.0	152.6	144.6	180.9	182.8	61.2	134.1	138.5	51.5	124.6	62.0
1919	3	170.7	117.2	146.8	141.2	189.9	198.6	94.6	158.3	153.3	67.1	139.6	81.9
1919	4	161.9	94.6	126.3	124.3	173.1	192.0	115.7	162.8	150.5	80.9	143.3	98.7
1920	1	152.0	136.8	151.3	145.2	197.3	218.6	127.1	183.8	171.5	86.9	154.1	110.8
1920	2	150.1	151.1	161.6	154.6	172.9	168.9	119.5	150.3	154.0	92.8	142.9	110.7
1920	3	151.1	153.8	163.4	157.4	160.7	144.6	113.1	133.0	145.2	100.8	137.2	112.4
1920	4	177.2	89.8	124.0	120.4	117.3	110.3	93.8	104.7	112.4	80.2	106.7	93.6
1921	1	149.2	109.1	131.3	126.4	131.9	127.0	63.3	100.8	109.7	72.7	102.9	76.2
1921	2	147.2	111.7	133.2	127.5	145.8	140.6	70.8	112.3	117.9	83.9	112.6	81.7
1921	3	98.1	81.0	89.7	89.1	122.3	137.9	75.2	112.9	105.1	91.9	106.0	85.5
1921	4	147.1	104.7	126.1	124.1	148.2	155.3	90.7	129.9	128.5	96.5	124.1	97.5
1922	1	136.6	158.2	156.6	150.1	166.5	158.3	97.2	134.7	139.7	100.2	133.1	100.4
1922	2	136.4	168.8	162.6	155.5	168.5	158.6	113.7	141.7	146.5	107.0	139.4	112.6
1922	3	107.6	144.7	133.0	129.8	159.4	181.5	125.2	160.0	150.3	98.2	139.3	121.2
1922	4	163.4	101.3	132.2	128.9	188.6	230.5	152.9	200.7	177.3	117.3	165.5	140.3
1923	1	154.5	157.3	166.6	158.3	210.1	228.8	157.6	201.8	187.0	120.3	173.8	140.5
1923	2	137.3	147.2	153.1	146.0	191.4	206.8	158.1	188.7	175.0	127.6	165.3	142.6
1923	3	115.2	96.9	108.8	105.8	135.1	154.9	131.7	146.8	133.5	130.3	134.4	132.9
1923	4	184.1	100.2	138.3	134.6	152.4	156.8	132.0	148.0	144.3	140.0	144.7	134.9

TABLE A-28

QUARTERLY VALUES,
SELECTED MAJOR EXPORT CLASSES
(MILLIONS OF DOLLARS)

YEAR	Q	201	203	205	207	209	212	213	215	217	218	220	222
1879	1	35	49	82	83	156	76	8	17	84	168	188	29
1879	2	47	41	86	88	114	30	8	22	38	126	149	33
1879	3	82	38	119	120	137	21	7	23	28	149	173	34
1879	4	66	47	111	113	210	101	7	23	107	221	245	33
1880	1	47	47	92	94	169	78	8	19	86	181	201	30
1880	2	69	54	120	122	172	54	8	19	62	185	205	31
1880	3	83	52	133	135	169	40	7	24	47	182	207	36
1880	4	59	60	117	119	226	111	8	23	119	239	263	35
1881	1	43	63	104	106	187	85	8	20	93	200	221	32
1881	2	55	44	97	99	150	56	10	26	66	166	193	41
1881	3	60	48	106	109	143	41	9	30	50	159	190	44
1881	4	42	45	85	87	166	84	9	29	93	180	210	42
1882	1	28	46	73	75	140	69	10	25	80	155	180	38
1882	2	23	35	56	58	108	51	10	30	63	122	154	47
1882	3	60	42	100	102	128	34	10	29	44	147	176	46
1882	4	36	46	81	82	199	121	9	27	130	213	240	40
1883	1	37	53	89	90	179	93	10	26	103	194	220	40
1883	2	30	41	69	71	118	53	11	31	65	136	168	48
1883	3	42	52	92	94	119	31	11	29	42	137	165	46
1883	4	34	50	82	84	178	100	11	28	111	195	225	44
1884	1	25	41	64	66	146	86	10	25	96	163	187	40
1884	2	29	46	72	75	99	33	10	28	44	120	148	47
1884	3	36	49	81	85	110	37	11	27	47	133	160	49
1884	4	27	49	74	77	192	123	11	27	134	212	238	45
1885	1	33	50	80	82	142	65	10	23	76	159	182	38
1885	2	26	51	76	77	103	32	10	26	42	120	146	41
1885	3	21	41	61	63	89	34	11	27	44	108	135	44
1885	4	21	43	61	64	168	111	10	26	120	185	211	42

YEAR	Q	201	203	205	207	209	212	213	215	217	218	220	222
1886	1	26	37	61	63	124	65	9	23	74	137	160	36
1886	2	32	40	71	72	118	52	10	26	61	134	160	41
1886	3	33	45	77	78	110	39	10	27	49	128	155	44
1886	4	29	45	72	74	183	114	10	26	124	198	224	40
1887	1	29	45	73	74	151	81	10	24	91	165	189	37
1887	2	34	39	72	73	92	25	11	26	36	109	135	42
1887	3	35	44	78	80	113	41	10	26	51	132	157	43
1887	4	17	44	60	62	176	122	10	27	132	195	222	44
1888	1	18	39	55	56	124	73	12	25	85	143	167	41
1888	2	15	39	53	54	91	44	12	27	56	111	137	45
1888	3	26	42	65	67	92	34	11	28	45	113	141	48
1888	4	23	42	63	65	187	130	11	28	141	207	234	46
1889	1	23	44	66	68	150	90	12	29	102	171	199	47
1889	2	26	44	67	69	105	43	12	30	55	126	156	49
1889	3	29	53	80	82	116	45	13	33	59	142	174	56
1889	4	30	57	84	87	230	152	13	32	165	252	285	53
1890	1	35	57	90	91	171	85	12	26	97	189	216	43
1890	2	38	53	90	91	116	32	14	32	45	137	171	51
1890	3	28	54	81	82	122	48	13	33	61	144	177	53
1890	4	23	58	79	81	225	152	13	35	165	247	283	55
1891	1	24	60	82	83	177	102	14	29	116	200	230	51
1891	2	31	49	78	80	126	54	15	33	69	150	183	55
1891	3	74	55	127	128	158	38	16	32	53	183	215	55
1891	4	71	61	130	132	275	150	13	33	163	297	330	53
1892	1	67	68	133	135	215	87	13	29	100	236	265	48
1892	2	50	62	111	112	153	49	14	30	63	176	206	51
1892	3	43	64	105	107	133	34	12	29	46	154	183	48
1892	4	43	68	109	111	214	112	13	32	125	237	269	53

YEAR Q	201	203	205	207	209	212	213	215	217	218	220	222
1893 1	32	55	85	86	142	63	13	28	75	163	191	46
1893 2	35	57	90	92	129	47	15	34	61	154	188	57
1893 3	44	68	110	112	142	41	19	34	59	173	208	62
1893 4	29	59	85	88	208	130	18	33	148	237	268	60
1894 1	30	62	90	92	161	77	17	29	94	187	216	53
1894 2	29	59	86	88	118	39	17	32	56	145	177	56
1894 3	26	58	80	83	109	36	17	32	53	137	169	58
1894 4	24	55	77	79	186	116	16	33	132	211	245	57
1895 1	23	54	76	77	145	75	15	31	90	168	199	53
1895 2	25	52	76	77	115	46	18	38	64	142	180	64
1895 3	25	51	74	76	98	30	20	39	51	128	167	67
1895 4	33	60	91	93	190	106	18	43	124	219	261	69
1896 1	37	56	92	93	167	81	21	40	102	196	236	67
1896 2	33	49	81	82	117	43	24	48	66	150	199	79
1896 3	40	55	94	95	134	47	24	47	72	168	216	79
1896 4	56	65	118	121	249	138	26	49	164	286	336	84
1897 1	45	58	102	103	174	78	25	48	103	207	256	79
1897 2	39	54	91	93	130	44	31	54	76	170	224	91
1897 3	72	63	133	135	165	39	28	49	67	203	252	84
1897 4	79	72	149	151	264	120	25	49	145	298	347	80
1898 1	65	75	139	140	224	90	28	51	118	259	311	84
1898 2	88	71	158	160	203	50	30	59	79	240	300	93
1898 3	54	64	116	118	147	38	30	57	67	186	244	94
1898 4	72	86	155	159	282	132	30	57	162	322	379	94
1899 1	55	81	135	137	205	76	33	61	109	247	308	100
1899 2	50	70	118	119	156	45	35	71	79	200	273	112
1899 3	66	75	139	140	185	54	37	71	91	233	304	116
1899 4	60	85	142	144	242	108	39	73	147	293	368	122

YEAR Q	201	203	205	207	209	212	213	215	217	218	220	222
1900 1	45	77	120	122	226	116	43	80	160	283	364	137
1900 2	55	79	132	134	189	66	46	85	113	248	374	140
1900 3	55	76	129	131	183	63	44	74	107	239	314	128
1900 4	63	87	145	150	312	175	42	70	217	369	440	125
1901 1	63	85	146	148	245	108	36	72	144	293	366	118
1901 2	66	84	148	149	208	70	37	80	107	258	340	127
1901 3	68	80	146	148	199	63	31	73	95	244	319	115
1901 4	50	93	139	143	291	160	35	73	195	339	413	119
1902 1	33	77	108	110	206	107	36	74	144	255	330	121
1902 2	34	76	108	110	158	61	40	80	101	212	293	120
1902 3	45	69	112	114	174	70	38	74	108	224	299	121
1902 4	49	95	139	143	284	154	36	75	190	335	411	123
1903 1	51	83	133	134	257	136	38	74	173	308	383	123
1903 2	42	72	113	114	160	60	39	83	99	216	299	135
1903 3	36	70	105	106	151	59	41	77	100	208	285	131
1903 4	46	90	132	136	348	226	44	81	270	408	490	138
1904 1	35	83	115	118	227	122	52	81	174	293	374	144
1904 2	20	60	78	80	131	66	49	89	115	196	286	151
1904 3	19	56	73	75	147	86	54	88	140	217	305	155
1904 4	29	79	103	107	294	200	54	95	255	364	460	162
1905 1	42	75	114	116	203	99	50	92	149	267	361	154
1905 2	29	69	97	98	182	99	60	106	159	258	365	179
1905 3	30	68	95	98	179	96	55	103	152	251	356	172
1905 4	56	97	150	154	337	198	56	107	254	409	518	176
1906 1	62	93	153	155	262	124	60	110	183	340	452	186
1906 2	33	79	110	112	195	98	65	116	162	275	393	193
1906 3	35	78	111	113	180	83	67	108	150	264	374	189
1906 4	50	85	131	134	357	238	67	111	305	441	554	192
1907 1	44	89	131	133	307	189	66	113	255	389	505	193
1907 2	41	83	122	124	207	100	72	121	172	297	421	208
1907 3	40	76	114	116	171	74	68	122	142	259	384	207
1907 4	71	83	151	154	375	239	73	115	312	467	586	206

YEAR Q		201	203	205	207	209	212	213	215	217	218	220	222
1908	1	54	95	148	150	310	177	66	112	243	394	509	193
1908	2	26	69	93	95	159	81	64	111	146	242	356	191
1908	3	43	64	105	107	170	81	55	101	135	244	347	172
1908	4	47	89	132	136	340	223	57	97	279	417	516	170
1909	1	30	80	108	110	236	142	55	107	196	307	416	176
1909	2	18	62	79	80	154	91	69	114	161	242	359	199
1909	3	29	58	84	86	169	101	67	109	167	255	366	193
1909	4	41	78	113	119	351	254	67	115	321	442	560	203
1910	1	26	63	86	89	195	126	67	119	193	283	404	205
1910	2	17	55	70	71	153	102	69	133	171	243	380	221
1910	3	21	58	76	78	180	120	77	131	196	276	409	225
1910	4	31	73	99	104	399	315	80	131	396	501	636	231
1911	1	33	70	101	103	282	197	77	147	274	378	527	241
1911	2	23	73	94	96	167	92	88	163	180	277	442	271
1911	3	31	67	96	99	198	124	86	149	210	309	460	258
1911	4	30	92	117	122	355	260	89	155	349	473	630	269
1912	1	30	86	113	115	327	234	87	161	321	438	599	269
1912	2	13	65	76	78	166	109	104	187	213	292	481	311
1912	3	35	62	94	97	185	117	110	181	227	325	508	318
1912	4	67	86	147	153	459	335	99	184	434	588	774	310
1913	1	51	89	138	141	273	159	107	189	266	409	599	322
1913	2	34	73	105	107	201	125	111	203	236	345	547	343
1913	3	56	69	122	125	238	146	104	181	251	377	559	316
1913	4	31	86	110	117	428	341	97	186	438	557	743	311
1914	1	25	73	94	98	271	198	96	164	293	393	557	283
1914	2	28	58	84	87	171	109	102	172	210	299	471	296
1914	3	98	63	159	161	190	54	71	124	125	288	412	218
1914	4	124	111	229	235	366	148	90	156	237	474	631	261
1915	1	160	143	298	302	527	235	103	207	338	642	850	319
1915	2	124	132	251	256	384	149	130	284	279	537	823	433
1915	3	85	122	202	207	309	128	143	334	270	479	816	501
1915	4	92	148	231	240	388	174	156	428	330	571	1003	609

YEAR	Q	201	203	205	207	209	212	213	215	217	218	220	222
1916	1	106	155	255	261	405	165	195	506	360	623	1128	720
1916	2	95	162	253	257	399	167	253	646	419	679	1324	921
1916	3	91	145	230	236	400	193	290	735	483	721	1455	1051
1916	4	126	166	282	292	552	289	303	631	592	887	1516	959
1917	1	133	190	316	323	482	189	355	748	544	871	1620	1130
1917	2	173	226	394	398	514	151	384	700	535	939	1636	1115
1917	3	80	171	247	251	429	217	297	530	514	768	1304	864
1917	4	109	220	318	330	555	274	391	621	665	1000	1609	1056
1918	1	83	324	396	407	603	230	301	476	531	944	1418	804
1918	2	87	442	519	529	686	201	288	488	489	1026	1508	813
1918	3	167	326	487	493	687	240	287	543	527	1030	1562	867
1918	4	198	315	505	512	773	300	246	501	545	1064	1561	779
1919	1	126	486	596	613	924	346	248	568	594	1217	1778	840
1919	2	215	655	857	870	1197	355	273	679	628	1507	2181	971
1919	3	156	430	571	586	895	349	293	546	642	1237	1773	869
1919	4	152	397	526	549	1074	569	263	629	832	1399	2018	918
1920	1	111	384	471	496	1077	640	295	699	935	1443	2143	1040
1920	2	163	321	474	485	808	414	305	806	719	1215	2015	1191
1920	3	311	180	485	491	681	344	248	722	592	1093	1805	1114
1920	4	300	241	530	541	875	475	238	857	713	1262	2117	1226
1921	1	185	204	383	389	592	265	161	662	426	823	1481	876
1921	2	168	153	318	321	458	205	86	367	291	616	983	518
1921	3	227	190	413	417	579	213	89	275	303	723	998	411
1921	4	95	128	217	223	483	301	107	284	407	636	917	426
1922	1	94	145	234	238	401	204	114	284	318	563	844	433
1922	2	107	151	253	258	451	218	119	342	337	602	941	477
1922	3	159	136	290	295	445	177	107	319	284	586	900	446
1922	4	101	146	242	247	585	395	105	328	500	753	1080	484
1923	1	71	154	219	225	435	262	130	347	392	622	966	523
1923	2	65	139	200	204	333	196	149	388	345	556	940	597
1923	3	71	124	191	195	393	260	142	375	402	604	975	571
1923	4	52	157	202	209	658	496	148	354	643	858	1209	542

TABLE A-29

QUARTERLY VALUES,
SELECTED MAJOR IMPORT CLASSES
(MILLIONS OF DOLLARS)

YEAR	Q	201	203	205	207	209	212	213	215	216	220	221	223
1879	1	20	18	37	38	52	18	12	30	68	37	111	52
1879	2	20	31	50	51	65	18	16	35	86	24	116	43
1879	3	22	18	38	39	53	19	19	38	78	43	129	66
1879	4	41	16	55	56	81	31	29	60	117	32	158	65
1880	1	24	25	49	50	80	35	33	68	118	56	182	92
1880	2	21	45	65	66	94	35	43	78	145	46	200	95
1880	3	22	23	44	46	61	22	30	52	98	59	167	94
1880	4	36	17	51	53	74	27	24	51	104	35	149	64
1881	1	23	25	47	48	68	24	22	47	95	49	154	75
1881	2	25	46	70	72	92	27	27	55	127	37	174	70
1881	3	22	22	42	44	62	25	31	56	101	58	170	94
1881	4	41	19	58	60	83	30	29	60	120	43	173	77
1882	1	27	29	54	55	79	30	30	60	116	61	184	97
1882	2	28	52	79	80	105	33	34	66	147	43	197	84
1882	3	27	30	55	57	77	29	35	64	122	67	195	109
1882	4	34	22	54	56	83	34	31	65	122	47	176	84
1883	1	23	25	47	49	74	31	28	59	109	59	174	92
1883	2	22	47	68	69	94	31	29	60	130	42	178	76
1883	3	20	29	46	49	65	24	31	55	105	54	167	92
1883	4	36	24	58	61	83	30	28	59	120	41	168	76
1884	1	24	32	54	56	81	32	23	55	111	55	170	84
1884	2	24	40	63	64	87	30	28	58	123	37	162	70
1884	3	20	22	40	42	62	27	27	54	97	57	157	90
1884	4	34	15	47	49	69	28	23	51	101	34	139	64
1885	1	21	24	43	44	65	26	18	44	90	44	137	67
1885	2	22	36	57	58	79	27	24	51	110	30	144	59
1885	3	20	23	41	43	63	27	25	52	96	49	150	80
1885	4	33	19	50	52	81	37	25	62	115	38	157	69

YEAR Q	201	203	205	207	209	212	213	215	216	220	221	223
1886 1	22	27	48	49	78	35	25	60	110	51	164	80
1886 2	21	37	57	58	83	31	30	62	121	39	164	75
1886 3	22	28	48	50	73	31	29	59	110	55	170	89
1886 4	31	17	46	48	80	39	28	68	117	42	165	76
1887 1	28	22	49	50	76	31	29	61	112	57	174	90
1887 2	31	37	67	68	96	35	36	70	139	39	183	80
1887 3	26	20	44	46	72	34	34	68	114	59	178	99
1887 4	35	18	50	53	83	39	29	67	121	46	173	81
1888 1	29	27	55	56	87	38	28	65	123	59	188	92
1888 2	31	38	67	69	97	36	31	67	136	42	184	79
1888 3	25	25	48	50	70	29	29	58	108	58	172	94
1888 4	38	22	58	60	93	41	28	69	130	45	181	79
1889 1	30	25	53	55	91	44	31	75	131	60	197	97
1889 2	33	45	77	78	109	38	32	70	149	40	195	78
1889 3	25	37	59	61	87	34	31	65	127	58	191	95
1889 4	35	22	55	58	93	44	30	75	134	48	188	85
1890 1	29	30	57	59	91	39	29	67	127	61	194	95
1890 2	39	41	78	80	115	43	35	78	159	52	217	94
1890 3	31	30	59	62	94	43	38	80	143	63	215	109
1890 4	38	27	62	65	95	40	34	74	140	48	197	90
1891 1	32	36	66	68	105	46	34	79	148	54	206	95
1891 2	39	61	99	100	131	40	44	84	185	37	227	89
1891 3	29	36	64	65	92	36	31	67	133	52	195	91
1891 4	39	34	70	73	107	45	28	73	147	44	201	81
1892 1	34	33	66	67	103	44	29	73	141	56	215	92
1892 2	34	40	72	74	108	43	36	79	153	40	217	83
1892 3	30	36	64	66	95	40	34	73	140	57	204	100
1892 4	36	30	63	66	106	51	34	85	152	47	205	90

YEAR	C	201	203	205	207	209	212	213	215	216	220	221	223
1893	1	37	38	73	75	121	55	36	91	167	63	235	107
1893	2	35	45	78	79	114	46	43	89	169	45	223	98
1893	3	28	33	59	61	79	29	24	53	114	49	168	82
1893	4	35	36	67	71	87	26	19	45	116	28	151	55
1894	1	37	38	74	75	100	31	19	51	127	35	165	60
1894	2	33	45	76	77	102	34	25	59	137	26	167	59
1894	3	34	31	63	65	88	32	25	57	122	40	168	73
1894	4	33	20	49	53	89	46	28	73	127	42	173	76
1895	1	36	21	56	57	94	44	26	70	128	63	195	94
1895	2	36	32	66	68	107	48	29	77	145	46	196	82
1895	3	32	22	50	54	96	53	33	86	140	63	209	104
1895	4	37	22	55	59	102	54	28	82	142	53	201	91
1896	1	31	30	57	60	99	47	25	72	133	59	198	91
1896	2	29	41	66	70	93	33	25	59	130	37	172	72
1896	3	27	27	51	54	67	22	23	45	100	47	152	78
1896	4	34	23	53	56	87	39	22	61	118	37	159	65
1897	1	33	25	55	58	103	53	22	74	133	50	187	78
1897	2	33	53	81	86	145	71	32	103	190	70	266	112
1897	3	23	14	34	37	66	38	23	61	99	32	136	63
1897	4	31	17	44	48	85	46	24	70	118	31	154	62
1898	1	23	23	44	46	87	48	23	72	118	44	165	73
1898	2	26	32	56	57	94	45	24	69	126	31	161	63
1898	3	19	23	40	42	73	39	25	64	107	38	149	71
1898	4	24	27	48	51	85	44	23	67	119	37	160	68
1899	1	28	31	57	59	109	59	26	85	144	44	191	78
1899	2	27	43	67	70	113	55	33	88	158	35	197	78
1899	3	21	36	55	57	98	53	38	91	149	44	197	93
1899	4	24	31	51	56	111	70	38	108	164	45	213	95

YEAR Q	201	203	205	207	209	212	213	215	216	220	221	223
1900 1	29	28	54	57	124	79	38	117	174	52	231	101
1900 2	22	38	58	60	110	64	38	102	162	41	208	92
1900 3	22	28	47	50	83	47	35	82	133	48	185	95
1900 4	32	31	59	63	103	56	35	91	155	45	205	93
1901 1	25	31	53	56	104	63	34	97	154	49	210	98
1901 2	29	35	61	64	120	74	40	114	179	42	224	98
1901 3	27	26	49	53	96	61	40	101	155	52	213	109
1901 4	33	26	54	59	112	73	42	115	174	53	234	112
1902 1	30	20	47	50	114	82	38	120	170	56	232	110
1902 2	28	24	49	52	106	71	46	117	170	49	225	112
1902 3	30	30	57	60	108	63	53	116	177	62	246	128
1902 4	31	30	55	61	126	84	55	139	202	59	267	130
1903 1	27	24	49	52	123	91	50	142	194	63	264	132
1903 2	27	32	56	59	117	75	56	131	191	51	249	123
1903 3	30	25	52	55	107	68	49	117	173	63	246	128
1903 4	35	25	55	60	114	70	45	115	175	56	237	115
1904 1	38	32	66	70	142	88	43	130	201	59	263	115
1904 2	28	37	61	65	129	81	46	127	193	48	245	109
1904 3	34	32	62	67	119	70	45	115	182	56	243	116
1904 4	48	31	73	79	155	94	49	144	224	56	285	121
1905 1	35	46	78	81	176	113	50	163	245	63	312	128
1905 2	28	36	61	64	145	101	53	154	219	54	278	124
1905 3	28	38	61	65	130	83	58	142	208	68	282	143
1905 4	45	34	73	80	154	95	57	152	233	68	307	143
1906 1	32	31	59	63	159	116	62	178	242	77	324	158
1906 2	28	39	63	67	149	104	68	172	240	66	313	154
1906 3	29	33	58	62	132	90	69	159	223	81	311	168
1906 4	46	37	77	84	178	118	79	197	282	83	372	182
1907 1	36	41	72	77	190	136	78	213	291	85	383	184
1907 2	38	48	81	86	179	118	77	195	281	79	369	179
1907 3	38	33	65	70	149	103	78	181	252	93	357	193
1907 4	41	32	67	73	145	94	56	150	225	83	315	158

YEAR	Q	201	203	205	207	209	212	213	215	216	220	221	223
1908	1	31	34	61	65	128	81	39	120	186	68	259	124
1908	2	35	49	80	84	147	79	42	122	207	51	264	108
1908	3	34	35	64	69	138	86	51	138	207	53	276	130
1908	4	42	34	70	76	162	109	62	171	248	64	318	147
1909	1	47	40	83	88	194	127	63	191	279	70	355	153
1909	2	41	57	92	97	196	124	65	189	288	68	363	157
1909	3	32	36	62	67	163	121	71	191	260	81	351	172
1909	4	50	33	76	83	203	149	80	229	314	85	407	182
1910	1	33	52	80	85	226	168	83	251	338	82	427	187
1910	2	29	60	84	89	188	125	78	203	294	68	373	168
1910	3	41	43	78	84	169	114	78	192	277	81	373	182
1910	4	53	33	78	85	192	131	81	212	299	84	391	178
1911	1	42	43	79	85	198	138	84	222	308	76	391	177
1911	2	44	52	91	96	196	126	75	200	297	67	372	162
1911	3	43	42	80	85	174	117	80	197	284	77	369	179
1911	4	64	40	96	104	199	122	76	198	304	87	400	174
1912	1	57	56	108	113	243	155	76	231	345	82	435	171
1912	2	66	58	119	123	258	165	83	248	373	72	449	178
1912	3	52	50	96	101	218	149	88	237	340	101	449	202
1912	4	68	41	100	108	238	166	95	261	371	108	485	212
1913	1	56	51	102	107	246	173	93	266	374	88	468	206
1913	2	46	48	89	94	203	145	90	235	331	75	411	197
1913	3	48	50	92	98	199	138	93	231	331	107	449	223
1913	4	81	42	114	123	242	152	79	231	355	104	465	202
1914	1	68	53	115	121	260	168	81	250	371	105	485	207
1914	2	62	73	129	135	284	178	83	261	397	91	496	199
1914	3	55	76	124	131	239	134	67	201	333	88	429	176
1914	4	62	46	100	108	199	118	62	180	290	83	379	163
1915	1	59	63	117	122	246	145	59	204	327	72	405	148
1915	2	58	91	145	149	302	179	66	245	395	60	461	148
1915	3	58	63	115	121	254	167	78	245	367	62	436	169
1915	4	75	46	114	122	282	200	75	275	398	70	477	176

YEAR Q	201	203	205	207	209	212	213	215	216	220	221	223
1916 1	59	78	131	137	369	280	100	380	518	72	592	212
1916 2	68	114	175	181	422	291	132	423	606	81	693	257
1916 3	58	72	123	130	295	217	112	329	460	81	546	239
1916 4	82	65	137	146	317	214	110	324	473	84	560	229
1917 1	88	84	164	172	438	311	131	443	616	89	712	256
1917 2	110	112	215	222	535	364	155	519	742	93	841	292
1917 3	81	98	169	179	449	315	143	458	639	83	730	269
1917 4	102	48	142	150	392	285	135	420	572	91	670	264
1918 1	88	94	174	182	420	281	127	408	591	87	684	253
1918 2	92	133	220	225	547	367	155	522	750	107	862	303
1918 3	84	88	165	172	435	306	171	477	651	121	777	333
1918 4	74	75	140	149	398	281	158	439	590	113	709	299
1919 1	96	122	211	219	439	267	125	392	614	92	716	259
1919 2	120	168	283	288	652	412	95	507	798	89	895	227
1919 3	166	144	301	310	748	490	154	644	957	121	1086	319
1919 4	171	123	280	295	759	528	206	734	1033	161	1207	416
1920 1	158	249	397	406	961	635	227	861	1271	175	1465	470
1920 2	153	366	511	519	936	502	223	725	1247	200	1479	498
1920 3	139	429	557	568	862	378	221	599	1171	217	1414	511
1920 4	148	178	315	326	482	237	173	410	741	163	920	403
1921 1	88	117	198	205	360	220	99	319	527	133	675	291
1921 2	82	104	181	187	354	214	91	306	493	135	645	269
1921 3	56	59	106	115	270	196	87	283	399	133	552	255
1921 4	91	69	150	160	335	225	98	323	485	134	636	273
1922 1	84	82	159	166	368	257	111	367	534	140	689	297
1922 2	88	98	179	186	384	254	131	385	572	146	730	328
1922 3	71	103	165	174	390	293	143	437	613	141	763	356
1922 4	105	80	176	185	486	381	178	558	746	168	931	411
1923 1	101	134	230	235	578	415	194	609	846	172	1031	430
1923 2	92	166	253	259	601	405	202	607	868	179	1057	438
1923 3	71	100	164	172	390	282	167	450	623	181	817	404
1923 4	113	104	207	216	451	301	164	465	684	192	888	407

TABLE A–30

COMPOSITION OF MAJOR CLASSES

Major Class	Major, Intermediate, and Minor Class Composition
A. EXPORTS	
201[a] Crude foodstuffs, excluding tobacco	101[b]–102
202 Crude foodstuffs, including tobacco	101[b] and 103
203[a] Manufactured foodstuffs, excluding tobacco	108 and 111[b]
204 Manufactured foodstuffs, including tobacco	108 and 112
205[a] Agricultural foodstuffs, excluding tobacco	104 and 113
206 Agricultural foodstuffs, including tobacco	105 and 113
207[a] Foodstuffs, excluding tobacco and products	201 and 203
208 Foodstuffs, including tobacco and products	202 and 204
209[a] Agricultural products	206, 132, and 041
210 Products of animal or vegetable origin, excluding printed matter and rubber products	208, 135, and 041
211 Crude materials, excluding tobacco	129 and 144
212[a] Crude materials, including tobacco	130 and 144
213[a] Semimanufactured products	*1899–1923:* 131 and 145
	1895–98: 131, 058, 060, 141, 063[c], and 074[c]
	1882–94: 131, 060, 141, 063[c], and 074[c]
	1879–81: 131, 141, 063[c], and 074[c]
214 Manufactured products, excluding tobacco manufactures	041, 137, and 147
215[a] Manufactured products, including tobacco manufactures	214 and 026
216 Crude materials and semimanufactures, excluding tobacco	211 and 213
217[a] Crude materials and semimanufactures, including tobacco	212–213
218[a] Crude materials, semimanufactures and foods, including tobacco and products	208 and 216
219 Total exports, excluding "all other articles, n.e.s."	214 and 218
220[a] Grand total	219 and "all other articles n.e.s."
221 Total products other than those of animal or vegetable origin	144–145, and 147
222[a] Total nonagricultural products	002, 013, 020, 024, 137, 134, and 221

(continued)

TABLE A-30 (concluded)

Major Class	Major, Intermediate, and Minor Class Composition

B. IMPORTS

201ᵃ Crude foodstuffs, excluding tobacco — 101ᵈ and 104
202 Crude foodstuffs, including tobacco — 101ᵈ and 105
203ᵃ Manufactured foodstuffs, excluding tobacco — 108 and 111ᵈ
204 Manufactured foodstuffs, including tobacco — 108 and 112
205ᵃ Agricultural foodstuffs, excluding tobacco — 106 and 113
206 Agricultural foodstuffs, including tobacco — 107 and 113
207ᵃ Foodstuffs, excluding tobacco and products — 201 and 203
208 Foodstuffs, including tobacco and products — 202 and 204
209ᵃ Agricultural products — 206, 131, and 044
210 Products of animal or vegetable origin — 208, 141, 139, and 044
211 Crude materials, excluding tobacco — 136 and 148
212ᵃ Crude materials, including tobacco — 211 and 024
213ᵃ Semimanufactured products — *1879–1914:* 033, 039, 138, and 149
1915–23: 033, 039, 042, 138, and 149
214 Crude materials and semimanufactured products — 211 and 213
215ᵃ Crude materials, including tobacco; and semimanufactured products — 214 and 024
216ᵃ Crude materials, semimanufactured products, and foods, including tobacco and products — 208 and 214
217 Manufactured products, excluding tobacco — *1914–23:* 044, 071 (excluding *1915–16*), 076, 087, 091 (excluding *1914–15*), 139, 082, 084, 079ᶜ, 083ᶜ, 088ᶜ, 071ᶜ (*1915–16* only)
1889–1913: 044, 071 (*1913* only), 076, 087, 139, 147, 088ᶜ
1879–88: 044, 076, 139, 147, 087ᶜ, 088ᶜ
218 Manufactured products, including tobacco — 217 and 025
219 Total, excluding "all other articles n.e.s." and art works — 216–217
220ᵃ Manufactured products, including tobacco products and art works — 218 and 089ᶜ
221ᵃ Grand total — 219 and "all other articles, n.e.s." and art works
222 Total products of mineral origin — 148–150, 091 (*1916–23* only)
223ᵃ Total nonagricultural products — 002, 013, 020 (excluding *1913–15*), 022, 139, 140 and 222

ᵃ Basic tables include annual Fisher price and quantity indexes and annual values. For classes noted, additional data are presented: annual Paasche and Laspeyres price indexes, quarterly Fisher price and quantity indexes, and quarterly values.

ᵇ See notes for Export Classes 101 and 111, Appendix B.

ᶜ These are uncovered classes.

ᵈ See notes for Import Classes 101 and 111, Appendix B.

Appendix B

Indexes and Values for Intermediate Classes, 1879–1923

THIS appendix presents annual price and quantity indexes and values for selected intermediate classes. We list in Tables B-7 and B-8 the composition of all intermediate classes; the reader must refer to Appendix C for the commodity detail. In making up the intermediate classes, some uncovered minor classes were deflated by price indexes for specific covered classes rather than by the average of all covered minor classes within the intermediate class. We made the selection of these specific deflators by a comparison of the behavior of the price indexes during periods for which there was an overlap. For example, Export Class 037 was an uncovered class for 1879-88 and 1913-23. We found that during the period 1889-1912, when prices were available, they followed quite well the fluctuations of the index for Export Class 038. We therefore used the price indexes for 038 to deflate 037 during the 1879-88 and 1913-23 periods.

APPENDIX B

TABLE B-1

ANNUAL FISHER PRICE INDEXES,
SELECTED INTERMEDIATE EXPORT CLASSES
(1913=100)

YEAR	104	106	107	108	113	114	120	121	122	125	128
1879	93.0	56.4	58.0	62.4	74.0	82.5	83.6	107.0	61.4	79.5	65.3
1880	95.6	62.0	67.1	72.2	83.3	92.0	93.8	122.8	66.5	88.5	72.3
1881	102.2	73.5	79.4	85.2	94.0	86.0	90.4	115.8	69.4	86.0	76.0
1882	108.5	86.0	89.8	95.7	103.1	86.3	90.5	121.4	71.2	87.3	76.4
1883	103.5	81.9	82.8	89.3	95.7	85.3	84.2	114.0	72.0	80.9	74.3
1884	91.0	79.3	77.8	84.3	88.3	88.4	85.2	106.3	68.0	82.6	70.1
1885	85.0	66.9	66.2	72.2	77.0	87.6	82.7	95.7	65.1	79.8	68.9
1886	80.0	61.7	61.3	67.4	72.2	81.7	76.7	94.2	64.8	74.0	67.1
1887	81.3	64.6	65.3	67.2	72.5	81.0	77.1	97.0	68.9	69.1	69.1
1888	85.7	69.3	70.6	72.6	80.4	72.6	80.0	103.8	70.7	76.6	68.6
1889	75.1	62.1	63.4	65.4	75.8	68.8	80.4	108.1	69.6	76.4	68.1
1890	76.4	59.4	60.3	62.1	72.6	69.1	81.0	104.0	68.7	77.1	68.1
1891	99.7	61.4	62.4	64.1	76.7	70.4	74.8	95.4	68.0	72.2	67.2
1892	86.3	64.0	65.5	67.3	85.1	71.6	67.1	90.7	65.0	66.2	64.4
1893	77.4	77.2	80.0	81.7	73.5	67.7	67.1	93.1	64.1	65.2	63.1
1894	69.1	67.6	69.1	70.7	68.5	64.3	53.5	84.9	63.4	52.8	62.1
1895	69.1	65.7	64.8	71.8	62.5	79.3	55.6	78.9	58.5	54.4	63.9
1896	63.3	58.6	55.8	57.4	65.9	74.5	61.9	81.2	58.0	59.0	62.6
1897	63.3	57.9	54.0	55.4	67.0	72.9	52.7	73.7	58.8	51.9	62.7
1898	76.5	60.7	57.5	59.1	67.0	77.4	45.2	70.0	58.8	46.2	62.8
1899	73.9	61.6	59.0	60.7	65.9	78.6	51.8	72.8	64.4	52.5	68.6
1900	73.8	66.5	64.7	66.5	70.1	79.8	72.4	85.7	70.4	71.0	72.6
1901	77.3	71.2	72.3	77.2	75.4	75.6	66.5	79.5	69.8	66.0	69.0
1902	81.9	80.1	83.0	84.2	81.3	79.7	66.6	80.6	75.1	67.4	75.2
1903	81.2	79.0	80.4	81.4	81.1	83.0	80.6	81.3	78.7	80.3	80.4
1904	80.1	75.0	71.0	71.2	77.1	82.9	84.9	88.3	77.4	83.8	82.1
1905	82.4	72.6	75.9	71.8	75.2	85.9	74.9	89.7	77.2	74.2	85.4
1906	81.5	76.6	82.4	76.7	80.2	89.6	84.1	95.0	91.5	83.3	95.6
1907	94.9	81.7	81.4	82.9	86.1	96.3	88.0	103.3	97.1	87.1	100.7
1908	99.7	79.6	88.3	89.2	87.4	88.7	79.0	90.6	92.1	78.7	91.7
1909	104.1	82.1	88.3	89.2	93.2	93.2	91.9	86.6	88.9	91.5	92.7
1910	98.5	89.8	104.0	104.5	107.2	92.3	112.4	95.7	90.8	110.8	92.8
1911	97.7	89.9	88.3	89.6	92.6	96.3	91.1	94.3	91.6	91.0	101.0
1912	104.0	91.3	93.5	94.4	96.5	99.4	87.7	92.8	94.7	88.0	100.2
1913	100.0	100.0	100.0	100.0	100.0	100.0	100.0	100.0	100.0	100.0	100.0
1914	114.3	102.3	99.8	100.4	102.9	102.5	84.1	101.1	93.8	86.1	107.3
1915	133.6	98.3	96.2	97.2	106.1	136.0	78.9	110.4	93.8	85.2	125.6
1916	144.0	109.7	109.8	110.4	118.4	180.1	119.1	129.7	98.2	119.8	158.4
1917	214.7	154.0	156.5	157.1	171.0	237.2	180.4	178.8	120.2	178.3	188.6
1918	243.3	199.8	201.7	201.7	238.4	259.7	252.2	247.0	166.7	242.5	243.2
1919	241.4	232.2	233.7	233.6	217.4		269.7	264.1	198.7	260.6	276.9
1920	267.9	188.4	191.5	193.2			296.4	323.6	265.5	294.0	
1921	155.3	134.9	126.0	128.1	135.2	143.4	134.3	182.3	180.2	149.4	151.3
1922	127.0	127.8	117.0	118.4	120.1	128.7	171.6	182.5	158.4	176.5	146.2
1923	128.7	108.8	112.4	115.0	122.0	131.3	229.6	201.7	183.3	227.4	163.0

227

147	146	145	144	143	142	141	140	139	136	133	YEAR
125.6	121.6	94.4	90.3	121.6		86.6	123.8	131.4	76.9	79.6	1879
139.6	133.8	103.0	107.1	133.8		89.6	139.7	146.6	85.5	88.7	1880
131.0	121.4	106.1	104.9	121.4		92.1	134.6	140.5	83.8	86.3	1881
127.6	127.5	107.5	106.2	127.5		93.9	126.3	131.1	85.1	87.5	1882
127.2	124.9	106.9	102.6	124.9		93.8	127.4	132.5	79.5	81.2	1883
129.6	128.4	103.1	97.5	128.4		86.0	128.1	134.3	80.4	82.9	1884
123.6	119.0	97.4	89.2	118.0		73.6	124.7	131.2	77.7	80.0	1885
115.2	112.7	93.1	83.8	112.7		70.0	114.6	120.0	72.8	74.1	1886
110.5	110.8	93.2	84.4	110.8		70.9	109.3	113.5	72.6	73.8	1887
115.0	112.5	104.7	102.0	112.5		100.4	116.0	120.5	75.1	76.8	1888
109.2	111.4	92.8	91.8	111.4		77.7	108.7	112.4	74.9	76.6	1889
106.9	110.1	95.7	96.3	110.1		85.0	104.7	107.0	75.4	77.2	1890
102.7	108.4	94.3	97.0	108.4		83.5	99.7	100.4	71.5	72.3	1891
92.7	102.0	93.2	90.3	100.4		78.5	87.7	86.1	65.8	66.3	1892
86.1	100.4	75.9	83.7	100.4		68.5	75.3	71.8	64.8	65.4	1893
81.2	95.4	67.7	85.7	95.4		61.7	70.1	67.3	54.4	53.1	1894
95.0	99.6	74.5	85.9	99.6		67.3	89.9	92.6	55.8	54.7	1895
102.4	110.8	75.6	87.5	110.8		71.8	92.2	94.5	59.2	59.0	1896
92.3	98.8	75.0	85.7	98.8		72.1	84.3	84.9	53.4	51.9	1897
85.2	91.6	77.0	82.8	91.6		73.9	76.9	76.4	48.8	46.3	1898
94.4	95.6	102.2	86.7	95.6	107.5	102.9	92.2	95.6	55.1	52.7	1899
102.6	103.4	105.4	92.7	101.4	106.0	103.7	101.1	106.0	70.6	71.1	1900
98.2	101.4	105.6	93.1	101.4	104.2	103.7	95.0	95.7	66.1	66.2	1901
97.8	102.1	90.2	95.3	102.1	105.1	85.5	94.7	91.9	68.3	67.8	1902
103.5	103.9	94.2	99.5	101.6	104.6	90.0	105.5	105.8	79.6	80.3	1903
102.3	101.9	89.5	99.7	100.3	103.3	86.2	106.2	107.3	82.4	83.6	1904
96.8	100.3	101.0	97.1	100.3	101.0	99.2	93.3	90.9	75.3	74.1	1905
99.2	103.3	116.0	99.2	107.5	103.5	117.4	93.9	92.0	84.5	83.3	1906
107.3	107.1	118.3	100.8	107.1	104.9	119.9	97.4	96.8	88.6	87.2	1907
103.1	107.1	93.1	97.6	107.1	105.5	91.4	97.9	97.6	80.2	78.8	1908
100.1	107.0	89.7	95.6	105.1	105.1	86.6	93.1	91.3	91.2	91.5	1909
100.3	107.0	88.6	94.6	107.0	107.4	88.1	88.3	85.1	108.0	110.8	1910
95.2	102.0	87.2	95.0	102.0	103.4	86.5	85.7	80.7	92.5	91.3	1911
93.0	101.2	100.5	98.6	101.2	107.9	101.1	92.4	89.1	90.4	88.2	1912
100.0	100.0	100.0	100.0	100.0	100.0	100.0	100.0	100.0	100.0	100.0	1913
94.0	94.4	95.5	96.3	94.7	96.1	92.7	95.1	92.8	89.1	86.5	1914
101.3	98.7	112.2	93.0	96.6	96.7	107.6	92.8	89.5	88.5	85.8	1915
131.4	119.1	135.8	97.6	108.3	99.9	160.1	113.1	117.0	120.1	120.3	1916
147.5	135.8	201.9	126.8	129.2	111.1	202.8	141.1	143.5	172.6	178.8	1917
163.6	151.6	197.7	141.5	149.2	131.4	187.8	177.9	187.4	228.1	242.4	1918
164.7	159.2	172.0	163.2	159.2	144.5	156.0	188.7	189.9	256.1	262.2	1919
182.3	170.6	179.3	254.2	170.9	155.7	152.2	245.4	226.3	285.6	292.3	1920
161.0	154.0	138.1	190.7	155.5	142.1	114.0	198.2	186.4	146.4	148.4	1921
132.8	127.7	116.4	186.7	128.5	121.7	101.1	168.6	147.3	167.8	175.0	1922
129.1	132.0	125.4	174.2	132.4	120.5	117.4	147.9	125.3	208.9	224.9	1923

ANNUAL FISHER PRICE INDEXES,
SELECTED INTERMEDIATE IMPORT CLASSES
(1913=100)

YEAR	102	103	104	106	108	109	110	111	113	114	115	118
1879	93.6	124.7	119.2	115.7	49.5	93.1	157.0	152.7	152.8		96.5	86.4
1880	98.0	136.1	129.0	124.7	55.1	92.8	189.2	183.8	180.0		108.5	96.7
1881	114.9	112.6	116.2	113.7	57.2	88.0	187.3	182.0	182.1		105.9	94.2
1882	116.5	95.9	105.9	106.2	68.0	79.3	187.9	182.5	182.4		109.2	112.7
1883	107.5	86.1	94.6	95.5	65.1	79.3	171.1	166.5	166.5		105.7	97.8
1884	103.6	91.0	97.1	96.3	69.1	78.8	136.0	131.0	130.8		107.0	71.3
1885	104.5	82.3	90.2	89.1	65.0	77.5	120.0	117.6	117.3		103.2	63.7
1886	95.7	83.4	89.0	88.0	65.1	73.6	122.9	120.5	119.9		95.8	68.6
1887	103.0	125.0	122.7	120.1	68.4	68.7	110.6	108.6	108.2		85.7	70.7
1888	99.1	111.3	111.4	109.2	80.7	68.5	124.8	122.3	121.8		76.0	64.5
1889	84.7	123.3	115.7	113.3	81.3	69.5	150.9	147.5	146.8	62.8	71.6	62.8
1890	98.3	135.6	127.3	124.6	80.9	79.0	129.0	126.3	125.9	59.5	63.8	74.7
1891	107.3	130.3	125.9	123.4	80.8	78.7	131.5	129.3	128.5	57.2	60.1	74.7
1892	104.5	134.0	116.4	114.2	77.8	73.0	127.7	125.7	124.6	59.1	56.0	68.0
1893	93.1	134.7	126.9	124.6	75.6	67.4	139.5	137.1	135.9	64.7	54.0	74.7
1894	75.2	126.6	117.9	115.5	75.6	62.3	114.5	113.0	111.9	67.8	55.5	70.7
1895	71.7	122.5	115.6	112.6	82.9	65.5	86.6	88.0	87.1	67.7	60.6	69.1
1896	72.7	109.0	102.7	100.3	77.1	72.8	105.6	104.3	103.1	74.7	63.8	69.3
1897	78.2	85.4	84.3	82.3	75.2	74.8	94.2	93.2	92.3	67.7	64.2	75.9
1898	77.6	68.4	69.5	68.7	79.7	74.8	103.1	102.2	101.0	74.7	71.9	85.8
1899	76.0	65.6	66.8	66.4	84.2	73.3	110.2	109.4	107.7	75.6	73.4	90.7
1900	77.1	75.3	73.8	70.4	81.1	81.2	111.2	109.2	107.4	80.1	77.5	86.4
1901	73.1	65.6	66.6	66.1	83.1	82.1	99.8	98.0	98.5	81.6	79.2	79.8
1902	72.6	67.2	68.0	67.9	87.0	73.1	79.5	79.4	86.0	81.9	79.6	75.4
1903	75.3	66.6	67.7	67.3	87.6	75.8	87.5	88.0	87.4	84.2	79.8	90.5
1904	71.7	73.2	73.5	73.0	87.6	76.2	94.5	94.7	93.6	86.9	82.1	99.4
1905	81.5	75.5	74.9	74.5	91.4	90.3	117.9	116.9	116.3	92.4	85.1	107.4
1906	90.2	75.4	76.4	75.9	95.4	97.4	97.1	97.3	96.9	96.3	92.6	107.8
1907	78.9	76.0	78.6	78.1	100.5	92.6	102.2	102.1	101.8	80.4	97.4	107.2
1908	78.2	71.4	72.8	72.6	94.0	89.7	108.6	107.9	107.5	84.9	84.7	90.8
1909	87.3	68.8	70.6	71.0	90.3	91.5	107.3	106.8	106.2	88.3	89.0	125.8
1910	91.8	78.7	80.3	80.6	93.1	98.7	119.0	117.7	117.0	86.8	84.7	156.0
1911	96.1	96.2	95.3	94.7	98.8	101.3	112.7	111.9	111.5	91.1	88.7	130.9
1912		107.1	104.8	104.2	104.7		123.1	121.9	121.4		90.4	126.3
1913	100.0	100.0	100.0	100.0	100.0	100.0	100.0	100.0	100.0	100.0	100.0	100.0
1914	95.1	87.8	89.3	90.6	104.4	98.6	110.3	110.1	111.3	103.4	97.7	79.6
1915	99.2	85.8	88.4	89.4	110.2	106.4	151.2	150.5	145.9	104.4	92.7	87.6
1916	116.6	93.1	97.7	98.1	126.6	133.9	184.5	183.0	176.7	120.4	92.8	100.1
1917	161.9	87.9	104.3	105.7	164.5	163.7	205.0	204.2	200.8	172.5	154.1	111.4
1918	170.5	90.0	106.5	109.0	198.1	177.8	217.9	219.0	217.6	158.6	139.9	95.7
1919	181.2	152.2	158.3	158.7	220.0	246.9	262.5	263.8	257.0	240.8	189.5	94.8
1920	205.7	153.7	165.9	165.6	184.0	278.5	541.2	543.1	483.9		219.0	76.8
1921	149.8	87.4	99.7	99.5	152.6	169.1	183.9	184.0	179.9	105.1	90.3	46.0
1922	132.4	104.5	110.2	109.5	144.5	151.5	125.6	126.2	127.8	109.2	95.3	42.8
1923	114.2	108.5	109.7	109.0	146.4	147.7	219.0	220.0	208.2	120.8	106.5	60.6

137	132	131	130	128	127	126	125	124	122	121	120	YFAR
74.0	97.7	98.8	98.1	92.9	101.9	96.8	107.2	101.4	125.2	102.3	77.3	1879
85.7	106.4	107.9	107.2	104.1	104.7	97.8	115.6	101.2	134.5	105.1	82.5	1880
83.2	102.8	103.9	103.5	101.5	102.2	96.5	108.2	102.6	125.7	99.7	82.1	1881
86.9	109.5	111.5	110.2	112.6	103.7	96.7	113.7	102.1	128.4	101.2	88.4	1882
85.6	100.2	102.1	100.7	103.6	100.8	95.8	104.1	99.8	115.1	102.1	85.6	1883
81.4	94.1	94.7	94.2	91.5	94.4	89.5	98.2	96.2	111.1	91.1	77.8	1884
76.0	87.0	87.1	87.0	84.7	88.1	84.5	90.8	92.0	102.7	84.6	68.5	1885
73.7	86.7	86.7	87.0	84.3	86.3	81.9	90.8	90.6	105.2	80.1	65.1	1886
71.4	89.1	89.1	89.5	79.8	90.0	83.1	100.9	91.5	114.9	81.7	77.2	1887
72.6	83.3	82.6	83.6	71.6	86.6	80.2	96.1	89.0	104.0	78.1	82.5	1888
74.8	84.4	83.9	84.8	68.3	89.8	82.2	102.6	89.8	108.0	81.8	92.7	1889
71.0	83.6	82.9	83.8	68.7	88.1	80.2	101.9	88.8	116.4	78.9	79.6	1890
67.5	77.8	77.6	82.1	66.5	84.4	80.3	89.9	86.8	98.2	79.9	76.1	1891
69.2	75.0	74.5	75.0	62.1	83.6	79.5	88.7	87.8	101.4	78.2	68.6	1892
69.3	75.9	75.1	76.0	62.2	84.6	80.5	90.3	90.7	105.1	77.4	68.3	1893
73.4	68.5	66.8	68.4	62.2	75.0	76.6	71.5	84.2	83.0	74.7	53.5	1894
68.0	70.5	69.5	70.6	64.7	77.2	75.6	76.8	86.7	94.4	71.6	48.8	1895
67.6	72.2	71.4	72.3	66.5	74.7	76.2	73.7	86.5	89.6	73.3	51.5	1896
67.6	73.1	71.4	77.4	69.5	74.7	75.2	73.7	85.2	90.6	71.8	47.0	1897
72.6	78.8	77.1	79.2	78.1	75.8	74.7	76.5	83.3	90.6	71.6	55.6	1898
65.4	85.2	83.6	85.8	80.9	82.6	78.4	87.9	91.2	99.0	73.5	70.3	1899
75.8	89.0	88.2	89.3	81.5	89.1	83.1	96.6	91.5	110.0	79.9	85.2	1900
77.7	82.0	81.2	82.1	79.6	83.9	84.3	83.1	88.1	103.1	82.6	75.1	1901
82.1	83.3	83.2	82.4	78.0	85.1	81.8	88.9	91.2	90.4	78.2	86.6	1902
87.3	89.4	89.6	89.7	84.8	88.4	83.7	95.2	90.7	96.4	81.0	87.4	1903
81.4	91.9	92.1	92.3	90.2	89.4	84.4	95.2	90.5	104.4	82.2	93.2	1904
84.2	95.9	96.2	96.6	93.4	92.6	85.7	100.8	91.9	104.9	83.5	94.4	1905
92.2	103.0	102.7	103.7	99.6	97.9	90.2	107.8	97.0	113.9	89.3	97.0	1906
93.7	109.4	108.9	110.2	102.8	105.5	95.6	118.2	93.9	130.5	95.2	99.1	1907
92.8	90.2	88.4	96.9	85.7	90.2	88.1	92.5	93.9	99.2	86.2	81.0	1908
96.7	96.1	95.6	96.7	102.8	86.1	82.9	89.3	92.6	99.2	79.8	73.1	1909
94.6	106.9	107.2	107.8	121.0	87.8	83.0	92.7	92.8	98.3	79.8	82.3	1910
96.7	101.8	101.2	107.8	107.0	90.9	88.0	93.4	96.3	97.1	85.5	82.2	1911
95.4	100.8	100.4	100.8	107.2	93.1	93.9	92.2	98.0	95.5	92.7	86.6	1912
100.0	100.0	100.0	100.0	100.0	100.0	100.0	100.0	100.0	100.0	100.0	100.0	1913
100.4	93.2	92.9	93.0	86.1	97.3	89.6	103.2	84.4	110.0	91.7	87.3	1914
97.0	89.7	89.2	89.5	87.1	91.6	89.1	94.1	86.4	103.1	90.1	75.4	1915
103.4	112.8	112.5	112.6	103.8	120.6	113.6	126.4	108.9	139.7	115.3	97.4	1916
121.5	143.2	142.3	142.7	126.0	155.4	134.8	169.3	119.6	176.7	140.9	163.5	1917
148.5	149.8	149.2	143.3	111.2	199.2	200.2	204.7	151.4	212.7	212.0	202.3	1918
161.3	161.8	160.4	159.8	122.6	210.5	208.7	213.8	197.4	234.1	212.9	181.7	1919
227.4	179.5	178.7	177.5	130.5	241.6	227.5	246.0	206.7	272.0	235.9	181.7	1920
175.3	92.4	88.4	91.0	58.0	138.0	147.3	131.4	137.3	147.4	151.5	103.6	1921
150.0	100.9	98.3	100.3	57.4	155.7	148.7	160.4	142.9	188.4	150.7	101.3	1922
156.9	119.7	117.1	119.0	74.8	166.0	143.0	181.4	138.8	215.1	144.5	106.8	1923

YEAR	134	137	139	140	142	144	145	146	147	148	149	150
1879		94.8	101.1	62.0	87.4			68.3	169.8	95.5	85.8	117.5
1880		104.5	102.3	69.7	95.8			84.7	176.5	85.4	101.8	126.4
1881		99.0	101.0	67.5	92.4			71.6	171.2	77.6	91.6	120.7
1882		105.0	101.4	70.1	97.7			73.1	164.0	98.1	90.8	119.7
1883		97.0	100.4	68.8	91.3			71.6	151.6	95.4	85.7	114.1
1884		91.7	93.8	69.3	87.6			66.5	149.3	96.1	84.5	117.5
1885		84.4	88.7	61.2	80.0			62.3	145.0	90.4	76.2	105.9
1886		84.5	85.9	65.1	81.2			61.9	134.3	86.0	76.0	100.3
1887		85.9	87.2	61.7	81.7			61.2	123.7	85.5	75.1	95.9
1888		80.8	84.2	60.1	77.2			63.2	126.4	91.8	72.9	95.2
1889	80.2	82.7	86.3	66.6	80.1		94.9	60.9	133.3	90.3	74.4	99.8
1890	77.7	81.7	84.1	62.1	78.2		97.1	66.8	126.9	91.3	80.8	100.6
1891	73.3	75.9	83.6	60.6	73.5		118.1	66.4	114.7	104.7	79.2	97.0
1892	75.2	73.3	83.7	59.4	71.2		110.2	61.4	116.2	101.5	77.9	93.2
1893	75.9	74.4	80.5	61.4	72.5		92.2	60.0	113.2	93.2	77.9	89.0
1894	78.8	67.7	79.6	58.6	66.2		74.4	51.1	103.0	81.4	67.9	81.4
1895	71.6	69.8	80.7	60.0	68.0		67.4	47.8	109.4	74.7	65.0	85.0
1896	67.6	71.2	79.2	59.7	69.2		58.5	46.1	110.2	68.8	66.9	84.9
1897	65.2	71.5	78.7	56.3	69.0		62.2	46.9	101.8	70.3	65.9	81.6
1898	65.1	76.5		57.2	73.5		63.5	45.8	96.7	72.3	61.8	83.8
1899	68.5	83.2	82.1	64.7	80.2	68.6	76.8	71.3	93.7	83.0	76.5	87.0
1900	78.9	87.5	86.8	74.1	85.5	81.6	84.4	81.0	97.0	89.0	85.5	92.2
1901	80.0	80.2	87.8	71.2	79.4	88.2	95.4	78.2	99.9	94.6	85.3	96.0
1902	83.2	81.7	87.9	74.5	81.2	89.9	87.4	71.6	100.0	91.6	80.5	93.3
1903	83.5	88.0	88.3	79.5	87.1	91.1	82.4	73.7	97.4	91.8	83.0	90.0
1904	83.9	89.2	89.9	76.4	88.2	95.1	82.4	72.5	99.5	89.4	83.6	89.1
1905	87.1	93.9	94.0	80.0	92.2	92.0	89.6	78.5	98.9	90.5	86.2	93.9
1906	93.5	106.9	98.5	87.3	99.3	106.3	102.8	98.5	97.5	99.5	99.8	92.4
1907	94.6	106.6	91.0	91.9	105.0	93.1	112.9	109.0	94.3	103.6	105.1	92.9
1908	95.7	89.7	85.5	89.5	90.0	46.1	97.4	79.2	89.6	89.3	80.7	89.1
1909	95.5	96.6	85.7	94.1	95.7	57.7	91.5	75.4	88.5	86.6	77.2	88.6
1910	96.5	107.6	89.7	101.0	105.6	68.7	92.7	78.4	90.0	88.9	80.8	87.7
1911	94.6	101.1	94.6	94.6	100.1	79.7	91.8	86.6	91.2	91.9	88.2	89.7
1912	95.4	100.6		97.0	100.0	93.0	100.1	97.1	96.4	98.5	97.1	94.4
1913	100.0	100.0	100.0	100.0	100.0	100.0	100.0	100.0	100.0	100.0	100.0	100.0
1914	100.4	92.5	91.5	97.6	94.1	83.5	102.6	87.1	78.2	96.7	89.9	87.9
1915	98.1	88.3	90.2	92.2	90.7	118.5	112.0	96.0	78.2	103.8	101.5	90.0
1916	114.6	111.6	109.8	119.1	114.6	94.1	155.1	130.1	94.7	125.8	128.8	121.9
1917	153.5	140.7	134.4	157.7	147.1	109.5	165.0	157.9	115.0	134.7	151.9	144.7
1918	161.6	148.0	181.6	179.0	156.9	123.9	183.4	168.5	146.2	143.0	170.0	191.7
1919	178.9	164.5	196.8	227.9	175.3	184.0	166.9	145.5	153.5	141.4	158.1	206.2
1920	256.6	185.4	230.9	292.2	201.1	223.6	157.1	141.1	136.7	142.9	162.6	214.5
1921	168.5	98.3	168.6	188.3	109.7	151.5	107.0	87.8	136.6	110.8	115.4	167.7
1922	150.0	105.9	155.1	173.7	114.7	142.6	107.1	85.0	116.7	109.0	106.8	145.5
1923	160.2	123.5	153.4	181.0	131.6	135.0	137.0	101.5	114.6	121.8	118.0	144.1

TABLE B-3

ANNUAL FISHER QUANTITY INDEXES, SELECTED INTERMEDIATE EXPORT CLASSES
(1913=100)

YEAR	104	106	107	108	113	114	120	121	122	125	128
1879	151.4	174.6	126.7	115.7	77.3	14.5	37.4	18.2	21.8	41.7	20.8
1880	165.5	194.6	141.1	128.2	83.3	15.4	42.4	16.1	22.8	46.8	22.0
1881	120.0	155.0	112.6	109.4	69.8	16.8	41.7	20.0	26.0	44.9	23.8
1882	83.0	94.4	73.9	69.4	53.4	18.9	41.7	18.3	33.3	45.5	28.8
1883	84.3	119.6	93.3	85.3	66.0	17.9	44.6	18.7	30.7	49.0	28.3
1884	78.6	103.0	81.2	74.5	66.0	19.1	43.8	17.5	28.7	47.2	28.4
1885	72.3	123.2	94.1	85.7	77.3	19.3	37.8	22.3	26.0	42.4	26.6
1886	90.7	118.4	93.1	83.8	75.0	19.0	47.6	26.1	26.2	51.1	26.1
1887	86.9	112.4	88.4	85.1	74.1	21.8	47.2	23.3	30.8	51.0	28.5
1888	57.8	103.8	79.3	77.6	64.3	22.8	46.7	17.5			29.5
1889	87.5	157.9	119.6	115.3	83.6	31.5	54.6	16.8	36.3	60.3	37.0
1890	98.3	187.4	145.5	138.5	99.5	31.6	51.9	18.2	35.6	57.7	36.6
1891	121.2	176.3	130.4	124.6	96.6	33.3	61.6	23.5	31.8	66.6	35.8
1892	143.3	190.0	141.4	100.7	111.3	27.8	53.9	23.9	35.7	58.5	36.6
1893	109.7	137.0	105.9	124.1	90.5	39.2	51.2	28.4	36.9	58.3	37.7
1894	98.9	166.2	130.3	142.8	101.6	43.8	63.0	30.5	38.8	69.5	41.3
1895	93.6	170.4	130.6	159.2	102.6	42.7	58.1	40.4	43.4	64.1	45.2
1896	159.2	201.0	151.1	161.7	117.0	48.3	64.8	42.5	51.7	72.0	50.4
1897	201.1	220.7	169.5	144.4	125.3	45.4	69.6	48.0	59.9	74.3	54.8
1898	222.1	249.5	187.6	160.8	144.3	47.0	88.6		57.2	92.5	55.8
1899	189.6	257.0	190.5	177.5	153.4	55.7	66.3	59.7	61.6	71.6	61.3
1900	179.6	240.4	177.5	179.7	146.7	56.2	73.7	43.4	64.5	80.6	64.1
1901	185.3	246.1	171.5	169.3	146.6	62.9	78.1	56.0	60.8	82.5	64.9
1902	113.3	190.1	137.1	171.5	122.6	62.9	77.2	70.2	59.8	79.2	61.7
1903	124.5	180.1	140.0	133.6	126.2	66.5	79.9	59.9	69.7	81.3	66.8
1904	73.2	176.5	142.8	138.4	115.4	73.3	79.2	67.6	69.0	76.9	70.0
1905	109.1	200.8	166.0	159.2	135.2	73.6	95.2	104.9	67.3	89.9	68.0
1906	126.8	202.0	168.5	161.7	124.8	83.4	85.9	78.0	73.5	88.0	76.8
1907	118.8	176.0	146.5	140.8	117.1	72.1	89.3	48.8	77.2	93.1	76.3
1908	99.0	159.9	137.8	132.6	95.3	75.1	93.4	54.2	67.5	95.7	71.7
1909	65.2	123.5	106.7	104.6	73.8	82.1	85.6	70.3	70.9	86.3	74.2
1910	54.9	81.5	78.0	77.2	104.0	98.0	79.8	65.1	82.5	80.8	84.5
1911	68.6	108.9	112.6	109.3	98.0	100.5	97.9	86.3	91.5	97.7	92.3
1912	79.4	99.2	98.7	96.8		108.8	122.0	102.6	97.5	120.3	99.7
1913	100.0	100.0	100.0	100.0	100.0	100.0	100.0	100.0	100.0	100.0	100.0
1914	141.5	95.1	89.3	89.4	93.1	110.4	74.2	102.1	69.6	74.8	79.6
1915	203.1	256.6	181.3	180.1	161.4	218.4	103.1	214.0	50.9	109.2	85.0
1916	170.9	247.2	179.9	179.3	165.5	190.8	89.8	210.7	51.8	91.6	90.3
1917	136.2	244.0	175.2	173.7	148.1	111.3	64.5	158.5	49.8	58.8	67.6
1918	134.7	458.3	295.2	287.2	207.3	81.2	53.7	136.7	46.4	52.0	51.2
1919	158.2	412.2	311.0	306.1	259.1	210.2	82.0	190.2	59.3	84.9	101.9
1920	194.7	203.2	177.6	175.6	157.7	120.2	82.2	209.7	61.1	74.5	75.1
1921	256.7	159.7	169.6	164.1	151.1	71.6	76.8	113.4	43.3	78.0	50.6
1922	213.4	150.9	149.4	146.7	147.1	81.5	75.0	131.4	54.5	73.0	68.6
1923	118.1	194.6	185.5	179.5		84.3	65.2	120.1	70.0	66.3	79.6

Year											
1879	8.3	3.5	3.9	6.0	3.5		2.3	14.5	18.8	38.1	41.3
1880	7.3	3.6	2.7	5.7	3.6		.9	12.2	15.6	42.3	46.3
1881	10.1	4.9	3.2	7.1	4.8		1.5	17.7	22.0	40.9	44.3
1882	10.7	5.7	2.8	8.4	5.7		1.1	17.3	22.0	42.2	44.9
1883	11.3	6.1	3.4	12.9	6.1		2.2	18.7	23.4	44.6	48.3
1884	10.5	4.4	4.1	17.8	5.0		2.6	19.8	24.1	43.5	46.5
1885	10.3	5.0	3.8	15.9	4.3		3.1	19.8	24.9	39.1	41.9
1886	10.7	6.0	3.8	18.3	4.9		1.9	20.9	24.9	46.6	51.3
1887	11.3		4.8	20.6	4.9		1.5	22.0	27.4	46.7	50.6
1888	11.7				5.8		3.1	21.8	26.5	46.6	50.4
1889	14.5	7.7	4.2	25.0	7.6		1.7	25.2	31.4	55.5	59.6
1890	15.3	8.6	4.5	21.8	8.6		1.3	26.4	32.8	53.3	57.3
1891	15.6	9.4	8.7	24.7	9.4		6.2	26.0	31.7	59.8	65.9
1892	16.0	9.1	6.6	27.1	9.0		3.1	28.0	34.6	53.9	57.8
1893	18.4	10.6	15.2	30.9	10.3		12.3	34.5	41.1	53.7	57.5
1894	18.9	12.0	17.1	26.4	10.4		14.3	35.2	42.0	62.7	68.4
1895	20.1	14.6	14.8	28.6	11.6		10.7	35.6	42.3	59.8	63.3
1896	22.6	20.4	24.9	27.6	14.4		22.5	37.9	45.8	67.5	71.6
1897	27.6	27.6	30.0	29.7	20.1		22.6	40.0	48.9	70.3	74.1
1898	33.5	28.9	32.5		28.9		29.3	41.6	49.7	83.9	92.1
1899	37.9	35.1	29.9	36.8	35.0	28.5	25.9	42.9	49.0	69.8	71.6
1900	40.2	38.0	38.7	42.6	37.8	33.0	36.2	45.8	49.5	77.7	80.5
1901	39.5	34.5	24.9	43.6	34.2	30.9	19.4	48.1	53.6	78.9	82.3
1902	39.8	33.7	33.8	38.2	33.8	35.1	29.2	44.9	44.9	75.0	78.6
1903	39.1	35.3	32.0	45.6	34.8	37.5	26.3	46.3	46.3	79.0	81.0
1904	44.3	41.4	53.7	47.1	40.2	44.6	52.1	49.3	52.6	75.6	76.6
1905	51.5	47.4	51.9	50.3	46.3	54.2	49.5	55.8	61.1	86.1	89.7
1906	58.1	55.5	49.1	54.4	54.4	54.6	45.6	59.6	65.0	89.7	87.8
1907	62.5	60.6	53.2	63.1	59.3	47.4	48.6	65.2	66.7	90.8	93.0
1908	55.4	47.6	59.2	61.7	46.9	46.6	58.1	69.3	75.3	84.0	86.1
1909	58.1	49.7	66.6	62.4	49.0	59.4	64.1	72.1	77.5	81.2	80.3
1910	67.5	62.5	73.0	67.3	61.4	75.2	70.1	72.4	75.7	96.7	97.4
1911	82.8	79.2	88.3	82.9	77.9	90.1	85.7	86.3	88.9	115.4	119.8
1912	94.3	92.6	96.9	86.3	91.5		94.1	91.6	95.4		
1913	100.0	100.0	100.0	100.0	100.0	100.0	100.0	100.0	100.0	100.0	100.0
1914	82.7	73.9	93.9	78.8	73.4	74.9	91.1	93.5	100.0	75.5	74.6
1915	155.1	145.1	132.0	79.7	206.7	131.6	118.6	104.4	111.2	103.0	108.8
1916	266.4	244.1	202.5	89.7	205.1	182.1	184.0	112.3	117.7	90.7	90.7
1917	245.1	222.7	239.4	107.0	150.2	197.1	226.6	120.8	119.4	60.5	58.8
1918	157.1	150.7	187.5	97.6	188.1	161.0	177.0	119.3	123.3	52.0	57.1
1919	172.5	188.0	136.7	95.6	218.6	212.0	120.9	115.2	123.7	89.6	87.5
1920	203.4	218.0	151.1	163.7	134.5	254.7	132.2	157.8	163.2	76.0	75.8
1921	130.4	135.1	163.7	109.1	105.1	123.5	77.4	124.8	134.0	74.0	78.7
1922	119.0	105.4	90.0	70.1	132.6	121.6	91.1	113.1	146.1	73.1	73.7
1923	144.1	132.5	106.8	118.0		162.1	87.3	155.6	182.2	69.9	67.1

APPENDIX B

TABLE B-4

ANNUAL FISHER QUANTITY INDEXES, SELECTED INTERMEDIATE IMPORT CLASSES (1913=100)

YEAR	102	103	104	106	108	109	110	111	113	114	115	118
1879	35.1	40.6	39.4	38.7	24.3	19.2	34.1	34.1	31.8		23.0	18.9
1880	36.8	37.1	37.0	36.7	27.8	22.2	37.9	37.8	35.4		31.9	18.7
1881	43.4	43.3	43.2	42.8	30.7	26.2	38.0	38.8	36.4		31.0	21.8
1882	55.6	44.7	47.2	46.0	33.0	31.4	45.5	45.2	44.0		27.7	21.5
1883	43.7	45.7	45.5	44.8	32.4	34.5	47.1	46.9	44.7		24.4	25.0
1884	42.0	46.5	45.6	45.9	28.8	29.7	52.1	51.6	48.7		23.1	26.0
1885	45.0	49.1	47.1	46.7	27.2	30.8	54.2	56.1	50.7		23.1	30.6
1886	45.0	49.9	48.5	48.0	27.7	27.8	56.9	56.1	53.3		30.0	28.2
1887	52.0	41.9	44.1	43.7	25.3	32.2	55.6	54.8	52.0		30.9	31.4
1888	56.6	48.1	50.0	49.2		44.3	57.1	56.6	53.5		35.9	
1889	49.8	49.2	49.3	48.2	24.5	38.8	53.6	53.0	50.2		34.7	32.5
1890	57.7	48.4	50.4	48.9	30.8	47.2	61.3	60.7	57.4		43.8	32.6
1891	44.0	53.8	52.1	50.1	25.8	41.0	81.2	79.6	75.4	48.7	42.1	31.9
1892	39.0	58.0	54.4	52.3	31.3	39.5	67.7	66.9	63.2	57.0	48.1	32.1
1893	45.5	51.6	50.4	48.2	30.0	32.9	68.0	67.3	63.4	50.8	41.1	32.6
1894	47.3	57.1	54.9	52.5	28.5	39.5	72.7	72.0	67.6	39.4	32.8	34.1
1895	43.9	60.4	54.2	52.5	29.0	40.3	65.5	66.8	60.7	64.7	59.0	37.8
1896	46.3	56.3	64.9	52.5	31.7	34.2	67.8	69.9	63.3	37.5	33.1	29.5
1897	39.0	71.5	60.1	64.3	27.9	36.0	67.2	69.2	62.9	54.4	50.3	34.5
1898	34.3	66.7		59.1		36.1	60.6	60.6	56.6	54.7	52.0	
1899	38.9	77.5	69.6	67.5	32.2	39.5	76.8	75.8	71.8	66.3	63.8	42.1
1900	38.1	73.2	80.5	76.4	34.0	33.3	66.1	66.5	62.1	64.5	60.8	39.0
1901	43.1	90.2	77.4	77.4	37.4	36.8	66.6	68.9	62.2	65.3	64.4	46.6
1902	53.4	92.4	82.7	78.8	43.3	48.4	71.7	66.8	63.2	67.1	66.8	44.2
1903	49.1	105.4	81.4	79.1	44.6	49.4	66.8	78.7	74.3	62.4	62.3	46.6
1904	57.4	93.4	95.6	90.2	47.3	52.0	79.0	74.5	70.8	64.8	64.7	50.9
1905	57.2	92.1	86.0	81.6	50.8	53.2	77.4	79.3	75.0	79.1	78.5	54.6
1906	53.7	97.8	84.0	79.8	52.9	63.5	79.1	82.2	78.2	87.0	83.5	57.9
1907	69.2	98.5	91.6	87.1	60.0	69.9	81.3	77.3	74.0	79.8	74.6	58.2
1908	69.2	119.1	92.3	87.4	61.8	65.3	76.6	84.8	80.6	68.5	68.5	58.5
1909	93.3	93.2	113.4	107.0	71.3	72.5	83.1	87.2	85.1	112.5	114.9	70.1
1910	78.1	96.4	90.0	85.7	79.4	78.3	87.0	84.5	84.8	92.6	93.4	81.1
1911	88.0	107.3	94.7	90.7	78.4	78.4	84.6	90.5	87.7	88.2	89.0	82.1
1912	110.6		108.0	103.3	74.4	88.5	90.1			121.4	123.3	103.7
1913	100.0	100.0	100.0	100.0	100.0	100.0	100.0	100.0	100.0	100.0	100.0	100.0
1914	116.6	114.4	115.1	117.8	186.5	98.2	106.1	105.0	120.0	105.9	104.0	119.8
1915	82.5	131.5	119.9	120.7	108.3	75.3	96.6	94.4	99.9	109.5	121.3	162.6
1916	96.7	127.7	120.3	116.7	81.3	68.4	102.0	100.3	100.6	129.0	137.9	187.0
1917	179.1	149.6	159.4	155.1	77.1	70.5	93.3	91.6	92.4	109.3	118.3	237.7
1918	128.1	133.7	133.2	133.2	114.9	65.2	94.1	89.0	99.5	64.1	69.0	208.9
1919	139.2	147.0	145.4	150.6	87.6	92.0	123.8	116.8	120.8	124.8	139.7	299.5
1920	198.1	144.3	158.3	155.5	140.3	93.3	138.6	131.1	143.9	92.6	98.0	340.2
1921	124.4	144.3	139.7	134.1	98.2	81.2	106.4	101.1	107.6	69.3	68.8	239.6
1922	130.0	143.5	140.5	134.7	115.2	81.5	160.8	151.9	157.2	94.6	99.7	344.2

234

Year	(1)	(2)	(3)	(4)	(5)	(6)	(7)	(8)	(9)	(10)	(11)	(12)
1879	28.7	16.6	17.0	17.0	20.8	31.7	49.6	15.0	104.4	14.7	28.7	15.5
1880	41.3	21.1	21.6	21.6	25.3	42.2	66.2	19.7	139.3	20.2	38.3	18.2
1881	41.1	19.2	19.5	19.7	24.9	38.1	61.7	16.3	124.5	14.1	37.3	21.6
1882	47.1	20.6	20.8	21.1	24.5	45.5	74.8	18.7	160.3	17.4	42.3	21.8
1883	42.1	21.2	20.7	20.7	22.7	44.6	70.2	20.0	153.6	19.1	39.8	21.8
1884	46.5	21.5	21.9	21.9	23.8	44.3	65.3	20.3	146.7	18.5	40.9	24.3
1885	41.5	23.7	23.4	24.2	23.8	43.9	77.2	24.0	128.9	23.0	40.9	25.9
1886	44.4	28.1	28.0	28.0	28.2	48.9	78.6	24.7	154.0	29.7	47.6	25.5
1887	51.2	27.8	27.3	28.4	29.3	52.5	81.9	26.7	161.7	26.3	46.8	27.5
1888	52.2	30.3	30.6	31.1	33.5	56.7	84.7	29.7	176.5	28.3	49.8	32.8
1889	53.3	33.7	33.0	34.6	33.3	60.2	86.2	34.4	188.4	32.1	47.3	39.2
1890	57.6	34.6	32.7	35.5	38.2	61.5	96.6	29.3	207.1	25.8	54.1	37.1
1891	63.5	36.7	37.3	37.7	37.0	65.6	73.4	39.6	153.1	36.5	44.2	46.5
1892	69.1	41.1	40.6	42.0	40.0	60.5	80.3	42.9	160.2	40.9	50.7	46.5
1893	65.1	34.6	34.8	34.7	37.0	52.9	74.4	32.1	141.9	25.1	49.1	49.1
1894	48.2	36.0	36.8	36.8	33.8	47.9	59.7	37.4	101.4	35.7	44.4	40.6
1895	62.6	50.9	50.9	52.1	48.2	78.5	100.5	56.4	204.3	56.8	61.1	52.6
1896	61.4	50.2	34.2	34.8	31.3	56.7	75.1	38.5	130.1	33.8	54.8	49.5
1897	61.6	52.3	53.6	53.6	42.3	81.9	81.9	72.7	138.2	76.3	61.0	59.0
1898	48.6	39.7	41.4	40.5	43.1	52.3	64.7	41.5	96.4	35.7	53.3	55.5
1899	55.0	48.5	50.3	49.4	52.8	58.8	69.6	49.9	93.1	46.6	61.1	56.6
1900	50.7	46.7	47.3	47.7	50.4	58.7	73.1	46.3	98.6	41.4	64.6	56.3
1901	56.0	53.8	54.8	55.0	55.8	64.0	74.8	55.6	101.1	51.0	66.2	64.4
1902	63.3	60.1	60.8	60.6	56.1	76.9	89.2	67.1	119.1	61.7	79.5	76.8
1903	61.2	57.6	57.3	57.6	54.4	74.2	80.9	61.7	117.8	55.1	78.8	74.5
1904	62.5	62.4	62.4	63.1	57.5	75.5	92.5	71.8	103.8	73.5	83.2	78.0
1905	70.4	70.6	71.8	71.6	66.2	85.1	106.0	80.6	120.9	81.9	100.3	73.3
1906	81.6	71.3	71.5	72.2	70.3	88.6	117.7	75.0	124.0	75.9	106.7	91.7
1907	90.5	70.0	71.0	70.7	66.3	93.4	86.0	78.1	132.0	71.2	84.0	76.6
1908	71.7	67.5	68.4	68.0	63.4	79.0	109.5	75.0	90.5	74.2	107.0	94.7
1909	86.4	93.6	95.9	94.8	90.4	106.4	108.0	105.8	117.0	111.2	84.0	107.0
1910	93.3	86.5	88.1	85.1	86.2	97.8	116.3	87.5	116.3	91.2	105.3	80.3
1911	88.2	84.0	84.5	83.8	85.2	88.0	94.2	82.5	88.5	81.1	96.1	85.2
1912	99.2	108.0	109.7	108.9	112.6	102.8	96.7	108.7	83.5	106.7	100.9	112.4
1913	107.0	100.0	100.0	100.0	100.0	100.0	100.0	100.0	100.0	100.0	100.0	100.0
1914	96.4	112.2	113.3	113.3	114.3	113.6	121.8	111.8	197.7	111.4	101.5	117.9
1915	89.4	134.4	140.9	137.4	141.7	112.5	84.9	143.1	110.3	149.2	77.3	133.7
1916	99.5	151.1	158.5	152.9	162.5	116.6	80.1	154.4	107.2	159.2	72.9	150.0
1917	96.1	159.6	167.5	159.2	177.2	112.7	73.0	151.9	110.2	165.2	62.9	120.0
1918	85.0	149.6	154.6	144.5	132.8	100.2	52.1	149.3	75.7	165.9	45.5	110.0
1919	89.5	191.4	198.2	191.7	223.4	110.7	53.9	170.4	82.4	190.9	46.1	170.8
1920	110.3	165.2	156.3	164.5	208.1	112.8	93.0	133.9	144.6	124.6	79.8	172.0
1921	83.4	150.5	152.9	152.3	146.1	118.2	86.2	152.9	157.3	177.4	67.8	91.5
1922	177.0	191.2	197.2	190.8	211.0	133.3	97.1	174.0	148.3	196.6	83.1	117.2
1923	152.6	198.2	208.0	197.3	232.6	146.7	118.3	178.4	174.7	198.7	102.7	129.8

YEAR	134	137	139	140	142	144	145	146	147	148	149	150
1879		18.7	42.0	43.2	20.9			35.1	21.9	10.9	26.4	36.5
1880		23.9	55.7	56.4	26.9			60.7	59.9	14.2	38.7	65.6
1881		22.1	52.5	58.2	25.5			48.7	63.5	20.5	34.8	69.1
1882		23.6	63.0	61.7	27.3			59.0	59.3	20.4	40.4	70.2
1883		24.2	59.6	57.6	27.2			47.6	39.8	18.5	37.8	57.7
1884		26.3	58.7	56.2	27.2			41.2	30.2	18.3	32.3	47.5
1885		30.7	55.0	57.5	29.4			39.5	22.1	18.6	33.0	47.6
1886		30.8	65.2	58.4	33.4			54.4	32.0	24.6	41.0	55.4
1887		33.5	66.7	64.5	34.0			68.7	48.0	23.3	48.1	67.7
1888			72.0	68.7	36.8			53.7	41.9	23.3	42.7	65.9
1889	42.0	36.6	73.4	66.2	39.4		32.0	54.1	38.4	25.5	43.9	60.4
1890	44.8	37.7	82.3	70.9	40.8		51.3	54.6	41.8	28.2	45.9	65.0
1891	49.4	40.1	65.5	71.4	42.8		29.8	57.3	40.3	28.4	47.9	61.6
1892	53.9	45.0	71.5	76.2	47.3		35.5	51.3	39.0	32.7	46.6	66.6
1893	51.4	37.9	66.7	70.9	40.6		49.3	47.6	34.5	29.2	41.8	62.1
1894	37.1	53.7	53.0	61.0	40.6		37.0	39.4	25.0	29.2	37.8	50.5
1895	48.6	37.1	86.7	78.7	56.1		28.5	51.0	38.4	26.4	44.2	70.8
1896	48.6	54.0	65.9	60.8	39.1		25.3	39.2	36.8	26.4	37.2	65.5
1897	47.6	54.0	54.0	72.7	56.2		29.8	36.9	29.5	28.3	38.2	57.0
1898	38.1	42.6	57.7	56.3	42.8		25.0	43.1	29.0	27.3	27.3	48.8
1899	44.4	50.5	62.3	59.7	50.8	62.6	37.3	46.7	37.8	35.2	50.1	56.8
1900	42.2	48.8	65.5	57.1	48.9	39.0	55.0	48.2	47.1	40.3	48.6	60.4
1901	45.5	56.5	67.0	59.7	55.1	63.5	48.3	50.4	47.5	57.0	42.5	62.9
1902	53.7	56.4	78.4	70.2	62.3	66.0	75.0	78.3	66.8	57.9	58.1	75.8
1903	53.0	59.1	79.3	65.0	58.9	67.9	46.2	80.9	73.4	55.2	70.2	85.0
1904	54.2	65.0	72.8	70.5	64.2	62.7	39.1	64.9	62.0	45.8	60.5	78.2
1905	60.9	65.2	83.3	77.2	72.1	85.6	50.1	74.8	69.0	52.0	71.3	81.5
1906	70.8	73.0	98.3	83.2	73.8	88.1	48.5	86.2	87.4	53.1	80.0	97.1
1907	81.4	73.9	106.7	87.6	73.7	76.6	54.4	79.8	93.1	56.0	77.0	101.9
1908	65.2	68.6	82.7	68.2	67.6	69.5	54.4	65.0	69.8	47.6	64.5	76.7
1909	81.8	93.8	103.9	90.1	93.0	162.3	76.1	89.8	102.2	69.2	97.0	96.5
1910	92.0	85.7	103.0	92.7	87.8	137.1	93.6	101.0	111.9	84.3	103.2	107.6
1911	89.7	84.7	91.8	94.3	86.4	115.7	69.9	91.4	104.4	73.6	96.4	102.2
1912	99.0	108.0	94.7	101.0	106.4	98.6	91.3	99.8	102.3	84.0	96.3	98.2
1913	100.0	100.0	100.0	100.0	100.0	100.0	100.0	100.0	100.0	100.0	100.0	100.0
1914	103.1	110.4	117.9	96.9	108.6	5.3	74.3	77.3	118.9	78.7	79.8	109.1
1915	102.7	133.4	86.4	92.1	123.7	48.5	95.6	74.6	84.9	84.1	71.7	71.2
1916	102.3	148.1	88.4	104.0	139.4	116.9	139.2	95.9	75.1	123.1	92.5	61.2
1917	96.5	153.0	79.7	96.6	143.1	79.7	132.6	102.2	63.5	124.5	90.8	53.0
1918	87.6	137.6	79.2	80.3	130.8	41.8	150.9	133.0	57.7	133.0	85.6	47.6
1919	93.6	179.3	62.0	87.4	161.7	122.0	113.2	81.2	70.2	123.0	78.7	52.0
1920	123.6	157.9	96.5	111.2	150.6	72.4	140.1	69.6	116.2	117.7	107.8	85.5
1921	94.0	141.1	92.2	84.1	130.6	53.7	78.6	132.8	108.8	132.8	63.8	88.4
1922	155.8	181.4	108.8	123.8	172.4	101.7	95.9	143.4	143.1	187.0	113.5	117.7
1923	179.9	191.4	132.5	152.6	187.0	122.8	108.3	158.2	162.9	155.8	132.6	150.3

APPENDIX B

TABLE B-5

ANNUAL VALUES, SELECTED INTERMEDIATE EXPORT CLASSES
(MILLIONS OF DOLLARS)

Year											
1879	21	216	15	13	197	8	168	118	114	71	230
1880	25	271	17	14	251	9	204	151	147	86	258
1881	28	253	21	16	236	9	193	144	139	82	200
1882	34	260	27	16	238	10	163	109	103	59	147
1883	33	259	25	15	237	10	190	125	120	71	142
1884	31	255	23	13	232	11	174	104	99	60	117
1885	31	221	21	15	197	11	178	102	98	60	101
1886	28	251	19	18	230	10	162	94	90	53	119
1887	27	246	21	16	230	11	167	95	91	53	116
1888	30	256	25	13	236	10	155	94	88	53	81
1889	39	302	29	13	277	14	189	125	119	72	108
1890	39	291	28	13	265	14	216	143	138	81	123
1891	37	314	25	16	291	15	219	133	128	79	198
1892	37	253	26	15	230	13	255	150	146	89	203
1893	37	249	27	16	217	17	230	137	133	77	139
1894	40	240	28	17	215	18	223	146	141	82	109
1895	45	228	29	17	204	20	210	138	132	82	106
1896	49	278	35	23	253	22	219	137	132	86	165
1897	54	252	40	22	231	21	240	149	145	94	235
1898	55	280	38	24	253	23	290	175	171	111	279
1899	67	246	45	31	217	28	304	182	178	116	229
1900	74	375	52	26	337	28	310	188	182	117	217
1901	71	356	48	32	328	30	333	210	204	128	246
1902	74	349	51	40	325	32	308	188	181	112	159
1903	86	427	63	34	407	35	308	183	178	105	174
1904	92	421	61	42	404	38	269	169	163	97	101
1905	92	436	50	66	450	40	302	191	187	107	154
1906	118	480	77	52	456	47	328	207	203	113	178
1907	123	531	86	36	496	44	325	195	191	105	194
1908	105	492	71	35	466	42	309	182	178	93	117
1909	110	516	72	43	496	48	268	156	149	74	93
1910	134	585	85	44	566	57	239	135	128	60	115
1911	150	582	96	58	663	61	293	164	157	71	142
1912	161	693	105	67	676	68	288	153	146	66	
1913	160	654	114	69	631	63	305	167	158	73	169
1914	126	421	74	71	394	71	293	150	140	71	274
1915	146	608	54	152	513	161	523	292	276	184	459
1916	182	718	58	191	675	163	604	330	312	198	416
1917	172	686	68	206	734	126	781	455	435	274	495
1918	155	825	86	247	855	93	1373	967	938	668	534
1919	397	1448	135	368	1410	314	1904	1194	1149	698	646
1920	334	1433	185	496	1538	197	1077	566	538	279	883
1921	123	763	89	153	651	66	657	351	338	157	673
1922	161	843	99	175	812	66	559	290	276	141	459
1923	208	987	147	177	945	70	553	345	330	154	257

YFAR	133	136	139	140	141	142	143	144	145	146	147
1879	218	246	37	39	4		16	5	7	17	62
1880	272	303	35	37	2		18	6	6	19	61
1881	253	288	49	52	3		22	7	7	23	79
1882	261	301	45	49	2		27	9	8	28	82
1883	260	298	49	54	4		29	13		30	87
1884	256	294	51	56	4		24	17	10	25	82
1885	223	256	52	56	4		19	15	10	20	77
1886	253	285	50	54	3		18	13		19	74
1887	248	286	49	54	2		20	15	9	22	75
1888	257	294	50	57	6		25	20	13	26	81
1889	304	351	56	62	2		32	22	8	34	97
1890	294	338	55	62	2		36	20	9	37	100
1891	317	360	50	59	10		38	23	18	40	98
1892	255	297	47	56	5		35	24	13	36	91
1893	251	294	46	59	16		39	25	25	42	97
1894	242	288	45	56	17		37	22	25	47	94
1895	230	281	62	73	14		44	24	25	47	117
1896	281	337	68	80	32		60	24	43	63	142
1897	316	316	65	77	39		75	23	52	79	155
1898	285	346	60	73	42		100	24	57	104	174
1899	251	325	74	90	53	78	125	30	72	130	217
1900	381	464	83	106	74	89	147	37	96	153	250
1901	363	441	81	104	40	80	130	38	62	136	235
1902	354	437	77	97	49	85	127	34	72	134	230
1903	433	530	82	112	47	94	136	42	71	142	245
1904	426	527	89	119	89	99	153	44	113	162	275
1905	442	545	88	119	98	115	174	45	123	185	302
1906	487	616	94	128	106	140	211	50	134	223	350
1907	540	673	102	145	115	157	239	57	147	253	391
1908	500	617	116	155	105	127	189	56	130	198	348
1909	524	649	111	153	112	125	193	56	140	203	361
1910	592	743	101	146	121	163	246	60	152	260	422
1911	591	757	113	169	145	199	298	75	181	314	504
1912	703	884	134	193	189	237	347	82	229	364	587
1913	663	844	161	231	203	251	370	97	251	380	625
1914	429	568	149	206	172	180	257	73	225	265	486
1915	619	770	160	224	260	319	489	73	375	544	983
1916	729	920	221	294	617	456	829	86	847	1105	2203
1917	698	882	275	394	963	549	980	134	1243	1147	2273
1918	838	1003	371	491	681	531	833	136	954	874	1624
1919	1522	1937	377	503	395	770	1108	154	605	1145	1795
1920	1470	1833	593	953	421	995	1382	410	715	1425	2340
1921	775	915	401	572	185	547	774	205	307	796	1327
1922	856	1039	346	441	172	371	500	129	271	515	1001

TABLE B-6

ANNUAL VALUES,
SELECTED INTERMEDIATE IMPORT CLASSES
(MILLIONS OF DOLLARS)

118	115	114	113	111	110	109	108	106	104	103	102	YEAR
15	20	30	78	79	77	3	4	102	98	79	19	1879
17	31	43	104	105	103	4	5	104	99	79	21	1880
17	30	42	106	107	105	4	5	111	105	76	28	1881
25	27	40	126	126	124	5	7	115	105	67	39	1882
21	23	35	118	119	117	5	6	101	91	62	29	1883
18	29	33	103	103	101	5	6	100	93	66	27	1884
17	27	34	96	96	94	5	5	94	90	63	26	1885
21	33	38	104	103	101	4	5	96	91	65	26	1886
20	31	35	91	91	89	5	6	119	114	82	32	1887
21	31	37	106	105	103	6	6	122	117	84	34	1888
22	29	34	123	123	121	9	5	122	118	99	19	1889
26	32	39	120	121	118	11	7	137	133	107	26	1890
25	29	38	161	162	159	10	6	138	136	114	22	1891
23	32	43	131	132	129	9	6	134	131	113	19	1892
26	26	36	143	145	141	7	6	134	133	113	19	1893
26	21	29	126	128	124	8	6	136	134	118	16	1894
28	42	52	88	91	86	8	6	139	136	121	16	1895
22	25	32	109	115	107	7	6	118	115	100	15	1896
28	38	46	96	102	94	8	6	119	114	100	14	1897
31	44	51	96	98	94	9	6	91	87	74	12	1898
41	56	63	131	133	128	11	9	99	95	83	12	1899
37	56	65	115	117	111	10	9	103	100	87	12	1900
40	61	67	104	108	101	11	10	113	110	97	13	1901
36	63	69	92	92	86	13	12	118	115	99	16	1902
46	59	65	94	94	88	14	13	118	144	100	15	1903
57	63	68	118	119	113	15	13	145	132	126	18	1904
64	80	86	138	139	133	15	15	134	142	115	17	1905
71	92	102	123	123	116	22	16	134	147	113	18	1906
60	87	97	135	134	126	26	19	150	137	121	26	1907
101	66	69	134	133	135	23	18	140	164	115	23	1908
144	116	120	145	145	157	24	20	168	148	134	30	1909
123	99	103	169	164	144	27	23	153	185	120	28	1910
149	92	96	157	151	168	29	26	190	233	151	34	1911
	132	139	183	177		34	27	239		187	46	1912
117	119	126	169	157	149	36	34	226	210	164	46	1913
111	121	138	226	182	174	35	66	242	216	165	51	1914
157	134	144	247	223	217	29	40	244	223	185	38	1915
219	179	195	306	291	282	36	37	259	247	195	52	1916
309	218	237	319	296	287	45	45	371	350	216	134	1917
234	115	128	372	309	308	50	81	327	298	198	101	1918
330	316	335	534	488	487	88	69	542	484	368	116	1919
385	256	280	1197	1129	1125	101	92	583	552	364	188	1920
129	74	92	333	296	294	53	54	302	293	207	86	1921
171	113	130	345	304	303	48	59	334	326	246	79	1922
282	127	147	490	430	429	43	74	365	358	285	73	1923

239

YEAR	120	121	122	124	125	126	127	128	130	131	132	133
1879	8	42	23	55	31	97	128	35	70	68	71	12
1880	10	58	33	73	44	131	175	48	97	94	99	20
1881	12	54	22	66	34	120	154	46	85	82	87	19
1882	13	62	27	85	41	146	188	52	98	95	101	23
1883	13	59	27	79	40	138	179	44	93	86	95	20
1884	13	57	25	73	38	130	169	47	92	88	94	21
1885	12	53	29	61	41	114	156	44	94	88	96	18
1886	11	58	38	72	50	131	183	54	112	106	114	18
1887	14	58	37	76	52	135	189	51	113	105	116	21
1888	19	59	36	81	55	140	198	52	116	110	119	21
1889	25	57	43	85	68	143	220	50	132	121	135	22
1890	21	63	37	92	58	156	220	58	134	118	137	23
1891	25	55	44	67	69	122	194	54	132	127	135	24
1892	22	62	51	71	73	132	209	55	142	132	146	27
1893	23	59	33	65	56	124	182	51	119	111	122	25
1894	15	51	37	43	52	94	148	46	113	102	117	20
1895	18	68	64	89	82	157	245	70	166	155	171	24
1896	18	62	39	57	57	119	180	46	114	107	118	22
1897	19	68	84	59	104	127	240	65	178	173	182	22
1898	22	59	40	41	61	100	163	76	146	141	150	17
1899	28	68	57	40	85	109	216	97	194	188	199	21
1900	34	78	53	43	86	121	222	93	195	186	201	21
1901	34	83	55	42	89	125	271	101	206	197	213	25
1902	47	94	69	51	115	146	273	99	231	226	242	30
1903	46	98	68	50	114	136	279	106	237	230	247	29
1904	45	91	87	44	132	157	326	121	269	263	279	30
1905	52	105	105	52	157	190	358	124	320	312	330	35
1906	50	136	106	54	156	214	407	163	346	331	358	44
1907	64	154	115	60	178	150	295	157	360	349	373	50
1908	44	111	91	40	134	180	378	126	285	272	297	39
1909	49	129	134	51	183	178	355	217	425	415	440	48
1910	46	127	110	51	157	165	333	243	424	426	451	53
1911	52	125	97	40	149	181	396	214	395	386	418	49
1912	68	142	125	39	194			281	508	498	531	55
1913	70	153	123	43	193	196	414	236	465	453	489	58
1914	72	142	151	65	223	207	457	232	490	477	511	57
1915	71	106	189	37	260	143	426	291	572	569	590	51
1916	103	127	274	44	377	171	582	398	801	808	835	60
1917	138	135	359	50	497	185	725	527	1057	1085	1119	68
1918	156	150	434	43	590	196	826	349	991	1045	1097	74
1919	154	285	550	61	704	211	964	646	1425	1440	1515	87
1920	219	157	417	113	636	398	1128	641	1359	1370	1451	146
1921	67	191	322	82	388	239	675	203	646	626	681	85
1922	83	227	456	80	539	271	859	285	890	877	943	112
1923	97		528	92	625	318	1008	409	1091	1102	1160	140

Year												
1879	25	62	2	9	31			98	27	106	83	
1880	48	108	2	25	67			139	40	142	118	
1881	48	87	7	26	46			127	40	132	104	
1882	50	103	6	24	57			146	45	161	119	
1883	39	91	6	15	45			136	41	150	111	
1884	36	77	6	11	36			135	41	141	111	
1885	30	71	7	8	33			133	37	125	129	
1886	37	88	7	11	45			153	40	144	132	
1887		102	7	15	56			157	41	149	135	
1888	42	90		13	45			162	43	155		
1889	40	89	9	13	42	3		188	53	158	152	24
1890	43	101	10	14	47	5		190	53	173	155	25
1891	40	103	13	12	49	6		187	54	140	153	26
1892	41	97	13	12	40	7		200	52	152	166	29
1893	36	88	14	10	37	8		175	52	143	142	28
1894	27	69	11	7	26	5		160	43	109	132	21
1895	40	77	10	11	31	4		227	57	177	189	25
1896	37	67	9	11	23	3		161	43	136	133	23
1897	31	67	10	8	22	4		231	49	145	198	22
1898	27	72	11	7	25	4		189	39	117	166	18
1899	32	98	22	9	42	8	21	251	52	129	215	23
1900	36	106	27	12	49	12	16	258	57	148	218	25
1901	39	117	41	12	49	23	27	270	57	148	232	27
1902	46	140	40	18	70	18	29	312	71	170	261	33
1903	50	149	38	19	75	10	30	318	71	161	267	34
1904	48	130	33	16	59	11	29	353	73	189	300	39
1905	52	157	38	18	74	15	39	414	84	232	353	49
1906	61	207	43	22	107	17	46	457	99	264	385	58
1907	65	206	49	23	111	21	35	485	111	189	402	46
1908	47	133	36	16	65	18	16	382	85	223	319	58
1909	59	191	52	24	85	24	46	558	118	222	470	66
1910	65	213	65	26	100	30	45	581	130	206	474	63
1911	65	217	58	25	122	23	46	542	124	205	444	70
1912	67	238	72	26		32	45	668	137		564	
1913	81	245	86	31	123	37	47	632	143	247	522	74
1914	77	176	65	29	82	28	20	651	139	261	533	77
1915	52	178	75	21	88	39	26	715	125	188	615	68
1916	65	298	139	22	154	85	52	1020	186	221	863	87
1917	66	345	150	23	201	86	41	1345	226	259	1125	110
1918	79	364	172	26	213	108	24	1311	214	272	1064	105
1919	93	311	156	34	146	74	105	1811	296	300	1541	236
1920	159	438	222	62	203	86	76	1934	483	538	1529	125
1921	128	184	132	47	76	33	38	916	235	375	724	175
1922	148	203	183	52	151	40	68	1262	318	407	1002	214
1923	188	391	170	58	198	58	78	1570	410	491	1234	

TABLE B–7

LIST OF INTERMEDIATE EXPORT CLASSES

Export Class	Class Composition

CRUDE FOODS

101	Animal	001–002ᵃ
102	Vegetable, excluding tobacco	*1901–23:* 003–007
		1879–1900: 003, 005–007
103	Vegetable, including tobacco	102 and 025
104†	All agricultural, excluding tobacco	102 and 001
105	All agricultural, including tobacco	103 and 001

MANUFACTURED FOODS

106†	Meats	008–010*
107†	Animal, agricultural	106 and 011–012
108†	Animal, all	107 and 013
109	Vegetable, agricultural, excluding beverages and tropical products	*1899–1923:* 014–016, 018, 017*
		1879–98: 014–015, 018, 017*
110	Vegetable, agricultural	109, 019, and 021–023
111	Vegetable, all	110, 020ᵇ, 024
112	Vegetable, including tobacco products	111 and 026
113†	All agricultural	107 and 110

NONFOOD ANIMAL PRODUCTS

114†	Hides, leather, and products, crude, semimanufactured and manufactured	027–029
115	All agricultural, crude and semimanufactured except fibers	027 and 032–033
116	All crude and semimanufactured, except fibers	*1913–23:* 028, 030–031ᶜ, 034, 115
		1879–1912: 028, 030, 034, 115
117	All, except textiles	116 and 029

NONFOOD VEGETABLE PRODUCTS

118	All agricultural, crude and semimanufactured, except textiles	037ᵈ–039
119	All crude and semimanufactured, except textiles	*1899–1923:* 118 035, 040
		1879–98: 118 and 040
120†	Cotton textiles, crude, semimanufactured and manufactured	*1899–1923:* 042–044
		1879–88: 042 and 044
121†	Manufactured textiles	*1913–23:* 044–045, 048–049
		1889–1912: 044–045, 048, 049*
		1882–88: 044–045 and 048*–049*
		1879–81: 044–045 and 048*
122†	Wood and manufactures, except paper	051–053

PRODUCTS OF ANIMAL OR VEGETABLE ORIGIN

Agricultural

123	Crude, excluding textiles and tobacco	027, 032, 037, and 039
124	Crude, excluding tobacco	*1916–23:* 123, 042, 046, and 050*
		1899–1915: 123, 042, and 050*
		1889–98: 123, 042, 046, and 050*
		1879–88: 123, 042, 046, and 050*
125†	Crude, including tobacco	124 and 025
126	Semimanufactures	033 and 038

(continued)

TABLE B-7 (concluded)

Export Class	Class Composition
PRODUCTS OF ANIMAL OR VEGETABLE ORIGIN (continued)	
Nonagricultural	
127 Crude	030 and 051ᵉ
128† Semimanufactures	*1913–23:* 028, 031ᶜ, 034, 035, 040, 043, 047, 052, and 054
	1899–1912: 028, 034, 035, 040, 043, 052, and 054
	1898: 028, 034, 040, 052, 054
	1879–97: 028, 034, 040, and 052
Agricultural and Nonagricultural	
129 Crude, excluding tobacco	124 and 127
130 Crude, including tobacco	125 and 127
131 Semimanufactures	126 and 128
Crude and Semimanufactured Materials	
132 Agricultural, excluding tobacco	124 and 126
133† Agricultural, including tobacco	125–126
134 Nonagricultural	127–128
135 All, excluding tobacco	132, 134
136† All, including tobacco	133–134
Nonagricultural Products	
137 Manufactures of animal or vegetable origin, excluding rubber	*1899–1923:* 029, 053, 121, 055
	1879–98: 029, 053, 121, 055*
PRODUCTS OF OTHER THAN ANIMAL OR VEGETABLE ORIGIN	
138 Crude fuels	057–059
139† Petroleum and products	*1882–1923:* 059, 060, 061
	1879–81: 059, 061
140† Fuels	*1895–1923:* 057, 058, 139
	1879–94: 057, 139
141† Semimanufactured metals	066, 069
142† Machinery and automobiles and parts	*1899–1923:* 071, 072
143† Manufactured iron and steel products including machinery and vehicles	*1899–1923:* 142, 070
	1879–98: 070, 071
144† Crude materials	*1907–23:* 138, 062, 065ᶠ, 068ᵍ, 073
	1895–1906: 138, 065, 068, 073
	1889–94: 135, 065, 078
	1882–88: 138, 065, 068, 073*
	1879–81: 138, 065, 073*
145† Semimanufactures	*1899–1923:* 058, 060, 063, 141, 074
	1895–98: 058, 060, 141, 063*, 074*
	1882–94: 060, 141, 063*, 074*
	1879–81: 141, 063*, 074*
146† Manufactured metal products	*1913–23:* 143, 067
	1879–1912: 143, 067*
147† Manufactured products, including rubber, books, and other printed matter	*1913–23:* 036, 061, 064, 146, 075, 076*, 056*, 077*
	1899–1912: 061, 064, 146, 075, 036*, 056*, 077*
	1879–98: 061, 146, 075, 036*, 056*, 064*, 077*

Notes to Table B–7

† Annual Fisher price and quantity indexes and values are presented for these classes in Tables B–1 to B–6 inclusive.

* Designates uncovered classes.

ᵃ Class 002 is an uncovered class (see Appendix C), deflated here by price indexes for Class 013.

ᵇ Class 020 is an uncovered class (see Appendix C), deflated here by price indexes for Class 019.

ᶜ Class 031 is an uncovered class deflated here by price indexes for Class 030. Before 1913, Class 030 included commodities later listed in 031 (see Appendix C).

ᵈ Class 037 is an uncovered class for 1879–88 and 1913–23. During the 1889–1912 period, its price behavior was similar to that of Export Class 038. The indexes for class 038 were therefore used to deflate the values for 037 in 1879–88 and 1913–23.

ᵉ Class 051 is uncovered because of difficulty in finding foreign prices for wood in log. It is deflated here by indexes for Class 052.

ᶠ Class 065 is an uncovered class, deflated here by price indexes for Class 066.

ᵍ Class 068 is an uncovered class for the period 1882–88 and 1895–98. Price indexes for Class 069 were used as deflators.

TABLE B-8

LIST OF INTERMEDIATE IMPORT CLASSES

Import Class	Class Composition
CRUDE FOODS	
101 Animal	001–002[a]
102† Vegetable, except tropical	*1912–23:* 003–005, 007
	1879–1911: 004–005, 007
103† Vegetable, tropical	*1889–1923:* 006, 008–011
	1879–88: 006, 008–010
104† Vegetable, all	102–103
105 Vegetable, including tobacco	104, 024
106† Agricultural, all	104, 001
107 Agricultural, including tobacco	105, 001
MANUFACTURED FOODS	
108† Animal	012–013
109† Vegetable, agricultural, excluding sugar and beverages	*1899–1923:* 014–018
	1898: 014–016, 018, and 017*
	1889–97: 014–016 and 017*
	1882–88: 014, 016
	1879–81: 014, 016, 017*
110† Vegetable, agricultural	*1919–23:* 109, 019, and 021*
	1913–18: 109, 019, 021
	1889–1912: 109, 019, 021, 023
	1879–88: 109, 019, 021
111† Vegetable, all	*1916–23:* 110, 020[b], 022
	1913–15: 110 and 022
	1879–1912: 110, 020[b], 022
112 Vegetable, including tobacco products	111, 025
113† Manufactured foodstuffs, agricultural	110, 012
NONFOOD ANIMAL PRODUCTS	
114† Hides, leather and products	*1891–1923:* 026, 027[c], 028
	1879–90: 026, 027[c], 028*
115† Crude, agricultural, excluding fibers	*1899–1923:* 026, 031
	1884–98: 026, 031*
	1879–83: 026
116 Crude, all, except fibers	*1882–1923:* 115, 029, 032
	1879–81: 115, 029
117 Crude and semimanufactured, except fibers	*1899–1923:* 116, 027, 030[d], 033, 034
	1879–98: 116, 027, 030, 033, 034*
NONFOOD VEGETABLE PRODUCTS	
118† Crude, agricultural, except fibers	036, 038, 040
119 Crude and semimanufactured, agricultural, except fibers	*1915–23:* 118, 039, 042
	1879–1914: 118, 039
ANIMAL AND VEGETABLE FIBERS	
120† Crude, vegetable	*1889–1923:* 045, 048, 051
	1879–88: 045, 051
121† Manufactured, vegetable	*1891–1923:* 047, 049, 050, 053
	1889–90: 049, 050, 053, 047*
	1879–88: 053, 047

(continued)

245

TABLE B–8 (continued)

	Import Class	Class Composition
	Animal and Vegetable Fibers (continued)	
122†	Crude, animal	054, 057, 060*
123	Semimanufactured, all	*1913–23, 1889–98:* 046, 052[e], 055, 058[f]
		1899–1912: 046, 052[e], 058[f]
		1882–88: 055, 058
		1879–81: 055
124†	Manufactured, animal	*1910–23, 1879–1904:* 056, 059, 061*
		1905–09: 056, 059
125†	Crude, all	120, 122
126†	Manufactured, all	121, 124
127†	All fibers	125, 123, 126
	Agricultural Products	
128†	Crude, except fibers and tobacco	115, 118
129	Crude materials	125, 128
130†	Crude, including tobacco	129, 024
131†	Crude and semimanufactured	*1915–23:* 129, 033, 039, 042
		1879–1914: 129, 033, 039
132†	Crude and semimanufactured, including tobacco	131, 024
133†	Wood and products, except paper and pulp	062, 063, 064[g]
134†	Wood and products, including pulp	*1889–1923:* 133, 065
135	Nonagricultural crude materials of animal or vegetable origin	*1882–1923:* 029, 041, 062, 032
		1879–81: 029, 041, 062
	Products of Animal or Vegetable Origin	
136	Crude	129, 135
137†	Crude, including tobacco	136, 024
138	Nonagricultural semimanufactured	*1899–1923:* 027[c], 030[d], 034, 043, 063, 065, 123
		1889–98: 027[c], 030[d], 123, 043, 063, 065, 034*
		1879–88: 027[c], 030[d], 063, 123, 034*
139†	Nonagricultural manufactures	*1899–1923:* 028, 064[g], 066, 126, 035*, 037*
		1891–98: 126, 064[g], 028, 035*, 037*, 066*
		1882–90: 126, 064[g], 037*, 028*, 066*, 035*
		1879–81: 126, 064[g], 037*, 028*, 066*
140†	Nonagricultural crude and semimanufactured	135, 138
141	Crude and semimanufactured	131, 140
142†	Crude and semimanufactured, including tobacco	132, 140
	Products of Mineral Origin	
143	Crude fuels	*1913–23:* 067, 069
144†	Precious stones, crude and semimanufactured	*1899–1923:* 072, 073[h]
145†	Crude metals	*1882–1923:* 077[i], 080
		1879–81: 077

(continued)

TABLE B–8 (concluded)

Import Class	Class Composition
PRODUCTS OF MINERAL ORIGIN (continued)	
146† Semimanufactured metals	078, 081
147† Manufactured metal products	*1899–1913, 1923:* 079, 082, 084, 083*
	1879–98: 082, 079*, 083*
148† Crude materials	*1913–23:* 143, 072, 074, 145, 085ʲ
	1899–1912: 067, 072, 074, 145, 085, 069*
	1882–98: 067, 074, 145, 085
	1879–81: 067, 145, 085
149† Semimanufactures	*1906–23:* 068, 070, 073ʰ, 075, 146, 086
	1889–1905: 070, 073ʰ, 075, 146, 086
	1884–88: 073ʰ, 075, 146, 086, 070*
	1879–83: 073ʰ, 075, 146, 086
150† Manufactured products	*1917–23, 1914:* 087, 076, 071, 082, 084, 079*, 083*, 088*
	1915–16: 087, 076, 082, 084, 079*, 083*, 088*, 071*
	1913: 087, 076, 071, 147, 088*
	1889–1912: 147, 076, 087, 088*
	1879–88: 147, 076, 087*, 088*

NOTES TO TABLE B–8

† Annual Fisher price and quantity indexes and values are presented for these classes in Tables B–1 to B–6 inclusive. Data for import class 145 for 1879–88 are not included.

* Designates uncovered classes.

ᵃ Class 002 is an uncovered class for the period 1879–88. We used the indexes for Class 013 as a deflator.

ᵇ Class 020 is an uncovered class for 1879–88 and 1916–23. We used price indexes for Class 019 as deflators.

ᶜ Class 027 is an uncovered class for the years 1889–1912. We used price indexes for Class 026 as deflators.

ᵈ Class 030 is an uncovered class, deflated here by price indexes for Class 029.

ᵉ Class 052 is an uncovered class for the period 1889–98. We used price indexes for Class 051 as deflators.

ᶠ Class 058 is an uncovered class for the period 1882–98. In the 1899–1913 period, when all three indexes were available, those for Class 059, silk textiles, manufactured, resembled the ones for 058 much more than did the indexes for Class 057, silk textiles, crude. We therefore used the former as deflators.

ᵍ Class 064 is an uncovered class for 1879–98. The price index for Class 063 followed that for 064 very closely from 1899 to 1923, and was therefore used as a deflator during the earlier years.

ʰ Class 144 extends back only to 1899 because there is no Class 072 before then. But the figures for Class 073, 1879–98, include semimanufactured precious stones and are therefore comparable with Class 144. Class 073 is an uncovered class, 1899–1912. We used the price indexes for Class 072 as deflators.

ⁱ Class 077 is an uncovered class for the period 1879–88. We used price indexes for Class 078 as deflators.

ʲ Class 085 is an uncovered class for the period 1879–98. We used as deflators the indexes for Class 086 whose movements were very similar to those of 085 during 1899–1912, although not during 1913–23.

Appendix C

Indexes and Values for Minor Classes, 1879–1923, and Description of Composition and Sources of Data

THIS appendix presents our new annual price and quantity indexes and values for selected minor groups, 1879-1923, together with descriptions of the composition and source notes for all minor groups.

The minor groups vary a great deal in size, both as to value and number of commodities included. They are by no means all minor in importance, including, as they do, such items as imports of unmanufactured cotton (Import Class 045), exports of pork and related meat products (Export Class 009), and exports of grain (Export Class 005). They range from one-commodity classes such as exports of green coffee (Export Class 004) to imports of semimanufactured chemicals (Import Class 086) with commodity numbers for over 100 items.

Despite their differences in size and importance, these groups are the basic sampling units or blocks on which the various economic classifications were built (see Chapter 3). Some of the smaller classes were distinguished only to provide the flexibility necessary for various combinations: economic class, commodity group, or agricultural vs. nonagricultural. Others were distinguished for sampling reasons: their price behavior was distinctive and should not be applied to any uncovered commodities. For the most important groups, annual Fisher "ideal" price and quantity indexes and values are presented in Tables C-1 to C-6. Tables C-7 and C-8 list all minor classes and show the commodities included in each class, the years for which these commodities were covered or uncovered, the sources of price and quantity data, and other notes on the selection of commodities. Where no source notes are given, the data were obtained entirely from the official United States customs records (other sources are described in the notes). The customs records are published in the following sources:

Title	Dates	Agency
Monthly data:		
Monthly Summary of Foreign Commerce of the U.S.	July 1914—Dec. 1923	Bureau of Foreign and Domestic Commerce
Monthly Summary of Commerce and Finance of the U.S.	July 1912—June 1914	Bureau of Foreign and Domestic Commerce

Title	Dates	Agency
Monthly Summary of Commerce and Finance of the U.S.	July 1903— June 1912	Bureau of Statistics, Department of Commerce and Labor
Monthly Summary of Commerce and Finance of the U.S.	July 1898— June 1903	Bureau of Statistics, Treasury Department
Monthly Summary of Finance and Commerce of the U.S.	Jan. 1896— June 1898	Bureau of Statistics, Treasury Department
Finance, Commerce, and Immigration of the U.S.	Jan. 1895— Dec. 1895	Bureau of Statistics, Treasury Department
Summary Statement of the Imports and Exports of the U.S.	Jan. 1879— Dec. 1894	Bureau of Statistics, Treasury Department
Quarterly:		
Quarterly Report of the Chief of the Bureau of Statistics showing the imports and exports of the U.S.	1879— June 1893	Bureau of Statistics, Treasury Department
Annual:		
Foreign Commerce and Navigation of the U.S.	Fiscal years 1912–1918, Calendar years 1919–1923	Bureau of Foreign and Domestic Commerce
Foreign Commerce and Navigation of the U.S.	Fiscal years 1904–1911	Bureau of Statistics, Department of Commerce and Labor
Foreign Commerce and Navigation of the U.S.	Fiscal years 1893–1903	Bureau of Statistics, Treasury Department
Annual Report and Statement of the Chief of the Bureau of Statistics on the Foreign Commerce and Navigation, Immigration and Tonnage of the U.S.	Fiscal years 1885–1892	Bureau of Statistics, Treasury Department
Annual Report and Statement of the Chief of the Bureau of Statistics on the Commerce and Navigation of the U.S.	Fiscal years 1879–1884	Bureau of Statistics, Treasury Department

Additional official data compiled from the above sources were published in various issues of the *Statistical Abstract of the United States* and publications of *Imports and Duties,* giving data on imports for consumption for long periods. The latter were compiled under the direction of the House Ways and Means Committee by William W. Evans.

We also used a great variety of price data sources, both for comparison with unit values and as a substitute where unit values were not available. Some of the most frequently useful sources, with the abbreviations used in the notes to Tables C-7 and C-8 (which follow the tables), were :

Abbreviation in notes	Source
BLS	U.S. Department of Labor, Bureau of Labor Statistics, *Wholesale Prices: 1890 to 1923* (BLS Bulletin 367), Washington, D.C., 1925 and earlier volumes.

Abbreviation in notes	Source
BLS File	A file of published and unpublished price series copied for the National Bureau from the files of the BLS by the Works Progress Administration.
WIB	U.S. War Industries Board, *History of Prices During the War* (WIB Price Bulletins), Washington, D.C., 1919.
Aldrich	*Wholesale Prices, Wages, and Transportation,* Report by Nelson W. Aldrich from the U.S. Senate Committee on Finance, Washington, D.C., 1893.
Bezanson	Anne Bezanson, *Wholesale Prices in Philadelphia: 1852–1896,* Philadelphia, 1954.
The Economist	*Commercial History and Review,* Supplement of *The Economist,* London, various issues from 1890.
Canadian prices: 1890–1917 1918–23	Dominion of Canada, Department of Labour, *Wholesale Prices,* Ottawa. Dominion of Canada, Bureau of Statistics, Prices Branch, *Prices and Price Indexes,* Ottawa, Canada.
U.K. export and import unit values	Statistical Office of the Customs and Excise Department, *Annual Statement of the Trade and Navigation of the United Kingdom,* London; and Great Britain Board of Trade, *Statistical Abstract of the United Kingdom,* London.

One difficulty in the use of customs data is that of insuring the consistency of commodities over time. In the original source there are many changes of commodity title which do not involve changes in content; in other cases, titles remain the same while content changes. We have endeavored to correct for these inconsistencies by examining the unit values, watching for sudden changes in value, origin, or destination, and comparing general import figures with the more detailed imports for consumption data. For our covered commodities we expended considerable effort in this direction, but we were less energetic for uncovered commodities, where shifts did not appear to cross minor group lines. As long as the contents of a commodity title appeared consistent, or showed only insignificant shifts, we retained the same commodity number throughout; otherwise, a new number was given.

TABLE C-1

ANNUAL FISHER PRICE INDEXES,
SELECTED MINOR EXPORT CLASSES
(1913=100)

YEAR	001	005	008	009	011	012	014	015	075	028	042	044	052
1879	56.2	105.7	70.1	52.1	65.3	54.5	115.2	87.1	64.6	85.8	81.2	106.7	60.1
1880	53.8	111.4	69.1	60.1	77.8	74.6	122.3	94.5	69.1	93.6	91.0	122.1	65.7
1881	68.9	114.6	76.4	73.1	100.2	72.1	124.4	96.4	72.8	87.5	87.7	113.0	70.1
1882	79.4	119.0	83.4	87.9	110.2	72.8	129.0	101.0	72.1	86.3	87.7	118.8	71.8
1883	74.0	114.0	80.2	83.1	94.8	69.0	122.0	89.8	71.8	86.8	81.6	112.5	72.5
1884	75.2	97.7	79.0	79.9	82.8	65.6	110.8	92.7	71.9	90.9	82.8	105.0	67.8
1885	65.1	92.4	72.8	64.5	71.4	55.9	101.2	85.1	79.1	90.3	80.8	94.7	65.0
1886	64.5	86.4	62.8	59.5	64.4	57.4	95.9	77.7	77.2	83.5	74.7	94.7	64.0
1887	57.9	89.8	62.3	66.1	68.7	66.6	96.7	80.6	69.2	83.5	74.1	94.1	69.1
1888	64.2	93.7	65.6	71.4	80.3	61.5	99.6	81.6	74.8	74.3	77.7	101.3	71.6
1889	52.2	83.2	58.9	63.9	70.7	58.6	102.0	81.0	71.3	71.0	78.0	103.3	70.7
1890	55.8	83.5	58.9	59.9	65.7	55.3	98.8	77.8	71.3	70.6	78.9	100.3	69.9
1891	60.0	108.9	63.1	61.0	67.4	60.5	100.8	78.3	71.5	71.5	72.8	94.1	69.5
1892	60.2	93.9	63.1	64.9	71.6	63.5	100.7	77.7	73.3	73.4	65.6	87.1	65.8
1893	64.7	80.2	67.6	69.4	90.9	66.8	92.9	86.4	74.5	71.6	64.7	85.7	65.4
1894	59.0	69.7	64.7	69.4	75.1	66.8	78.6	75.8	76.1	68.1	50.8	81.3	60.4
1895	64.0	70.6	67.3	65.2	66.2	56.8	74.4	63.8	71.5	81.0	53.3	83.8	52.7
1896	56.4	65.9	61.2	57.8	52.2	55.5	76.5	60.5	68.8	83.7	59.4	74.0	62.2
1897	63.5	73.5	60.7	56.9	47.7	57.2	89.2	58.4	69.4	72.9	59.6	74.9	69.1
1898	65.0	79.0	64.5	59.2	52.9	57.9	91.6	58.1	76.0	77.7	43.2	67.9	61.4
1899	71.1	74.9	66.2	59.9	55.2	63.2	79.8	60.1	73.7	78.4	50.2	68.3	67.0
1900	70.6	75.4	68.7	65.2	62.1	66.9	76.7	72.5	75.0	79.5	71.7	80.6	72.2
1901	73.1	77.9	69.7	70.7	74.2	64.7	80.3	75.2	74.3	72.9	65.9	76.4	71.7
1902	84.7	87.4	79.4	79.6	88.5	71.4	82.7	83.7	80.1	78.1	80.9	73.9	81.5
1903	74.2	89.8	71.9	81.5	81.6	69.9	90.1	79.7	76.1	81.6	84.8	76.2	80.2
1904	76.3	89.6	68.3	75.5	69.5	62.3	92.1	74.3	77.8	82.9	73.7	86.0	80.3
1905	77.5	84.4	69.0	72.6	69.4	70.6	82.1	72.4	80.3	86.9	73.6	86.5	97.4
1906	78.9	88.6	69.3	77.6	75.4	73.2	86.9	81.4	82.1	86.5	87.3	90.5	107.4
1907	81.2	98.9	74.5	82.7	83.2	81.9	90.9	88.0	87.5	93.7	83.6	99.9	96.3
1908	80.9	107.2	81.2	79.1	82.2	81.0	100.9	86.7	90.4	86.6	78.1	89.6	92.6
1909	89.9	112.5	81.1	82.1	94.4	91.3	109.3	90.6	88.2	93.6	92.3	87.8	94.0
1910	91.7	104.4	88.3	101.6	108.3	95.0	106.5	103.7	92.5	92.1	113.4	99.8	93.3
1911	84.4	99.4	80.3	89.8	87.8	83.2	92.4	98.8	95.9	99.4	90.3	99.8	95.9
1912	99.0	106.1	89.7	91.4	95.1	99.1	98.3	98.2	96.1	99.3	87.0	96.2	
1913	100.0	100.0	100.0	100.0	100.0	100.0	100.0	100.0	100.0	100.0	100.0	100.0	100.0
1914	112.4	119.3	94.7	105.0	97.4	98.4	107.4	99.8	105.8	106.8	81.5	107.8	94.1
1915	108.5	144.1	101.2	100.9	96.3	92.4	131.4	107.8	101.6	118.3	74.4	133.4	92.5
1916	122.4	153.2	106.0	112.5	117.5	101.9	129.4	129.4	109.5	147.8	116.5	176.9	93.9
1917	170.4	237.6	126.0	162.4	179.1	143.5	207.4	169.5	151.2	216.7	180.9	273.2	117.8
1918	192.5	254.2	177.9	210.5	231.6	155.9	242.9	229.0	253.3	216.1	247.0	306.4	163.9
1919	224.5	256.5	197.7	237.2	273.3	175.4	241.7	264.1	282.6	260.7	263.0	390.0	195.3
1920	214.6	287.2	146.4	193.3	209.0	190.5	248.5	243.4	437.0	287.8	278.4	202.0	259.2
1921	133.1	158.0	117.9	135.4	114.7	163.4	144.7	145.5	331.5	146.3	124.6	207.9	167.3
1922	121.1	126.0	109.2	128.1	105.8	135.5	121.8	152.6	282.7	128.3	166.3	207.9	152.6
1923	126.0	129.2	118.6	108.3	112.6	156.0	117.7	156.4	267.8	131.1	229.2	235.2	183.1

251

YEAR	055	057	059	060	061	066	067	069	070	071	072	074	075
1879		81.1	124.7		127.4	79.9		169.0	124.2	116.2			98.2
1880		106.9	130.2		143.5	80.1		232.5	138.7	123.4			105.1
1881		109.6	131.7		136.5	83.4		194.0	126.6	112.1			104.3
1882		109.2	129.2	186.7	127.0	83.1		202.1	125.4	122.6			106.3
1883		108.2	129.7	195.8	128.4	86.1		176.0	116.9	124.3			103.0
1884		100.9	132.0	206.3	130.1	79.5		146.1	119.2	128.5			100.5
1885		93.0	127.9	212.6	126.9	68.2		125.8	113.0	116.9			89.4
1886		90.9	114.4	193.9	116.2	64.6		117.8	102.0	113.3			87.5
1887		95.1	109.9	178.4	109.8	65.0		125.1	102.0	111.5			87.5
1888		100.0	121.3	174.8	116.6	96.8		121.7	97.5	116.7			87.3
1889	126.0	97.5	124.1	161.2	107.5	73.2		114.6	96.1	115.8	155.0	87.9	95.9
1890	123.4	100.8	116.7	141.2	103.1	79.6		115.1	97.9	112.9	153.5	95.7	89.4
1891	103.4	102.5	95.6	176.5	95.1	81.2		117.8	94.6	111.8	151.6	95.1	89.3
1892	107.8	102.2	77.5	171.8	80.6	74.1		122.3	89.1	105.9	151.9	91.4	86.7
1893	109.2	95.9	59.4	132.6	68.3	66.0		102.9	87.5	104.8	138.5	91.7	89.4
1894	114.0	87.0	70.0	111.3	63.7	60.2		84.9	79.7	102.3	134.4	92.4	81.5
1895	113.2	81.6	93.3	113.8	90.8	65.4		96.4	81.1	109.1	131.4	92.0	75.6
1896	104.1	86.1	88.0	117.1	93.4	69.5		90.2	81.7	109.1	129.0	100.6	79.1
1897	109.0	87.0	71.4	112.1	84.1	71.5		78.5	81.7	127.5	134.0	101.6	76.5
1898	108.9	82.5	71.8	110.4	74.1	74.5		72.8	70.0	114.5	130.7	87.4	76.8
1899		82.0	87.3	121.4	94.4	105.6		92.4	77.1	105.2			78.5
1900		87.7	91.6	150.4	104.3	103.3		105.1	99.0	103.2			84.4
1901		91.8	81.9	151.5	103.9	103.4		104.6	96.5	101.5			79.5
1902		100.9	75.1	138.3	90.1	79.3		120.8	96.3	102.6			82.6
1903		103.1	82.5	135.7	105.6	85.7		114.6	102.5	101.5			86.3
1904		102.2	92.5	136.6	106.5	83.4		97.5	98.4	101.0			96.4
1905		98.9	78.1	141.3	88.8	97.2		106.3	107.4	98.6			88.3
1906		98.6	83.8	140.8	89.6	119.1		109.7	116.0	99.1			92.1
1907		98.5	83.4	142.0	94.6	119.3		121.9	111.9	101.2			93.0
1908		98.5	82.0	141.1	96.4	86.0		118.3	104.2	102.6			93.6
1909	93.6	97.4	77.3	121.1	90.5	85.4		102.9	106.0	103.2			92.1
1910	92.9	96.1	70.7	105.8	84.7	83.0		102.8	99.2	103.4	146.0	85.4	98.5
1911	92.9	97.7	70.8	95.1	80.5	81.9		98.3	97.7	101.4	120.4	94.2	101.6
1912	97.0	100.4	84.4	94.1	89.0	102.4		97.6		102.6	105.3	97.7	96.5
1913	100.0	100.0	100.0	100.0	100.0	100.0	100.0	100.0	100.0	100.0	100.0	100.0	100.0
1914	95.0	98.6	87.8	100.7	91.2	89.5	80.8	95.6	92.1	99.0	84.6	101.7	99.9
1915	94.6	100.2	66.3	96.9	88.5	115.6	131.3	98.0	99.7	97.9	77.7	163.8	161.7
1916	124.9	97.6	102.3	104.6	119.5	174.3	228.0	152.3	138.9	110.4	72.5	239.6	199.2
1917	169.4	134.7	110.7	150.3	142.0	192.1	237.7	257.4	192.4	129.5	74.7	252.0	208.0
1918	180.5	145.8	147.2	214.4	181.4	163.6	191.5	270.5	216.8	158.8	81.4	266.5	224.7
1919	196.8	175.0	147.5	213.1	188.6	138.5	152.7	226.7	212.6	170.0	96.9	223.0	186.1
1920	284.9	301.4	201.9	240.6	224.3	129.0	154.2	233.0	226.2	177.5	109.2	247.8	218.4
1921	233.8	225.9	124.8	180.5	191.7	88.6	106.7	198.6	204.4	163.5	98.6	192.5	167.7
1922	171.1	224.8	117.0	122.2	153.6	89.9	101.5	141.2	151.1	144.0	78.4	170.5	147.1
1923	203.6	212.8	94.2	102.9	131.3	100.8	115.2	175.8	175.7	146.8	73.3	171.5	143.7

APPENDIX C

TABLE C-2

ANNUAL FISHER PRICE INDEXES, SELECTED MINOR IMPORT CLASSES
(1913=100)

Year										
1879	94.0	144.3	101.2	157.1	184.9	87.8	95.6	74.6		
1880	102.1	144.4	114.6	110.8	226.6	93.3	107.5	86.0		
1881	107.9	137.7	89.0	102.9	224.7	94.3	104.9	87.1	84.6	
1882	114.9	131.2	73.8	104.8	224.8	92.3	108.2	108.2	81.1	
1883	109.1	111.3	67.2	100.4	203.7	88.5	106.7	99.3	80.7	
1884	108.4	106.1	73.3	103.8	153.7	90.8	106.0	66.1	77.7	
1885	109.9	106.9	63.9	108.1	125.6	90.5	102.2	58.6	76.9	
1886	99.7	101.7	65.2	106.9	129.5	89.4	94.9	69.9	76.3	
1887	108.4	94.3	113.9	109.0	123.4	93.6	84.9	71.1	74.6	
1888	96.2	84.8	100.3	106.3	147.1	94.3	75.1	63.4	75.3	
1889	86.6	81.3	115.8	94.9	155.8	176.9	94.3	71.0	59.7	
1890	105.7	85.5	133.6	101.4	165.0	146.0	96.2	63.2	74.2	
1891	113.1	87.6	124.2	116.7	165.0	147.9	76.4	59.5	74.8	
1892	114.1	85.2	113.7	114.3	137.5	143.9	83.2	56.3	67.3	
1893	101.2	86.3	132.3	129.2	146.7	159.8	89.6	53.5	73.7	
1894	73.1	74.1	125.9	94.0	165.0	128.0	93.7	55.0	69.6	
1895	69.0	73.8	122.4	84.5	137.5	94.7	85.4	60.0	70.2	
1896	66.0	69.5	103.4	77.1	165.0	116.3	102.2	63.3	58.6	
1897	79.4	73.2	76.5	85.7	110.0	100.7	106.1	63.6	70.4	
1898	87.8	75.3	54.3	114.0	119.2	111.9		71.2	78.6	
1899	77.5	67.8	52.0	108.3	119.2	121.2	108.7	72.6	96.2	75.5
1900	81.3	66.3	61.7	112.7	137.5	121.0	100.3	88.6	88.6	81.4
1901	71.8	69.6	53.3	105.5	126.7	104.8	93.0	79.4	78.0	87.6
1902	70.8	72.7	55.3	101.9	121.9	78.5	85.5	79.4	75.7	83.8
1903	73.1	89.8	51.3	96.7	125.0	89.5	87.0	80.4	94.1	87.8
1904	69.0	85.8	64.0	95.5	114.0	99.6	89.0	81.9	105.7	88.0
1905	66.0	84.0	68.6	89.0	99.5	134.6	91.4	84.7	113.0	88.4
1906	79.4	85.2	62.2	92.7	95.5	99.7	107.4	92.6	119.3	88.1
1907	87.8	91.2	62.3	138.7	91.6	105.5	116.2	96.4	113.2	90.5
1908	74.9	88.0	61.8	87.1	89.3	116.9	113.4	79.4	137.5	87.0
1909	72.2	86.0	74.7	82.4	89.9	116.0	103.7	83.8	169.2	84.0
1910	84.9	92.0	98.9	85.9	92.6	133.2	83.8	87.2	132.8	86.8
1911	91.6	95.4	112.8	87.5	97.1	119.2	102.9	85.7	125.2	90.2
1912	91.1	98.7			101.4	134.2	105.4	90.7		92.1
1913	100.0	100.0	100.0	100.0	100.0	100.0	100.0	100.0	100.0	100.0
1914	94.2	101.2	84.4	85.3	99.0	115.2	98.3	102.4	91.3	76.0
1915	89.8	108.6	75.4	107.5	97.0	166.3	89.2	99.9	82.5	91.5
1916	99.7	99.6	82.9	110.7	99.2	201.7	102.6	116.8	97.6	89.2
1917	105.4	121.0	77.6	84.0	109.0	220.5	124.0	168.8	131.7	70.1
1918	129.5	133.8	77.0	83.5	121.4	229.5	153.8	151.1	194.0	63.1
1919	169.2	149.6	159.6	117.3	123.4	275.1	177.6	204.7	214.5	67.2
1920	171.3	153.4	158.5	125.1	140.8	616.0	189.1	240.5	226.1	27.9
1921	126.8	109.2	86.7	60.0	126.3	193.5	182.4	94.2	155.5	23.7
1922	120.5	142.0	105.1	73.5	123.0	127.3	155.5	101.7	157.5	41.9
1923	100.2	166.5	109.9	64.6	132.5	242.1	171.0	114.9	137.8	

253

YEAR	049	051	053	054	056	057	059	062	063	065
1879		91.9	117.4	86.0	89.7	144.0	108.3	121.8	51.5	149.5
1880		99.0	120.5	104.1	90.8	137.4	105.9	141.3	58.9	165.6
1881		98.1	114.4	94.6	91.2	133.3	108.8	126.6	63.3	166.3
1882		105.9	116.1	91.3	91.6	142.5	107.1	117.8	72.0	171.3
1883		101.8	117.1	85.7	86.9	122.8	108.3	115.8	72.0	177.7
1884		91.1	104.8	82.8	86.6	118.4	100.3	109.0	68.6	161.1
1885		81.5	97.1	75.4	83.3	111.1	94.7	103.0	64.5	108.6
1886		78.4	91.9	72.4	81.0	120.6	94.8	90.5	66.7	74.3
1887		93.6	93.8	85.5	83.4	122.7	93.6	83.7	67.2	77.3
1888		99.9	89.6	78.6	79.9	109.6	92.6	88.3	66.3	75.6
1889	63.9	112.2	93.8	81.4	78.6	114.1	97.0	93.6	66.8	
1890	59.8	90.9	91.5	83.3	77.8	126.3	95.8	91.4	63.5	
1891	56.8	90.3	91.5	75.4	78.6	109.0	91.4	84.8	59.9	
1892	60.5	84.8	89.5	69.7	75.3	112.3	96.2	86.0	62.9	
1893	55.3	79.2	90.2	70.6	74.8	117.6	101.9	86.9	62.4	
1894	54.8	56.9	86.6	63.4	77.8	88.5	91.2	90.9	66.2	
1895	52.8	49.7	78.9	66.2	75.3	97.3	93.6	85.8	60.4	
1896	54.1	50.3	84.5	71.1	79.3	97.2	89.0	82.0	58.1	
1897	53.5	45.5	83.0	69.6	75.2	89.5	90.7	79.7	55.2	
1898	49.5	65.5	83.8	67.9	73.6	89.2	90.9	80.4	54.9	
1899	56.5	83.8	85.0	64.2	77.7	112.8	100.3	84.5	57.2	92.5
1900	61.5	103.3	93.7	75.7	81.9	120.7	97.7	88.3	67.2	98.1
1901	64.8	84.8	92.6	60.7	82.3	105.2	93.1	85.4	74.8	96.1
1902	56.4	108.6	91.3	59.9	82.1	105.8	96.1	87.5	80.2	90.2
1903	57.9	99.3	91.9	74.3	82.5	115.3	96.3	86.2	82.2	90.2
1904	58.3	106.2	95.7	82.1	83.2	105.2	95.0	84.9	83.7	96.8
1905	64.6	108.5	93.3	94.7	84.7	110.1	95.7	93.9	84.6	99.2
1906	81.5	107.2	97.7	101.7	88.9	119.8	95.9	94.4	91.2	100.3
1907	92.4	106.7	104.4	106.6	91.3	142.6	100.7	84.3	103.5	101.7
1908	70.2	83.5	100.9	79.6	80.2	106.9	96.6	85.0	104.2	102.8
1909	61.0	75.3	91.3	87.1	87.5	103.8	97.0	92.0	101.5	99.2
1910	54.5	76.2	94.7	97.8	86.6	99.4	97.0	95.8	102.9	95.8
1911	65.3	77.2	97.8	89.8	95.3	90.8	97.0	95.3	97.6	94.5
1912	87.4	82.7	98.1	91.2	99.1	97.4	97.4	96.9	95.9	95.5
1913	100.0	100.0	100.0	100.0	100.0	100.0	100.0	100.0	100.0	100.0
1914	90.3	92.2	93.7	100.8	86.2	109.1	87.6	98.8	105.5	101.3
1915	80.7	87.7	111.1	105.0	81.3	97.2	92.0	95.4	103.5	101.7
1916	112.7	97.7	142.4	122.6	104.4	130.0	109.8	105.3	107.7	143.6
1917	122.4	179.2	177.1	184.6	120.2	157.3	117.6	123.4	127.6	234.7
1918	204.5	270.3	262.1	238.9	161.6	170.9	142.4	155.0	152.6	196.5
1919	165.2	171.0	295.2	219.1	216.0	220.0	178.9	162.0	175.2	208.4
1920	173.8	151.4	348.3	210.0	222.6	229.4	196.2	215.5	224.1	324.1
1921	96.9	94.6	237.8	81.7	169.7	170.0	113.3	174.0	182.6	188.3
1922	105.1	209.2	209.2	109.3	157.4	224.8	131.3	134.9	154.0	155.1
1923	124.4	87.6	182.8	145.3	157.9	246.9	122.6	138.8	164.2	169.6

YEAR	066	069	072	073	076	077	078	081	082	086
1879				63.6	87.5	73.9	44.3	108.2	175.0	132.3
1880				67.7	97.1	94.8	56.8	132.2	189.2	154.5
1881				81.3	89.2	97.2	58.1	106.7	182.7	138.2
1882				69.7	90.4	106.9	64.1	107.0	175.3	136.3
1883				53.3	92.3	98.1	58.9	106.8	161.4	131.6
1884				56.6	84.7	84.9	50.0	101.6	159.0	134.7
1885				46.5	79.7	86.8	52.1	92.7	153.5	119.5
1886				50.8	76.4	101.1	60.6	87.1	143.6	119.2
1887				53.8	74.0	103.8	62.3	85.3	133.0	115.6
1888				47.1		112.5	67.5	85.8	135.3	106.8
1889				66.0	79.1	90.3	54.2	88.6	142.5	103.8
1890				74.6	85.4	92.5	57.2	102.5	137.2	106.7
1891				57.6	88.9	123.2	54.5	107.8	122.3	113.3
1892				57.8	80.5	121.7	55.1	90.8	124.1	114.2
1893				67.1	74.2	103.2	55.1	88.0	121.0	112.6
1894				54.2	64.5	81.7	42.8	84.3	100.1	98.4
1895				58.5	68.6	72.7	39.8	80.8	100.1	91.9
1896				57.9	68.3	59.6	38.8	79.1	100.1	98.9
1897				56.5	68.6	67.1	39.8	84.4	110.1	94.7
1898				59.2	69.2	69.3	39.3	84.9	100.1	83.1
1899	129.2		68.6	68.6	77.8	84.1	66.9	99.6	100.1	87.5
1900	124.0		82.4	82.6	82.2	95.5	75.2	117.4	107.7	93.5
1901	126.8		88.0	88.0	90.5	105.5	74.3	99.4	111.9	93.9
1902	132.7		89.8	89.8	85.9	90.7	66.6	88.1	107.1	91.4
1903	130.0		90.7	90.7	80.6	84.1	69.3	86.8	101.3	94.8
1904	130.0		95.1	95.1	80.2	87.5	70.4	86.8	98.1	95.5
1905	135.5		91.9	91.9	89.4	90.9	76.6	89.5	101.1	95.0
1906	129.2		106.3	106.3	88.2	104.4	96.3	101.1	99.2	99.6
1907	127.4		93.0	93.0	87.5	113.3	109.0	114.3	102.6	104.0
1908	118.4		44.8	44.8	87.2	97.1	77.3	92.9	97.9	98.2
1909	102.6		58.1	58.1	85.6	92.9	73.4	88.9	94.5	91.4
1910	98.2		68.7	68.7	88.5	91.5	76.4	90.9	99.5	90.0
1911	101.4		79.6	79.6	92.5	91.8	86.0	91.7		94.0
1912	100.8		93.2	93.2		102.5	96.8	99.2		98.9
1913	100.0	100.0	100.0	100.0	100.0	100.0	100.0	100.0	100.0	100.0
1914	98.9	91.9	78.1	86.9	94.2	103.2	86.6	91.7	106.8	94.2
1915	96.2	88.8	105.6	121.3	115.8	114.2	93.4	113.7	132.4	101.3
1916	103.3	93.8	82.7	97.3	142.2	160.3	125.8	160.5	174.5	149.7
1917	145.3	83.7	97.2	100.0	164.6	168.1	148.5	232.8	194.5	160.0
1918	154.0	87.6	108.8	117.2	199.5	184.2	157.5	275.0	188.0	187.8
1919	182.3	77.9	164.7	188.8	218.0	164.4	138.2	204.1	201.0	163.6
1920	243.2	81.5	205.0	231.0	258.1	159.3	131.3	232.4	188.4	173.6
1921	253.3	82.3	147.4	159.3	238.6	102.9	80.5	166.2	133.8	143.4
1922	179.9	85.8	136.1	147.2	193.8	98.1	79.9	128.5	131.2	128.7
1923	192.1	101.9	87.2	148.9	202.1	133.9	96.6	141.4		133.0

255

APPENDIX C

TABLE C-3

ANNUAL FISHER QUANTITY INDEXES, SELECTED MINOR EXPORT CLASSES (1913=100)

YEAR	001	005	008	009	011	012	014	015	025	028	042	044	052
1879	305.2	155.1	613.6	167.2	48.8	1237.3	48.5	21.0	41.6	17.5	39.9	20.3	19.3
1880	579.2	160.3	696.2	182.3	59.3	1180.7	52.9	23.2	49.5	19.7	45.7	18.3	19.9
1881	297.7	122.6	592.1	141.7	45.6	1058.1	51.2	15.9	47.8	20.3	43.9	23.8	22.2
1882	131.8	87.0	423.4	81.7	35.5	693.4	55.8	14.1	49.4	22.4	44.5	22.0	28.1
1883	419.4	80.9	622.1	98.5	44.1	881.4	68.6	19.7	52.5	20.7	47.9	21.6	26.8
1884	332.5	77.2	587.7	81.7	36.4	876.2	71.1	21.0	44.9	22.8	46.5	20.3	24.3
1885	375.6	67.7	668.3	99.9	45.8	762.8	72.6	24.1	63.5	22.9	39.7	26.6	25.6
1886	303.2	91.1	529.4	103.5	50.6	660.7	73.0	27.8	69.4	24.5	50.1	31.9	23.0
1887	277.0	86.7	542.7	95.8	47.7	536.1	88.6	23.0	57.2	28.6	50.0	28.7	23.0
1888	359.7	51.5	640.4	79.6	40.3	576.3	78.3	22.4	47.2	29.8	50.4	20.8	26.1
1889	881.7	69.2	1007.2	119.8	60.9	821.5	77.4	28.9	58.2	40.2	59.4	19.3	31.7
1890	1056.3	77.3	1254.3	138.5	84.8	797.4	84.0	37.9	56.0	40.6	56.0	21.4	30.2
1891	740.4	114.4	1168.0	130.3	71.5	614.0	95.5	34.1	53.8	43.8	66.1	28.3	26.0
1892	1024.0	130.0	1276.8	139.4	80.5	600.9	126.9	44.4	56.0	35.2	57.5	26.9	31.4
1893	613.3	105.7	938.0	99.7	64.6	475.5	119.4	37.7	60.4	44.1	54.8	32.7	29.3
1894	978.3	68.4	1054.5	125.0	83.9	511.3	154.9	38.3	67.7	50.1	68.6	34.6	32.7
1895	812.0	75.7	989.3	133.9	84.8	389.5	117.4	50.1	65.3	51.6	62.0	35.8	36.1
1896	1180.1	137.2	1376.4	141.7	90.7	555.8	121.6	55.1	66.0	57.7	67.8	46.7	40.7
1897	1114.2	189.7	1205.8	174.3	103.7	700.0	111.0	72.9	62.0	58.3	73.1	53.2	48.5
1898	924.9	224.7	1156.4	207.4	122.4	425.3	133.0	96.0	59.1	62.6	93.8	55.8	46.8
1899	793.2	189.6	1382.0	198.6	116.5	543.1	151.5	106.7	57.9	73.3	66.4	70.4	50.9
1900	877.1	171.9	1421.7	178.1	108.1	522.9	155.6	99.4	67.7	69.7	76.5	64.7	55.1
1901	936.4	188.3	1508.7	179.0	109.6	517.8	156.1	105.9	68.3	77.0	76.9	86.2	53.4
1902	531.0	107.5	1198.5	153.4	88.9	259.0	144.9	93.6	80.6	76.0	76.9	65.9	50.1
1903	904.4	100.2	1340.6	119.5	100.0	266.8	154.9	83.5	70.1	75.5	75.7	74.6	60.0
1904	990.0	34.6	1222.8	123.0	105.1	362.5	96.5	90.1	78.3	83.8	92.7	126.0	62.4
1905	966.5	80.5	1310.2	142.4	129.8	309.7	110.6	113.8	65.0	84.9	85.9	88.6	59.0
1906	886.8	106.7	1220.1	161.8	129.6	468.3	117.3	117.3	73.9	99.2	93.5	99.2	67.1
1907	773.8	105.6	1105.3	133.7	118.2	216.2	123.1	104.2	70.9	78.4	97.6	46.7	72.5
1908	559.1	87.9	670.9	106.1	115.4	240.6	103.4	114.4	68.2	84.2	86.9	53.2	62.2
1909	343.1	53.8	470.3	71.0	93.3	91.3	79.3	96.1	66.2	92.3	81.3	72.0	66.8
1910	209.9	41.1	302.3	103.6	74.6	88.5	71.2	71.6	73.7	105.8	99.5	62.8	77.0
1911	364.6	52.9	238.3	98.1	113.3	198.3	101.5	98.0	83.0	104.9	124.4	83.3	88.0
1912	149.4	71.0	130.7		97.2	128.3	87.3	112.9	92.3	114.8		98.9	94.8
1913	100.0	100.0	100.0	100.0	100.0	100.0	100.0	100.0	100.0	100.0	100.0	100.0	100.0
1914	94.2	149.8	305.1	82.8	82.0	133.1	101.8	80.4	78.4	112.9	73.3	87.6	68.3
1915	125.6	216.8	1258.4	192.1	90.2	825.1	131.3	114.7	87.5	177.5	97.3	167.0	48.8
1916	122.3	179.4	931.4	210.5	80.4	1339.5	128.9	89.1	108.4	176.8	81.3	180.0	49.8
1917	90.4	140.0	1190.7	195.8	63.2	1775.0	142.0	42.0	56.9	98.8	55.2	163.6	49.9
1918	88.3	140.3	2458.0	356.8	91.4	2331.8	203.9	25.0	91.7	65.7	47.3	120.3	43.5
1919	200.6	157.7	912.2	393.5	135.7	3124.3	248.5	64.2	173.8	220.3	75.1	162.3	56.4
1920	203.4	205.7	477.4	191.4	103.0	1602.5	182.4	47.7	106.1	101.0	70.9	191.5	59.2
1921	312.5	282.0	124.2	160.2	144.6	1014.2	172.6	73.6	116.9	58.1	74.5	107.8	42.6
1922	237.8	236.6	86.0	155.1	127.0	695.3	148.0	39.1	97.9	94.7	70.4	122.0	55.0
1923	151.8	112.1	71.7	202.1	159.4	661.5	152.2	35.1	108.2	87.3	61.2	105.4	70.9

Year	(1)	(2)	(3)	(4)	(5)	(6)	(7)	(8)	(9)	(10)	(11)	(12)	(13)
1879	12.4			4.1	3.5	.2		3.0	19.6		19.6		
1880	13.0			4.1	3.8	.2		1.1	15.7		24.3	3.6	
1881	15.0			5.7	5.1	.4		1.8	23.6		27.7	3.5	
1882	16.9			6.9	5.7	.5		1.3	23.1	4.9	30.8	4.6	
1883	18.0			7.8	5.4	.4		2.8	23.9	7.0	40.4	5.3	
1884	15.7			6.2	4.7	.4		3.4	29.6	8.4	54.6	7.3	
1885	15.4			5.1	4.3	.5		4.0	24.4	10.7	55.8	6.6	
1886	17.6			5.0	4.8	.7		2.3	26.3	11.6	52.3	6.8	
1887	18.9			5.7	5.3	.5		1.7	27.0	14.0	55.3	8.5	
1888	19.3			6.6	6.5	1.2		3.6	26.0	14.7	53.2	10.2	
1889	22.6			9.5	7.1	.8		2.0	31.1	17.4	58.4	9.8	
1890	24.4			10.4	8.5	1.1		1.3	31.5	25.3	66.2	10.7	
1891	23.4			11.5	9.1	1.0		7.6	30.5	27.6	66.3	12.6	
1892	24.0			12.0	10.9	1.7		3.8	33.5	29.0	71.5	12.7	
1893	23.3			11.3	12.4	2.1		15.3	39.4	42.0	78.9	18.9	
1894	26.9			12.4	14.4	3.8		17.6	40.8	36.0	78.7	19.3	
1895	34.3			14.0	20.6	17.3		13.0	39.7	48.4	79.6	18.9	
1896	33.8			19.1	29.3	19.5		28.1	43.8	47.7	80.9	19.0	
1897	37.1			27.6	42.3			30.3	46.4	57.7	83.5	22.3	
1898	38.7							31.8	46.4	70.5	82.5		
1899	49.6		.4	33.4	51.3	22.0		26.9	45.2	77.1	80.8	28.4	39.7
1900	48.2		.8	38.8	48.5	32.6		37.2	45.7	66.5	94.9	36.4	50.7
1901	50.7	57.2	1.4	35.1	43.6	12.7		21.3	50.8	64.3	87.2	35.6	63.0
1902	51.7	58.9	2.1	37.0	36.4	7.9		26.9	49.0	74.3	99.7	26.6	59.8
1903	54.8	59.6	3.2	40.8	34.2	8.2		32.3	44.3	86.5	97.3	39.1	59.0
1904	60.0	59.7	4.1	43.2	46.2	31.6		58.6	49.5	74.0	81.3	41.5	61.5
1905	68.1	61.6	6.0	51.7	50.2	27.1		56.5	56.8	68.1	92.2	43.5	69.0
1906	70.4	67.4	10.1	61.7	54.9	34.9		48.4	61.8	73.5	109.2	46.2	88.2
1907	78.9	75.3	13.4	67.4	59.1	32.5		53.2	65.8	87.9	89.9	60.3	70.8
1908	74.1	80.1	11.0	53.6	46.0	27.3		68.5	75.3	60.0	94.1	60.5	59.3
1909	77.1	77.1	17.9	51.4	54.1	40.3		71.4	76.8	76.8	92.3	58.5	83.2
1910	83.3	88.2	27.1	65.2	65.7	54.5		75.0	74.3	84.7	90.5	64.9	90.8
1911	89.4	105.3	47.8	79.1	83.4	86.6		85.4	88.0	90.7	103.0	79.2	98.8
1912	99.7	103.7	80.7	91.5	94.6	130.1		84.3	93.7	124.8	95.0	83.1	105.5
1913	100.0	100.0	100.0	100.0	100.0	100.0	100.0	100.0	100.0	100.0	100.0	100.0	100.0
1914	98.5	106.8	121.3	67.9	69.9	64.2	100.5	101.5	97.9	133.6	66.8	81.7	104.7
1915	539.5	213.0	431.1	97.5	142.8	169.1	437.8	101.5	107.6	195.9	76.4	90.7	133.4
1916	1615.6	349.0	499.7	139.7	224.0	340.5	1171.0	134.1	107.1	232.0	81.4	103.8	205.1
1917	1416.0	373.0	483.6	152.3	188.0	374.1	677.8	168.5	111.2	228.2	82.0	121.6	181.1
1918	568.7	293.0	356.7	125.6	117.1	352.1	160.5	96.4	121.4	143.7	97.1	109.8	206.8
1919	211.3	297.0	470.0	167.3	133.6	237.4	181.9	68.7	158.6	200.2	118.9	102.0	308.2
1920	261.3	347.2	820.4	180.3	143.6	252.2	213.1	75.8	126.2	174.2	169.9	172.2	200.6
1921	111.8	137.3	249.6	130.7	93.2	102.1	155.3	64.8	141.8	126.2	185.6	110.5	107.8
1922	136.9	150.1	375.6	87.2	71.5	90.2	112.7	77.0		159.2		60.2	122.4
1923	156.0	180.3	681.7	101.3	76.5	89.9	128.9	86.4	168.4	252.2	290.4	107.4	109.5

APPENDIX C

TABLE C-4

ANNUAL FISHER QUANTITY INDEXES, SELECTED MINOR IMPORT CLASSES
(1913=100)

YEAR	007	008	009	010	011	019	024	026	036	047
1879	26.4	83.9	52.5	4.3		37.5	11.3	19.7	1.4	
1880	27.8	79.9	47.3	4.3		41.5	14.9	27.4	1.5	
1881	30.0	95.5	54.7	6.9		41.9	14.7	26.8	2.6	51.1
1882	35.1	80.2	59.4	6.4		49.2	17.4	23.8	2.1	60.7
1883	35.0	84.0	61.7	7.3		50.7	25.9	20.9	1.9	61.1
1884	34.1	84.9	61.1	7.3		58.6	19.4	20.0	1.9	52.9
1885	32.2	83.3	66.4	6.8		61.1	25.9	20.8	2.1	74.4
1886	34.9	95.1	64.6	8.9		64.7	23.8	26.6	2.6	66.4
1887	39.5	94.6	51.9	8.4		62.5	31.8	26.4	2.6	70.7
1888	42.8	98.7	61.4	11.2		62.8	26.7	31.5	2.8	63.6
1889	39.1	89.6	64.3	10.2	15.8	58.5	40.2	29.8	2.6	78.2
1890	46.9	100.8	57.6	13.2	22.0	66.0	52.6	39.0	2.8	82.8
1891	37.6	98.8	68.2	12.8	20.4	94.8	29.9	41.1	3.1	75.2
1892	39.1	102.6	72.4	15.8	23.8	76.2	45.6	47.2	3.3	93.2
1893	42.2	92.6	63.7	13.6	23.9	78.5	35.4	40.2	4.2	96.1
1894	44.7	114.7	71.0	13.3	19.5	84.6	44.3	31.8	2.9	85.9
1895	45.0	110.0	75.3	19.2	21.4	73.6	48.7	57.3	2.5	99.1
1896	53.3	94.3	73.9	21.4	16.5	79.7	33.9	30.9	2.8	124.9
1897	39.5	112.0	94.6	17.5	25.2	78.3	44.7	49.4	3.0	138.6
1898	37.4	77.3	94.3	18.2	23.8	69.4	22.3	52.9	3.7	103.3
1899	46.5	98.3	103.0	24.6	36.0	90.3	29.0	66.4	4.5	
1900	40.5	108.6	92.2	29.1	26.7	76.3	40.8	63.1	4.1	
1901	46.1	76.6	125.7	32.4	35.1	75.3	48.0	66.1	4.6	
1902	52.1	122.2	110.9	36.4	42.4	78.6	52.9	68.7	4.2	
1903	56.0	115.8	114.3	40.2	45.4	69.8	54.7	62.6	47.0	
1904	62.1	120.0	130.5	47.3	46.7	86.2	51.5	66.4	51.1	
1905	65.2	108.7	104.9	51.2	64.2	73.6	56.2	81.8	53.9	
1906	65.6	100.5	100.5	55.8	79.4	77.8	68.1	85.5	55.9	
1907	88.1	111.3	110.3	55.5	84.2	80.6	57.5	76.1	56.9	
1908	71.8	102.1	110.1	62.5	77.6	80.6	59.5	68.6	59.4	
1909	89.6	117.4	133.7	77.9	85.9	79.8	68.8	116.8	71.7	128.0
1910	92.0	110.2	94.4	74.4	87.3	87.5	66.1	93.3	76.9	116.8
1911	93.1	117.0	93.9	86.3	98.6	86.2	80.8	89.8	78.0	109.4
1912	92.0	110.9	110.6	98.3	90.9	90.0	86.5	126.2	104.6	112.3
1913	100.0	100.0	100.0	100.0	100.0	100.0	100.0	100.0	100.0	100.0
1914	103.9	107.0	118.6	113.9	103.3	113.3	97.4	103.6	115.7	101.4
1915	84.5	109.6	144.1	148.0	85.0	110.0	64.9	120.4	175.6	77.4
1916	103.8	109.1	136.9	155.7	79.8	118.0	72.1	139.5	211.9	76.9
1917	98.9	129.8	150.9	250.1	82.5	106.8	74.3	117.3	316.2	54.1
1918	80.5	134.6	123.4	251.3	82.6	111.4	93.6	67.5	250.5	29.6
1919	106.5	82.1	156.4	220.6	83.9	146.5	116.5	141.4	413.9	35.4
1920	120.5	96.9	155.2	195.7	88.1	167.9	118.8	95.8	436.1	82.3
1921	108.9	79.5	157.3	221.4	99.7	124.1	81.8	67.7	319.4	76.8
1922	124.0	102.3	146.2		101.1	201.9	116.9	99.4	514.7	83.2

YEAR	049	051	053	054	056	057	059	062	063	065
1879						8.6	76.5	19.7	40.6	7.3
1880						9.3	103.9	30.1	57.1	6.5
1881						9.4	95.2	28.0	59.6	8.3
1882						11.5	119.6	35.9	62.0	8.1
1883						12.3	100.5	31.2	57.0	9.1
1884						12.3	101.8	37.1	60.5	4.3
1885						14.2	82.4	32.4	54.8	5.9
1886						17.4	96.4	34.9	57.0	8.7
1887						17.5	108.1	42.5	63.6	8.1
1888						19.8	110.0	42.9	64.6	5.7
1889	23.4	46.8	55.5	79.8	358.1	21.0	115.7	41.1	69.8	8.4
1890	24.5	42.6	60.8	64.6	381.2	16.4	132.5	43.5	73.6	14.8
1891	26.9	50.3	48.7	86.6	246.4	25.3	112.2	47.3	78.0	10.7
1892	24.7	51.3	56.3	105.6	284.5	27.9	107.7	55.8	78.0	20.0
1893	24.6	54.6	52.2	68.7	230.7	16.2	105.0	52.9	74.4	24.3
1894	22.4	41.5	49.0	72.7	130.6	28.1	88.1	41.5	50.5	26.4
1895	28.2	53.1	67.7	177.3	431.6	32.7	104.4	49.2	70.6	28.6
1896	29.3	51.3	58.4	109.6	250.6	18.1	75.3	47.5	70.1	31.4
1897	38.0	61.4	54.5	266.7	257.3	35.9	85.7	49.7	69.7	49.5
1898	34.4	55.2	54.5	59.3	118.5	30.2	85.9	43.2	45.6	42.6
1899	38.2	55.8	59.1	63.1	108.3	42.3	85.8	37.1	73.2	65.3
1900	43.0	53.9	58.4	88.2	111.3	29.4	92.3	41.4	59.1	87.1
1901	57.3	61.9	61.3	80.2	109.3	43.9	97.6	44.5	63.6	95.5
1902	63.1	71.6	72.0	113.7	131.8	49.2	113.5	47.9	76.5	97.9
1903	57.3	83.6	76.3	106.7	134.9	41.7	109.6	51.1	65.3	
1904	58.3	76.6	80.6	124.3	111.7	59.3	107.1	52.6	65.3	
1905	52.5	83.9	91.8	171.9	144.4	55.5	110.9	50.8	79.9	
1906	74.5	77.9	95.0	131.1	146.2	60.2	122.9	63.5	97.5	
1907	75.1	77.0	74.7	129.4	147.8	56.1	84.8	84.2	91.3	
1908	65.1	73.0	95.0	101.8	100.4	66.9	100.7	63.0	74.6	
1909	80.8	90.0	100.7	221.6	145.6	79.4	99.3	76.0	96.2	
1910	94.1	84.5	99.1	128.3	143.6	77.1	82.4	84.7	100.6	
1911	81.5	82.0	91.7	98.6	98.1	74.7	78.3	79.2	93.6	
1912	86.1	111.8	101.2	160.9	92.2	88.6		93.9	104.0	
1913	100.0	100.0	100.0	100.0	100.0	100.0	100.0	100.0	100.0	100.0
1914	95.3	113.3	105.9	200.9	326.4	91.7	107.7	90.7	92.0	126.4
1915	88.4	111.5	66.0	314.5	138.4	110.6	87.7	71.4	98.7	104.4
1916	83.5	145.0	58.1	355.9	107.5	116.0	100.5	76.0	117.4	118.0
1917	105.5	123.1	43.8	323.0	128.5	130.5	59.6	72.4	113.4	112.2
1918	94.5	123.5	26.8	366.2	96.6	117.7	58.0	62.6	110.0	100.5
1919	95.8	107.7	24.2	343.8	46.7	160.4	98.4	65.7	108.4	111.5
1920	123.7	117.7	47.0	210.1	149.7	107.5	121.2	93.2	133.8	173.1
1921	102.8	74.1	36.5	257.4	136.2	162.2	142.8	67.1	83.0	131.3
1922	112.7	86.6	60.7	275.2	182.7	181.3	103.7	90.7	152.7	256.0
1923	129.5	106.6	78.6	310.2	222.1	177.0	126.0	112.4	189.4	275.3

YFAR	066	069	072	073	076	077	078	081	082	086
1879				16.8	66.4	4.5	9.5	166.3	27.1	19.2
1880				26.8	87.5	12.1	13.1	301.9	80.9	20.6
1881				24.2	93.1	7.5	9.4	250.2	84.8	23.4
1882				29.3	101.5	8.7	11.8	304.0	73.5	25.8
1883				38.9	100.5	7.3	11.9	231.9	44.9	26.8
1884				29.1	85.7	20.0	11.7	193.5	33.8	23.5
1885				36.0	82.3	22.2	11.4	184.8	25.2	24.4
1886				43.6	96.7	18.6	14.5	262.1	34.4	26.3
1887				46.9	111.9	10.4	14.3	355.9	56.8	28.0
1888				52.9	117.5	19.9	15.2	253.5	47.4	29.0
1889				43.3	106.4	23.4	17.0	246.2	38.6	31.4
1890				41.1	111.2	42.5	19.4	228.4	42.3	35.6
1891				50.5	113.5	27.3	25.3	210.9	34.4	33.1
1892				54.5	128.5	37.6	25.2	185.6	37.0	35.2
1893				36.3	123.4	62.0	23.4	170.8	31.7	33.9
1894				31.2	116.2	50.5	20.5	128.7	28.1	34.3
1895				28.1	155.3	32.2	30.4	145.4	47.8	40.2
1896				21.4	134.7	25.2	27.1	95.1	46.1	37.1
1897				28.2	112.3	34.6	31.2	64.6	30.4	39.5
1898				42.7	92.2	31.2	41.1	55.4	27.4	41.9
1899	21.6		56.3	64.8	95.9	42.5	44.4	60.7	35.4	45.2
1900	24.7		35.5	41.0	101.7	63.1	45.2	65.6	36.2	47.1
1901	26.5		58.8	65.3	101.1	107.2	46.2	77.8	38.7	50.5
1902	26.8		71.9	64.0	111.0	89.4	58.1	213.3	62.1	53.2
1903	30.7		89.1	60.8	132.7	51.6	63.2	199.9	72.0	56.7
1904	30.8		88.2	53.6	124.3	46.2	63.1	77.3	54.4	55.5
1905	35.5		89.1	84.5	118.0	56.8	70.0	109.6	55.4	60.3
1906	46.5		87.7	88.2	135.5	57.9	79.4	134.4	64.2	66.7
1907	62.8		75.5	75.6	142.3	58.5	71.0	145.5	74.0	69.5
1908	54.3		44.0	81.3	100.3	63.4	63.9	72.4	49.7	57.9
1909	72.7		123.6	174.6	106.6	79.9	86.9	109.9	69.9	79.6
1910	78.6		107.0	147.8	127.0	92.9	94.8	144.2	90.9	89.8
1911	75.1		97.6	122.3	109.6	69.5	93.0	79.5	85.7	93.8
1912	77.6		83.5	103.7	97.3	93.6	103.5	72.2	85.5	88.1
1913	100.0	100.0	100.0	100.0	100.0	100.0	100.0	100.0	100.0	100.0
1914	114.5	98.8	33.9	56.8	98.0	80.2	77.1	78.3	86.9	91.6
1915	105.2	102.8	59.3	47.1	47.3	108.4	79.2	48.1	62.0	80.1
1916	117.6	126.8	113.9	118.8	34.6	162.3	100.4	69.9	44.6	78.2
1917	130.1	199.0	115.0	70.9	30.7	158.7	114.6	44.9	34.6	82.0
1918	133.0	235.1	97.5	128.5	23.6	185.2	117.4	28.3	34.6	84.5
1919	130.1	332.3	106.0	76.7	25.9	141.5	87.0	49.0	33.7	55.7
1920	145.9	649.4	58.6	64.2	46.2	165.8	125.9	67.2	73.3	111.7
1921	150.5	776.8	17.7	115.3	55.0	100.7	80.9	18.7	56.3	55.9
1922	205.6	837.2	57.6	134.8	78.1	116.9	148.6	113.2	97.0	79.2
1923	258.4	538.9	84.2		119.6	113.6	163.4	127.2	86.4	98.0

APPENDIX C

TABLE C-5

ANNUAL VALUES,
SELECTED MINOR EXPORT CLASSES
(MILLIONS OF DOLLARS)

YEAR	001	005	008	009	011	012	014	015	025	028	042	044	052
1879	10.1	217.5	16.6	53.8	25.6	17.8	37.7	8.2	14.2	5.8	186.5	11.0	10.6
1880	18.3	236.8	18.6	67.7	37.1	23.2	43.7	9.8	18.1	7.1	239.3	11.3	12.2
1881	12.0	185.7	17.5	64.0	37.0	20.1	43.1	6.8	18.4	6.8	222.1	11.6	14.2
1882	6.1	138.4	13.7	44.9	31.5	13.3	48.6	6.4	18.9	7.2	222.6	13.2	18.4
1883	18.2	122.3	19.3	51.1	33.6	16.1	56.5	7.9	20.0	6.9	224.7	12.3	17.7
1884	14.7	100.0	18.0	40.8	24.3	15.2	55.2	8.7	20.0	8.0	221.6	12.7	16.2
1885	14.3	83.1	18.8	40.3	26.3	11.3	49.6	9.1	26.6	8.0	184.4	12.7	15.1
1886	11.5	104.4	14.0	38.5	26.2	10.0	47.3	9.6	28.3	7.8	215.4	14.9	13.4
1887	9.4	103.4	12.6	39.5	26.4	11.4	57.9	8.3	20.9	8.2	216.0	13.7	14.7
1888	13.5	64.0	16.2	35.5	26.0	9.4	52.7	8.2	18.7	8.5	225.1	10.7	17.1
1889	27.0	76.4	22.9	47.9	34.6	12.7	53.0	10.4	22.0	11.0	266.6	10.4	20.5
1890	34.6	85.6	28.6	51.9	44.9	11.6	56.0	13.2	21.2	11.0	254.3	11.1	19.3
1891	29.5	164.4	28.5	49.7	38.7	9.8	68.2	11.9	20.4	12.0	277.0	11.0	18.4
1892	36.1	161.9	31.1	56.5	46.5	10.1	86.1	15.3	21.7	12.0	217.1	12.7	18.7
1893	23.3	112.5	24.5	51.9	47.3	8.4	74.9	14.5	23.8	12.1	204.1	13.0	17.6
1894	39.4	63.3	26.4	54.2	50.6	8.6	62.3	13.0	25.8	13.1	200.4	14.0	19.4
1895	30.5	70.9	25.7	54.5	45.2	5.8	54.4	14.3	24.7	16.2	189.9	14.0	19.9
1896	39.0	120.0	32.5	51.2	38.1	8.2	62.8	14.9	24.1	16.3	233.4	19.8	19.3
1897	41.5	185.1	28.0	61.9	40.8	10.6	57.9	19.0	22.8	16.3	212.9	18.6	23.3
1898	35.3	235.5	28.8	76.8	53.4	6.5	82.5	24.9	23.8	18.7	233.3	19.6	26.7
1899	33.1	188.8	35.3	74.3	53.1	9.1	76.9	28.6	30.0	22.1	191.8	24.5	31.1
1900	36.3	172.3	37.7	73.2	55.4	9.2	75.9	32.2	26.9	21.3	315.9	19.7	36.8
1901	40.1	152.2	40.6	81.1	67.1	8.8	78.6	35.6	34.6	21.8	301.9	25.2	34.8
1902	26.4	116.0	36.8	69.1	64.9	4.9	74.0	34.8	29.8	22.1	291.5	37.6	35.3
1903	39.4	114.9	37.3	62.4	67.9	6.0	81.5	29.7	31.5	23.7	379.6	25.6	44.6
1904	44.3	41.3	34.2	59.6	60.3	6.0	55.7	30.6	26.8	26.7	370.4	32.2	45.6
1905	43.0	94.9	34.9	66.3	74.3	9.1	64.8	37.7	32.1	28.0	393.3	39.3	43.2
1906	41.0	119.8	32.7	75.4	80.6	4.7	71.2	38.8	32.6	33.0	413.1	40.9	59.6
1907	36.9	138.8	31.8	68.3	81.1	5.2	66.3	41.9	36.8	28.2	469.8	23.7	67.7
1908	26.5	125.5	21.7	67.8	79.1	2.2	55.2	45.3	36.1	28.4	438.8	24.3	54.6
1909	18.1	80.5	14.7	55.9	72.7	2.2	48.2	39.8	34.2	33.2	461.9	32.2	56.4
1910	11.3	57.1	10.3	46.2	66.6	2.4	59.6	33.9	36.8	37.5	530.8	32.0	66.7
1911	18.0	69.9	7.4	59.7	82.1	4.4	54.6	44.3	42.2	39.3	517.1	42.3	74.9
1912	9.4	100.1	4.5	57.5	76.3	3.4	54.6	50.7	46.9	43.8	623.1	48.5	82.9
1913	6.3	133.0	3.9	64.1	82.5	2.6	64.5	45.8	52.9	37.4	575.5	49.4	88.0
1914	6.7	237.6	11.2	55.7	65.9	3.5	70.6	36.7	43.9	44.2	347.9	44.9	57.0
1915	8.5	415.4	49.2	124.3	71.7	20.1	111.2	56.6	52.5	78.4	417.0	88.6	40.0
1916	9.5	365.6	38.2	161.8	78.0	36.1	110.5	52.8	62.8	97.7	545.2	118.0	41.5
1917	9.8	442.4	58.0	203.8	93.4	67.3	195.1	33.3	45.6	77.8	576.3	143.0	49.0
1918	10.8	474.3	169.0	481.4	174.7	96.1	328.0	26.2	122.9	53.0	674.1	162.4	63.2
1919	78.5	537.9	69.7	598.2	305.9	144.9	398.0	77.7	260.0	214.5	1137.4	245.7	97.5
1920	27.7	785.7	27.0	223.1	177.5	80.7	300.2	53.2	245.5	108.6	1137.6	369.0	136.1
1921	26.4	592.9	5.7	139.1	136.8	43.8	165.5	49.1	205.1	31.7	534.2	107.6	63.1
1922	18.3	396.4	3.6	127.3	110.8	24.9	119.5	27.3	146.5	45.4	673.2	125.4	74.9
1923	12.1	192.6	3.3	140.3	148.1	27.3	118.7	25.1	153.4	42.7	807.1	122.5	115.2

YEAR	075	074	072	071	070	069	067	066	061	060	059	057	055
1879	1.6	3.4		10.0	5.9	.1		3.7	35.2		2.1	2.0	1.2
1880	1.8	3.8		10.7	7.2	.2	.7	1.4	31.8		2.7	2.5	1.2
1881	2.0	4.1		13.4	8.7	.3	.8	2.3	45.5	.8	3.4	3.4	1.3
1882	2.4	4.1		17.6	8.4	.3	1.1	1.6	41.2	1.4	4.4	3.9	1.7
1883	2.2	4.1		20.2	8.4	.3	1.1	3.7	43.3	1.9	4.4	5.1	1.4
1884	2.0	4.0		16.5	6.6	.2	1.3	4.1	43.4	1.8	6.0	5.0	1.3
1885	1.8	4.6		12.5	6.6	.3	1.0	4.1	43.6	1.8	5.1	4.2	1.5
1886	2.0	4.6		11.8	6.3	.3	1.0	2.3	43.1	1.8	5.1	4.5	1.5
1887	2.1	5.0		13.2	7.3	.3	1.3	1.7	41.8	2.0	5.1	5.5	1.5
1888	2.2	4.8		16.2	8.5	.5	1.5	5.3	42.6	2.1	5.5	6.9	1.6
1889	4.2	3.3	.2	22.9	9.2	3.3	1.4	2.2	47.2	2.3	6.1	6.4	1.2
1890	4.7	4.1	.4	24.6	11.2	.4	1.6	1.6	45.7	2.9	6.5	7.3	1.2
1891	4.5	3.8	.7	26.7	11.6	.4	1.6	9.3	40.8	4.0	5.4	8.7	1.3
1892	4.5	4.2	1.6	23.3	11.4	.4	1.5	4.2	38.0	4.6	4.7	12.3	1.5
1893	4.5	4.6	1.6	26.3	12.8	.6	2.5	15.2	37.9	4.5	4.0	18.2	1.7
1894	4.7	5.0	2.7	24.0	13.7	.7	2.4	15.9	36.6	3.5	6.3	27.0	2.1
1895	5.8	5.7	4.4	28.2	15.7	1.6	2.7	13.1	50.8	4.6	6.1	28.9	2.4
1896	5.8	6.3	5.8	39.7	20.6	5.6	3.2	30.1	57.6	4.6	6.0	30.2	2.8
1897	6.2	6.5	4.9	48.6	26.6	7.3	3.6	33.2	55.0	7.3	5.0	36.9	4.5
1898	6.2	7.6	7.8	63.9	36.2	5.8	3.5	36.4	48.4	6.4	5.0	38.4	5.6
1899	7.9	10.3	13.2	77.9	47.4	8.8	5.0	44.0	60.1	18.2	6.0	41.5	5.6
1900	8.1	11.6	34.2	89.0	57.5	14.7	7.7	59.6	67.2	24.5	7.3	54.3	7.0
1901	8.9	11.6	111.0	79.0	50.4	5.8	7.7	34.2	66.7	34.5	6.3	61.2	7.3
1902	8.6	11.1	120.7	84.4	42.0	4.1	6.8	45.3	62.3	41.8	6.8	68.3	7.3
1903	10.5	12.0	120.3	92.0	42.0	4.0	6.8	42.9	65.8	63.5	6.4	110.7	7.9
1904	12.1	13.9	83.8	96.9	54.4	13.3	10.3	75.7	74.3	88.0	6.1	107.9	8.8
1905	13.1	15.5	151.7	112.3	59.4	12.4	12.1	85.1	73.6	55.6	6.7	120.4	10.7
1906	14.8	16.6	82.3	135.8	70.6	16.5	13.7	89.4	78.0	87.5	6.3	349.8	8.7
1907	15.0	15.4	298.2	151.4	82.2	17.1	9.4	98.3	85.0	57.1	6.5	168.2	7.3
1908	15.6	15.8	81.0	121.9	61.7	13.9	10.0	91.6	102.3	57.1	6.5	91.2	8.8
1909	15.6	20.3	98.1	117.6	67.6	17.9	13.2	94.6	97.8	35.4	6.2	154.1	8.5
1910	17.8	20.7	19.2	149.5	83.7	24.2	16.0	96.5	88.7	47.1	6.8	91.2	10.3
1911	19.7	20.3	166.3	179.7	99.2	36.8	16.0	108.4	99.8	47.1	6.8	154.1	11.5
1912	21.5	20.7	28.3	208.2	110.8	54.9	16.9	133.7	117.4	9.6	6.8	56.2	11.5
1913	21.2	20.9	33.3	217.6	119.1	44.0	9.5	159.4	134.0	18.2	8.4	67.4	11.2
1914	20.7	22.0	34.2	146.3	76.6	27.0	7.7	144.8	119.6	24.5	5.0	54.3	14.2
1915	185.0	73.0	111.7	207.8	169.6	72.9	54.9	187.5	121.0	34.5	4.3	61.2	29.5
1916	686.4	179.4	120.7	335.6	372.2	228.0	276.8	389.7	172.4	41.8	7.7	68.3	35.3
1917	628.4	201.7	120.3	429.2	430.8	423.4	166.8	439.1	204.0	63.5	7.7	110.7	43.1
1918	272.6	164.3	83.8	434.1	302.5	418.6	41.1	262.7	270.2	88.9	12.1	107.9	65.9
1919	83.8	140.2	151.7	618.8	337.8	236.6	37.0	158.4	306.7	55.6	14.8	120.4	65.8
1920	121.7	184.6	298.2	696.4	386.9	258.5	43.9	162.9	476.4	87.5	20.2	349.8	29.0
1921	40.0	95.7	81.0	465.2	727.0	89.2	72.2	95.6	323.9	57.1	20.2	168.2	24.1
1922	43.0	54.9	98.1	273.2	128.6	56.4	15.3	115.4	291.8	35.4	18.3	91.2	24.1
1923	47.8	66.4	166.3	322.6	160.1	69.5	19.8	145.1	296.2	47.1	23.1	154.1	25.7

TABLE C-6

ANNUAL VALUES,
SELECTED MINOR IMPORT CLASSES
(MILLIONS OF DOLLARS)

YEAR	007	008	009	010	011	019	024	026	036	047
1879	11.7	19.9	55.6	1.3		68.4	3.6	20.0	8.2	22.9
1880	13.4	18.6	56.8	0.9		92.8	5.0	31.2	10.2	32.7
1881	15.3	21.6	50.9	1.4		92.8	5.0	29.8	10.9	31.6
1882	20.0	17.3	43.4	1.3		109.1	5.8	27.2	17.6	37.2
1883	19.0	15.8	46.9	1.4		101.8	8.3	23.1	14.8	34.3
1884	18.5	14.8	44.4	1.5		88.8	6.4	22.5	10.7	30.2
1885	17.4	14.6	44.1	1.4		81.7	8.5	22.6	9.7	27.9
1886	17.4	15.9	44.1	1.9		89.0	7.7	26.7	14.2	30.7
1887	21.4	10.8	61.9	1.8		76.0	10.8	23.7	14.4	30.2
1888	20.6	13.7	64.4	2.4		88.0	9.1	25.1	14.2	28.6
1889	11.0	12.0	77.9	1.9	3.8	102.1	13.8	22.4	12.5	27.8
1890	16.1	14.1	80.6	2.6	5.8	95.0	18.4	26.1	16.7	33.0
1891	13.8	14.2	88.6	2.9	5.2	138.2	8.3	25.9	18.5	25.8
1892	14.5	14.4	88.2	3.5	5.4	109.1	11.5	28.1	16.7	29.4
1893	13.9	13.1	93.5	3.0	5.0	123.7	15.2	22.8	19.2	29.5
1894	11.4	13.9	96.5	2.5	5.0	107.1	10.5	18.5	16.2	24.5
1895	11.6	14.0	80.0	3.2	4.2	68.7	9.1	36.4	19.3	45.2
1896	12.8	16.7	75.7	2.6	4.3	91.3	8.6	20.7	15.8	34.2
1897	10.1	16.6	53.7	2.9	4.4	77.7		33.2	21.8	30.3
1898	9.5	9.5		4.1		76.5		39.9	26.1	31.5
1899	10.6	10.9	56.1	5.2	6.6	107.9	11.8	51.1	34.4	35.3
1900	11.3	11.8	59.5	6.5	9.1	91.0	14.2	51.6	28.7	40.3
1901	9.7	8.7	70.2	6.7	6.8	77.8	16.2	55.6	28.3	39.4
1902	10.8	14.6	64.2	7.3	8.7	60.9	16.2	57.7	25.4	46.7
1903	12.5	17.1	61.3	7.6	8.2	61.5	17.3	53.3	35.8	50.4
1904	12.6	16.9	87.4	8.0	9.8	84.7	16.7	57.6	45.5	45.2
1905	15.3	14.0	75.3	9.0	11.7	103.1	18.7	73.4	51.2	52.4
1906	22.7	16.7	72.3	10.2	11.9	79.5	26.6	83.9	56.0	65.8
1907	15.8	14.9	71.8	15.2	10.7	83.8	24.3	77.7	54.2	75.0
1908	18.9	16.6	86.5	13.0	11.9	89.4	24.5	57.7	46.2	53.8
1909	22.9	16.6	73.7	13.4	12.4	91.3	25.9	103.7	83.7	64.3
1910	25.0	18.3	97.2	12.1	14.6	114.9	24.7	86.1	110.4	60.6
1911	24.5	17.9	130.5	14.6	14.2	101.3	32.1	81.5	87.9	59.0
1912				16.9		119.6	33.1	121.2	111.2	61.8
1913	27.1	16.4	104.7	19.7	15.4	98.8	36.3	105.9	84.9	59.8
1914	26.5	17.8	104.8	19.1	15.9	129.0	34.8	112.3	74.7	55.3
1915	20.5	19.6	113.8	31.3	12.7	181.4	21.0	127.4	115.5	38.2
1916	28.0	19.4	118.8	33.8	12.0	235.3	26.9	172.6	164.5	44.9
1917	28.2	25.8	122.6	41.4	14.0	232.7	33.5	209.7	239.5	42.6
1918	28.2	29.5	99.4	38.0	16.4	252.7	52.1	108.0	149.2	34.3
1919	48.8	20.1	261.3	58.0	15.9	398.4	75.1	306.5	221.6	45.4
1920	55.9	24.4	252.5	54.3	19.1	1022.0	81.6	243.9	248.9	111.2
1921	37.4	14.2	142.8	23.1	19.4	237.4	56.2	67.6	75.7	71.4
1922	40.4	23.8	160.9	32.0	19.1	254.0	66.0	107.0	103.7	78.4
1923	38.6	29.7	190.2	33.8	19.7	384.8	57.2	118.9	188.5	87.8

263

YEAR	049	051	053	054	056	057	059	062	063	065
1879		7.6	19.3	10.8	27.1	11.1	27.0	6.2	4.6	
1880		9.0	25.4	20.9	36.0	11.5	35.9	10.9	7.4	
1881		11.0	22.6	9.7	31.6	11.1	33.8	9.1	8.4	
1882		12.3	24.6	11.5	41.9	14.6	41.8	10.9	10.0	
1883		11.8	24.3	11.8	39.3	13.5	35.5	10.3	9.1	
1884		11.4	26.6	10.5	39.3	13.1	33.3	10.4	9.2	
1885		11.4	24.7	12.9	35.6	14.1	25.5	8.6	7.8	
1886		10.8	27.3	17.4	42.4	18.9	29.8	8.1	8.4	
1887		13.8	28.1	15.6	43.2	19.3	33.0	9.2	9.5	
1888		18.0	30.6	14.5	47.8	19.5	33.3	9.7	9.5	
1889	6.2	20.8	22.1	18.7	48.3	21.5	36.6	9.9	10.3	1.7
1890	6.1	15.4	23.6	15.5	50.9	18.6	41.4	10.2	10.3	1.7
1891	6.4	18.0	21.6	18.8	33.2	23.1	33.5	10.3	10.4	1.9
1892	6.2	16.2	24.4	21.2	36.7	28.1	33.8	12.2	10.9	2.6
1893	5.7	17.1	22.0	14.0	29.6	17.1	34.9	11.7	10.3	2.0
1894	5.1	9.4	20.5	13.3	16.5	22.3	26.2	10.7	7.4	1.1
1895	6.2	10.5	25.8	33.8	55.7	28.6	31.9	10.9	9.4	1.0
1896	6.6	10.2	23.9	22.4	34.1	15.8	21.9	10.0	9.0	
1897	8.4	11.1	25.9	53.4	32.2	28.9	25.5	10.2	8.5	.6
1898	7.1	14.3	22.1	11.6	15.0	26.6	25.5	9.0	5.5	.7
1899	9.0	18.6	22.6	11.7	14.6	42.8	25.3	8.1	9.3	1.2
1900	11.0	22.1	24.6	19.2	15.8	31.8	26.6	9.4	8.8	2.3
1901	15.4	20.8	25.5	14.0	15.6	39.5	26.8	10.8	10.5	1.6
1902	14.8	30.9	29.6	19.6	18.8	46.7	32.4	11.4	13.6	2.9
1903	13.8	32.9	31.5	22.8	19.3	43.1	31.1	11.5	11.9	3.5
1904	14.1	32.2	30.3	29.4	21.4	54.9	28.1	12.3	15.0	4.1
1905	16.8	36.1	33.8	46.8	22.7	54.8	30.6	15.5	19.7	4.5
1906	25.3	31.5	40.3	38.4	23.6	64.7	31.3	18.3	20.9	5.0
1907	28.8	33.0	44.6	39.7	15.6	71.8	36.5	13.8	17.2	8.0
1908	19.0	24.2	33.9	23.3	22.1	64.2	24.2	18.0	21.6	7.0
1909	20.5	26.9	41.0	55.5	21.6	74.1	28.6	20.9	22.9	10.3
1910	21.3	25.5	42.2	36.1	16.2	68.1	28.2	19.5	20.2	13.3
1911	22.1	25.1	40.3	25.5	15.8	67.0	23.3	23.4	22.1	14.4
1912	31.3	35.7	44.9	42.2		77.5	22.5			14.9
1913	41.6	39.7	46.0	28.8	17.3	89.8	25.9	25.8	22.7	15.9
1914	35.8	41.4	45.8	58.3	39.7	89.2	24.7	23.1	22.0	20.4
1915	29.7	38.6	33.9	95.0	15.1	91.7	20.9	17.6	23.2	16.9
1916	39.1	56.2	38.2	125.5	15.7	144.8	28.6	20.6	32.7	27.0
1917	53.7	87.5	35.4	171.6	20.7	184.4	28.5	23.0	38.2	42.0
1918	80.3	107.9	32.4	251.6	20.9	180.5	21.5	25.0	43.2	31.5
1919	65.8	77.4	33.0	216.8	13.5	329.8	45.6	27.4	68.1	37.0
1920	89.4	70.7	75.6	127.0	44.7	285.2	61.6	51.8	34.4	89.4
1921	41.4	27.8	40.0	60.5	30.9	259.2	42.1	30.1	53.4	39.4
1922	49.3	27.2	58.7	86.5	38.5	365.9	35.3	31.5	70.7	63.3
1923	67.0	37.0	66.3	129.7	47.0	392.3	40.0	40.2		74.4

TABLE C-6 (concluded)

Year										
1879	3.4			5.0	10.3	.1	5.2	26.2	6.4	24.8
1880	4.8			8.5	15.0	.2	9.1	58.1	20.7	31.0
1881	5.2			9.2	14.7	.1	6.7	38.9	21.0	31.6
1882	6.0			9.7	16.6	.2	9.8	47.4	17.4	34.4
1883	5.1			9.8	16.0	.1	9.1	36.1	9.8	34.4
1884	5.0			7.8	14.0	.3	7.7	28.6	7.3	30.9
1885	4.8			7.9	12.3	.4	7.7	24.9	5.2	28.5
1886	5.5			10.5	13.6	.3	11.3	33.2	6.7	30.6
1887	6.3			12.0	15.1	.2	11.5	44.2	10.2	31.6
1888	6.5			11.8	15.5	.4	13.3	31.7	8.7	30.2
1889	6.6			13.6	14.9	.9	10.5	31.8	7.4	29.7
1890	7.1			14.5	16.7	1.7	12.7	34.1	7.8	34.6
1891	7.2			13.8	17.8	3.7	15.7	33.1	5.7	34.1
1892	7.5			15.0	18.3	5.1	14.8	24.6	5.2	36.6
1893	5.9			11.5	16.2	7.1	10.0	21.9	3.8	34.8
1894	6.6			8.0	13.2	4.6	13.4	15.8	6.8	30.7
1895	6.2			7.8	18.8	3.3	11.6	17.1	6.2	33.6
1896	6.1			5.9	16.2	2.1	13.7	11.0	4.5	33.4
1897	6.0			7.6	13.6	3.3	17.9	7.9	3.7	34.1
1898				12.0	12.0	4.0		6.9		31.7
1899	7.2	*	5.0	16.1	13.2	6.6	32.9	8.8	4.8	36.0
1900	7.9	*	3.8	12.2	14.8	11.2	37.7	11.2	5.3	40.1
1901	8.6	*	6.6	20.8	16.2	21.0	38.1	11.3	5.9	43.1
1902	9.1	*	8.3	20.8	16.8	15.1	42.8	27.4	9.0	44.3
1903	10.3	*	10.8	20.0	18.9	8.1	48.4	26.3	9.9	48.9
1904	10.3	*	10.6	18.5	18.1	9.6	59.8	9.8	7.2	48.3
1905	12.4	.1	12.0	28.2	19.2	12.9	85.4	14.3	7.6	52.1
1906	15.5	.1	9.1	34.0	21.8	13.8	86.4	21.8	8.6	60.5
1907	20.6	.4	2.5	25.5	22.7	16.6	55.1	24.2	10.0	64.1
1908	16.6	.4	13.8	13.2	15.9	15.7	71.2	9.8	6.9	50.5
1909	19.2	.2	9.4	36.8	16.9	19.4	80.9	14.2	9.3	64.6
1910	19.9	1.4	9.0	36.8	19.0	22.2	89.2	19.1	11.7	72.2
1911	19.6	2.4	10.0	34.3	17.7	16.7	111.8	10.6	11.0	78.8
1912	20.1	6.0	10.0	35.0	16.8	25.3		10.4	11.5	77.2
1913	25.2	11.5	12.8	33.9	18.7	28.3	107.9	14.6	12.9	85.4
1914	28.5	10.4	3.0	16.8	17.3	23.4	72.0	10.5	12.0	73.6
1915	25.5	10.5	7.1	19.4	10.2	35.1	79.8	8.0	8.7	69.3
1916	30.5	13.7	12.4	39.2	9.3	80.0	137.8	15.2	7.6	100.0
1917	47.6	19.2	14.7	26.2	9.6	82.1	185.7	11.3	7.7	112.1
1918	51.6	23.7	13.9	10.3	8.9	104.9	201.6	14.6	8.7	135.5
1919	59.7	29.7	22.9	82.3	10.8	71.6	131.5	22.8	9.0	77.8
1920	89.4	61.0	15.8	60.1	22.6	81.2	180.3	4.5	19.0	165.1
1921	96.0	73.7	3.4	34.7	24.9	31.9	71.0	21.2	13.4	68.5
1922	93.2	82.7	40.3	57.6	28.7	35.3	129.4	26.2	16.8	87.1
1923	125.0	63.3	9.6	68.1	45.9	46.8	172.2		14.7	111.3

*Less than $50,000.

TABLE C-7

COMPOSITION AND COVERAGE OF MINOR EXPORT CLASSES

Export Class and Commodity Composition	Covered	Uncovered	Export Class and Commodity Composition	Covered	Uncovered
001ᵃ *Crude animal foods, agricultural*			006 *Vegetables*		
1. Cattle	1879–1923		1. Potatoes, white	1879–1923	
2. Hogs	1879–1923		2. Onions	1879–1923	
3. Sheep	1879–1923		3. Peas, dried	1918–23	
4. Eggs in shell	1879–1923		4. Beans, dried	1918–23	
5. Poultry, live	1922–23	1912–21	5. Items 3, 4	1884–1917	
6. Milk and cream	1922–23	1922–23	6. Dried or dehydrated vegetables		1922–23
7. Other live animals		1879–1921	7. Other fresh veg.		1922–23
8. Items 5, 7			8. Items 6, 7		1913–21
002 *Crude animal foods, nonagricultural*			9. Item 8, and pickles and sauces		1879–1912
1. Salmon, fresh		1922–23	007 *Fruits*		
2. Salmon, smoked or dry-cured		1922–23	1. Apples in barrels	1922–23	
3. Items 1, 2		1918–21	2. Apples in boxes	1922–23	
4. Salmon, pickled		1918–23	3. Items 1, 2	1879–1921	
5. Items 3, 4		1884–1917	4. Oranges	1908–23	1898–1907
6. Other fresh fish		1884–1909, 1912–17	5. Lemons	1913–23	
7. Items 5, 6		1879–83	6. Peanuts	1906–23	
003 *Hay*			7. Pears		1906–23
1. Hay	1879–1923		8. Berries		1913–23
004 *Coffee, green*			9. Grapefruits		1922–23
1. Coffee, green	1901–23		10. Pineapples		1922–23
005ᵃ *Grains*			11. Grapes		1922–23
1. Barley, grain	1879–1923		12. Peaches		1922–23
2. Buckwheat, grain	1913–23	1899–1912	13. Other fresh fruits		
3. Corn, grain	1879–1923		14. Other subtropical fruits		1922–23
4. Oats, grain	1879–1923		15. Items 9–14		1920–21
5. Rye, grain	1879–1923		16. Fruit pulp and cannery waste		1920–23
6. Wheat, grain	1879–1923		17. Items 15, 16		1918–19

007 Fruits (CONT.)

18. Other dried fruits	1918–23
19. Items 17, 18	1913–17
20. Other nuts	1906–23
21. Apricots, dried	1902–12
22. Peaches, dried	1906–12
23. Items 5, 8, 19	1906–12
24. Items 7, 22–23	1902–05
25. Items 21, 24	1898–1901
26. Items 6, 20	1889–1905
27. Prunes	1898
28. Raisins and other dried grapes	1898
29. Items 4, 25, 27–28	1879–97

008ᵃ Beef

1. Beef, fresh	1879–1923
2. Beef, pickled or cured	1879–83, 1910–23
3. Beef, canned	1887–1923
4. Beef, other cured	1884–1909
5. Beef, pickled	1884–1909

009ᵃ Pork and related products

1. Pork carcasses, fresh	1922–23
2. Loins and other fresh pork	1922–23
3. Items 1, 2	1891–1921
4. Hams and shoulders, cured	1881–1923
5. Bacon	1881–1923
6. Pickled pork	1884–1923
7. Pork, canned	1900–23
8. Sausage, not canned	1913–23
9. Sausage, canned	1913–23
10. Sausage casings	1882–1923
11. Items 8, 9	1901–12
12. Items 3, 6	1879–83
13. Items 4, 5	1879–80

010 Other meats and products

1. Mutton and lamb	1879–1923
2. Poultry and game, fresh	1884–1923
3. Poultry, canned	1922–23
4. Other canned meats	1922–23
5. Items 3, 4	1900–21
6. Veal, fresh	1922–23
7. Meat extracts and bouillion cubes	1922–23
8. Other meats and products n.e.s.	1922–23
9. Items 6–8	1901–21
10. Item 9 and sausage, canned and uncanned	1900
11. Items 5, 10	1884–99

011ᵃ Lard, oleo, and related products

1. Oleo oil	1911–23
2. Lard	1879–1923
3. Neutral lard	1911–23
4. Items 8, 9	1897–1921
5. Items 10, 11	1882–1921
6. Items 1, 3	1882–1910
7. Items 5, 6	1879–81
8. Lard compounds	1922–23
9. Vegetable oil-lard compounds	1922–23
10. Oleo containing animal fats	1922–23
11. Vegetable oleo	1922–23

012ᵃ Dairy products, manufactured

1. Butter	1879–1923
2. Cheese	1879–1923

(continued)

TABLE C-7 (continued)

Export Class and Commodity Composition	Covered	Uncovered
012ª *Dairy products, manufactured* (CONT.)		
3. Milk, condensed	1920–23	
4. Milk, evaporated	1920–23	
5. Milk, powdered	1920–23	
6. Items 3–5	1910–19	1879–1909
013 *Manufactured animal foods, nonagricultural*		
1. Canned salmon	1879–1923	
2. Cod, salted or dry-cured	1922–23	
3. Haddock, hake, and pollock, salted or dry-cured	1922–23	
4. Items 2, 3	1884–1909, 1911–21	
5. Herring, salted or dry-cured	1888, 1915–23	1889–1909, 1911–14
6. Other fish, salted or dry-cured	1888	1889–1909 1911–23
7. Items 15, 19, 20	1879–83	1909–23
8. Other canned fish, including tuna		1922–23
9. Canned sardines		1922–23
10. Items 8, 9		1888–1921
11. Oysters, canned or fresh		1879–1923

Export Class and Commodity Composition	Covered	Uncovered
013 *Manufactured animal foods, nonagric.* (CONT.)		
12. Other shellfish		1884–1923
13. Items 17 and 18		1888–93, 1909–23
14. Items 4–6	1879–83	1910
15. Pickled mackerel	1884–88	1889–1908
16. Items 19 and 20	1884–87	1894–1908
17. Caviar		1898–1908
18. Other fish products, except caviar		1898–1908
19. Pickled herring	1888	1889–93
20. Other pickled fish, excluding herring and mackerel	1888	1889–93
21. Items 5, 6	1884–87	1889–93
014ª *Flour and other grain products*		
1. Wheat flour	1879–1923	
2. Corn meal and flour	1879–1923	
3. Oatmeal and rolled oats	1884–1923	
4. Rye flour	1913–23	1879–1912
5. Rice flour, meal and broken rice	1922–23	
6. Rice grain	1922–23	
7. Buckwheat flour		1922–23
8. Corn hominy and grits		1922–23

014ᵃ Flour and other grain products (CONT.)

Item	Period(s)
9. Other corn preparations for table use	1922–23
10. Wheat macaroni and spaghetti	
11. Other wheat products	1922–23
12. Cereal and breakfast foods, n.e.s.	1922–23
13. Other grains and flour	1922–23
14. Rice bran and polish	1895–1916
15. Items 13, 14	1922–23
16. Cereal and breakfast foods, n.e.s.	1898–1921
17. Other grains and flours	1919–21
18. Barley flour	1919–23
19. Items 17, 18	1917–18
20. Item 19 less 14	1913–16
21. Wheat bread, biscuits, cakes, crackers	1879–1923
22. Rice, including flour, meal and grain	1899–1921, 1879–90, 1898
23. Barley malt	1916–23
24. Bran, middlings, other mill feeds	1898
25. Other breadstuffs, including dried grains and malt sprouts	1898
26. Items 16, 24–25	1897
27. Buckwheat	1897–98
28. Items 26, 27	1884–96
29. Items 3, 28	1879–83

015ᵃ Vegetable oil, cake, and meal

Item	Period	Period
1. Cottonseed oil, crude	1922–23	1913–23
2. Cottonseed oil, refined	1922–23	1920–23
3. Items 1, 2	1879–1921	1922–23
4. Cottonseed cake	1915–23	1922–23
5. Cottonseed meal	1915–23	1922–23
6. Items 4, 5	1894–1914	1920–21
7. Linseed cake	1918–23	1913–1⟩
8. Linseed meal	1918–23	
9. Items 7, 8	1894–1917	
10. Corn cake	1904–12	
11. Coconut cake		
12. Peanut cake		
13. Other oil cake meal		
14. Other oil cake		
15. Items 12–14		
16. Items 11, 15		
17. Items 6, 9	1879–93	
18. Vegetable stearin		1916–23

016 Other feeds

Item	Period
1. Bran and middlings	1913–23
2. Screenings	1922–23
3. Corn feed	1922–23
4. Sorghum, Kafir, and milo maize	
5. Other mill feeds	1922–23
6. Items 2–5	1922–23
7. Dried grains and malt sprouts	1913–21
8. Prepared feeds, not medicinal	1922–23

(continued)

269

TABLE C-7 (continued)

Export Class and Commodity Composition	Years Covered	Years Uncovered
016 Other feeds (CONT.)		
9. Items 7, 8	1901–21	
10. Items 1, 6	1899–1912	
11. Other breadstuffs		1901–12
12. Items 9, 11		1899–1900
017 Vegetables and products, manufactured		
1. Canned asparagus		1922–23
2. Canned beans		1922–23
3. Canned peas		1922–23
4. Other canned vegetables, n.e.s.		1922–23
5. Items 1–4		1918–21
6. Canned corn		1918–23
7. Canned soups		1918–23
8. Canned tomatoes		1918–23
9. Items 5–8		1879–1917
10. Pickles and sauces		1913–23
11. Vinegar		1879–98, 1916–23
12. Yeast		1916–23
018 Canned and dried fruits		
1. Raisins and other dried grapes	1899–1923	
2. Prunes	1899–1923	
3. Apricots, dried	1913–23	
4. Apples, dried	1879–1923	
5. Peaches, dried	1913–23	
6. Canned peaches	1918–23	
7. Canned pineapples	1920–23	
018 Canned and dried fruits (CONT.)		
8. Canned pears		1920–23
9. Canned cherries		1922–23
10. Canned plums		1922–23
11. Canned apricots		1923
12. Other canned fruit		1923
13. Items 11, 12		1922
14. Items 9, 10, 13		1920–21
15. Items 7, 8, 14		1918–19
16. Items 6, 15		1884–1917
17. Preserved fruit, jellies, and jams		1884–1923
18. Fruit juices and flavoring extracts		1916–23
19. Items 16, 17		1879–83
019 Sugar and related products, agricultural		
1. Refined sugar	1899–1923	
2. Glucose	1908–23	
3. Grape sugar	1908–23	
4. Syrup, including maple	1898–1923	
5. Molasses	1898	1899–1923
6. Honey		1882–1908, 1916–23
7. Items 2, 3	1883–1907	
8. Refined sugar, except brown (Item 1 less 9)		
9. Brown sugar	1879–98	1879–98
10. Items 4, 5	1879–97	

Category / Item	Years
020 Sugar and related products, nonagricultural	
1. Confectionery	1879–1923
2. Chewing gum	1916–23
021 Coffee, chocolate, and spices	
1. Coffee, roasted	1902–23
2. Cocoa, powdered, and chocolate, including sweetened	1902–23
3. Spices	1884–88, 1916–23
4. Items 1, 2	1884–1901
5. Items 3, 4	1879–83
022 Malt beverages	
1. Malt extracts and beverages in bottles	1879–1920
2. Malt extracts and beverages in other coverings	1879–98, 1921–23
3. Items 1, 2	1899–1920
023 Wines	
1. Wines	1879–83, 1910–23
2. Wine in bottles	1884–1909
3. Wine in other coverings	1884–1909
024 Alcoholic beverages, nonagricultural	
1. Rum	1879–1921
2. Rye	1884–1921
3. Bourbon	1884–94, 1913–21
024 Alcoholic beverages, nonagricultural (CONT.)	
4. Items 9, 10	1884–90, 1909–21
5. Total distilled liquors (Items 1-4)	1922–23
6. Mineral waters	1922–23
7. Other beverages, n.e.s.	1922–23
8. Items 6, 7	1913–21
9. Other distilled liquors, n.e.s., excluding brandy (Item 4 less 10)	1891–1908
10. Brandy	1891–1908
11. Alcohol	1884–88
12. Pure, neutral, and cologne spirits	1884–88
13. Items 2–4, 11–12	1879–83
025a Crude tobacco	
1. Leaf tobacco	1884–1923
2. Stems, trimmings, scrap	1884–1923
3. Tobacco, leaf, stems, trimmings, scrap	1879–83
026 Manufactured tobacco products	
1. Cigarettes	1884–1923
2. Plug tobacco	1898–1923
3. Smoking tobacco	1913–23
4. Cigars and cheroots	1879–88
5. Other tobacco manufactures	1889–1923, 1913–23

(continued)

271

TABLE C-7 (continued)

Export Class and Commodity Composition	Years Covered	Years Uncovered
026 *Manufactured tobacco products* (CONT.)		
6. Items 3, 5	1898–1912	
7. Items 2, 6	1884–97	
8. Items 1, 7	1879–83	
027 *Hides, leather, and manufactures, crude*		
1. Cattle hides	1913–23	
2. Calfskins	1913–23	
3. Sheep and goat skins		1922–23
4. Items 5, 6		1923
5. Other hides and skins, excluding furs		1922
6. Horse, colt, and ass skins		1913–22
7. Items 3, 5		1913–21
8. Items 1, 2, 6, 7	1879–1912	
028ᵃ *Hides, leather, and products, semimanufactured*		
1. Upper leather, cal and whole kip	1911–23	
2. Upper leather, goat and kid, including glazed kid	1911–23	1898–1910
3. Patent upper leather	1913–23	1898–1912
4. Sole leather	1884–1923	
5. Upper leather, cattle, grain and finished splits	1920–23	

Export Class and Commodity Composition	Years Covered	Years Uncovered
028ᵃ *Hides, leather, and products, semimanufactured* (CONT.)		
6. Upper leather, cattle, wax and rough splits	1920–23	
7. Items 5, 6	1918–19	
8. Upper leather, sheep and lamb		1922–23
9. Upper leather, horse and colt		1922–23
10. Upper leather, other		1922–23
11. Items 8–10		1918–21
12. Items 7, 11	1911–12	1913–17
13. Belting leather		1911–12
14. Glove leather		1913–23
15. Upholstery and auto leather		1911–23
16. Rough tanned leather		1922–23
17. Harness, collar and saddle leather		1922–23
18. Fancy leather		1922–23
19. Case, bag, and strap leather		1922–23
20. Other leather and tanned skins		1922–23
21. Items 16–20		1913–21
22. Items 1, 12	1884–1910	
23. Items 14, 21		1911–12
24. Items 13, 15, 23		1884–1910
25. Items 2, 3		1884–97
26. Items 4, 22, 24, 25	1883	

028a Hides, leather and products, semimanufactured—(CONT.)

27. Sole, upper, and other leather excluding morocco and other fine leather
28. Morocco and other fine leather — 1879–82

029 Hides, leather, and products, manufactured

1. Boots and shoes, men's and boys' — 1913–23
2. Boots and shoes, women's — 1913–23
3. Boots and shoes, children's — 1913–23
4. Leather belting — 1920–23
5. Belting leather — 1913–19
6. Items 4, 5 — 1913–23
7. Slippers — 1879–1923
8. Harness and saddles — 1918–23
9. Leather gloves — 1922–23
10. Athletic shoes, etc. — 1922–23
11. Pocketbooks and purses
12. Other manufactures of leather — 1922–23
13. Items 10–12 — 1918–21
14. Items 9, 13 — 1879–1917
15. Items 1–3, 7 — 1879–1912

030 Furs, unmanufactured

1. Furs, undressed — 1913–23
2. Furs, undressed and dressed, and manufactures of — 1879–1912

031 Furs, semimanufactured

1. Dressed fur, fox — 1922–23
2. Dressed fur, muskrat — 1922–23
3. Dressed fur, skunk and civet cat — 1922–23
4. Dressed fur, opossum — 1922–23
5. Dressed fur, other — 1922–23
6. Fur apparel, except hats — 1922–23
7. Other fur manufactures, including waste — 1922–23
8. Items 1–7 — 1913–21

032 Other animal products, crude, agricultural

1. Horses — 1889–1923, 1879–88
2. Tallow, edible — 1922–23
3. Tallow, inedible — 1922–23
4. Items 2, 3 — 1879–1921
5. Mules, asses, and burros — 1879–1912, 1915–21, 1913–14, 1922–23
6. Bones, hoofs, and horns, unmanuf. — 1883–1909, 1913–23
7. Feathers, crude, not dressed — 1922–23
8. Feathers, dressed and manufactures of — 1922–23
9. Items 7, 8 — 1922–23
10. Bones and bone dust — 1898–1921, 1879–82

033 Other animal products, semimanufactured, agricultural

1. Glue of animal origin — 1922–23

(continued)

TABLE C-7 (continued)

Export Class and Commodity Composition	Covered	Uncovered
033 *Other animal products, semimanufactured, agricultural* (CONT.)		
2. Vegetable glue	1922–23	
3. Items 1, 2	1889–1909, 1912–21	1879–88
4. Neat's foot oil	1922–23	
5. Whale oil	1922–23	
6. Other animal oils	1922–23	
7. Items 4–6	1908–21	
8. Grease stearin	1922–23	
9. Oleic acid or red oil	1922–23	
10. Stearic and other fatty acids	1922–23	
11. Oleo and lard stearin	1922–23	
12. Items 8–11	1913–21	
13. Oleo stock	1922–23	
14. Other animal greases, oils, and fats	1922–23	
15. Vegetable soap stock	1922–23	
16. Items 13–15	1913–21	
17. Lard oil	1879–1912	1913–23
18. Beeswax		1879–92, 1898–1907, 1916–23
19. Wax manufactures		
20. Other animal products, n.e.s.		1916–23
21. Grease, including lubricating, and soap stock	1884–1912	1922–23
22. Whale oil	1899–1907	
23. Other animal oils	1879–1907	

Export Class and Commodity Composition	Covered	Uncovered
034 *Other animal products, semimanufactured, nonagricultural*		
1. Cod and cod liver oil	1922–23	
2. Other fish oils	1922–23	
3. Items 1 and 2	1879–1921	
4. Shells, unmanufactured		1916–23
5. Whale oil	1879–98	
035 *Rubber and products, semimanufactured*		
1. Reclaimed rubber	1906–23	
2. Scrap and old rubber	1899–1923	
036 *Rubber and products, manufactured*		
1. Tires, tubes, etc. for automobiles	1913–23	1911–12
2. Other tires and tubes	1913–23	1911–12
3. Rubber boots	1913–23	
4. Rubber belting		1920–23
5. Rubber hose		1920–23
6. Rubber packing		1920–23
7. Items 4–6		1900–19
8. Druggists' rubber sundries		
9. Rubber soles and heels		1918–23
10. Battery jars and accessories		1920–23
11. Other electrical supplies		1922–23
12. Other hard rubber goods		1922–23

036 Rubber and products, manufactured (CONT.)

13. Tire accessories and repair materials	1922–23	
14. Rubber thread	1922–23	
15. Other manufactures of rubber		
16. Items 10–15	1922–23	
17. Items 9, 16	1920–21	
18. Items 8, 17	1918–19	
19. Rubber shoes	1911–17	
20. Canvas shoes with rubber soles	1922–23	
21. Items 19, 20	1922–23	
22. Items 1, 2, 18	1913–21	
23. Items 7, 22	1900–10	
24. Items 3, 21	1879–99 1879–1912	

037 Oilseeds, crude

1. Items 2, 3	1923	
2. Cottonseed	1889–1912	1879–88, 1913–22
3. Flaxseed	1889–1912	1913–22

038 Vegetable oils, expressed, and fats, semimanufactured

1. Linseed oil	1879–1923	
2. Corn oil	1898–1923	
3. Soya bean oil	1920–23	
4. Coconut oil	1920–23	
5. Cocoa butter	1920–23	
6. Peanut oil	1920–23	
7. Other vegetable fats and oils		
8. Items 3–7	1913–19	1920–23
9. Items 2, 8	1898–1912 1884–97	

039 Other vegetable products, crude, agricultural

1. Red clover seed	1922–23	
2. Other clover seed	1922–23	
3. Items 1 and 2	1880–1921	
4. Timothy seed	1889–1923	1884–88
5. Alfalfa	1922–23	
6. Other grass seed	1922–23	
7. Items 5, 6	1913–21	1898–1912
8. Hops	1879–1923	
9. Ginseng	1879–1923	
10. Other field and forage plant seeds	1922–23	
11. Vegetable and flower seeds	1922–23	
12. Other oilseeds, n.e.s.	1922–23	
13. Items 10–12	1898–1921	
14. Fruit stock, cuttings, seedlings	1922–23	
15. Other nursery or greenhouse stock	1922–23	
16. Items 14, 15	1898–1921	
17. Broom corn	1882–1909 1912–23	
18. Other crude vegetable drugs	1889–1923,	
19. Items 7, 13	1889–97	
20. Other seeds, including flaxseed		
21. Items 4, 20	1884–88	
22. Items 3, 21	1880–83 1879	

040 Other vegetable products, semimanufactured, nonagricultural

1. Rosin	1884–1923

(continued)

TABLE C-7 (continued)

Export Class and Commodity Composition	Years	
	Covered	Uncovered
040 *Other vegetable products, semimanufactured, nonagricultural* (CONT.)		
2. Spirits of turpentine	1879–1923	
3. Chestnut extract	1922–23	
4. Other tanning extracts	1922–23	1906–12
5. Items 3, 4	1913–21	1922–23
6. Wood turpentine		1922–23
7. Tar and pitch, wood		1909–21
8. Items 6, 7		1916–23
9. Moss		1889–1908
10. Tar	1884–88	
11. Turpentine and pitch	1884–88	1889–1908
12. Bark for tanning		1906–08
13. Items 5, 12		1889–1905
14. Items 1, 10, 11	1883	
15. Item 1 and turpentine	1879–82	
16. Item 10 and pitch	1879–82	
041 *Other vegetable products, manufactured, agricultural*		
1. Cornstarch	1918–23	
2. Other starch	1918–23	
3. Items 1, 2	1879–1917	
4. Peppermint oil	1891–1923	
5. Other essential oils		1891–1923
6. Items 4, 5	1879–90	
042ª *Cotton textiles, crude*		
1. Cotton, unmanufactured	1889–97, 1905–23	
2. Cotton linters	1898–1904	
3. Unmanufactured cotton except linters	1898–1904	
4. Sea Island cotton	1879–88	
5. Unmanufactured cotton except Sea Island	1879–88	
043 *Cotton textiles, semimanufactured*		
1. Cotton mill waste	1899–1923	
2. Carded yarn, not combed	1922–23	
3. Combed yarn	1922–23	
4. Items 2, 3	1913–21	
5. Cotton, rags, except paper stock		1913–23
044ª *Cotton textiles, manufactured*		
1. Duck, unbleached	1917–23	
2. Other cloth, unbleached	1917–23	
3. Items 1, 2	1907–16	
4. Duck, bleached	1917–23	
5. Other cloth, bleached	1917–23	
6. Items 4, 5	1907–16	

044ᵃ Cotton textiles, manufactured (CONT.)

7. Duck, colored	1917–23
8. Other cloth, yarn or stock dyed	1917–23
9. Items 7, 8	1915–16
10. Other cloth, printed	1915–23
11. Other cloth, piece dyed	1915–23
12. Items 9–11	1879–1914
13. Knit goods, hosiery	1918–23
14. Knit goods, underwear	1918–23
15. Gloves	1922–23
16. Sweaters, shawls, and other outerwear	1922–23
17. Items 15, 16	1918–21
18. Items 13, 14, 17	1913–17
19. Corsets	1908–12
20. Collars and cuffs	1913–23
21. Overalls	1918–23
22. Underwear, not knit, for men and boys	1922–23
23. Shirts	1922–23
24. Other wearing apparel, for men and boys	1922–23
25. Items 21–24	1918–21
26. Dresses and skirts	1922–23
27. Shirt waists and blouses	1922–23
28. Underwear, not knit, for women and children	1922–23
29. Other wearing apparel for women and children	1922–23

044ᵃ Cotton textiles, manufactured (CONT.)

30. Items 26–29		1918–21
31. Items 25, 30		1913–17
32. Laces and embroideries		1913–23
33. Blankets		1918–23
34. Sewing thread		1922–23
35. Crochet, darning, and embroidery cotton		1922–23
36. Twine and cordage		1922–23
37. Items 34–36		1918–21
38. Damasks		1922–23
39. Pile fabrics, plushes, etc.		1922–23
40. Tapestries and other upholstery goods		1922–23
41. Other cotton fabrics, n.e.s.		1922–23
42. Handkerchiefs		1922–23
43. Lace window curtains		1922–23
44. Cotton bags		1922–23
45. Mattresses		1922–23
46. Quilts and comforters		1922–23
47. Sheets and pillow-cases		1922–23
48. Towels and bathmats		1922–23
49. Cotton belting		1923
50. Other manufactures of cotton, n.e.s.		1923
51. Items 49, 50		1922
52. Items 38, 48, 51		1918–21
53. Items 33, 37, 52		1913–17
54. Items 19, 31		1908–12
55. Items 13, 54		1889–1907
56. Items 3, 6	1879–1906	
57. Cotton yarn	1904–12	

(continued)

TABLE C-7 (continued)

Export Class and Commodity Composition	Years Covered	Years Uncovered
044ª *Cotton textiles, manufactured* (CONT.)		
58. Other manufactures of cotton, n.e.s., including rags, laces and embroideries, and typewriter ribbons		
59. Items 57, 58	1904–12	1898–1903
60. Cotton waste, cop and mill		1898
61. Items 59, 60		1879–97
045 *Other vegetable textiles, manufactured*		
1. Binder twine	1910–23	
2. Manila cordage	1923	
3. Sisal or henequen cordage	1923	
4. Items 2 and 3	1922	
5. Other cordage except jute	1922–23	
6. Jute, yarn, cordage, and twine	1922–23	
7. Cordage	1884–1921	
8. Twine, excluding binder twine	1910–21	
9. Bags of jute	1882–1923	
10. Artificial silk hosiery	1918–23	
11. Other manufactures of artificial silk		1918–23
12. Items 10, 11		1917
13. Linoleum, inlaid		1922–23
14. Linoleum, other		1922–23

Export Class and Commodity Composition	Years Covered	Years Uncovered
045 *Other vegetable textiles, manufactured* (CONT.)		
15. Felt base and oil cloth floor coverings		1922–23
16. Items 13–15		1898–1921
17. Oil cloth, except for floors		1898–1923
18. Leather cloth and artificial leather		1913–23
19. Jute burlaps		1922–23
20. Jute bagging for cotton		1922–23
21. Other manufactures of jute		1922–23
22. Flax, hemp, and ramie manufactures		1922–23
23. Window shade, book cloth, etc.		1922–23
24. Water proofed auto cloth, etc.		1922–23
25. Water proofed clothing		1922–23
26. Other manufactures of vegetable fiber		1922–23
27. Other textile manuf.		1922–23
28. Items 19–27		1879–1921
29. Hats of straw, palm leaf		1922–23
30. Hat braid of straw, etc.		1922–23
31. Items 29, 30		1879–1921
32. Oakum		1882–88, 1916–23
33. Hat trimmings		1918–23
34. Wool felt hats		1922–23
35. Fur felt hats		1922–23

045 Other vegetable textiles, manufactured (CONT.)

36. Items 34, 35	1918–21
37. Items 38–40	1922–23
38. Other hats and caps, men's and boys'	
39. Hats, for women and children, untrimmed	1918–21
40. Hats, for women and children, trimmed	1918–21
41. Items 33, 36, 37	1916–17
42. Garters and arm bands	
43. Suspenders and braces	1922–23
44. Items 42, 43	1922–23
45. Items 1, 8	1884–1909 / 1918–21
46. Items 7, 45	1883
47. Hemp cables and cordage	1879–82
48. Other cordage, rope and twine	1879–82

046 Wool textiles, crude

1. Wool and mohair, unmanuf.	1889–99, 1916–23

047 Wool textiles, semimanuf.

1. Wool rags	1913–23

048 Wool textiles, manufactured

1. Wool cloth and dress goods	1918–23
2. Other wool manuf., except wearing apparel	1918–23

048 Wool textiles, manufactured (CONT.)

3. Items 1, 2	1913–17	
4. Wool wearing apparel, incl. knit goods	1889–1923	1884–88 / 1910–12
5. Items 6–9		1898–1909
6. Wool dress goods	1894–98	1879–92, 1899–1909
7. Carpets		
8. Flannels and blankets		1884–1909
9. Other wool manuf., incl. rags		1898–1909
10. Items 6, 9		1884–97
11. Cotton wearing apparel		1884–88
12. Items 4, 11		1879–83
13. Items 8, 10		1879–83

049 Silk textiles, manufactured

1. Silk wearing apparel	1918–23
2. Broad silk dress goods	1918–23
3. Thrown silk, spun silk, etc.	1922–23
4. Sewing, embroidery and crochet silk	1922–23
5. Velvets, plushes, etc., incl. ribbons	1922–23
6. Ribbons, except velvet and plush	1922–23
7. Silk bandings, bindings, etc.	1922–23
8. Laces, veils, and embroideries	1922–23
9. Other manuf. of silk	1922–23
10. Items 3–9	1918–21
11. Items 1, 2, 10	1882–1912 / 1913–17

(continued)

TABLE C-7 (continued)

Export Class and Commodity Composition	Years Covered	Years Uncovered
050 *Other animal textiles, crude*		
1. Cattle hair, unmanuf.		1922–23
2. Other hair, unmanuf.		1922–23
3. Items 1, 2		1879–82, 1913–21
4. Manuf. of hair, n.e.s.		1879–82, 1913–23
5. Items 3, 4		1883–1912
051 *Wood and related products, crude*		
1. Logs, southern pine		1918–23
2. Logs, Douglas fir		1918–23
3. Logs, cedar		1922–23
4. Logs, other softwood		1922–23
5. Items 3, 4		1918–21
6. Logs, hardwoods		1918–23
7. Pulpwood		1922–23
8. Firewood and other unmanuf. wood		1922–23
9. Items 7, 8		1909–21
10. Items 1, 2, 5, 6		1909–11, 1916–17
11. Logs, except hickory, oak, and walnut		1912–15
12. Logs, hickory		1912–15
13. Logs, oak		1912–15
14. Logs, walnut		1912–15
15. Items 9, 10		1893–1908
16. Firewood		1879–92
17. Items 18, 19		1883–92
051 *Wood and related products, crude* (CONT.)		
18. Logs, masts, spars, and other whole timber		1879–82
19. Other unmanuf. wood, excl. firewood		1879–82
052ª *Wood and related products, semimanuf.*		
1. Timber, sawed, southern pine	1912–23	
Boards, planks, and scantlings (Items 2–14) of:		
2. Cypress	1913–23	
3. Douglas fir	1912–23	
4. Yellow pine, southern	1922–23	
5. Yellow pine, western	1922–23	
6. Yellow pine, pitch or long leaf	1912–21	
7. Yellow pine, short leaf	1912–21	
8. Yellow pine, other	1912–21	
9. Redwood	1913–23	
10. White pine	1913–23	
11. Gum	1912–23	
12. Oak	1912–23	
13. Poplar	1912–23	
14. Spruce	1912–23	
15. Staves, tight	1922–23	
16. Staves, slack	1922–23	
17. Items 15 and 16	1898–1921	

052ᵃ *Wood and related products, semimanuf.* (CONT.)

18.	Timber, hewn or sawed, Douglas fir	1922–23	
19.	Timber, hewn or sawed, cedar	1922–23	
20.	Timber, hewn or sawed, softwood other than southern pine, Douglas fir and cedar		1922–23
21.	Items 18–20		1920–21
22.	Softwoods, hewn		1918–19
23.	Softwoods, sawed, excl. southern pine		1918–19
24.	Timber, hewn or sawed, oak		1922–23
25.	Timber, hewn or sawed, hardwoods except oak		1922–23
26.	Items 24, 25		1920–21
27.	Hardwoods, hewn		1918–19
28.	Hardwoods, sawed		1918–19
29.	Items 22, 27		1889–98, 1913–17
30.	Items 23, 28	1884–88, 1899–1912	1913–17
	Boards, planks, and scantlings (Items 31–41) of:	1912	
31.	Hemlock		1923
32.	Other softwood		1923
33.	Items 31, 32		1918–22
34.	Chestnut		1922–23
35.	Hickory		1922–23
36.	Walnut		1922–23

052ᵃ *Wood and related products, semimanuf.* (CONT.)

37.	Ash		1923
38.	Other hardwood		1923
39.	Items 37, 38		1922
40.	Items 34–36, 39		1918–21
41.	Items 33, 40		1913–17
42.	Piling		1922–23
43.	Telegraph, trolley, electric light poles		1922–23
44.	Lath		1922–23
45.	Other lumber		1922–23
46.	Items 42–45		1913–21
47.	Box shooks, southern pine		1923
48.	Box shooks, other		1923
49.	Items 47, 48		1879–1922
50.	Heading		1898–1923
51.	Railroad ties, softwood	1922–23	
52.	Railroad ties, hardwood	1922–23	
53.	Items 51, 52	1913–21	
54.	Items 1, 30	1884–1911	
55.	Boards and planks, other, excl. joists and scantlings	1912	
56.	Items 3, 6–8, 11–14, 55		
57.	Joists and scantlings	1884–1911	
58.	Shooks, except box	1884–1912	1884–98
59.	Items 46, 53	1899–1912	1893–1912
60.	Items 17, 50		1884–97
61.	Pickets, palings, bed slats		1884–92

(continued)

TABLE C-7 (continued)

Export Class and Commodity Composition	Years Covered	Years Uncovered
052ª *Wood and related products, semimanuf.* (CONT.)		
62. Hoops and hoop poles		1879–92
63. Laths		1884–92
64. Item 59, less Items 61–63		1879–92
65. Items 29, 54	1879–83	
66. Items 36, 57	1879–83	
67. Items 58, 60		1879–83
68. Items 61, 63		1879–83
053 *Wood and related products, manufactured*		
1. Shingles	1879–1923	
2. Wood chairs	1918–23	
3. Other wood furniture	1918–23	
4. Items 2, 3	1879–1917	
5. Doors, sash, and blinds	1884–1923	
6. Shooks, tight	1922–23	
7. Shooks, slack	1922–23	
8. Items 6, 7	1918–21	
9. Other manuf. of wood, n.e.s., incl. Item 14		
10. Hardwood flooring		1923
11. Items 9, 10		1923
12. Cane and reed manuf., n.e.s.		1922
13. Veneers and plywood		1922–23
14. Shooks, other		1922–23
15. Items 11–13		1918–21
		1918–21

Export Class and Commodity Composition	Years Covered	Years Uncovered
053 *Wood and related products, manufactured* (CONT.)		
16. Boats, oars, and paddles		1918–23
17. Handles for agric. implements		
18. Handles for tools		1923
19. Items 17, 18		1923
20. Items 8, 14		1918–22
21. Items 15, 16, 19	1913–17	
22. Barrels, casks, and hogsheads		1913–17
23. Trimmings and mouldings		1879–1909, 1912–23
24. Woodenware		1884–1923
25. Cork discs, washers, and wafers		1879–1923
26. Cork stoppers		1922–23
27. Other manuf. of cork		1922–23
28. Items 25–27		1922–23
29. Other manuf. of wood, incl. incubators and brooders		1916–21
30. Items 22, 29		1884–1909, 1912
31. Items 5, 23, 29		1910–11
		1879–83
054 *Paper and related products, semimanuf.*		
1. Sulphite wood pulp	1922–23	
2. Soda wood pulp	1922–23	

054 Paper and related products, semimanuf. (CONT.)

3. Other wood pulp — 1922–23
4. Items 1–3 — 1898–1921
5. Rags and other paper stock — 1910–23

055ᵃ Paper and related products, manuf.

1. Newsprint paper — 1911–23
2. Book paper, not coated — 1911–23
3. Wrapping paper, Kraft — 1922–23
4. Wrapping paper, other — 1922–23
5. Items 3, 4 — 1913–21
6. Writing paper, excl. papeteries — 1922–23
7. Envelopes — 1922–23
8. Papeteries — 1922–23
9. Items 6–8 — 1913–21 / 1884–1912
10. Paperboard and strawboard — 1915–23
11. Cover paper — 1922–23
12. Surface coated paper — 1922–23
13. Bristols and bristol board — 1922–23
14. Sheathing and building paper — 1922–23
15. Cigarette paper and books — 1922–23
16. Photographic paper — 1922–23
17. Other paper and products, n.e.s. — 1922–23

055ᵃ Paper and related products, manuf. (CONT.)

18. Items 11–17 — 1918–21
19. Grease proof and waterproof paper — 1918–23
20. Tissue and crepe paper — 1922–23
21. Toilet paper — 1922–23
22. Items 20, 21 — 1918–21
23. Paper towels and napkins — 1918–23
24. Cash register and adding machine paper — 1918–23
25. Items 18, 19, 22–24 — 1918–23
26. Items 10, 25 — 1915–17
27. Paper hangings — 1913–14
28. Paper bags — 1882–1923
29. Boxes and cartons — 1913–23
30. Carbon paper — 1913–23
31. Playing cards — 1913–23
32. Wall board (plaster board) — 1904–23
33. Items 5, 26, 28–30 — 1916–23 / 1899–1910
34. Items 1, 2 — 1904–12
35. Items 31, 33 — 1898
36. Items 34, 35 — 1898–1903
37. Stationery other than paper — 1884–97
38. Items 9, 36, 37 — 1884–88 / 1879–83

056 Books and other printed matter

1. Books and pamphlets — 1922–23
2. Maps and charts — 1922–23

(continued)

283

TABLE C-7 (continued)

Export Class and Commodity Composition	Years Covered	Uncovered
056 Books and other printed matter (CONT.)		
3. Music, in books and sheets		1922–23
4. Souvenir post cards		1922–23
5. Lithographically printed matter, n.e.s.		1922–23
6. Other printed matter		1922–23
7. Items 1–6		1879–1921
057ª Coal and products, crude		
1. Anthracite coal	1879–1923	
2. Bituminous coal	1879–1923	
058 Coal and products, semimanufactured		
1. Coke	1895–1923	
059ª Petroleum and products, crude		
1. Crude petroleum	1879–1923	
060ª Petroleum and products, semimanufactured		
1. Gas and fuel oil	1913–23	
2. Paraffin wax, unrefined	1918–23	
3. Paraffin wax, refined	1918–23	
4. Items 2, 3	1882–1917	

Export Class and Commodity Composition	Years Covered	Uncovered
061ª Petroleum and products, manufactured		
1. Illuminating oil (kerosene)	1879–1923	
2. Items 3, 4	1879–1917, 1922–23	
3. Paraffin lubricating oil	1918–21	
4. Other lubricating oil	1918–21	
5. Items 6, 7	1879–1912, 1921–23	
6. Gasoline	1913–20	
7. Naptha and other light products	1913–20	
8. Lubricating greases		1913–23
9. Residuum		1913–23
10. Petroleum jelly		1913–23
11. Gas and fuel oil and Item 9		1879–1912
062 Other nonmetallic minerals, crude		
1. Asphalt and bitumen, unmanuf.	1912–23	
2. Sulphur or brimstone	1907–23	
3. Fire clays	1916–23	
4. Other clays		1916–23
5. Plaster, builders' and patent	1916–23	
6. Graphite, unmanuf.		1913–23
7. Asbestos, unmanuf.		1916–23

063 Other nonmetallic minerals, semimanufactured

1.	Cement, hydraulic	1899–1923	1896–98
2.	Sand and gravel	1916–23	
3.	Lime	1916–23	1896–98
4.	Marble in blocks, rough or dressed		1922–23
5.	Other building or monumental stone	1922–23	1922–23
6.	Items 4, 5		1879–1921
7.	Precious stones, incl. pearls	1899–1923	
8.	Other nonmetallic minerals, n.e.s.	1922–23	1922–23
9.	Items 1, 3		1879–95

064 Other nonmetallic minerals, manufactured

1.	Glass containers	1913–23	
2.	Window glass, common	1899–1923	1884–98
3.	Plate glass, unsilvered	1913–23 1911–23	1908–12
4.	Fire-clay bricks	1899–1923	1884–98
5.	Roofing slate	1899–1923	1879–98
6.	Building bricks	1913–23	
7.	Tile: wall, floor, and hollow	1899–1923	1879–90, 1898
8.	Salt	1899–1923	
9.	Table glassware, plain		
10.	Other window and plate glass	1922–23	1922–23

064 Other nonmetallic minerals, manufactured (CONT.)

11.	Lamp chimneys and lantern globes		1922–23
12.	Globes and shades for light fixtures		1922–23
13.	Lamps and other illuminating devices		1922–23
14.	Electrical glassware except lighting		1922–23
15.	Other glassware, n.e.s.		1922–23
16.	Items 9–15		1918–21
17.	Table or other glassware, cut or engraved		1918–23
18.	Chemical glassware		1918–23
19.	Items 16–18		1913–17
20.	China and porcelain table, toilet, and kitchenware		1922–23
21.	Electric porcelain		1922–23
22.	Other china and porcelain ware		1922–23
23.	Earthen and stoneware, table, toilet, and kitchenware		1922–23
24.	Other earthen and stoneware, except sanitary		1922–23
25.	Other refractory bricks		1922–23
26.	Refractory shapes		1922–23
27.	Chinaware	1913–18	1884–1912, 1919–21
28.	Earthen and stoneware		1884–1921

(continued)

TABLE C-7 (continued)

Export Class and Commodity Composition	Years Covered	Years Uncovered
064 Other nonmetallic minerals, manufactured (CONT.)		
29. Other earthenware, stoneware, china-ware and crockery		
30. Sanitary earthenware		1916–21
31. Items 29, 30		1916–23
32. Asbestos paper, mill board, etc.		1913–15
33. Asbestos pipe covering and cement		1922–23
34. Asbestos textiles, yarn, and packing		1922–23
35. Other asbestos manuf.		1922–23
36. Items 32–35		1912–21
37. Graphite crucibles		1922–23
38. Other graphite manuf.		1922–23
39. Items 37, 38		1912–21
40. Manuf. of asphalt and bitumen		1912–23
41. Wheels of emery and corundum		1922–23
42. Wheels of artificial abrasives		1922–23
43. Items 41, 42		1913–21
44. Hones, whetstones, etc.		1922–23
45. Artificial abrasives, crude or grains		1922–23
46. Artificial abrasives, other		1922–23
47. Items 44–46		1913–21
48. Marble manufs.		1922–23
49. Other manufs. of stone		1922–23
50. Items 48, 49		1913–21
064 Other nonmetallic minerals, manufactured (CONT.)		
51. Grindstones		1913–23
52. Manufs. of chalk		1916–23
53. Mica and manufs. of		1916–23
54. Gypsum and manuf. of		1922–23
55. Sulphur, refined		1922–23
56. Magnesia and manuf. of		1922–23
57. Manuf. of cement		1922–23
58. Items 7, 31		1911–12
59. Items 4, 58		1882–1910
60. Items 1, 19		1908–12
61. Items 3, 60		1884–1907
62. Items 50, 51		1884–1912
63. Items 43, 47		1910–12
64. Items 2, 61		1879–83
65. Items 5, 62		1879–83
66. Items 27, 28		1879–83
065 Nonferrous metals, crude		
1. Items 2, 3		1879–1915, 1921–23
2. Copper ores		1916–20
3. Copper concentrates, matte, and regulus		1916–20
4. Items 5, 6		1922–23
5. Zinc ore and concentrates		1879–1921
6. Zinc dross		1906–21
7. Bauxite and other aluminum ores and concentrates		1915–23

066ᵃ Nonferrous metals, semimanufactured

1. Copper plates and sheets	1913–23	
2. Unrefined black, blister, and converter copper	1916–23	
3. Refined copper in ingots, bars, etc.	1922–23	
4. Copper rods	1922–23	
5. Copper wire	1916–21	
6. Items 3, 4	1915	
7. Items 2, 9	1915	
8. Items 2, 3	1913–14	
9. Items 4, 5	1913–14	
10. Brass ingots, plates, sheets, bars, rods	1913–23	
11. Brass, scrap and old	1913–23	
12. Zinc sheets, strips, etc.	1916–23	
13. Zinc slabs, blocks, and pigs, from foreign ore	1916–23	
14. Zinc slabs, blocks, and pigs, from domestic ore	1916–23	
15. Items 12–14	1892–1915	1884–91
16. Lead in pigs, bars, etc., from domestic ore	1914–23	
17. Lead in pigs, bars, etc., from foreign ore	1916–23	
18. Tin in bars, blocks, and pigs	1916–23	

066ᵃ Nonferrous metals, semimanufactured (CONT.)

19. Aluminum ingots, scraps, alloys	1918–23	
20. Aluminum plates, sheets, bars, strips, rods	1918–23	
21. Aluminum, table, kitchen, and hospital ware		1922–23
22. Aluminum tubes, moldings, castings, etc.		1922–23
23. Other manufs. of aluminum		1922–23
24. Items 21–23		1918–21
25. Items 19, 20, 24	1913–17	1899–1912
26. Nickel oxide and matte		1922–23
27. Nickel, monel metal, and alloys		1922–23
28. Items 26, 27	1895–1919	1920–21
29. Other manufs. of lead, n.e.s.		1914–23
30. Items 16, 29		1913
31. Old and scrap copper		1913–23
32. Quicksilver or mercury	1879–98	1899–1909, 1912–23
33. Ferrovanadium		1913–23
34. Babbitt metal		1915–1923
35. Platinum ingots, sheets, etc.		1916–23
36. Ferrotungsten and tungsten metal and wire		1916–23

(continued)

287

TABLE C-7 (continued)

Export Class and Commodity Composition	Covered	Uncovered
066ª Nonferrous metals, semimanufactured (CONT.)		
37. Nickel or German silver		
38. Items 1, 8, 9, 31	1884–1912	1916–23
39. Copper sheets		1884–88
40. Items 38, 39	1879–83	1884–88
41. Manufs. of zinc		1879–83
42. Items 15, 41		
067ª Nonferrous metals, manufactured		
1. Brass and bronze manufs.	1913–23	
2. Type	1913–23	1898–1909, 1912
3. Composition metal, copper chief value	1918–23	
4. Copper pipes and tubes	1918–23	
5. Other manufs. of copper	1918–23	
6. Items 3–5	1913–17	1889–1912
7. Zinc dust		1922–23
8. Other zinc manufs.		1922–23
9. Items 7, 8		1889–1921
10. Plated ware, silver: tableware		1922–23
11. Plated ware, silver: other		1922–23
12. Items 10, 11		1917–21
13. Plated ware, gold		1922–23

Export Class and Commodity Composition	Covered	Uncovered
067ª Nonferrous metals, manufactured (CONT.)		
14. Other plated ware		1922–23
15. Items 13–14		1917–21
16. Items 12, 15		1879–1916
17. Manufs. of gold		1922–23
18. Sterling silver tableware		1922–23
19. Other manufs. of silver		1922–23
20. Items 17–19		1899–21
21. Tin and galvanized iron hollow ware		1918–23
22. Tin cans, finished or unfinished		1922–23
23. Tin manufs.		1923
24. Other manufs. of metal or metal composition		1923
25. Other metals and alloys, n.e.s.		1922–23
26. Items 23, 24		1922
27. Items 22, 23		1918–21
28. Items 24, 25		1918–21
29. Items 21, 27		1879–1917
30. Other manufs. of bronze		1916–23
31. Nickel manufs.		1916–23
32. Platinum manufs.		1916–23
33. Items 35, 36		1899–1912
34. Brass and manufs. of		1879–1912
35. Lead manufs., except type and pigs, bars and old		1898

067ª Nonferrous metals, manufactured (CONT.).

36. Lead pigs, bars, and old	1895–98	
37. Items 2, 35	1895–97	
38. Items 36, 37	1879–94	
39. Manufs. of copper, except sheets	1879–88	

068 Iron and steel products, crude

1. Iron ore	1899–1923	1882–98

069ª Iron and steel products, semimanufactured

1. Steel sheets	1913–23	
2. Steel ingots, blooms, billets, slabs	1899–1923	
3. Tinplate, terneplate, and taggers' tin	1899–1923	
4. Hoop, band, and scroll iron and steel	1913–23	1884–98
5. Wire rods	1898–1923	
6. Iron and steel scrap	1897–1923	1896
7. Iron bars	1879–1921, 1923	
8. Steel bars	1923	
9. Items 7, 8	1922	
10. Alloy steel bars	1922–23	
11. Items 8, 10	1898–1921	
12. Boiler plates	1922–23	
13. Other plates, not fabricated	1922–23	1879–82
14. Iron and steel sheets, galvanized	1922–23	

069ª Iron and steel products, semimanufactured (CONT.)

15. Iron sheets, black	1922–23	
16. Iron sheets and plates, galvanized	1913–21	
17. Iron sheets and plates, other	1913–21	
18. Steel plates	1913–21	
19. Pig iron, not containing alloys	1922–23	
20. Tungsten, manganese, and other ferro-alloying ores		1922–23
21. Other ferro-alloys, except ferro-manganese and ferrosilicon		1922–23
22. Items 19–21	1918–21	
23. Ferromanganese		1918–23
24. Ferrosilicon		1918–23
25. Items 22–24	1879–1917	
26. Items 16, 17	1897–1912	1884–96
27. Items 1, 18	1898–1912	1884–97
28. Items 5, 11	1897	1884–96
29. Items 27, 28	1879–83	
30. Items 4 and 26 or 12 and 31		1883
31. Iron sheet, band, and hoop		1879–82

070ª Iron and steel products, manufactured

1. Railroad spikes	1913–23	
2. Rails, steel	1879–1923	
3. Wire, except barbed	1909–23	

(continued)

289

TABLE C–7 (continued)

Export Class and Commodity Composition	Years Covered	Years Uncovered
070ª *Iron and steel products, manufactured* (CONT.)		
4. Barbed wire	1909–23	
5. Cut nails	1889–1923	
6. Wire nails	1898–1923	
7. Bolts, nuts, rivets, and washers, except railway	1913–23	
8. Axes	1913–23	
9. Saws	1899–1923	
10. Hammers and hatchets	1913–23	
11. Shovels and spades	1913–23	
12. Locks	1913–23	
13. Structural iron and steel	1899–1923	
14. Casing and oil pipe-line	1922–23	
15. Welded black pipe	1922–23	
16. Welded galvanized pipe	1922–23	
17. Malleable iron pipe fittings	1922–23	
18. Items 14–17	1915–21	
19. Cast iron pipe	1922–23	
20. Cast iron pipe fittings	1922–23	
21. Items 19, 20	1915–21	
22. Items 18, 21	1899–1914	
23. Table and kitchen cutlery	1913–23	1899–1909, 1912

Export Class and Commodity Composition	Years Covered	Years Uncovered
070ª *Iron and steel products, manufactured* (CONT.)		
24. Augers and bits, woodworking	1918–23	
25. Files and rasps	1918–23	
26. Mechanics' and other tools, n.e.s.	1918–23	
27. Items 24–26	1913–17	
28. Hinges and other builders' hardware	1913–23	
29. Stoves, ranges, and parts of	1913–23	1879–1912
30. Railway track material	1913–23	
31. Ship and tank plates, punched and pressed	1918–23	
32. Wood screws	1918–23	
33. Horseshoe nails		1922–23
34. Other nails, incl. tacks		1922–23
35. Items 33, 34		1918–21
36. Items 32, 35		1913–17
37. Woven wire fencing		1913–23
38. Wire rope		1918–23
39. Wire cloth and screening		1922–23
40. Insulated iron and steel wire and cable		1922–23
41. Other wire and manufs. of		1922–23
42. Items 39–41		1918–21

070ᵃ Iron and steel products, manufactured (CONT.)

43.	Items 38, 42	1913–17
44.	Iron castings	1922–23
45.	Steel castings	1922–23
46.	Items 44, 45	1879–1921
47.	Car wheels and axles 1879–88	1889–1923
48.	Razors, straight blade	1920–23
49.	Razors, safety	1920–23
50.	Items 48, 49	1913–19
51.	Safety razor blades	1922–23
52.	Scissors and shears	1922–23
53.	Other cutlery and parts of	1922–23
54.	Items 51–53	1913–21
55.	Bathtubs	1913–23
56.	Closet bowls, lavatories, and sinks	1913–23
57.	Other household enamelware	1913–23
58.	Safes	1899–1923
59.	Filing cases	1922–23
60.	Other office furniture and fixtures	1922–23
61.	Items 59, 60	1918–21
62.	Other metal furniture	1918–23
63.	Items 61–62	1899–1917
64.	Heating boilers and radiators	1911–23
65.	Scales and balances	1879–1923
66.	Horseshoes	1913–23
67.	Items 68, 69	1922–23
68.	Iron and steel forgings	1918–21

070ᵃ Iron and steel products, manufactured (CONT.)

69.	Shells and projectiles, empty	1918–21
70.	Furniture hardware	1922–23
71.	Saddlery and harness hardware	1922–23
72.	Car and marine hardware	1922–23
73.	Other hardware	1922–23
74.	Items 70–73	1918–21
75.	Sprockets and other power transmission	1922–23
76.	Other chains	1922–23
77.	Items 75, 76	1918–21
78.	Needles, hand and machine	1918–23
79.	Railroad bolts, nuts, washers, etc.	1922–23
80.	Ball and roller bearings and parts of	1922–23
81.	Sheet and tin plate bars	1922–23
82.	Skelp iron and steel	1922–23
83.	Strip steel, cold rolled	1922–23
84.	Other manuf. of iron and steel	1922–23
85.	Items 79–84	1918–21
86.	Items 31, 68, 69, 74, 77, 78, 85	1915–17
87.	Refrigerators	1915–23
88.	Items 86, 87	1913–14
89.	Items 3, 4	1884–1908
90.	Items 8, 10, 11, 27	1899–1912

(continued)

TABLE C-7 (continued)

Export Class and Commodity Composition	Years Covered	Years Uncovered
070ª Iron and steel products, manufactured (CONT.)		
91. Items 12, 28	1884–1912	
92. Items 1, 36		1898–1912
93. Items 50, 54		1899–1909, 1912
94. Items 23, 93		1879–98, 1910–11
95. Items 7, 30, 37, 43, 55, 56, 57, 66, 88		
96. Items 64, 95		1911–12
97. Other iron and steel manufs. except hoop, band and scroll iron (Item 95 less 98)		1910
98. Hoop, band, and scroll iron		1905–09
99. Other iron and steel manufs. except iron rails (Item 97 less 100)		1899–1909
100. Iron rails		1899–1904
101. Items 9 and 90	1879–98	1879–1904
102. Items 6 and 92		1889–97
103. Items 13, 22, 58, 68 and 99		1896–98
104. Items 5 and 102	1879–88	
105. Items 89, 91, 108		1883
106. Other manufs. of iron, n.e.s.		1879–82
107. Other manufs. of steel, n.e.s.		1879–82
070ª Iron and steel products, manufactured (CONT.)		
108. Item 103 plus cycles and parts of		1884–95
071ª Machinery and vehicles, except automobiles		
1. Plows and cultivators	1879–99, 1913–23	
2. Planters and seeders	1913–23	
3. Hay rakes and tedders	1913–23	
4. Mowers and reapers	1879–1923	
5. Cream separators	1913–23	
6. Seed separators, threshers		
7. Other agricultural machinery, exc. tractors	1913–23	
8. Tractors	1922–23	
9. Items 7, 8	1922–23	
10. Electric fans	1913–21	
11. Electric lamps, incand., carbon filament	1913–23	
12. Electric lamps, incand., metal filament	1913–23	
13. Generators and parts	1913–23	
14. Motors and parts	1913–23	

071ª *Machinery and vehicles, except automobiles* (CONT.)

Item	Years
15. Pumps and pump machinery	1913–23
16. Railway cars, passenger (steam)	1898–1912
17. Railway cars, freight	1913–23
18. Wagons and drays	1913–23
19. Bicycles	1913–23
20. Motor cycles	1913–23
21. Cash registers	1900
22. Sewing machines	1901–23
23. Steam engines, locomotives	1879–1923
24. Electric locomotives	1913–23
25. Machine tools	1913–23
26. Other metalworking machinery	1918–23
27. Items 25, 26	1918–23
28. Woodworking machinery exc. sawmill	1898–1917
29. Telephones	1913–23
30. Engines, n.e.s., incl. kerosene	1913–23
31. Engines, n.e.s. excl. kerosene	1918–23
32. Insulated copper wire and cable	1913–17
33. Transformers	1914–23
34. Mechanical stokers and boilers	1914–23
35. Incubators and brooders	1918–23
36. Cotton gins and parts of	1913–23, 1913–23

071ª *Machinery and vehicles, except automobiles* (CONT.)

Item	Years
37. Windmills	1907–23
38. Railway cars; passenger (electric railway)	1922–23
39. Mine cars	1922–23
40. Items 38, 39	1898–1921
41. Aircraft	1913–23
42. Aircraft parts, exc. engines and tires	1913–23
43. Motorboats	1908–23
44. Carriages, coaches, and buggies	1913–23
45. Wheelbarrows	1922–23
46. Pushcarts and hand trucks	1922–23
47. Items 45, 46	1904–21
48. Station and warehouse motor trucks	1918–23
49. Parts of railway cars, exc. axles and wheels	1920–23
50. Other vehicles and parts of	1920–23
51. Items 49, 50	1918–19
52. Items 48, 51	1913–17
53. Elevators and elevator machinery	1913–23
54. Mining and quarrying machinery	1915–23
55. Oil well machinery	1915–23
56. Items 54, 55	1907–14
57. Textile machinery	1913–23
58. Shoe machinery, exc. sewing	1898–1923

(continued)

TABLE C-7 (continued)

Export Class and Commodity Composition	Years Covered	Years Uncovered
071ª *Machinery and vehicles, except automobiles* (CONT.)		
59. Flour-mill and grist-mill machinery		1913–23
60. Sugar-mill machinery		1911–23
61. Paper and pulp-mill machinery		1913–23
62. Sawmill machinery		1913–23
63. Brewing machinery		1911–23
64. Refrigerating and ice-making machinery		1911–23
65. Air compressors		1913–23
66. Adding and calculating machines		1911–23
67. Typewriters	1897–1923	
68. Power laundry machinery		1914–23
69. Other laundry equipment		1914–23
70. Items 68, 69		1900–13
71. Typesetting machines		1913–23
72. Printing presses		1879–1923
73. Meters, gas and water		1915–23
74. Parts of cash registers		1915–23
75. Concrete mixers		1918–23
76. Excavating machinery		1918–23
77. Road making machinery		1918–23
78. Other machinery, n.e.s.		1918–23
79. Lawn mowers		1913–23

Export Class and Commodity Composition	Years Covered	Years Uncovered
071ª *Machinery and vehicles, except automobiles* (CONT.)		
80. Items 75–78		1915–17
81. Items 73, 74, 80		1913–14
82. Steam engines, stationary, exc. turbine		1913–23
83. Steam engines, marine, exc. turbine		1913–23
84. Internal combustion engines, marine		1913–23
85. Internal combustion engines, auto and truck		1913–23
86. Other engines, turbines, etc.		1918–23
87. Item 86 and kerosene engines		1913–17
88. Boiler tubes		1918–23
89. Other parts of boilers		1918–23
90. Items 34, 88, 89		1913–17
91. Electric lamps except incandescent: arc		1913–23
92. Telegraph, radio, and wireless apparatus		1913–23
93. Batteries		1914–23
94. Wiring supplies and fixtures		1914–23
95. Volt, watt, watt-hour, and other meters		1915–23
96. Starting and controlling equipment		1918–23

071ᵃ Machinery and vehicles, except automobiles (CONT.)

No.	Description	Years
97.	Domestic heating and cooking devices	1918–23
98.	Spark plugs and other ignition apparatus	1918–23
99.	Carbons, brushes, and electrodes	1918–23
100.	Switches, switchboard panels, fuses, etc.	1918–23
101.	Other electrical apparatus	1918–23
102.	Items 96–101	1915–17
103.	Items 95, 102	1914
104.	Items 32, 33, 93, 94, 103	1913
105.	Items 1, 2, 3, 6, 9, less item 110	1899–1912
106.	Items 28, 62	1904–12
107.	Items 16, 17	1910–12
108.	Items 5, 36, 53, 57, 59, 61, 65, 71, 79, 81	1898–1909
109.	Items 60, 63, 64, 66, 108	1911–12
110.	Tractors, exc. agricultural	1909–10
111.	Items 109, 110	1909–12
112.	Items 37, 56, 111	1907–08
113.	Items 106, 112	1904–06
114.	Items 21, 70, 113	1900–03
115.	Stationary engines and parts of	1898–99
116.	Items 117, 118	1879–1912, 1910–12
117.	Other engines, exc. fire engines	1879–1909

071ᵃ Machinery and vehicles, except automobiles (CONT.)

No.	Description	Years
118.	Fire engines	1879–1909
119.	Items 13, 14	1898–1912
120.	Items 10–12, 29, 91, 92, 104	1902–12
121.	Medical, optical, and scientific instruments	1910–12
122.	Phonographs	1910–12
123.	Items 121, 122	1902–09
124.	Items 120, 123	1879–1901
125.	Bicycles and motor cycles	1896–1912
126.	Items 18, 41, 42, 44, 52	1908–12
127.	Items 43, 126	1904–07
128.	Items 47, 127	1899–1903
129.	Item 105 less item 1	1879–98
130.	Items 15, 27, 58, 114, 119	1897
131.	Items 67, 130	1879–96
132.	Items 40, 107	1879–97
133.	Item 128 and automobiles	1879–98

072ᵃ Automobiles and parts

No.	Description	Years
1.	Items 2, 3	1899–1906, 1913–23
2.	Motor vehicles: commercial and passenger	1907–12
3.	Parts of automobiles, not incl. engines or tires	1907–12

(continued)

TABLE C-7 (continued)

Export Class and Commodity Composition	Years Covered	Years Uncovered
073 Chemicals and allied products, crude		
1. Phosphate rock: high grade hard	1913–23	
2. Phosphate rock: land pebble	1913–23	
3. Other phosphate rock		1913–23
4. Other gums and resins, n.e.s.		1922–23
5. Items 1–3	1899–1912	
6. Items 8, 9	1889–98	1883–88
7. Bark and extracts of, for tanning		1879–88
8. Guano		1879–82
9. Manures other than guano		1879–82
074ᵃ Chemicals and allied products, semimanufactured		
1. Wood and denatured alcohol	1899–1923	1898
2. Acetate of lime	1899–1923	1898
3. Copper sulphate	1899–1923	1898
4. Zinc oxide	1899–1923	
5. White lead, carbonate	1913–23	
6. Superphosphates	1918–23	
7. Sulphate of ammonia	1921–23	
8. Prepared fertilizer mixtures	1922–23	
9. Other nitrogenous fertilizers, n.e.s.	1922–23	

Export Class and Commodity Composition	Years Covered	Years Uncovered
074ᵃ Chemicals and allied products, semimanufactured (CONT.)		
10. Other fertilizers, n.e.s.	1922–23	
11. Items 8–10	1921	
12. Items 7, 11	1918–20	
13. Items 6, 12	1899–1917	
14. Carbolic acid	1918–23	
15. Nitric acid	1918–23	
16. Acetic acid	1922–23	
17. Boric acid	1922–23	
18. Items 16 and 17 and other acids exc. picric	1918–21	
19. Other acids, incl. picric	1922–23	
20. Picric acid	1918–21	
21. Items 14, 15, 18, 20	1909–17	
22. Coal-tar dyes, colors, and stains	1918–23	
23. Logwood extract	1918–23	
24. Other dye extracts	1918–23	
25. Items 22–24	1899–1917	1879–98
26. Calcium carbide	1910–23	
27. Other dry colors, n.e.s., incl. mineral earths	1913–23	
28. Bone black, carbon and lampblack	1899–1923	
29. Alcohol, exc. wood and denatured	1913–23	1898–1912

074ᵃ Chemicals and allied products, semimanufactured (CONT.)

#	Item	Years
30.	Celluloid and manufs. of	1898–1912
31.	Soda ash	1913–23
32.	Sodium silicate	1918–23
33.	Sal soda	1918–23
34.	Caustic soda	1918–23
35.	Borax	1920–23
36.	Sodium bicarbonate	1920–23
37.	Other sodium compounds, n.e.s., incl. cyanide	1920–23
38.	Items 35–37	1918–19
39.	Items 31–34, 38	1915–17
40.	Crude tar and pitch	1916–23
41.	Benzol	1918–23
42.	Chlorinated lime (bleaching powder)	1918–23
43.	Formaldehyde	1918–23
44.	Glycerin	1918–23
45.	Infants' food, malted milk, etc.	1918–23
46.	Crude coal tar distillates, n.e.s.	1918–23
47.	Chlorate of potash	1918–23
48.	Bichromate of potash	1922–23
49.	Other potash, n.e.s.	1922–23
50.	Items 48, 49	1918–21
51.	Other chemicals, n.e.s.	1918–23
52.	Items 41–47, 50, 51	1915–17
53.	Items 39, 52	1913–14
54.	Sulphuric acid	1909–12 1913–23
55.	Items 21, 54	1899–1908 1879–98
56.	Item 53 and petrol. jelly	1910–12

074ᵃ Chemicals and allied products, semimanufactured (CONT.)

#	Item	Years
57.	Washing powder and fluid	1902–12
58.	Items 26, 56	1909
59.	Item 58 less 60	1902–08
60.	Ashes, pot and pearl	1879–1908
61.	Items 57, 59	1901
62.	Items 1, 29	1889–97
63.	Baking powder	1901–23
64.	Items 61, 63	1898–1900
65.	Items 2, 3, 64	1884–97
66.	Medicines	1884–88
67.	Roots, herbs, etc.	1884–88
68.	Items 65–67	1879–83

075ᵃ Chemicals and allied products, manuf.

#	Item	Years
1.	Washing powder and fluid	1913–23
2.	Enamel paints	1922–23
3.	Other ready-mix paints	1922–23
4.	Items 2, 3	1913–21
5.	Varnishes	1879–1923
6.	Powder, smokeless and other	1879–1923
7.	Dynamite	1908–23
8.	Laundry and other soap exc. toilet or fancy	1879–1923
9.	Red lead and litharge	1918–23
10.	Other paints	1918–23
11.	Items 9, 10	1913–17
12.	Soap, toilet or fancy	1913–23 1879–1912

(continued)

TABLE C–7 (continued)

Export Class and Commodity Composition	Years Covered	Years Uncovered	Export Class and Commodity Composition	Years Covered	Years Uncovered
075ª Chemicals and allied products, manuf. (CONT.)			075ª Chemicals and allied products, manuf. (CONT.)		
13. Coal tar medicinals		1922–23	29. Metal polishes		1916–23
14. Quinine sulphate and all alkaloids or salts from cinchona bark			30. Items 4, 11, and white lead and other dry colors	1899–1912	
15. Antitoxins, serums, vaccines		1922–23	31. Stove polish		1899–1908
16. Other medicinal and pharmaceutical preparations		1922–23	32. Other blacking and polishes		1899–1908
17. Items 13–16		1922–23	33. Item 30 and carbon black and zinc oxide	1879–98	
18. Perfumery and toilet water		1889–1921	076 Misc. items, covered		
19. Talcum and other toilet powder		1922–23	1. Organs	1913–23	
20. Creams, rouges, and other cosmetics		1922–23	2. Player pianos	1913–23	
21. Dentifrices		1922–23	3. Other pianos	1913–23	
22. Other toilet preparations		1922–23	4. Metallic pens, except gold	1913–23	
23. Items 18–22		1879–1921	5. Fountain pens	1913–23	
24. Items 31, 32		1879–98, 1909–23	6. Penholders	1913–23	
25. Fuses		1918–23	7. Candles	1913–23	
26. Explosive shells and projectiles		1918–23	8. Phonographs	1915–23	
27. Other ammunition, explosives, fireworks, etc.		1918–23	9. Matches	1916–23	
28. Items 25–27		1913–17	077 Misc. items, uncovered		
			1. Cameras		1913–23
			2. Motion picture films, exposed		1913–23
			3. Motion picture films, sensitized, not exposed		1913–23

077 *Misc. items, uncovered* (CONT.)

Item	Years
4. Other sensitized films, not exposed, incl. dry plates	1913–23
5. Other photo apparatus	1913–23
6. Optical goods	1913–23
7. Dental instruments and supplies	1913–23
8. Teeth	1913–23
9. Surgical and medical instruments	1913–23
10. Surgical appliances, artificial limbs, etc.	1913–23
11. Scientific instruments and equipment	1913–23
12. Dolls and parts of	1918–23
13. Mechanical toys	1918–23
14. Other toys	1918–23
15. Items 12–14	1912–17
16. Buttons, pearl or shell	1918–23
17. Other buttons	1918–23
18. Items 16, 17	1910–17
19. Brushes	1913–23
20. Athletic and sporting goods	1912–23
21. Roofing	1908–23
22. Gas lighting appliances	1918–23
23. Incandescent mantles	1918–23
24. Other lamps and lighting devices	1918–23
25. Items 22–24	1879–1917
26. Art works, painting, and statuary	1882–1923

077 *Misc. items, uncovered* (CONT.)

Item	Years
27. Clocks	1879–1923
28. Watches	1879–1923
29. Jewelry	1899–1923
30. Rifles, shotguns, and parts of	1918–23
31. Revolvers and pistols	1918–23
32. All other firearms	1918–23
33. Items 30–32	1879–1917
34. Cartridges, loaded	1908–23
35. Perforated music rolls	1913–23
36. Piano players	1904–20
37. Other musical instruments	1913–20
38. Items 36, 37	1921–23
39. Pencils	1904–09, 1913–23
40. Printers' and lithographers' ink	1899–1923
41. Typewriter ribbons	1913–23
42. Writing and other ink	1899–1923
43. Brooms	1913–23
44. Sponges	1912–23
45. Phonographs	1923
46. Phonograph records	1915–23
47. Items 45, 46	1913–14
48. Household and personal effects	1911–23
49. Manufs. of vulcanized fiber, incl. trunks	1922–23
50. Manufs. of vulcanized fiber, excl. trunks	1912–21
51. Bags and suitcases, incl. trunks	1889–98, 1912–21

(continued)

299

TABLE C-7 (concluded)

Export Class and Commodity Composition	Years Covered	Years Uncovered	Export Class and Commodity Composition	Years Covered	Years Uncovered
077 *Misc. items, uncovered* (CONT.)			077 *Misc. items, uncovered* (CONT.)		
52. Bags and suitcases, excl. trunks		1922–23	68. Gelatin		1922–23
53. Umbrellas and parasols		1879–88, 1916–23	69. Items 35, 37		1904–12
54. Flowers, cut		1916–23	70. Items 36, 69		1879–1903
55. Dyeing and tanning materials, crude		1916–23	71. Items 15, 20		1884–1911
56. Notions		1916–23	72. Candles		1879–1912
57. Fire extinguishers		1916–23	73. Organs		1879–1912
58. Flypaper and fly traps			74. Pianos, incl. player pianos		1879–1912
59. Plates and cuts, electrotype, halftone, etc.		1916–23	75. Explosives, n.e.s.		1908–12
60. Paste and mucilage		1916–23	76. Items 34, 75 and dynamite		1879–1907
61. Shoe findings		1916–23	77. Items 19, 43		1889–1912
62. Billiard tables and accessories			78. Items 1–5		1909–12
63. Paper clips, binders, etc.		1918–23	79. Items 7, 8		1909–12
64. Pipes and smokers' articles, n.e.s.		1922–23	80. Items 40, 42		1882–98
65. Other vegetable products, n.e.s.		1922–23	81. Item 29 and manufs. of gold and silver		1879–98
66. Coffee extracts, and substitutes		1922–23	82. Matches		1889–98
67. Other vegetable preparations		1922–33	83. Stereotype and electrotype plates		1889–98
			84. Ice		1879–98
			85. Ores, gold and silver bearing		1879–88
			86. Fancy articles, exc. toys and perfumery		1884–88
			87. Items 71, 86		1879–83

ᵃ Price and quantity indexes and values presented for these classes in Tables C–1 through C–6.

APPENDIX C

NOTES TO TABLE C-7

Export Class
001
    Items:
1. 1890–1923: BLS, Cattle, steers, good to choice.
     1889: Aldrich, Beeves, live weight, Chicago.
     1879–89: Aldrich, Beeves, good to prime, live weight, New York City.
2. 1890–1923: BLS, Hogs, good to choice, light butchers.
     1889: Aldrich, Hogs, live weight, Chicago.
     1879–89: Aldrich, Hogs, good to prime, live weight, New York City.
3. 1907–23: BLS, Lambs.
     1890–1906: BLS, Sheep, native wethers.
     1879–89: Aldrich, Sheep, good to prime, New York City.

003
    Hay was separated from other vegetable foods because of differences in price behavior.

004
    The series on green coffee begins with the inclusion of Puerto Rico in the U.S. customs area.

011
    Before July 1882, commodities 5–7 were not listed separately in the published quarterly and monthly trade statements, but fiscal year annuals were available. We used these to estimate quarterly values by assuming that the ratio of these commodities to "all other articles" remained constant throughout each fiscal year. We obtained quarterly quantities from the published fiscal annual quantities by interpolating the unit values, using import unit values for lard as a guide.

013
    Items:
1. Unit values were extrapolated back from fiscal 1887 by Bezanson price of salmon, Halifax.
5. Herring, salted or dry-cured was used as a covered item, 1915–23, when almost all of it consisted of shipments from New York to Latin America and the unit values moved similarly to BLS and WIB prices. Shipments in 1913–14 were mainly from the State of Washington to the Far East and at much lower unit values. We considered these to be non-comparable with later years and treated the item as uncovered.

014
    Items 16 and 17 equal items 7–15.

018
    Items:
6. BLS file, unpublished series, Peaches, cannery.
7. BLS file, unpublished series, Pineapples, cannery.

021
    Items:
3. 1916–23: BLS price of pepper, black, Singapore, 1918 annual through 1923, extrapolated to 1918 quarterlies and 1916 by unweighted average of WIB prices for cassia, cloves, ginger, nutmeg, and black pepper, Singapore.
     1884–88: Unweighted index of cloves and cassia from Bezanson, and nutmegs and Singapore pepper from Aldrich report.
4. Laspeyres price index of import unit values of coffee and cocoa with 1902 export weights.
5. Laspeyres price index combining price indexes used for items 3 (1884–88) and 4 (1884 weights).

APPENDIX C

Notes to Table C-7 (continued)

024

To a considerable extent, 1879–89 based on outside price data. Export unit values for alcoholic beverages became very erratic after 1918–19. The methods of obtaining them (shown below) are crude, but preferable to leaving a fairly large item incompletely covered or leaving the whole group uncovered from 1913 on.

Items:

1. 1919 export unit value extrapolated to 1920 by unit value of exports to all countries except Canada and China; to 1921 by unit value of exports to Canada, and to 1923 by the Canadian import unit value for imports of rum from the United States.
2. First half of 1919 export unit values extrapolated to 1923 by U.K. annual export unit values of spirits.
3. BLS price for bourbon, straight, four years in bond, in barrels, used for 1913 through first quarter of 1919. These were extrapolated to the rest of 1919 by U.S. export unit values and to 1920, 1921, and 1923 by U.K. export unit values of spirits.
5. U.K. annual export unit values for spirits.
13. Price per gallon of "whiskey, 32 u.p." in Toronto from *Statistical Contributions to Canadian Economic History*, Vol. II by K. W. Taylor and H. Michell, Toronto, 1931. The movements of this series followed closely those of the unit values of the main U.S. export item, bourbon, in the rest of this period.

026

To a considerable extent, 1879–98 based on outside price data.

Items:

3. BLS, smoking tobacco.
6. BLS, smoking tobacco.
7. 1889–97: Index of BLS, smoking tobacco, weighted 1 and BLS, tobacco, plug, smooth, weighted 3, 1890 to 1897. This was extrapolated back to 1889 by Aldrich, tobacco: plug, navy, best grade.
   1884–88: Aldrich, tobacco: plug, navy, best grade.
8. Index of Aldrich, tobacco: plug, navy, best grade and same, medium grade, and low grade, weighted equally.

027

To a considerable extent, 1879–89 based on outside price data.

Item:

8. 1890–94, BLS, hides: steer, green salted.
   1879–89, Aldrich, hides: green salted.

028

To a considerable extent, 1879–1910 based on outside price data.

Items:

3. Prices for first and second quarters of 1920 were estimated from the unit value for the first half of 1920 and prices for 1919 were extrapolated from 1920, both by use of the average of patent chrome side upper leather and smooth black chrome side-upper leather prices from Federal Trade Commission, *Report on Shoe and Leather Costs and Prices*, June 10, 1921. Prices for 1913–18 and earlier years from WIB, cattle, side-upper leather, patent chrome.
12. Prices for 1911 and 1912 are unit values for commodity 1. of this class.
22. 1908–10: BLS, calf, chrome, range of first commercial grades;
    1890–1907: calf, wax, 30–40 lbs. to doz.;
    1884–89: Aldrich, leather: calfskins, tanned and dressed, domestic, No. 1.
26. Combination of Aldrich, upper leather and sole leather prices.
27. Base price derived by extrapolating unit values by index used for item 26.

029

Items:

6. WIB prices for leather belting, 1913–18, extrapolated to 1919 quarterly, by

302

BLS, men's shoes, vici calf. To obtain a base year price, the 1919 unit value is extrapolated to 1920 by the same BLS series, and from 1920–23, by export unit values for leather belting.

15. Interpolated between export unit values for 1896 and 1903 by an unweighted average of four BLS shoe prices.

030

Based to a considerable extent on outside price data. Quarterly indexes are largely interpolated.

Items:

1. Prices are a Laspeyres index (with 1923 weights derived from export values) of prices of skunk, muskrat, and opposum from *Fur News Magazine*, Columbus, Ohio. The source gave data for only the first and fourth quarters of each year, figures for the intervening quarters were interpolated.

2. 1907–12: Same index as for item 1.

   1899–1907: To extrapolate the above index we used a Laspeyres index of Canadian prices of muskrat and skunk, still with 1923 U.S. export value weights. It seems likely that both of these indexes for 1899–1913 overweight skunk, whose price was increasing faster than that of the other furs.

   1889–98: Unweighted index of prices of beaver, red fox, muskrat, raccoon, and skunk, from *Fur Trade Review*, New York, extrapolated by prices for the same furs from Bezanson.

   1879–89: Unweighted index of Bezanson prices for beaver, red fox, gray fox, muskrat, raccoon, and skunk.

032

Based to a considerable extent on outside price data. Quarterly indexes were largely interpolated.

Items:

1. 1913–23: U.S. farm price of horses, U.S. Department of Agriculture, *Yearbook of Agriculture*, 1924, p. 985.

   1899–1913: For 1899–1907, the price of draft horses at Omaha (USDA, *Yearbook*, 1907). The calculated calendar year 1907 average price was extrapolated to calendar year 1910 by the average farm price of horses two years and older, and for quarterly 1910–13, was extrapolated from calendar 1910 by average farm prices of all horses, from the 1924 USDA *Yearbook*. For 1908–09, first quarter prices were estimated by interpolating between first quarter 1907 and first quarter 1910 by the average value of all horses on farms, January, from the 1911 USDA *Yearbook*. The remaining quarters of 1908–09 were filled in by straight line interpolation.

   1889–99: Omaha price of horses for 1897 to 1899. First quarter figures were extrapolated back to 1889 by average price of horses on farms in the U.S. and remaining quarters were interpolated on a straight line between Januaries.

5. 1915–21, 1923: Average prices of mules, St. Louis, USDA *Yearbook*, 1916, 1918, 1920, 1921, 1924.

033

Based to a considerable extent on outside price data.

Items:

5. Price of whale oil, crude no. 1: Av. price per pound, sellers' tanks, f.o.b. Pacific coast. Compiled from the *Oil, Paint, and Drug Reporter* and published in U.S. Dept. of Agriculture, Statistical Bulletin No. 59 (May 1937), *Fats, Oils, and Oleaginous Raw Materials—Production, Prices, Trade, Disappearance in the U.S., 1912–35 and Available Data for Earlier Years.* We used the Pacific Coast price because most of the whale oil was exported from West Coast ports.

14. Grease, white, average price per pound in tierces, New York. Same source as item 5.

16. Same as item 14.

NOTES TO TABLE C-7 (continued)

21. 1899–1912: BLS price for tallow, New York, extrapolated by Aldrich, tallow. 1884–88: Aldrich price of tallow.

034

Based to a considerable extent on outside price data.

Items:

1. Prices are cod oil, Newfoundland tanked: av. price per pound in barrels, New York, compiled from the *Oil, Paint, and Drug Reporter* and published in U.S. Dept. of Agriculture, Statistical Bulletin No. 59, *Fats, Oils, and Oleaginous Raw Materials.*
2. Prices are Menhaden oil, light, refined: av. price per pound, in barrels, New York, compiled from the *Oil, Paint, and Drug Reporter* and published in the same source as above.
3. Unit values extrapolated from 1920 to 1921 and 1923 by price of cod oil (see item 1).

035

To a considerable extent, 1899–1906 based on outside price data.

Item:

2. 1907 annual unit value extrapolated back to 1899 by BLS, rubber, Para Island, fine.

036

The 1913–23 period is based on outside price data to a considerable extent.

Items:

1 and 2. BLS, automobile tires, fabric.

038

Item:

8. 1913–19 and 1923. Price index composed of coconut oil, weighted four times and soya bean oil weighted once. Weights were taken from earliest available values, those for the last half of 1919. Prices were from WIB and BLS.

040

Item:

5. Unweighted index of prices of chestnut extract, hemlock extract, and oak extract, from the *Oil, Paint, and Drug Reporter.*

041

Item:

6. Unweighted average of Bezanson prices of bergamot, cassia, and lemon oil, on 1889 base.

043

Item:

4. Unit values extrapolated from 1918 to 1913–17 by BLS, cotton, yarn, white, mule-spun, northern, cones, 22/1.

044

Items:

14. Index composed of BLS underwear: men's, cotton drawers and shifts, flat fleece; and BLS underwear: women's cotton union suits, weighted equally with 1923 as base.
18. Index composed of underwear price index used for item 14, weighted once, and hosiery index weighted five times. The hosiery index is a combination of BLS, hosiery: cotton, men's; BLS, hosiery: cotton, women's mercerized; and BLS, hosiery: cotton, women's, rib top.
57. BLS, Cotton yarns: corded, white, mule-spun, northern, cones, 22/1.

045

The 1884–1909 period is based on outside price data to a considerable extent.

Items:

2–6, and 8. BLS, rope: manila, 1st grade, ⅜″ and large.

304

NOTES TO TABLE C–7 (continued)

9. BLS, jute: raw, native firsts, actuals, extrapolated back from 1890 by Aldrich, jute, raw.

45. Export unit values for binder twine (item 1.) extrapolated back from 1910 to 1890 by BLS, rope, and to 1879–89 by export unit values of cordage (item 7.).

046

Based to a considerable extent on outside price data.

Item:

1. Data are not available for 1900–16. Quantities for 1916–23 are estimated from an index composed of BLS prices of wool: Ohio, fine, clothing, unwashed; and wool: Ohio, ¼ and ⅜ grades, unwashed (med. grade), weighted equally, on a 1923 base. Quantities for 1889–99 are estimated from an index of the same two prices, on an 1899 base, extrapolated to 1889 by Aldrich price for wool: Ohio, fine fleece, scoured; and wool: Ohio, med. fleece, scoured. No quantities were estimated for 1879–88.

048

Based to a considerable extent on outside price data.

Items:

1–4. 1913–23: Quantities derived from a price index composed of BLS series for, overcoating: heavy; suiting: serge, 11 oz.; suiting: clay worsted, diagonal 16 oz.; uniform serge: wool-dyed, blue, 55–56″, 16 oz.; suiting: serge, 9½ oz., 55–57″; dress goods: women's broadcloth; dress goods: storm serge, all wool, double wrap. These were weighted equally, with 1923 as a base.

4. 1899–1913: Quantities derived from a price index composed of BLS series for overcoating: soft faced, black, 24 oz.; suiting: serge, 11 oz., 56–58″; suiting: clay worsted, diagonal, 16 oz.; uniform serge: all wool, indigo blue, 14 oz., 54″; suiting: serge, 9½ oz., 55–57″; dress goods: women's, cashmere, cotton warp; dress goods: Panama cloth, 50″. These were weighted equally, with 1913 as a base.

1892–99: Quantities derived from price index composed of BLS series for suiting: serge, 11 oz., 56–58″, weighted twice; uniform serge: all wool, indigo blue, 14 oz., 54″, weighted twice; dress goods: women's, cashmere, cotton warp, weighted once; and dress goods: Franklin sackings, 54″, weighted once.

1890–91: Quantities derived from price index composed of BLS series for uniform serge: all wool, indigo blue, 14 oz., 54″, weighted four times and the two series for dress goods used for the succeeding period, weighted once each.

1889: Quantities derived from Aldrich series for suiting: flannel, all wool, indigo blue, 6–4 Assabet, weighted six times; women's dress goods: all wool, ladies' cloth, 25″, Assabet, opera, weighted once; and women's dress goods: all wool, ladies' cloth, 6–4, Assabet, weighted once.

049

Based to a considerable extent on outside price data.

Items:

1. BLS, hosiery: silk, women's, 39–42 gauge, full-fashioned, 7 thread.

11. 1913–17: Quantities estimated from index composed of WIB prices weighted by 1918 and 1922 export values. The price series used, and their weights, were as follows:

Price Series	*Weight*
Average of 3 series for ladies' hose	Fiscal 1918 export value, wearing apparel.
Average of 23 series for broad silk	Fiscal 1918 export value, broad silk dress goods.
Spun silk yarn, domestic, 60/1; and spun silk yarn, domestic, gray spun, 60/2, No. 1	Fiscal 1918 export value, other manuf. of silk multiplied by ½ of the 1922 ratio of export values of thrown silk, spun silk, etc. to export values of other manufs. of silk.

Price Series	Weight
Average of 2 velvet series, and average of 3 plush series	Fiscal 1918 export value, other manuf. of silk, multiplied by ½ of the 1922 ratio of export values of velvets, plushes, etc. to other manuf. of silk.
Average of 2 ribbon series	Fiscal 1918 export value, other manuf. of silk, multiplied by 1922 ratio of export values of ribbons exc. velvet and plush to other manuf. of silk.
Average of 2 thread and embroidery silk series	Fiscal 1918 export value, other manuf. of silk, multiplied by 1921 ratio of export values of sewing, embroidery, crochet silk to other manuf. of silk.

053

Based to a considerable extent on outside price data.

Items:

2. Price index for wooden chairs composed of BLS, bedroom chairs: all gum, cane seat, weighted four times; BLS, bedroom chairs: bedroom rockers, quartered oak, weighted twice; and BLS, dining room chairs: set of six (composite), weighted fourteen times.

3. Price index for other wood furniture composed of BLS, kitchen tables, weighted once, and BLS, bedroom sets, weighted six times.

4. 1913–17: Combination of index for item 2, weighted once and index for item 3, weighted twice.

1899–1912: Price index composed of BLS, chairs: bedroom, weighted twice; BLS, bedroom sets, weighted twelve times; BLS, kitchen chairs, weighted once, and BLS, kitchen tables, weighted twice.

1889–98: Price index composed of BLS, bedroom chairs, maple, cane seat, N.Y., weighted twice; BLS, kitchen chairs, weighted once; BLS, kitchen tables, weighted twice; and BLS, bedroom sets, weighted twelve times. BLS series were extrapolated from 1890 to 1889 by corresponding Aldrich report series.

1879–88: Price index composed of four Aldrich report series, weighted equally. The series were: bedroom set, painted, five pieces; chairs, bedroom, maple, cane seat; chairs, kitchen, common spindle; tables, kitchen, pine, 3½ foot.

5. 1890–1923: BLS, doors, ponderosa pine.

1884–89: Aldrich report, doors, pine, unmoulded.

055

The 1889–1910 period is based on outside price data to a considerable extent.

Items:

9. Price index composed of envelopes, manila writing paper, medium writing paper, good writing paper, and medium bond paper, weighted equally, on 1922 base. Data are originally from *Paper Trade Journal*, quoted in U.S. Tariff Commission, *Tariff Information Survey, Paragraphs 326 and 327 of 1913* (1922).

10. Price index composed of BLS series for boxboard: chip, no. 90 to 50; boxboard: chip, manila lined, single; boxboard: liner, 85 lb. test; and, for 1918 to 1923, boxboard: manila lined, chip. All are weighted equally, on a 1923 base.

34. Price index composed of BLS, newsprint, weighted six times, and three book paper prices weighted once each. The book paper prices, which were compiled from the *Paper Trade Journal*, are for book paper, sized and super calendared, book paper, machine finish, and book paper, lithographing.

059

Quarterly indexes are largely interpolated.

The published export unit values for total crude petroleum could not be used for the last two periods, because they contain a strong downward bias which is due to the shift from high-quality, high-priced Pennsylvania crude to the cheaper crudes of

306

NOTES TO TABLE C–7 (continued)

other regions. This phenomenon has been noted before in studies of mining output. For example, Harold Barger and Sam H. Schurr, in *The Mining Industries, 1899–1939: A Study of Output, Employment and Productivity* (NBER, New York, 1944, p. 191), separated Pennsylvania-grade oil from all other for the period 1899–1919 for this reason. Spencer and Wardwell in U.S. Bureau of the Census, *Raw Materials in the U.S. Economy: 1900–52,* Bureau of the Census Working Paper No. 1, Washington, D.C., 1954, p. 71, calculated that adjusting for the shift from Pennsylvania-grade crude between 1900 and 1925 would cut the growth of the index of petroleum output almost in half.

No data on the origin of crude petroleum exports are available to measure the shift, but its effects are observable: the unit value of crude petroleum exports fell by 25 per cent between 1902 and 1923, while the export unit value of illuminating oil, the BLS price of refined petroleum, for export, and the BLS price of Pennsylvania crude all rose by 40 per cent or more.

While there is no direct link between production and export data, we did find that the shift away from Pennsylvania-grade petroleum was reflected in a shift in customs area of shipment of crude petroleum exports. From East Coast districts, which were the natural outlets for Pennsylvania petroleum, and which had virtually a monopoly of crude exports in 1902, the trade shifted to Great Lakes, Pacific, and Gulf Coast districts. The hypothesis that this shift in port of export reflected a shift in origin was reinforced by the observation that unit values of crude exports from East Coast ports were considerably higher than the others. We attempted to correct for this bias by treating exports from each major area as a separate commodity, and then combining all of them in a Fisher "ideal" price index for the 1902–23 period. There were probably some shifts in the origin of crude petroleum exports before that, since the Lima-Indiana field became important in output as far back as the late 1880's. But we could not extend our procedure back any further because practically all exports went through East Coast ports before 1902. It is possible that Pennsylvania-grade crude maintained its dominance in exports longer than in domestic production for transportation reasons.

One possible indication of bias in the two earlier periods is the sharp fall, particularly between 1879 and 1893, in the margin between the export price of crude petroleum and the price (at the field) of Appalachian crude. This fall, however, may have been due to other factors, such as a decline in transportation cost; this is supported by the fact that there was a considerable fall also in the margin between the field price of Pennsylvania crude and the price at East Coast ports of refined oil for export.

Our index for 1902 to 1923 was an annual one, because the port data are not available quarterly. We converted the index to quarterly form by a freehand interpolation using the fluctuations of the original export unit values of crude and refined petroleum.

For 1879–98, unit values were used as published.

063

Item:
2. BLS price of gravel.

064

The 1899–1923 period is based on outside price data to a considerable extent.
Items:
1. Price index for 1918–23 composed of four BLS series weighted equally: fruit jars, quart, self-sealing; fruit jars, pint, self-sealing; fruit jars, quart, mason; and milk bottles, quart size. This index was extrapolated back to 1913 by WIB, glass milk bottles.
2. For 1899–1912, BLS price for glass, window, single B, 25″ bracket. The same series was used for 1913–14 to extrapolate back the 1915 annual export unit value.

NOTES TO TABLE C-7 (continued)

4. 1911–12: Average value per unit of fire bricks, from U.S. Interior Dept., *Mineral Resources of the U.S., 1912* and *1913*.
5. 1913–23: BLS price for roofing slate.
   1899–1913: Annual data for average value per unit of roofing slate from U.S. Interior Dept., *Mineral Resources of the U.S., 1913*. We estimated quarterly prices by a freehand interpolation of these annual unit values.
6. 1899–1912: BLS, brick: red, common building, domestic.
7. BLS and WIB prices for hollow building tile.
8. BLS, salt, American, medium.
9. BLS, tumblers, table, price per dozen, f.o.b. factory.
27. Index composed of two WIB series: dinnerware sets, best commercial grade; and dinnerware sets, decorated in cheap standard treatments, weighted equally. The 1918 price was extrapolated to 1923 by BLS, plates: white granite.

066

Items:

2. Unit values of 3 and 6 used.
10. BLS prices for brass sheets.
19, 20, 25. BLS prices for aluminum: 98–99 per cent.

067

The 1913–23 period is based on outside price data to a considerable extent.
Items:
1. BLS price for brass sheets.
5 and 6. Unit values for Items 6–8, class 066 were used.

068

The 1899–1912 period is based on outside price data to a considerable extent.
Import quantities and unit values are used for the period from 1913 to 1923, but for the years 1899 to 1912, we used the price of iron ore, mesabi, non-Bessemer, from the *Iron Trade Review*.

069

Items:

3. 1899–1903: BLS prices of tinplate, domestic, coke, at New York.
10. Price of steel bars, quarterly averages, from American Metal Market, *Metal Statistics, 1938*, New York, 1938.

070

Based to a considerable extent on outside price data.
Items:

2. 1879–88: Prices of steel rails, at works in Pennsylvania, from U.S. Commissioner of Labor, *Sixth Annual Report*, 1890.
9. BLS price for saws: crosscut, Champion, 6 ft., f.o.b. factory.
10. BLS price for hammers: 1½ lbs., f.o.b. New York.
11. BLS price for shovels: Ames, No. 2.
12. BLS price for locks: common mortise.
13. 1913–23: BLS prices for structural steel: structural shapes, beams, etc., 3″ to 15″, f.o.b. mill.
22. Unit values extrapolated back from 1906 to 1899–1905 by annual BLS series for cast iron pipe, lagged one year. Quarterly prices were estimated by a freehand interpolation.
23. 1913–23: BLS prices for knives and forks: cocobolo handles.
24. BLS price for augers: regular, 1-inch.
25. BLS price for files: 8-inch mill, bastard.
26. Price index composed of equally weighted BLS series for planes, trowels, vises, and chisels, on 1923 base.
27. Price index composed of equally weighted BLS series for planes, trowels, vises, chisels, augers, and files, on 1923 base.

NOTES TO TABLE C-7 (continued)

28. Price index for 1918–23 composed of equally weighted BLS series for knobs: door; and butts, wrought iron, on a 1923 base. This is linked at 1918 to an index for 1913–17 on a 1918 base, composed of equally weighted WIB series for butts: wrought iron; hinges: spring hold back; lock sets; knobs: door; and hooks and eyes.

29. Price index composed of equally weighted BLS series for stoves: cooking, coal; stoves: cooking, gas, and stoves: cooking, oil.

30. For 1915–23, annual price index for "other track materials" from Engineering News-Record, *Construction Costs, 1935 edition*, p. 23. We extrapolated this index back to 1913 by an index made up of equally weighted prices for No. 9 Eureka spring frog, split switch, No. 9 rapid frog, and Positive rail anchors, from Presidents' Conference Committee, Western Group Office, *Material and Labor Index Numbers* (1927). Quarterly price indexes were estimated from these annual ones by a freehand interpolation.

90. Price index composed of equally weighted BLS series for planes, trowels, vises, chisels, shovels, augers, files, and hammers, on a 1913 base.

91. 1899–1912: Price index composed of equally weighted BLS series for knobs: door; locks: common mortise; and butts, on a 1913 base.

    1889–98: Same as 1899–1912, but on an 1899 base, extrapolated from 1890 to 1889 by corresponding Aldrich series.

    1884–88: Price index composed of equally weighted Aldrich series for door knobs, locks, and butts, on an 1889 base.

101. 1889–98: Price index composed of equally weighted BLS series (extrapolated from 1890 to 1889 by corresponding Aldrich series), for planes, trowels, vises, chisels, shovels, augers, files, hammers, and saws, on an 1899 base.

    1879–88: Price index composed of equally weighted Aldrich series for same items as 1889–98, on an 1889 base.

071

Most of the coverage was achieved by the use of outside price data rather than by using the published quantity data from Commerce and Navigation reports. Since most of the price data were available only annually, we did not attempt to use available quarterly series. Instead, we computed only annual price indexes and converted them (by a freehand interpolation) to quarterly indexes. The latter were used only for combining with other groups.

Items:

1. 1913–23: Price index composed of the average of six BLS series for cultivators, weighted once, and the average of twenty BLS series for plows, weighted five times, with 1923 as a base.

    1879–99: Our first step was the computation of a price index on a 1900 base for the years 1895, 1890, and 1880, from data in George K. Holmes, *Course of Prices of Farm Implements and Machinery for a Series of Years*, Department of Agriculture, Division of Statistics, Miscellaneous Series, Bulletin 18, 1901. This index was an equally weighted combination of a price index for plows, composed of 72 series for individual types, and a price index for cultivators, composed of 19 series. The second step was to interpolate this index between 1880 and 1900 and extrapolate to 1879 by an annual price series for plows given in T. S. Adams, *Prices Paid by Vermont Farmers for Goods and Services and Received by Them for Farm Products, 1790–1940; Wages of Vermont Farm Labor, 1780–1940*, Vermont Agricultural Experiment Station, Bulletin 507, February 1944.

2. Price index composed of price of planters (average of two BLS series), weighted once, and price of grain drills (average of four BLS series), weighted five times, on a 1923 base.

3. Average of six BLS series for rakes, weighted equally, on a 1923 base.

4. 1913–23: Average of three BLS series for mowers, weighted equally, on a 1923 base.

APPENDIX C

NOTES TO TABLE C–7 (continued)

1899–1913: For 1911–13 we used the index of prices paid by farmers for farm machinery except tractors, from Department of Agriculture, Bureau of Agricultural Economics, *Income Parity for Agriculture*, Part III, 1939. We extrapolated this back to 1903 by an index made up of equally weighted price relatives, on a 1911 base, for the following items: Deere grain binder, 6 ft., 7 ft., and 8 ft.; International Harvester grain binder, 5, 6, 7, and 8 ft.; Deere corn binder; International Harvester corn binder; Deere mower, 5 ft. regular, 5 ft. vertical, and 6 ft.; and International Harvester mower. These data were from U.S. Bureau of Corporations, *The International Harvester Company*, 1913. We then extrapolated the index back to 1899 by an equally weighted average of series for mowing machines and plows from Adams, *Prices Paid by Vermont Farmers*.

1879–99: Indexes covering 1895, 1890, and 1880 on a 1900 base for mowers (composed of twelve series, equally weighted) and for reapers (composed of seven series, equally weighted) were constructed from data in Holmes, *Prices of Farm Implements* and were combined, again with equal weights. We then interpolated between 1880 and 1900 and extrapolated to 1879 by the price series for mowing machines from Adams, *Prices Paid by Vermont Farmers*.

5. Average of three BLS price series for cream separators.
6. Average of two BLS price series for threshers.
7. Price index composed of: (1) An average, weighted three times, of thirteen BLS series for harrows and manure spreaders; (2) an average, weighted three times, of one BLS series for grain binders, three series for corn binders, one series for hay loaders (itself an average of three), one series for potato diggers (itself an average of two), three series for ensilage cutters, and one series for a cornpicker-husker; (3) an average, weighted once, of four BLS series for milking machines; (4) an average, weighted three times, of two BLS series for spraying outfits and four series for wagons.
8. An equally weighted average of seven BLS tractor series.
9. An index composed of all the series used for item 7, with the same weights, combined with the index used for 8, weighted twice.
13. Price index for turbogenerators from William W. Handy, *The Yardstick of Public Utility Operations and Construction Costs*, Baltimore, 1929.
14. Price index for motors from *ibid.*
15. Price index for pumps from *ibid.*
16. ICC index of price of passenger train cars, 1915–23, published in *Railway Age*, July 25, 1936, Vol. 101, No. 4, extrapolated back to 1913 by corresponding index from Presidents' Conference Committee, Eastern Group Pamphlet 138–6, *Trend of Prices for Locomotives, Freight and Passenger Train Cars and Floating Equipment*, August 15, 1930.
17. ICC index for freight train cars extrapolated by PCC index (see item 16).
18. BLS price for wagons, 2-horse, with bed, no brake-composite.
19. Value per unit of bicycles produced in the U.S., 1914, 1919, 1921, and 1923 interpolated by export unit values for motorcycles. Bicycle prices are Census of Manufactures data reproduced in Solomon Fabricant, *The Output of Manufacturing Industries, 1899–1937*, NBER, New York, 1940, p. 590.
22. 1913–23: BLS price for sewing machines, foot treadle.
1879–1913: Canadian import unit values for sewing machines from the U.S., centered to approximate calendar year figures. Data are from various issues of the *Canada Yearbook*, the *Report of the National Revenue Department of Canada*, and the *Sessional Papers of the Canadian Parliament*.
23. 1913–23: ICC index for steam engines extrapolated to 1913 by PCC indexes (see note to item 16).
1899–1913: Export unit values, 1899 to 1910, extrapolated to 1913 by PCC index.
24. ICC index for locomotives other than steam, 1915 to 1923, extrapolated to 1913 by PCC index for steam locomotives.

APPENDIX C

NOTES TO TABLE C-7 (continued)

25. Machine tool price index from Presidents' Conference Committee, Western Group Office, *Materials and Labor Indexes*, p. 61.

26. ICC index of railroad shop machinery costs.

27. For 1900 to 1917 and 1923, price index for shop machinery and machine tools, equally weighted. The index for shop machinery is the ICC index extrapolated back from 1915 by the Presidents' Conference Committee series, published in Presidents' Conference Committee, Eastern Group Pamphlet 314, *Trend of Cost of Shop Machinery*, Jan. 1926. The machine tool price index is from the source listed for 26. For 1898 and 1899, this index was extrapolated back by the shop machinery price index alone.

28. Index of the cost of woodworking machinery, from same source as item 25.

29. Price index for "substation apparatus" from Federal Communications Commission, *Telephone Investigation, Special Investigation Docket #1, Exhibit #2091, Western Electric Co. Profits and Price Trends*, June 14, 1937, p. 270.

30 and 31. Price index composed of the following BLS series for engines, on a 1923 base: 3 hp single cylinder, horizontal hopper cooled, weighted once; less than 5 hp hopper cooled, weighted once; 5-10 hp inclusive, weighted twice; more than 10 hp weighted six times.

32. Index composed of four equally weighted price series for insulated wire and cable from Handy, *Yardstick*.

33. Price index for power transformers from *ibid*.

34. Price index for boilers from *ibid*.

67. Canadian import unit values for typewriters from the U.S., centered to approximate calendar years. For sources, see item 22.

105. For 1911-12, index of prices paid by farmers for farm machinery other than tractors, from Department of Agriculture, Bureau of Agricultural Economics, *Income Parity for Agriculture*, Part III, 1939. We extrapolated this series back to 1903 by an unweighted average of prices for rakes, tedders, disk harrows, and manure spreaders, from U.S. Bureau of Corporations, *The International Harvester Company*, 1913, and from 1903 back to 1899 using an unweighted average of the Adams series for mowing machines and plows (see notes to item 1).

106. PCC index of the cost of woodworking machinery. For source, see item 25.

107. A combination of PCC indexes for freight cars, weighted five times, and passenger cars, weighted once. For source, see item 16.

125. Canadian import unit values for bicycles from the U.S. centered to approximate calendar year figures. For source, see item 22.

129. Price index for 1895, 1890, and 1880 on a 1900 base, composed of equally weighted series for harvesters, tedders, and rakes, from Holmes, *Prices of Farm Implements*. This index was interpolated between 1880 and 1900 and extrapolated to 1879 by a price index for farm machinery other than motor vehicles from Adams, *Prices Paid by Vermont Farmers* which is itself extrapolated from 1881 back to 1879 by the Adams series for plows.

072

Based to a considerable extent on outside price data. Quarterly indexes are largely interpolated.

Items:

1. 1913-23: BLS index for passenger automobiles.

1. 1899-1906 and 2, 1907-12: The annual index for the periods was constructed in several segments as follows:

1910-13: Index composed of prices of Ford 4.22 hp, weighted four times; Buick-7 passenger, weighted twice; Buick-5 passenger, weighted twice; and Overland 4.18 hp, weighted once. Prices are from U.S. Tariff Commission, *Tariff Information Surveys, Automobiles, Bicycles, Motor Cycles, and Axles*, GPO, 1921.

1909: Index for 1910 extrapolated back to 1909 by price of Ford Model T touring car (same one used for 1910-13) from Federal Trade Commission, *Report on the Motor Vehicle Industry*, p. 632, quoting U.S. Board of Tax Appeals Reports, Vol. 11, p. 1116.

311

NOTES TO TABLE C-7 (continued)

1904–08: We constructed a Fisher "ideal" index for 1904 on a 1909 base for open passenger cars: 2-door, and open passenger cars: 4-door, using Census of Manufactures data on unit values of cars produced in the U.S. as quoted in Solomon Fabricant, *The Output of Manufacturing Industries, 1899–1937*, NBER, New York, 1940. We then interpolated this index between 1904 and 1909 by an equally weighted combination of our indexes for mowers and reapers (item 4, class 071) and other agricultural machinery (item 105, class 071).

1900–03: The index for 1904 was extrapolated back to 1900 using the unit value of passenger cars produced in the U.S., from Automobile Manufacturers Association, *Automobile Facts and Figures*, 1952.

1899: The 1904 index was extrapolated back by the unit value of complete vehicles and chassis, produced in the U.S. These are Census of Manufactures data quoted in Fabricant, *Output of Manufacturing Industries*, p. 578.

Quarterly indexes, used only for combining with other groups, were estimated by a freehand interpolation. Values for 1899 to June 1901 were included with "cars, carriages, and other vehicles and parts of" in the published figures. We made very crude estimates of these values to complete the period.

073

Items:

5 and 6. Export unit values for crude fertilizers moved very differently from domestic prices between 1889 and 1913; they changed only slightly during the whole period, particularly after 1899, while domestic prices fell by over 50 per cent between 1890 and 1897 and then rose by 50 per cent or more by 1907–08. By contrast, the total range of the export unit values, between 1898 and 1912, was from $7.41 to $8.42 per ton. Exports through individual customs districts were still steadier in price. Exports through the Fernandina, Florida district, for example, were reported at exactly $10.00 per ton for every year checked between 1899 and 1912. The same was true of Brunswick, Georgia, and, with a few exceptions, of Jacksonville, Florida and Savannah, Georgia. Another important customs district, Tampa, Florida, reported exactly $6.00 per ton for many years. The contrast between the movements of export and domestic prices and the peculiar stability of the customs district unit values would have led us to discard the export unit values if there had been no information to confirm them. But we found that United Kingdom import unit values of crude fertilizers exhibited very similar stability during this period and therefore accepted the U.S. figures.

074

Based to a considerable extent on outside price data.

Items:

5. Values for 1923 estimated from values of white and sublimed lead, using 1922 ratio. Prices estimated by extrapolation from 1922 using BLS series for lead, carbonate of (white lead): American, in oil.

13. 1899–1912: Price series for ammonia sulphate from E. E. Vial, *Prices of Fertilizer Materials and Factors Affecting the Fertilizer Tonnage*, New York State, Cornell University Agricultural Experiment Station, Mim. 119.

14. BLS price series for benzol.

15. BLS, nitric acid.

16. BLS, acetic acid.

17. BLS, boric acid.

18. Index, on a 1923 base, of BLS prices for muriatic acid, weighted once; stearic acid, weighted once; oleic acid, weighted once; acetic acid, weighted once; and boric acid, weighted twice.

19. Index, on a 1923 base, of equally weighted BLS prices for muriatic acid, stearic acid, and oleic acid.

20. BLS, picric acid.

21. 1913–17: Index composed of BLS, picric acid, weighted five times; BLS, carbolic acid, weighted once; and the index for item 19, weighted once.

APPENDIX C

NOTES TO TABLE C–7 (continued)

1909–12: Index composed of equally weighted series for muriatic acid, from BLS, and nitric and stearic acid, from the *Oil, Paint, and Drug Reporter.*

22. 1918–23: Index composed of equally weighted BLS series for jet nigrosine, water soluble #845; direct black, #582; sulphur brown, #1177; and indigo, 20% paste, #1177; on a 1923 base.

    1913–17: The above index was extrapolated back to 1913 by one composed of the same series plus WIB series for chrysoidine Y and chrysoidine R, all on a 1918 base.

23. BLS price of logwood extract, solid.

24. Index composed of equally weighted *Oil, Paint, and Drug Reporter* series for fustic extract, solid, and quercitron extract, 51º.

25. 1913–17: Index composed of equally weighted series in items 23 and 24.

    1899–1912: Index composed of equally weighted *Oil, Paint, and Drug Reporter* series for logwood extract, solid, and synthetic indigo, on a 1913 base.

27. The price index is composed of equally weighted indexes for mineral earth pigments and chemical pigments which were constructed as follows: The mineral earth pigment index was composed, for 1918 annual and 1919–23, of BLS series for barytes and whiting, equally weighted; and for 1913–17 and 1918 quarterly, of the same two plus WIB series for ocher, umber, venetian red, and paris green, also weighted equally. The chemical pigment index was composed, for 1918 annual and 1919–23, of equally weighted BLS series for lithopone and cadmium sulphide; for 1918 quarterly, of the same two plus WIB series for chrome yellow, chrome green, prussian blue, and ultramarine; and for 1913–17, of the same series with the exception of cadmium sulphide, all equally weighted.

28. 1913–23: BLS price for lampblack.

    1899–1912: Index composed of equally weighted prices of carbon black, lampblack, and bone black, from the *Oil, Paint, and Drug Reporter.*

30. Price of collodion, flexible, New York spot, from the *Oil, Paint, and Drug Reporter,* Sept. 1915 through 1923. The 1918 fiscal annual was extrapolated to fiscal years 1913–15, and interpolated freehand for quarterly estimates.

37, 38 and 39. Index composed of equally weighted BLS series for soda ash and caustic soda.

40. BLS, tar.

41. BLS, benzol.

43. BLS, formaldehyde.

54. BLS, sulphuric acid, 66º.

55. Index composed of equally weighted BLS series for sulphuric acid and muriatic acid, and *Oil, Paint, and Drug Reporter* series for nitric acid and stearic acid, on a 1913 base.

075

To a considerable extent, 1879–99 based on outside price data.

Items;

10. Index composed of equally weighted BLS series for white lead, putty, and zinc oxide, on a 1923 base.

11. Index composed of the index for item 10, weighted five times, and an index made up of equally weighted WIB prices for red lead and litharge, weighted once.

12. WIB toilet soap, 1913–18, extrapolated to 1923 by export unit value for item 8.

30. Index, on a 1913 base, composed of equally weighted BLS series for lead: white, in oil, basic carbonate; and zinc oxide: leaded grades, 5% pigment.

33. 1889–99: Same as item 30; 1890–99, extrapolated to 1889 by corresponding Aldrich series.

    1879–89: Index, on an 1889 base, composed of equally weighted Aldrich series for zinc oxide and Bezanson series for lead: white, dry; lead: white, in oil; and lead: red, dry.

076

Includes items not classified elsewhere. Values range from $2.5 million to $16.3 million.

313

THE HUNT LIBRARY
CARNEGIE INSTITUTE OF TECHNOLOGY

TABLE C-8
Composition and Coverage of Minor Import Classes

Import Class and Commodity Composition	Covered	Uncovered
001 Crude animal foods, agricultural		
1. Cattle	1884–1923	
2. Items 8, 9	1913–23	
3. Poultry eggs in shell	1879–98, 1914–23	
4. Swine		1916–21
5. Other live food animals, free		1916–21
6. Items 4, 5		1884–1915, 1922–23
7. Other live food animals, dutiable		1884–1923
8. Sheep, free	1884–1912	
9. Sheep, dutiable	1884–1912	
10. All live animals, free and dutiable		1882–83
11. All live animals, dutiable		1879–81
002 Crude animal foods, nonagricultural		
1. Lobsters, other than canned	1913–23	
2. Crabmeat	1913–23	
3. Halibut	1919–23	
4. Whitefish	1919–23	
5. Mackerel	1919–23	
6. Herring	1919–23	

Import Class and Commodity Composition	Covered	Uncovered
002 Crude Animal foods, nonagricultural (CONT.)		
7. Salmon, fresh	1889–1908	1884–88, 1919–23
8. Other shellfish: crabs, shrimps, lobsters		1913–23
9. Items 3, 7	1913–18	
10. Items 4, 7	1913–18	
11. Items 5, 7	1913–18	
12. Items 6, 7	1913–18	
13. Items 3–7	1909–12	
14. Fresh fish exc. salmon	1889–1908	
15. Items 1, 2, and 8		1903–12
003 Hay		
1. Hay	1912–23	
004 Grains		
1. Wheat	1879–1923	1889–98
2. Oats	1879–88, 1899–1923	1879–98
3. Corn	1913–23	1922–23
4. Rice uncleaned	1913–21	
5. Barley	1879–98	1879–98
6. Rye		
005 Vegetables, crude		
1. Onions	1897–1923	
2. Beans, dried	1910–23	

005 Vegetables, crude (CONT.)

3. Peas, dried	1912–23	1914–16
4. Potatoes, dutiable	1917–18	1914–18
5. Potatoes, free	1879–94,	1895–1900,
6. Items 4, 5	1901–02	1903
	1904–06	1907
	1908–09	1910
	1911–12	1913
	1919–20	1921–23
7. Garlic		1919–23
8. Potatoes, sweet, dried, prepared		1919–23
9. Other fresh vegetables		1919–23
10. Items 7–9		1897–1908, 1912–18
11. Item 2 and ½ of item 3	1909	1909
12. Items 2, 3	1879–1908	
13. Item 10 and ½ of item 3		
14. Items 10, 3		1910–11
15. Items 1, 10		1882–96

006 Spices, crude

1. Pepper, unground	1884–1923	
2. Vanilla beans	1889–1923	
3. Ginger root, unground, not preserved	1913–23	1912
4. Cassia and cassia vera, unground	1913–23	1912
5. Capsicum or red pepper, ground	1919–23	
6. Capsicum or red pepper, unground	1919–23	
7. Cloves, unground	1919–23	

006 Spices, crude (CONT.)

8. Mustard seed, ground or prepared	1919–23	
9. Item 15 and cayenne pepper and sage		1884–90
10. Nutmeg, unground	1884–1908, 1919–23	
11. Other spices, n.e.s.		1919–23
12. Items 5–8, 10, 11		1913–18
13. Other unground spices		1912
14. Items 3, 4, 13		1909–11
15. Item 14, excl. 10		1891–1908
16. Spices, ground, dutiable		
17. Spices, total	1879–83	1884–88

007ᵃ Fruits and nuts, crude, except bananas

1. Peanuts, shelled	1913–23	
2. Peanuts, not shelled	1913–23	
3. Almonds, shelled	1913–23	
4. Almonds, not shelled	1913–23	
5. Filberts, shelled	1913–23	
6. Filberts, not shelled	1913–23	
7. Walnuts, shelled	1913–23	
8. Walnuts, not shelled	1913–23	
9. Brazil and cream nuts	1907–23	
10. Coconuts	1907–23	1882–1906
11. Chestnuts		1919–23
12. Olives	1907–20	1921–23
13. Lemons	1884–1912	1913–23
14. Pineapples		1910–23
15. Grapes		1907–23
16. Other nuts, n.e.s.		1919–23
17. Items 11, 16		1912–18

(continued)

TABLE C-8 (continued)

Import Class and Commodity Composition	Years Covered	Years Uncovered
007ᵃ *Fruits and nuts, crude, except bananas* (CONT.)		
18. Oranges	1884-1906	1907-21
19. Item 18 and limes		1922-23
20. Other fruits, incl. apples and berries		
21. Item 20 and limes		1922-23
22. Grapefruit		1919-21
23. Items 21, 22		1919-23
24. Items 3, 4	1879-1912	1910-18
25. Items 7, 8	1903-12	
26. Copra, not prepared	1907-12	
27. Items 1, 2	1910-12	
28. Items 5, 6	1910-12	
29. Coconut meat, dessicated or prepared		1912
30. Items 17, 29		1910-11
31. Items 27, 28, 30		1907-09
32. Items 9, 26, 31		1903-06
33. Items 10, 25, 32		1889-1902
34. Items 14, 23, 35, 36		1909
35. Other fruits, n.e.s., exc. plums and prunes		
36. Plums and prunes	1879-94	1907-08
37. Items 15, 35	1879-88, 1891-98	1895-1908
38. Currants		1891-1906
39. Dates		1889-90
40. Items 37-39	1891-98	
41. Raisins	1879-88	
42. Bananas	1879-88	
007ᵃ *Fruits and nuts, crude, except bananas* (CONT.)		
43. Figs	1884-88	
44. Other fruits, canned or preserved		1884-88
45. Other fruits, incl. fruits from Hawaii and Brazil nuts		
46. Items 13, 18	1879-83	1884-88
47. Items 43-45, exc. Brazil nuts		1879-83
008ᵃ *Tea*		
1. Tea from the U.K.	1913-23	
2. Tea from Canada	1913-23	
3. Tea from British East Indies	1916-23	
4. Tea from China	1913-23	
5. Tea from Japan	1913-23	
6. Tea from Dutch East Indies	1916-23	
7. Other tea, n.e.s.		1913-23
8. Items 3, 6	1913-15	
9. Items 1-2, 4-5, 7-8	1879-1912	
009ᵃ *Coffee*		
1. Coffee	1879-1923	
010ᵃ *Cocoa or Cacao Beans*		
1. Cocoa or Cacao beans	1879-1923	

011a Bananas
1. Bananas from Jamaica — 1913–23
2. Bananas from Cuba — 1913–23
3. Bananas from Central America — 1913–23
4. Bananas from Colombia — 1913–23
5. Bananas from other countries — 1913–23
6. Items 1–5 — 1889–1912

012 Manuf. animal foods, agricultural
1. Butter and substitutes — 1879–1923
2. Milk and cream, fresh, condensed, etc. — 1913–23
3. Cheese from Italy — 1913–23
4. Cheese from Switzerland — 1921–23
5. Cheese from France — 1921–23
6. Cheese from Netherlands — 1921–23
7. Cheese from Greece — 1921–23
8. Cheese from Argentina — 1921–23
9. Cheese from other countries — 1921–23
10. Items 3–9 — 1879–1920
11. Beef and veal, fresh — 1913–23
12. Pork, fresh — 1913–23
13. Mutton, fresh — 1913–23
14. Lamb, fresh — 1913–23
15. Eggs and yolks, preserved — 1916–23
16. Bologna sausage — 1912–20

012 Manuf. animal foods, agricultural (CONT.)
17. Bacon and ham — 1914–20
18. Other meat, preserved and prepared — 1914–20
19. Items 16–18 — 1921–23
20. Other meat products — 1919–23
21. Tallow — 1919–21
22. Oleo stearin — 1912–21
23. Items 21, 22 — 1922–23
24. Items 20, 21 — 1914–18
25. Items 17, 18, 24 — 1913
26. Sausage casings — 1898–1923
27. Cream — 1911–12, 1909–12
28. Items 11–14, 25 — 1884–1908
29. Meat and meat extracts — 1884–1908
30. Other meat products — 1884–1906, 1912
31. Milk, fresh and condensed — 1879–83
32. Items 29–31

013 Manuf. animal foods, nonagricultural
1. Items 7, 8
2. Mackerel, cured or preserved — 1909–23
3. Cod, haddock, hake, and pollock, cured or preserved — 1879–1923
4. Lobster, canned — 1884–1923
5. Fish, packed in oil — 1912–23, 1879–1912
6. Other cured and preserved, n.e.s. — 1913–23, 1909–23

(continued)

TABLE C-8 (continued)

Import Class and Commodity Composition	Years Covered	Uncovered
013 Manuf. animal foods, nonagricultural (CONT.)		
7. Herring, dried or smoked	1884–1908	
8. Herring, pickled or salted	1879–1908	
9. Lobsters, fresh	1912	
10. Items 4, 9	1899–1911	1884–88
11. Salmon, pickled or salted	1884–1908	
12. Item 6 minus item 11		1879–1908
13. All other fish, exc. fresh		1884–88
14. Items 3, 7, 10, 11, 13		1879–83
014 Flour and other grain products		
1. Rice, cleaned, exc. patina	1912–23	
2. Wheat flour	1905–23	1879–1904
3. Macaroni, vermicelli, etc.	1903–23	
4. Rice flour, meal, etc.	1884–1923	
5. Biscuits, wafers, and other breadstuffs		1913–23
6. Rice, uncleaned	1912	
7. Items 1, 6	1899–1911	
8. Other breadstuffs, exc. oatmeal		1903–07
9. Oatmeal		1884–1907

Import Class and Commodity Composition	Years Covered	Uncovered
014 Flour and other grain products (CONT.)		
10. Barley		1899–1907
11. Corn		1899–1907
12. Rye		1899–1907
13. Items 8–12		1908–12
14. Items 3, 8		1891–1902
15. Rice, exc. under treaty with Hawaii	1884–98	
16. Rice, under treaty with Hawaii	1880–98	
17. Barley malt	1879–98	
18. Other breadstuffs, exc. macaroni and vermicelli		1884–90
19. Items 4, 15	1880–83	
20. Items 16, 19	1879	
21. Other farinaceous substances		1884–88
22. Items 9, 18, 21, exc. tapioca, sago, and sago flour		1879–83
015 Fruits, processed		
1. Currants	1899–1923	
2. Dates	1899–1923	
3. Figs	1889–1923	
4. Raisins and other dried grapes		1899–1923
5. Fruits, canned and processed	1889–98	1889–1923

016 Vegetable oil, cake, and meal, edible

1. Olive oil exc. salad oil	1879–81	
2. Coconut meat, desiccated or prepared	1913–23	
3. Olive oil, edible (salad oil)	1879–81, 1891–1923	
4. Peanut oil	1913–23	
5. Cottonseed oil	1913–20	1921–23
6. Cocoa butter	1913–16, 1920–23	1917–19
7. Oil cake and meal		1916–23
8. Items 1, 3	1882–90	

017 Vegetables and products, manuf.

1. Mushrooms and truffles	1910–23	
2. Farinaceous substances	1899–1923	1891–98, 1882–1923
3. Pickles and sauces		1910–23
4. Other prepared and preserved vegetables		1916–21
5. Vinegar		1916–21
6. Other edible substances		1922–23
7. Items 5, 6		1882–1909
8. Items 1, 4		1889–90
9. Item 2 and macaroni		

018 Cocoa and chocolate, prepared

1. Items 2, 3	1902–23	
2. Cocoa, prepared	1898–1901	

018 Cocoa and chocolate, prepared (CONT).

3. Chocolate, prepared, exc. confectionery	1898–1901	

019ª Sugar, except refined, and related products

1. Cane sugar, total	1914–23	
2. Maple sugar and syrup	1914–23	
3. Items 1, 2	1913	
4. Beet sugar	1888–1908, 1911–12	1909–10, 1913–23
5. Items 7, 8		1891–94, 1899–1923
6. Cane and maple sugar, exc. refined	1888–1912	
7. Molasses, exc. item 8	1880–88	1889–90, 1895–98
8. Molasses, under treaty with Hawaii	1880–88	1889–90, 1895–98
9. Sugar, #13 to #20	1884–88	
10. Items 4, 6	1884–87	
11. Items 9, 10	1879–83	
12. Items 7, 8	1879	

020 Sugar, refined, and related products

1. Honey	1916–23	
2. Candy and confectionery		
3. Refined sugar	1889–1912	1879–98, 1916–23
4. Sugar, over #20	1879–88	

(continued)

319

TABLE C-8 (continued)

Import Class and Commodity Composition	Years Covered	Uncovered
021 Beverages, agricultural		
1. Malt liquors, in bottles or jugs	1884–1918	1919–20
2. Malt liquors, in other coverings	1884–1918	1919–23
3. Still wines in casks	1879–1918	1919–21
4. Still wines in other coverings	1884–1918	1919–21
5. Champagne and other sparkling wines	1884–1912	1913–23
6. Items 3, 4		1922–23
7. Items 1, 2	1879–83	
8. Other beverages and fruit juices		1910–23
9. Ginger ale and ginger beer	1898–1909	
10. Items 4, 5	1879–83	
022 Beverages, nonagricultural		
1. Mineral waters	1889–1923	
2. Brandy	1884–1917	1918–21
3. Whiskey	1910–17	1918–21
4. Gin	1910–17	1918–21
5. Cordials, liqueurs, etc.	1912	1913–21
6. Other distilled liquors	1912	1913–21
7. Items 2–6		1922–23
8. Items 5, 6	1910–11	
9. Items 3, 4, 8	1884–1909	
10. Items 2, 9	1879–83	
023 Spices, ground		
1. Spices, ground	1891–1912	
023 Spices, ground (CONT.)		
2. Spices, ground, exc. sage and red pepper	1889–90	
024a Tobacco, crude		
1. Leaf suitable for cigar wrapping	1891–1923	
2. Other leaf, from Cuba	1913–20	
3. Other leaf, from Greece	1916–20	
4. Other leaf, from Turkey in Asia	1913–14, 1919–20	
5. Items 2–4, 6	1921–23	
6. Other leaf, from other countries		1919–20
7. Items 4, 6, 10		1916–18
8. Items 3, 7		1915
9. Item 8 less item 4		1913–14
10. Tobacco from Philippines		1919–23
11. Other leaf, from all countries	1891–1912	
12. Items 1, 11	1879–90	
025 Manufactured tobacco products		
1. Cigars and cheroots, exc. item 2	1912–23	
2. Cigars and cheroots from Philippines	1912–23	
3. Cigarettes, exc. item 4		1912–23

025 Manufactured tobacco products (CONT.)

Item	Years
4. Cigarettes from Philippines	1912–23
5. Other uses of tobacco	1879–1923
6. Items 1, 3	1910–11
7. Items 2, 4	1910–11
8. Items 6, 7	1879–1909

026ᵃ Hides, leather, and products, crude

Item	Years
1. Cattle hides, dry and dry-salted	1911–23
2. Cattle hides, wet-salted	1911–23
3. Buffalo hides, dry	1911–23
4. Calfskins, incl. kip, dry	1911–23
5. Calfskins, wet-salted	1911–23
6. Horse, colt, and ass skins, dry	1911–23
7. Horse, colt, and ass skins, green or pickled	1911–23
8. Goat and kid skins, dry	1911–23
9. Goat and kid skins, green or pickled	1911–23
10. Sheep and lamb skins, dry	1911–21
11. Sheep and lamb skins, green	1911–21
12. Items 10, 11	1909–10, 1922–23

026ᵃ Hides, leather, and products, crude (CONT.)

Item	Years
13. Kangaroo and wallaby skins	1913–23
14. All other hides and skins	1913–23
15. Items 1, 2	1898–1910
16. Items 8, 9	1894–1910
17. Items 4, 5	1910
18. Items 6, 7	1910
19. Items 13, 14	1911–12
20. Item 19 exc. buffalo hides, green or wet	1910
21. Items 17, 18, 20	1909
22. Items 12, 21	1898–1908
23. Items 15, 22	1884–97
24. Items 16, 23	1879–83

027 Hides, leather and products, semimanufactured

Item	Years
1. Sole leather	1918–23
2. Goatskins, tanned (skins for morocco)	1913–23
3. Upper leather, calf and kip	1916–23
4. Harness and saddle leather	1916–23
5. Items 6, 7	1922–23
6. Other leather	1918–21
7. Chamois skins	1884–1912
8. Patent, japanned, etc.	1914–21
9. Upper leather, goat and kid	1916–23
10. Upper leather, sheep and lamb	1916–23

(continued)

321

TABLE C-8 (continued)

Import Class and Commodity Composition	Years		Import Class and Commodity Composition	Years	
	Covered	Uncovered		Covered	Uncovered
027 *Hides, leather and products, semimanufactured* (CONT.)			**029** *Furs, unmanufactured*		
11. Upper leather, other incl. cattle		1916–23	1. Beaver	1923	
12. Upper leather, dressed and finished		1909–15	2. Fox, exc. silver or black	1923	
13. Glove leather		1912–23	3. Hare, coney, and rabbit	1923	
14. Item 6 exc. belting	1916–17		4. Marten	1923	
15. Items 4, 14	1914–15		5. Mink	1923	
16. Sole, band and belting leather	1913–17	1884–1908, 1912	6. Mole	1923	
17. Items 7, 15	1913		7. Muskrat	1923	
18. Calfskins, tanned or tanned and dressed		1909–12	8. Squirrel	1923	
19. Skins, chamois, kangaroo, etc., dressed and finished, n.e.s.		1909–12	9. Other undressed furs		1923
20. Other leather, incl. patent, japanned, etc.		1912	10. Items 1–9	1879–1912, 1919–22	
21. Items 13, 16, 20		1909–11	11. Furs from U.K. and Australia	1913–18	
22. Item 18 and patent, japanned, etc.	1884–88	1889–1908	12. Furs from Canada	1913–18	
23. Items 12, 19, 21	1884–88	1889–1908	13. Furs other than items 11–12		1913–18
24. Items 2, 16, 22, 23	1879–83		**030** *Furs, semimanufactured*		
028 *Hides, leather, and products, manufactured*			1. Furs dressed on the skin, not advanced beyond drying		1911–23
1. Gloves	1891–1923	1879–90	2. Cut fur, plates, mats, and other manuf.		1912–23
2. Boots and shoes	1918–23	1912–17	3. Hats, caps, bonnets of fur		1912–23
3. Other manufs. of leather		1912–23	4. Items 2, 3		1911
4. Items 2, 3		1879–1911	5. Items 1, 3, 4		1879–1910

031 Other animal products, crude, agricultural
1. Ostrich feathers, crude — 1912–23
2. Horses, from England, France, and Belgium — 1913–16
3. Glue stock, hide cuttings, etc. — 1916–23, 1899–1915
4. Bones, hoofs, horns, unmanufactured — 1919–23, 1899–1918
5. Bristles, crude, not sorted — 1899–1908, 1912–23
6. Other feathers — 1912–23
7. Items 2, 8 — 1917–23
8. Horses, other countries — 1913–16
9. Rennets — 1916–21
10. Grease and oils, n.e.s., free — 1913–22
11. Grease and oils, dutiable, inc. items free before 1922, and exc. seal oil — 1923
12. Grease and oils, n.e.s., dutiable — 1916–22
13. Items 1, 6 — 1899–1911, 1895–98
14. Horses, free — 1899–1912, 1884–98
15. Horses, dutiable — 1884–1912
16. Feathers, advanced — 1895–98
17. Items 13, 16 — 1884–94
18. Grease, n.e.s., dutiable — 1898–1909

031 Other animal products, crude, agricultural (CONT.)
19. Grease and oil (tallow) n.e.s. — 1898
20. Items 18, 19 — 1895–97

032 Other animal products, crude, nonagricultural
1. Ivory tusks in natural state — 1882–1923
2. Shells, unmanuf. mother of pearl — 1913–23
3. Other unmanuf. shells — 1904–12, 1898–1923
4. Fish sounds — 1916–21

033 Other animal products, semimanuf., agricultural
1. Glue and glue size — 1898–1923
2. Casein or lactarene — 1913–23
3. Bristles, sorted, bunched, or prepared — 1895–1923
4. Beeswax and other animal wax — 1916–23
5. Gelatin, unmanuf. — 1917–23
6. Bristles, not sorted — 1913–16, 1895–98
7. Items 3, 6 — 1879–94

034 Other animal products, semimanuf., nonagric.
1. Cod and cod-liver oil — 1914–23
2. Whale oil — 1923
3. Other fish oil — 1923
4. Seal oil — 1923
5. Items 2–4 — 1914–22

(continued)

TABLE C-8 (continued)

Import Class and Commodity Composition	Years Covered	Years Uncovered
034 Other animal products, semimanuf., nonagric. (CONT)		
6. Items 1, 5	1907–13	
7. Whale and fish oil	1899–1906	1885–98
8. All other animal oil		1882–1906
9. Whale and fish oil, free		1879–84
10. Whale and fish oil, dutiable		1879–84
035 Other animal products, manuf., nonagricultural		
1. Brushes		1882–1923
2. Sponges		1882–1909, 1915–23
3. Shells, manuf.		1904–08, 1916–23
4. Bone and horn, manuf.		1898–1908, 1916–23
5. Feathers, advanced, not for millinery and quilts, etc.		1914–23
6. Feathers, advanced		1899–1913
036ª Rubber and related gums, crude		
1. Rubber, crude and milk of	1911–23	
2. Jelutong and Pontianak	1903–23	
3. Gayule	1911–1920	1921
4. Other crude, scrap, and reclaimed		1904–21

Import Class and Commodity Composition	Years Covered	Years Uncovered
036ª Rubber and related gums, crude (CONT.)		
5. Items 3, 4		1922–23
6. Balata		1909–23
7. Gutta-percha		1891–1923
8. Rubber and gayule, exc. Mexican	1903–10	
9. Rubber and gayule, Mexican	1903–10	
10. Items 8, 9	1891–1902	
11. Crude rubber and gutta-percha	1879–90	
037 Rubber and related gums, manufactured		
1. Manuf. of rubber		1879–1921
2. Rubber substitutes		1912–21
3. Items 1, 2		1922–23
038 Oilseeds, crude		
1. Copra, not prepared	1913–23	
2. Flaxseed	1879–1923	
3. Castor beans	1913–23	
039 Vegetable oils, expressed, and fats, semimanufactured		
1. Chinese wood or nut oil		1912
2. Linseed oil	1912–23	
3. Soya bean oil	1913–23	
4. Coconut oil	1907–23	
5. Items 6, 7	1922–23	

039 Vegetable oils, expressed, and fats, semimanuf. (CONT.)

6. Olive foots oil	1913–21	
7. Denatured olive oil	1906–21	
8. Palm oil	1907–23	
9. Rape oil	1912–23	
10. Palm kernel oil	1912–14	1915–21
11. Other vegetable oils, free		
12. Items 10, 11		1912–21
13. Other vegetable oils, dutiable		1922–23
14. Peanut oil	1912	1912–23
15. Nut oils, incl. items 1, 14	1907–11	
16. Cottonseed oil	1912	
17. Items 3, 10, 11, 16	1909–11	
18. Cocoa butter	1910–12	
19. Rape oil and hemp oil	1910–11	
20. Items 18, 19, 26		1909
21. Items 16, 20		1891–1908
22. Items 3, 10, 11	1907–08	
23. Items 4, 8, 15, 22	1906	
24. Items 7, 23	1891–1905	
25. Greases, incl. olive foots oil		1899–1912
26. Items 2, 13		1910–11
27. Vegetable oil, free	1884–90	
28. Vegetable oil, dutiable, incl. cocoa butter	1888	1889–90
29. Vegetable oil, dutiable, exc. cocoa butter	1884–87	

039 Vegetable oils, expressed, and fats, semimanuf. (CONT.)

30. Vegetable oil, free	1879–83	
31. Item 28 and poppy seed oil	1879–83	

040 Other vegetable products, crude, agricultural

1. Licorice root	1889–1923	
2. Opium, crude	1884–1923	
3. Clover seed, red	1913–23	
4. Clover seed, other	1913–23	
5. Grass seeds	1912–23	
6. Sugar beet seeds	1910–23	
7. Vegetable ivory	1882–1923	
8. Hops	1882–1915, 1920–23	1916–19
9. Cinchona bark	1879–1923	
10. Bulbs, roots, and corns	1913–23	1909–12
11. Mustard seed, whole, dutiable	1919–23	
12. All other free seeds		1919–23
13. Items 11, 12		1912–18
14. Other dutiable seeds		1910–23
15. Trees, roots, cuttings, and seedlings		1919–23
16. Other nursery and greenhouse stock, dutiable		1919–23
17. Items 15, 16		1909–18
18. Nursery and greenhouse stock, free		1919–23
19. Broom corn		1912–23, 1912–21
20. Palm leaf fans		1916–21

(continued)

TABLE C-8 (continued)

Import Class and Commodity Composition	Years Covered	Years Uncovered
040 Other vegetable products, crude, agricultural (CONT.)		
21. Clover seed	1907–12	
22. Castor beans	1910–12	
23. Items 5, 13		1910–11
24. Items 6, 23, exc. canary seed		1907–09
25. Items 21, 24		1879–1906
26. Items 14, 22, and canary seed		1879–1909
27. Items 10, 17		1899–1908
28. Opium, less than 9%	1884–1908	1909–12
29. Vegetable wax	1913–23	
30. Items 2, 28	1879–83	
041 Other vegetable products, crude, nonagricultural		
1. Chicle, crude	1899–1923	
2. Gambier	1891–1923	
3. Logwood	1884–1909, 1912–23	
4. Sumac, ground and unground	1913–23	
5. Copal, damar, kauri	1899–1923	
6. Mangrove bark	1908–12	1912–23
7. Quebracho wood	1884–98	1913–23
8. Arabic		1899–1909, 1919–23
9. Other gums, dutiable		1919–23
10. Items 8, 9		1913–18
11. Asafetida, turpentine and other varnishes, resins, and gums, free		1913–23

Import Class and Commodity Composition	Years Covered	Years Uncovered
041 Other vegetable products, crude, nonagricultural (CONT.)		
12. Items 13, 14		1922–23
13. Other crude dyewoods		1884–1908, 1912–21
14. All other crude tanning material		1912–21
15. Moss and seaweed, crude		1916–23
16. Items 8, 17		1910–13
17. Other gums and resins, free, incl. amber and senegal, but exc. arabic		
18. Items 6, 14		1899–1909
19. Hemlock bark		1911
20. Sumac, ground	1889–1909, 1912–13	1879–1906
21. All other gums, free, incl. cutch	1891–98	
22. Gambier and cutch	1879–90	
23. All other gums, exc. cutch		
24. Shellac	1884–90	
25. Items 8, 23, 24	1884–89	
26. Items 3, 13	1879–83	
27. All other moss and seaweed	1879–83	1916–21
042 Other vegetable products, semimanuf., agricultural		
1. Starch	1915–23	

043 Other vegetable product, semimanuf., nonagric.
1. Shellac — 1889–1923
2. Quebracho extract — 1907–23
3. Other tanning extracts — 1913–23
4. Other tanning and dyeing extracts — 1889–1912

044 Other vegetable products, manuf., agricultural
1. Lemon oil — 1910–23
2. Items 3, 5 — 1913–23
3. Other essential and distilled oils, free, incl. oils from P.I. — 1910–12
4. Items 1, 3, and orange oil, exc. other essential oils from P.I. — 1884–1909
5. Item 6, and orange oils, exc. other essential oils from P.I. — 1910–12
6. Essential and distilled oils, dut., exc. orange and lemon oil, incl. other essential oils from P.I. — 1884–1909
7. Item 4, exc. orange and lemon oil — 1879–83
8. Item 6, and orange and lemon oil — 1879–83

045 Cotton textiles, crude
1. Cotton, long staple — 1921–23

045 Cotton textiles, crude (CONT.)
2. Cotton, short staple — 1921–23
3. Items 1, 2 — 1879–1920

046 Cotton textiles, semimanuf.
1. Cotton yarns and warps — 1889–1923
2. Cotton waste — 1899–1923

047ª Cotton textiles, manufactured
1. Cotton cloth unbleached — 1889–1923
2. Cotton cloth, bleached — 1911–23
3. Items 4–6 — 1911–15, 1923
4. Cotton cloth, dyed in the piece — 1916–22
5. Cotton cloth, printed — 1916–22
6. Cotton cloth, other colored, dyed — 1916–22
7. Cotton pile fabrics, exc. terry cloth — 1891–1923
8. Sewing thread, embroidery cotton, etc. — 1913–23
9. Cotton gloves — 1914–16, 1920–23; 1917–19
10. Cotton hosiery — 1910–15, 1920–23; 1916–19
11. Cotton underwear, and other knit goods — 1914–23

(continued)

TABLE C-8 (continued)

Import Class and Commodity Composition	Covered	Uncovered
047ᵃ Cotton textiles, manufactured (CONT.)		
12. Other cotton wearing apparel, product of P.I.		1919–23
13. Other cotton wearing apparel		
14. Items 12, 13		1919–23
15. Cotton handkerchiefs and mufflers		1889–1918
16. Handmade laces		1912–23
17. Machine made laces		1912–23
18. Items 19, 20		1912–23
19. Nets and netting		1921–23
20. Veils and veilings		1912–20
21. Lace window curtains		1912–20
22. Embroideries		1912–23
23. Lace etc., product of P.I.		1912–23
24. Other laces		1919–23
25. Items 23, 24		1919–23
26. Cotton tapestries, etc.		1912–18
27. Other manufs. of cotton, incl. terry		1919–23
28. Items 26, 27		1919–23
29. Other manufs. of cotton, incl. thread		1913–18
30. Items 2, 3	1889–1910	1912
31. Items 10, 32	1891–1909	1879–90
32. Other cotton knit goods, incl. gloves		1910–13
33. Items 16, 17, 19–22, and 25		1884–1911
047ᵃ Cotton textiles, manufactured (CONT.)		
34. Items 15, 29		1891–1911
35. Items 7, 34	1919–23	1884–90
36. Cotton cloth, total		1879–88
37. Cotton yarns, etc.		1884–88
38. Other cotton wearing apparel		
39. Corsets		1884–88
40. Items 33, 35, 37–39		1884–88
048 Jute and products, crude		
1. Jute and jute butts, unmanufactured	1889–1923	1879–83
049ᵃ Jute textiles, semimanufactured		
1. Items 2, 3	1889–1913, 1923	
2. Burlaps, unbleached	1914–22	
3. Burlaps, bleached	1914–22	
050 Jute textiles, manufactured		
1. Jute bags or sacks	1895–1923	
2. Bagging for cotton, gunny cloth, etc.	1895–23	
3. Items 1, 2	1889–94	
051ᵃ Other vegetable fibers, crude		
1. Sisal	1884–1923	
2. Manilla or abaca	1891–1923	

051ª Other vegetable fibers, crude (CONT.)

3. Hemp, unmanuf.	1891–1923	
4. Istle or tampico	1891–1923	
5. Flax, hackled	1919–23	
6. Other flax		1919–23
7. Items 5, 6	1879–1912	1913–18
8. Kapok	1911–23	
9. Items 10, 11		1922–23
10. New Zealand flax	1910–21	
11. Maguey and other vegetable fibers		
12. Items 8, 11		1911–21
13. Items 10, 12		1910
14. Items 2, 3	1879–90	1891–1909
15. Items 4, 13	1884–89	
16. Jute	1879–83	1888–90
17. Items 1, 16		

052 Other vegetable fibers, semimanufactured

1. Yarns of jute, flax, hemp, etc.	1913–23	1889–1912
2. Materials for hats of straw, etc.	1899–1923	
3. Artificial silk, threads and filaments	1913–23	

053ª Other vegetable textiles, manufactured

1. Binding twine	1899–1923	1895–98
2. Matting and mats of China, Japan, and India straw	1899–1923	1891–98

053ª Other vegetable textiles, manufactured (CONT.)

3. Linoleum and floor oilcloth	1899–1917, 1920–23	1918–19
4. Coir yarn	1889–1923	1882–88
5. Items 6, 7	1922–23	
6. Plain woven fabrics of flax, hemp, and ramie		
7. Other woven fabrics of flax, hemp, and ramie	1903–1921	
8. Handkerchiefs	1919–21	
9. Hats, bonnets, and hoods of straw, grass, etc., not blocked	1919–23	1899–1918
10. Hats, etc., of straw, blocked	1919–23	1919–23
11. Items 9, 10		1899–1918
12. Hats, etc., product of Philippines		1912–23
13. Laces and embroideries		
14. Items 15, 16		1910–23
15. Straw and grass, manufactures		1922–23
16. Other manufs. of fibers, grasses, etc.		1899–1921
17. Woven articles and manufs. of flax, incl. damasks		1919–21
18. Items 16, 17	1919–23	1916–18
19. Wearing apparel		1916–23

(continued)

329

TABLE C-8 (continued)

Import Class and Commodity Composition	Years	
	Covered	Uncovered
053ª Other vegetable textiles, manufactured (CONT.)		
20. Items 18, 19		1910-15
21. Manufs. of artificial horsehair		
22. Manufs. of artificial silk		1913-23
23. Hat trimmings, incl. artificial and ornamental feathers		1913-23
24. Hat trimmings, exc. artificial and ornamental feathers		1914-23
25. Items 13, 20, minus item 26		1889-1913
26. Cables, cordage, threads, and twine		1905-09
27. Carpets and carpeting		1895-1909
28. Item 25 minus item 27		1899-1904
29. Items 6, 28	1899-1902	
30. Items 34, 35	1879-81	1903-04
31. Manufs. of flax, hemp, and ramie, n.e.s.		
32. Hats of straw, etc., and materials for	1889-98	
33. Items 1, 26		1884-98
34. Jute bags and baggings		1879-94
35. Burlaps, total	1884-88	
36. Yarns of flax, hemp, and ramie, not incl. thread	1884-88	

Import Class and Commodity Composition	Years	
	Covered	Uncovered
053ª Other vegetable textiles, manufactured (CONT.)		
37. Brown or bleached linens, ducks, etc. (manuf. of flax, by the yard)	1879-81, 1884-88	
38. Items 40-42		1884-88
39. Items 34-38, 43	1882-83	
40. Manufs. of flax		1879-81
41. Manufs. of hemp, by the yard		1879-81
42. Other manufs. of hemp		1879-81
43. Thread and twine		1884-88
054ª Wool textiles, crude		
1. Carpet wool	1884-1923	
2. Clothing wool	1884-1923	
3. Combing wool	1914-23	
4. Hair of angora, goat, alpaca, etc.	1914-23	
5. Combing wool; incl. angora, goat, etc.	1884-1913	
6. Items 1, 2, 5	1879-83	
055 Wool textiles, semimanufactured		
1. Woolen yarns	1889-98, 1913-23	
2. Wool and hair, advanced; incl. tops 1919-23		1916-18

055 Wool textiles, semimanufactured (CONT.)

3. Items 4, 5 — 1879–88 — 1889–94, 1898, 1914–23
4. Rags, noils, waste — 1895–97
5. Shoddy, mungo, flocks, and carbonized wool — 1895–97

056ᵃ Wool textiles, manufactured

1. Items 4, 5 — 1922–23
2. Worsteds — 1919–21
3. Woolens — 1919–21
4. Items 2, 3 — 1879–1918
5. Dress goods — 1879–1921
6. Items 7, 8 — 1879–1915, 1922–23
7. Carpets and carpeting, woven whole — 1916–21
8. Carpets and carpeting, other — 1916–21
9. Cloth of angora, alpaca, etc. — 1914–23
10. Items 11, 12 — 1922–23
11. Other manufs. of wool — 1916–21
12. Other manufs. of hair, exc. human hair — 1913–21
13. Item 11, incl. wool and hair, advanced, and tops — 1914–15
14. Items 9, 13 — 1913
15. Wool wearing apparel — 1913–23
16. Items 18–21 — 1908–12

056ᵃ Wool textiles, manufactured (CONT.)

17. Items 18, 19 — 1906–07
18. Items 11, 15 — 1899–1905
19. Shawls — 1879–1905
20. Flocks, noils, waste, etc. — 1899–1907
21. Wool yarns — 1884–88 — 1899–1907
22. Wool wearing apparel — 1884–98
23. Knit fabrics — 1879–98
24. Other manufs. of wool — 1884–98
25. Items 21, 22, 24 — 1879–83

057ᵃ Silk textiles, crude

1. Raw silk — 1879–1923
2. Silk cocoons — 1882–1908, 1912–23

058 Silk textiles, semimanufactured

1. Spun silk or schappe silk yarn — 1899–1923
2. Silk waste — 1913–23 — 1882–1912

059ᵃ Silk textiles, manufactured

1. Fabrics, broad, exc. pile fabrics — 1879–1923 — 1879–1909, 1912–23
2. Pile fabrics — 1899–1923
3. Bolting cloths
4. Silk ribbons — 1879–1912 — 1913–23
5. Banding, belting, etc. — 1910–23
6. Wearing apparel, incl. hats, caps, etc. — 1890–1923

(continued)

TABLE C-8 (continued)

Import Class and Commodity Composition	Years Covered	Uncovered
059ᵃ Silk textiles, manufactured (CONT.)		
7. Laces, embroideries, etc.	1879–1912	1913–23
8. Handkerchiefs and mufflers		1919–23
9. Other manufs. of silk		1919–23
10. Items 8, 9		1911–18
11. Artificial silk yarns, threads, etc.		
12. Artificial silk, other manufs.		1912
13. Items 11, 12		1912
14. Items 10–12		1911
15. Items 5, 14		1910
16. Spun silk, silk yarn, and items 2, 15		1899–1909
17. Item 6 minus item 21		1890–98
18. Items 16, 21		1884–89
19. Items 17, 18		1884–89
20. Items 16, 17		1883
21. Hosiery		1879–82
060 Other animal fibers, crude		1879–82
1. Human hair, uncleaned		1910–23
2. Horse hair		1910–23
3. Other animal hair		1910–23
4. Items 1–3		1879–1909
061 Other animal fibers, manufactured		
1. Human hair, cleaned		1923

Import Class and Commodity Composition	Years Covered	Uncovered
061 Other animal fibers, manufactured (CONT.)		
2. Nets and netting of human hair		1923
3. Other manufs. of human hair		1923
4. Items 1–3		1912–22
5. Other manufs. of hair		1912
6. Items 4, 5		1910–11
7. Manufs. of artificial horse hair		1910–12
8. Items 6, 7		1879–1904
062ᵃ Wood and products, crude		
1. Pulpwood, rough	1910–23	
2. Pulpwood, peeled	1910–23	
3. Pulpwood, rossed	1910–23	
4. Logs and round timber, exc. cabinet wood	1895–1923	
5. Cabinet woods in the log, mahogany	1895–1923	
6. Cabinet woods in the log, cedar	1910–23	
7. Rags for paper stock	1879–1923	
8. Cabinet woods in the log, other	1879–1923	
9. Paper stock other than rags	1879–98	1899–1923
10. Rattan, unmanuf.		1910–23
11. Briar root, wood, ivy, etc.		1910–23

062ª Wood and products, crude (CONT.)

12. Other unmanuf. wood, free		1910–23,
13. Items 18, 19		1889–97, 1905–23
14. Items 1–3	1907–09	1895–1909
15. Items 6, 8		1907–09
16. Items 10–12		1895–1906
17. Items 14, 16		
18. Other unmanuf. wood, dutiable		1898–1904
19. Timber, hewn, squared, and sided		1879–88, 1898–1904
20. Items 4, 5, 15, 17	1889–94	1879–88

063ª Wood and products, exc. paper, semimanufactured

1. Boards, planks, deals, etc.	1914–23	
2. Sawed cabinet woods	1914–23	
3. Cork bark or wood, unmanufactured	1919–23	
4. Cork waste and shavings	1919–23	
5. Items 3, 4	1913–18	1879–1912
6. Chair cane or reed		1913–23
7. Other lumber, free		1914–23
8. Other lumber, dutiable		1914–23
9. Items 7, 8	1879–1913	1879–1913
10. Items 1, 2		1879–98

064 Wood and products, exc. paper, manufactured

1. Laths	1899–1923
2. Shingles	1899–1923

064 Wood and products, exc. paper, manufactured (CONT.)

3. Furniture	1884–1923
4. Baskets	1916–23
5. Other manufs. of wood incl. osier and willow	1919–23
6. Timbers, other than sawed	1919–23
7. Items 5, 6	1916–18
8. Items 4, 7	1910–15
9. Cork disks, wafers, and washers, etc.	1919–23
10. Other manufs. of cork	1919–23
11. Items 9, 10	1898–1918
12. Chair cane or reed	1910–12
13. Items 8, 12	1884–1909
14. Other unmanuf. wood, dutiable	1884–88
15. Items 3, 13, 14	1879–83

065ª Paper and related products, semimanufactured

1. Wood and other pulp, mechanically ground	1909–23
2. Chemical wood pulp, sulphite, unbleached	1917–23
3. Chemical wood pulp, sulphate, unbleached	1917–23
4. Items 2, 3	1909–16
5. Chemical wood pulp, sulphite, bleached	1917–23

(continued)

333

TABLE C-8 (continued)

Import Class and Commodity Composition	Years	
	Covered	Uncovered
065ª Paper and related products, semimanufactured (CONT.)		
6. Chemical wood pulp, sulphate, bleached	1920–23	1917–19
7. Items 5, 6	1909–16	
8. Items 1, 4, 7	1889–1908	
066ª Paper and products, manufactured		
1. Standard newsprint	1911–23	
2. Wrapping paper	1913–23	1912
3. Surface coated paper	1910–23	
4. Pulp boards in rolls	1919–23	
5. All other paper, exc. printed matter		1919–23
6. Items 4, 5		1914–18
7. Decals, not printed		1914–23
8. Items 6, 7		1912–13
9. Other printing paper	1911–12	1913–23
10. Cigarette paper, books, covers		1913–23
11. Photographic paper	1910–12	1913–23
12. Hanging paper		1911–23
13. Books and other printed matter, free		1879–1923
14. Books and other printed matter, dutiable		1879–1923
15. Post cards, lithographed		1913–23
16. Lithographic printed matter, n.e.s.		1913–23

Import Class and Commodity Composition	Years	
	Covered	Uncovered
066ª Paper and products, manufactured (CONT.)		
17. Items 1, 9	1909–10	
18. Items 2, 8		1911
19. Items 12, 18		1910
20. Items 3, 11, 19	1909	
21. Items 17, 20	1905–08	
22. Parchment paper		1899–1904
23. Item 21 minus item 22	1899–1904	
24. Cigarette paper, pipes, smokers' articles		1899–1922
25. Post cards and other lithographic printed matter	1899–1912	
26. Other paper and products, manuf.		1879–98
067 Coal, crude		
1. Bituminous coal	1879–1923	
2. Anthracite coal	1918–23	1898–1909, 1912–17
068 Coal, semimanufactured		
1. Coke	1906–23	
069ª Petroleum and related products, crude		
1. Petroleum, crude	1913–23	
2. Lubricating, illuminating, and fuel oils, tops, and other unfinished products		1913–23

069a Petroleum and related products, crude (CONT.)

3. Items 4, 5 — 1909–12
4. Mineral oil, free — 1899–1908
5. Mineral oil, dutiable — 1899–1908

070 Petroleum and related products, semimanuf.

1. Asphalt and bitumen — 1889–1923 | 1884–88
2. Paraffin wax and paraffin — 1916–23

071 Petroleum and related products, manufactured

1. Gasoline, naptha, and other light finished products — 1913–14, 1917–23 | 1915–16

072a Precious stones, crude

1. Diamonds, rough, uncut — 1914–23
2. Diamonds, glaziers', engravers', etc. — 1916–23
3. Other precious stones incl. bort — 1916–23 | 1899–1915
4. Item 3, exc. bort — 1899–1913
5. Items 1, 2 — 1904–09
6. Diamond dust and bort

073a Precious stones, semimanufactured

1. Diamonds, cut, but not set — 1898, 1913–23 | 1899–1912
2. Pearls, not strung or set — 1911–23

073a Precious stones, semimanufactured (CONT.)

3. Imitation precious stones — 1912–23
4. Other precious and semiprecious stones, cut, but not set — 1898–1900, 1912–23
5. Gold and silver jewelry — 1908–12
6. Other manufs. of gold and silver — 1908–12
7. Items 3, 4 — 1911
8. Items 2, 7 — 1901–10
9. Items 5, 6 — 1901–07
10. Items 8, 9 — 1898–1900
11. Diamonds, miners', glaziers', etc., and rough and uncut — 1898
12. Other precious stones, rough, uncut — 1898
13. Items 1, 11 — 1897 | 1897
14. Items 3, 4, 12
15. Jewelry, gold and silver manufs., pearls — 1879–97
16. Items 13, 14, minus item 17 — 1879–96
17. Diamonds, miners', glaziers', etc.

074 Other nonmetallic minerals, crude

1. Asbestos, unmanuf. — 1907–23
2. Kaolin, china, or paper clay — 1911–23 | 1882–96

(continued)

335

TABLE C-8 (continued)

Import Class and Commodity Composition	Years Covered	Years Uncovered
074 *Other nonmetallic minerals, crude* (CONT.)		
3. Other clay	1911–23	
4. Mica, crude, unmanuf.	1913–23	1908–12
5. Pyrites or sulphuret of iron	1899–1923	
6. Graphite or plumbago	1882–1923	
7. Gypsum or plaster rock		1916–23
8. Flint and flint stones		1912–23
9. Mineral wax or ozokerite		1913–23
10. Lithographic stones, not engraved		1912–23
11. Emery ore		1916–23
12. Corundum		1916–23
13. Chalk, unmanuf.		1916–23
14. Monazite sand and thorite		
15. Fluorspar		1916–23
16. Items 2, 3	1882–1910	1916–23
075 *Other nonmetallic minerals, semimanufactured*		
1. Artificial abrasives, crude	1916–23	
2. Cement, Portland and other hydraulic	1882–1912, 1920–23	1913–19

Import Class and Commodity Composition	Years Covered	Years Uncovered
075 *Other nonmetallic minerals, semimanufactured* (CONT.)		
3. Marble, breccia, onyx, crude	1919–23	
4. Manufs. of marble, breccia, onyx		1919–23
5. Items 3, 4	1884–1918	
6. Other building and monumentalstone, etc.		1914–23
7. Cement, exc. Portland		1916–23
8. Mica, cut, split, manuf.		1916–23
9. Talcum, steatite, etc., ground, prepared		1916–23
10. Other stone and manuf.		
11. Items 5, 10	1879–83	1884–1913
076a *Other nonmetallic minerals, manufactured*		
1. Earthenware, crockery, stoneware, total	1914–23	
2. Chinaware, exported from U.K.	1914–23	
3. Glass: cylinder, crown, sheet, unpolished	1879–1923	
4. Salt	1879–1923	
5. Plate glass, unsilvered	1879–1914, 1920–23	1915–19

076ª Other nonmetallic minerals, manufactured (CONT.)

6. Chinaware except from U.K. — 1914-23
7. Glass containers, bottles, etc. — 1884-1923
8. Items 9, 10 — 1922-23
9. Glass plates or disks for optical purposes — 1904-21
10. Other glassware — 1912-21
11. Optical instruments, incl. lenses and spectacles
12. Glass bottles, decanters, etc., cut or ornamented — 1912-23
13. Other stones, free — 1911-23
14. Asbestos, manuf. — 1912-23
15. Manuf. of carbon — 1912-23
16. Carbon for electric lights — 1922-23
17. Electrodes, brushes, etc. — 1916-21
18. Other manufs. of carbon — 1916-21
19. Chalk manuf. — 1916-21
20. Other natural abrasives — 1916-23
21. Artificial abrasives, manuf., incl. pumice, diamond dust, etc. — 1916-23
22. Meerschaum, crude — 1916-23
23. Other earthen, stone, and chinaware, incl. bricks and tiles — 1920-23 ... 1899-1913 ... 1884-98

076ª Other nonmetallic minerals, manufactured (CONT.)

24. China, earthenware, etc., from U.K — 1899-1913
25. China and earthenware except from U.K. — 1899-1913
26. Items 10, 11 — 1911
27. Items 12, 26 — 1910
28. Glass: cylinder, crown, and sheet, polished, unsilvered — 1889-1909 ... 1885-88, 1909
29. Item 27 minus item 28 — 1889-1908
30. Plate glass, fluted, etc. — 1879-88 ... 1907-08
31. Item 29 minus item 30
32. Plate glass, cast, polished, silvered — 1879-88 ... 1889-1906
33. Glass: cylinder, crown, sheet, polished, silvered — 1889-98 ... 1885-88, 1899-1906
34. Other glassware — 1884-1906
35. China, earthenware, etc., not decorated — 1884-98
36. China, earthenware, etc., decorated — 1884-98
37. Items 28, 33 — 1879-84
38. Items 7, 34 — 1879-83
39. Items 23, 35, 36 — 1879-83

077ª Nonferrous metals, crude

1. Manganese ores — 1898-1923
2. Chrome ore or chromite — 1909-12 ... 1913-23

(continued)

TABLE C-8 (continued)

077ᵃ Nonferrous metals, crude (CONT.)

Import Class and Commodity Composition	Years Covered	Years Uncovered
3. Copper ore	1889–94, 1909–23	1879–88
4. Copper concentrates	1916–23	
5. Copper regulus, etc.	1916–23	
6. Items 4, 5	1909–15	
7. Lead ore and matte	1910–23	
8. Lead bullion or base bullion	1910–23	
9. Platinum, unmanuf.	1913–23	
10. Nickel ore and matte	1904–23	
11. Zinc ore	1908–23	
12. Tin ore	1916–23	
13. Aluminum ore or bauxite		1912–23
14. Cobalt ore and metal		1916–23
15. Gold and silver sweepings		1916–23
16. Tungsten		1916–23
17. Other crude minerals, incl. vanadium ore and other ferro-alloy ores		1916–23
18. Items 7, 8	1898–1909	
19. Items 3, 6	1895–1908	
20. Lead: pigs, bars, old		1898
21. Lead, other manuf.		1894–98
22. Items 18, 20, and lead in silver ore	1894–97	
23. Items 21, 22	1891–93	
24. Item 23, exc. lead in silver ore	1889–90	

078ᵃ Nonferrous metals, semimanufactured

Import Class and Commodity Composition	Years Covered	Years Uncovered
1. Copper, unrefined, in pigs, bars, etc.	1916–23	
2. Copper refined, in pigs, bars, etc.	1916–23	
3. Items 1, 2	1913–15	
4. Copper, old, and clippings, for remanuf.	1913–23	
5. Brass, old, and clippings, for remanuf.	1913–23	1904–12
6. Tin bars, blocks, pigs	1879–1923	
7. Aluminum metal, scrap, and alloys	1912–23	
8. Platinum ingots, bars, etc.	1912–23	
9. Antimony, liquidated, regulus, or metal	1899–1908, 1914–23	
10. Antimony ore	1899–1908	1898
11. Items 9, 10	1909–13	1895–97
12. Lead: pigs, bars, old, etc.	1899–1912, 1916–23	
13. Tungsten and other ferro-alloys		1913–15
14. Zinc: blocks, pigs, old, etc.		1911–23
15. Composition metal, copper chief value	1884–1912	1913–23

078ª Nonferrous metals, semimanufactured (CONT.)

16. Brass manufs.		1899–1905, 1919–23
17. Nickel manufs.		1919–23
18. Platinum manufs. dutiable		1919–23
19. Tin manufs.		1919–23
20. Other manufs. of metal, incl. quicksilver and type metal		1919–23
21. Items 16–20		1913–18
22. Platinum metals and native combinations thereof		1916–23
23. Other metals and alloys, free		1916–23
24. Copper ingots, bars, plates, etc., and old and composition metal	1895–1912	
25. Platinum, unmanuf.	1912	
26. Items 8, 25	1882–1911	
27. Manufs. of aluminum		1912
28. Other metals and alloys, etc., incl. elect. lamps		1912
29. Items 7, 27, 28		1911
30. Items 13, 29		1906–10
31. Item 30 minus item 16		1895–1905
32. Item 24, and copper regulus, etc.		1879–94
33. Items 11, 31		1884–94

078ª Nonferrous metals, semimanufactured (CONT.)

34. Item 35, and other manufs. of lead	1883–88	
35. Lead: pigs, bars, old, etc.	1879–82	
36. Zinc sheets and other manufs. of zinc		1884–88
37. Items 14, 36		1883
38. Zinc bars, blocks, pigs, and manufs. of zinc		
39. Zinc sheets	1879–82	1884–88
40. Brass and manufs.	1879–82	
41. Metals, alloys, metal composition and manufs.		
42. Items 40, 41		1879–82
43. Lead manufs.		1879–82
44. Other manufs. of tin		1879–82

079 Nonferrous metals, manufactured

1. Watches and watch movements	1913	1919–23
2. Cases and parts of watches, incl. jewels, exc. dials		1913, 1919–23
3. Items 1, 2	1899–1912	1879–98, 1914–18
4. Items 5, 6		1889–1912, 1922–23
5. Zinc dust		1913–21
6. Other manufs. of zinc		1913–21

(continued)

TABLE C-8 (continued)

Left panel:

Import Class and Commodity Composition	Covered	Uncovered
079 Nonferrous metals, manufactured (CONT.)		
7. Chronometers, clocks, and parts of		1882–1923
8. Jewelry; gold, silver, and other		1913–23
9. Gold and silver threads, braids, fabrics, and laces		1919–23
10. Other manufs. of gold and silver		1919–23
11. Items 9, 10		1913–18
12. Copper manufs., n.e.s.		1879–1923
13. Bronze and manufs. of		1889–1923
14. Lead manufs., n.e.s.		1899–1923
15. Manufs. of aluminum		1913–23
16. Platinum manufs., other dutiable		1912–23
17. Brass manufs.		1879–98
080 Iron and steel products, crude		
1. Iron ore, exc. from Sweden	1909–23	
2. Iron ore, from Sweden		1909–23
3. Items 1, 2	1882–1908	
4. Chromate of iron		1909–12
081ᵃ Iron and steel products, semimanufactured		
1. Bar iron	1879–1923	

Right panel:

Import Class and Commodity Composition	Covered	Uncovered
081ᵃ Iron and steel products, semimanufactured (CONT.)		
2. Scrap iron and steel	1899–1923	1889–98
3. Ferromanganese	1913–23	
4. Ferrosilicon	1913–23	
5. Other pig iron	1913–23	
6. Tin plates, terne-plates, and taggers' tin	1879–1914, 1923	1915–22
7. Items 8–10		1884–1913, 1922–23
8. Steel ingots, blooms, etc., free		1914–21
9. Steel ingots, etc., bessemer or open hearth, dutiable		1919–21
10. Steel ingots, etc., crucible, electric, or cementation process		1919–21
11. Items 9, 10		1914–18
12. Iron and steel sheets and plates	1891–98	1899–1923
13. Wire rods	1883–1912	1913–23
14. Pig iron, incl. ferro-manganese and ferrosilicon	1879–1912	
15. Items 17, 18		1891–98
16. Sheet, plate, and taggers' iron	1879–90	
17. Item 12 and hoops, strips, etc. of steel	1884–88	1889–90

081ᵃ Iron and steel products, semimanufactured (CONT.)

18. Hoop, band, and scroll of iron		1889-90
19. Iron scrap	1879-88	
20. Items 7, 17		1883
21. Items 13, 20		1879-82

082ᵃ Iron and steel and products, manuf.

1. Rails for railways	1879-88, 1899-1907, 1913-23	1889-98, 1908-09, 1912
2. Structural shapes, and building forms	1913-23	1904-09, 1912
3. Wire and manufs. of	1879-1923	
4. Pen and pocket knives	1913-15, 1919-23	1916-18
5. Scissors and shears	1913-15, 1919-23	1916-18
6. Needles, hand and sewing, darning, shoe machine, etc.	1919-23	1891-1918
7. Razors and parts of	1913-23	
8. Other cutlery	1913-23	
9. Antifriction balls and bearings	1912-23	
10. Table and kitchen-ware, etc.	1907-23	
11. Other needles	1919-23	
12. Other manufs. of iron and steel, dutiable	1919-23	
13. Items 11, 12	1914-18	

082ᵃ Iron and steel and products, manuf. (CONT.)

14. Other manufs. of iron and steel, free		1914-16, 1923
15. Shotgun barrels		1891-1916, 1923
16. Items 14, 15		1917-22
17. Items 13, 14		1913
18. Cutlery	1889-1912	1879-88
19. Aeroplanes		1912
20. Bicycles, motor-cycles, etc.		1912
21. Other vehicles and parts		1912
22-23, 25-26, 28-29, 33-34, 36-37, 41-42. All other manufs. of iron and steel (varying content)		1879-1912
24. Firearms, dutiable	1899-1909	1879-98
27. Hoop, band, and scroll		1899-1908
30. Files		1879-1904
31. Chains	1889-98	1884-1904
32. Anvils		1884-88
35. Hoops, bands, ties, for baling cotton	1884-88	1889-96
38. Item 6, and other needles		1884-88
39. Steel scrap		1884-90
40. Hoop, band, and scroll of iron		1884-88
43. Anchors, chains, cables, of all types	1879-88	1879-82

(continued)

341

TABLE C-8 (continued)

Import Class and Commodity Composition	Years Covered	Years Uncovered
082ᵃ Iron and steel and products, manuf. (CONT.)		
44. Saws and tools		1879–82
45. Hardware		1879–82
46. Castings		1879–82
083 Machinery		
1. Electric lamps, incandescent, carbon filaments		1913–23
2. Electric lamps, incandescent, metal filaments		1913–23
3. Agricultural machinery and implements		1915–23
4. Metalworking machine tools		1915–13
5. Sewing machines and parts		1915–23
6. Textile machinery		1915–23
7. Cream separators, valued not over $50.00		
8. Other machinery, free		1919–23
9. Other machinery, dutiable		1919–23
10. Other electric lamps		1915–23
11. Items 7, 8		1916–23
12. Items 3–6, 9, 11		1915–18
084 Vehicles		
1. Autos	1899–1923	1879–1914
084 Vehicles (CONT.)		
2. Chassis	1913–23	
3. Items 4, 5		1922–23
4. Parts of automobiles		1913–21
5. Items 6, 7		1917–21
6. Bicycles, motorcycles, other cycles and parts		1913–16
7. Items 8–10		1915–16
8. Aeroplanes		1913–14
9. Parts of aeroplanes		1913–14
10. Other vehicles and parts		1913–14
11. Parts of autos, incl. chassis		1899–1912
085 Chemicals and allied products, crude		
1. Guano	1899–1912	1879–98, 1913–23
2. Bone phosphates, dust, ash, and meal	1906–1923	
3. Item 12 and other fertilizers	1913–23	1911–12
4. Manure salts	1913–17, 1919–23	1911–12, 1918
5. Kainite	1910–15, 1919–23	1916–18
6. Dried blood	1919–23	1916–18
7. Calcium cyanamid	1910–12	
8. Other fertilizers, inc. manure salts and crude phosphates		1910

APPENDIX C

085 Chemicals and allied products, crude (CONT.)

9. Kainite, keiserite, kyanite, etc.	1899–1909	
10. Items 7, 8	1909	
11. Item 10, exc. 12	1906–08	
12. Crude phosphates	1882–1908	
13. Items 2, 11	1899–1905	
14. Other fertilizers	1882–98	

086ª Chemicals, semimanufactured

1. Sodium nitrate	1879–1923	
2. Calcium cyanamid	1913–23	
3. Sulphate of ammonia	1907–23	
4. Potassium chloride	1884–1923	
5. Potassium sulphate	1907–23	
6. Dead or creosote oil	1899–1923	
7. Arsenic sulphide	1910–23	
8. Glycerin	1884–1923	
9. Muriate of ammonia	1912–23	
10. Iodine, crude	1907–23	
11. Potassium bitartrate, crude, argols, or wine lees	1879–1923	
12. Oxalic acid	1913–23	1912
13. Potassium carbonate	1907–23	
14. Potassium compounds, n.e.s.	1913–23	1912
15. Other acids, free	1913–23	
16. Other acids, dutiable	1917–23	
17. Item 16 and benzoic acid	1913–16	
18. Indigo, natural	1899–1921	1922–23
19. Indigo, synthetic	1899–1921	1922–23

086ª Chemicals, semimanufactured (CONT.)

20. Potassium nitrate, crude, or saltpeter	1879–1912	1913–23
21. Potassium hydrate (hydroxide)	1907–12	1913–23
22. Potassium cyanide		1912–23
23. Citrate of lime	1910–12	1913–23
24. Chlorinated lime or bleaching powder	1879–1912	1913–23
25. Benzine and toluene		1919–23
26. Napthalene		1919–23
27. Items 28, 30		1922–23
28. Other crude coal tar products, incl. toluol		1919–21
29. Cresol		1919–21
30. Carbolic acid, crude		1917–21
31. Items 25, 26, 28, 29		1907–18
32. Carbolic acid, semimanuf. (phenol)		1917–23
33. Items 30, 32		1912–16
34. Alizarin and derivatives	1889–98	1884–88, 1899–1923
35. Colors or dyes, n.e.s.		1884–1923
36. Items 37, 38		1922–23
37. Analine salts		1907–21
38. Other coal tar intermediates		1919–21
39. Benzoic acid and other coal tar intermediate acids		1919–23
40. Coal tar medicinals		1919–23
41. Other finished coal tar chemicals		1919–23
42. Items 38–41		1917–18

(continued)

343

TABLE C-8 (continued)

Import Class and Commodity Composition	Years Covered	Years Uncovered
086ᵃ *Chemicals, semimanufactured* (CONT.)		
43. Item 42, exc. benzoic acid		1907–16
44. Fusil oil, or amylic and butyl alcohol	1910–23	
45. Camphor, natural, crude	1899–1923	1879–98
46. Magnesite, not purified	1920–23	1918–19
47. Magnesite, calcined, not purified	1910–12	1913–17
48. Other sodium compounds, free		1915–23
49. Other sodium compounds, dutiable		1915–23
50. Items 48, 49		1908–14
51. Sulphur or brimstone	1879–1912	1913–23
52. Lithopone and other zinc pigments		1919–23
53. Pigments other than zinc, and varnish		1919–23
54. Items 52, 53		1883–1918
55. Sodium cyanide		1915–23
56. Egg albumen		1919–23
57. Balsams, crude		1919–23
58. Extracts for dyeing and coloring		1919–23
59. Other chemicals, dutiable		1919–23
60. Items 56–59		1915–18
61. Items 55, 60		1913–14
62. Other chemicals, free		1919–23
086ᵃ *Chemicals, semimanufactured* (CONT.)		
63. Calcium acetate, carbide, chloride, crude, and nitrate		1919–23
64. Items 62, 63		1918
65. Item 64 and magnesite, not purified, crude		1913–17
66. Tar and pitch		1916–23
67. Items 5, 13, 21	1899–1906	1891–98
68. Other chemicals, n.e.s., dutiable		1912
69. Items 9, 68		1911
70. Medicinal preparations, n.e.s., dutiable		1911–12
71. Other gums, dutiable		1911–12
72. Other acids, dutiable		1912
73. Items 12, 72		1911
74. Items 69–71, 73		1910
75. Items 14, 21		1910–11
76. All other chemicals, dutiable		1909
77. Gelatin		1909–12
78. Camphor, refined, synthetic	1909–12	
79. All other chemicals, dutiable; incl. gelatin and ref. synthetic camphor		1907–08
81. Items 3, 43, 79, and quebracho extract		1905–06

086ᵃ Chemicals, semimanufactured (CONT.)

82. All other chemicals, n.e.s., dutiable		
83. Potassium chlorate	1891–98	
84. Other acids, free		1891–1904
85. Items 33, 84		1899–1904
86. Other chemicals, n.e.s., free		1912
87. Item 86 and other crude dyewoods and logwood		1910–11
88. Items 85, 87, minus logwood		1909
89. Item 88 minus other crude dyewoods		1907–08
90. Vegetable wax		1910–12
91. Mineral wax		1910–12
92. Items 90, 91		1907–09
93. All other chemicals, free		1905–06
94. Other chemicals, free, exc. cochineal		1884–1904
95. Cochineal		1879–1904
96. Items 98–100		1905–07
97. Soda ash	1893–98	1899–1907
98. Other sodium compounds		
99. Sal soda	1893–98	1889–1904
100. Caustic soda	1879–98	1899–1904
101. Items 97, 99	1879–92	1899–1904
102. Items 18, 19	1879–98	
103. Mineral oil, free	1895–98	
104. Mineral oil, dutiable	1895–98	
105. Items 103, 104	1879–94	
106. Items 67, 82, 83	1884–90	

086ᵃ Chemicals, semimanufactured (CONT.)

107. Licorice root	1884–88	1884–88
108. Quinine	1884–88	1884–88
109. Logwood and other dye extracts		1884–88
110. Ground sumac		1884–88
111. Other chemicals, dutiable		1879–83
112. Items 34, 94		1879–83
113. Sodium bicarbonate		1879–88
114. Other sodium compounds		1879–88
115. Whiting and paris white		1879–82
116. Red lead and litharge		1879–82
117. Other paints, colors, etc.		1879–82
118. White lead		1879–82

087 Chemicals and allied products, manufactured

1. Quinine sulphate and other alkalies and salts from cinchona	1889–1923	
2. Camphor, refined, synthetic	1913–23	
3. Soap, castile	1913–23	
4. Other explosives, n.e.s.	1913–15, 1919–23	1916–18
5. Fulminates, gunpowder, etc.	1916–23	1913–15
6. Other soap	1919–23	1913–18

(continued)

345

TABLE C-8 (concluded)

Import Class and Commodity Composition	Years Covered	Years Uncovered
087 *Chemicals and allied products, manufactured* (CONT.)		
7. Perfumery and cosmetics		1879–1923
8. Medicinal preparations, n.e.s.		1913–23
9. Soap, medicated, and perfumed, incl. castile	1909–12	
10. Other soap, exc. item 11		1909–12
11. Soap, medicated and perfumed	1889–1908	1882–88
12. Other soap		1882–1908
13. Explosives		1910–12
14. Collodion and manufactures		1916–23
088 *Miscellaneous*		
1. Motion picture films, positives		1911–23
2. Motion picture films, sensitized, not exposed		1914–23
3. Motion picture films, negatives		1912–23
4. Other films, sensitized, not exposed		1914–23
5. Items 2, 4		1911–13
6. Other toys		1913–23
7. Dolls and parts of		1913–23
8. Matches		1912–23

Import Class and Commodity Composition	Years Covered	Years Uncovered
088 *Miscellaneous* (CONT.)		
9. Buttons, pearl or shell		1919–23
10. Buttons, all other		1919–23
11. Items 9, 10		1879–1918
12. Pipes and smokers articles, exc. cigarette paper, books, etc.		1884–1898, 1913–23
13. Beads and bead ornaments		1884–88, 1904–23
14. Pencils		1904–23
15. Other musical instruments, parts, and accessories		1879–1923
16. Household and personal effects		1879–1923
17 to 21. Not used		
22. Photographic goods, exc. paper		1916–23
23. Other photographic goods		1916–23
24. Pens and penholders		1916–23
25. Toys: fishing rods, etc.		
26. Scientific and professional instruments		1916–23
27. Phonographs		1916–23
28, 29. Not used		

088 *Miscellaneous* (CONT.)

30. Articles imported under bond for export within 6 months	1916–23
31. Products of Philippine Islands	1916–23
32. Products of Virgin Islands	1919–23
33. Products of Cuba	1923
34. Other toys and dolls	1884–1912
36. Feathers, artificial	1884–88

089 *Art works*

1. Art works, the products of American artists	1879–1894, 1897–1923
2. All other art works	1910–23
3. Items 4, 9	1910–18
4. 100-year old works of art	1919–23

089 *Art works* (CONT.)

5. Works of art for exhibition	1916–23
6. Statuary, regalia, etc. for religious and educational purposes	1916–23
7. Items 2, 3	1879–94, 1897–1909
8. Items 1, 7	1895–96
9. Original paintings, statuary, etc.	1919–23

090 *U.S. exports returned*

1. Automobiles	1911–23
2. All other exc. automobiles	1911–23
3. Items 1, 2	1879–87, 1909–10
4. Item 3, exc. distilled spirits	1888–1908
5. Distilled spirits	1888–1908

[a] Price and quantity indexes and values presented for these classes in Tables C–1 through C–6.

NOTES TO TABLE C–8

Import Class:

001

Based to a considerable extent on outside price data.

Items:

1. 1890–1923: Canadian price of butcher's cattle: choice steers, price per cwt. at Toronto, from various issues of Canada, Dominion Bureau of Statistics, Internal Trade Branch, *Prices and Price Indexes*, and Canada, Dept. of Labour, *Wholesale Prices in Canada.*

   1884–89: Canadian price of cattle, live—1st quality (export steers), price per cwt. in Toronto, from K. W. Taylor and H. Michell, *Statistical Contributions to Canadian Economic History*, Vol. II, Toronto, 1931.

2, 8, and 9. Canadian price of sheep, price per cwt. at Toronto. For sources see item 1.

3. 1889–99: Canadian wholesale price of eggs: storage, in case lots, at Toronto, 1890–99; and of eggs (new laid), 1889. For sources see item 1.

002

To a considerable extent, 1889–1923 based on outside price data. Quarterly values for items 9–12 for 1913–18 were estimated from quarterly data for imports of total fresh fish including salmon and annual data on Canadian exports, by type of fish. In order to simplify index computations, imports for item 7 were not estimated separately (we had no price index to use for fresh salmon) but were distributed proportionately among the other types.

Canadian price data are from *Prices and Price Indexes* and *Wholesale Prices in Canada.*

Items:

3 and 9. Canadian price of halibut, fresh, white, at Canso, N.S.

4 and 10. Canadian price of whitefish, at Toronto.

5. Canadian price of mackerel, salted, at Halifax.

6. Canadian price of herring, salted, at Halifax.

11. Same as item 5, for 1913. Extrapolated to 1918 by mackerel, at Montreal.

12. Same as item 6, for 1913. Extrapolated to 1918 by herring, salted, at Canso, N.S.

13 and 14. Canadian price of whitefish, at Toronto.

004

To a considerable extent, 1889–1913 based on outside price data.

Items:

1. 1913–23: Imports of wheat, mainly from Canada, were responsible for the growth of this class. Approximately half of the $45 million of wheat grain imported in 1922–23 were for milling in bond and export as flour. The rest, imported for U.S. consumption despite the $.30 a bushel tariff (roughly 30 per cent) imposed in 1921, was apparently hard red spring wheat, superior to most U.S. wheat (see Henry C. Wallace, *The Wheat Situation: A Report to the President*, Washington D.C., 1922, pp. 13, 27, 31–32).

   1889–1913: Canadian wholesale prices of wheat, Ontario, No. 2, White.

2. 1899–1913: Canadian wholesale price of oats, Western, No. 2, White.

3. Instead of following domestic prices, the import unit values for corn used here follow those from Argentina; these in turn resemble the spot price of corn in Buenos Aires (U.S. Department of Agriculture, *Yearbook*, 1924, p. 615).

4. Rice has been treated as a covered item from 1913 through 1921, but we have used as a base the 1923 import unit value from Japan only. It was not clear that the fall in price from 1921 to 1923 occasioned by the shift from Japanese to Mexican rice, was a price, rather than quality, change. As we have used it, the unit values follow fairly closely the Tokyo price of average quality brown rice (see V. D. Wickizer and M. K. Bennett, *The Rice Economy of Monsoon Asia*, Food Research Institute, Stanford University, California, 1941).

348

NOTES TO TABLE C–8 (continued)

5. For a few quarters in 1896 and 1898, when quantities imported were small and unit values showed violent fluctuations unrelated to price movements, we discarded the unit values and interpolated by the Canadian wholesale price of barley, Ontario No. 2.

005

Items:

4. Potatoes were imported mainly from Canada during 1917–18; we therefore used these imports alone for the 1923 base.

6. 1919–20: The 1923 import unit value of potatoes from Canada was used to estimate base-year quantity because Canada was the main source of imports in 1919 and 1920.

1899–1913: In this period, fluctuations in import unit values for potatoes were violent and largely inverse to those of the American domestic price. Imports of potatoes were of two distinct types: those from the United Kingdom, which came in large amounts, but sporadically, mainly in years when the American domestic price was high, and more stable import quantities from Bermuda, with unit values about three times as high as those from the U.K. Thus, when U.S. prices were high, imports were dominated by low-priced potatoes from the U.K., and the unit value was therefore low, but when U.S. prices were low, imports were dominated by the high-priced imports from Bermuda, and the unit values were therefore high. Since we were more interested in coverage for the years when imports were large, we tried to put together a series that would be consistent for those years and would follow the movements of U.K. export unit values which are shown in U.K. Statistical Abstracts. We did not use the unit values for each quarter of every year, but only those, mainly the large ones, which followed the pattern of the U.K. export prices. We then applied these quarterly unit values to the rest of their respective years, in place of the actual ones. For this reason, the quarterly movements of the series are somewhat arbitrary.

1879–99: The procedure used here was similar to that for the 1899–1913 period, but the annual fluctuations followed U.K. prices much better and fewer of the quarterly changes had to be smoothed out.

006

The 1879–83 period based on outside price data.

Item:

17. Prices are a weighted index (with fiscal 1883 imports-for-consumption weights) of Bezanson series for pepper, pimiento, cassia, cloves, and nutmeg, with fiscal 1883 as 100. To arrive at a base year price, the index is extrapolated to 1889 by a Fisher "ideal" index of the import unit values of pepper and nutmeg.

007

To a considerable extent, 1879–99 based on outside price data.

Items:

10. Import unit values extrapolated back from 1919 to 1907 by import unit values of copra, not prepared.

13. 1889–99: The 1899 U.S. import unit value is extrapolated back to 1895 by United Kingdom import unit values, and from 1895 back to 1889 by Bezanson prices of lemons from Sicily. Italy was the main source of lemon imports.

1884–89: Bezanson prices of lemons.

18. 1889–99: The U.S. annual 1900 import unit value was extrapolated back to 1893 annually by U.K. import unit values. Approximate quarterly values were obtained by using British values, roughly deseasonalized and then multiplied by a crude American seasonal index derived from import unit values for 1899–1905. The resulting quarterly series was then adjusted to the level of the

Notes to Table C–8 (continued)

annual series. The 1893 annual unit value was then extrapolated back to 1890 by a similar process using U.K. values for lemons and oranges combined, and to 1889 by U.S. imports-for-consumption unit values for oranges in boxes, 1.5 to 2.5 cubic feet.

1884–88: U.S. imports-for-consumption unit values averaged to estimate calendar year prices and multiplied by the seasonal index mentioned above to get quarterly prices.

24. 1879–89: Import unit values extrapolated back to 1879 from 1884 by Bezanson prices of almonds.

25. The trend in general import unit values of walnuts was biased upwards because of a shift from unshelled to shelled nuts. We were able to construct a fiscal annual Fisher "ideal" index from imports-for-consumption data for the two types separately, and we adjusted the quarterly general import unit values to the movements of this index.

36. Import unit values extrapolated from 1884 back to 1879 by Aldrich prices of prunes, Turkish.

38. Aldrich prices of currants, Zante.

41. Import unit values extrapolated back from 1884 to 1879 by Bezanson price of raisins, Valentia.

42. Annual export unit values of bananas from Jamaica, D. W. Rodriquez, *Bananas: An Outline of the Economic History of Production and Trade With Special Reference to Jamaica*, Department of Agriculture, Commodity Bulletin No. 1, Kingston, Jamaica, 1955. These were multiplied by a seasonal index derived from 1908–11 U.S. import unit values. Quarterly values for 1879–83 were estimated by annual imports-for-consumption ratios from general imports data for all other fruits.

46. Price index for lemons and oranges, with 1884 weights consisting of the Bezanson price of lemons and an orange price series constructed from Jamaican annual export unit values multiplied by the seasonal price index described above (Item 18). The Jamaica export unit values are from Great Britain, Parliament, *Sessional Papers*, 1892. Quarterly import values for oranges and lemons were estimated from quarterly import values for all fruits by the use of annual ratios from imports-for-consumption data.

008

Tea imports were broken down by country in 1913–23 to eliminate the effects of shifts among qualities and types of tea. There was a wartime shift, partially reversed afterwards, in the origin of black tea, from Great Britain to the British and Dutch East Indies, and there was a long-term trend, in evidence since the 1890's, away from green tea (mostly from China) to black tea (from India and Great Britain). We were not able to make the same breakdown of quarterly import data in the 1899–1913 period, and the price index for those years is therefore biased upwards, since black tea was more expensive than green tea.

011

To a considerable extent, 1899–1907 based on outside price data.

1913–23: Import unit values for bananas are dubious on two counts. First, they did not follow closely the price of bananas in New York during 1913–23, the only period for which we could make a comparison. Second, they involve, to some extent, transactions by American companies with their own subsidiaries in a product for which the market is not developed in the producing country. For these reasons there is considerable doubt as to the meaning of any price that might have been reported. We decided to use the unit values, however, because the figures for different countries of origin show similar movements and because they agree quite well with export unit values reported by the countries of origin, where we could make the comparison.

350

Notes to Table C-8 (continued)

1899–1913: Quarterly import unit values were used for 1908–13. The U.S. import value was then extrapolated back from 1908 to 1900 by United Kingdom import unit values multiplied by the seasonal pattern for U.S. import values, 1908–11. The series was then extended back to 1899 by the export unit value of bananas from Jamaica, also multiplied by the U.S. seasonal pattern.

1889–99: Jamaica export unit values multiplied by U.S. seasonal price pattern, 1908–13. Jamaica export unit values are from D. W. Rodriquez, *Bananas: An Outline of the Economic History of Production and Trade with Special Reference to Jamaica.*

012

To a considerable extent, 1879–83 based on outside price data.

Items:

1. Unit value extrapolated back from fiscal 1884 by Canadian wholesale price of butter (dairy prints) in Toronto. Values estimated from values for provisions using annual ratios from imports-for-consumption data.
2. Canadian wholesale price of milk: prices paid to producers, Montreal.
10. Unit values extrapolated back from fiscal 1884 by Canadian wholesale price of cheese (new large) in Toronto. Values estimated as for item 1.
11 and 12. 1913 figures are derived from imports-for-consumption data.
13 and 14. General import data give only the combination of mutton and lamb. We separated them using annual ratios derived from imports-for-consumption data.

013

Item:

5. Unit values extrapolated back to 1913 by using the last half of 1918 ratio, by the WIB price for sardines, ¼ oils, keyless, canned.

017

To a considerable extent, 1899–1918 based on outside price data.

Item:

2. 1913–23: Import unit values extrapolated back from 1919 to 1914–18 by export unit values for pearl tapioca from the Straits Settlements. These data are from Straits Settlements, Import, Export, and Statistical Office, *Return of Imports and Exports.* These prices were extrapolated to 1913 by Canadian wholesale prices of tapioca, medium pearl, at Toronto.
1899–1913: Canadian wholesale prices of tapioca.

020

Item:

3. Import unit values extrapolated back from 1891 to 1889 by import unit values for class 019, item 6. The very sharp rise in imports of refined sugar after 1890 is due to the cut in tariffs under the 1890 Act. The rate dropped from 3-3.5 cents per pound (roughly 60 to 90% ad valorem), to .5-.6 cents (about 12 to 17% ad valorem).

021

1923 import unit values for malt liquors estimated from U.K. export unit values and for still wines, from U.K. import unit values.

022

Items:

2. Import unit value for 1923 estimated by using Canadian import unit value for countries other than the U.S. and the U.K.
3 and 4. Import unit values for 1923 estimated by using U.K. export unit values.

351

NOTES TO TABLE C–8 (continued)

023

Items:

1. Quarterly import quantities were adjusted to the level determined by a fiscal year Laspeyres index, on a calendar 1913 base, of imports-for-consumption unit values for capsicum, or red pepper; mustard seed, ground; and sage.

2. Quarterly import quantities were adjusted to the level determined by fiscal year imports-for-consumption unit values for mustard seed, ground or prepared, which was, by far, the main component of the group.

024

Item:

12. 1889–90: General import data combined leaf suitable for cigar wrapping with all other leaf before 1891. Since the former was almost twice as expensive as the latter, we adjusted the published quarterly quantities to the level implied by a fiscal year index of the two types separately, computed from imports-for-consumption data. The earlier figures were not adjusted because tobacco for cigar wrapping was of minor importance before 1889. We did, however, set the 1889 base-year price at the 1888 level to eliminate the effect of the shift to tobacco for cigar wrapping.

025

Cigars, cheroots and cigarettes from the Philippine Islands were much lower in price than those from other countries and were admitted free of duty. Before they became free, in 1909, imports from this source were negligible. We therefore used as a base the unit value for imports from countries other than the Philippine Islands.

026

Items:

4. Adjusted for shifts among countries of origin 1913–June 1917. A fiscal Fisher index using general imports country data was computed on a calendar 1923 base for "calfskins, dry and dry salted" from two groups of countries. Group 1: Finland, France, Germany, Latvia, Norway, Russia, and Dutch East Indies. Group 2: England, Canada, Argentina, Uruguay, New Zealand, British India, and Denmark. Quarterly quantities were adjusted to level of new fiscal quantities.

10 and 11. 1923 annual value estimated from "total sheep and lamb skins" by the ratio for the nine-months ending September 1922. 1923 annual quantity figure obtained by using a price extrapolated from that of the nine-months ending September 1922 by "total sheep and lamb skins."

027

To a large extent, 1883–89 and 1916–23 based on outside price data.

Items:

1. 1919 unit value extrapolated back to 1918 by Canadian wholesale price of sole leather, green hide crops.

2. Prices extrapolated back from 1919 and forward from 1921 by BLS, leather: glazed kid, black, top grade from Brazilian skins, No. 3030.

3. 1919–23 prices are Canadian wholesale prices of box sides "B", extrapolated back to 1916–18 by Canadian wholesale prices of upper leather, waxed.

4. Prices extrapolated back from 1919 to 1916 by Canadian wholesale prices of harness leather.

5. 1922–23 prices obtained by computing an index of leather prices obtained from *The Economist*, "Commercial History and Review." The items used in the index are shoulders from dry salted hides, shoulders from wet salted hides, bellies from dry salted hides, and bellies from wet salted hides.

NOTES TO TABLE C–8 (continued)

6. 1918–21 and 1923, see item 5.
14. 1916–17 and 1923, see item 5.
16. 1923 price is taken from 1923 price of item 1.
17. 1913 and 1923, see item 5.
22. 1884–89: Quantities obtained using prices from the Aldrich report—calfskins, tanned and dressed, French, J. Griffon and Co., for years 1885–89 and 1883. Prices were extrapolated back to 1884 by Aldrich report price for calfskins, tanned and dressed, French (E. Ogerau).
23. See item 22.
24. 1883 and 1889 prices extrapolated from Aldrich Report leather prices: calfskins, tanned and dressed, French, J. Griffon and Co.

028

Quarterly indexes are largely interpolated.
Items:
1. 1899–1913: Prices obtained by computing a fiscal year index for glove prices on a calendar 1913 base with imports-for-consumption unit values for gloves, Schmäschen, of sheep origin, under 14″, unlined; gloves, lamb, or sheep, "glacé" finish, not over 14″, unlined; gloves, same as preceding description, piqué or prix seam; gloves, same, over 17″, unlined; gloves, goat, kid, etc., "glacé" finish, not more than 14″, unlined; gloves, same, piqué or prix seam, and gloves, same, over 17″, unlined. Quarterly prices were obtained by a straight line interpolation.
   1891–99: Quarterly prices used are interpolated freehand from an average of price relatives on a calendar 1899 base of imports-for-consumption fiscal unit values for gloves: "Schmäschen," "Lamb or Sheep" and "Goat or Kid."

029

To a considerable extent, 1879–1918 based on outside price data. Quarterly indexes are largely interpolated.
Items:
10. 1919–23: Prices obtained by straight line interpolation of a calendar annual Fisher "ideal" index on a 1923 base for undressed furs. This index was computed from imports-for-consumption value and quantity data for fox, hare and rabbit, marten, mink, mole, muskrat, and squirrel.
    1899–1913: Prices obtained by straight line interpolation of a calendar annual Fisher "ideal" index on a 1911 base for undressed furs. This index was computed from value and quantity data of Hudson's Bay Company fur sales for silver fox, white fox, lynx, marten, mink, land otter, and muskrat as given in J. W. Jones, *Fur-Farming in Canada* (Canada, Commission of Conservation, Ottawa, 1914). 1913 prices obtained by extrapolation.
    1879–98: Prices obtained by interpolation of a calendar annual Fisher "ideal" index on an 1899 base using the same furs (excluding white fox) and the same source as for the 1899–1913 period.
11. Quarterly prices of "001 H hair, best," from WIB Price Bulletin No. 27, *Prices of Hatter's Fur and Fur Felt Hats* for 1913–18. The 1923 figure obtained by extrapolating above to 1919 by import unit values of "furs, undressed total" (1919 and 1918 third and fourth quarters) and to 1923 by the fur price index used for item 10.
12. Weighted average of price relatives of Canadian wholesale prices for mink, weighted once, and muskrat, weighted twice.

031

To a considerable extent, 1899–1911 based on outside price data.
Items:
1. 1912–23: Prices are Union of South Africa export unit values for ostrich feathers

NOTES TO TABLE C–8 (continued)

taken from reports of the Customs and Excise Department and converted to dollars.

13. 1899–1911: Same as for item 1, and for earlier years, similar records of the Cape of Good Hope, published in the *Government Gazette*.

032

To a considerable extent, 1913–17 based on outside price data.
Item:
2. Price for last half of 1918 extrapolated back through 1913 by WIB price of West Australia pearl shells.

036

The period 1892 and first half of 1893 based on outside price data.
Item:
10. 1892 and first half of 1893 prices obtained by interpolating between fourth quarter 1891 and third quarter 1893 by BLS Para Island rubber prices. These prices were multiplied by the published quantity figures to obtain new values. The adjustment of values for this period was made in order to correct for a depreciation in the value of Brazilian paper money not reflected in the published values (see *Foreign Commerce and Navigation of the U.S.*, 1893).

039

To a considerable extent, 1894–1906 based on outside price data.
Items:
6 and 7. Unit values interpolated between 1917, third quarter and 1919, second quarter, by Italian olive oil price. (*Annuario Statistico Italiano*).
17, 22, and 23. Quarterly prices are U.K. prices of palm oil, Lagos, from *The Economist*.
24. 1894–99: Prices obtained by extrapolating the fiscal 1893 unit value by U.K. price of palm oil, Lagos, from *The Economist*.
1899–1905: See item 17.

040

The years 1879–83 based on outside price data.
Item:
30. Prices for 1879–83 are Aldrich report price for opium.

041

To a considerable extent, 1891–99 based on outside price data. In the same period, quarterly indexes are largely interpolated.
Items:
21. Price used is Bezanson price for cutch, 1891–96, extrapolated to calendar 1899 by imports-for-consumption unit value of copal, damar, and kauri. Prices for 1897–98 are interpolated on a straight line between 1896, fourth quarter, and 1899.
22. Prices for 1890 and 1889 are Bezanson prices for cutch. 1899 price is assumed to be the same as for item 21.

044

Based to a considerable extent on outside price data. Quarterly indexes are largely interpolated.
Items:
2. 1918–23: Prices are a quarterly Laspeyres index computed from prices for bergamot, cassia, citronella, orange, lavender, and spike lavender, taken from *Perfumery and Essential Oil Record (Supplement: Market Prices)*, New York; and weights taken from 1923 values given in imports for consumption.

NOTES TO TABLE C-8 (continued)

1913–17: Prices are a quarterly Laspeyres index computed from WIB prices for oils of bergamot, cassia, orange, lavender, and rose, linked to 1923 and weighted by 1923 imports-for-consumption values.

3. Prices are a fiscal Laspeyres index on a calendar 1913 base computed from imports-for-consumption unit values for oils of bergamot, cassia, citronella, lavender, and rose, and weighted by imports-for-consumption values. Quarterly prices obtained by straight line interpolation.

4. 1884–1909: Same as item 3 except that lemon and orange have been included in the index.

7. 1879–83: See item 3.

8. 1879–83: Bezanson price for lemon oil.

047

Items:

1. 1917, third and fourth quarters, 1918, and 1919, first quarter, extrapolated by U.K. prices for cotton cloth, 38 in. shirtings, taken from *The Economist*.

7. 1899–1913: Fiscal year Fisher "ideal" index on a calendar 1913 base, using U.S. imports-for-consumption data for cotton pile fabrics: dyed, colored, stained, painted or printed; not bleached; dyed, etc.; all on which duty does not amount to 40–47.5 per cent; corduroy weighing 7 oz. or over per sq. yd. Quarterly prices estimated by straight line interpolation. Values for 1899-June 1906 were obtained by finding the ratio for each fiscal year of "cotton pile fabric" (imports-for-consumption value) to "all other manufactures of cotton" (general imports value) and assuming that the ratio remained constant for the four quarters within each fiscal year.

1891–99: Quarterly prices obtained by straight line interpolation of fiscal imports-for-consumption unit values for total cotton pile fabrics. Values obtained as for the 1899–June 1906 period.

8. 1913–June 1918: Prices used are BLS quarterly prices of "cotton thread, J. & P. Coats, 200 yd. spools."

9. 1914–June 1918: Values were calculated from quarterly figures for "total knit goods, cotton, excluding hosiery," using fiscal imports-for-consumption ratios of "gloves, cotton" to total "knit goods, cotton, excluding hosiery."

1914–16: Quantities obtained by straight line interpolation of fiscal imports-for-consumption unit values for "cotton gloves."

1920: Prices affected by shift from Japanese to German gloves during 1920. We estimated the annual price by extrapolating from 1921 by the import unit value from Germany alone, and interpolated the quarterly unit values by using those for hosiery.

31. 1902–09: Prices are BLS quarterly prices for "hosiery: cotton, women's mercerized 200 needle seamless, 50/2 yarn in leg, 30/2 yarn in heel and toe, 8/1 C.P., double sole and spliced heel, 8½-10, all colors, f.o.b. mill."

1898–1901: Prices are BLS annual prices for hosiery (see 1902–09 above) interpolated freehand to obtain a quarterly price series.

1893–97: Prices are BLS annual prices for hosiery (same as above) assuming quarterly prices are identical with annual.

1891–92: Quantities computed by extrapolating 1893 BLS price back by imports-for-consumption unit value for stockings valued at $.60- $2.00.

048

Item:

1. 1913–23: Quarterly unit values interpolated freehand from a Fisher "ideal" Index for jute and jute butts on a calendar 1923 base using U.S. imports-for-consumption data. British quarterly and annual wholesale prices of "jute, native firsts" from *The Economist* and U.S. quarterly and annual import unit values for "jute and jute butts" were used as guides in the interpolation.

Notes to Table C–8 (continued)

1901–13: Quarterly U.K. wholesale prices of "jute, native firsts" from *The Economist*.

1899–1900: Prices extrapolated back to 1899 from 1901 annual price by French quarterly wholesale prices of "jute" from *La Réforme Économique*.

1889–99: Quarterly unit values interpolated from a fiscal annual Fisher "ideal" index for jute and jute butts on a calendar 1899 base, using U.S. imports-for-consumption data. U.S. annual and quarterly import unit values for "jute and jute butts" and BLS annual and quarterly prices for "raw jute" were used as guides in the interpolation.

049
Item:
1. 1889: Prices extrapolated by Bezanson prices for gunny cloth.
1890–99: BLS series for jute.
1899–1904: Unit values extrapolated back from 1905 by Canadian wholesale price of jute.

051
Items:
3. 1913–23: Italian prices of hemp, 1914–23, from various volumes of *Annuario Statistico Italiano*, converted to dollars and extrapolated back to 1913 by United States import unit values.
17. 1879–83: Fisher "ideal" price index on a calendar 1889 base from imports-for-consumption data for jute, jute butts, and sisal, interpolated freehand.

052
Items:
1. Prices for 1919–23 extrapolated from 1918 unit value by imports-for-consumption unit values of "single yarns of flax, hemp, and ramie," interpolated freehand. Prices for 1913–14 extrapolated from 1915 import unit value by Canadian wholesale prices for "flax sewing twine."
2. Prices from 1899–1913 are general import unit values of "matting and mats of China, Japan and India straw." (item 2, class 053). For 1913–18 the same items are used to extrapolate from 1919.

053
To a considerable extent, 1879–99 and 1922–23 based on outside price data. Quarterly indexes for 1899–1902 are largely interpolated.
Items:
5. Quarterly British export unit values to U.S. of "linen piece goods," converted to dollars.
29. Fiscal imports-for-consumption unit values of "plain-woven fabrics of vegetable fiber," interpolated freehand.
30. Quarterly British export unit values of "jute piece goods."
31. Quarterly British export unit values of "linen piece goods, plain, bleached or unbleached."
34. 1884–89: Quarterly British export unit values of ' jute piece goods."
35. Quarterly British export unit values of "jute piece goods."
37 and 39. Quarterly British export unit values of "linen piece goods, plain, bleached or unbleached."

054
Item:
2. The sudden spurt in imports of "clothing wool" in the second quarter of 1897 was in anticipation of the imposition of a ten cents per pound (over 60% ad valorem) tariff in July 1897. Imports fell off sharply immediately afterwards.

NOTES TO TABLE C–8 (continued)

055

Quarterly indexes for 1913-June 1915 are largely interpolated.

Item:

1. 1913-June 1915 prices are interpolated from imports-for-consumption fiscal unit values of "woolen yarns."

056

To a considerable extent, 1879–99 based on outside price data.

Items:

4. 1879–89: Aldrich prices for "suitings, flannel: all wool, indigo blue, 6–4 Assabet." A few slight adjustments were made on these prices to make them conform better to imports-for-consumption unit values of "wool cloth."

   1889–99: Annual U.K. export unit values of "worsted tissues, coatings, broad, all wool," other than to U.S., interpolated freehand, using as a guide, quarterly U.K. export unit values of "worsted tissues," other than to U.S.

5. 1899–1901: Prices obtained by extrapolating 1902 unit values back by quarterly U.K. export unit values of "worsted stuffs, mixed."

6. 1879–99: Quarterly U.K. export unit values of "carpets, not being rugs," other than to U.S.

9. 1914–June 1918: Fiscal import-for-consumption unit values of "woven fabrics, wholly or in chief value of mohair, alpaca, etc.," interpolated freehand.

059

To a considerable extent, 1879–1913 based on outside price data. Quarterly indexes for 1913–18 are largely interpolated.

Items:

1. 1913–18: Unit values extrapolated back from 1919 by imports-for-consumption unit values of "total silk fabrics, woven in the piece, etc." Quarterly unit values were obtained by freehand interpolation using WIB quarterly price series for "imported broad silk, Japanese habutai, 3½ momme, 36″ wide" and "imported broad silk, Japanese habutai, 6 momme, 36″ wide" as guides.

   1879–1913: Quarterly prices are interpolated from annual French export unit values for "tissus de soie pure, unis," Commerce Spécial, in *Annuaire Statistique*, Bureau de la Statistique Générale, and Direction Générale des Douanes, *Tableau Général du Commerce et de la Navigation*. All of these French export unit values are open to considerable suspicion because they are official, rather than declared, values (R. G. D. Allen and J. Edward Ely, *International Trade Statistics*, New York, 1953, pp. 94, 354–355). However, they were revised annually, and did not show the sudden large jumps which are characteristic of official values when revised only occasionally. We compared them with other series, such as those for average export given in Lyons, Chambre de Commerce, *Compte Rendu de Lyons*, and fragmentary U.S. imports-for-consumption unit values, and found them fairly similar.

4. 1879–1913: Quarterly prices are interpolated from annual French export unit values for "rubans de soie ou de bourre de soie pure, autre". See item 1, 1879–1913 for source.

7. 1879–1913: Quarterly prices are interpolated from annual French export unit values for "Passementerie de soie ou de bourre de soie pure." See item 1, 1879–1913 for source.

062

To a considerable extent, 1889–94, 1899 based on outside price data. Quarterly indexes for 1883–99 are largely interpolated.

Items:

9. 1883–99: Fiscal year prices were obtained by using imports-for-consumption quantity figures for "waste and other paper materials, including all grasses,

NOTES TO TABLE C-8 (continued)

fibers, waste, etc., fit only to be converted into papers" and general import value figures for "paper stock, all other." Quarterly prices were obtained by freehand interpolation from fiscal year prices.

20. 1890–94 and 1899: Prices used are quarterly Canadian wholesale prices of "New Brunswick merchantable spruce deals."

1889: Annual price obtained by extrapolating back from 1890 by Canadian export price index for lumber. (*Statistical Contributions to Canadian Economic History*, Vol. II, by K. W. Taylor and H. Michell.)

063

Items:

5. 1913–18 and 1923: Fisher "ideal" index using imports-for-consumption data for "cork, bark or wood, unmanufactured" and "cork waste and shavings, etc.," interpolated freehand.

9. 1899-June 1909: Estimated quarterly values for "laths" (obtained by using the imports-for-consumption ratio of "laths" to "all other lumber, dutiable,") have been subtracted out of "all other lumber, dutiable."

064

To a considerable extent, 1899-June 1909 based on outside price data.

Item:

1. 1899-June 1909: See item 9, class 063 for method of obtaining quarterly values for "laths." Prices are quarterly Canadian wholesale prices of "lath No. 1 white pine, 1⅜ inch," adjusted to level of fiscal 1910 U.S. import unit value of "laths."

065

Quarterly indexes for 1899–1908 are interpolated.

Item:

8. 1899–1908 and 1913: Quarterly prices were obtained by freehand interpolation of a fiscal Fisher "ideal" price index on a calendar 1913 base for imports-for consumption quantities and values of "wood pulp, mechanically ground," "wood pulp, chemical, bleached," and "wood pulp, chemical, unbleached."

066

Quarterly indexes for 1899–1913 are largely interpolated.

Items:

2. Prices extrapolated back from 1914 by quarterly Canadian wholesale prices of "wrapping paper, manila #1."

11. 1910–13: Quarterly prices were interpolated from annual German export unit values for "photographic paper, sensitized-#663" taken from various years of *Statistik des Deutschen Reichs*, Statistisches Amt.

17. 1913: Annual price obtained by extrapolating from fiscal 1911 general import unit value for "total printing paper" by Fisher "ideal" price index for "printing paper," computed from general import values and quantities for "newsprint" and "other printing paper."

20. 1909: Same as for item 21 except that index was computed excluding "printing paper, valued above 5 cents per pound."

21. 1905–08: Quarterly prices were interpolated freehand from a Fisher "ideal" fiscal price index for paper computed on a calendar 1913 base using imports-for-consumption values and quantities for "copying, stereotype paper, etc., less than 6 pounds," "copying, stereotype paper, etc., 6–10 pounds," "crepe and filtering paper," "photographic paper, plain basic," "printing paper, valued above 5 cents per pound," and "surface coated paper, other n.s.p.f."

23. 1899–1904: Same as for item 21.

25. 1899–1913: Quarterly prices for 1910–13 were interpolated freehand from a Fisher fiscal price index on a calendar 1913 base using imports-for-consumption

NOTES TO TABLE C–8 (continued)

data for "articles lithographically printed: not exceeding $\frac{8}{1000}$ inch in thickness, not exceeding 35 square inches, die cut or embossed, exceeding 35 square inches, and exceeding $\frac{20}{1000}$ inch in thickness;" "souvenir postcards, lithographically printed: exceeding $\frac{8}{1000}$ inch, and not exceeding $\frac{20}{1000}$ inch in thickness, die cut or embossed;" "decalcomanias, in ceramic colors, not over 100 lbs.;" "booklets decorated in whole or in part by hand or by spraying;" and "booklets, all other."

Quarterly prices for 1899–1909 were interpolated freehand from a Fisher "ideal" fiscal price index on a calendar 1913 base, using imports-for-consumption values and quantities for articles lithographically printed (first four items listed above for 1910–13 index)—the index being adjusted to the level of the 1910–13 index.

072

To a considerable extent, 1899–1918 based on outside price data.
Items:
1. 1914–18: Prices obtained by extrapolating 1919 U.S. import unit value back to 1914 by quarterly South African export unit values of diamonds taken from *Trade of the Union of South Africa* (Union of South Africa, Customs and Excise Department).
5. 1913, 1923: Quarterly prices for 1913 are South African export unit values of diamonds. 1923 annual price was obtained by extrapolating the fiscal 1919 South African export unit value of diamonds, by U.S. import unit value of "diamonds, rough, uncut" (item 1) for fiscal 1919 and calendar 1923.
1899–1913: South African export unit values for diamonds (see item 1 for source).

073

Based to a considerable extent on outside price data.
Items:
1. 1913–18: Quarterly prices prior to July 1918 obtained by extrapolation of unit values from calendar year 1919 by South African export unit values of diamonds (see Import Class 072, Item 1 for source).
1898–99: Quarterly prices are South African export unit values of diamonds (source same as for 1913–18).
11. 1898–99: See item 1, 1898–99, above.
13. 1897: Prices used are quarterly export unit values of diamonds exported from Kimberly division, taken from *Statistical Register*, Cape of Good Hope, Colonial Secretary's Dept.
16. 1884–96, 1899: See item 13.
1879–84: Annual prices extrapolated back to 1879 by obtaining export unit values from figures for values of diamonds exported through Customs and Post Office and quantity of diamonds exported through Post Office at Kimberly, taken from the *Blue Book*, Cape of Good Hope.

074

Items:
1. 1907–June 1908: Fiscal prices extrapolated back from 1909 by imports-for-consumption unit value of "asbestos, unmanufactured". Quarterly prices obtained by freehand interpolation.
1922 (fourth quarter)–1923: The sum of imports-for-consumption value figures for "Keene's cement or other gypsum cement, the same valued at: $14 or less per ton, over $14 and not over $20 per ton, and over $20 and not over $40 per ton," have been subtracted from general imports, and new quarterly values estimated for 1923.
10. 1922 (fourth quarter)–1923: Quarterly values estimated from imports-for-consumption annual values for "lithographic stones" and general imports quarterly values for "other stones."

NOTES TO TABLE C–8 (continued)

15. 1922 (fourth quarter)–1923: Quarterly values estimated from imports-for-consumption annual value for "fluorspar" and general imports quarterly values for "other nonmetallic minerals, dutiable."

075

Quarterly indexes are largely interpolated.

Items:

1. 1916–23: Quarterly prices interpolated freehand from an annual price index on a calendar 1923 base obtained by computing an unweighted average of price relatives of silicon carbide, aluminum oxide, and metallic abrasives, taken from U.S. Bureau of Mines, *Minerals Yearbook*.

5. 1879–1918, 1923: Quarterly prices interpolated freehand from U.S. imports-for-consumption unit values of "marble veined and all other, in block, rough, or squared" (1879–83); "marble in block, rough or squared only" (1884–99); "marble, breccia, and onyx in block, rough, or squared only" (1899–1907); and "marble, breccia and onyx, total" (1908–18).

076

To a considerable extent, 1899–1923 based on outside price data.

Items:

1. 1914–23: Prices are U.K. quarterly export unit values (converted to dollars) of "jet, Rockingham, samian, and all other glazed earthenware; excl. terracotta."

2. 1914–23: Prices are U.K. quarterly export unit values (converted to dollars), of porcelain, chinaware, and parian.

    1914–first half 1915: Quarterly values estimated from total quarterly values for "china, parian and porcelain, decorated and not decorated" and from fiscal year totals of general imports from the U.K. taken from *Annual Report of the Commerce and Navigation of the U.S.*

    1922 and 1923 (fourth quarter): Quarterly values obtained by adding quarterly general imports for "china and porcelain" and estimated quarterly values of imports from U.K. of "bisque and parian" (obtained by using annual figures from *Annual Report of Commerce and Navigation* of imports from U.K. and quarterly figures for total imports).

3. 1898–99: Prices are U.S. import unit values of "glass-cylinder and crown, polished, unsilvered" multiplied by the ratio of 1897 unit value of "cylinder and crown, polished, unsilvered" to the 1897 unit value of cylinder and crown, polished, silvered.

23. 1923, 1908–13: Prices are quarterly British export unit values of "floor tiles for tesselated pavement."

    1904–07: 1908 prices extrapolated back by quarterly British export unit values of "other earthenware; incl. semi-porcelain, majolica, and tiles."

    1899–1903: 1904 prices extrapolated back by quarterly unit values of U.S. imports of "china, parian, porcelain, etc., from U.K." (see item 24 for source of prices).

24. 1908–13: Prices are U.K. quarterly export unit values of "other earthenware; incl. semi-porcelain and majolica."

    1904–07: 1908 prices extrapolated back by U.K. quarterly export unit values of "other earthenware; incl. semi-porcelain, majolica, and tiles."

    1899–1903: 1904 prices extrapolated back by annual German export unit values of porcelain ware, taken from *Greifswalder Staatswissenschaftliche Abhandlungern 51*, p. 161–2. Quarterly prices obtained by interpolation.

077

To a considerable extent, 1899–1903 based on outside price data.

Quarterly indexes for 1889–93 are largely interpolated.

NOTES TO TABLE C–8 (continued)

Items:

3. 1894 (Sept.) and 1899 (fourth quarter), annual: Prices extrapolated by Canadian wholesale price of "copper, casting ingot" from eight-month period ending August 1894.

11. 1922–23: Prices extrapolated by BLS price for "zinc sheets" from 1921 annual U.S. import unit value.

19. 1899–1903: Prices extrapolated back from 1904 by U.S. import unit values of "unrefined copper."

    1895–99: Prices used are U.S. import unit values of Import Class 078, item 24.

23. 1891–93: Prices used are interpolated freehand from a Fisher "ideal" price index on a fiscal 1895 base using imports-for-consumption data on "lead contained in silver ore" and "lead pigs and bars, etc."

24. 1889–90: Quarterly prices interpolated from imports-for-consumption fiscal unit values for "lead ore, pigs, bars, etc., excluding lead in silver ore."

078

Items:

8. 1922 (fourth quarter)–1923: Quarterly values and quantities estimated from general imports quarterly data for "platinum, unmanufactured" and imports-for-consumption data for platinum in ingots, bars, sheets or plate, not less than $\frac{1}{8}$ inch thick.

34. 1883–89: Quarterly quantities obtained by freehand interpolation of imports-for-consumption fiscal unit values for "lead, pigs and bars."

079

Items:

1. 1913, 1923: Quantities for 1913 obtained by interpolation of a fiscal 1913 and 1st quarter fiscal 1914 Fisher price index on a calendar 1923 base computed from U.S. imports-for-consumption values and quantities for watches "having not more than 7 jewels;" "having more than 11 and not more than 15 jewels"; "having more than 15 and not more than 17 jewels;" and "having more than 17 jewels."

3. 1899–1913: Same as item 1, except that index is on a fiscal 1913 base.

081

To a considerable extent, 1913–June 1916 based on outside price data.

Quarterly indexes for 1899–1913 are largely interpolated.

Items:

3. 1922 (fourth quarter)–1923: Quantities obtained by using British export unit values (converted to dollars) of "iron and steel and manufactures thereof; incl. pig iron and ferro alloys—ferro alloys including Spiegeleisen and ferromanganese, etc."

   1916 (first half): Prices are U.S. import unit values for six months ending June interpolated by U.K. export unit values (see above).

   1913–15: Prices used are U.K. export unit values (see above) extrapolated from U.S. calendar 1916 import unit value.

5. Prices extrapolated back from calendar 1916 by U.S. quarterly wholesale prices of "basic pig iron" taken from WIB.

14. 1899–1913: Quarterly prices are interpolated from a fiscal Fisher price index on a calendar 1913 base computed with imports-for-consumption data on "ferromanganese," "ferrosilicon," "Spiegeleisen" and "all other pig iron."

082

To a considerable extent, 1913–23 based on outside price data.

Quarterly indexes for 1889–1913 are largely interpolated.

Notes to Table C–8 (continued)

Items:

3. 1913–23: Prices are a quarterly Laspeyres price index computed from U.K. export unit values, converted to dollars, of "wire for fencing," "other sorts of wire," and "wire cables and ropes."

   1899–1913: Prices are a quarterly interpolation of U.S. imports-for-consumption unit values of "total round iron or steel wire."

   1879–June 1883: Values estimated using annual imports-for-consumption totals for "iron wire and steel wire" and annual and quarterly general imports data on "steel ingots, bars, sheets, and wire" and "all other iron and steel manufactures."

   1879–June 1884: Unit values were extrapolated back from fiscal 1885 by a Fisher "ideal" price index on a fiscal 1885 base computed from imports-for-consumption data on "iron wire, bright, coppered, etc., not less than No. 16," "iron wire, rope, strand, chain, not less than No. 16," "steel wire, less than $\frac{1}{4}$ inch, not less than No. 16," "steel wire, less than $\frac{1}{4}$ inch, less than No. 16," "steel wire, rope, strand, chain, less than $\frac{1}{4}$ inch, not less than No. 16," "steel wire, rope, strand, chain, less than $\frac{1}{4}$ inch, less than No. 16." Extrapolated fiscal unit values were interpolated freehand to yield quarterly unit values.

18. 1899–1913: Quarterly unit values interpolated freehand from a fiscal Fisher "ideal" price index on a calendar 1913 base computed from imports-for-consumption data for "pens and pocket knives," "scissors and shears,": and "razor blades, etc."

    1889–99: Quarterly unit values for 1892–99 interpolated freehand from a fiscal Laspeyres price index on a calendar 1899 base computed from imports-for-consumption data for "penknives," and "razors." Annual unit values for 1889–91 extrapolated back from calendar 1892 by average annual price of "pocket knives" as noted in Aldrich Report. Quarterly unit values were interpolated.

24. 1899–1909, 1913: Quarterly prices interpolated from imports-for-consumption unit values for "shotguns, etc., valued at not more than five dollars each."

084

Quarterly indexes are largely interpolated.

Items:

1. 1913–23: Quarterly prices for 1913 (fourth quarter)–1922 (third quarter) interpolated freehand from imports-for-consumption unit values for "automobiles valued at more than $2,000." Quarterly prices for first, second and third quarters of 1913 extrapolated back from 9 months ending June 1914 by general imports quarterly unit values for "automobiles." Quarterly prices for 1922 (fourth quarter)–1923 extrapolated from 9 months ending September 1922 by quarterly prices used for "auto chassis" (item 2).

   July 1900–June 1905: Quarterly prices interpolated freehand from imports-for-consumption unit values for "autos and chassis."

   1899–June 1900: Quantities obtained by using 1901 fiscal unit value.

2. 1913 (fourth quarter)–1923: Quarterly values for auto chassis estimated from imports-for-consumption data for "auto chassis"; general imports data for "autos and chassis", 1923 and 1922 (fourth quarter); and general imports data for "parts of autos", 1913 (fourth quarter)–1922 (third quarter). Quarterly prices obtained by freehand interpolation of imports-for-consumption unit values for "auto chassis."

   1913 (first, second, and third quarters): Quarterly unit values obtained by extrapolating back from 9 months ending June 1914 by general imports unit values for "automobiles." Quarterly values estimated by multiplying the value of general imports of parts of autos by the ratio of: imports-for-consumption (value), autos and chassis (new tariff, fiscal 1914) to gen. imports (value) auto parts (9 months ending June 1914).

4. 1913–23: Estimated quarterly values of "chassis" (item 2) subtracted out.

NOTES TO TABLE C–8 (continued)

085

To a considerable extent, 1899–1913 based on outside price data.

Quarterly indexes for 1913–June 1918 are largely interpolated.

Items:

1. 1899–1913: Quantities obtained by using *Oil, Paint, and Drug Reporter* price quotations for fish guano (adjusted for changes in methods of quoting).

2. 1906-June 1911: Quarterly values estimated from "all other fertilizers" using imports-for-consumption values for "bone phosphates" to obtain fiscal year ratios. Quarterly quantities obtained by freehand interpolation of imports-for-consumption unit values for "bone phosphates."

3. 1913-June 1918: Estimates of quarterly values for "calcium cyanamid" have been subtracted out and imports-for-consumption unit values for "other fertilizers" have been interpolated freehand to obtain quarterly unit values.

5. 1910–13: Prices of kainite taken from *Oil, Paint, and Drug Reporter*.

   1910–June 1911: Values estimated from imports-for-consumption values of kainite and general imports quarterly values of "kainite and manure."

7. 1910–13: Quarterly values estimated from general imports values for "other fertilizers" and imports-for-consumption fiscal values for "calcium cyanamid." Quarterly quantities obtained by freehand interpolation of imports-for-consumption unit values for "calcium cyanamid."

9. 1899–1909, 1913: Prices of kainite from *Oil, Paint, and Drug Reporter*.

086

Items:

2. 1913–June 1918: Quarterly values estimated from imports-for-consumption fiscal values for "calcium cyanamid" and general imports values for "other fertilizers." Quarterly quantities obtained by freehand interpolation of imports-for-consumption fiscal unit values for "calcium cyanamid."

6. 1899–June 1907: Quarterly values estimated from imports-for-consumption fiscal values for "dead or creosote oil" and general imports values for "mineral oil." Quarterly quantities obtained by freehand interpolation of imports-for-consumption fiscal unit values for "dead or creosote oil."

15. 1913–23: Quarterly quantities obtained by freehand interpolation of a Fisher "ideal" price index on a calendar 1923 base for fiscal years 1913–18 and calendar years 1919–22. The index was computed using imports-for-consumption values and quantities for "arsenic or arsenious acid," "phosphoric acid," "sulphuric acid," and "acetic or pyroligneous acid."

16. 1917–23: Quarterly quantities obtained by freehand interpolation of a Fisher "ideal" price index on a calendar 1923 base for fiscal years 1917–18 and calendar years 1919–22. The index was computed using imports-for-consumption values and quantities for "citric acid," "tartaric acid," and "boric (boracic) acid."

17. 1913–16: See item 16.

18 and 19: Before July 1916, U.S. import data did not separate natural from synthetic indigo although the latter was much cheaper. Since synthetic indigo did not drive the natural product completely out of the market, the two were treated here as separate commodities and it was therefore necessary to break down reported imports into the two types. The only data available for this purpose were the annual reports of imports by country of origin. Since synthetic indigo came mainly from Germany and to some extent from Switzerland, we took imports of indigo from these countries to represent imports of synthetic indigo and the rest to represent natural indigo. Quarterly imports were estimated by assuming that the ratio of synthetic to natural was constant throughout the year.

   1913–June 1916: Quarterly prices of natural indigo were extrapolated back from fiscal 1917 by U.K. wholesale prices of "indigo, Bengal, good consuming," from *The Economist*. Quarterly prices of synthetic indigo were extrapolated back by WIB, "synthetic indigo."

NOTES TO TABLE C–8 (concluded)

1899–1913: Quarterly prices of natural indigo, 1901–13, are U.K. wholesale prices of "indigo, Bengal, good to fine," from *The Economist*. These were extrapolated back to 1899 by annual U.K. wholesale prices of "indigo, Bengal, good consuming," from *The Economist* and interpolated freehand. Synthetic indigo prices are from the *Oil, Paint, and Drug Reporter* quotations for "J (synthetic) indigo."

087

To a considerable extent, 1913–23 based on outside price data.

Items:

1. 1913–23: BLS prices for "quinine sulphate."
4. 1913–15, 1919–23: Quarterly prices obtained by freehand interpolation of imports-for-consumption unit values for "firecrackers."
5. 1916–19: Quarterly prices obtained by freehand interpolation of imports-for-consumption unit values for "gunpowder, etc."
   1920–23: Quarterly prices obtained by freehand interpolation of imports-for-consumption unit values for "fulminates."

Appendix D

Construction of Quarterly Interpolating Series for
U.S. Department of Commerce Annual Import Price Indexes

THE indexes described here were computed to fill a gap in the quarterly import indexes between the end of the National Bureau's indexes in 1923 and the beginning of the official Department of Commerce indexes in 1929. On the export side, the gap is bridged adequately by Cowden's indexes, which are available monthly from 1923 through 1930.[1] For imports, the only series available were the annual Department of Commerce indexes and an inadequate monthly volume index published by the American Tariff League. We accepted the annual Commerce series and constructed quarterly series from them by interpolation. The interpolating series were quarterly and annual indexes constructed in such a way that the annual indexes closely matched the Commerce series.

The Commerce series are Fisher "ideal" price indexes, but, unlike ours, are constructed with constantly changing bases, the index for each year using the previous year as a base. The interpolating indexes we prepared are of the same type as the Commerce indexes, but we attempted to roughly duplicate the annual movements of the Commerce series with a smaller number of commodities. The two sets of annual indexes are shown in Table D-1.

The year-to-year changes in the two sets of indexes are very similar. Of thirty comparisons, twenty-five show either no difference or a difference of only one percentage point; only one discrepancy is as high as 4 per cent.

Because of the similarity of the two series we considered it safe to use a fairly crude method of interpolation. Each quarterly interpolating index was multiplied by the ratio, for that year, of the Commerce index to the annual interpolating index. The interpolated Commerce price indexes derived in this way, with 1923 equal to 100, are given in Table D-2.

We did not, in most cases, make any attempt to improve on the Commerce indexes. The published export and import values were used[2] without the introduction of outside price data which might have improved the coverage or representativeness of the indexes. All the series were examined, however, by comparing them with price data or by making country breakdowns.

[1] Dudley J. Cowden, *Measures of Exports of the United States*, New York, 1931.
[2] From U.S. Department of Commerce, *Monthly Summary of Foreign Commerce of the United States,* various issues, 1924 to 1930.

TABLE D-1

PRICE INDEXES: DEPARTMENT OF COMMERCE AND NBER INTERPOLATING SERIES, ANNUAL DATA

(each year on previous year base)

	Crude Foodstuffs		Manufactured Foodstuffs		Crude Materials		Semi-manufactures		Manufactured Products	
	Comm.	NBER	Comm.	NBER	Comm.	NBER	Comm.	NBER	Comm.	NBER
1924	120	119	90	90	97	96	96	97	97	97
1925	122	125	69	68	123	127	104	103	108	108
1926	99	98	93	92	99	99	100	100	95	97
1927	93	93	119	122	84	82	99	98	96	96
1928	108	108	89	88	91	90	95	94	105	106
1929	94	93	86	85	93	92	103	103	91	90

SOURCE: For Commerce series see *Foreign Trade of the United States 1936–1949.*

TABLE D–2

QUARTERLY PRICE INDEXES FOR U.S. IMPORTS
(1923 = 100)

		Crude Food-stuffs	Manufactured Foodstuffs	Crude Materials	Semi-manufactures	Manufactured Products
1924	I	103	103	103	97	94
	II	119	94	99	98	95
	III	119	74	95	94	99
	IV	141	83	96	95	102
1925	I	155	66	104	100	104
	II	145	70	120	101	105
	III	142	61	119	99	106
	IV	143	55	135	101	106
1926	I	147	56	139	100	105
	II	149	58	122	101	101
	III	146	57	104	99	98
	IV	140	62	106	100	96
1927	I	141	71	102	101	94
	II	134	71	100	100	96
	III	133	67	100	98	96
	IV	134	65	95	97	99
1928	I	143	63	100	96	99
	II	148	66	94	94	100
	III	150	60	90	93	103
	IV	143	54	81	93	103
1929	I	142	52	85	95	101
	II	144	54	86	100	94
	III	138	53	83	97	88
	IV	128	54	83	96	87

Tables D-3 to D-7 show the list of commodities included in our interpolating indexes, the extent to which they cover the commodities in the
Commerce indexes, and the extent to which they cover all of the commodities in each economic class. Notes to these tables indicate differences
in composition between the Commerce indexes and ours and describe
peculiarities and inadequacies in the individual commodity data.

TABLE D-3

VALUE OF COMMODITIES IN NBER INTERPOLATING INDEXES, CRUDE FOODSTUFFS

(in thousands of dollars)

	1923	1924	1925	1926	1927	1928	1929
A. NBER covered items							
Wheat	19,229	15,590	19,343	19,553	15,344	22,040	16,219
Bananas	19,739	22,074	29,693	31,684	34,269	35,381	36,048
Cocoa or cacao beans	33,807	29,425	38,246	42,749	56,816	47,205	49,493
Coffee from Brazil	116,086	158,007	184,793	199,663	164,773	189,839	178,356
Coffee from Colombia	37,325	49,255	54,915	74,279	65,585	69,592	78,811
Coffee from Venezuela	8,569	12,844	13,364	12,829	9,621	12,190	13,799
Coffee from Mexico	6,177	5,070	7,049	7,206	6,162	10,193	7,858
Tea from UK	5,482	7,384	9,334	8,173	8,267	8,534	8,162
Tea from British East Indies	7,947	8,466	9,249	9,143	8,680	9,015	8,739
Tea from Japan	9,172	6,202	6,456	6,898	5,890	5,250	5,152
B. Total of covered commodities	263,533	314,317	372,442	412,177	375,407	409,239	402,637
C. Total of items in Commerce index	279,865	328,276	399,882	445,139	412,316	440,469	432,506
D. Total crude foodstuffs	363,032	424,873	494,800	539,818	504,686	549,891	538,560
B. as % of C.	94.2	95.7	93.1	92.6	91.0	92.9	93.1
B. as % of D.	72.6	74.0	75.3	76.4	74.4	74.4	74.8

Notes to Table D-3

Commerce indexes include the following additional items:

1924–29: cream, fresh; milk, fresh; fresh water fish and eels; halibut, fresh or frozen; lobsters, not canned; beans, dried; potatoes,white or Irish; turnips; onions; grapes; coconuts in the shell; walnuts, not shelled; cloves, unground; pepper, unground, white.

1925–1929: smelts, fresh or frozen; tuna fish, fresh or frozen; tomatoes, natural state.

1926–1929: chestnuts.

Commerce excludes coffee from Venezuela and Mexico.

As indicated, the NBER indexes divide tea by country instead of using total tea as Commerce does. This was done because of large and persistent differences among teas imported from the three countries, apparently due to differences in grade or type of tea and possibly to differences in transport cost.

Unit values for bananas, which are used in both Commerce and NBER indexes, do not inspire much confidence. They remained quite stable from 1925 through 1929 while the BLS price series for bananas of a specific size and country of origin, at New York, fell by more than a quarter. Furthermore, the import unit values differ among themselves in both level and movement. There are several plausible explanations for these differences. A letter from the BLS suggests that changes in the unit value reflect changes in the average size of bunches of bananas, since prices are in terms of dollars per bunch. A letter from the Commerce Dept. points out this possibility and the additional fact that bananas imported from foreign branches or subsidiaries of American firms have often "been declared at arbitrarily fixed prices for a good many years."

Despite large differences in the levels of unit values, by country of origin, the total unit value gives a fairly good representation of the individual country unit value series.

TABLE D-4

VALUE OF COMMODITIES IN NBER INTERPOLATING INDEXES, MANUFACTURED FOODSTUFFS

(in thousands of dollars)

	1923	1924	1925	1926	1927	1928	1929
A. NBER covered items							
Canned and preserved meats	1,295	1,697					
Canned meats	10,427	959	1,189	2,743	4,311	6,644	11,433
Cheese from Italy	5,687	8,906	8,576	10,348	12,176	12,833	10,130
Cheese from Switzerland	1,588	4,809	5,571	5,218	5,938	5,963	6,051
Cheese from France	2,581	1,400	1,548	1,349	1,414	1,758	1,934
Sardines	2,299	4,490	3,451	4,500	5,235	5,139	5,521
Crabmeat	1,716	1,493	3,112	3,770	3,784	5,042	5,112
Canned tomatoes	12,218	2,320	4,076	4,082	5,306	5,198	9,005
Olive oil	380,090	12,585	15,656	13,901	17,577	14,951	16,408
Sugar (cane)	5,613	363,513	246,008	232,530	258,158	207,026	209,277
Almonds, shelled	4,219	5,855	6,342	7,709	6,470	5,869	6,437
Walnuts, shelled	2,989	4,868	6,636	5,688	6,454	4,210	4,944
Wheat by-products		4,968	6,109	4,429	5,104	8,019	7,398
B. Total of covered commodities	430,722	416,904	308,274	296,267	331,927	282,652	293,650
C. Total of items in Commerce index	445,002	434,921	330,624	320,036	358,930	309,638	322,226
D. Total manufactured foods	530,208	521,600	433,246	417,817	450,849	405,815	423,622
B. as % of C.	96.8	95.9	93.2	92.6	92.5	91.3	91.1
B. as % of D.	81.2	79.9	71.2	70.9	73.6	69.7	69.3

Notes to Table D-4

Commerce indexes include the following additional items:

1924–29: beef, fresh; veal, fresh (beef and veal combined, 1924–25); butter; lobsters, canned; currants; dates; coconut meat, dessicated or prepared, free; coconut meat, dessicated or prepared, dutiable.

1925–29: egg yolk, dried; egg albumen, dried; tomato paste.

1929: pork hams; pork shoulders; bacon; herring, pickled or salted.

As indicated, NBER indexes separate cheese by country, whereas Commerce has a total cheese series.

Commerce separates wheat by-products into those of "direct importation" and those "withdrawn from bonded mills" for 1926–29; it uses the combined series only for 1924–25.

Commerce separates olive oil into "packages less than 40 lbs." and "packages 40 lbs. or over;" it separates free cane sugar from dutiable. We did not follow Commerce on this last breakdown because it is an artificial distinction created by the tariff act rather than one based on differences in the type or grade of commodity. The shift brought about by the tariff differential from lower priced (in country of origin) Cuban sugar to higher priced (in country of origin) Philippine sugar represented a rise in the price paid by the United States rather than a change in taste.

TABLE D–5

VALUE OF COMMODITIES IN NBER INTERPOLATING INDEXES, CRUDE MATERIALS

(in thousands of dollars)

	1923	1924	1925	1926	1927	1928	1929
A. NBER covered items							
Cattle hides, wet salted (over 25 lbs.)	39,895	22,240	23,353	19,863	37,085	57,456	39,819
Goat and kid skins, dry or dry-salted	32,845	18,444	31,103	35,643	32,058	37,050	42,878
Sheep and lamb skins	17,587	16,039	23,459	18,791	16,148	20,731	21,905
Coney and rabbit furs				24,403	26,314	20,270	19,611
Rubber, crude or milk of	185,060	174,231	429,705	505,818	339,859	244,855	240,966
Copra	13,477	12,857	18,081	23,513	20,641	22,778	24,195
Flaxseed	48,957	30,038	39,683	41,383	38,059	31,245	46,549
Tobacco leaf for cigar wrappers	18,134	15,100	15,077	14,747	12,438	13,630	15,750
Cigar leaf (filler), unstemmed	11,544	11,315	8,067	7,266	6,460	5,765	5,010
Cigar leaf (filler), stemmed	12,609	14,911	14,244	15,395	13,719	13,996	13,883
Cigarette leaf	13,773	33,134	33,281	22,519	41,207	20,614	18,072
Cotton, long staple	17,163	23,201	20,500	18,582	19,624	14,178	17,687
Cotton, short staple	32,280	25,396	32,275	27,657	26,044	28,620	35,646
Jute	10,235	7,235	11,997	13,968	11,319	8,773	8,058
Sisal and henequen	10,923	16,274	23,329	21,762	18,219	19,533	21,088
Manila or abaca	13,785	14,345	18,195	18,282	13,138	9,588	13,496
Carpet wool, dutiable: On the skin or in the grease and washed and scoured	23,820	30,555	29,795	16,119	22,402	22,807	27,476
On the skin or in the grease only		24,011					
Carpet wool, free: On the skin or in the grease and washed and scoured	2,484	3,619	4,688	3,400	2,217	3,097	4,424
On the skin or in the grease only		2,574					
Clothing wool: On the skin or in the grease and washed and scoured	11,406	8,129	8,376	5,163	5,657	7,450	6,453
On the skin or in the grease only		5,104					
Combing wool: On the skin or in the grease and washed and scoured	89,181	48,393	79,132	64,798	37,451	30,814	31,266
On the skin or in the grease only		44,900					
Raw silk from Japan	275,874	285,923	317,753	328,903	334,160	318,124	356,122
Raw silk from China	83,395	26,131	54,339	50,118	49,775	45,949	61,597

Crude petroleum from:							
Venezuela			1,585	6,870	14,946	21,275	32,609
Colombia				7,264	13,559	17,210	18,490
Netherlands W. Indies			4,740	9,690	14,229	27,370	12,165
Mexico			64,646	46,778	30,442	19,400	11,388
All countries	53,882	73,842	75,407				
Copper ore	11,735	12,807	13,582	13,452	10,757	11,589	15,358
	910,052	1,320,985	1,382,147				
B. Total of covered commodities	1,030,044	924,159	1,325,421	1,350,480	1,207,927	1,094,167	1,161,961
C. Total items in Commerce index	1,139,743	1,051,584	1,502,487	1,550,906	1,370,541	1,257,495	1,351,774
D. Total crude materials	1,407,000	1,258,000	1,747,233	1,792,292	1,600,809	1,466,733	1,558,620
B. as % of C.	90.4	87.9	88.2	87.1	88.1	87.0	86.0
B. as % of D.	73.2	73.5	75.9	75.3	75.5	74.6	74.6

NBER index includes only carpet, clothing, and combing wool on the skin or in the grease, 1925–29, while Commerce combines these with corresponding wools washed and scoured. In 1924, both series use the combinations. The NBER index separates carpet wool, free, from carpet wool, dutiable, throughout.

NBER uses raw silk from China and raw silk from Japan as separate commodities. Commerce uses total raw silk.

Instead of the division by country for crude petroleum, Commerce uses total crude petroleum throughout as does NBER for 1924–25. The total petroleum series was separated by country of origin, because the unit values moved very differently from changes in domestic petroleum prices and from several of the country import unit value series. It seemed possible that these differences could be caused by shifts among the sources of petroleum, since there were some substantial differences in the level of unit values that were at least partly due to differences in specific gravity.

Commerce includes the following additional items:

1924–29: Cattle hides, dry or dry-salted; kip skins, wet-salted; calf skins, wet-salted; horse, colt, and ass hides, wet-salted; bones, hoofs, and horns, unmanufactured; mother of pearl; chicle, crude; gum arabic or senegal; cinchona bark or other from which quinine may be extracted; pyrethrum flowers; licorice root; castor beans; sugar beet seed; bulbs, hyacinth; vegetable ivory; flax, unmanufactured, hackled; flax, unmanufactured, all other; hemp, unmanufactured; kapok; istle or tampico; logs of fir, spruce, or western hemlock; cork wood or bark, unmanufactured; pulpwood, rough; pulpwood, peeled; rags for paper stock; anthracite coal; bituminous coal; china clay or Kaolin; pyrites or sulphide of iron; iron ore; manganese ore (dutiable); chrome ore or chromite; aluminum, bauxite, crude; copper concentrates; lead ore and matte; lead bullion and base bullion; nickel ore and matte; Kainite; manure salts. 1925–29: guano. 1927–29: platinum grains, nuggets, sponge, and scrap. 1928–29: furs, beaver. 1929: furs, fitch; furs, kolinski; furs, weasel; carnauba wax.

TABLE D-6

VALUE OF COMMODITIES IN NBER INTERPOLATING INDEXES, SEMIMANUFACTURES
(in thousands of dollars)

	1923	1924	1925	1926	1927	1928	1929
A. NBER covered items							
Bristles, sorted, bunched, or prepared	10,444	8,515	8,233	7,680	6,969	6,576	8,327
Shellac	22,955	13,139	10,164	10,515	10,395	10,210	12,789
Chinese wood oil or nut oil (tung oil)	13,397	11,092	11,386	9,148	11,810	13,419	14,972
Coconut oil, free	13,009	17,288	19,650	22,088	22,900	23,061	29,552
Palm oil	9,339	7,002	11,040	10,112	11,040	11,067	17,500
Rayon yarns, threads, or filaments	6,738	2,295	8,171	9,051	13,664	10,902	12,147
Sawed boards, planks, and deals—softwood	57,011	48,333	50,431	48,776	43,180	35,409	36,520
Wood pulp, mechanically ground	9,297	7,190	8,517	8,278	5,962	5,443	6,246
Chemical wood pulp:							
sulphite, unbleached	26,548	30,082	31,542	37,032	34,263	32,587	35,329
sulphite, bleached	22,246	21,006	22,528	23,678	24,225	23,368	25,339
sulphate (kraft pulp) unbleached	15,229	15,915	18,257	21,193	20,684	21,171	20,519
Diamonds, cut but not set	52,020	47,268	49,621	51,362	40,736	42,396	42,010
Pig iron	9,005	3,741	7,951	7,709	2,254	2,232	2,398
Ferromanganese and other manganese alloys	8,605	4,055	6,533	4,138	3,405	—	—
Aluminum metal, scrap, and alloys	8,518	6,307	10,180	17,108	15,316	7,736	8,973
Unrefined copper	56,564	59,462	48,870	56,101	51,954	67,595	104,306
Refined copper	19,120	18,556	13,831	23,336	13,105	12,634	23,757
Nickel, manufactures of	5,564	5,136	6,541	7,857	7,721	12,346	16,448
Nickel, alloys in pigs, ingots, and other forms		4,950					
Tin in bars, blocks, and pigs	61,092	68,953	95,121	104,793	100,865	86,983	91,839
Dead or creosote oil	10,071	13,464	10,973	11,720	15,437	13,928	10,119
Sodium nitrate	41,956	47,169	52,531	42,781	30,132	36,991	34,913
B. Total of covered commodities	478,728	455,968	502,071	534,456	486,017	476,054	554,003
C. Total items in Commerce index	501,049	487,603	548,686	582,543	541,524	550,449	634,532
D. Total semimanufactures	720,729	655,887	768,947	804,333	749,801	762,832	885,051
B. as % of C	95.5	93.5	91.5	91.7	89.7	86.5	87.3
B. as % of D	66.4	69.5	65.3	66.4	64.8	62.4	62.6

APPENDIX D

NOTES TO TABLE D-6

Commerce includes the following additional items:

1924–29: potassium carbonate; potassium hydroxide (caustic potash); sodium cyanide; lithopone and zinc pigments, including zinc oxide and leaded zinc; ammonium sulphate; calcium cyanide; bone ash, dust, and meal; chloride of potash, crude; potassium sulphate, crude; sole leather; calf and kip upper leather; goat and kid leather; cod oil and cod-liver oil (combined, 1924–28 and separately for 1929); casein or lactarene; camphor, crude; quebracho extract; cotton yarns, bleached, dyed, etc.; wool noils; poles, telegraph, telephone, etc.; sawed boards and lumber, hardwood; cork waste and shavings; marble, onyx, and breccia, in blocks; cement, hydraulic; steel ingots; tinplate, terneplate and taggers' tin; antimony, liquidated, regulus; coal tar colors, dyes, etc.; arsenious or white arsenic; tartaric acid; argols and wine lees.

1925–29: potassium chlorate and perchlorate; olive oil, sulphured or foots.

1926–29: iodine, crude.

1927–29: calf and kip lining leather; glycerin, crude; ferromanganese and other manganese alloys.

1928–29: platinum ingots, bars, etc.

1929: perilla oil; asbestos, mill fiber; asbestos, stucco and other.

Commerce excludes the following items: bristles, sorted, bunched, or prepared; coconut oil, free; and rayon yarns, threads, or filaments.

TABLE D-7

VALUE OF COMMODITIES IN NBER INTERPOLATING INDEXES, MANUFACTURED PRODUCTS
(in thousands of dollars)

	1923	1924	1925	1926	1927	1928	1929
A. NBER covered items							
Women's and children's gloves in leather	6,772	6,389	7,352	8,764	10,367	10,982	16,432
Cigars and cheroots, free	5,543	4,692	5,133	5,047	4,142	4,190	3,341
Cigars and cheroots, dutiable	3,716	3,383	4,331	3,309	3,742	3,350	3,111
Cotton knit gloves	4,034	4,247	5,488	6,514	6,544	8,230	5,809
Burlaps	66,971	59,396	85,028	82,238	67,249	80,087	77,377
Flax, hemp, and ramie, plain woven fabrics less than 9½ oz. per sq. yd.	6,344	9,769	6,618	3,925	4,942	4,842	5,671
Other woven fabrics, flax chief value	10,161	15,372	11,578	9,764	9,411	7,523	7,390
Woolens weighing over 4 oz. per sq. yd.	19,155	17,140	17,353	16,766	16,992	14,169	13,977
Woolens and worsteds over 4 oz. per sq. yd.	18,778	18,778					
Carpets, rugs, oriental, axminster, etc.:							
from Persia	4,371	4,585	6,059	7,356	6,845	8,275	7,906
from China	3,264	4,578	5,410	5,485	4,042	2,960	2,983
Laths	9,332	10,152	10,608	9,748	7,250	6,322	3,562
Shingles	9,812	9,328	9,992	8,907	6,693	7,657	6,850
Standard newsprint	98,021	101,297	103,717	123,982	131,489	139,433	144,493
Gasoline and naptha	14,859	13,135	15,978	24,553	22,773	31,516	43,335
B. Total of covered commodities	262,355	265,101	294,645	316,358	302,481	329,536	342,237
C. Total items in Commerce index	325,445	337,151	368,816	394,986	385,871	408,641	442,701
D. Total finished manufactures	771,299	749,346	794,316	876,628	878,597	906,173	993,508
B. as % of C	80.6	78.6	79.9	80.1	78.4	80.6	77.3
B. as % of D	34.0	35.4	37.1	36.1	38.4	36.4	34.4

NOTES TO TABLE D-7

Commerce includes the following additional items:

1924–29: footwear with textile uppers, from Czechoslovakia; footwear with textile uppers, from Japan; camphor, refined, and camphor, synthetic (combined, 1924; separate, 1925–29); citronella and lemon grass oil; cotton sewing thread; cotton cloth, bleached; cotton cloth, printed, dyed, colored, etc.; jute bags or sacks; flax fabrics, 4 to 12 oz. per square yard; handkerchiefs, linen, not embroidered or of lace; handkerchiefs, of lace or embroidered; binding twine; wool hosiery; silk bolting cloths; silk pile fabrics; Kraft wrapping paper (combined with "all other wrapping paper" in 1924); pulp board in rolls; cigarette paper, books, etc.; plate glass; flat wire and steel strip n.e.s.; nails (nails and screws after 1925); electric lamps other than carbon; quinine sulphate; firecrackers; soap, castile; golf balls; other balls for games; watches and watch movements; tooth brushes.

1924–26: table damask and manufactures.

1925–29: geranium oil; worsted fabrics over 4 oz. per square yard; tracing cloths; menthol; soap, toilet.

1927–29: china and porcelain table and kitchen ware, domestic and household, from Germany; same, from Japan; earthenware crockery, and stoneware, table, toilet, and kitchen ware, domestic and household, from U.K.; same, from Japan; barbed wire; glycerine, refined.

Commerce excludes: cigars and cheroots, free; cigars and cheroots, dutiable.

The NBER index separated carpets and rugs from Persia and China because the increase in unit value of total carpets and rugs seemed to arise from a shift in type from Chinese and other lower priced rugs to the more expensive Persian rugs.

Cotton cloth was omitted from the NBER interpolating index because the import unit values, even those for imports from the U.K. alone, moved so differently from both U.S. and U.K. prices, and because there were such large differences among the import unit value changes for the various countries of origin.

Silk fabrics, broad, except pile fabrics were not used in the NBER index because the steep decline in their unit values would have caused the index to fall steadily relative to the Commerce index. On the other hand, gasoline, naptha, etc. were added to the NBER index, despite great disparities in the unit value movements of the country-of-origin components, and between the total and the components, in order to give the interpolating series a shape closer to that of the Commerce index.

We omitted watches and watch movements from the NBER index because our study of the earlier data showed that quality changes were often the predominant causes of the unit value changes in the total group.

It is clear that the index for this group is the least satisfactory of the five. The coverage is low, never rising above 40 per cent, and more than half of the coverage is provided by two items, burlap and newsprint, which could be considered semimanufactures, and were in fact removed from the manufactured group in the Federal Reserve Bank study, *The Pattern of United States Import Trade Since 1923*, by John H. Adler, Eugene R. Schlesinger, and Evelyn Van Westerborg.

Appendix E

Data on Variability, Sampling Error, and Coverage

The first part of this Appendix presents the basic data on the variability of price movements within and among minor classes and estimates of sampling error for minor and major classes. The second contains detailed information on coverage and shifts in coverage.

VARIABILITY AND SAMPLING ERRORS

Two assumptions must be kept in mind as the basis for these measurements and their interpretation. One is that the commodities which are covered in the minor class indexes are completely covered—the prices for individual commodities are assumed to be known precisely and not subject to sampling error. The other is that commodities and minor classes have been selected for the sample randomly, either with equal probabilities or with probability proportional to size.

Table E-1 gives weighted and unweighted standard deviations for minor classes, where they were computed. They could not be calculated for uncovered classes or for classes in which there was only one covered commodity. The latter are divided into two groups: those with only one commodity, for which, by our assumption, there is no variance, and those with one covered commodity and one or more uncovered ones, for which we cannot measure the variance. These standard deviations are measures of the homogeneity of classes rather than of the accuracy of the indexes, although homogeneity does, of course, affect accuracy. They are descriptive of the covered commodities within each class and do not require any assumption of randomness in the sampling procedure. A large standard deviation implies a heterogeneous stratum but it may not, if coverage is high, imply inaccuracy in the estimation of the mean. The two standard deviations in Table E-1 are:

$$\text{Unweighted: } \sigma_u = \sqrt{\frac{\Sigma\left(\frac{P_1}{P_0}\right)^2}{N} - \left(\frac{\Sigma\frac{P_1}{P_0}}{N}\right)^2}$$

$$\text{Weighted: } \sigma_w = \sqrt{\frac{\Sigma P_0 Q_0\left(\frac{P_1}{P_0}\right)^2}{\Sigma P_0 Q_0} - \left(\frac{\Sigma P_1 Q_0}{\Sigma P_0 Q_0}\right)^2}$$

The σ_u is appropriate for an unweighted index or for an assumption that the commodity weights among the covered items are irrelevant to the uncovered ones; that is, each commodity, no matter how large, is only a single observation of the mean. The weighted standard deviation is appropriate for use with a weighted index and, in general, for the assumption that the importance of different price behavior patterns in the uncovered items would match that among the covered commodities. Equality of the two standard deviations implies no correlation between the weight or importance of a commodity and its distance from the mean. The usual case—namely that σ_u is greater than σ_w means that the correlation is negative; and σ_w greater than σ_u implies that the importance of a commodity is positively correlated with exceptional behavior (distance from the mean).

Standard errors of the mean (the mean being the Laspeyres price index) are given in Table E-2. These do involve inference from the standard deviations. They are measures of the accuracy of the minor class indexes, under the assumption that the commodities sampled are representative of all commodities in their groups. In other words, samples are treated as if they had been drawn randomly. Since only the weighted standard errors are shown here, the assumption implied is that the sample was drawn with probability proportional to size (value) rather than, as in the unweighted indexes, equal probability of representation for each commodity.

Two sets of standard errors are computed. The first, with no finite sampling adjustment, takes account of the number of commodities drawn from each class but not of the proportion of total value covered. It treats the samples as if they included only a small part of the whole class. It answers the question, "How accurate an estimate of the mean could be made with a sample of this size from a large population?" The second set takes account not only of the number of items but also of their share in the total value of the class. It makes use of the fact (or assumption) that the mean is known precisely for a substantial part of the total (the sample) and that, in effect, the estimation applies only to the remaining, often small, fraction of the total value.

The two measures of standard error can be described in terms of the standard deviations of Table E-1, where N is the number of covered commodities in the minor class.

Without finite sampling adjustment:

$$\sigma_m \text{ (unadjusted)} = \frac{\sigma_w}{\sqrt{N-1}}$$

With finite sampling adjustment (where f is the coverage ratio):

$$\sigma_m \text{ (adjusted)} = \frac{\sigma_w}{\sqrt{N-1}} \sqrt{1-f}$$

Coefficients of variation, presented in Table E-3, are the ratios of standard errors to the means they apply to. In this case the means are the Laspeyres price indexes. Only the weighted measures are shown, but the relationship between weighted and unweighted coefficients would be the same as in Table E-1.

The variance of a major class mean can be calculated from the variance within minor classes (already computed) and the variance among minor classes, as follows:

$$Var_{\bar{\bar{Y}}} = \frac{1}{n-1}\left[\left(\frac{V-v}{V}\right)\sum_{i=1}^{n}\frac{V_i(\bar{Y}_i-\bar{\bar{Y}})^2}{v} + \sum_{i=1}^{n}\frac{1}{m_i}\cdot\frac{V_i}{v}\left(\frac{V_i-v_i}{V}\right)S_i^2\right]$$

where:

n = number of sampled minor classes

N = number of minor classes

m_i = number of sampled commodities in minor class i

M_i = number of commodities in minor class i

V_{ij} = value of commodity j in minor class i

v_i = value of sampled commodities in minor class $i = \sum_{j=1}^{m_i} V_{ij}$

V_i = value of all commodities in minor class $i = \sum_{j=1}^{M_i} V_{ij}$

v = value of sampled minor classes $= \sum_{i=1}^{n} V_i$

V = value of all minor classes $= \sum_{i=1}^{N} V_i$

Y_{ij} = value of price relative for commodity j in minor class i

$\bar{Y}_i$ = means of minor class $i = \sum_{j=1}^{m_i}\frac{V_{ij} Y_{ij}}{v_i}$

$\bar{\bar{Y}}$ = major class mean $= \sum_{i=1}^{n}\frac{V_i \bar{Y}_i}{v}$

S_i^2 = minor class variance $= \frac{1}{v_i}\sum_{j=1}^{m_i} V_{ij}(Y_{ij}-\bar{Y}_i)^2$

The S_i^2 is the square of the weighted standard deviation of Table E-1.

These computations are carried out in Table E-4 and the coefficients of variation derived from these variances are shown in Chapter 5, Table 18.

MEASURES OF COVERAGE AND CHANGE IN COVERAGE

Tables E-5 through E-8 give basic data on coverage for all major and intermediate classes. The figures show, for the earliest year of each period, the ratio of the value of covered commodities to the value of all commodities in the class. For the last year of each period they show the ratio of the value of those commodities which were covered in the first year to the value of all the commodities which were part of the class in the first year. Thus, for within-period comparisons, changes in coverage due to increasing availability of data are eliminated.

For each period, the table reveals whether the commodities covered in the initial year grew in value at a faster or slower rate than the uncovered ones. In order to see the trend of coverage as a whole (not just that for fixed groups of commodities) one must follow the movement from the right-hand column of one period to the right-hand column of the next. Export Class 115 in Table E-5 illustrates the two uses of the table. By 1889, the commodities covered in 1879 had fallen from 91 to 89 per cent of the total value of the class. But those commodities which actually were covered in 1889 formed 97 per cent of the total value of the class in that year.

It should be noted that these tables show the proportion of total value in covered commodities, not that contained in covered minor classes. These changes in coverage do not indicate the possibility of bias in the total or major class indexes, because they include the effects of both shifts in the weight or importance of minor classes and shifts within them. Only the latter, as is pointed out in Chapter 5, would suggest bias because they indicate that covered commodities possessed different characteristics (possibly different price changes) from uncovered products. Tables E-9 through E-12 are intended to reveal such shifts. They show the actual end-year coverage ratios for commodities covered in the initial year (first columns of Tables E-5 through E-8) as percentages of the ratios that would have existed if values of covered and uncovered items had grown at the same rate within each minor class.[1] Thus, a ratio over 100 per cent indicates that covered commodities grew at a more rapid rate than uncovered commodities.

[1] The computation of the hypothetical ratios is performed by applying the initial year coverage ratio to the end-year value for each minor class.

TABLE E-1

STANDARD DEVIATIONS FOR MINOR CLASS PRICE INDEXES

Minor Class	Weighted Standard Deviations				Unweighted Standard Deviations			
	1879	1889	1899	1913	1879	1889	1899	1913
				A. EXPORTS				
001	.057	.076	.092	.091	.152	.195	.163	.181
002a								
003b								
004	c	c	c	b	c	c	c	b
005	.133	.052	.041	.053	.107	.113	.077	.091
006	.067	.294	.216	.090	.081	.258	.215	.107
007	d	d	d	.075	d	d	d	.220
008	0	.029	.079	.181	0	.057	.080	.207
009	.029	.032	.066	.087	.047	.031	.064	.206
010a								
011	.078	.030	.043	.034	.119	.068	.153	.114
012	.035	0	.032	.029	.037	0	.034	.040
013	.027	.022	.073	.008	.058	.030	.191	.017
014	.040	.038	.083	.058	.119	.133	.263	.185
015	.057	.268	.110	.047	.065	.270	.108	.044
016	c	c	d	.079	c	c	d	.087
017a								
018	d	d	.072	.100	d	d	.068	.102
019	.077	.150	.235	.051	.077	.196	.224	.091
020a								
021	b	b	b	.320	b	b	b	.326
022	0	.019	d	d	0	.033	d	d
023	b	.124	.063	b	b	.259	.096	b
024	d	.094	.066	.118	d	.117	.094	.300
025	b	d	d	d	b	d	d	d
026	.045	.304	.118	.122	.159	.310	.112	.187
027	b	b	b	.129	b	b	b	.153
028	d	.039	.081	.135	d	.040	.081	.129
029	d	d	d	.083	d	d	d	.120
030b								
031	c	c	c	a	c	c	c	a
032	.122	.304	.121	.424	.233	.270	.115	.488
033	.254	.117	.045	.010	.257	.155	.144	.016
034	.060	.288	b	b	.068	.393	b	b
035	c	c	b	.494	c	c	b	.498
036	a	a	a	.242	a	a	a	.539
037	a	.169	.248	a	a	.337	.248	a
038	b	d	.196	.373	b	d	.200	.403
039	.385	.222	.052	.265	.438	.289	.094	.203
040	.326	.030	.378	.315	.297	.031	.390	.293
041	.158	.008	.201	.082	.166	.009	.300	.173
042	.024	b	.009	b	.148	b	.071	b
043	c	c	b	.007	c	c	b	.005
044	.012	.089	.055	.057	.010	.098	.055	.052
045	.046	.148	.138	.144	.053	.183	.201	.207
046	a	b	c	c	a	b	c	c
047	c	c	c	b	c	c	c	b

(continued)

Minor Class	Weighted Standard Deviations				Unweighted Standard Deviations			
	1879	1889	1899	1913	1879	1889	1899	1913
048	a	d	d	.003	a	d	d	0
049	c	a	a	b	c	a	a	b
050a								
051a								
052	.030	.046	.163	.180	.032	.070	.238	.207
053	.017	.073	.114	.199	.049	.200	.129	.175
054	c	c	b	.221	c	c	b	.225
055	a	a	d	.020	a	a	d	.018
056a								
057	.144	.194	.349	.010	.145	.195	.080	.010
058	c	c	b	b	c	c	b	b
059b								
060	c	b	b	.018	c	b	b	.021
061	.079	.093	.181	.122	.228	.158	.187	.120
062	c	c	c	.098	c	c	c	.128
063	a	a	d	d	a	a	d	d
064	a	a	.168	.173	a	a	.169	.188
065a								
066	.210	.056	.095	.017	.345	.230	.157	.140
067	a	a	a	.049	a	a	a	.105
068	c	a	b	b	c	a	b	b
069	.305	.191	.119	.102	.426	.303	.122	.113
070	.218	.251	.127	.106	.303	.246	.157	.106
071	.161	.155	.150	.211	.152	.158	.336	.220
072	c	c	b	b	c	c	b	b
073	a	b	b	.174	a	b	b	.176
074	a	a	.325	.345	a	a	.336	.362
075	.174	.065	.137	.080	.185	.064	.237	.092
076	c	c	c	.084	c	c	c	.159
077a								

B. IMPORTS

Minor Class	1879	1889	1899	1913	1879	1889	1899	1913
001	d	.254	.007	.051	d	.226	.029	.107
002	a	.089	.032	.346	a	.154	.067	.349
003	c	c	c	b	c	c	c	b
004	.031	.038	.090	.045	.278	.046	.136	.113
005	.168	.121	.195	.174	.181	.121	.265	.160
006	b	.413	.622	.315	b	.533	.578	.362
007	.173	.099	.088	.295	.165	.119	.105	.265
008	b	b	b	.114	b	b	b	.119
009b								
010b								
011	c	b	b	.145	c	b	b	.123
012	.019	0	.011	.064	.089	.014	.021	.093
013	.237	.115	.249	.123	.237	.126	.276	.129
014	.041	.056	.129	.169	.109	.084	.130	.274
015	c	.120	.250	.138	c	.120	.238	.135
016	.037	b	b	.046	.042	b	b	.190
017	c	a	d	.011	c	a	d	.013

(continued)

TABLE E-1 (continued)

Minor Class	Weighted Standard Deviations				Unweighted Standard Deviations			
	1879	1889	1899	1913	1879	1889	1899	1913
018	c	c	.222	b	c	c	.222	b
019	.024	.121	.018	d	.055	.187	.101	d
020	a	d	b	c	a	d	b	c
021	.191	.058	.147	.072	.270	.073	.127	.142
022	b	.147	.083	.290	b	.155	.099	.275
023	c	b	b	c	c	b	b	c
024	b	b	.194	.051	b	b	.225	.070
025	d	d	d	.146	d	d	d	.149
026	b	d	.162	.231	b	d	.176	.295
027	b	a	a	.137	b	a	a	.295
028	a	a	d	d	a	a	d	d
029	b	b	b	.028	b	b	b	.030
030[a]								
031	c	a	.094	1.246	c	a	.126	1.273
032	c	b	d	.106	c	b	d	.107
033	b	b	.012	.136	b	b	.015	.277
034	a	a	d	b	a	a	d	b
035	c	a	a	a	c	a	a	a
036	b	b	d	.130	b	b	d	.819
037[a]								
038	b	b	b	.271	b	b	b	.305
039	.135	d	d	.322	.140	d	d	.241
040	.520	.139	.206	.332	.676	.189	.261	.386
041	.216	.476	.340	.087	.210	.450	.284	.115
042	c	c	c	c	c	c	c	c
043	c	d	d	.196	c	d	d	.264
044	.205	d	d	.563	.223	d	d	1.338
045[b]								
046	c	b	.035	.012	c	b	.038	.012
047	a	a	.125	.101	a	a	.118	.118
048	c	b	b	b	c	b	b	b
049	c	b	b	b	c	b	b	b
050	c	b	.118	.185	c	b	.155	.197
051	.260	.112	.215	.344	.275	.119	.167	.310
052	c	a	d	.202	c	a	d	.178
053	.056	.035	.069	.074	.059	.195	.121	.133
054	b	.072	.060	.019	b	.102	.088	.028
055	b	d	c	b	b	d	c	b
056	.019	.154	.068	.119	.025	.147	.066	.170
057	b	d	d	b	b	d	d	b
058	c	a	d	.024	c	a	d	.026
059	.065	.068	.136	.077	.063	.093	.123	.085
060[a]								
061[a]								
062	.210	.174	.131	.108	.211	.173	.124	.142
063	d	d	d	.113	d	d	d	.245
064	a	a	.205	.107	a	a	.206	.107
065	c	b	b	.030	c	b	b	.042

(continued)

TABLE E–1 (concluded)

Minor Class	Weighted Standard Deviations				Unweighted Standard Deviations			
	1879	1889	1899	1913	1879	1889	1899	1913
066	a	a	.108	.023	a	a	.165	.094
067	b	b	d	d	b	b	d	d
068	c	c	c	b	c	c	c	b
069	c	c	a	d	c	c	a	d
070	c	b	b	b	c	b	b	b
071	c	c	c	b	c	c	c	b
072	c	c	d	d	c	c	d	d
073	d	d	a	d	d	d	a	d
074	c	.268	.153	.379	c	.296	.147	.651
075	b	.136	.018	d	b	.169	.031	d
076	.261	.390	.155	.180	.296	.335	.170	.230
077	a	.174	.221	.342	a	.244	.357	.590
078	.117	.108	.224	.124	.162	.176	.301	.256
079	a	a	d	d	a	a	d	d
080	c	b	b	d	c	b	b	d
081	.142	.188	.091	.221	.256	.170	.150	.388
082	.206	.233	.151	.147	.266	.286	.259	.144
083a								
084	c	c	b	.013	c	c	b	.014
085	a	a	.134	.056	a	a	.170	.060
086	.206	.538	.314	.232	.234	.205	.388	.303
087	a	.076	.062	.056	a	.090	.177	.135
088a								
089a								
090a								
091	c	c	c	c	c	c	c	c

a Uncovered class.
b One-commodity class, complete coverage.
c Class not listed separately in this year.
d One covered commodity, incomplete coverage.

TABLE E–2

STANDARD ERRORS OF MEAN FOR WEIGHTED MINOR CLASS PRICE INDEXES

Minor Class	Without Finite Sampling Adjustment				With Finite Sampling Adjustment			
	1879	1889	1899	1913	1879	1889	1899	1913
	A. EXPORTS							
001	.033	.044	.053	.053	.001	.003	.006	.020
002a								
003	b	b	b	b	0	0	0	0
004	c	c	c	b	c	c	c	0
005	.067	.026	.020	.024	0	0	.001	0
006	.067	.208	.153	.064	.025	.092	.070	.039
007	d	d	d	.043	d	d	d	.025

(continued)

TABLE E–2 (continued)

Minor Class	Without Finite Sampling Adjustment				With Finite Sampling Adjustment			
	1879	1889	1899	1913	1879	1889	1899	1913
008	0	.017	.046	.128	0	0	0	0
009	.029	.022	.038	.035	0	.002	.006	.009
010a								
011	.078	.021	.025	.017	0	0	0	0
012	.035	0	.032	.021	.003	0	.012	0
013	.019	.022	.073	.008	.007	.012	.045	.004
014	.028	.022	.041	.026	.007	.003	.007	.006
015	.057	.268	.078	.033	0	0	0	0
016	c	c	d	.056	c	c	d	0
017a								
018	d	d	.051	.050	d	d	.037	.028
019	.077	.106	.166	.029	0	.019	.045	.005
020a								
021	b	b	b	.320	0	0	0	0
022	0	.019	d	d	0	0	d	d
023	b	.124	.063	b	0	0	0	0
024	d	.066	.066	.083	d	.020	.033	.034
025	b	d	d	d	0	d	d	d
026	.045	.304	.084	.086	0	.043	.011	.017
027	b	b	b	.129	0	0	0	.065
028	d	.039	.081	.078	d	.008	.029	.036
029	d	d	d	.048	d	d	d	.018
030	b	b	b	b	0	0	0	0
031	c	c	c	a	c	c	c	a
032	.122	.215	.086	.424	.038	.042	.016	.201
033	.254	.068	.023	.006	.067	.007	.003	.001
034	.060	.288	b	b	0	0	0	0
035	c	c	b	.494	c	c	0	0
036	a	a	a	.171	a	a	a	.133
037	a	.169	.248	a	a	0	0	a
038	b	d	.196	.264	0	d	.125	0
039	.385	.128	.030	.132	.258	.040	.011	.049
040	.230	.030	.378	.223	0	.007	.083	.034
041	.158	.008	.201	.082	0	0	.052	.023
042	.024	b	.009	b	0	0	0	0
043	c	c	b	.007	c	c	0	.002
044	.012	.089	.055	.033	.004	.036	.024	.018
045	.046	.105	.098	.083	.038	.031	.046	.039
046	a	b	c	c	a	b	c	c
047	c	c	c	b	c	c	c	0
048	a	d	d	.003	a	d	d	0
049	c	a	a	b	c	a	a	0
050a								
051a								
052	.030	.033	.073	.050	.020	.019	.026	.020
053	.017	.052	.081	.115	.013	.036	.056	.077
054	c	c	b	.221	c	c	0	0
055	a	a	d	.011	a	a	d	.008
056a								

(continued)

Table E–2 (continued)

Minor Class	Without Finite Sampling Adjustment				With Finite Sampling Adjustment			
	1879	1889	1899	1913	1879	1889	1899	1913
057	.144	.194	.349	.010	0	0	0	0
058	c	c	b	b	c	c	0	0
059	b	b	b	b	0	0	0	0
060	c	b	b	.018	c	0	0	0
061	.056	.065	.128	.070	.005	.003	.013	.013
062	c	c	c	.098	c	c	c	.043
063	a	a	d	d	a	a	d	d
064	a	a	.097	.061	a	a	.080	.050
065a								
066	.210	.056	.067	.006	.035	.008	009.	.001
067	a	a	a	.035	a	a	a	.020
068	c	a	b	b	c	a	0	0
069	.216	.191	.042	.031	.135	.067	0	0
070	.126	.125	.045	.025	.107	.084	.026	.013
071	.080	.078	.061	.041	.064	.056	.044	.027
072	c	c	b	b	c	c	0	0
073	a	b	b	.174	a	0	0	.006
074	a	a	.123	.096	a	a	.090	.062
075	.100	.037	.079	.030	.055	.028	.060	.021
076	c	c	c	.034	c	c	c	0
077a								
B. IMPORTS								
001	d	.147	.005	.051	d	.048	.001	.015
002	a	.089	.032	.155	a	0	.032	.057
003	c	c	c	b	c	c	c	0
004	.022	.038	.090	.026	.006	.003	0	0
005	.168	.121	.195	.123	0	.056	.133	.080
006	b	.292	.440	.182	0	.142	.232	.096
007	.077	.057	.062	.093	.031	.034	.038	.063
008	b	b	b	.057	0	0	0	.006
009	b	b	b	b	0	0	0	0
010	b	b	b	b	0	0	0	0
011	c	b	b	.084	c	0	0	.022
012	.019	0	.011	.026	.012	0	.007	.013
013	.237	.057	.112	.062	.197	.033	.060	.024
014	.041	.032	.129	.097	.017	.010	.064	.046
015	c	.120	.177	.098	c	.064	.126	.053
016	.037	b	b	.023	0	0	0	0
017	c	a	d	.011	c	a	d	.009
018	c	c	.222	b	c	c	0	0
019	.024	.121	.018	d	0	.028	.002	d
020	a	d	b	c	a	d	0	c
021	.135	.029	.066	.042	0	0	0	.025
022	b	.104	.059	.167	0	0	0	.070
023	c	b	b	c	c	0	0	c
024	b	b	.194	.036	0	0	0	.017
025	d	d	d	.146	d	d	d	.031
026	b	d	.115	.070	0	d	0	.010

(continued)

TABLE E–2 (continued)

Class Class	Without Finite Sampling Adjustment				With Finite Sampling Adjustment			
	1879	1889	1899	1913	1879	1889	1899	1913
027	b	a	a	.097	0	a	a	.051
028	a	a	d	d	a	a	d	d
029	b	b	b	.028	0	0	0	.022
030[a]								
031	c	a	.094	.881	c	a	.067	.568
032	c	b	d	.106	c	0	d	.046
033	b	b	.012	.096	0	0	0	.031
034	a	a	d	b	a	a	d	0
035	c	a	a	a	c	a	a	a
036	b	b	d	.092	0	0	d	.020
037[a]								
038	b	b	b	.192	0	0	0	0
039	.135	d	d	.114	0	d	d	.017
040	.520	.062	.092	.105	.215	.031	.053	.049
041	.153	.238	.170	.044	.041	.057	.090	.023
042	c	c	c	c	c	c	c	c
043	c	d	d	.196	c	d	d	.028
044	.205	d	d	.563	0	d	d	0
045	b	b	b	b	0	0	0	0
046	c	b	.035	.012	c	0	0	0
047	a	a	.072	.045	a	a	.055	.038
048	c	b	b	b	c	0	0	0
049	c	b	b	b	c	0	0	0
050	c	b	.118	.185	c	0	0	0
051	.184	.079	.107	.154	0	.014	.020	.053
052	c	a	d	.143	c	a	d	0
053	.056	.035	.034	.037	.024	.015	.017	.026
054	b	.051	.042	.013	0	0	0	0
055	b	d	c	b	0	d	c	0
056	.014	.109	.048	.084	.006	.059	.019	.038
057	b	d	d	b	0	d	d	0
058	c	a	d	.024	c	a	d	0
059	.046	.048	.078	.077	.020	.038	.033	.053
060[a]								
061[a]								
062	.210	.123	.093	.044	.128	.004	.072	.025
063	d	d	d	.113	d	d	d	.029
064	a	a	.205	.107	a	a	.167	.088
065	c	b	b	.022	c	0	0	0
066	a	a	.108	.016	a	a	.078	.013
067	b	b	d	d	0	0	d	d
068	c	c	c	b	c	c	c	0
069	c	c	a	d	c	c	a	d
070	c	b	b	b	c	0	0	0
071	c	c	c	b	c	c	c	0
072	c	c	d	d	c	c	d	d
073	d	d	a	d	d	d	a	d
074	c	.268	.108	.170	c	0	0	.048
075	b	.136	.018	d	0	.056	.004	d
076	.131	.195	.069	.090	.102	.162	.052	.078

(continued)

TABLE E–2 (concluded)

Minor Class	Without Finite Sampling Adjustment				With Finite Sampling Adjustment			
	1879	1889	1899	1913	1879	1889	1899	1913
077	a	.174	.156	.129	a	0	0	.022
078	.067	.076	.091	.051	.032	.040	.032	.014
079	a	a	d	d	a	a	d	d
080	c	b	b	d	c	0	0	d
081	.071	.094	.046	.099	.018	.030	.020	.056
082	.206	.164	.087	.073	.182	.123	.058	.063
083a								
084	c	c	b	.013	c	c	0	.006
085	a	a	.134	.032	a	a	.099	.008
086	.078	.170	.095	.053	.055	.106	.070	.032
087	a	.076	.062	.032	a	.047	.037	.027
088a								
089a								
090a								
091	c	c	c	c	c	c	c	c

a Uncovered class.
b One-commodity class, complete coverage.
c Class not listed separately in this year.
d One covered commodity, incomplete coverage.

TABLE E–3

COEFFICIENTS OF VARIATION FOR WEIGHTED MINOR CLASS INDEXES

Minor Class	Without Finite Sampling Adjustment				With Finite Sampling Adjustment			
	1879	1889	1899	1913	1879	1889	1899	1913
				A. EXPORTS				
001	.030	.060	.067	.064	.001	.004	.007	.025
002a								
003	b	b	b	b	0	0	0	0
004	c	c	c	b	c	c	c	0
005	.054	.023	.027	.031	0	0	.001	0
006	.053	.180	.182	.102	.020	.079	.083	.063
007	d	d	d	.053	d	d	d	.031
008	0	.015	.047	.146	0	0	0	0
009	.036	.021	.063	.038	0	.002	.010	.010
010a								
011	.083	.017	.045	.019	0	0	0	0
012	.037	0	.051	.032	.003	0	.018	0
013	.006	.019	.066	.013	.002	.010	.041	.006
014	.025	.017	.052	.030	.006	.002	.009	.007
015	.053	.189	.127	.051	0	0	0	0
016	c	c	d	.079	c	c	d	0
017a								
018	d	d	.050	.072	d	d	.036	.040

(continued)

TABLE E–3 (continued)

Minor Class	Without Finite Sampling Adjustment					With Finite Sampling Adjustment			
	1879	1889	1899	1913		1879	1889	1899	1913
019	.075	.075	.181	.052		0	.013	.049	.009
020a									
021	b	b	b	.245		0	0	0	0
022	0	.017	d	d		0	0	d	d
023	b	.084	.055	b		0	0	0	0
024	d	.082	.064	.236		d	.025	.032	.096
025	b	d	d	d		0	d	d	d
026	.037	.245	.083	.096		0	.035	.011	.019
027	b	b	b	.116		0	0	0	.058
028	d	.043	.105	.098		d	.009	.038	.045
029	d	d	d	.068		d	d	d	.025
030	b	b	b	b		0	0	0	0
031	c	c	c	a		c	c	c	a
032	.087	.149	.169	.416		.027	.029	.032	.197
033	.233	.061	.032	.008		.006	.006	.005	.001
034	.045	.234	b	b		0	0	0	0
035	c	c	b	.226		c	c	0	0
036	a	a	a	.079		a	a	a	.062
037	a	.152	.372	a		a	0	0	a
038	b	d	.293	.176		0	d	.187	0
039	.340	.121	.055	.148		.228	.038	.019	.055
040	.253	.030	.651	.319		0	.007	.144	.048
041	.144	.004	.244	.106		0	0	.063	.030
042	.024	b	.018	b		0	0	0	0
043	c	c	b	.015		c	c	0	.004
044	.012	.058	.079	.078		.004	.024	.035	.042
045	.057	.075	.099	.097		.047	.022	.047	.046
046	a	b	c	c		a	0	c	c
047	c	c	c	b		c	c	c	0
048	a	d	d	.006		a	d	d	0
049	c	a	a	b		c	a	a	0
050a									
051a									
052	.035	.031	.107	.091		.024	.018	.038	.036
053	.018	.044	.148	.187		.013	.031	.012	.126
054	c	c	b	.236		c	c	0	0
055	a	a	d	.023		a	a	d	.016
056a									
057	.169	.158	.423	.021		0	0	0	0
058	c	c	b	b		c	c	0	0
059	b	b	b	b		0	0	0	0
060	c	b	b	.018		c	0	0	0
061	.047	.057	.142	.089		.004	.003	.015	.016
062	c	c	c	.085		c	c	c	.038
063	a	a	d	d		a	a	d	d
064	a	a	.118	.099		a	a	.097	.081
065a									
066	.164	.082	.064	.006		.027	.012	.009	.001
067	a	a	a	.040		a	a	a	.022
068	c	a	b	b		c	a	0	0
069	.134	.155	.045	.053		.084	.054	0	0

(continued)

TABLE E–3 (continued)

Minor Class	Without Finite Sampling Adjustment				With Finite Sampling Adjustment			
	1879	1889	1899	1913	1879	1889	1899	1913
070	.094	.093	.057	.025	.080	.062	.033	.013
071	.080	.069	.060	.057	.064	.050	.033	.038
072	c	c	b	b	c	c	0	0
073	a	b	b	.177	a	0	0	.006
074	a	a	.137	.166	a	a	.101	.108
075	.087	.034	.098	.044	.048	.026	.074	.030
076	c	c	c	.039	c	c	c	0
077ᵃ								
				B. IMPORTS				
001	d	.129	.008	.050	d	.042	.002	.015
002	a	.112	.049	.238	a	0	.049	.088
003	c	c	c	b	c	c	c	0
004	.019	.030	.106	.030	.005	.003	0	0
005	.177	.133	.321	.158	0	.062	.218	.102
006	b	.248	.278	.173	0	.121	.147	.092
007	.067	.051	.083	.092	.027	.030	.050	.062
008	b	b	b	.097	0	0	0	.011
009	b	b	b	b	0	0	0	0
010	b	b	b	b	0	0	0	0
011	c	b	b	.111	c	0	0	.028
012	.017	0	.015	.038	.010	0	.010	.018
013	.430	.061	.117	.093	.357	.035	.063	.037
014	.030	.034	.199	.110	.013	.010	.098	.052
015	c	.140	.186	.174	c	.075	.132	.093
016	.027	b	b	.021	0	0	0	0
017	c	a	d	.025	c	a	d	.019
018	c	c	.189	b	c	c	0	0
019	.023	.083	.015	d	0	.019	.001	d
020	a	d	b	c	a	d	0	c
021	.151	.030	.063	.050	0	0	0	.031
022	b	.158	.058	.228	0	0	0	.096
023	c	b	b	c	c	0	0	c
024	b	b	.170	.060	0	0	0	.028
025	d	d	d	.154	d	d	d	.032
026	b	d	.163	.081	0	d	0	.011
027	b	a	a	.099	0	a	a	.052
028	a	a	d	d	a	a	d	d
029	b	b	b	.075	0	0	0	.058
030ᵃ								
031	c	a	.116	.350	c	a	.083	.226
032	c	b	d	.103	c	0	d	.044
033	b	b	.014	.172	0	0	0	.056
034	a	a	d	b	a	a	d	0
035	c	a	a	a	c	a	a	a
036	b	b	d	.037	0	0	d	.008
037ᵃ								
038	b	b	b	.261	0	0	0	0
039	.119	d	d	.140	0	d	d	.021
040	.304	.065	.138	.151	.126	.033	.080	.071
041	.138	.206	.255	.053	.037	.049	.135	.028

(continued)

TABLE E–3 (concluded)

Minor Class	Without Finite Sampling Adjustment				With Finite Sampling Adjustment			
	1879	1889	1899	1913	1879	1889	1899	1913
042	c	c	c	c	c	c	c	c
043	c	d	d	.581	c	d	d	.084
044	.140	d	d	.553	0	d	d	0
045	b	b	b	b	0	0	0	0
046	c	b	.052	.023	c	0	0	0
047	a	b	.096	.059	a	a	.073	.050
048	c	b	b	b	c	0	0	0
049	c	b	b	b	c	0	0	0
050	c	b	.196	.181	c	0	0	0
051	.221	.059	.124	.139	0	.011	.024	.048
052	c	a	d	.281	c	a	d	0
053	.045	.032	.040	.067	.019	.014	.020	.047
054	b	.040	.065	.019	0	0	0	0
055	b	d	c	b	0	d	c	0
056	.012	.106	.062	.122	.005	.057	.025	.055
057	b	d	d	b	0	d	d	0
058	c	a	d	.040	c	a	d	0
059	.041	.050	.080	.094	.018	.039	.033	.065
060[a]								
061[a]								
062	.167	.113	.109	.062	.101	.004	.085	.035
063	d	d	d	.188	d	d	d	.048
064	a	a	.427	.184	a	a	.347	.151
065	c	b	b	.036	c	0	0	0
066	a	a	.082	.031	a	a	.059	.024
067	b	b	d	d	0	0	d	d
068	c	c	c	b	c	c	c	0
069	c	c	a	d	c	c	a	d
070	c	b	b	b	c	0	0	0
071	c	c	c	b	c	c	c	0
072	c	c	d	d	c	c	d	d
073	d	d	a	d	d	d	a	d
074	c	.437	.112	.244	c	0	0	.070
075	b	.172	.022	d	0	.071	.005	d
076	.110	.195	.087	.188	.087	.162	.065	.164
077	a	.134	.171	.177	a	0	0	.030
078	.082	.093	.126	.048	.039	.048	.045	.014
079	a	a	d	d	a	a	d	d
080	c	b	b	d	c	0	0	d
081	.056	.108	.044	.136	.015	.034	.020	.077
082	.146	.112	.087	.097	.130	.084	.058	.084
083[a]								
084	c	c	b	.012	c	c	0	.006
085	a	a	.139	.037	a	a	.102	.009
086	.061	.149	.108	.072	.043	.093	.080	.043
087	a	.072	.044	.070	a	.044	.026	.059
088[a]								
089[a]								
090[a]								
091	c	c	c	c	c	c	c	c

[a] Uncovered class.   [b] One-commodity class, complete coverage.
[c] Class not listed separately in this year.   [d] One covered commodity, incomplete coverage.

TABLE E–4

CALCULATION OF VARIANCE FOR SELECTED MAJOR ECONOMIC CLASSES

Major Class	Year	$\sum_{i=1}^{n} \dfrac{V_i(\bar{Y}-\bar{\bar{Y}})^2}{v}$ (1)	$\dfrac{V-v}{V}$ (2)	$\sum_{i=1}^{n} \dfrac{1}{m_i}\dfrac{V_i}{v}\left(\dfrac{V_i-v_i}{V_i}\right)S_i^2$ (3)	$n-1$ (4)	$Var\ \bar{\bar{Y}}$ $\dfrac{[(1) \times (2)] + (3)}{(4)}$ (5)
			A. EXPORTS			
201						
	1879	.00595	.00087	0	4	.00000(25)
	1889	.01744	.00210	.00009	4	.00003
	1899	.00049	.01496	.00016	4	.00004
	1913	.00185	.00800	.00018	5	.00004
203						
	1879	.12518	.00233	.00002	12	.00003
	1889	.02966	.02446	.00002	12	.00006
	1899	.02277	.03139	.00021	13	.00007
	1913	.01601	.03475	.00008	13	.00005
212						
	1879	.00547	.03661	.00101	7	.00017
	1889	.05346	.02114	.00012	10	.00012
	1899	.01756	.01207	0	10	.00002
	1913	.02282	.00675	.00027	10	.00004
213						
	1879	.02750	.11096	.00053	7	.00051
	1889	.04235	.06460	.00038	8	.00039
	1899	.03400	0	.00116	14	.00008
	1913	.05038	.00693	.00069	15	.00007
215						
	1879	.01364	.12558	.00199	9	.00041
	1889	.02915	.10623	.00271	10	.00058
	1899	.03786	.08254	.00120	13	.00033
	1913	.11291	.05923	.00096	17	.00045
			B. IMPORTS			
201						
	1879	.07929	.00741	.00013	7	.00010
	1889	.30417	0	.00110	9	.00012
	1899	.07049	0	.00242	9	.00027
	1913	.05021	0	.00104	10	.00010
203						
	1879	.01413	.00032	.00129	6	.00022
	1889	.05025	.01446	.00071	9	.00016
	1899	.04656	0	.00100	11	.00009
	1913	.02292	0	.00011	9	.00001
212						
	1879	.04212	.02196	.00211	12	.00025
	1889	.05316	.03042	.00012	17	.00010
	1899	.04198	.02998	.00082	20	.00010
	1913	.45021	.00416	.00201	21	.00018
213						
	1879	.04602	.04597	.00108	9	.00036
	1889	.02628	.09265	.00391	12	.00053
	1899	.01264	.14743	.00183	13	.00028
	1913	.04009	.01267	.00056	17	.00006
220						
	1879	.00522	.29233	.00307	6	.00077
	1889	.01685	.41095	.00523	9	.00135
	1899	.04916	.17995	.00263	15	.00077
	1913	.02942	.13589	.00156	16	.00035

TABLE E–5
COVERAGE RATIOS FOR INTERMEDIATE EXPORT CLASSES: EARLIEST AND BASE YEARS
OF EACH PERIOD
(per cent)

Export Class	1913–1923		1899–1913		1889–1899		1879–1889	
	1923	1913	1913	1899	1899	1889	1889	1879
101	81.5	61.0	69.9	98.6	97.5	99.2	99.2	98.6
102	94.6	95.6	91.3	98.1	97.7	98.5	98.5	99.8
103	96.4	96.7	93.5	98.2	97.8	98.4	98.8	99.8
104	94.7	95.2	91.6	98.5	97.8	98.7	98.8	99.8
105	96.4	96.3	93.6	98.4	98.0	98.6	99.0	99.8
106	90.3	87.7	85.1	92.9	90.9	97.8	91.4	88.4
107	96.7	96.9	92.2	94.7	93.3	98.5	94.6	92.7
108	95.4	95.9	91.5	93.9	92.6	97.1	94.2	92.5
109	85.4	90.8	90.5	93.4	90.6	97.0	96.2	93.7
110	87.7	91.3	91.0	93.4	91.3	97.1	96.3	94.6
111	86.8	90.3	90.2	92.7	90.9	96.6	93.5	91.0
112	88.1	90.6	90.6	92.9	91.2	96.7	93.9	91.4
113	93.1	94.2	91.6	94.1	92.5	98.0	95.3	93.3
114	79.9	81.2	57.2	85.8	85.8	92.0	90.3	83.8
115	82.3	85.1	95.0	96.8	98.3	97.4	89.1	91.2
116	79.5	84.2	66.7	91.9	94.3	97.3	93.7	93.2
117	81.1	84.7	71.3	90.5	91.0	95.2	91.6	91.1
118	79.0	84.4	84.6	87.9	88.8	89.8	48.7	54.0
119	90.0	92.5	90.3	91.7	92.0	92.7	79.0	71.6
120	97.0	97.7	97.0	97.8	97.6	99.4	99.5	99.4
121	75.3	74.6	63.4	78.1	77.5	83.9	81.7	76.1
122	63.4	75.9	80.9	71.6	59.3	60.3	63.7	49.6
123	70.8	79.4	86.5	94.4	96.0	94.3	72.6	76.1
124	99.0	98.9	99.2	99.1	99.3	99.6	98.6	98.0
125	99.0	99.0	99.3	99.1	99.2	99.5	98.7	98.1
126	99.3	99.0	96.0	86.5	69.9	96.1	92.1	93.2
127	78.1	79.8	80.6	44.4	44.4	77.0	77.0	89.1
128	77.1	85.3	79.2	88.9	80.2	81.3	84.9	71.5
129	98.4	98.3	98.6	97.3	97.5	99.0	98.1	97.7
130	98.5	98.4	97.2	97.5	97.6	99.0	98.2	97.9
131	78.4	86.0	80.3	88.8	79.4	82.1	85.1	72.7
132	99.0	98.9	99.1	98.8	98.6	99.6	98.6	98.0
133	99.0	99.0	99.2	98.8	98.7	99.5	98.7	98.1
134	77.2	84.7	79.4	84.4	76.5	80.6	83.6	75.8
135	94.3	95.7	94.6	95.2	93.1	96.9	96.5	95.3
136	94.9	95.9	95.0	95.5	93.7	97.0	96.7	95.6
137	67.9	71.0	62.4	69.0	64.2	67.5	63.2	63.7
138	100.0	100.0	100.0	100.0	100.0	100.0	100.0	100.0
139	98.6	96.9	92.9	99.1	99.1	99.8	99.8	99.2
140	99.0	98.2	95.1	99.3	99.3	99.8	99.8	99.3
141	99.1	99.1	99.5	98.3	91.1	96.6	95.6	96.2
142	62.7	62.0	44.4	47.5	—	—	—	—
143	62.6	65.7	51.5	54.8	34.4	41.9	35.0	38.2
144	99.2	85.2	96.2	96.1	95.9	62.5	56.0	76.9
145	91.6	95.5	93.8	90.9	80.0	55.6	30.6	49.2
146	62.5	65.8	49.7	52.7	33.2	40.1	33.5	36.6
147	66.3	64.5	55.0	61.3	48.9	64.2	63.4	67.7

TABLE E–6

COVERAGE RATIOS FOR MAJOR EXPORT CLASSES: EARLIEST AND BASE YEARS
OF EACH PERIOD
(per cent)

Export Class	1913–1923		1899–1913		1889–1899		1879–1889	
	1923	1913	1913	1899	1899	1889	1889	1879
201	93.9	93.9	90.2	98.2	97.6	98.6	98.7	99.8
202	95.9	95.3	92.6	98.2	97.8	98.6	91.2	99.8
203	92.0	93.3	90.9	93.4	91.9	96.9	93.9	92.0
204	92.3	93.3	91.0	93.5	92.0	96.9	94.1	92.1
205	93.6	94.6	91.6	96.0	94.8	98.2	96.5	97.1
206	94.5	95.1	92.5	96.1	95.0	98.2	96.8	97.2
207	92.6	93.5	90.7	95.4	94.3	97.5	95.6	96.4
208	93.8	94.1	91.7	95.6	94.6	97.6	96.0	96.6
209	96.6	97.1	96.1	96.9	96.0	98.9	97.6	97.4
210	94.0	94.7	93.4	95.5	94.1	97.2	96.2	96.1
211	98.5	96.5	98.3	97.1	97.3	96.4	95.0	97.2
212	98.6	96.8	97.1	97.3	97.4	96.5	95.4	97.4
213	86.3	91.7	88.1	89.8	79.7	77.7	76.2	66.8
214	66.7	65.7	56.4	63.1	52.3	65.0	63.6	67.1
215	67.2	66.0	56.8	63.8	53.1	66.0	64.7	67.9
216	94.3	94.7	94.6	94.5	91.1	93.8	92.5	93.5
217	94.7	95.0	94.0	94.8	91.7	94.0	92.9	93.9
218	94.1	94.5	93.6	95.2	93.2	95.6	94.2	95.4
219	84.5	85.7	82.3	88.2	84.2	91.1	89.7	92.3
220	83.2	85.6	80.3	87.5	83.3	90.7	88.3	91.5
221	75.1	74.6	68.9	71.2	60.0	63.4	60.0	66.5
222	74.3	75.5	69.6	72.9	63.2	68.1	65.9	67.6

TABLE E–7

COVERAGE RATIOS FOR INTERMEDIATE IMPORT CLASSES: EARLIEST AND BASE YEARS
OF EACH PERIOD
(per cent)

Import Class	1913–1923		1899–1913		1889–1899		1879–1889	
	1923	1913	1913	1899	1899	1889	1889	1879
101	84.1	91.7	94.4	94.4	94.4	91.2	32.3	19.9
102	73.6	67.1	49.1	63.5	57.4	76.5	84.9	87.2
103	97.5	99.0	99.0	98.6	98.5	99.2	100.0	100.0
104	94.1	91.2	88.8	94.1	92.7	95.5	96.9	97.6
105	89.7	89.3	90.5	94.7	93.5	95.9	97.3	97.6
106	92.2	91.3	89.1	94.0	92.7	95.3	94.3	94.6
107	89.4	89.5	90.7	94.7	93.5	95.7	94.9	94.8
108	71.1	79.6	84.7	80.7	69.2	66.4	49.5	39.3
109	78.5	76.5	50.5	64.4	63.4	68.9	83.8	85.8
110	96.8	89.1	86.6	96.5	96.6	93.3	99.4	99.4
111	96.8	88.8	87.3	96.6	96.7	93.4	99.3	99.4
112	96.8	89.0	87.7	96.6	96.7	93.6	99.3	99.3
113	93.7	87.6	88.0	96.6	96.3	92.9	98.8	99.0

(continued)

TABLE E-7 (concluded)

Import Class	1913–1923		1899–1913		1889–1899		1879–1889	
	1923	1913	1913	1899	1899	1889	1889	1879
114	91.6	95.0	91.4	89.9	47.8	42.1	83.0	85.9
115	93.8	93.6	96.6	95.8	55.8	49.9	100.0	100.0
116	74.1	87.8	96.6	94.8	60.8	54.9	100.0	100.0
117	72.5	83.3	86.2	81.5	˙52.7	42.4	85.6	89.6
118	95.9	82.0	88.0	94.1	96.2	92.6	93.5	94.4
119	96.0	84.0	86.8	91.8	94.6	91.4	93.8	94.8
120	94.1	93.2	96.2	97.6	96.1	97.4	100.0	100.0
121	65.1	56.2	62.8	61.8	39.5	44.4	40.9	37.5
122	98.8	96.3	96.3	95.9	95.9	93.8	94.1	96.9
123	100.0	100.0	82.6	83.4	51.0	37.2	100.0	100.0
124	57.3	63.0	70.7	83.0	73.8	57.2	55.6	79.9
125	98.1	95.2	96.2	96.5	95.9	95.2	96.3	97.8
126	62.6	57.7	64.7	69.6	52.8	52.1	49.9	61.4
127	86.5	77.7	80.4	81.5	71.3	64.8	65.3	70.2
128	95.3	87.9	92.5	95.1	73.1	68.3	97.0	97.5
129	97.0	91.1	94.2	95.7	83.9	83.8	96.6	97.6
130	95.7	90.1	94.7	96.0	84.9	85.5	96.9	97.8
131	96.8	91.4	93.7	99.4	90.3	83.8	96.5	97.7
132	95.5	90.4	94.1	99.4	90.9	85.4	97.0	97.8
133	82.0	71.8	51.9	54.2	73.3	79.8	61.7	64.9
134	88.2	77.8	62.2	56.7	74.9	81.3	—	—
135	54.5	66.6	65.1	65.8	98.6	98.0	78.2	80.4
136	91.8	88.3	90.9	92.6	85.4	85.7	93.8	94.7
137	90.9	87.6	91.6	93.0	86.2	85.7	94.4	94.9
138	92.3	86.1	68.2	52.2	42.2	41.3	69.0	69.7
139	67.6	55.9	64.7	68.2	45.3	46.8	45.2	56.2
140	78.7	78.4	69.5	57.8	67.0	62.5	73.0	75.1
141	92.1	88.3	87.4	92.0	85.6	77.3	89.9	91.3
142	91.3	87.7	88.2	90.8	86.3	78.9	90.7	91.6
143	97.2	99.9	—	—	—	—	—	—
144	78.0	80.5	26.1	23.5	—	—	—	—
145	91.7	92.6	100.0	100.0	100.0	100.0	—	—
146	90.3	89.3	86.5	86.0	59.8	85.7	79.6	90.7
147	20.1	19.2	29.7	49.0	19.8	24.3	7.4	15.5
148	88.9	95.0	68.3	96.2	85.8	80.8	83.0	85.2
149	80.8	78.0	61.5	57.3	60.5	77.9	70.6	74.5
150	26.3	9.8	20.4	36.7	18.2	22.5	13.3	21.3

TABLE E-8

COVERAGE RATIOS FOR MAJOR IMPORT CLASSES: EARLIEST AND BASE YEARS
OF EACH PERIOD
(per cent)

Import Class	1913–1923		1899–1913		1889–1899		1879–1889	
	1923	1913	1913	1899	1899	1889	1889	1879
201	92.2	91.2	89.3	94.1	92.8	95.3	93.6	94.3
202	89.5	89.5	90.8	94.7	93.5	95.8	94.2	94.5
203	93.2	87.1	86.8	95.6	95.3	92.3	97.0	96.8
204	93.2	87.4	87.2	95.6	95.3	92.5	97.0	96.8
205	93.1	89.7	88.6	95.5	94.7	94.1	96.5	96.5
206	91.7	88.8	89.6	95.7	95.0	94.6	96.7	96.6
207	92.8	89.4	88.1	95.0	94.2	93.8	95.3	95.4
208	91.5	88.6	89.2	95.2	94.5	94.2	95.6	95.5
209	94.5	90.2	91.6	97.2	91.0	90.0	95.6	96.1
210	87.6	82.1	83.4	88.1	82.2	77.5	81.1	84.4
211	91.6	89.3	87.8	92.9	85.4	85.5	93.4	94.5
212	90.7	88.6	88.6	93.3	86.2	86.7	94.1	94.7
213	86.2	81.2	64.6	57.1	57.8	68.3	70.9	74.2
214	89.7	86.2	78.6	79.5	74.6	77.6	82.9	84.6
215	89.2	85.9	79.4	80.2	75.5	78.7	83.8	85.0
216	90.3	87.0	82.1	86.1	83.1	85.9	89.4	90.6
217	58.5	46.3	54.8	61.0	40.3	42.2	39.7	49.9
218	59.0	47.1	55.6	61.6	41.1	43.3	40.9	50.7
219	84.4	79.1	77.0	80.8	73.9	74.1	75.9	79.5
220	56.7	42.7	50.2	60.6	40.4	42.9	40.5	50.1
221	81.8	76.0	72.7	78.6	68.8	71.7	70.4	74.7
222	69.4	68.2	56.0	58.6	53.0	62.1	55.4	59.8
223	71.1	66.4	60.8	62.4	54.6	55.7	52.9	59.8

TABLE E-9

INTERMEDIATE EXPORT CLASS COVERAGE AT END OF EACH PERIOD AS PER CENT OF
CALCULATED COVERAGE ASSUMING NO CHANGE WITHIN MINOR CLASSES

Export Class	Per Cent			
	1923	1913	1899	1889
101	102.7	101.1	99.4	99.7
102	101.4	100.1	98.9	99.2
103	100.6	100.3	99.2	99.4
104	101.8	100.2	99.0	99.4
105	100.9	100.4	99.2	99.5
106	103.4	96.3	96.9	108.5
107	102.9	97.7	97.4	104.6
108	102.1	98.7	97.4	104.2
109	98.3	101.1	93.7	103.6
110	98.9	101.3	94.3	103.4
111	98.8	101.6	94.4	103.7
112	99.3	101.6	94.7	103.5

(continued)

TABLE E–9 (concluded)

Export Class	Per Cent			
	1923	1913	1899	1889
113	101.3	99.3	96.1	104.1
114	98.9	67.8	97.3	105.7
115	94.7	97.9	101.4	96.7
116	98.1	72.1	95.7	101.3
117	98.1	79.8	99.0	101.7
118	89.2	101.0	101.3	89.8
119	95.6	100.5	100.7	97.2
120	101.0	98.6	99.5	99.9
121	100.2	83.8	93.0	107.7
122	83.0	103.1	102.0	129.0
123	86.9	95.4	100.9	94.5
124	99.7	99.8	100.1	99.8
125	99.6	99.9	100.2	99.8
126	100.3	107.4	84.4	98.7
127	100.0	100.0	100.0	100.0
128	91.4	89.1	97.2	116.2
129	99.7	99.8	100.1	99.9
130	99.6	98.4	100.2	99.8
131	92.0	90.3	96.2	115.5
132	99.7	100.0	99.8	99.8
133	99.8	100.0	99.9	99.8
134	92.2	90.2	97.3	113.5
135	98.3	98.0	99.3	101.3
136	98.4	98.1	99.4	101.2
137	95.3	90.0	98.8	107.0
138	100.0	100.0	100.0	100.0
139	101.1	93.9	99.3	100.5
140	100.8	95.8	99.4	100.5
141	99.9	101.1	94.4	103.2
142	88.4	81.7	—	—
143	87.4	88.5	77.5	86.5
144	104.6	100.0	100.0	100.0
145	87.6	100.6	95.2	103.2
146	87.4	88.5	77.5	86.5
147	94.4	90.2	89.3	97.6

APPENDIX E

TABLE E–10

MAJOR EXPORT CLASS COVERAGE AT END OF EACH PERIOD AS PER CENT OF
CALCULATED COVERAGE ASSUMING NO CHANGE WITHIN MINOR CLASSES

Export	Per Cent			
Class	1923	1913	1899	1889
201	101.8	100.1	99.0	99.3
202	100.9	100.4	99.2	99.5
203	100.9	100.0	96.2	104.0
204	101.0	100.0	96.2	104.0
205	101.5	99.6	97.4	102.3
206	101.2	99.8	97.6	102.1
207	101.2	100.0	97.4	102.3
208	102.1	100.2	97.6	102.1
209	100.4	99.9	98.2	101.0
210	100.1	98.8	98.2	101.7
211	100.6	99.9	100.1	99.8
212	100.4	98.6	100.1	99.8
213	97.2	96.4	95.7	114.6
214	94.6	90.2	91.5	99.2
215	94.8	90.4	91.7	99.3
216	99.5	98.7	98.7	101.3
217	99.5	97.9	98.9	101.2
218	100.4	99.1	98.0	101.7
219	101.3	97.1	97.1	101.4
220	98.1	97.1	97.2	101.4
221	97.2	94.8	92.4	98.2
222	96.4	93.9	94.1	103.3

TABLE E–11

INTERMEDIATE IMPORT CLASS COVERAGE AT END OF EACH PERIOD AS PER CENT
OF CALCULATED COVERAGE ASSUMING NO CHANGE WITHIN MINOR CLASSES

Import	Per Cent			
Class	1923	1913	1899	1889
101	94.7	100.5	102.9	174.6
102	107.1	73.7	87.3	97.6
103	99.2	100.1	99.7	100.0
104	100.4	96.3	98.5	99.6
105	99.3	96.9	98.6	99.6
106	99.9	96.6	98.7	100.3
107	98.8	97.1	98.9	100.3
108	91.3	131.5	104.1	120.0
109	103.6	74.7	92.2	97.6
110	101.6	94.6	103.7	99.9
111	101.5	95.0	104.1	99.9
112	101.5	95.2	104.0	99.9
113	100.6	100.0	103.8	99.9
114	97.5	99.6	92.1	100.0

(continued)

399

TABLE E–11 (concluded)

Import Class	Per Cent			
	1923	1913	1899	1889
115	98.1	102.4	92.0	100.0
116	99.6	102.6	91.2	100.0
117	99.3	102.5	91.6	100.0
118	101.6	94.5	99.8	95.8
119	100.9	98.0	100.2	96.0
120	98.7	98.2	98.2	100.0
121	113.3	90.3	95.2	102.9
122	99.9	100.0	100.4	100.0
123	115.0	90.8	102.2	100.0
124	87.0	86.2	147.7	69.1
125	99.7	99.4	99.6	100.0
126	104.1	89.1	117.9	77.2
127	101.6	94.7	106.4	86.8
128	100.5	98.6	96.3	98.1
129	100.0	99.0	98.0	99.2
130	99.6	99.1	98.2	99.2
131	99.9	99.8	105.7	99.3
132	99.6	99.8	105.3	99.4
133	111.7	99.3	98.9	93.2
134	106.8	99.5	99.1	—
135	101.9	104.1	95.5	99.7
136	100.1	99.4	97.8	99.3
137	99.7	99.4	97.9	99.4
138	102.7	98.4	100.3	96.6
139	125.7	93.7	117.9	77.2
140	102.5	100.6	97.1	98.1
141	100.5	99.9	104.3	99.0
142	100.2	99.9	104.0	99.0
143	101.5	—	—	—
144	102.0	101.1	—	—
145	98.6	100.0	100.0	—
146	101.5	99.8	78.1	89.3
147	125.0	66.3	87.5	56.3
148	93.9	91.5	100.0	100.0
149	102.7	102.9	81.6	93.0
150	117.6	61.1	78.3	63.4

TABLE E–12

Major Import Class Coverage at End of Each Period as Per Cent of Calculated Coverage Assuming No Change Within Minor Classes

Import Class	Per Cent			
	1923	1913	1899	1889
201	100.1	103.5	98.7	100.3
202	99.1	97.2	98.8	100.3
203	100.3	99.4	104.1	100.3
204	100.3	99.5	104.1	100.4
205	100.3	98.0	101.5	100.1
206	99.8	98.2	101.5	100.1
207	100.2	97.9	101.8	100.3
208	99.8	98.1	101.7	100.3
209	99.9	99.0	101.0	98.7
210	102.9	98.3	106.1	96.4
211	99.4	98.5	97.9	99.3
212	99.1	98.5	98.1	99.4
213	102.2	103.0	84.7	93.9
214	100.3	99.9	93.5	97.0
215	100.1	99.9	93.8	97.3
216	100.1	99.2	97.3	98.8
217	129.4	90.1	112.0	76.4
218	128.6	90.5	111.5	77.4
219	103.3	97.9	98.8	94.9
220	128.6	90.5	111.5	77.4
221	103.3	98.1	99.3	95.0
222	101.1	96.1	83.2	90.5
223	107.5	96.1	96.1	86.2

Appendix F

Adjustments for Changes in the U.S. Customs Area

THE incorporation of Hawaii and Puerto Rico into the United States customs area in 1900 introduced a degree of incomparability into the official foreign trade records. The official figures, which include the effect of the annexations, are appropriate for the calculation of the balance of payments but not for the comparison of foreign trade with domestic prices and production.

The only way to achieve consistent territorial coverage would have been to include or exclude Hawaii and Puerto Rico for the entire period studied; but this would have been too laborious. Instead, we only included the two territories back through 1899. This made the 1899-1913 period internally consistent and provided an overlap in 1899 to which the earlier data excluding the two possessions could be spliced.

Recalculating the value of trade involved the subtraction from the published data for the United States of the trade of Puerto Rico and Hawaii with the United States, and the addition of the trade of the two territories with the rest of the world. This computation is described in detail in Table F-1.

The change in total exports and imports is small. For exports, it was 6/10 of one per cent in calendar years 1899 and 1900 and no higher than 1.3 per cent in any quarter; for imports it was 2.3 per cent in calendar 1899 and 1 per cent in calendar 1900, the greatest change being 3.7 per cent in one quarter.

Imports into Puerto Rico and Hawaii were scattered widely over the commodity list but exports from them were extremely concentrated. Almost all their exports were accounted for by green coffee from Puerto Rico and sugar from both territories; most of the latter was exported to the United States. As a result of this commodity concentration the effect of the adjustment is almost entirely on two of our minor classes, Export Class 004 (green coffee) and Import Class 019 (sugar and related products, agricultural).

Since all U.S. exports of green coffee were from Puerto Rico, Export Class 004 was empty before July 1900 in the official records. Furthermore, because no commodity data were used for parts of years in which data for the full year were not available, the recorded exports of green coffee for the last half of 1900 were thrown into "all other articles." The inclusion of Puerto Rico makes it possible to carry this class back to 1899, as is shown in Table F-2. Only one price index is given because this is a one-commodity class. All indexes are reduced to the ratio of the given year price to the base year price.

The adjustments in Export Class 004 require some changes in the intermediate and major classes of which it is a component. These are shown in Tables F-3 and F-4. Adjustments in the price index were carried through Export Class 205; after that they were negligible and only the quantity indexes and dollar values were altered.

On the import side, shifting Puerto Rico and Hawaii across the customs frontier lowered the price, quantity and value indexes for Import Class 019 to the levels given in Table F-5. The reductions in 1899, the only year in which all four quarters were affected, were about 9 per cent in price, 15 per cent in quantity, and 23 per cent in value.[1]

As these changes were carried into the intermediate and major classes (see Table F-6) the reduction in the price index for Import Class 019 tended to lower the indexes for the classes into which it was combined. In addition, the adjustments lowered quantities and values for Class 019 and therefore reduced its weight in these combinations. Since the 1899 price index for this class was high compared with those of the classes with which it was combined, its loss of weight further lowered the price indexes for combined groups.

Table F-7 gives adjusted and unadjusted quantity indexes for total exports and imports. The adjustment in the export index reflects only changes in the value series while that in imports reflects changes in the price index as well.

[1] The eliminated Hawaiian and Puerto Rican sugar imports had much higher average unit values than those from all other countries, 59 per cent higher in fiscal 1899 for example (*Foreign Commerce and Navigation of the United States*, 1899, Vol. II, pp. 366–368). Most of this was duty-free sugar from Hawaii, with an average unit value of 3.7 cents per pound in 1899. The average unit value for dutiable sugar was 2.2 cents per pound and the duty on it was 1.7 cents.

TABLE F-1

ADJUSTMENT OF VALUE OF U.S. DOMESTIC EXPORTS AND IMPORTS TO INCLUDE PUERTO RICO AND HAWAII IN U.S. CUSTOMS AREA, 1899-JUNE 1900

(dollar figures in thousands)

	Published U.S. Exports or Imports (1)	U.S. Exports to or Imports from[a] Puerto Rico (2)	U.S. Exports to or Imports from[a] Hawaii (3)	Exports to or Imports from other Countries (4)	(5)	Adjusted U.S. Exports and Imports (cols. 1, 4 and 5 minus cols. 2 and 3) (6)	Adjusted U.S. Export and Import Value Indexes (1913 = 100) (7)
EXPORTS				(from Puerto Rico)[b]	(from Hawaii)[c]		
1899 I	308,291	825	2,144	2,513	20	307,855	50.297
II	272,558	962	2,815	2,355	33	271,170	44.303
III	304,455	653	2,897	869	44	301,818	49.311
IV	367,628	1,030	2,907	933	13	364,638	59.575
Calendar Year	1,252,932	3,470	10,763	6,670	111	1,245,481	50.872
1900 I	364,435	806	4,045	1,252	14	360,850	58.956
II	334,245	1,771	3,229	557	28	329,829	53.887
Calendar Year	1,453,010	2,578	7,274	1,808	42	1,445,009	59.021
IMPORTS				(to Puerto Rico)[b]	(to Hawaii)[c]		
1899 I	191,319	538	4,080	1,264	209	188,174	41.989
II	197,126	2,244	6,654	1,474	274	189,977	42.391
III	197,458	579	8,763	1,759	282	190,157	42.432
IV	213,065	56	2,691	1,354	283	211,955	47.296
Calendar Year	798,967	3,417	22,188	5,852	1,049	780,263	43.527
1900 I	231,253	92	3,054	1,335	846	230,289	51.387
II	208,165	2,352	6,200	628	675	200,917	44.833
Calendar Year	829,150	2,444	9,254	1,963	1,521	820,937	45.796

APPENDIX F

NOTES TO TABLE F-1

ᵃ From various issues of U.S. Treasury Department, Bureau of Statistics, *Monthly Summary of Commerce and Finance of the United States*, 1899, 1900, and 1901.

ᵇ July 1899 to April 1900 from U.S. Customs and Insular Affairs Division, *Monthly Summary of Commerce of the Island of Puerto Rico*. Calendar year 1899 and Jan. to June 1900 totals including coin and bullion, from the *Statistical Abstract of the United States, 1906*, p. 487, were used, after adjustment for gold and silver imported and exported July 1899–April 1900, to estimate the remaining quarters. Therefore the figures for Jan. to June 1899 and May and June 1900 may include some coin and bullion. The Jan. to June 1899 total for exports was distributed between the two quarters in the same proportion as exports of green coffee (see Table F-2); for imports—the same proportion as U.S. exports to Puerto Rico (See col. 2).

ᶜ Calendar 1899 and Jan.-June 14, 1900 totals from the *Statistical Abstract of the United States, 1906*, p. 488, were distributed for exports among the quarters in the same proportions as imports, col. 3, and for imports, in the same proportion as exports, col. 3.

TABLE F-2

ADJUSTMENT OF EXPORT CLASS 004, GREEN COFFEE, TO INCLUDE PUERTO RICO
IN U.S. CUSTOMS AREA, 1899–JUNE 1900

	Value of Exports ($000)	Price Index (1913 = 100)	Quantity Index (1913 = 100)	Value Index (1913 = 100)
1899 I	2,028	77.057	125.701	96.862
II	1,901	56.206	161.531	90.790
III	510	59.008	41.327	24.386
IV	585	74.422	37.524	27.926
Calendar Year	5,023	65.548	91.520	59.990
1900 I	817	86.769	44.968	39.018
II	328	82.137	19.105	15.692
III	14	100.915	.648	.654
IV	26	91.614	1.376	1.261
Calendar Year	1,185	85.669	16.524	14.156

SOURCE: Data are from various issues of U.S. Customs and Insular Affairs Division, *Monthly Summary of Commerce of the Island of Puerto Rico*. Figures for May and June 1899 include exports to the U.S., but these were assumed to be small since U.S. imports of coffee from Puerto Rico were only $222,000 during the whole of fiscal 1899. We estimated figures for the second quarter of 1900 by multiplying the April values and quantities by three.

TABLE F-3

ADJUSTMENT OF EXPORT VALUES AND PRICE AND QUANTITY INDEXES FOR INTERMEDIATE AND MAJOR CLASSES TO INCLUDE COFFEE EXPORTS FROM PUERTO RICO, 1899-JUNE 1900

(dollar figures in thousands)

EXPORT CLASS	Year or Quarter	Value of Exports		FISHER INDEXES (1913 = 100)			
				Price		Quantity	
		Unadjusted	Adjusted	Unadjusted	Adjusted	Unadjusted	Adjusted
104	1899	229,339	234,362	73.9	73.6	189.6	185.1
	1900	216,760	217,946	73.8	74.1	179.6	171.1
201	1899 I	55,031	57,058	77.5	77.5	170.9	168.8
	II	49,589	51,490	76.1	75.2	156.9	157.0
	III	65,663	66,174	73.5	73.0	215.2	207.7
	IV	59,540	60,124	72.8	72.8	197.1	189.5
	Calendar Year	229,823	234,846	74.2	73.2a	186.5	183.9
	1900 I	44,998	45,815	72.1	72.5	150.4	144.9
	II	54,952	55,281	76.8	76.9	172.2	164.8
	Calendar Year	217,324	218,509	74.1	74.4a	176.6	168.4
202	1899	259,809	264,832	74.0	73.7	160.3	158.0
	1900	244,210	245,396	74.2	74.4	150.3	145.0
205	1899 I	135,085	137,112	69.8	69.9	166.5	165.8
	II	117,875	119,774	68.4	68.2	148.3	148.5
	III	138,964	139,474	68.6	68.5	174.3	172.1
	IV	141,692	142,276	69.4	69.5	175.7	173.2
	Calendar Year	533,616	538,640	68.9	68.9a	166.7	165.4
	1900 I	120,012	120,829	69.4	69.6	148.8	146.8
	II	131,966	132,294	72.1	72.2	157.6	155.0
	Calendar Year	526,475	527,600	71.5	71.6a	158.5	155.7

a Adjusted Paasche and Laspeyres Annual Price Indexes for these classes:

	201		205	
	1899	1900	1899	1900
Paasche	71.8	73.3	67.8	70.8
Laspeyres	76.0	75.5	69.9	72.5

TABLE F-4

ADJUSTMENT OF EXPORT VALUES AND QUANTITY INDEXES FOR MAJOR CLASSES TO INCLUDE COFFEE EXPORTS FROM PUERTO RICO, 1899–JUNE 1900

(dollar figures in thousands)

EXPORT CLASS	Year or Quarter	Value of Exports		Fisher Quantity Index (1913 = 100)	
		Unadjusted	Adjusted	Unadjusted	Adjusted
206	1899	563,602	568,625	157.3	156.1
	1900	553,361	554,547	149.0	147.0
207	1899 I	136,514	138,541	161.7	161.3
	II	119,187	121,087	144.1	143.9
	III	140,485	140,995	168.9	166.6
	IV	144,427	145,011	171.5	169.2
	Calendar Year	540,613	545,637	161.9	160.6
	1900 I	122,032	122,849	145.0	143.5
	II	133,581	133,909	153.3	151.1
	Calendar Year	536,435	537,620	154.7	152.4
208	1899	575,800	580,823	152.2	151.2
	1900	569,059	570,245	145.2	148.4

TABLE F-5

ADJUSTMENT OF IMPORT CLASS 019, SUGAR AND RELATED PRODUCTS, AGRICULTURAL, TO
INCLUDE PUERTO RICO AND HAWAII IN U.S. CUSTOMS AREA, 1899–JUNE 1900

	Value of Imports ($000)	Price Indexes (1913 = 100)			Fisher Quantity Index (1913 = 100)	Value Index (1913 = 100)
		Paasche	Laspeyres	Fisher "ideal"		
1899 I	19,906	103.770	105.380	104.572	77.234	80.765
II	26,235	116.626	118.449	117.534	90.564	106.443
III	20,245	112.789	112.635	112.712	72.876	82.140
IV	17,120	102.285	102.940	102.612	67.693	69.461
Calendar Year	83,506	109.299	110.606	109.951	77.036	84.702
1900 I	17,907	105.429	113.097	109.196	66.536	72.654
II	22,636	115.615	118.383	116.991	78.504	91.842
Calendar Year	79,846	111.656	114.937	113.285	71.492	80.990

SOURCE: Data are from various issues of U.S. Treasury Dept., Bureau of Statistics, *Monthly Summary of Commerce and Finance of the United States*, 1899 and 1900.

TABLE F-6

ADJUSTMENT OF IMPORT VALUES AND PRICE AND QUANTITY INDEXES FOR INTERMEDIATE
AND MAJOR CLASSES TO EXCLUDE SUGAR IMPORTED FROM HAWAII AND PUERTO RICO,
1899–JUNE 1900

(dollar figures in thousands)

| IMPORT CLASS | Year or Quarter | Value of Imports | | FISHER INDEXES (1913 = 100) | | | |
| | | | | Price | | Quantity | |
		Unadjusted	Adjusted	Unadjusted	Adjusted	Unadjusted	Adjusted
111	1899	132,607	108,178	109.4	101.4	75.8	67.7
	1900	116,768	105,645	109.9	104.6	66.5	63.2
113	1899	131,074	106,645	107.7	99.8	71.8	63.0
	1900	114,540	103,418	108.7	103.5	62.1	58.9
203	1899 I	31,200	26,920	101.1	95.0	64.3	59.0
	II	42,591	34,160	108.8	101.8	81.9	69.9
	III	36,042	26,894	112.7	101.9	66.6	55.0
	IV	31,462	28,891	100.9	96.7	65.0	62.2
	Calendar Year	141,295	116,866	106.3	99.1[a]	69.2	61.4
	1900 I	28,157	25,111	105.8	99.5	55.5	52.6
	II	38,125	30,049	112.8	102.4	70.4	61.2
	Calendar Year	125,614	114,492	106.1	101.4[a]	61.7	58.8
204	1899	143,635	119,206	105.9	98.9	68.5	60.9
	1900	128,000	116,878	105.6	101.1	61.2	58.4
205	1899 I	56,615	52,336	81.2	79.0	70.6	67.9
	II	67,297	58,866	89.4	85.4	77.1	70.6
	III	54,805	45,656	88.0	81.7	63.8	57.3
	IV	51,447	48,875	76.8	74.6	68.6	67.1
	Calendar Year	230,164	205,735	84.3	80.2[a]	70.0	65.7

(continued)

TABLE F-6 (continued)

IMPORT CLASS	Year or Quarter	Value of Imports		FISHER INDEXES (1913=100)			
				Price		Quantity	
		Unadjusted	Adjusted	Unadjusted	Adjusted	Unadjusted	Adjusted
	1900 I	54,282	51,236	84.9	81.8	65.5	64.1
	II	57,779	49,703	95.4	89.4	62.1	57.0
	Calendar Year	217,843	206,721	88.1	85.7a	63.3	61.8
206	1899	241,954	217,525	85.9	82.1	66.0	62.1
	1900	232,711	221,589	89.0	86.8	61.2	59.8
207	1899 I	58,903	54,622	82.0	79.0	69.2	66.6
	II	69,578	61,148	88.9	85.1	75.3	69.2
	III	57,484	48,336	88.2	82.2	62.7	56.6
	IV	55,602	53,030	78.2	76.2	68.4	67.0
	Calendar Year	241,567	217,139	84.6	80.8a	68.8	64.7
	1900 I	56,686	53,640	84.9	82.0	64.3	63.0
	II	59,931	51,854	94.6	88.9	61.0	56.2
	Calendar Year	230,248	219,126	87.8	85.5a	63.1	61.7
208	1899	255,697	231,268	86.1	82.5	64.9	61.2
	1900	247,502	236,379	88.7	86.6	60.9	59.6
209	1899 I	108,600	104,319	83.0	81.5	59.6	58.3
	II	113,293	104,862	86.4	84.2	59.8	56.8
	III	98,095	88,946	85.1	81.9	52.5	49.5
	IV	111,486	108,914	83.7	82.7	60.7	60.0
	Calendar Year	431,474	407,046	84.6	82.6a	58.1	56.1

1900 I	123,830	120,784	89.8	88.4	62.2	62.8
II	110,442	102,365	92.7	89.8	51.9	54.3
Calendar Year	420,673	409,551	88.4	87.3[a]	53.5	54.2
210 1899	625,804	601,376	82.1	80.7	57.5	58.9
1900	635,287	624,165	86.5	85.7	56.2	56.7
216 1899 I	144,354	140,073	77.9	76.9	53.2	54.1
II	157,753	149,321	81.5	79.9	54.5	56.6
III	148,808	139,658	81.5	79.4	51.4	53.3
IV	164,324	161,751	83.1	82.4	57.3	57.7
Calendar Year	615,239	590,810	81.2	79.9[a]	54.0	55.3
1900 I	174,095	171,049	86.8	85.9	58.2	58.6
II	162,313	154,237	89.2	87.3	51.6	53.2
Calendar Year	623,858	612,735	86.5	85.7[a]	52.2	52.7
219 1899	777,901	753,472	81.5	80.4	55.4	56.5
1900	804,771	793,648	86.7	86.1	54.5	54.9

[a] Adjusted Paasche and Laspeyres Annual Price Indexes for these classes:

	203		205		207		209		216	
	1899	1900	1899	1900	1899	1900	1899	1900	1899	1900
Paasche	100.3	98.0	77.8	83.3	78.2	83.0	80.5	84.7	77.3	83.1
Laspeyres	101.7	101.2	82.7	88.1	83.4	88.1	84.8	89.9	82.5	88.4

TABLE F–7

ADJUSTMENT OF QUANTITY INDEXES[a] FOR TOTAL EXPORTS AND IMPORTS FOR INCLUSION OF PUERTO RICO AND HAWAII IN U.S. CUSTOMS AREA, 1899–JUNE 1900
(1913 = 100)

		Exports[b]		*Imports*[c]	
		Unadjusted	Adjusted	Unadjusted	Adjusted
1899	I	73.4	73.3	54.0	53.7
	II	61.9	61.6	54.0	52.9
	III	67.2	66.6	53.9	53.0
	IV	80.1	79.4	57.1	57.2
	Calendar Year	70.8	70.3	54.7	54.1
1900	I	75.5	74.7	59.5	59.7
	II	66.2	65.3	52.4	51.5
	Calendar Year	73.2	72.8	53.4	53.2

[a] Fisher "ideal" indexes.
[b] Export Class 220.
[c] Import Class 221.

Appendix G

Source Notes and Underlying Data for Charts and Tables

TABLE G–1

U.S. EXPORT AND IMPORT PRICE INDEXES, FISCAL YEARS, 1879–1916
(Calendar Year 1913 = 100)

Year Ending June 30	Exports		Imports	
	Kreps (1)	NBER (2)	Kreps (3)	NBER (4)
1879	88.2		120.2	
1880	100.0	99.7	131.7	109.3
1881	100.9	101.4	122.1	109.2
1882	105.5	106.8	118.3	109.8
1883	93.6	105.8	111.5	104.8
1884	92.7	100.6	101.0	99.6
1885	86.4	94.3	91.3	89.5
1886	79.1	88.5	92.3	87.8
1887	82.7	85.5	105.8	88.8
1888	88.2	87.5	103.8	91.3
1889	83.6	88.8	111.5	91.0
1890	88.2	84.2	113.5	94.1
1891	80.9	87.6	108.7	93.8
1892	72.7	85.2	103.8	89.0
1893	74.5	82.0	108.7	90.5
1894	64.5	75.6	93.3	88.8
1895	62.7	69.4	81.7	79.3
1896	66.4	73.4	86.5	81.6
1897	62.7	69.5	80.8	77.5
1898	61.8	69.9	76.0	75.4
1899	66.4	68.7	83.7	78.2
1900	78.2	77.6	90.4	85.1
1901	77.3	81.2	82.7	84.8
1902	78.2	80.6	80.8	80.8
1903	86.4	84.0	84.6	82.6
1904	91.8	90.1	89.4	85.1
1905	80.9	82.3	97.1	88.9
1906	90.0	88.6	98.1	91.4
1907	96.4	92.6	102.9	98.2
1908	90.0	94.9	91.3	94.0
1909	93.6	89.2	90.4	86.8
1910	107.3	100.0	99.0	91.9
1911	99.1	100.1	101.0	95.4
1912	94.5	92.4	108.7	98.7
1913	100.9	99.5	102.9	101.3
1914	99.1	98.3	97.1	96.7
1915	99.1	99.3	96.2	93.9
1916	122.7	118.3	113.5	108.7

413

APPENDIX G

NOTES TO TABLE G-1

SOURCE: Columns 1 and 3: Theodore J. Kreps, "Export and Import Prices in the United States and the Terms of International Trade, 1880–1914," *Quarterly Journal of Economics*, August 1926, p. 714. We converted the Kreps index from fiscal 1903–13 = 100 to calendar 1913 = 100, estimating calendar 1913 as the average of fiscal years 1913 and 1914.

Columns 2 and 4: Table A–24, Export Class 220, and Table A–25, Import Class 221. Fiscal year indexes are unweighted averages of four quarterly figures.

TABLE G-2

U.K. EXPORT AND IMPORT PRICE INDEXES, 1870–1913
(1913 = 100)

	Exports		Imports	
	Imlah (1)	Schlote (2)	Imlah (3)	Schlote (4)
1870	122.3	104	138.8	120
1871	121.8	104	129.4	115
1872	134.8	117	138.6	123
1873	139.5	121	138.4	123
1874	131.8	113	135.3	120
1875	123.8	106	128.9	116
1876	114.0	98	125.7	113
1877	109.6	93	129.3	113
1878	105.6	89	119.8	106
1879	99.5	85	113.7	102
1880	103.2	88	119.9	107
1881	98.9	85	118.8	106
1882	100.8	85	117.6	105
1883	97.4	84	114.9	103
1884	93.8	81	109.1	98
1885	90.2	77	102.3	92
1886	86.3	74	96.0	86
1887	86.1	73	94.0	86
1888	85.6	75	97.1	88
1889	87.3	78	98.4	89
1890	91.1	82	97.0	88
1891	90.3	82	97.7	89
1892	86.3	78	93.6	86
1893	86.1	77	91.5	85
1894	81.7	74	85.3	78
1895	78.6	72	82.5	75
1896	79.4	73	83.2	77
1897	78.4	72	82.9	77
1898	78.6	72	83.6	77
1899	82.4	77	85.3	79
1900	94.6	89	91.6	85
1901	90.1	85	88.6	82
1902	86.0	81	87.5	82
1903	85.9	82	88.7	84

(continued)

TABLE G–2 (concluded)

	Exports		Imports	
	Imlah (1)	Schlote (2)	Imlah (3)	Schlote (4)
1904	86.9	83	89.1	85
1905	86.7	84	89.4	86
1906	91.8	89	93.3	90
1907	96.4	94	97.5	94
1908	92.7	91	93.9	90
1909	89.3	88	94.8	92
1910	93.1	92	100.2	99
1911	94.7	94	97.7	97
1912	96.4	96	99.5	98
1913	100.0	100	100.0	100

SOURCE: Columns 1 and 3: Albert H. Imlah, *Economic Elements in the Pax Britannica*, Cambridge, 1958, pp. 96–98. We converted Imlah's index from 1880 = 100 to 1913 = 100.

Columns 2 and 4: Charles P. Kindleberger, *The Terms of Trade: A European Case Study*, New York, 1956, pp. 22–25. The current account indexes were adjusted as indicated in the source to calculate the commodity trade indexes. The Schlote indexes were taken from this source to insure their comparability with the indexes for industrial Europe in Table G–4. They were originally published in Werner Schlote, *British Overseas Trade from 1700 to the 1930's*, Oxford, England, 1952.

TABLE G–3

U.K. EXPORT AND IMPORT PRICE INDEXES, 1920–38, 1948–60
(1913 = 100)

	Exports (1)	Imports (2)
1920	270	214
1921	213	151
1922	182	138
1923	180	140
1924	173	141
1925	183	154
1926	173	142
1927	165	136
1928	162	137
1929	159	134
1930	151	117
1931	126	88
1932	91	64
1933	110	74
1934	132	93
1935	130	93
1936	135	98
1937	145	111
1938	147	103

(continued)

TABLE G–3 (concluded)

	Exports (1)	Imports (2)
1948	296	245
1949	283	229
1950	221	194
1951	260	258
1952	273	253
1953	263	231
1954	260	228
1955	265	235
1956	276	240
1957	289	244
1958	286	226
1959	283	224
1960	289	226

SOURCE: 1920–51: Kindleberger, *Terms of Trade*, pp. 22–23. These are a linking of U.K. Board of Trade Indexes.

1952–60: Extrapolated from 1951 by U.K. Board of Trade Indexes published in U.K., Central Statistical Office, *Monthly Digest of Statistics,* June 1961, p. 146, and *Annual Abstract of Statistics,* No. 96, 1959, p. 214.

TABLE G–4

INDUSTRIAL EUROPE EXPORT AND IMPORT PRICE INDEXES, 1870–1913

(1913 = 100)

Calendar Year	Export Prices		Import Prices	
	Including U.K. (1)	Excluding U.K. (2)	Including U.K. (3)	Excluding U.K. (4)
1870	119	126	119	118
1871	120	128	116	116
1872	130	136	123	123
1873	131	136	123	123
1874	124	130	119	118
1875	117	122	115	114
1876	110	116	115	116
1877	108	116	112	112
1878	103	110	106	106
1879	101	109	103	104
1880	103	110	107	107
1881	101	109	107	108
1882	101	109	105	105
1883	98	105	102	102
1884	93	99	97	96

(continued)

APPENDIX G

TABLE G-4 (concluded)

Calendar Year	Export Prices		Import Prices	
	Including U.K. (1)	Excluding U.K. (2)	Including U.K. (3)	Excluding U.K. (4)
1885	88	94	90	89
1886	85	90	87	88
1887	84	90	87	88
1888	87	93	88	88
1889	90	96	90	90
1890	90	94	90	91
1891	89	92	89	89
1892	85	88	85	84
1893	85	89	84	84
1894	80	83	78	78
1895	79	82	77	78
1896	80	84	78	78
1897	81	86	78	78
1898	82	87	79	80
1899	87	92	82	84
1900	94	96	87	88
1901	88	90	83	84
1902	87	90	83	84
1903	88	91	85	86
1904	89	92	86	86
1905	91	94	88	89
1906	95	98	92	93
1907	98	100	95	96
1908	95	97	90	90
1909	93	96	92	92
1910	95	96	96	94
1911	97	98	97	97
1912	99	100	99	100
1913	100	100	100	100

SOURCE: Columns 1 and 3: Kindleberger, *Terms of Trade.*
Columns 2 and 4: Estimated roughly from U.K. and total industrial Europe indexes in Kindleberger, *ibid.*, pp. 22–23, 316, by assuming that the U.K. represented one-third of the total weight.

417

TABLE G–5

INDUSTRIAL EUROPE EXPORT AND IMPORT PRICE INDEXES, 1920–38, 1948–52

(1913 = 100)

Calendar Year	Export Prices		Import Prices	
	Including U.K. (1)	Excluding U.K. (2)	Including U.K. (3)	Excluding U.K. (4)
1920	188	147	196	187
1921	129	87	137	130
1922	134	110	123	116
1923	147	130	130	125
1924	146	132	131	126
1925	149	132	141	134
1926	139	122	130	124
1927	138	124	128	124
1928	136	123	128	124
1929	133	120	125	120
1930	125	112	109	105
1931	105	94	85	84
1932	85	82	65	66
1933	99	94	76	77
1934	122	117	94	94
1935	120	115	95	96
1936	119	111	98	98
1937	123	112	108	106
1938	124	112	100	98
1948	269	256	231	224
1949	248	230	216	210
1950	204	196	198	200
1951	251	246	257	256
1952	258	250	245	241

SOURCE: See Table G–4.

TABLE G–6

PRODUCTIVITY INDEXES FOR AGRICULTURE AND MANUFACTURING, 1879–1957

(1913 = 100)

Calendar Year	Agriculture		Manufacturing	
	Net Output Per Manhour (1)	Total Factor Productivity (2)	Net Output Per Manhour (3)	Total Factor Productivity (4)
1879	84.3	91.2	52.9	62.4
1889	90.0	96.2	67.0	75.8
1890	87.3	93.2	69.2	
1891	90.0	95.9	69.4	
1892	84.7	89.8	70.1	
1893	81.7	86.6	65.6	
1894	83.8	88.6	68.9	
1895	88.3	93.3	73.6	
1896	93.8	99.0	69.7	
1897	100.0	104.9	72.6	
1898	103.5	108.0	80.4	
1899	102.7	106.8	77.4	84.7
1900	102.7	105.8	75.0	
1901	101.4	104.4	79.8	
1902	100.0	103.9	83.7	
1903	102.3	105.0	81.0	
1904	104.4	107.6	85.0	
1905	104.9	107.2	85.2	
1906	109.8	111.8	86.4	
1907	104.3	106.1	83.3	
1908	105.7	107.5	77.9	
1909	102.9	104.2	88.1	91.0
1910	105.1	106.1	86.9	
1911	97.3	97.9	83.2	
1912	113.6	114.4	95.6	
1913	100.0	100.0	100.0	
1914	108.3	109.3	100.5	
1915	118.3	117.1	113.4	
1916	104.7	103.1	111.6	
1917	112.4	111.6	103.7	
1918	100.7	100.1	103.6	
1919	103.3	101.4	98.6	93.7
1920	100.2	99.2	104.6	
1921	102.3	98.3	120.7	
1922	105.6	103.4	136.7	
1923	112.0	110.7	131.6	
1924	105.1	104.6	140.0	
1925	110.5	110.8	149.1	
1926	109.1	109.3	152.0	
1927	116.9	115.0	155.6	
1928	112.3	110.9	162.6	
1929	116.8	114.7	170.1	157.2
1930	109.8	107.7	171.3	
1931	120.3	118.6	176.7	

(continued)

TABLE G-6 (concluded)

Calendar Year	Agriculture		Manufacturing	
	Net Output Per Manhour (1)	Total Factor Productivity (2)	Net Output Per Manhour (3)	Total Factor Productivity (4)
1932	119.4	115.7	165.1	
1933	122.9	119.8	179.8	
1934	118.0	111.5	187.8	
1935	125.0	120.2	200.0	
1936	120.2	114.6	201.5	
1937	124.8	122.2	198.8	183.5
1938	140.0	133.9	195.4	
1939	139.6	133.6	213.9	
1940	140.1	132.7	224.3	
1941	154.9	144.7	232.5	
1942	159.7	149.5	236.6	
1943	153.6	142.9	239.8	
1944	156.5	145.2	237.1	
1945	160.4	145.9	233.8	
1946	169.9	152.5	215.0	
1947	170.7	151.0	227.6	
1948	188.4	163.8	235.7	217.6
1949	193.8	165.0	244.4	
1950	213.2	175.5	264.1	
1951	210.6	169.5	260.7	
1952	221.6	175.2	267.2	
1953	254.3	196.3	278.7	246.5
1954	271.8	207.7	286.6	
1955	280.7	215.3	305.6	
1956	295.0	222.6	311.6	
1957	310.3	227.1	318.2	

SOURCE: Columns 1 and 2: John W. Kendrick, *Productivity Trends in the United States*, Princeton University Press for the NBER, 1961, Table B–I. Figures converted to 1913 base.

Column 3: *Ibid.*, Table D–II.

Column 4: *Ibid.*, Table D–I. 1913 base estimated by interpolating between 1909 and 1919 via the "output per unit of labor input" in Table D–II.

TABLE G–7

(1913 = 100)

| Calendar Year | Agricultural Productivity Index as a Percentage of Manufacturing Productivity Index | |
	Output Per Manhour (1)	Total Factor Productivity (2)
1879	159.4	146.2
1889	134.3	126.9
1890	126.2	
1891	129.7	
1892	120.8	
1893	124.5	
1894	121.6	
1895	120.0	
1896	134.6	
1897	137.7	
1898	128.7	
1899	132.7	126.1
1900	136.9	
1901	127.1	
1902	119.5	
1903	126.3	
1904	122.8	
1905	123.1	
1906	127.1	
1907	125.2	
1908	135.7	
1909	116.8	114.5
1910	120.9	
1911	116.9	
1912	118.8	
1913	100.0	
1914	107.8	
1915	104.3	
1916	93.8	
1917	108.4	
1918	97.2	
1919	104.8	108.2
1920	95.8	
1921	84.8	
1922	77.2	
1923	85.1	
1924	75.1	
1925	74.1	
1926	71.8	
1927	75.1	
1928	69.1	
1929	68.7	73.0
1930	64.1	

(continued)

421

TABLE G–7 (concluded)

Calendar Year	Agricultural Productivity Index as a Percentage of Manufacturing Productivity Index	
	Output Per Manhour (1)	Total Factor Productivity (2)
1931	68.1	
1932	72.3	
1933	68.4	
1934	62.8	
1935	62.5	
1936	59.7	
1937	62.8	66.6
1938	71.6	
1939	65.3	
1940	62.5	
1941	66.6	
1942	67.5	
1943	64.1	
1944	66.0	
1945	68.6	
1946	79.0	
1947	75.0	
1948	79.9	75.3
1949	79.3	
1950	80.7	
1951	80.8	
1952	82.9	
1953	91.2	79.6
1954	94.8	
1955	91.9	
1956	94.7	
1957	97.5	

SOURCE: Column 1: Table G–6, col. 1 ÷ col. 3.
Column 2: Table G–6, col. 2 ÷ col. 4.

TABLE G–8

GROSS NATIONAL PRODUCT IN CURRENT AND 1913 DOLLARS AND IMPLICIT PRICE INDEX UNDERLYING DEFLATED GNP

Calendar Year	Gross National Product (millions of dollars)		Implicit Price Index Underlying Deflated GNP 1913 = 100 (3)
	Current Dollars (1)	1913 Dollars (2)	
1869			127.1
1870			120.6
1871			124.9
1872			116.9
1873			114.3

(continued)

TABLE G–8 (continued)

Calendar Year	Gross National Product (millions of dollars)		Implicit Price Index Underlying Deflated GNP 1913 = 100
	Current Dollars (1)	1913 Dollars (2)	(3)
1874			111.1
1875			107.2
1876			101.4
1877			97.6
1878			90.6
1879			86.5
1880			95.3
1881			93.0
1882			95.7
1883			93.8
1884			88.8
1885			83.2
1886			82.1
1887			82.8
1888			84.0
1889	11,944	14,137	84.5
1890	12,560	15,234	82.4
1891	12,918	15,928	81.1
1892	13,649	17,520	77.9
1893	13,172	16,593	79.4
1894	11,904	16,007	74.4
1895	13,202	18,078	73.0
1896	12,519	17,658	70.9
1897	13,804	19,341	71.4
1898	14,418	19,567	73.1
1899	16,381	21,488	76.2
1900	17,705	22,171	79.9
1901	19,638	24,814	79.1
1902	20,450	25,039	81.7
1903	21,615	26,274	82.3
1904	21,618	25,893	83.5
1905	23,739	27,752	85.5
1906	27,252	31,121	87.6
1907	28,726	31,499	91.2
1908	25,734	28,426	90.5
1909	30,361	32,315	94.0
1910	31,453	32,674	96.3
1911	31,891	33,351	95.6
1912	34,883	35,097	99.4
1913	36,713	36,713	100.0
1914	33,864	33,548	100.9
1915	36,031	34,544	104.3
1916	47,250	39,956	118.3
1917	57,191	38,842	147.2
1918	65,580	38,175	171.8
1919	74,013	42,132	175.7

(continued)

TABLE G–8 (concluded)

| Calendar Year | Gross National Product (millions of dollars) | | Implicit Price Index Underlying Deflated GNP 1913 = 100 |
	Current Dollars (1)	1913 Dollars (2)	(3)
1920	85,340	42,583	200.4
1921	68,700	40,675	168.9
1922	69,536	43,735	159.0
1923	81,242	49,690	163.5
1924	81,814	50,701	161.4
1925	85,975	52,396	164.1
1926	92,006	55,817	164.8
1927	90,356	56,322	160.4
1928	92,235	57,079	161.6
1929	98,379	60,918	161.5
1930	87,938	56,268	156.3
1931	70,056	49,844	140.6
1932	51,532	41,245	124.9
1933	50,526	40,820	123.8
1934	58,672	44,282	132.5
1935	63,557	48,944	129.9
1936	72,548	53,981	134.4
1937	81,269	59,774	136.0
1938	76,557	56,321	135.9
1939	82,482	61,035	135.1
1940	90,844	66,511	136.6
1941	109,551	74,531	147.0
1942	120,239	72,303	166.3
1943	130,005	71,674	181.4
1944	138,947	74,381	186.8
1945	146,574	76,219	192.3
1946	183,819	88,874	206.8
1947	200,403	89,517	233.9
1948	228,400	92,611	246.6
1949	222,944	89,505	249.1
1950	252,494	100,657	250.8
1951	281,369	104,166	270.1
1952	288,221	105,121	274.2
1953	299,488	107,870	277.6
1954	302,639	108,617	278.6
1955	330,950	117,944	280.6
1956	349,044	120,407	289.9
1957	368,695	122,719	300.4
1958	370,110	120,527	307.1
1959	402,000	128,666	312.4
1960	419,985	132,390	317.2

SOURCES: Columns 1 and 2: Simon Kuznets, *Capital in the American Economy: Its Formation and Financing*, Tables R–1 and R–2, extrapolated, for years since 1955, by Department of Commerce data in *U.S. Income and Output*, 1958 Supplement to *The Survey of Current Business*, and in *The Survey of Current Business*, July 1961. Before 1919, figures were taken from unpublished data.

Col 3: col. 1 ÷ col. 2.

TABLE G–9

FARM GROSS PRODUCT IN CURRENT AND 1913 DOLLARS AND IMPLICIT
PRICE INDEX UNDERLYING FARM GROSS PRODUCT

CALENDAR YEAR	FARM GROSS PRODUCT		Implicit Price Index (1913 = 100) (3)
	Millions of:		
	Current Dollars (1)	1931 Dollars (2)	
1869	2,423	2,157	112.3
1870	2,333	2,332	100.0
1871	2,151	2,373	90.6
1872	2,206	2,490	88.6
1873	2,238	2,525	88.6
1874	2,316	2,527	91.7
1875	2,415	2,649	91.2
1876	2,298	2,854	80.5
1877	2,464	3,127	78.8
1878	2,100	3,292	63.8
1879	2,167	3,350	64.7
1880	2,754	3,589	76.7
1881	2,758	3,325	82.9
1882	3,293	3,594	91.6
1883	3,023	3,662	82.6
1884	2,987	3,873	77.1
1885	2,610	3,860	67.6
1886	2,511	3,865	65.0
1887	2,638	3,808	69.3
1888	2,873	3,931	73.1
1889	2,754	4,195	65.6
1890	2,779	4,129	67.3
1891	3,007	4,293	70.0
1892	2,751	4,076	67.5
1893	2,828	3,970	71.2
1894	2,509	4,109	61.1
1895	2,612	4,373	59.7
1896	2,468	4,689	52.6
1897	2,817	5,039	55.9
1898	3,110	5,263	59.1
1899	3,218	5,263	61.1
1900	3,595	5,309	67.7
1901	3,818	5,276	72.4
1902	4,077	5,237	77.8
1903	4,070	5,395	75.4
1904	4,248	5,533	76.8
1905	4,284	5,599	76.5
1906	4,656	5,896	79.0
1907	4,801	5,632	85.2
1908	4,928	5,744	85.8
1909	5,462	5,626	97.1
1910	5,916	5,784	102.3
1911	5,162	5,592	92.3
1912	6,325	6,364	99.4
1913	5,685	5,685	100.0

(continued)

TABLE G–9 (concluded)

	FARM GROSS PRODUCT		
	Millions of:		Implicit
CALENDAR	Current	1913	Price Index
YEAR	Dollars	Dollars	(1913 = 100)
	(1)	(2)	(3)
1914	6,133	6,169	99.4
1915	6,323	6,515	97.1
1916	6,812	5,952	114.4
1917	10,998	6,364	172.8
1918	12,069	6,154	196.1
1919	12,755	6,179	206.4
1920	12,206	6,161	198.1
1921	7,020	5,574	125.9
1922	7,842	6,037	129.9
1923	8,676	6,373	136.1
1924	8,416	6,101	137.9
1925	10,194	6,518	156.4
1926	9,470	6,356	149.0
1927	9,198	6,629	138.8
1928	9,485	6,402	148.2
1929	9,817	6,715	146.2
1930	7,733	6,143	125.9
1931	6,192	7,184	86.2
1932	4,448	6,748	65.9
1933	4,588	6,662	68.9
1934	4,331	5,516	78.5
1935	6,944	6,725	103.3
1936	6,263	5,749	108.9
1937	8,089	7,189	112.5
1938	6,726	7,252	92.7
1939	6,498	7,242	89.7
1940	6,843	7,118	96.1
1941	9,363	7,656	122.3
1942	13,388	8,332	160.7
1943	15,288	7,644	200.0
1944	15,658	7,834	199.9
1945	16,230	7,389	219.7
1946	19,280	7,491	257.4
1947	20,747	6,885	301.3
1948	23,821	7,855	303.3
1949	19,295	7,473	258.2
1950	20,537	7,883	260.5
1951	23,552	7,357	320.1
1952	22,759	7,663	297.0
1953	20,895	7,926	263.6
1954	20,344	8,290	245.4
1955	19,612	8,725	224.8
1956	19,313	8,527	226.5
1957	19,361	8,396	230.6
1958	21,349	8,509	250.9
1959	19,933	8,468	235.4
1960	20,838	8,853	235.4

NOTES TO TABLE G-9

SOURCE: Column 1, 1956–60: *Survey of Current Business,* July 1961, p. 32.

1910–55: *Ibid.,* October 1958, p. 13.

1869–1909: Extrapolated from 1910 by Frederick Strauss and Louis H. Bean, *Gross Farm Income and Indices of Farm Production and Prices in the United States, 1869–1937,* U.S. Dept. of Agriculture, Technical Bulletin No. 703, p. 24, Table 8, column headed "Total (gross income) adjusted for changes in inventory values of meat animals."

Column 2, 1910–1960: *SCB,* same issues as for column 1, converted to 1913 dollars.

1869, 1879 and 1889–1909: Extrapolated from 1910 by John W. Kendrick, *Productivity Trends in the United States,* Table B–I, "net output."

1870–78 and 1880–88: Interpolated by Strauss and Bean, *Gross Farm Income,* p. 126, Table 61, Calendar year "ideal index" of farm production.

Column 3: Col. 1 ÷ col. 2.

TABLE G–10

RATIO OF FARM TO TOTAL U.S. GROSS PRODUCT, CURRENT AND CONSTANT DOLLARS

Calendar Year	Ratio of Farm Gross Product to Gross National Product	
	Current Dollars (1)	Constant (1913) Dollars (2)
1869	.390	.442
1870	.397	.479
1871	.349	.481
1872	.297	.392
1873	.296	.382
1874	.313	.379
1875	.330	.388
1876	.306	.385
1877	.313	.388
1878	.268	.381
1879	.259	.346
1880	.259	.322
1881	.263	.295
1882	.285	.298
1883	.266	.303
1884	.268	.309
1885	.248	.305
1886	.228	.288
1887	.230	.275
1888	.252	.289
1889	.231	.297

(continued)

TABLE G–10 (continued)

Calendar Year	Ratio of Farm Gross Product to Gross National Product	
	Current Dollars (1)	Constant (1913) Dollars (2)
1890	.221	.271
1891	.233	.270
1892	.202	.233
1893	.215	.239
1894	.211	.257
1895	.198	.242
1896	.197	.266
1897	.204	.261
1898	.216	.269
1899	.196	.245
1900	.203	.239
1901	.194	.213
1902	.199	.209
1903	.188	.205
1904	.196	.214
1905	.180	.202
1906	.171	.189
1907	.167	.179
1908	.191	.202
1909	.180	.174
1910	.188	.177
1911	.162	.168
1912	.181	.181
1913	.155	.155
1914	.181	.184
1915	.175	.189
1916	.144	.149
1917	.192	.164
1918	.184	.161
1919	.172	.147
1920	.143	.145
1921	.102	.137
1922	.113	.138
1923	.107	.128
1924	.103	.120
1925	.119	.124
1926	.103	.114
1927	.102	.118
1928	.103	.112
1929	.100	.110
1930	.088	.109
1931	.088	.144
1932	.086	.164
1933	.091	.163
1934	.074	.125
1935	.109	.137
1936	.086	.107

(continued)

TABLE G–10 (concluded)

Calendar Year	Ratio of Farm Gross Product to Gross National Product	
	Current Dollars (1)	Constant (1913) Dollars (2)
1937	.100	.120
1938	.088	.129
1939	.079	.119
1940	.075	.107
1941	.085	.103
1942	.111	.115
1943	.118	.107
1944	.113	.105
1945	.111	.097
1946	.105	.084
1947	.099	.077
1948	.104	.085
1949	.087	.083
1950	.081	.078
1951	.084	.071
1952	.079	.073
1953	.070	.073
1954	.067	.076
1955	.059	.074
1956	.055	.071
1957	.053	.068
1958	.058	.071
1959	.050	.066
1960	.050	.067

SOURCE: *1889–1960*, Column 1: Table G–9, col. 1 ÷ Table G–8, col. 1.
Column 2: Table G–9, col. 2 ÷ Table G–8, col. 2.
1869–88: See Table G–8.

TABLE G–11

U.S. EXPORTS AND IMPORTS AS A PERCENTAGE OF GNP, CURRENT AND 1913 DOLLARS

Calendar Year	Exports		Imports	
	Current Dollars (1)	Constant (1913) Dollars (2)	Current Dollars (3)	Constant (1913) Dollars (4)
1869	5.2		7.1	
1870	6.6		7.8	
1871	7.2		9.3	
1872	6.1		8.8	
1873	7.3		7.9	
1874	7.5		7.6	
1875	6.8		6.9	
1876	7.7		5.7	
1877	7.7		6.1	
1878	9.2		5.5	
1879	9.0	8.4	6.1	4.9
1880	8.2	7.7	6.6	5.3
1881	7.8	6.9	6.4	5.3
1882	6.5	5.8	6.5	5.5
1883	6.9	6.3	6.1	5.3
1884	6.6	6.0	5.7	5.0
1885	6.4	5.8	5.6	5.0
1886	6.4	6.0	6.0	5.4
1887	6.1	5.9	6.2	5.4
1888	6.0	5.5	6.4	5.7
1889	6.8	6.6	6.5	5.5
1890	6.7	6.5	6.6	5.5
1891	7.4	6.8	6.4	5.4
1892	6.8	6.4	6.2	5.2
1893	6.5	6.4	5.9	4.8
1894	6.8	7.1	5.7	5.0
1895	6.1	6.2	6.1	5.5
1896	7.9	7.8	5.4	4.7
1897	7.8	8.0	5.4	5.0
1898	8.6	9.2	4.4	4.2
1899	7.6	8.0	4.9	4.5
1900	8.2	8.0	4.7	4.3
1901	7.3	7.3	4.5	4.3
1902	6.5	6.5	4.7	4.8
1903	6.7	6.4	4.6	4.5
1904	6.6	6.3	4.8	4.7
1905	6.7	6.9	5.0	4.7
1906	6.5	6.3	4.8	4.5
1907	6.6	6.3	5.0	4.6
1908	6.7	6.8	4.3	4.5
1909	5.6	5.6	4.9	5.2
1910	5.8	5.5	5.0	5.0
1911	6.5	6.6	4.8	4.8
1912	6.8	7.0	5.2	5.1
1913	6.7	6.7	4.9	4.9
1914	6.1	6.3	5.3	5.7
1915	9.7	9.6	4.9	5.3

(continued)

TABLE G–11 (concluded)

Calendar Year	Exports		Imports	
	Current Dollars (1)	Constant (1913) Dollars (2)	Current Dollars (3)	Constant (1913) Dollars (4)
1916	11.5	10.0	5.1	5.0
1917	10.8	9.0	5.2	5.2
1918	9.2	7.7	4.6	4.9
1919	10.5	8.5	5.3	5.1
1920	9.5	8.2	6.2	5.7
1921	6.4	6.8	3.7	4.9
1922	5.4	6.0	4.5	5.9
1923	5.0	5.3	4.7	5.6
1924	5.5	5.8	4.4	5.3
1925	5.6	6.0	4.9	5.6
1926	5.1	6.0	4.8	5.6
1927	5.3	6.4	4.6	5.7
1928	5.5	6.6	4.4	5.6
1929	5.2	6.4	4.5	6.1
1930	4.3	5.7	3.5	5.6
1931	3.4	5.2	3.0	5.5
1932	3.1	4.8	2.6	5.3
1933	3.3	5.0	2.9	5.9
1934	3.6	4.9	2.8	5.4
1935	3.5	4.7	3.2	6.0
1936	3.3	4.4	3.3	6.0
1937	4.1	5.1	3.7	6.1
1938	4.0	5.5	2.5	4.6
1939	3.8	5.3	2.8	4.9
1940	4.3	5.7	2.8	4.7
1941	4.6	6.0	2.9	5.0
1942	6.7	8.1	2.3	3.8
1943	9.9	12.0	2.6	4.3
1944	10.3	11.1	2.8	4.5
1945	7.0	7.4	2.8	4.5
1946	5.4	6.6	2.6	4.1
1947	7.2	8.8	2.7	3.8
1948	5.5	6.6	3.1	4.2
1949	5.4	7.0	3.0	4.3
1950	4.0	5.5	3.5	4.6
1951	5.3	6.8	3.8	4.4
1952	5.2	6.8	3.7	4.6
1953	5.2	6.9	3.6	4.7
1954	5.0	6.7	3.4	4.3
1955	4.7	6.3	3.4	4.4
1956	5.4	7.3	3.6	4.7
1957	5.6	7.5	3.5	4.7
1958	4.8	6.6	3.5	5.0
1959	4.3	6.1	3.7	5.6
1960	4.8	6.8	3.5	5.2

SOURCE: *1889–1960,* Column 1: Table A–6, col. 1 ÷ Table G–8, col. 1.
Column 2: Table A–6, col. 2 ÷ Table G–8, col. 2.
Column 3: Table A–6, col. 3 ÷ Table G–8, col. 1.
Column 4: Table A–6, col. 4 ÷ Table G–8, col. 2.
Years prior to 1889. See note to Table G–8.

TABLE G–12

U.S. AGRICULTURAL EXPORTS AND IMPORTS AS A PERCENTAGE OF GNP, CURRENT AND 1913 DOLLARS

Calendar Year[a]	Exports		Imports	
	Current Dollars (1)	1913 Dollars (2)	Current Dollars (3)	1913 Dollars (4)
1869	4.9	5.0		
1870	5.5	7.2		
1871	4.9	5.8		
1872	5.3	6.3		
1873	6.1	7.2		
1874	5.3	6.1		
1875	5.5	6.6		
1876	5.7	6.7		
1877	6.8	7.6		
1878	6.9	8.0		
1879	7.5	8.0	3.0	2.3
1880	7.0	7.6	2.9	2.2
1881	6.3	6.4	2.9	2.2
1882	5.0	5.0	2.9	2.3
1883	5.3	5.6	2.7	2.3
1884	5.0	5.2	2.6	2.3
1885	4.8	5.1	2.7	2.4
1886	4.9	5.4	2.8	2.5
1887	4.7	5.2	2.8	2.3
1888	4.4	4.7	3.0	2.5
1889	5.1	5.7	3.1	2.5
1890	5.1	5.7	3.0	2.4
1891	5.7	5.9	3.3	2.6
1892	5.3	5.6	2.9	2.4
1893	4.8	5.1	2.9	2.3
1894	4.9	5.8	3.1	2.5
1895	4.2	4.9	2.9	2.5
1896	5.4	6.4	2.7	2.2
1897	5.3	6.4	2.8	2.5
1898	6.0	7.4	2.2	2.1
1899	4.8	6.0	2.5	2.3
1900	5.1	5.8	2.3	2.1
1901	4.8	5.3	2.2	2.2
1902	4.0	4.4	2.2	2.4
1903	4.2	4.3	2.1	2.2
1904	3.7	3.8	2.5	2.5
1905	3.8	4.3	2.5	2.3
1906	3.6	3.9	2.3	2.1
1907	3.7	3.8	2.3	2.1
1908	3.8	4.1	2.2	2.3
1909	3.0	3.0	2.5	2.6
1910	2.9	2.6	2.5	2.3
1911	3.1	3.3	2.4	2.3
1912	3.3	3.5	2.7	2.6
1913	3.1	3.1	2.4	2.4
1914	2.9	2.9	2.9	3.1
1915	4.5	4.3	3.0	3.2
1916	3.7	3.4	3.0	2.9

(continued)

TABLE G–12 (concluded)

Calendar Year[a]	Exports		Imports	
	Current Dollars (1)	1913 Dollars (2)	Current Dollars (3)	1913 Dollars (4)
1917	3.5	2.6	3.2	3.2
1918	4.2	2.9	2.7	3.1
1919	5.5	3.6	3.5	3.5
1920	4.0	3.0	3.8	3.4
1921	3.1	3.4	1.9	3.0
1922	2.7	2.8	2.3	3.5
1923	2.2	2.1	2.5	3.1
1924	2.6	2.3	2.3	3.1
1925	2.5	2.2	2.7	3.2
1926	2.0	2.1	2.6	3.2
1927	2.1	2.2	2.5	3.3
1928	2.0	2.1	2.3	3.2
1929	1.7	1.8	2.3	3.5
1930	1.4	1.7	1.7	3.2
1931	1.2	1.8	1.4	3.5
1932	1.3	2.4	1.3	3.6
1933	1.4	2.2	1.4	3.9
1934	1.2	1.6	1.4	3.5
1935	1.2	1.3	1.7	3.8
1936	1.0	1.1	1.7	3.5
1937	1.0	1.2	1.9	3.4
1938	1.1	1.4	1.2	2.8
1939	0.8	1.1	1.4	2.9
1940	0.6	0.7	1.4	3.0
1941	0.6	0.6	1.5	3.2
1942	1.0	0.8	1.1	2.0
1943	1.6	1.1	1.2	2.1
1944	1.5	1.0	1.3	2.2
1945	1.5	1.1	1.2	2.0
1946	1.7	1.3	1.2	2.0
1947	1.9	1.4	1.3	2.0
1948	1.5	1.1	1.4	2.1
1949	1.6	1.4	1.3	2.1
1950	1.1	1.1	1.6	2.0
1951	1.4	1.3	1.8	1.9
1952	1.2	1.1	1.6	1.9
1953	1.0	0.9	1.4	1.8
1954	1.0	1.0	1.3	1.6
1955	1.0	1.0	1.2	1.5
1956	1.2	1.3	1.1	1.6
1957	1.2	1.4	1.1	1.5
1958	1.0	1.3	1.0	1.6
1959	1.0	1.3	1.0	1.6
1960	1.2	1.6	0.9	1.5

SOURCE: *1889–1960*, Column 1: Table A–7, col. 1 ÷ Table G–8, col. 1.
Column 2: Table A–7, col. 2 ÷ Table G–8, col. 2.
Column 3: Table A–7, col. 3 ÷ Table G–8, col. 3.
Column 4: Table A–7, col. 4 ÷ Table G–8, col. 4.
1869–88, See note to Table G–8.
a 1869–78 are years beginning July. 1879–1960 are calendar years.

TABLE G–13

U.S. Manufactured Exports and Imports as a Percentage of GNP, Current and 1913 Dollars

Calendar Year	Exports		Imports	
	Current Dollars (1)	1913 Dollars (2)	Current Dollars (3)	1913 Dollars (4)
1879	1.0	0.8	1.6	1.4
1880	0.8	0.6	1.8	1.8
1881	1.0	0.8	1.8	1.7
1882	1.0	0.8	1.9	1.8
1883	1.0	0.8	1.7	1.7
1884	1.0	0.7	1.6	1.5
1885	1.0	0.7	1.5	1.4
1886	0.9	0.7	1.7	1.6
1887	0.9	0.7	1.7	1.7
1888	0.9	0.7	1.8	1.8
1889	1.0	0.8	1.7	1.7
1890	1.0	0.8	1.8	1.8
1891	1.0	0.8	1.4	1.4
1892	0.9	0.8	1.5	1.4
1893	1.0	0.9	1.4	1.3
1894	1.1	1.0	1.2	1.1
1895	1.1	0.9	1.7	1.6
1896	1.5	1.1	1.4	1.3
1897	1.5	1.2	1.3	1.2
1898	1.5	1.4	1.0	1.0
1899	1.7	1.5	1.0	1.0
1900	1.7	1.4	1.0	1.0
1901	1.5	1.3	1.0	0.9
1902	1.5	1.3	1.1	1.1
1903	1.5	1.2	1.1	1.0
1904	1.6	1.4	1.0	1.0
1905	1.7	1.6	1.1	1.0
1906	1.6	1.5	1.1	1.1
1907	1.6	1.5	1.2	1.1
1908	1.6	1.5	1.0	1.0
1909	1.5	1.4	1.0	1.1
1910	1.6	1.6	1.0	1.1
1911	1.9	1.9	1.0	1.0
1912	2.0	2.1	1.0	1.1
1913	2.1	2.1	1.0	1.0
1914	1.8	1.9	1.1	1.2
1915	3.5	3.6	0.7	0.9
1916	5.3	4.8	0.7	0.7
1917	4.5	4.4	0.6	0.7
1918	3.1	3.0	0.6	0.6
1919	3.3	3.2	0.6	0.6
1920	3.6	3.6	0.9	0.8
1921	2.3	2.3	0.8	0.8
1922	1.8	2.1	0.9	0.9
1923	1.8	2.1	0.9	1.0

(continued)

TABLE G–13 (concluded)

Calendar Year	Exports		Imports	
	Current Dollars (1)	1913 Dollars (2)	Current Dollars (3)	1913 Dollars (4)
1924	1.9	2.2	0.9	1.0
1925	2.1	2.5	0.9	0.9
1926	2.1	2.5	1.0	1.0
1927	2.2	2.8	1.0	1.0
1928	2.4	3.2	1.0	1.0
1929	2.6	3.3	1.0	1.1
1930	2.2	2.9	0.9	1.0
1931	1.6	2.3	0.8	1.0
1932	1.2	1.7	0.7	0.9
1933	1.2	1.8	0.6	0.9
1934	1.5	2.2	0.6	0.9
1935	1.6	2.2	0.6	0.9
1936	1.6	2.3	0.6	1.0
1937	2.0	2.8	0.7	1.0
1938	2.0	2.9	0.6	0.8
1939	2.0	2.9	0.5	0.8
1940	2.6	3.4	0.4	0.6
1941	3.1	4.3	0.4	0.5
1942	4.7	6.1	0.4	0.5
1943	7.3	9.1	0.5	0.7
1944	7.7	8.6	0.5	0.7
1945	4.3	4.9	0.6	0.7
1946	2.7	3.9	0.5	0.5
1947	4.1	5.6	0.5	0.5
1948	3.1	4.2	0.6	0.6
1949	2.9	4.2	0.6	0.6
1950	2.3	3.4	0.6	0.6
1951	3.0	4.3	0.7	0.7
1952	3.2	4.7	0.7	0.7
1953	3.6	5.3	0.7	0.8
1954	3.2	4.7	0.7	0.8
1955	2.8	4.1	0.8	0.9
1956	3.2	4.6	0.9	1.0
1957	3.2	4.6	1.0	1.1
1958	3.0	4.2	1.1	1.2
1959	2.6	3.7	1.3	1.5
1960	2.7	3.9	1.2	1.5

SOURCE: *1889–1960,* Col. 1: Table A–8, col. 5 ÷ Table G–8, col. 1.
Col. 2: Table A–9, col. 5 ÷ Table G–8, col. 2.
Col. 3: Table A–10, col. 5 ÷ Table G–8, col. 3.
Col. 4: Table A–11, col. 5 ÷ Table G–8, col. 4.
1879–89, See note to Table G–8.

TABLE G–14

RATIO OF U.S. AGRICULTURAL EXPORTS AND IMPORTS TO FARM GROSS PRODUCT,
CURRENT AND 1913 DOLLARS

Calendar Year[a]	Ratio of Agricultural Exports to Farm Gross Product		Ratio of Agricultural Imports to Farm Gross Product	
	Current Dollars (1)	Constant (1913) Dollars (2)	Current Dollars (3)	Constant (1913) Dollars (4)
1869	.125	.111		
1870	.147	.148		
1871	.153	.134		
1872	.178	.161		
1873	.199	.192		
1874	.164	.156		
1875	.174	.172		
1876	.183	.173		
1877	.233	.197		
1878	.261	.220		
1879	.289	.232	.116	.067
1880	.271	.236	.112	.068
1881	.238	.217	.110	.076
1882	.176	.169	.102	.078
1883	.199	.184	.102	.077
1884	.185	.168	.098	.076
1885	.194	.166	.108	.080
1886	.215	.189	.122	.086
1887	.203	.188	.121	.084
1888	.173	.161	.118	.088
1889	.220	.192	.134	.083
1890	.230	.209	.137	.089
1891	.246	.219	.140	.097
1892	.262	.242	.145	.102
1893	.221	.214	.137	.095
1894	.231	.225	.146	.098
1895	.211	.204	.148	.105
1896	.272	.239	.135	.083
1897	.262	.247	.137	.098
1898	.277	.275	.104	.078
1899	.245	.247	.128	.095
1900	.253	.241	.115	.090
1901	.247	.251	.113	.103
1902	.202	.210	.111	.112
1903	.225	.210	.113	.105
1904	.188	.177	.128	.115
1905	.210	.212	.141	.116
1906	.213	.205	.133	.112
1907	.221	.213	.138	.119
1908	.199	.202	.116	.114
1909	.167	.172	.138	.149
1910	.157	.148	.131	.132
1911	.194	.194	.149	.136
1912	.180	.193	.151	.143
1913	.201	.201	.157	.157
1914	.163	.160	.160	.167
1915	.254	.230	.171	.169
1916	.258	.226	.206	.196

(continued)

TABLE G–14 (concluded)

Calendar Year[a]	Ratio of Agricultural Exports to Farm Gross Product		Ratio of Agricultural Imports to Farm Gross Product	
	Current Dollars (1)	Constant (1913) Dollars (2)	Current Dollars (3)	Constant (1913) Dollars (4)
1917	.180	.159	.165	.197
1918	.228	.179	.149	.193
1919	.321	.249	.204	.236
1920	.282	.204	.266	.233
1921	.301	.245	.188	.219
1922	.240	.205	.208	.253
1923	.210	.164	.233	.241
1924	.251	.192	.227	.255
1925	.210	.175	.230	.261
1926	.192	.186	.255	.285
1927	.205	.191	.241	.279
1928	.196	.184	.221	.286
1929	.172	.163	.226	.315
1930	.155	.153	.190	.289
1931	.133	.128	.163	.242
1932	.149	.144	.150	.221
1933	.151	.133	.160	.238
1934	.169	.124	.190	.277
1935	.108	.096	.155	.278
1936	.113	.105	.198	.328
1937	.099	.095	.195	.286
1938	.123	.108	.142	.219
1939	.101	.093	.172	.242
1940	.076	.070	.188	.276
1941	.071	.058	.178	.308
1942	.088	.067	.095	.170
1943	.136	.102	.099	.195
1944	.134	.090	.116	.207
1945	.139	.113	.105	.202
1946	.163	.159	.119	.237
1947	.191	.178	.133	.260
1948	.146	.130	.132	.245
1949	.185	.169	.150	.250
1950	.140	.142	.194	.254
1951	.172	.178	.220	.269
1952	.151	.146	.199	.261
1953	.136	.124	.200	.248
1954	.150	.128	.195	.205
1955	.163	.137	.203	.208
1956	.216	.189	.205	.219
1957	.233	.208	.205	.220
1958	.181	.180	.183	.224
1959	.198	.192	.206	.245
1960	.233	.231	.183	.220

SOURCE: Col. 1: Table A–7, col. 1 ÷ Table G–9, col. 1. (Farm gross product for years beginning July, 1869–78, interpolated from Table G–9, col. 1.)

Col. 2: Table A–7, col. 2 ÷ Table G–9, col. 2. (Farm gross product for years beginning July, 1869–78, interpolated from Table G–9, col. 2.)

Col. 3: Table A–7, col. 3 ÷ Table G–9, col. 1.

Col. 4: Table A–7, col. 4 ÷ Table G–9, col. 2.

a 1869–78 are years beginning July. 1879–1960 are calendar years.

TABLE G–15
RATIO OF U.S. MANUFACTURED TO AGRICULTURAL QUANTITY INDEXES FOR
EXPORTS AND IMPORTS
(1913 = 100)

Year	Ratio of Manufactured to Agricultural Quantity Indexes		Year	Ratio of Manufactured to Agricultural Quantity Indexes	
	Exports (1)	Imports (2)		Exports (1)	Imports (2)
1879	.142	1.490	1920	1.837	.558
1880	.117	1.927	1921	1.050	.632
1881	.184	1.806	1922	1.101	.618
1882	.227	1.882	1923	1.507	.751
1883	.213	1.709	1924	1.458	.742
1884	.207	1.565	1925	1.743	.664
1885	.215	1.387	1926	1.758	.726
1886	.200	1.544	1927	1.858	.746
1887	.209	1.719	1928	2.300	.739
1888	.234	1.666	1929	2.789	.771
1889	.221	1.646	1930	2.579	.784
1890	.216	1.725	1931	1.915	.679
1891	.207	1.251	1932	1.106	.605
1892	.203	1.368	1933	1.263	.569
1893	.264	1.397	1934	2.130	.607
1894	.255	1.062	1935	2.553	.584
1895	.284	1.472	1936	3.150	.678
1896	.260	1.385	1937	3.694	.713
1897	.281	1.127	1938	3.099	.656
1898	.286	1.102	1939	3.959	.628
1899	.364	.998	1940	6.959	.472
1900	.377	1.099	1941	10.876	.388
1901	.369	.990	1942	11.796	.637
1902	.453	1.080	1943	12.573	.790
1903	.434	1.161	1944	13.570	.726
1904	.563	.957	1945	6.714	.850
1905	.561	1.049	1946	4.326	.632
1906	.583	1.217	1947	6.154	.582
1907	.594	1.271	1948	5.746	.664
1908	.555	1.014	1949	4.517	.672
1909	.714	1.030	1950	4.577	.780
1910	.920	1.159	1951	5.178	.844
1911	.884	1.084	1952	6.653	.931
1912	.888	1.005	1953	8.792	1.012
1913	1.000	1.000	1954	7.285	1.175
1914	.992	.950	1955	6.126	1.325
1915	1.246	.641	1956	5.222	1.561
1916	2.137	.573	1957	4.813	1.692
1917	2.540	.495	1958	5.017	1.851
1918	1.591	.476	1959	4.429	2.250
1919	1.337	.385	1960	3.772	2.396

SOURCE: Col. 1: Table A–2, col. 6 ÷ Table A–5, col. 2.
Col. 2: Table A–4, col. 6 ÷ Table A–5, col. 4.

TABLE G–16

RATIO OF U.S. EXPORT TO IMPORT QUANTITY INDEXES FOR MANUFACTURED
AND AGRICULTURAL PRODUCTS
(1913 = 100)

Year	Ratio of Export to Import Quantity Indexes		Year	Ratio of Export to Import Quantity Indexes	
	Manufactured Products (1)	Agricultural Products (2)		Manufactured Products (1)	Agricultural Products (2)
1879	.259	2.713	1920	2.249	.683
1880	.165	2.712	1921	1.450	.872
1881	.226	2.222	1922	1.126	.632
1882	.205	1.694	1923	1.065	.531
1883	.233	1.870	1924	1.157	.589
1884	.229	1.729	1925	1.372	.523
1885	.252	1.624	1926	1.231	.508
1886	.221	1.707	1927	1.329	.533
1887	.212	1.747	1928	1.565	.503
1888	.201	1.427	1929	1.464	.404
1889	.241	1.799	1930	1.355	.412
1890	.228	1.819	1931	1.163	.412
1891	.291	1.757	1932	.927	.507
1892	.273	1.846	1933	.966	.435
1893	.331	1.749	1934	1.228	.350
1894	.429	1.789	1935	1.175	.269
1895	.293	1.517	1936	1.155	.248
1896	.424	2.255	1937	1.347	.260
1897	.491	1.969	1938	1.814	.384
1898	.713	2.745	1939	1.887	.300
1899	.739	2.029	1940	2.898	.197
1900	.718	2.092	1941	4.105	.146
1901	.706	1.893	1942	5.700	.308
1902	.610	1.453	1943	6.495	.408
1903	.586	1.567	1944	6.344	.339
1904	.709	1.204	1945	3.439	.436
1905	.761	1.422	1946	3.581	.524
1906	.685	1.430	1947	5.624	.532
1907	.650	1.393	1948	3.582	.414
1908	.757	1.382	1949	3.547	.528
1909	.626	.903	1950	2.558	.436
1910	.692	.872	1951	3.158	.515
1911	.906	1.111	1952	3.115	.436
1912	.927	1.050	1953	3.384	.389
1913	1.000	1.000	1954	3.029	.489
1914	.780	.747	1955	2.371	.513
1915	2.063	1.061	1956	2.238	.669
1916	3.351	.898	1957	2.099	.738
1917	3.228	.629	1958	1.696	.626
1918	2.420	.724	1959	1.201	.610
1919	2.856	.822	1960	1.292	.821

SOURCE: Col. 1: Table A–2, col. 6 ÷ Table A–4, col. 6.
Col. 2: Table A–5, col. 2 ÷ Table A–5, col. 4.

TABLE G–17

EXPORTS OF MANUFACTURES: U.K. PRICE AND QUANTITY INDEXES AND RELATION
OF U.S. TO U.K. QUANTITY INDEXES
(1913 = 100)

Year	U.K. Indexes for Exports of Finished Manufactures		U.S. Export Quantity Index as Per Cent of U.K. Quantity Index	
	Price (1)	Quantity (2)	Finished Manufactures (3)	Textiles (4)
1879	88	46.4	20.9	28.4
1880	92	51.5	16.9	22.6
1881	87	57.0	20.4	25.7
1882	88	57.8	20.9	24.2
1883	86	58.8	21.4	24.5
1884	83	59.4	19.9	22.7
1885	80	56.5	21.4	30.2
1886	76	58.9	21.7	32.7
1887	76	61.8	21.2	28.7
1888	77	64.1	20.3	21.4
1889	77	65.8	23.7	20.6
1890	82	65.7	24.8	22.4
1891	82	61.6	27.8	30.8
1892	79	58.8	29.8	31.0
1893	78	57.3	34.4	33.1
1894	74	59.0	35.1	37.9
1895	72	64.4	34.5	37.5
1896	74	67.5	37.9	49.2
1897	73	64.8	47.2	55.3
1898	72	65.2	55.7	62.3
1899	76	68.7	60.3	74.4
1900	85	64.7	65.2	57.6
1901	84	64.9	66.1	74.7
1902	80	68.6	63.6	89.7
1903	82	69.3	62.3	76.4
1904	84	70.5	68.7	83.6
1905	85	77.0	76.0	120.4
1906	89	82.0	75.4	86.7
1907	94	86.9	71.9	52.0
1908	93	77.6	72.7	67.0
1909	90	79.7	76.2	81.0
1910	93	88.9	77.6	70.2
1911	96	91.8	91.5	88.9
1912	97	96.8	98.7	101.7
1913	100	100.0	100.0	100.0

SOURCES: Col. 1: Werner Schlote, *British Overseas Trade from 1700 to the 1930's*, p. 177.
Col. 2: *Ibid.*, pp. 153–154. Values in 1913 prices converted to quantity index.
Col. 3: Table A–2, col. 6 ÷ Table G–17, col. 2.
Col. 4: Table G–18, col. 2 ÷ Table G–18, col. 1.

TABLE G–18

U.S. AND U.K. PRICE AND QUANTITY INDEXES FOR TEXTILE EXPORTS
(1913 = 100)

Year	Quantity Index		Price Index	
	U.K. (1)	U.S. (2)	U.K. (3)	U.S. (4)
1879	64.0	18.2		
1880	71.3	16.1	89.0	122.8
1881	77.9	20.0	85.6	115.8
1882	75.5	18.3	84.9	121.4
1883	75.8	18.6	78.8	114.0
1884	77.0	17.5	78.1	106.2
1885	73.9	22.3	74.7	95.7
1886	79.4	26.0	71.9	94.2
1887	81.2	23.3	73.3	97.0
1888	81.8	17.5	74.7	103.8
1889	81.7	16.8	76.7	108.1
1890	81.4	18.2	78.1	104.0
1891	77.7	23.9	72.6	95.4
1892	75.9	23.5	67.1	90.7
1893	72.1	23.9	69.2	93.1
1894	75.0	28.4	63.0	84.9
1895	81.1	30.4	61.0	78.9
1896	82.1	40.4	63.0	81.2
1897	76.9	42.5	59.6	73.7
1898	77.1	48.0	59.6	70.0
1899	80.2	59.7	63.7	72.8
1900	75.4	43.4	74.7	85.6
1901	76.2	56.9	69.9	79.5
1902	78.3	70.2	69.2	80.6
1903	78.4	59.9	76.0	81.3
1904	80.9	67.6	81.5	88.3
1905	87.1	104.9	80.1	89.6
1906	90.0	78.0	86.3	95.0
1907	93.9	48.8	91.1	103.3
1908	80.9	54.2	81.5	90.6
1909	86.7	70.2	82.2	86.6
1910	92.8	65.1	95.2	95.7
1911	97.1	86.3	97.9	94.3
1912	100.9	102.6	96.6	92.8
1913	100.0	100.0	100.0	100.0

SOURCE: Col. 1: Derived from Werner Schlote, *British Overseas Trade from 1700 to the 1930's* Table 15, p. 150.

Col. 2: Table B–3, Export Class 121.

Col. 3: Derived from A. G. Silverman, "Monthly Index Numbers of British Export and Import Prices, 1880–1913," *Review of Economic Statistics*, 1930, p. 147.

Col. 4: Table B–1, Export Class 121.

Appendix H

Indexes of Terms of Trade and Other Price Ratios

TABLE H-1

INDEX OF TERMS OF TRADE OF THE UNITED STATES.
NBER-COMMERCE SERIES, 1879–1960
(1913 = 100)

Calendar Year	Terms of Trade Index
1879	90.3
1880	89.7
1881	96.4
1882	98.8
1883	99.6
1884	102.3
1885	103.8
1886	97.9
1887	94.1
1888	101.0
1889	91.6
1890	91.2
1891	95.5
1892	92.6
1893	87.2
1894	84.4
1895	90.3
1896	88.0
1897	91.0
1898	90.4
1899	88.7
1900	93.4
1901	96.1
1902	100.7
1903	103.1
1904	101.3
1905	92.4
1906	94.9
1907	96.0
1908	102.4
1909	107.2
1910	107.9
1911	97.3
1912	94.6
1913	100.0
1914	104.3
1915	108.1

(continued)

TABLE H–1 (concluded)
(1913 = 100)

Calendar Year	Terms of Trade Index
1916	112.7
1917	121.8
1918	127.8
1919	119.2
1920	106.1
1921	125.8
1922	120.2
1923	112.9
1924	113.2
1925	105.6
1926	99.2
1927	99.8
1928	105.2
1929	111.8
1930	120.9
1931	119.1
1932	132.4
1933	137.5
1934	141.4
1935	141.2
1936	135.2
1937	127.6
1938	133.8
1939	128.4
1940	128.7
1941	128.9
1942	135.6
1943	137.1
1944	146.4
1945	141.8
1946	121.0
1947	116.9
1948	112.7
1949	110.0
1950	98.1
1951	89.5
1952	93.9
1953	97.9
1954	94.0
1955	95.3
1956	97.4
1957	99.6
1958	103.6
1959	105.7
1960	105.6

SOURCE: Table A–1, col. 1 ÷ Table A–3, col. 1.

443

TABLE H–2

INDEXES OF TERMS OF TRADE OF THE UNITED STATES, 1879–1916
KREPS AND NBER COMPARED
(calendar 1913 = 100)

| Fiscal Year | Terms of Trade Index | |
	NBER (1)	Kreps (2)
1880	91.2	75.9
1881	92.9	82.6
1882	97.3	89.2
1883	101.0	83.9
1884	101.0	91.8
1885	105.4	94.6
1886	100.8	85.7
1887	96.4	78.2
1888	95.8	85.0
1889	97.7	75.0
1890	89.5	77.7
1891	93.4	74.4
1892	95.7	70.0
1893	90.6	68.5
1894	85.1	69.1
1895	87.5	76.7
1896	90.0	77.6
1897	89.7	77.6
1898	92.7	81.3
1899	87.9	79.3
1900	91.2	86.5
1901	95.8	93.5
1902	99.8	96.8
1903	101.7	102.1
1904	105.9	102.7
1905	92.6	83.3
1906	96.9	91.7
1907	94.3	93.7
1908	101.0	98.6
1909	102.8	103.5
1910	108.8	108.4
1911	104.9	98.1
1912	93.6	86.9
1913	98.2	98.1
1914	101.7	102.1
1915	105.8	103.0
1916	108.8	108.1

SOURCE: Column 1: Table G–1, col. 2 ÷ col. 4.
Column 2: Table G–1, col. 1 ÷ col. 3.

TABLE H-3

INDEXES OF TERMS OF TRADE OF INDUSTRIAL EUROPE AND THE
UNITED KINGDOM, 1870–1913
(1913 = 100)

Year	U.K. Imlah (1)	U.K. Schlote (2)	Industrial Europe Including U.K. (3)	Industrial Europe Excluding U.K. (4)	Industrial Europe Including U.K. but excluding intra-European trade (5)
1870	88.0	87	101	107	
1871	94.1	90	104	110	
1872	97.2	95	106	111	
1873	100.9	98	106	111	
1874	97.4	94	104	110	
1875	96.0	91	102	107	
1876	90.7	86	98	100	
1877	84.8	82	97	104	
1878	88.1	84	98	104	
1879	87.5	83	98	105	
1880	86.1	82	96	103	
1881	83.2	80	94	101	
1882	85.7	81	95	104	
1883	84.8	82	96	103	
1884	86.0	83	96	103	
1885	88.2	84	96	106	
1886	89.8	86	98	102	
1887	91.6	85	97	102	
1888	88.0	85	99	106	
1889	88.6	88	99	107	
1890	93.9	93	100	103	
1891	92.4	92	101	103	
1892	92.1	91	100	105	
1893	94.1	91	102	106	
1894	95.9	95	102	106	
1895	95.4	96	103	105	
1896	95.4	95	103	108	
1897	94.7	94	103	110	
1898	94.1	94	104	109	
1899	96.6	98	106	110	
1900	103.3	105	107	109	113
1901	101.6	104	107	107	113
1902	98.2	99	104	107	109
1903	96.7	98	104	106	109
1904	97.5	98	104	107	108
1905	96.9	98	103	106	107
1906	98.5	99	104	105	107
1907	98.9	100	103	104	106
1908	98.7	101	106	108	108
1909	94.1	96	101	104	103
1910	92.9	93	99	102	100
1911	96.9	97	100	101	101
1912	96.8	98	100	100	100
1913	100.0	100	100	100	100

SOURCE: Column 1: Albert H. Imlah, *Economic Elements in the Pax Britannica,* pp. 96–98.
We converted Imlah's terms of trade index from 1880 = 100 to 1913 = 100.

NOTES TO TABLE H–3 (continued)

Column 2: Kindleberger, *Terms of Trade*, p. 12, as computed from Werner Schlote, *British Overseas Trade from 1700 to the 1930's*, Oxford, 1952, pp. 176–177.

Columns 3 and 5: Kindleberger, *Terms of Trade*, p. 12.

Column 4: Table G–4, col. 2 ÷ col. 4.

TABLE H–4

INDEXES OF TERMS OF TRADE OF INDUSTRIAL EUROPE AND THE
UNITED KINGDOM, 1920–60
(1913 = 100)

CALENDAR YEAR	U.K. Board of Trade (1)	INDUSTRIAL EUROPE		Excluding U.K. (4)
		Including U.K.		
		Unadjusted (2)	Adjusted to Exclude Intra-Europe Trade (3)	
1920	126	96	96	79
1921	141	107	108	67
1922	132	109	110	95
1923	129	113	114	104
1924	123	112	113	105
1925	119	106	108	98
1926	122	107	109	98
1927	121	107	109	100
1928	118	106	108	99
1929	119	106	109	100
1930	129	115	119	107
1931	143	124	129	112
1932	142	130	136	124
1933	149	131	138	122
1934	142	129	137	124
1935	140	127	135	120
1936	138	121	130	113
1937	131	115	124	106
1938	143	124	134	114
1946	133			
1947	123	123	125	
1948	121	116	118	114
1949	124	115	118	110
1950	114	103	106	98
1951	101	98	102	96
1952	108	105	109	104
1953	114			
1954	114			
1955	113			
1956	115			
1957	118			
1958	127			
1959	126			
1960	128			

SOURCE: Column 1, 1920–51: Kindleberger, *Terms of Trade*, p. 13.
1952–60: Table G–3, col. 1 ÷ col. 2.
Columns 2 and 3: Kindleberger, *ibid.*, p. 13.
Column 4: Table G–5, col. 2 ÷ col. 4.

TABLE H–5

RELATION OF U.S. TO U.K. AND CONTINENTAL INDUSTRIAL
EUROPE EXPORT PRICES, 1870–1913
(1913 = 100)

| CALENDAR YEAR | U.S. EXPORT PRICE INDEX AS % OF EXPORT PRICE INDEX FOR | | | |
| | U.K. | | Industrial Europe | |
	Imlah (1)	Schlote (2)	Including U.K. (3)	Excluding U.K. (4)
1879	93.0	108.8	91.6	84.9
1880	98.4	115.3	98.5	92.3
1881	105.0	122.1	102.8	95.2
1882	106.2	125.9	105.9	98.2
1883	104.1	120.7	103.5	96.6
1884	104.1	120.5	104.9	98.6
1885	100.9	118.2	103.4	96.8
1886	99.3	115.8	100.8	95.2
1887	99.3	117.1	101.8	95.0
1888	104.8	119.6	103.1	96.5
1889	98.5	110.3	95.6	89.6
1890	93.3	103.7	94.4	90.4
1891	97.3	107.2	98.8	95.5
1892	94.9	105.0	96.4	93.1
1893	93.1	104.2	94.4	90.1
1894	86.3	95.3	88.1	84.9
1895	91.3	99.7	90.9	87.6
1896	89.4	97.3	88.8	84.5
1897	88.1	96.0	85.3	80.3
1898	87.0	95.0	83.4	78.6
1899	87.7	93.9	83.1	78.6
1900	85.6	91.0	86.2	84.4
1901	88.1	93.4	90.2	88.2
1902	94.7	100.5	93.6	90.4
1903	100.8	105.6	98.4	95.2
1904	100.0	104.7	97.6	94.5
1905	96.5	99.6	92.0	89.0
1906	97.9	101.0	94.6	91.7
1907	98.8	101.3	97.1	95.2
1908	97.2	99.0	94.8	92.9
1909	105.6	107.2	101.4	98.2
1910	109.7	111.0	107.5	106.4
1911	98.7	99.5	96.4	95.4
1912	99.1	99.5	96.5	95.5
1913	100.0	100.0	100.0	100.0

SOURCE: Column 1: Table A–1, col. 1 ÷ Table G–2, col. 1.
Column 2: Table A–1, col. 1 ÷ Table G–2, col. 2.
Column 3: Table A–1, col. 1 ÷ Table G–4, col. 1.
Column 4: Table A–1, col. 1 ÷ Table G–4, col. 2.

TABLE H–6

RELATION OF U.S. TO U.K. AND CONTINENTAL INDUSTRIAL EUROPE
EXPORT PRICES, 1920–60
(1913 = 100)

| CALENDAR YEAR | U.S. EXPORT PRICE INDEX AS % OF EXPORT PRICE INDEX FOR Industrial Europe | | |
	U.K. Board of Trade (1)	Including U.K. (2)	Excluding U.K. (3)
1920	86.1	123.7	158.2
1921	73.9	122.1	181.0
1922	79.0	107.3	130.7
1923	85.7	104.9	118.6
1924	87.3	103.5	114.5
1925	83.7	102.8	116.1
1926	81.4	101.3	115.4
1927	79.8	95.4	106.1
1928	83.1	99.0	109.5
1929	84.0	100.5	111.3
1930	78.9	95.4	106.4
1931	72.6	87.1	97.3
1932	87.0	93.2	96.6
1933	74.7	83.0	87.4
1934	73.2	79.2	82.6
1935	75.9	82.2	85.8
1936	74.6	84.6	90.7
1937	73.7	86.9	95.4
1938	67.8	80.4	89.0
1948	69.5	76.5	80.4
1949	67.6	77.1	83.2
1950	83.8	90.7	94.4
1951	81.5	84.4	86.1
1952	77.2	81.7	84.3
1953	79.8		
1954	79.5		
1955	78.8		
1956	78.6		
1957	77.6		
1958	77.7		
1959	78.9		
1960	78.3		

SOURCE: Column 1: Table A–1, col. 1 ÷ Table G–3, col. 1.
Column 2: Table A–1, col. 1 ÷ Table G–5, col. 1.
Column 3: Table A–1, col. 1 ÷ Table G–5, col. 2.

TABLE H–7

RELATION OF U.S. TO U.K. AND CONTINENTAL INDUSTRIAL
EUROPE IMPORT PRICES, 1879–1913
(1913 = 100)

CALENDAR YEAR	U.S. IMPORT PRICE INDEX AS % OF IMPORT PRICE INDEX FOR			
	U.K.		Industrial Europe	
	Imlah (1)	Schlote (2)	Including U.K. (3)	Excluding U.K. (4)
1879	90.1	100.4	99.4	98.5
1880	94.3	105.7	105.7	105.7
1881	90.7	101.6	100.7	99.7
1882	92.1	103.1	103.1	103.1
1883	88.6	98.8	99.8	99.8
1884	87.4	97.3	98.4	99.4
1885	85.7	95.3	97.4	98.5
1886	91.1	101.7	100.6	99.4
1887	96.7	105.7	104.5	103.3
1888	91.5	100.9	100.9	100.9
1889	95.4	105.5	104.3	104.3
1890	96.1	105.9	103.6	102.4
1891	94.2	103.4	103.4	103.4
1892	94.4	102.8	104.0	105.2
1893	100.5	108.2	109.5	109.5
1894	97.9	107.1	107.1	107.1
1895	96.4	106.0	103.2	101.9
1896	97.0	104.8	103.5	103.5
1897	91.6	98.6	97.3	97.3
1898	90.6	98.3	95.8	94.6
1899	95.5	103.2	99.4	97.0
1900	94.7	102.0	99.7	98.5
1901	93.2	100.7	99.5	98.3
1902	92.3	98.5	97.3	96.2
1903	94.7	100.0	98.8	97.7
1904	96.3	100.9	99.8	99.8
1905	101.3	105.3	103.0	101.8
1906	101.5	105.2	102.9	101.8
1907	101.7	105.5	104.4	103.3
1908	93.7	97.8	97.8	97.8
1909	92.8	95.7	95.7	95.7
1910	94.4	95.6	98.5	100.6
1911	98.4	99.1	99.1	99.1
1912	101.5	103.1	102.0	101.0
1913	100.0	100.0	100.0	100.0

SOURCE: Column 1: Table A–3, col. 1 ÷ Table G–2, col. 3.
Column 2: Table A–3, col. 1 ÷ Table G–2, col. 4.
Column 3: Table A–3, col. 1 ÷ Table G–4, col. 3.
Column 4: Table A–3, col. 1 ÷ Table G–4, col. 4.

TABLE H–8

RELATION OF U.S. TO U.K. AND CONTINENTAL INDUSTRIAL
EUROPE IMPORT PRICES, 1920–60
(1913 = 100)

| CALENDAR YEAR | U.S. IMPORT PRICE INDEX AS % OF IMPORT PRICE INDEX FOR | | |
| | U.K. Board of Trade (1) | *Industrial Europe* | |
		Including U.K. (2)	Excluding U.K. (3)
1920	102.4	111.8	117.2
1921	82.9	91.4	96.3
1922	86.7	97.2	103.1
1923	97.6	105.1	109.3
1924	94.7	101.9	106.0
1925	94.2	102.9	108.3
1926	100.0	109.2	114.5
1927	97.0	103.0	106.4
1928	93.5	100.1	103.3
1929	89.2	95.6	99.6
1930	84.3	90.5	93.9
1931	87.3	90.4	91.4
1932	93.4	92.0	90.6
1933	80.8	78.7	77.7
1934	73.4	72.7	72.7
1935	75.2	73.6	72.8
1936	76.0	76.0	76.0
1937	75.5	77.6	79.1
1938	72.3	74.5	76.0
1948	74.5	79.0	81.5
1949	75.9	80.5	82.8
1950	97.3	95.3	94.4
1951	91.8	92.1	92.5
1952	88.7	91.6	93.1
1953	92.8		
1954	96.4		
1955	93.2		
1956	92.9		
1957	92.3		
1958	94.8		
1959	94.3		
1960	94.8		

SOURCE: Column 1: Table A–3, col. 1 ÷ Table G–3, col. 2.
Column 2: Table A–3, col. 1 ÷ Table G–5, col. 3.
Column 3: Table A–3, col. 1 ÷ Table G–5, col. 4.

TABLE H-9

RELATION OF U.S. MANUFACTURED TO AGRICULTURAL PRODUCT PRICES, 1879–1960
(1913 = 100)

Calendar Year	Manufactured Export Price Index as % of Agricultural Export Price Index (1)	Manufactured Export Price Index as % of Agricultural Import Price Index (2)	Manufactured Import Price Index as % of Agricultural Export Price Index (3)	Manufactured Import Price Index as % of Agricultural Import Price Index (4)
1879	147.8	106.1	127.4	91.5
1880	150.3	104.7	119.6	83.3
1881	136.5	103.6	112.9	85.6
1882	129.5	102.4	108.8	86.0
1883	136.9	110.9	114.2	92.5
1884	143.5	122.8	112.8	96.5
1885	146.2	126.4	114.8	99.2
1886	147.7	118.6	118.4	95.1
1887	141.7	106.1	116.8	87.5
1888	141.3	113.5	108.4	87.1
1889	141.9	101.3	116.5	83.2
1890	140.9	101.0	116.6	83.6
1891	127.6	99.4	109.5	85.3
1892	125.8	95.8	116.1	88.5
1893	118.0	84.8	114.8	82.5
1894	131.0	90.1	128.4	88.4
1895	147.7	108.7	129.7	95.5
1896	161.6	112.6	135.6	94.4
1897	148.6	112.5	133.9	101.4
1898	138.8	104.7	133.4	100.6
1899	148.0	109.3	135.7	100.2
1900	138.7	113.3	122.6	100.1
1901	132.5	117.5	124.6	110.5
1902	125.7	120.4	116.2	111.3
1903	122.6	120.0	108.6	106.5
1904	121.7	114.2	108.0	101.4
1905	124.8	101.0	119.0	96.3
1906	118.9	103.2	113.7	98.6
1907	116.0	103.0	110.2	97.9
1908	119.1	113.6	107.1	102.1
1909	103.9	107.0	92.1	94.8
1910	91.2	96.8	79.9	84.8
1911	103.2	94.0	97.5	88.8
1912	105.2	92.3	103.2	90.6
1913	100.0	100.0	100.0	100.0
1914	93.6	99.1	90.0	95.3
1915	94.0	102.4	84.2	91.7
1916	100.5	109.2	86.3	93.8
1917	77.0	104.4	69.7	94.4
1918	68.1	112.2	72.3	119.1
1919	65.7	98.3	73.5	110.0
1920	72.4	87.8	81.8	99.2
1921	106.3	152.2	106.7	152.8
1922	90.9	129.8	98.5	140.7

(continued)

TABLE H-9 (concluded)

| Calendar Year | Manufactured Export Price Index as % of | | Manufactured Import Price Index as % of | |
	Agricultural Export Price Index (1)	Agricultural Import Price Index (2)	Agricultural Export Price Index (3)	Agricultural Import Price Index (4)
1923	79.1	104.6	85.8	113.4
1924	75.7	110.4	80.4	117.1
1925	73.8	100.3	84.1	114.3
1926	90.0	103.6	97.6	112.4
1927	84.1	104.3	96.7	119.9
1928	78.3	107.6	95.6	131.4
1929	79.5	116.7	88.9	130.6
1930	91.4	141.0	95.8	147.8
1931	104.7	161.3	116.9	180.0
1932	125.1	190.8	124.2	189.4
1933	103.1	174.9	101.7	172.5
1934	82.5	164.0	79.3	157.8
1935	76.8	154.9	71.7	144.6
1936	76.4	136.5	69.0	123.4
1937	81.5	123.2	73.0	110.4
1938	88.4	155.4	85.7	150.7
1939	95.6	145.6	91.9	139.9
1940	96.1	152.9	95.4	151.7
1941	68.9	146.9	68.7	146.4
1942	60.4	141.4	54.5	127.7
1943	53.5	139.8	48.1	125.7
1944	56.0	148.1	47.4	125.4
1945	60.9	143.5	53.7	126.4
1946	54.7	111.2	63.7	129.5
1947	52.2	109.8	65.0	136.7
1948	52.6	109.0	67.3	139.3
1949	60.3	109.8	78.1	142.4
1950	64.7	83.3	84.2	108.3
1951	59.6	70.3	82.3	97.1
1952	60.5	82.0	81.9	111.0
1953	64.3	87.5	84.9	115.5
1954	64.2	78.6	86.0	105.3
1955	69.6	84.9	90.2	109.9
1956	75.0	91.9	94.8	116.1
1957	80.6	96.6	97.5	117.0
1958	83.8	103.0	98.3	120.8
1959	88.8	109.1	101.5	124.9
1960	93.1	111.4	106.8	127.9

SOURCE: Column 1: Table A-1, col. 6 ÷ Table A-5, col. 1.
Column 2: Table A-1, col. 6 ÷ Table A-5, col. 3.
Column 3: Table A-3, col. 6 ÷ Table A-5, col. 1.
Column 4: Table A-3, col. 6 ÷ Table A-5, col. 3.

TABLE H-10

RELATION OF U.S. MANUFACTURED EXPORT TO PRIMARY IMPORT PRICES, BY
ECONOMIC CLASS, 1879–1960
(1913 = 100)

| Calendar Year | U.S. Manufactured Export Price Index as % of Import Price Index for | | | |
	Crude Foodstuffs (1)	Manufactured Foodstuffs (2)	Crude Materials (3)	Semi-manufactures (4)
1879	104.4	90.1	125.5	152.9
1880	107.4	83.4	127.1	145.3
1881	111.0	79.2	125.6	148.9
1882	117.2	77.3	118.0	145.2
1883	128.8	83.5	125.7	150.7
1884	128.1	104.9	133.1	152.7
1885	130.8	110.0	136.5	160.9
1886	124.9	101.5	129.0	149.1
1887	89.2	108.7	123.7	147.8
1888	102.3	100.7	136.4	159.6
1889	94.9	81.1	128.6	147.2
1890	84.4	92.1	127.0	138.6
1891	81.7	86.4	129.3	135.0
1892	80.7	81.5	122.6	126.8
1893	70.2	71.1	115.1	118.0
1894	71.4	80.6	119.7	125.8
1895	81.9	113.3	130.6	144.2
1896	97.3	102.7	136.3	149.2
1897	107.7	104.0	123.4	139.0
1898	120.8	89.2	108.4	135.9
1899	136.0	91.1	108.5	123.0
1900	135.7	97.5	112.8	119.6
1901	142.5	98.1	114.9	114.3
1902	138.4	116.8	113.3	117.5
1903	147.0	112.1	111.8	119.3
1904	135.3	105.4	110.8	118.5
1905	127.4	83.5	101.1	110.7
1906	128.5	100.4	96.8	100.1
1907	130.7	100.4	96.2	99.1
1908	138.0	95.0	112.0	119.8
1909	137.0	93.4	102.2	120.0
1910	122.0	86.7	94.2	115.2
1911	101.1	87.1	95.6	105.6
1912	93.5	81.7	96.8	100.3
1913	100.0	100.0	100.0	100.0
1914	103.5	85.2	101.6	101.1
1915	112.2	70.6	112.5	101.1
1916	132.3	75.8	115.5	102.0
1917	141.0	76.4	107.6	93.8
1918	153.6	78.4	115.2	94.1
1919	109.4	68.2	107.9	95.2
1920	118.8	41.9	110.4	96.8
1921	162.1	91.6	164.2	121.4

(continued)

TABLE H–10 (concluded)

| Calendar Year | U.S. Manufactured Export Price Index as % of Import Price Index for | | | |
	Crude Foodstuffs (1)	Manufactured Foodstuffs (2)	Crude Materials (3)	Semi-manufactures (4)
1922	124.8	107.0	129.8	110.0
1923	124.4	66.6	111.3	100.2
1924	103.5	73.3	113.4	102.5
1925	85.8	106.8	93.2	100.2
1926	86.7	114.7	94.5	100.2
1927	83.9	87.6	101.9	91.5
1928	76.6	97.4	110.4	94.8
1929	80.8	112.6	117.7	91.4
1930	104.4	129.9	141.5	101.9
1931	107.3	115.7	167.4	102.5
1932	115.7	128.3	215.5	117.2
1933	119.7	116.6	197.3	105.3
1934	114.4	114.0	180.6	96.5
1935	123.3	104.3	171.1	97.5
1936	119.4	97.2	147.4	97.6
1937	105.6	100.3	130.0	91.1
1938	128.3	113.3	153.3	99.5
1939	129.9	114.6	138.6	98.5
1940	146.8	129.6	137.7	96.4
1941	123.6	123.0	136.6	94.7
1942	113.6	111.3	148.2	105.5
1943	116.9	115.2	149.5	113.3
1944	123.8	132.0	163.7	128.6
1945	119.2	124.0	156.3	126.2
1946	82.6	94.8	135.1	99.0
1947	68.8	90.2	142.3	91.3
1948	65.9	93.7	134.1	84.7
1949	65.1	93.6	133.2	88.8
1950	46.2	90.5	118.9	88.5
1951	45.4	92.3	90.1	77.7
1952	45.5	92.2	109.9	77.5
1953	45.5	93.7	123.2	82.2
1954	37.5	94.0	124.7	83.0
1955	44.3	96.2	120.0	78.0
1956	48.0	99.6	122.3	76.6
1957	51.9	101.3	125.8	82.8
1958	55.7	104.1	136.8	92.2
1959	64.4	106.8	139.2	94.2
1960	66.6	110.6	136.9	93.8

SOURCE: Table A–1, col. 6 ÷ Table A–3, cols. 2, 3, 4, and 5.

TABLE H-11

RELATION OF U.S. MANUFACTURED EXPORT TO PRIMARY EXPORT PRICES, BY
ECONOMIC CLASS, 1879–1960
(1913 = 100)

	U.S. Manufactured Export Price Index as % of Export Price Index for			
Calendar Year	Crude Foodstuffs (1)	Manufactured Foodstuffs (2)	Crude Materials (3)	Semi-manufactures (4)
1879	127.5	155.5	148.9	150.4
1880	137.5	152.9	148.1	151.3
1881	121.3	127.9	143.8	135.5
1882	112.9	115.4	139.6	132.6
1883	116.9	122.2	148.4	134.1
1884	133.5	132.6	146.8	141.6
1885	134.9	142.8	144.0	138.0
1886	135.2	142.9	145.5	135.4
1887	129.7	139.1	142.4	129.1
1888	128.7	136.4	142.0	130.9
1889	141.3	139.1	137.7	130.3
1890	135.9	141.8	133.0	126.5
1891	100.0	130.8	135.4	122.8
1892	105.8	118.1	135.4	116.6
1893	111.7	101.6	131.0	121.2
1894	120.9	110.5	148.3	121.1
1895	131.5	131.5	161.2	127.5
1896	152.2	152.4	158.7	138.1
1897	123.2	136.0	162.2	126.6
1898	107.4	121.5	168.9	117.3
1899	123.4	135.0	163.9	106.4
1900	132.9	138.7	137.0	110.5
1901	121.7	123.9	138.7	109.5
1902	114.6	112.2	136.0	112.6
1903	121.5	120.9	122.1	113.3
1904	123.0	127.0	117.2	115.0
1905	114.7	124.8	125.0	101.0
1906	119.3	120.8	116.3	92.1
1907	107.6	118.2	116.9	93.0
1908	100.7	114.3	125.9	108.8
1909	93.5	103.9	106.6	107.0
1910	100.0	92.0	91.1	105.7
1911	97.5	102.4	105.1	102.5
1912	93.3	100.2	108.8	96.9
1913	100.0	100.0	100.0	100.0
1914	82.4	91.3	107.3	96.6
1915	75.4	94.7	117.3	89.1
1916	90.6	110.3	113.1	83.5
1917	70.0	88.2	90.2	75.8
1918	72.3	79.2	77.2	83.7
1919	72.2	73.5	72.3	87.4
1920	73.7	91.0	69.3	93.9
1921	105.3	120.3	104.8	114.2

(continued)

TABLE H-11 (concluded)

Calendar Year	U.S. Manufactured Export Price Index as % of Export Price Index for			
	Crude Foodstuffs (1)	Manufactured Foodstuffs (2)	Crude Materials (3)	Semi-manufactures (4)
1922	108.2	114.1	78.0	108.6
1923	106.1	111.0	63.8	99.1
1924	90.0	108.7	67.5	101.9
1925	78.7	92.8	75.7	98.3
1926	91.6	96.5	97.6	99.1
1927	83.0	95.3	91.1	95.1
1928	87.3	96.8	78.6	94.5
1929	90.5	96.1	80.6	88.5
1930	96.0	100.2	99.0	97.1
1931	111.5	102.8	117.0	95.7
1932	118.6	122.8	126.0	105.3
1933	114.9	111.3	102.2	97.0
1934	107.1	107.0	84.2	92.1
1935	103.9	92.7	84.2	94.1
1936	100.1	91.9	83.5	88.9
1937	96.9	90.2	89.5	77.2
1938	117.6	103.8	100.3	86.7
1939	138.8	110.0	100.4	85.9
1940	129.9	116.1	102.8	87.3
1941	114.4	102.0	92.1	82.5
1942	116.8	90.1	97.5	93.3
1943	104.8	94.0	98.1	100.9
1944	107.6	97.3	110.1	114.4
1945	98.0	98.0	107.7	115.6
1946	78.0	83.2	83.3	97.4
1947	79.5	78.7	83.9	88.4
1948	81.7	81.6	78.8	86.6
1949	88.4	97.5	78.4	87.3
1950	99.8	112.3	73.7	87.0
1951	99.5	99.3	68.8	78.2
1952	92.6	106.1	73.7	80.3
1953	99.4	103.7	78.6	82.8
1954	109.5	102.2	76.2	82.1
1955	115.3	113.8	77.3	78.5
1956	119.2	121.9	81.4	73.8
1957	128.0	124.4	85.8	80.1
1958	130.9	124.4	88.9	91.1
1959	135.2	137.5	94.1	90.4
1960	138.3	142.5	97.0	92.0

SOURCE: Table A-1, col. 6 ÷ Table A-1, cols. 2, 3, 4, and 5.

TABLE H–12

RELATION OF U.S. MANUFACTURED IMPORT TO PRIMARY EXPORT PRICES, BY
ECONOMIC CLASS, 1879–1960
(1913 = 100)

Calendar Year	U.S. Manufactured Import Price Index as % of Export Price Index for			
	Crude Foodstuffs (1)	Manufactured Foodstuffs (2)	Crude Materials (3)	Semi-manufactures (4)
1879	109.8	134.0	128.3	129.6
1880	109.4	121.7	117.9	120.5
1881	100.3	105.7	118.9	112.1
1882	94.9	97.0	117.3	111.4
1883	97.5	101.9	123.8	111.9
1884	104.9	104.2	115.4	111.2
1885	106.0	112.1	113.1	108.4
1886	108.4	114.5	116.7	108.6
1887	107.0	114.7	117.4	106.4
1888	98.7	104.7	109.0	100.5
1889	116.0	114.2	113.0	107.0
1890	112.5	117.4	110.1	104.7
1891	85.8	112.3	116.2	105.4
1892	97.7	109.1	125.1	107.8
1893	108.6	98.8	127.4	117.8
1894	118.6	108.4	145.4	118.8
1895	115.5	115.5	141.6	112.0
1896	127.7	127.9	133.1	115.8
1897	111.0	122.5	146.2	114.1
1898	103.3	116.8	162.4	112.8
1899	113.1	123.8	150.3	97.5
1900	117.5	122.6	121.1	97.7
1901	114.5	116.6	130.5	103.0
1902	106.0	103.7	125.8	104.1
1903	107.6	107.1	108.1	100.3
1904	109.2	112.7	104.0	102.1
1905	109.3	119.0	119.2	96.3
1906	114.1	115.5	111.2	88.0
1907	102.2	112.3	111.1	88.4
1908	90.6	102.8	113.3	97.8
1909	82.8	92.1	94.4	94.8
1910	87.6	80.6	79.8	92.6
1911	92.1	96.7	99.2	96.8
1912	91.6	98.4	106.8	95.1
1913	100.0	100.0	100.0	100.0
1914	79.2	87.8	103.2	92.9
1915	67.5	84.8	105.0	79.8
1916	77.8	94.8	97.1	71.7
1917	63.4	79.8	81.6	68.6
1918	76.8	84.1	81.9	88.8
1919	80.8	82.2	80.9	97.8
1920	83.3	102.9	78.3	106.2
1921	105.7	120.9	105.2	114.7

(continued)

TABLE H–12 (concluded)

Calendar Year	U.S. Manufactured Import Price Index as % of Export Price Index for			
	Crude Foodstuffs (1)	Manufactured Foodstuffs (2)	Crude Materials (3)	Semi-manufactures (4)
1922	117.4	123.7	84.6	117.7
1923	115.1	120.4	69.2	107.4
1924	95.5	115.3	71.6	108.1
1925	89.7	105.8	86.3	112.0
1926	99.4	104.7	105.8	107.4
1927	95.5	109.6	104.7	109.3
1928	106.6	118.3	96.0	115.4
1929	101.3	107.6	90.2	99.1
1930	100.7	105.0	103.8	101.8
1931	124.5	114.7	130.6	106.8
1932	117.8	121.9	125.1	104.6
1933	113.3	109.7	100.8	95.6
1934	103.1	102.9	81.0	88.6
1935	96.9	86.5	78.6	87.8
1936	90.5	83.0	75.5	80.3
1937	86.8	80.8	80.2	69.1
1938	114.1	100.7	97.3	84.1
1939	133.3	105.7	96.5	82.5
1940	128.9	115.2	102.0	86.6
1941	114.1	101.7	91.8	82.2
1942	105.5	81.4	88.1	84.3
1943	94.3	84.5	88.2	90.8
1944	91.1	82.4	93.2	96.8
1945	86.4	86.4	94.9	101.8
1946	90.8	96.9	97.0	113.4
1947	99.0	97.9	104.5	110.1
1948	104.5	104.4	99.5	110.8
1949	114.6	126.3	101.6	113.1
1950	129.8	146.1	95.9	113.2
1951	137.4	137.1	94.9	108.0
1952	125.4	143.6	99.8	108.6
1953	131.1	136.9	103.8	109.3
1954	146.6	136.9	102.0	109.9
1955	149.3	147.5	100.2	101.7
1956	150.7	154.0	102.9	93.3
1957	154.9	150.6	103.9	97.0
1958	153.6	146.0	104.3	106.8
1959	154.7	157.3	107.7	103.5
1960	158.8	163.6	111.4	105.6

SOURCE: Table A–3, col. 6 ÷ Table A–1, cols. 2, 3, 4, and 5.

TABLE H–13

RELATION OF U.S. MANUFACTURED IMPORT TO PRIMARY IMPORT PRICES, BY
ECONOMIC CLASS, 1879–1960
(1913 = 100)

Calendar Year	U.S. Manufactured Import Price Index as % of Import Price Index for			
	Crude Foodstuffs (1)	Manufactured Foodstuffs (2)	Crude Materials (3)	Semi-manufactures (4)
1879	89.9	77.6	108.2	131.8
1880	85.5	66.4	101.2	115.7
1881	91.8	65.5	103.9	123.2
1882	98.5	64.9	99.1	122.0
1883	107.4	69.7	104.9	125.7
1884	100.6	82.4	104.6	120.0
1885	102.7	86.4	107.2	126.3
1886	100.1	81.4	103.4	119.6
1887	73.6	89.7	102.0	121.9
1888	78.5	77.3	104.7	122.4
1889	77.9	66.6	105.5	120.8
1890	69.8	76.3	105.1	114.7
1891	70.1	74.2	111.0	115.9
1892	74.6	75.2	113.2	117.1
1893	68.3	69.1	111.9	114.8
1894	70.0	79.1	117.4	123.3
1895	72.0	99.5	114.7	126.7
1896	81.6	86.1	114.4	125.1
1897	97.1	93.7	111.2	125.2
1898	116.1	85.7	104.2	130.6
1899	124.7	83.6	99.5	112.8
1900	119.9	86.2	99.7	105.7
1901	134.0	92.3	108.0	107.5
1902	128.0	108.0	104.7	108.6
1903	130.2	99.3	99.0	105.7
1904	120.1	93.6	98.3	105.2
1905	121.4	79.6	96.4	105.5
1906	122.8	96.0	92.6	95.7
1907	124.2	95.4	91.4	94.2
1908	124.2	85.4	100.8	107.7
1909	121.4	82.7	90.6	106.3
1910	106.9	76.0	82.5	100.9
1911	95.4	82.2	90.3	99.8
1912	91.7	80.2	95.0	98.5
1913	100.0	100.0	100.0	100.0
1914	99.6	81.9	97.7	97.2
1915	100.4	63.2	100.7	90.5
1916	113.7	65.1	99.2	87.6
1917	127.6	69.1	97.4	84.9
1918	163.0	83.2	122.3	99.8
1919	122.5	76.3	120.8	106.6
1920	134.3	47.3	124.8	109.5
1921	162.8	92.0	164.9	121.9
1922	135.3	116.0	140.7	119.2

(continued)

| Calendar Year | U.S. Manufactured Import Price Index as % of Import Price Index for | | | |
	Crude Foodstuffs (1)	Manufactured Foodstuffs (2)	Crude Materials (3)	Semi-manufactures (4)
1923	134.9	72.2	120.7	108.7
1924	109.9	77.8	120.4	108.8
1925	97.8	121.7	106.3	114.3
1926	94.0	124.4	102.5	108.7
1927	96.5	100.7	117.1	105.2
1928	93.6	118.9	134.8	115.8
1929	90.5	126.0	131.8	102.3
1930	109.5	136.2	148.4	106.9
1931	119.7	129.1	186.8	114.5
1932	114.9	127.4	214.0	116.3
1933	118.1	115.0	194.6	103.8
1934	110.1	109.6	173.8	92.8
1935	115.1	97.3	159.7	90.9
1936	107.9	87.8	133.2	88.2
1937	94.6	89.9	116.5	81.6
1938	124.4	109.9	148.7	96.5
1939	124.9	110.1	133.1	94.6
1940	145.6	128.6	136.6	95.6
1941	123.3	122.7	136.2	94.4
1942	102.6	100.5	133.8	95.3
1943	105.1	103.6	134.4	101.9
1944	104.8	111.7	138.6	108.8
1945	105.0	109.3	137.7	111.2
1946	96.2	110.3	157.3	115.3
1947	85.6	112.3	177.2	113.6
1948	84.2	119.8	171.4	108.3
1949	84.3	121.4	172.7	115.1
1950	60.1	117.7	154.7	115.2
1951	62.7	127.4	124.3	107.3
1952	61.5	124.8	148.8	104.8
1953	60.0	123.6	162.6	108.5
1954	50.2	125.9	167.0	111.1
1955	57.4	124.6	155.5	101.1
1956	60.6	125.9	154.5	96.9
1957	62.8	122.7	152.4	100.3
1958	65.3	122.1	160.5	108.2
1959	73.7	122.2	159.2	107.8
1960	76.5	127.0	157.2	107.7

SOURCE: Table A–3, col. 6 ÷ Table A–3, cols. 2, 3, 4, and 5.

TABLE H–14

RELATION OF U.S. MANUFACTURED TO TOTAL EXPORT AND IMPORT PRICE
INDEXES, 1879–1960
(1913 = 100)

Calendar Year	Price Index for Manufactured Exports as % of Price Index for		Price Index for Manufactured Imports as % of Price Index for	
	Total Exports	Total Imports	Total Exports	Total Imports
1879	129.0	116.5	111.1	100.4
1880	130.4	117.1	103.8	93.2
1881	120.2	115.9	99.4	95.8
1882	115.2	113.9	96.8	95.7
1883	120.1	119.6	100.2	99.8
1884	125.3	128.2	98.5	100.7
1885	126.9	131.7	99.7	103.4
1886	127.2	124.6	102.0	99.9
1887	124.1	116.7	102.3	96.3
1888	123.6	124.9	94.9	95.8
1889	124.1	113.6	101.9	93.3
1890	122.8	112.0	101.6	92.7
1891	114.1	109.0	98.0	93.6
1892	112.1	103.8	103.5	95.9
1893	108.5	94.6	105.5	92.0
1894	116.3	98.2	114.0	96.3
1895	127.3	115.0	111.8	101.0
1896	136.3	120.0	114.4	100.6
1897	127.5	116.1	114.9	104.6
1898	120.8	109.1	116.1	104.9
1899	124.9	110.8	114.5	101.6
1900	122.1	114.1	107.9	100.8
1901	118.6	114.0	111.6	107.3
1902	115.5	116.3	106.8	107.5
1903	114.2	117.7	101.2	104.3
1904	113.7	115.2	100.9	102.2
1905	112.9	104.3	107.6	99.4
1906	108.5	103.0	103.7	98.4
1907	107.4	103.0	102.0	97.9
1908	111.5	114.2	100.3	102.7
1909	103.3	110.7	91.5	98.1
1910	96.7	104.3	84.7	91.4
1911	102.1	99.4	96.5	93.9
1912	101.8	96.2	99.9	94.5
1913	100.0	100.0	100.0	100.0
1914	96.5	100.6	92.8	96.8
1915	96.0	103.8	85.9	92.9
1916	96.4	108.7	82.8	93.3
1917	85.0	103.5	76.9	93.7
1918	82.3	105.2	87.4	111.7
1919	80.9	96.4	90.5	107.8
1920	85.0	90.2	96.1	102.0
1921	104.1	130.9	104.5	131.5
1922	95.8	115.2	103.9	124.9
1923	88.9	100.4	96.4	108.9

(continued)

TABLE H–14 (concluded)

Calendar Year	Price Index for Manufactured Exports as % of Price Index for		Price Index for Manufactured Imports as % of Price Index for	
	Total Exports	Total Imports	Total Exports	Total Imports
1924	89.5	101.3	95.0	107.6
1925	89.5	94.5	102.0	107.7
1926	97.4	96.5	105.6	104.7
1927	94.4	94.2	108.5	108.3
1928	90.9	95.6	111.0	116.7
1929	90.9	101.7	101.8	113.8
1930	97.2	117.5	101.9	123.2
1931	101.5	121.0	113.3	135.0
1932	106.9	141.6	106.2	140.6
1933	97.4	133.9	96.1	132.1
1934	90.5	128.0	87.1	123.1
1935	89.5	126.3	83.5	117.9
1936	88.7	119.9	80.1	108.3
1937	87.8	112.1	78.7	100.4
1938	93.2	124.7	90.4	120.9
1939	94.2	120.9	90.5	116.2
1940	94.8	122.0	94.0	121.0
1941	92.0	118.5	91.7	118.2
1942	92.2	125.0	83.3	112.9
1943	93.8	128.6	84.3	115.6
1944	95.9	140.4	81.2	118.8
1945	95.1	134.8	83.8	118.8
1946	87.9	106.4	102.4	123.9
1947	86.6	101.2	107.8	126.0
1948	86.0	97.0	110.0	124.0
1949	88.2	97.1	114.4	125.8
1950	89.0	87.3	115.8	113.6
1951	86.1	77.0	118.8	106.3
1952	87.2	81.9	118.0	110.9
1953	88.2	86.4	116.4	114.0
1954	88.2	83.0	118.2	111.1
1955	88.6	84.5	114.8	109.5
1956	89.1	86.7	112.6	109.6
1957	91.7	91.3	111.0	110.5
1958	94.2	97.6	110.5	114.5
1959	95.8	101.2	109.6	115.8
1960	96.1	101.4	110.3	116.5

SOURCE: Column 1: Table A–1, col. 6 ÷ Table A–1, col. 1.
Column 2: Table A–1, col. 6 ÷ Table A–3, col. 1.
Column 3: Table A–3, col. 6 ÷ Table A–1, col. 1.
Column 4: Table A–3, col. 6 ÷ Table A–3, col. 1.

TABLE H–15

RELATION OF AGRICULTURAL EXPORT TO TOTAL U.S. IMPORT PRICES
(1913 = 100)

Calendar Year	Agricultural Export Price Index as % of Total Import Price Index
1879	78.8
1880	77.9
1881	84.9
1882	87.9
1883	87.4
1884	89.3
1885	90.1
1886	84.3
1887	82.4
1888	88.4
1889	80.1
1890	79.5
1891	85.4
1892	82.6
1893	80.1
1894	75.0
1895	77.9
1896	74.2
1897	78.1
1898	78.6
1899	74.8
1900	82.2
1901	86.1
1902	92.6
1903	96.1
1904	94.6
1905	83.6
1906	86.6
1907	88.8
1908	95.9
1909	106.5
1910	114.4
1911	96.3
1912	91.5
1913	100.0
1914	107.6
1915	110.4
1916	108.2
1917	134.3
1918	154.5
1919	146.7
1920	124.6
1921	123.2
1922	126.8
1923	126.9
1924	133.8
1925	128.0
1926	107.3

(continued)

TABLE H–15 (concluded)

Calendar Year	Agricultural Export Price Index as % of Total Import Price Index
1927	111.9
1928	122.0
1929	127.9
1930	128.6
1931	115.5
1932	113.2
1933	129.9
1934	155.2
1935	164.5
1936	156.9
1937	137.5
1938	141.1
1939	126.4
1940	126.9
1941	172.1
1942	207.0
1943	240.5
1944	250.7
1945	221.4
1946	194.5
1947	193.9
1948	184.4
1949	161.1
1950	134.9
1951	129.3
1952	135.4
1953	134.3
1954	129.3
1955	121.5
1956	115.6
1957	113.3
1958	116.5
1959	114.1
1960	109.0

Source: Table A–5, col. 1 ÷ Table A–3, col. 1.

TABLE H–16

SINGLE FACTORAL TERMS OF TRADE FOR U.S. AGRICULTURAL AND
MANUFACTURED EXPORTS
(1913 = 100)

CALENDAR YEAR	TERMS OF TRADE OF AGRICULTURAL EXPORTS *Input Measured By:*		TERMS OF TRADE OF MANUFACTURED EXPORTS *Input Measured By:*	
	Manhours (1)	Total Factor Input (2)	Manhours (3)	Total Factor Input (4)
1879	66.4	71.9	61.6	72.7
1889	72.1	77.1	76.1	86.1
1890	69.4	74.1	77.5	
1891	76.9	81.9	75.6	
1892	69.9	74.1	72.8	
1893	65.4	69.4	62.1	
1894	62.8	66.4	67.7	
1895	68.8	72.7	84.6	
1896	69.6	73.5	83.6	
1897	78.1	81.9	84.3	
1898	81.4	84.9	87.7	
1899	76.8	79.9	85.8	93.8
1900	84.4	87.0	85.6	
1901	87.3	89.9	91.0	
1902	92.6	96.2	97.3	
1903	98.3	100.9	95.3	
1904	98.8	101.8	97.9	
1905	87.7	89.6	88.9	
1906	95.1	96.8	89.0	
1907	92.6	94.2	85.8	
1908	101.4	103.1	89.0	
1909	109.6	111.0	97.5	100.7
1910	120.2	121.4	90.6	
1911	93.7	94.3	82.7	
1912	103.9	104.7	92.0	
1913	100.0	100.0	100.0	
1914	116.5	117.6	101.1	
1915	130.6	129.3	117.7	
1916	113.3	111.6	121.3	
1917	151.0	149.9	107.3	
1918	155.6	154.7	109.0	
1919	151.5	148.8	95.1	90.3
1920	124.8	123.6	94.3	
1921	126.0	121.1	158.0	
1922	133.9	131.1	157.5	
1923	142.1	140.5	132.1	
1924	140.6	140.0	141.8	
1925	141.4	141.8	140.9	
1926	117.1	117.3	146.7	
1927	130.8	128.7	146.6	

(continued)

TABLE H–16 (concluded)

CALENDAR YEAR	TERMS OF TRADE OF AGRICULTURAL EXPORTS *Input Measured By:*		TERMS OF TRADE OF MANUFACTURED EXPORTS *Input Measured By:*	
	Manhours (1)	Total Factor Input (2)	Manhours (3)	Total Factor Input (4)
1928	137.0	135.3	155.4	
1929	149.4	146.7	173.0	159.9
1930	141.2	138.5	201.3	
1931	138.9	137.0	213.8	
1932	135.2	131.0	233.8	
1933	159.6	155.6	240.8	
1934	183.1	173.0	240.4	
1935	205.6	197.7	252.6	
1936	188.6	179.8	241.6	
1937	171.6	168.0	222.9	205.7
1938	197.5	188.9	243.7	
1939	176.5	168.9	258.6	
1940	177.8	168.4	273.6	
1941	266.6	249.0	275.5	
1942	330.6	309.5	295.8	
1943	369.4	343.7	308.4	
1944	392.3	364.0	332.9	
1945	355.1	323.0	315.2	
1946	330.5	296.6	228.8	
1947	331.0	292.8	230.3	
1948	347.4	302.0	228.6	211.1
1949	312.2	265.8	237.3	
1950	287.6	236.7	230.6	
1951	272.3	219.2	200.7	
1952	300.0	237.2	218.8	
1953	341.5	263.6	240.8	213.0
1954	351.4	268.6	237.9	
1955	341.1	261.6	258.2	
1956	341.0	257.3	270.2	
1957	351.6	257.3	290.5	

SOURCE: Column 1: Table H–15, col. 1 × Table G–6, col. 1.
Column 2: Table H–15, col. 1 × Table G–6, col. 2.
Column 3: Table H–14, col. 2 × Table G–6, col. 3.
Column 4: Table H–14, col. 2 × Table G–6, col. 4.

TABLE H–17

RATIO OF MANUFACTURED TO AGRICULTURAL EXPORT
VALUES PER UNIT OF INPUT
(1913 = 100)

Calendar Year	Input Measured by:	
	Manhours (1)	Total Factor Input (2)
1879	92.8	101.1
1889	105.5	111.7
1890	111.7	
1891	98.3	
1892	104.1	
1893	95.0	
1894	107.8	
1895	123.0	
1896	120.1	
1897	107.9	
1898	107.7	
1899	111.7	117.4
1900	101.4	
1901	104.2	
1902	105.1	
1903	96.9	
1904	99.1	
1905	101.4	
1906	93.6	
1907	92.7	
1908	87.8	
1909	89.0	90.7
1910	75.4	
1911	88.3	
1912	88.5	
1913	100.0	
1914	86.8	
1915	90.1	
1916	107.1	
1917	71.1	
1918	70.1	
1919	62.8	60.7
1920	75.6	
1921	125.4	
1922	117.6	
1923	93.0	
1924	100.9	
1925	99.6	
1926	125.3	
1927	112.1	
1928	113.4	
1929	115.8	109.0
1930	142.6	

(continued)

467

TABLE H–17 (concluded)

Calendar Year	Input Measured by:	
	Manhours (1)	Total Factor Input (2)
1931	153.9	
1932	172.9	
1933	150.9	
1934	131.3	
1935	122.9	
1936	128.1	
1937	129.9	122.4
1938	123.4	
1939	146.5	
1940	153.9	
1941	103.3	
1942	89.5	
1943	83.5	
1944	84.9	
1945	88.8	
1946	69.2	
1947	69.6	
1948	65.8	69.9
1949	76.0	
1950	80.2	
1951	73.7	
1952	72.9	
1953	70.5	80.8
1954	67.7	
1955	75.7	
1956	79.8	
1957	82.6	

SOURCE: Column 1: Table H–16, col. 3 ÷ col. 1.
Column 2: Table H–16, col. 4 ÷ col. 2.

TABLE H–18

U.S. Export Price Indexes as Percentage of Implicit Price Index
Underlying Deflated GNP

$(1913 = 100)$

| | Exports | | |
| | | | |
Calendar Year	Total (1)	Manufactured Products (2)	Agricultural Products (3)
1879	106.9	137.9	93.3
1880	106.5	138.9	92.4
1881	111.6	134.2	98.3
1882	111.8	128.8	99.5
1883	108.1	129.9	94.9
1884	109.9	137.7	95.9
1885	109.4	138.8	95.0
1886	104.4	132.8	89.9
1887	103.3	128.1	90.5
1888	106.8	132.0	93.5
1889	101.8	126.3	89.0
1890	103.2	126.7	89.9
1891	108.9	123.7	96.9
1892	105.1	117.8	93.7
1893	101.0	109.6	92.8
1894	94.8	110.2	84.1
1895	98.4	125.2	84.8
1896	100.1	136.5	84.5
1897	96.8	123.4	83.1
1898	92.8	112.1	80.7
1899	94.9	118.5	80.1
1900	101.4	123.8	89.2
1901	100.4	119.1	89.9
1902	99.6	115.1	91.6
1903	105.2	120.2	98.1
1904	104.1	118.3	97.2
1905	97.9	110.5	88.5
1906	102.6	111.3	93.6
1907	104.4	112.1	96.6
1908	99.6	111.0	93.3
1909	100.3	103.6	99.7
1910	106.0	102.5	112.4
1911	97.8	99.9	96.8
1912	96.1	97.8	93.0
1913	100.0	100.0	100.0
1914	96.8	93.5	99.9
1915	100.8	96.7	102.9
1916	114.5	110.4	109.9
1917	120.2	102.2	132.6
1918	120.0	98.8	145.1
1919	122.8	99.3	151.1
1920	116.0	98.7	136.3
1921	93.3	97.0	91.3

(continued)

TABLE H–18 (concluded)

Calendar Year	Exports		
	Total (1)	Manufactured Products (2)	Agricultural Products (3)
1922	90.4	86.7	95.3
1923	94.3	83.9	106.0
1924	93.6	83.8	110.7
1925	93.4	83.5	113.2
1926	85.4	83.2	92.5
1927	82.0	77.4	92.0
1928	83.4	75.7	96.7
1929	82.7	75.2	94.7
1930	76.3	74.2	81.1
1931	65.1	66.1	63.1
1932	63.4	67.8	54.2
1933	66.4	64.7	62.8
1934	72.9	66.0	80.0
1935	76.0	68.0	88.5
1936	74.9	66.4	87.0
1937	78.6	69.0	84.7
1938	73.4	68.4	77.3
1939	72.3	68.1	71.2
1940	76.8	72.8	75.7
1941	76.3	70.1	101.8
1942	82.3	75.8	125.6
1943	82.7	77.6	145.1
1944	91.9	88.2	157.4
1945	89.3	84.9	139.4
1946	78.6	69.1	126.3
1947	82.6	71.6	137.1
1948	83.4	71.8	136.5
1949	76.8	67.8	112.4
1950	73.8	65.7	101.5
1951	78.5	67.5	113.3
1952	76.9	67.0	110.8
1953	75.6	66.7	103.7
1954	74.2	65.5	102.0
1955	74.4	66.0	94.8
1956	74.9	66.7	88.9
1957	74.6	68.4	84.9
1958	72.3	68.1	81.3
1959	71.4	68.4	77.1
1960	71.3	68.5	73.6

SOURCE: Table A–1, columns 1 and 6, and Table A–5, column 1, as percentage of Table G–8, column 3.

TABLE H–19

U.S. Import Price Indexes as Percentage of Implicit Price Index
Underlying Deflated GNP

(1913 = 100)

Calendar Year	Imports		
	Total (1)	Manufactured Products (2)	Agricultural Products (3)
1879	118.4	118.8	129.9
1880	118.7	110.6	132.7
1881	115.8	111.0	129.6
1882	113.2	108.3	125.8
1883	108.5	108.3	117.1
1884	107.4	108.2	112.2
1885	105.4	109.0	109.9
1886	106.6	106.5	111.9
1887	109.8	105.7	120.8
1888	105.7	101.3	116.3
1889	111.1	103.7	124.6
1890	113.1	104.9	125.5
1891	113.4	106.2	124.4
1892	113.5	108.9	123.0
1893	115.9	106.5	129.2
1894	112.2	108.1	122.3
1895	108.9	110.0	115.2
1896	113.8	114.5	121.3
1897	106.3	111.2	109.7
1898	102.7	107.7	107.1
1899	107.0	108.7	108.4
1900	108.5	109.4	109.3
1901	104.4	112.0	101.4
1902	98.9	106.4	95.6
1903	102.1	106.4	100.1
1904	102.8	105.0	103.6
1905	106.0	105.4	109.5
1906	108.1	106.4	107.9
1907	108.8	106.5	108.8
1908	97.2	99.9	97.8
1909	93.6	91.8	96.8
1910	98.2	89.8	105.9
1911	100.5	94.4	106.3
1912	101.6	96.0	105.9
1913	100.0	100.0	100.0
1914	92.9	89.9	94.4
1915	93.2	86.6	94.4
1916	101.6	94.8	101.1
1917	98.7	92.5	97.9
1918	93.9	104.8	88.0
1919	103.0	111.1	101.0
1920	109.3	111.5	112.4
1921	74.1	97.5	63.8

(continued)

471

TABLE H-19 (concluded)

Calendar Year	Imports		
	Total (1)	Manufactured Products (2)	Agricultural Products (3)
1922	75.2	94.0	66.8
1923	83.5	90.9	80.2
1924	82.7	89.0	76.0
1925	88.4	95.2	83.3
1926	86.2	90.2	80.3
1927	82.2	89.0	74.3
1928	79.3	92.5	70.4
1929	74.0	84.2	64.5
1930	63.1	77.7	52.6
1931	54.6	73.8	41.0
1932	47.9	67.3	35.5
1933	48.3	63.8	37.0
1934	51.5	63.5	40.2
1935	53.8	63.4	43.9
1936	55.4	60.0	48.7
1937	61.6	61.8	56.0
1938	54.8	66.3	44.0
1939	56.3	65.4	46.8
1940	59.7	72.2	47.6
1941	59.2	69.9	47.8
1942	60.7	68.5	53.6
1943	60.4	69.8	55.5
1944	62.8	74.6	59.5
1945	63.0	74.8	59.2
1946	65.0	80.5	62.1
1947	70.7	89.1	65.2
1948	74.0	91.8	65.9
1949	69.8	87.8	61.7
1950	75.2	85.4	78.9
1951	87.7	93.2	96.0
1952	81.8	90.7	81.8
1953	77.2	88.0	76.2
1954	78.9	87.7	83.3
1955	78.0	85.5	77.7
1956	76.9	84.3	72.6
1957	75.0	82.8	70.8
1958	69.8	79.9	66.2
1959	67.6	78.3	62.7
1960	67.6	78.7	61.5

SOURCE: Table A-3, columns 1 and 6, and Table A-5, column 3, as percentage of Table G-8, column 3.

TABLE H–20

RATIO OF U.S. EXPORT TO IMPORT PRICE INDEXES FOR MANUFACTURED
AND AGRICULTURAL PRODUCTS
(1913 = 100)

Calendar Year	Ratio for Manufactured Products (1)	Ratio for Agricultural Products (2)
1879	1.161	.718
1880	1.256	.696
1881	1.209	.759
1882	1.190	.791
1883	1.199	.811
1884	1.273	.855
1885	1.273	.864
1886	1.247	.803
1887	1.213	.749
1888	1.303	.803
1889	1.218	.714
1890	1.208	.717
1891	1.165	.779
1892	1.083	.762
1893	1.028	.718
1894	1.020	.688
1895	1.138	.736
1896	1.192	.697
1897	1.110	.757
1898	1.040	.754
1899	1.091	.738
1900	1.132	.817
1901	1.063	.887
1902	1.082	.958
1903	1.129	.979
1904	1.127	.939
1905	1.049	.809
1906	1.046	.868
1907	1.053	.888
1908	1.112	.954
1909	1.129	1.030
1910	1.141	1.061
1911	1.059	.910
1912	1.019	.877
1913	1.000	1.000
1914	1.040	1.059
1915	1.117	1.089
1916	1.164	1.087
1917	1.105	1.355
1918	.942	1.648
1919	.893	1.496
1920	.885	1.213
1921	.996	1.432
1922	.922	1.427
1923	.922	1.322
1924	.942	1.458

(continued)

APPENDIX H

TABLE H–20 (concluded)

Calendar Year	Ratio for Manufactured Products (1)	Ratio for Agricultural Products (2)
1925	.877	1.359
1926	.922	1.152
1927	.870	1.239
1928	.819	1.373
1929	.893	1.469
1930	.954	1.543
1931	.896	1.540
1932	1.007	1.525
1933	1.014	1.697
1934	1.039	1.989
1935	1.072	2.018
1936	1.107	1.787
1937	1.117	1.512
1938	1.031	1.758
1939	1.041	1.522
1940	1.008	1.591
1941	1.003	2.132
1942	1.107	2.342
1943	1.112	2.615
1944	1.181	2.645
1945	1.135	2.356
1946	.859	2.033
1947	.803	2.104
1948	.782	2.072
1949	.771	1.822
1950	.769	1.287
1951	.724	1.180
1952	.739	1.355
1953	.758	1.360
1954	.747	1.224
1955	.772	1.220
1956	.791	1.225
1957	.826	1.199
1958	.852	1.229
1959	.874	1.230
1960	.871	1.197

SOURCE: Column 1: Table A–1, col. 6 ÷ Table A–3, col. 6.
Column 2: Table A–5, col. 1 ÷ Table A–5, col. 3.

TABLE H–21

U.S. EXPORT AND IMPORT PRICES AS PERCENTAGE OF U.K. EXPORT PRICES
FOR TEXTILES AND TOTAL FINISHED MANUFACTURES
(1913 = 100)

Calendar Year	As Percentage of U.K. Export Price Index for Manufactures		Export Price Indexes for Textiles: U.S. as Percentage of U.K. (3)
	U.S. Export Price, Manufactures (1)	U.S. Import Price, Manufactures (2)	
1879	135.6	116.8	
1880	143.9	114.6	138.0
1881	143.4	118.6	135.3
1882	140.1	117.7	143.0
1883	141.6	118.1	144.7
1884	147.3	115.8	136.0
1885	144.4	113.4	128.1
1886	143.4	115.0	131.0
1887	139.6	115.1	132.3
1888	144.0	110.5	139.0
1889	138.6	113.8	140.9
1890	127.3	105.4	133.2
1891	122.3	105.0	131.4
1892	116.2	107.3	135.2
1893	111.5	108.5	134.5
1894	110.8	108.6	134.8
1895	126.9	111.5	129.3
1896	130.8	109.7	128.9
1897	120.7	108.8	123.7
1898	114.7	110.3	117.4
1899	118.8	108.9	114.3
1900	116.4	102.8	114.6
1901	112.1	105.5	113.7
1902	117.5	108.6	116.5
1903	120.6	106.8	107.0
1904	117.6	104.4	108.3
1905	111.2	106.0	111.9
1906	109.6	104.7	110.1
1907	108.7	103.3	113.4
1908	108.1	97.2	111.2
1909	108.2	95.9	105.4
1910	106.1	93.0	100.5
1911	99.5	94.0	96.3
1912	100.2	98.4	96.1
1913	100.0	100.0	100.0

SOURCE: Column 1: Table A–1, col. 6 ÷ Table G–17, col. 1.
Column 2: Table A–3, col. 6 ÷ Table G–17, col. 1.
Column 3: Table G–18, col. 4 ÷ col. 3.

Author Index

Adams, T. S., 309, 310, 311
Adelman, Irma, 110n, 113n, 115
Adler, John H., 54n, 124n
Aldrich, Nelson W., 250
Allen, R. G. D., 91n, 357

Baldwin, Robert E., 17n, 18, 19n
Banerjee, K. S., 110n, 113n, 115, 124n
Barger, Harold, 307
Bean, Louis H., 427n
Bennett, M. K., 348
Bezanson, Anne, 250, 301, 303, 304, 313, 349, 350, 354, 355, 356
Blackwell, Carl P., 128n
Bowley, A. L., 115, 117
Brady, Dorothy S., 113n
Burgess, Robert W., 114n
Burns, Arthur F., 3n

Cochran, William G., 114n
Copeland, Morris A., 114n
Cowden, Dudley J., 3n, 82, 92n, 365

Deutsch, Karl W., 39f

Eckstein, Alexander, 39f
Ellsworth, P. T., 19n
Ely, J. Edward, 91n, 357

Fabricant, Solomon, 58n, 81n, 108n, 124n, 310, 312
Fisher, Irving, 89n, 116

Gallman, Robert E., 42f
Graham, Frank D., 3n

Haberler, Gottfried, 18, 19n
Handy, William W., 310, 311
Hansen, Morris H., 112n, 117n
Harris, Curtis C., Jr., 62n
Hilgerdt, Folke, 18, 39n, 63, 65, 74
Hirschman, Albert O., 37n, 39n
Holmes, George K., 309, 310, 311
Humphrey, Don, 5, 43n
Hurwitz, Abner, 113n
Hurwitz, William H., 112n, 117n

Imlah, Albert H., 14ff, 414-15, 445, 449

Jones, J. W., 353

Kendrick, John W., 26, 30n, 420n, 427n
Kindleberger, Charles P., 13, 15n, 17, 19, 23, 25n, 65n, 72n, 95n, 98, 102n, 415n, 416n, 417n, 446n
Kravis, Irving B., 58n
Kreps, Theodore J., 3f, 11, 13, 43n, 95n, 113n, 130-34, 413-14, 444
Kuznets, Simon, 40n, 41f, 44, 424n

Lerdau, E., 5
Letiche, J. M., 17n

MacDougall, G. D. A., 71n
Madow, William G., 112n, 117n
Martin, K., 12, 13
McCarthy, Philip J., 110n, 113n
Mears, Eliot G., 92n
Michell, H., 302, 348, 358
Mill, John Stuart, 17n
Mills, Frederick C., 112, 115, 117
Mitchell, Wesley C., 96f, 112
Montgomery, Sarah S., 19
Morgan, Theodore, 19
Mosteller, Frederick, 114n
Mudgett, Bruce D., 116

North, Douglass C., 3n, 4, 19n, 43n, 47n
Nourse, Edwin G., 45n

Olson, Mancur, Jr., 62n

Prebisch, Raul, 18n, 25

Rasmussen, Wayne D., 45n, 51
Robertson, D. H., 37
Rodriquez, D. W., 350, 351
Rostow, Walt W., 17n
Rutter, Frank R., 92n

Sauerbeck, A., 18, 96, 97n, 115
Schlesinger, Eugene R., 54n, 124n
Schlote, Werner, 14ff, 71, 73n, 414-15, 440n, 441n, 445f, 449
Schmeckebier, Lawrence F., 91n, 92n
Schurr, Sam H., 307
Shaw, William H., 40n, 41ff
Silverman, A. G., 73n, 95n, 441n
Simon, Matthew, 3n, 5
Singer, H. W., 25, 30n

477

Subject Index

Agricultural products:
  composition of class, 224-25
  coverage ratios, 395, 397, 399, 401
  European market for, 45, 47, 52
  export data:
    price indexes, 151-52, 172, 184, 186, 188-93
    quantity indexes, 151-52, 176, 200-05
    values in current and constant dollars, 157-58, 180, 212-17
  import data:
    price indexes, 151-52, 174, 185, 187, 194-99
    quantity indexes, 151-52, 178, 206-11
    values in current and constant dollars, 157-58, 182, 218-23
  manufactured foods as part of, 55-57
  price relationships:
    export to import, 69, 473-74
    foreign trade to domestic, 32, 34, 469-72
    to manufactured products, 21, 67-68, 451-52
    Paasche-Laspeyres ratios, 84-86
    to productivity, 25-30
    to quantity, 63-69, 88
    terms of trade, 25-28, 36-37, 463-68
  production expansion and migration, 46-47
  quantity relationships:
    export to import, 69, 439
    to manufactured products, 67-68, 438
  share in total exports, 54-56
  supply and demand, 45-46
  trade-output ratios, 49-52, 54-55, 432-33, 436-37
  value and quantity trends, 45-57
  See also Primary products and listings under specific commodities
American Tariff League, 3n, 365
Animals, live, exports:
  coverage and sources, 266, 301
  indexes and values, 251, 256, 261
Automobile exports:
  coverage and sources, 295, 311-12
  indexes and values, 252, 257, 262

Banana imports:
  coverage and sources, 317, 350-51

customs data on, 92, 350, 369
  indexes and values, 253, 258, 263
Basic data, NBER, 172-223, 227-41, 251-65
  See also Coverage
Beef exports, see Meat exports

Chemical exports:
  coverage and sources, 296-98, 312-13
  indexes and values, 252, 257, 262
  Paasche-Laspeyres ratios, 83-84
Chemical imports:
  coverage and sources, 342-46, 363-64
  indexes and values, 255, 260, 265
Coal exports:
  coverage, 284
  indexes and values, 252, 257, 262
  unit values compared to prices, 98-102
Cocoa imports:
  coverage, 316, 319
  indexes and values, 253, 258, 263
  timing relation of unit values and prices, 103, 105
Coffee exports:
  coverage, 266, 301
  customs area adjustment, 402-03, 405-07
Coffee imports:
  correction for overvaluation, 6
  coverage, 316
  effect on food import prices, 35
  indexes and values, 253, 258, 263
  unit values compared to prices, 97, 103, 105
Commodity classification:
  correspondence with Dept. of Commerce, 4, 80, 128, 241
  intermediate class composition, 242-47
  major class composition, 168-71, 224-25
  minor class composition and coverage, 266-300, 314-47
  procedures and problems, 4, 80-81, 141, 248, 250
  See also Sampling error; Sampling procedure
Copper exports:
  unit values compared to prices, 100, 103

479

quantity indexes, 148-49, 179, 206-11

values in current and constant dollars, 164-67, 183, 218-23

interpolating series for Commerce price indexes, 366-67, 376-77

price relationships:
to agricultural products, 21, 67-68, 451-52
export to import, 70, 473-74
foreign trade to domestic, 32-33, 469-72
Paasche-Laspeyres ratios, 83-84, 86
to primary products, 17-25, 36-37, 453-60
to productivity, 25-30
to quantity, 65-71
terms of trade, 17-28, 36-37, 461-62, 465-68
to total exports and imports, 21-22, 461-62
to United Kingdom, 71-74, 440, 475

quantity relationships:
to agricultural products, 67-68, 438
export to import, 70, 439
to United Kingdom, 71-74, 440

share in total trade, 57-62

trade-output ratios, 57-59, 61, 434-35

variability of price indexes, 120f, 393

weight in NBER and Kreps indexes, 133-34

Marshall-Edgeworth indexes, *see* Price indexes

Meat exports:
cost of materials related to value of product, 57
coverage, 242, 267
in European market, 47
indexes and values, 227, 232, 237, 251, 256, 261
influence on domestic output, 50-51
migration of production and, 46

Metal products exports:
coverage and sources, 125, 127, 243, 287-95, 308-12
indexes and values, 228, 233, 238, 252, 257, 262
share in manufactured exports, 60

Metal products imports:
coverage and sources, 125, 247, 338-42, 361-62
indexes and values, 231, 236, 241, 255, 260, 265

share in manufactured imports, 61

Minor classes:
composition and coverage, 266-300, 314-47
indexes and values, 251-65
sources of data, 248-50, 301-13, 348-64
variability of indexes, 118-20, 378-92

Nonferrous metal products exports, *see* Metal products exports

Nonferrous metal imports:
coverage and sources, 337-38, 360-61
indexes and values, 255, 260, 265
See also Metal products imports

Oats:
output, 46
timing relation of export unit values and prices, 103
See also Grain exports .

Output, *see* Farm gross product; Gross national product; Trade-output ratios

Paasche indexes, *see* Price indexes

Paasche-Laspeyres ratios, 80, 83-90

Paper products exports:
coverage and sources, 282-83, 306
indexes and values, 252, 257, 262

Paper products imports:
coverage and sources, 333-34, 358-59
indexes and values, 254-55, 259-60, 264-65
share in imports, 61

Petroleum exports:
coverage and sources, 243, 284, 306-07
indexes and values, 228, 233, 238, 252, 257, 262
quality change, 93n, 306-07
share in manufactured exports, 59f

Petroleum imports:
coverage, 334-35
customs data on, 92, 373
indexes and values, 255, 260, 265

Pork exports, *see* Meat exports

Potato imports:
domestic prices and, 349

Precious stone imports:
coverage and sources, 246, 335, 359
indexes and values, 231, 236, 241, 255, 260, 265

Price data:
description, 93-109
sources, 248-50, 301-13, 348-64

486